Principles of Computer Security

SECURITY + ™ AND BEYOND

D0206931

Principles of Computer Security

SECURITY+™ AND BEYOND

Wm. Arthur Conklin, Gregory B. White, Chuck Cothren, Dwayne Williams, Roger L. Davis

McGraw-Hill Technology Education

Boston   Burr Ridge, IL   Dubuque, IA   Emeryville, CA   Madison, WI
New York   San Francisco   St. Louis   Bangkok   Bogotá   Caracas   Kuala Lumpur   Lisbon
London   Madrid   Mexico City   Milan   Montreal   New Delhi   Santiago   Seoul
Singapore   Sydney   Taipei   Toronto

The McGraw·Hill Companies

Technology Education

1333 Burr Ridge Parkway
Burr Ridge, Illinois 60527
U.S.A..

Principles of Computer Security: Security+™ and Beyond

For information on translations or book distributors outside the U.S.A., please see the International Contact Information page immediately following the index of this book. Some ancillaries, including electronic and print components, may not be available to customers outside the United States.

1 2 3 4 5 6 7 8 9 0 DOC DOC 0 1 9 8 7 6 5 4

Book p/n 0-07-225643-5 and CD p/n 0-07-225644-3
parts of
ISBN 0-07-225509-9

Sponsoring Editor Christopher C. Johnson	**Indexer** Valerie Perry
Developmental Editor Laura Stone	**Interior Design** Peter F. Hancik
Project Editor Julie M. Smith	**Composition** Jean Butterfield
Technical Editor Steven Bale	**Illustrators** Kathleen Fay Edwards, Melinda Moore Lytle
Copy Editor Mike McGee	**Instructor's Manual** Dr. James Frost, Dr. John Springer
Proofreader Susie Elkind	

This book was composed with Corel VENTURA™ Publisher.

www.mhteched.com

This book is dedicated to the many
security professionals who daily work
to ensure the safety of our nation's
critical infrastructures.

We want to recognize the thousands
of dedicated individuals who strive
to protect our national assets but who
seldom receive praise and often are
only noticed when an incident occurs.

To you we say thank you for a job well done!

ABOUT THE AUTHORS

Wm. Arthur Conklin is a Senior Lecturer in the College of Business at The University of Texas at San Antonio and a Research Scientist at the Center for Infrastructure Assurance and Security. He is currently working on a Ph.D. specializing in Information Systems/Information Assurance. Mr. Conklin has an MBA from UTSA, and two graduate degrees in electrical engineering from the Naval Postgraduate School in Monterey, California. His current research interests are in the areas of steganography and in security implications of distributed computing. Mr. Conklin is a 10-year veteran of the U.S. Navy, serving as a surface warfare officer and engineering duty officer, and has over 10 years experience in software engineering and project management. He is a co-author of McGraw Hill's *Security+ Certification All-in-One Exam Guide*.

Dr. Gregory White has been involved in computer and network security since 1986. He spent 19 years on active duty with the United States Air Force and is currently in the Air Force Reserves assigned to the Air Force Information Warfare Center. He obtained his Ph.D. in computer science from Texas A&M University in 1995. His dissertation topic was in the area of computer network intrusion detection, and he continues to conduct research in this area today. He is currently the Interim Executive Director and Technical Director for the Center for Infrastructure Assurance and Security (CIAS) and is an associate professor of information systems at the University of Texas at San Antonio (UTSA). Dr. White has written and presented numerous articles and conference papers on security. He is also the coauthor for four other textbooks on computer and network security and has written chapters for two other security books. Dr. White continues to be active in security research. His current research initiatives include efforts in high-speed intrusion detection, infrastructure protection, and methods to calculate a return on investment and the total cost of ownership from security products.

Chuck Cothren, CISSP, is a research scientist at UTSA CIAS, and currently serves on the Information Systems Security Association (ISSA)'s Alamo Chapter Board of Directors. Mr. Cothren has a wide array of security experience including performing controlled penetration testing, network security policies, computer intrusion forensics, and computer security training. He is also well versed in wireless networking and wireless security assessments. Mr. Cothren joined UTSA CIAS in February 2003. He was previously employed as a senior network security engineer working with Fortune 100 clients to provide them with vulnerability assessments and other security services. Prior to that he was employed as a network administrator, and also as a trainer for an information technology firm. Mr. Cothren is a certified information systems security professional (CISSP) and has coauthored *Voice and Data Security* as well as *Security+ Certification All-in-One Exam Guide*. Mr. Cothren also holds a B.S. in industrial distribution from Texas A&M University.

Dwayne Williams, CISSP, joined the UTSA CIAS in 2002 as a senior researcher and has over ten years' experience in information systems and network security. Mr. Williams' experience includes six years of commissioned military service as a communications computer information systems officer in the United States Air Force specializing in network security, corporate information protection, intrusion detection systems, incident response, and VPN technology. Prior to joining the CIAS, he served as director of consulting for SecureLogix Corporation where he directed and provided security assessment and integration services to Fortune 100, government, public utility, oil and gas, financial, and technology clients. Mr. Williams graduated in May 1993 from Baylor University with a bachelor of arts in computer science. Mr. Williams is a certified information systems security professional (CISSP) and coauthor of *Voice and Data Security* and *Security+ Certification All-in-One Exam Guide*.

Roger L. Davis, CISSP, CISM, CISA, is senior internal audit manager at Nu Skin Enterprises, evaluating global business operations in over 35 countries. He has served as president of the Utah chapter of the Information Systems Security Association (ISSA) and various board positions for the Utah chapter of the Information Systems Audit and Control Association (ISACA). He is a retired Air Force lieutenant colonel with over 20 years of military and information security experience. Mr. Davis served on the faculty of Brigham Young University and the Air Force Institute of Technology. He coauthored McGraw-Hill's *Security+ Certification All-in-One Exam Guide* and *Voice and Data Security*, which was also translated into Chinese. He holds a master's degree in computer science from George Washington University, a bachelor's degree in computer science from Brigham Young University, and performed post-graduate studies in electrical engineering and computer science at the University of Colorado.

ABOUT THE SERIES EDITOR

Corey D. Schou, Ph.D., is the University Professor of Informatics and the Associate Dean of the College of Business at Idaho State University. He has been involved in establishing computer security and information assurance training and standards for 25 years. His research interests include information assurance, ethics, privacy, and collaborative decision making. He was responsible for compiling and editing computer security standards and training materials for the Committee on National Security Systems (CNSS).

Throughout his career, Dr. Schou has remained an active classroom teacher despite his research and service commitments. He is the founding director of the Informatics Research Institute and the National Information Assurance Training and Education Center (NIATEC), which was designated the National Center of Excellence in Information Assurance Education.

In 1996, his research center was cited by the Information Systems Security Association (ISSA) for Outstanding Contributions to the Security Profession and he was selected as the Educator of the Year by the Federal Information Systems Security Educators Association (FISSEA). In 1997, the Masie Institute and TechLearn Consortium recognized his contributions to distance education. In 2001, Dr. Schou was honored by the International Information Systems Security Certification Consortium [(ISC)^2] with the Tipton award for his work in professionalization of computer security and his development of the generally accepted common body of knowledge (CBK) used in the certification of information assurance professionals.

Dr. Schou serves as the chair of the Colloquium for Information Systems Security Education (CISSE). Under his leadership, the Colloquium creates an environment for exchange and dialogue among leaders in government, industry, and academia concerning information security and information assurance education. In addition, he is the editor of *Information Systems Security* and serves on the board of several professional organizations.

ABOUT THE TECHNICAL EDITORS

Steven C. Bale, JD, CISSP, is a Professor of Computer Technology at Truckee Meadows Community College in Reno, Nevada. Steve has more than 25 years in system design, implementation and network administration as well as network security in both the private and public sector, including having worked with various state and federal agencies. He is currently the program director for the Microsoft IT Academy and the MCSE program at Truckee Meadows Community College. In addition to being a Certified Information Systems Security Professional, he holds a variety of other industry certifications including, MCSA (2000 & 2003), MCSE (2000 & 2003), MCSAS, MCSES, MCSAM, MCDBA, MCT, CCNA, CCDA, A+, Network+, Security+, Server+, CTT+, and CNA. In addition to his law degree, he holds a MPA from the Graduate School of Management at Brigham Young University and is finishing a Ph.D. in public administration and public policy at the University of Nevada Reno.

ACKNOWLEDGMENTS

We, the authors of *Principles of Computer Security: Security+ and Beyond*, have so many individuals that we need to acknowledge—individuals without whom this effort would not have been successful.

The list needs to start with those folks at McGraw-Hill who worked tirelessly with the project's multiple authors to lead us successfully through the minefield that is a schedule, who took our rough chapters and drawings and turned them into a final, professional product we can be proud of: Chris Johnson, Laura Stone, Julie Smith, and Jean Butterfield. We also thank the copy editor Mike McGee; the proofreader, Susie Elkind; and the indexer, Valerie Perry for all their attention to detail that made this a finer work after they finished with it.

We also need to acknowledge our current employers who, to our great delight, have seen fit to pay us to work in a career field that we all find exciting and rewarding. There is never a dull moment in security because it is constantly changing.

We would like to thank Dr. James Frost and Dr. John Springer for their contributions to the Instructor's Resource Kit.

Finally, we would each like to individually thank those people who—on a personal basis—have provided the core support for us individually. Without these special people in our lives, none of us could have put this work together.

To Susan, my muse and inspiration–I send my thanks, my love, and my deepest appreciation.

Wm. Arthur Conklin

I would like to thank my wife, Charlan. No matter how many times I have sworn that I'll never get involved with another book project, only to return within months to yet another, you have always remained supportive and my constant source of inspiration.

I would also like to thank all of the individuals at the Center for Infrastructure Assurance and Security at UTSA for their dedication and tremendous work. You make it worth coming back each day to fight the bureaucracy that seems to constantly be placed in our way. Thanks to all of you for all that you do.

Gregory B. White, Ph.D.

Josie, thank you for all love and support you have given me, you make the things I do possible.

Chuck Cothren

I would like to thank my wife Leah and my family for all the support and love they've shown me on this and every other project I've undertaken.

Dwayne E. Williams

Special thanks to my wife and best friend, Geena, for her unfailing support and to my kids, Angee, Adam, and Reed.

Roger L. Davis

CONTENTS AT A GLANCE

CONTENTS

About the McGraw-Hill Information Security Series

A new century—a new set of problems and a new curriculum. In the past four years, our awareness of critical information infrastructure and the importance of these systems in our lives has increased. Colleges and universities world wide have been challenged to increase course offerings in computer security, information systems, and information assurance. The stumbling block has been a lack of trained faculty and of suitable teaching materials to provide literacy, awareness, training and education at all levels.

Welcome to the McGraw Hill series on Information Assurance. It will provide material to support an integrated curriculum in information assurance for both technical and non technical programs. The texts in this series support all aspects of the Committee on National Security Standards (CNSS) (http://www.nstissc.gov/html/library.html) as well as many of the national and international certification standards.

A stable technological economy demands a general populace who are at least aware and literate in information security and assurance.

The texts in this series are based on more than fifteen years of international progress across academia, government, and industry in the developing cognitive and pedagogic models for teaching information security and assurance. Collectively the series deals with the defense in depth model that relies on technology, operations, and finally literacy, awareness, training, and education.

Literacy, awareness, training, and education are the most cost-effective means of protecting organizational information assets. The following illustration shows the relationship among these countermeasures.

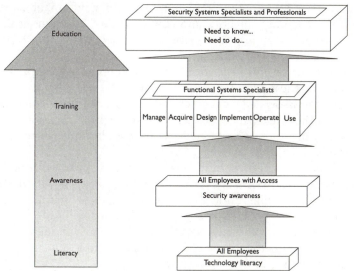

Based on a figure in Schou, C., W. V. Maconachy, et al. (1993). "Organizational Information Security: Awareness, Training, and Education to Maintain System Integrity." Proceedings of the 9th International Computer Security Symposium, Toronto, Canada, IFIP.

To learn about information assurance, one must first be literate in information technology. The second step in the process is making the learner aware. Awareness is frequently a passive activity that focuses on short-term memory and may be a component of other classes.

The training is the next step of the process. It requires active participation and focus more on long-term memory, job skills, tasks and methods. In eDACUM studies (http://www.nsa.gov/isso/programs/nietp/edacum.htm) performed throughout the '90s information assurance experts established a series of KSAs (knowledge, skill, and Ability) and determined that functional security specialists used their KSAs in at least five major areas, management, acquisition, design, implementation, operation, and testing of secure systems. Depending on the functions performed individual need different combinations and amounts of training in each of these areas. Of course, every functional specialist is ultimately a user and needs specific training.

The final stage in the learning pyramid is education. It focuses on internalization and accommodation of the KSAs through research, analysis, evaluation, and judgment. Pedagogically these KSAs fall into two major categories – things you need to know and things you need to do.

Information Assurance

Information assurance is a combination of both art and science. It is an interdisciplinary activity that protects the most complex organizational asset—its data and the ability to provide information. Most organizations profess an interest in some aspects of information security. All organizations should view this effort as a planned integrative systematic objective at the highest level.

The books in this series form the foundation for teaching information assurance – the combination of availability, integrity, and confidentiality. Throughout the series students are lead to examine appropriate measures to protect systems while data are being processed, stored or in transmission.

The texts will focus on three categories of the countermeasures triad—technology, operations, and awareness, training and education.

Hardware and the associated technology are the most obvious elements of the countermeasures triad. They are the most expensive means of protecting systems. At best they must be constantly maintained or patched and at worst they must be recapitalized if severely compromised.

In any case, they are ineffective countermeasures if good policies are not in place and the systems are operated incorrectly. Correctly operated systems will insure that availability will remain high while confidentiality and integrity are maintained.

Hardware, technology, policies, and sound operations will fail if the humans involved are not aware of the problems, technologically literate enough to communicate about the problems, trained to apply countermeasures, and well enough educated to think about avoiding the problem in the future.

Principles of Computer Security Security+ and Beyond

The hard work and dedication of the authors have created a book that shows the importance of developing a professional approach to computer security and information assurance. The book is unique in that it deals with both certification and academic issues at the same time. They make an excellence balance between technological and managerial issues.

The overall writing style and tone make the book readable and thorough.. The examples are sufficiently clear that a true beginner can rapidly learn the essentials while the more experienced will be able to find examples for practical use. The authors challenge the learner to learn more.

On a regular basis I teach computer security related courses at both the graduate and undergraduate level. My students constantly ask about preparation for certifications. This book can be used to teach a thorough fundamentals of information security and assurance at the sophomore level in technical courses. In the upper division, the text is suitable for survey and introductory courses. As a bonus, the book covers the learning requirements for several certifications including the ComTIA Security Plus (http://comptia.com/) and (ISC)^2 SSCP examination (https://www.isc2.org/cgi/content.cgi?category=20). In addition, it is a teaching resource for major portions of the contents of NSTISSC 4011.

This outstanding team of authors has created a unique text that makes it clear to the reader that information security is a process not just manipulation of tools. It covers a broad spectrum of materials for security specialist.s

This book and the entire series can be summed up by the motto of my research center:

Awareness—Training—Education

There is no patch for ignorance.

Corey D. Schou, PhD
University Professor of Informatics
Professor of Computer Information Systems
Director of the National Information Assurance Training and Education Center

PREFACE

Information and computer security has moved from the confines of academia to mainstream America in the last decade. The Slammer and SoBig attacks were heavily covered in the media and broadcast into the average American's home. It has increasingly become obvious to everybody that something needs to be done in order to secure not only our nation's critical infrastructure but the businesses we deal with on a daily basis. The question is, "Where do we begin?" What can the average information technology professional do in order to secure the systems that they are hired to maintain? One immediate answer is education and training. If we want to secure our computer systems and networks, our IT professionals need to know how to do this, and what security entails. Computer security education is an essential foundational element for today's computer science and information systems professionals.

Complacency is not an option in today's hostile network environment. While we once considered the insider to be the major threat to corporate networks, and the "script kiddie" to be the standard external threat (often thought of as only a nuisance), the highly interconnected network world of today is a much different place. The U.S. government identified eight critical infrastructures a few years ago that were thought to be so critical to the nation's daily operation that if one were to be lost, it would have a catastrophic impact on the nation. To this original set of eight sectors, more have recently been added. A common thread throughout all of these, however, is technology—especially technology related to computers and communication. Thus, if an individual, organization, or nation wanted to cause damage to this nation, it could attack it not just with traditional weapons but with computers through the Internet. It is not surprising to hear that among the other information seized in raids on terrorist organizations, computers and information about the Internet are present. While the insider can certainly still do tremendous damage to an organization, the external threat is again becoming the chief concern among many. While many may argue the source and credibility of specific threats, the fact remains that computer security plays an essential role in reducing risk to our national economy and way of life.

So, where do you, the IT professional seeking more knowledge on security, start your studies? The IT world is overflowing with certifications that can be obtained by those attempting to learn more about their chosen profession. The security sector is no different, and the Security+ exam offers a basic level of certification for security. In the pages of this introductory text on computer security can be found not only material that can help you build a solid foundation in computer security, but also prepare for taking the Security+ examination. The basic information that you will need in order to understand the issues involved in securing our computer systems and networks today will act as a foundational element in your education as a computer science or information systems professional. In no way is this textbook the final source you will need in order to learn all about protecting your organization's systems, but it serves as a point from which to launch your security studies and career.

One thing is certainly true about this field of study—it never gets boring. It constantly changes as technology itself advances. Something else you will find as you progress in your security studies is that no matter how much technology advances and no matter how many new security devices are developed, at its most basic level, the human is still the weak link in the security chain. If you are looking for an exciting area to delve into, then you have certainly chosen wisely. Security offers a challenging blend of technology and people issues. We, the authors of this textbook, wish you luck as you embark on an exciting and challenging career path.

Wm. Arthur Conklin
Gregory B. White, Ph.D.
Chuck Cothren
Dwayne Williams
Roger L. Davis

INTRODUCTION

Computer security is becoming increasingly important today as the number of security incidents steadily climbs. Many corporations are now spending significant portions of their budget on security hardware, software, services, and personnel. They are spending this money not because it increases sales or enhances the product they provide, but because of the possible consequences should they not take protective actions.

Why Focus on Security?

Security is not something that we want to have to pay for, it would be nice if we didn't have to worry about protecting our data from disclosure, modification, or destruction from unauthorized individuals, but that is not the environment that we find ourselves in. Instead, we have seen the cost of recovering from security incidents steadily rise along with the rise in the number of incidents themselves. Since September 11, 2001 this has taken on an even greater sense of urgency as we now face securing our systems not just from attack by disgruntled employees, juvenile hackers, organized crime, or competitors. We now have to also consider the possibility of attacks on our systems from terrorist organizations. If nothing else, the events of September 11, 2001 showed that anybody is a potential target, you do not have to be part of the government or a government contractor, being an American is sufficient reason to make you a target to some and with the global nature of the Internet, collateral damage from cyber attacks on one organization could have a worldwide impact.

A Growing Need for Security Specialists

In order to protect our computer systems and networks, we will need a significant number of new security professionals trained in the many aspects of computer and network security. This is not an easy task for the systems we connect to the Internet are becoming increasingly complex with software whose lines of codes number in the millions. It is not hard to understand why this is such a difficult problem to solve if one considers just how many errors might be present in a piece of software that is several million lines long. When you add the additional factor of how fast software is being developed, out of necessity as the market is constantly moving, it is easy to understand how errors occur.

Not every "bug" in the software will result in a security hole, but it doesn't take many to have a drastic affect on the Internet community. We can't just blame the vendors for this situation, because they are reacting to the demands of government and industry. Most vendors are fairly adept at developing patches for flaws found in their software and patches are constantly issued to protect systems from bugs that may introduce security problems. This introduces a whole new problem for managers and administrators to be concerned with—patch management. How important this has become is easily illustrated by how many of the most recent security events have been as a result of a security bug that had been discovered months prior to the security incident, and for which a patch has been available, but the community has not correctly installed the patch making the incident possible. One of the reasons for this is that many of the individuals who would be responsible for installing the patches are not trained to understand the security implications surrounding the hole or the ramifications of not installing the patch. Many of these individuals simply lack the necessary training.

Security training has become a foundation element of a complete education in information systems and computer science. As such, measurement of a new graduate's computer security knowledge and ability is of interest to many employers. It is for this reason, the need for an increasing number of security professionals who are trained to some minimum level of understanding, that certifications such as the Security+ certification have been developed. Prospective employers want to know that the individual they are considering hiring knows what to do in terms of security. The prospective employees in turn want to have a way to demonstrate their level of understanding, which can enhance their chances of being hired. The community as a whole just wants more trained security professionals. This book is designed not only to serve as an introductory textbook, but to give the students the necessary material to pass the Security+ exam at the completion of the course. When you pass it, you will demonstrate that you have that basic understanding of security that employers are looking for. Passing this certification exam will not be an easy task for there are many things that you will need to learn to acquire that basic understanding of computer and network security.

How This Book is Organized

The book is divided into chapters to cover essential aspects of computer security and cover the objectives of the Security+ exam. Some of the chapters are more technical than others—reflecting the nature of the security environment where you will be forced to deal with not only technical details but other issues such as security policies and procedures as well as training and education. While there are many individuals involved in computer and network security that have advanced degrees in math, computer science, information systems, or computer or electrical engineering, you do not need to be this technical to effectively address security in your organization. For example, you do not need to develop your own cryptographic algorithm—you simply need to be able to understand how cryptography is used along with its strengths and weaknesses. As you progress in your studies, you will learn that many of the problems in security are a result of the human element. The best technology in the world still ends up being placed in an environment where humans have the opportunity to foul things up—and they all too often do.

This book begins with an introduction of some of the basic elements of security. This begins with the Introduction (Chapter 1) then General Security Concepts (Chapter 2), then an introduction to operational concepts (Chapter 3) and finishes with the role of people in computer security (Chapter 4). It is recommended that these chapters be used in order in all classes as they are foundational to other elements in the book.

Chapters 5 through 9 represent various technical elements of a computer security class. The order of presentation is somewhat arbitrary, although it would be best to have cryptography (Chapter 5) prior to public key infrastructure (Chapter 6).

Chapters 10 through 17 cover the implementation of computer security aspects in remote access, email, web components, software engineering and specific types of vulnerabilities. These chapters are where the technical details meet the practical road of use in systems.

Chapters 18–24 address operational and organizational issues. This is where we depart from a discussion of technology again and will instead discuss how security is accomplished in an organization. Since we know that we will not be absolutely successful in our security efforts, attackers are always finding new holes and ways around our security defenses, one of the most important topics we will address is the subject of responses to security incidents and how to recover from them.

There are two appendixes in *Principles of Computer Security: Security+™ and Beyond*. Appendix A explains how best to use the CD-ROM bound into this book and Appendix B provides a cross reference of the text material with respect to the Security+ exam.

Located just before the Index of the book, you will find a useful glossary of security terminology, including many related acronyms and their meanings. We hope that you use the Glossary frequently and find it to be a useful study aid as you work your way through the various topics in this textbook.

Special Features of the Textbook

To make this textbook more useful and a pleasure to read, we have used the following special conventions.

Icons

To alert you to an important bit of advice, a shortcut, or a pitfall, you'll occasionally see Notes, Tips, Cautions, and Study Tips peppered throughout the text.

NOTE Notes offer nuggets of especially helpful stuff, background explanations and information, and they occasionally define terms.

TIP Tips provide suggestions and nuances to help you learn to finesse your job. Take a tip from me and read the Tips carefully.

CAUTION When you see a Caution, pay special attention. Cautions appear when you have to make a crucial choice or when you are about to undertake something that may have ramifications you might not immediately anticipate. Read them now so you don't have regrets later.

STUDY TIP Study Tips give you special advice or may provide information specifically relating to preparing for the Security+ exam itself.

> ## Sidebars
>
> From time to time you will find sidebars in this book. They may present informa-
> tion that is tangential to the main discussion, or may serve to highlight an impor-
> tant concept. Sidebars appear in screened boxes like this one.

End-of-Chapter Reviews and Chapter Tests

An important part of this book comes at the end of each chapter where you will find a
brief review of the high points of the chapter along with a series of questions followed by
the answers to those questions. There is a set of key terms and a vocabulary quiz. Then a
series of questions in a multiple-choice format. The last two sets of questions are essay
questions and lab projects designed to reinforce important issues from the chapter.

The CD-ROM

Principles of Computer Security: Security+ and Beyond also provides you with a CD-ROM of
even more test questions and their answers to help you prepare yourself for the certification exam. Read more about the companion CD-ROM in Appendix A.

Onward and Upward

At this point we hope that you are now excited about the topic of security, even if you
weren't in the first place. We wish you luck in your endeavors and welcome you to the exciting field of computer and network security.

Information Technology Skill Standards and Your Curriculum

Students in today's increasingly competitive IT career market are differentiated not only
by their technical skills, but by their communication, problem solving, and teaming
skills. More and more, these professional skills are the ones that guarantee career lon-
gevity and success. The National Workforce Center for Emerging Technologies
(NWCET) and McGraw-Hill Technology Education have partnered in an effort to help
you build technical *and* employability skills in the classroom.

Skill standards–aligned curriculum is becoming a *de facto* requirement for schools everywhere in the United States today. Programs are required to be standards aligned in order to show clearly that students are being taught and assessed consistently and to an
agreed upon set of skill and content standards. For those programs preparing students to
enter the workforce, skill standards provide an excellent skeleton upon which to build
courses.

Research has shown improved learning and retention of knowledge when learning takes place in a rich learning context. Students that learn in a real-world context are also better equipped to transfer their skills to the real world. IT skill standards provide the kind of real-world data that educators can use. Educators can draw from the skill standards to develop contextually rich assignments that help students to situate their learning in specific work contexts with complex and real-world problems to solve.

IT skill standards provide a common language between industry and education so that building bridges between these two groups can be more efficient. The more industry recognizes what educational programs are doing, the easier it is for education to gain industry support. Schools that use a skill standards–aligned program are better prepared to gain support from industry for technical advisory boards, student internships, job shadows, faculty internships, and a host of other support resources.

IT skill standards provide increased portability of skills because of the common language. Other institutions can clearly identify the content and skills that graduates of a skill standards–aligned curriculum have acquired. Programs that are skill standards based will effectively oil the wheels of articulation between programs that traditionally may have difficulty agreeing on what has been taught and assessed.

NWCET and McGraw-Hill in Partnership

McGraw-Hill Technology Education and the NWCET have partnered with the goal of helping IT educators meet these demands by making the IT skill standards more easily available and ready to use. McGraw-Hill Technology Education and the NWCET have developed four different products that will help you to address the IT skill standards in your Security+ programs and courses:

- A summary crosswalk that highlights the IT skill standards addressed by the McGraw-Hill *Principles of Computer Security: Security+ and Beyond:*

Chapter 1	Chapter 2	Chapter 3	Chapter 4	Chapter 5
Network Design and Administration	A2 Develop data/information assurance plans and implementation strategies	B2. Identify, analyze, and evaluate infrastructure and network vulnerabilities	E1. Identify and assess current and anticipated security risks and vulnerabilities	B1. Gather data and analyze security requirements
G1—Gather and document security requirements	B2. Identify, analyze, and evaluate infrastructure and network vulnerabilities			B2. Identify, analyze, and evaluate infrastructure and network vulnerabilities
G2—Design and document security plan				

Chapter 6	Chapter 7	Chapter 8	Chapter 9	Chapter 10
B1. Gather data and analyze security requirements B2. Identify, analyze, and evaluate infrastructure and network vulnerabilities	B2. Identify, analyze, and evaluate infrastructure and network vulnerabilities	E1. Identify and assess current and anticipated security risks and vulnerabilities	B2. Identify, analyze, and evaluate infrastructure and network vulnerabilities	B2. Identify, analyze, and evaluate infrastructure and network vulnerabilities A5 Monitor performance to ensure integrity and confidentiality

Chapter 11	Chapter 12	Chapter 13	Chapter 14	Chapter 15
B2. Identify, analyze, and evaluate infrastructure and network vulnerabilities C1. Perform research and analyze requirements	B2. Identify, analyze, and evaluate infrastructure and network vulnerabilities C1. Perform research and analyze requirements	B1. Gather data and analyze security requirements E4. Monitor, evaluate, and test security conditions and environment	B2. Identify, analyze, and evaluate infrastructure and network vulnerabilities	E1. Identify and assess current and anticipated security risks and vulnerabilities E4. Monitor, evaluate, and test security conditions and environment

Chapter 16	Chapter 17	Chapter 18	Chapter 19	Chapter 20
E1. Identify and assess current and anticipated security risks and vulnerabilities E4. Monitor, evaluate, and test security conditions and environment	B2. Identify, analyze, and evaluate infrastructure and network vulnerabilities	Programming and Software Development C8—Incorporate security requirements into design	B3. Develop critical situation contingency plans and disaster recovery plan C2. Develop, assess, and document security policies, practices, and procedures	E1. Identify and assess current and anticipated security risks and vulnerabilities

Chapter 21	Chapter 22	Chapter 23	Chapter 24
A2 Develop data/information assurance plans and implementation strategies	Network Design and Administration	C4. Implement, enforce, and monitor security policies, practices, and procedures	A2 Develop data/information assurance plans and implementation strategies
	E1—Set up and maintain user accounts		
A4 Implement data/information assurance plans and strategies	G2—Design and document security plan		F3. Evaluate organization¦s security strategies
	G3—Implement and enforce system and user security requirements		

- A detailed crosswalk listing Technical Knowledge, Employability Skills, and Performance Indicators addressed by the compliant curriculum (textbook, lab manual, and learning activities in the instructor pack CD)

- Twenty four skill standards–based activities with assessment rubrics that focus on technical and soft skills

- A training document that helps instructors understand and use the features of teaching a skill standards–aligned curriculum

NWCET Background and Mission

In 1995, the National Science Foundation (NSF) designated and funded the NWCET as a National Center of Excellence in Advanced Technological Education. The Center was created to advance IT education and improve the supply, quality, and diversity of the IT workforce.

The National Workforce Center for Emerging Technologies has since become a leader in new designs for Information Technology (IT) education developing products, services, and best practices that provide timely, relevant, and lasting solutions to meet the needs of IT educators and the IT workforce. The NWCET translates the rapidly changing demands of the technology workplace into programs, curricula, courseware, and assessments that prepare students for current and future IT careers.

The NWCET is perhaps best known for its IT skill standards. Skill standards provide an agreement of what is expected to be successful in a given career area. They provide a validated, industry-derived framework upon which educators can build curricula. Using industry skill standards as the foundation for curricula will result in a closer alignment between educational programs and workplace expectations, and result in a better-skilled workforce.

To support new and innovative IT programs and degrees, the NWCET (www.nwcet.org) provides other professional development opportunities for high school teachers and community college and university faculty. The Educator-to-Educator Institute (E2E) (http://e2e.nwcet.org), the training branch of the NWCET, is dedicated to helping IT educators achieve excellence in IT instruction. CyberCareers (www.cybercareers.org) is a web site oriented toward middle and high schools students and teachers and provides a wide variety of career education materials such as job descriptions and an IT Interest Inventory.

Instructor and Student Web Site

For instructor and student resources, check out www.mhteched.com/security. You'll find all sorts of stuff that will help you learn more about security.

Additional Resources for Teachers

Resources for teachers are provided via an instructor's resource kit that maps to the organization of the textbook. This manual includes the following:

- Answer keys to the end-of-chapter activities in the textbook
- ExamView® Pro testbank software that generates a wide array of paper- or network-based tests, and features automatic grading
- More than 1,000 questions, written by experienced IT instructors
- A wide variety of question types and difficulty levels, allowing teachers to customize each test to maximize student progress
- Engaging PowerPoint slides on the lecture topics
- WebCT and Blackboard cartridges

Introduction and Security Trends

Upon completion of this chapter, you will be able to:

- List and discuss recent trends in computer security
- Describe simple steps to take in order to minimize the possibility of an attack on a system
- Describe various types of threats that exist for computers and networks
- Discuss recent computer crimes that have been committed

Why should we be concerned about computer and network security? All you have to do is turn on the television or read the newspaper to hear about a variety of security problems that affect our nation and the world today. The danger to computers and networks may seem to pale in comparison to the threat of terrorist strikes, but in fact the average citizen is much more likely to be the target of an attack on their own personal computer, or a computer they use at their place of work, than they are to be the direct victim of a terrorist attack. This chapter will introduce the reader to a number of issues involved in securing our computers and networks from a variety of threats that may utilize any of a number of different attacks.

The Security Problem

Fifty years ago, few people had access to a computer system or network, thus securing them was a relatively easy matter. If you could secure the building that these early, very large systems were housed in, you could secure the data and information they stored and processed. With the rise of the personal computer, and at the same time the creation of what we now refer to as the Internet, computing and the machines required to access the World Wide Web have become commonplace. No longer are computers reserved for use by scientists and engineers, now children who are barely able to read can be taught to boot a computer in order to gain access to their own favorite games or educational software.

Fifty years ago, companies did not conduct business across the Internet. Online banking and shopping were only dreams in science fiction stories. Today, however, millions of people perform online transactions every day. Companies rely on the Internet to operate and conduct business. Vast amounts of money are transferred via networks, either in the form of bank transactions or simple credit card purchases. Wherever there are vast amounts of money, there are those who will try to take advantage of the environment to conduct fraud or theft. There are many different ways to attack computers and networks to take advantage of what has made shopping, banking, investment, and leisure pursuits a simple matter of "dragging and clicking" for many people. Identity theft is so common today that most everyone knows somebody who's been a victim of such crime, if they haven't been a victim themselves. This is just one type of criminal activity that can be conducted using the Internet. There are many others and all are on the rise.

Security Incidents

It is interesting to examine some of the crimes that have been committed over the last dozen or so years. By doing so, we can better understand the threats and security issues that surround our computer systems and networks. Electronic crime can take a number of different forms, but the ones we will examine here fall into two basic categories: crimes in which the computer was the target, and incidents in which a computer was used to perpetrate the act (for example, there are many different ways to conduct bank fraud, one of which uses computers to access the records they process and maintain).

We will start our tour of computer crimes with the 1988 Internet Worm (Morris Worm), one of the first real Internet crime cases. Prior to 1988, criminal activity was chiefly centered around unauthorized access to computer systems and networks owned by the telephone company and companies which provided dial-up access for authorized users. Virus activity also existed prior to 1988, having started in the early 1980s.

The Morris Worm (November, 1988)

Robert Morris, then a graduate student at Cornell University, released what has become known as The Internet Worm (or the Morris Worm). This was the first large-scale attack on the Internet, though it appears doubtful that Morris actually intended that his creation cause the impact that it did at the time. The worm infected roughly 10 percent of the machines then connected to the Internet (which amounted to approximately 6,000 infected machines) and caused an estimated $100 million in damage, though this number has been the subject of wide debate. The worm carried no malicious payload, the program being obviously a "work in progress," but it did wreak havoc due to it continually reinfecting computer systems until they could no longer run any programs. The worm took advantage of known vulnerabilities in several programs to gain access to new hosts and would then copy itself over. Morris was eventually convicted under Title 10 United States Code Section 1030 for releasing the worm and was sentenced to three years probation, a $10,000 fine, and 400 hours of community service.

Citibank and Vladimir Levin (June–October, 1994)

Starting about June of 1994 and continuing until at least October of the same year, a number of bank transfers were made by Vladimir Levin of St. Petersburg, Russia. By the time he and his accomplices were caught, they had transferred an estimated $10 million. Eventually all but about $400,000 was recovered. Levin reportedly accomplished the break-ins by dialing into Citibank's cash management system. This system allowed clients to initiate their own fund transfers to other banks. An estimated $500 billion were transferred daily during this period so the amounts transferred by Levin were very small in comparison to the overall total on any given day. He also conducted the transactions at night in Russia so that it coincided with normal business hours in New York to avoid detection. Levin was arrested in London in 1995 and, after fighting extradition for 30 months, eventually was turned over to U.S. authorities, was tried, and sentenced to three years in jail. Four accomplices of Levin pled guilty to conspiracy to commit bank fraud and received lesser sentences.

Kevin Mitnick (February, 1995)
Kevin Mitnick's computer activities occurred over a number of years during the 1980s and 1990s. He was arrested in February, 1995 (not his first arrest on computer criminal charges) for federal offenses related to what the FBI described as a two and a half-year computer hacking spree. He eventually pled guilty to four counts of wire fraud, two counts of computer fraud, and one count of illegally intercepting a wire communication and was sentenced to 46 months in jail. In the plea agreement, Mitnick admitted to having gained unauthorized access to a number of different computer systems belonging to companies such as Motorola, Novell, Fujitsu, and Sun Microsystems. He described using a number of different "tools" and techniques including social engineering, sniffers, and cloned cellular telephones. Kevin also admitted to having used stolen accounts at the University of Southern California to store proprietary software he had taken from various companies. He also admitted to stealing e-mails and impersonating employees of targeted companies in order to gain access to the software he was seeking.

Omega Engineering and Timothy Lloyd (July, 1996)
On July 30, 1996, a software "time bomb" went off at Omega Engineering, a New Jersey-based manufacturer of high-tech measurement and control instruments. Twenty days earlier, Timothy Lloyd, a computer network program designer, had been dismissed from the company after a period of growing tension between Lloyd and management at Omega. The program that ran on July 30 deleted all of the design and production programs for the company, severely damaging the small firm and forcing the layoff of 80 employees. The program was eventually traced back to Lloyd, who had left it in retaliation for his dismissal. In May of 2000, a federal judge sentenced Lloyd to 41 months in prison and ordered him to pay more than $2 million in restitution.

Jester and the Worcester Airport (March, 1997)
In March of 1997, airport services to the FAA control tower as well as the emergency services at the Worcester Airport and the community of Rutland, Massachusetts were cut off for a period of six hours. This disruption occurred as a result of a series of commands sent by a teenage computer "hacker" who went by the name "jester." The individual had gained unauthorized access to the "loop carrier system" operated by NYNEX. Loop carrier systems are programmable remote computer systems used to integrate voice and data communications. Jester was eventually caught and ordered to pay restitution to the telephone company, as well as complete 250 hours of community service.

Solar Sunrise (February, 1998)

In January of 1998, relations between Iraq and the United States again took a turn for the worse and it appeared as if the U.S. might take military action against the Arab nation. During this period of increased tension and military preparation, a series of computer intrusions occurred at a number of military installations in the U.S. At first the military thought that this might be the start of an information warfare attack—a possibility they had been discussing since the early 1990s. Over 500 domain name servers were compromised during the course of the attacks. Making it harder to track the actual origin of the attacks was the fact that the attackers made a number of "hops" between different systems, averaging eight different systems before arriving at the target. The attackers eventually turned out to be two teenagers from California and their mentor in Israel. The attacks, as it turned out, had nothing to do with the potential conflict in Iraq.

The Melissa Virus (March, 1999)

Melissa is the best known of the early macro type viruses that attach themselves to documents for programs that have limited macro programming capability. The virus, written and released by David Smith, infected about a million computers and caused an estimated $80 million in damages. Melissa, which clogged networks with the traffic it generated and caused problems for e-mail servers worldwide, was attached to Microsoft Word 97 and Word 2000 documents. If the user opened the file, the macro ran causing it to infect the current host and also send itself to the first 50 addresses in the individual's address book. The e-mail sent contained a subject line stating "Important Message From" and then included the name of the individual who was infected. The body of the document contained the text "Here is that document you asked for … don't show anyone else ;-)." The nature of both the subject line and the body of the document usually generated enough user curiosity that many people opened the document and thus infected their system, which in turn sent the same message to 50 of their acquaintances. As a final action, if the minute of the current hour when the macro was run matched the day of the month, the macro inserted "Twenty-two points, plus triple-word-score, plus fifty points for using all my letters. Game's over. I'm outta here." into the current document. Smith, who pled guilty, was ultimately fined $5,000 and sentenced to 20 months in jail for the incident. Being that the macro code is easily modified, there have been many variations of the Melissa virus. Avoiding infection by Melissa was a simple matter: users simply didn't open the attached file.

The Love Letter Worm (May, 2000)

Also known as the "ILOVEYOU" virus and the "Love Bug," the Love Letter Worm was written and released by a Philippine student named Onel de Guzman. The worm was spread via e-mail with the subject line of "ILOVEYOU." Estimates of the number of infected machines worldwide have been as high as 45 million, accompanied by a possible $10 billion in damages (it should be noted that figures like these are extremely hard to verify or calculate). Similar to the Melissa virus, the Love Letter Worm spread via an e-mail attachment, but in this case instead of utilizing macros, the attachments were VBScript programs. When the receiver ran the attachment, it searched the system for files with specific extensions in order to replace them with copies of itself. It also sent itself to everyone in the user's address book. Again, since the receiver generally knew the sender, most individuals opened the attachment without questioning it. Onel ultimately was not convicted for releasing the worm since the Philippines, at the time, did not have any laws denoting the activity as a crime. Again, users avoided infection from the worm simply by not opening the attachments.

The Code-Red Worm (2001)

On July 19, 2001, over 350,000 computers connected to the Internet were infected by the Code-Red worm. This infection took only 14 hours to occur. The cost estimate for how much damage the worm caused (including variations of the worm released on later dates) exceeded $2.5 billion. The vulnerability exploited by the Code-Red worm had been known for a month. The worm took advantage of a buffer-overflow condition in Microsoft's IIS web servers. Microsoft released a patch for this vulnerability and made an official announcement of the problem on June 18, 2001. The worm itself was memory resident so simply turning off an infected machine eliminated it. Unfortunately, unless the system was patched before being reconnected to the Internet, chances were good that it would soon become re-infected. Though the worm didn't carry a malicious pay-load designed to destroy data on the infected system, on some systems, however, the message "Hacked by Chinese" was added to the top-level page for the infected host's web site. If the date on the infected system was between the 1st and the 19th of the month, the worm would attempt to infect a random list of IP addresses it generated. If the date was between the 20th and the 28th of the month, the worm stopped trying to infect other systems and instead attempted to launch a Denial-of-Service attack against a web site owned by the White House. After the 28th, the worm would lay dormant until the 1st of the next month. This date scheme actually ended up helping to eliminate the worm since soon after it was released on the 19th, the worm stopped trying to infect systems. This provided a period of time when systems could be rebooted and patched before they were infected again.

Adil Yahya Zakaria Shakour (August, 2001–May, 2002)

On March 13, 2003, 19-year-old Adil Yahya Zakaria Shakour pled guilty to a variety of crimes including unauthorized access to computer systems and credit card fraud. Shakour admitted to having accessed several computers without authorization, including a server at Eglin Air Force Base (where he defaced the web site), computers at Accenture (a Chicago-based management consulting and technology services company), a computer system at Sandia National Laboratories (a Department of Energy facility), and a computer at Cheaptaxforms.com. During the break-in of Cheaptaxforms.com, Shakour admitted to having obtained credit card and personal information which he used to purchase items worth over $7,000 for his own use. Shakour was sentenced to one year and one day in federal prison, a three-year term of supervised release, and was ordered to pay $88,000 in restitution.

The Slammer Worm (2003)

On Saturday, January 25, 2003, the Slammer virus was released. It exploited a buffer-overflow vulnerability in computers running Microsoft's SQL Server or Microsoft SQL Server Desktop Engine. Like the vulnerability in Code-Red, this weakness was not new and, in fact, had been discovered in July of 2002; Microsoft issued a patch for the vulnerability before it was even announced. Within the first 24 hours of Slammer's release, the worm had infected at least 120,000 hosts and caused network outages and the disruption of airline flights, elections, and ATMs. At its peak, Slammer-infected hosts were generating a reported 1TB of worm-related traffic *every second*. The worm doubled its number of infected hosts every 8 seconds. It is estimated that it took less than ten minutes to reach global proportions and infect 90 percent of the possible hosts it could infect. Once a machine was infected, the host would start randomly selecting targets and sending packets to them to attempt infection at a rate of 25,000 per second. Slammer did not contain a malicious payload. The problems it caused were a result of the massively overloaded networks, which could not sustain the traffic being generated by the thousands of infected hosts. The worm sent its single packet to a specific UDP port, 1434, which provided an immediate fix to prevent further network access. Thus, the response of administrators was to quickly block all traffic to UDP port 1434, effectively curbing the spread of the worm to new machines.

Threats to Security

The incidents in the previous section provide a glimpse into the many different threats that face administrators as they attempt to protect their computer systems and networks. There is, of course, the normal natural disasters that organizations have faced for years. In today's highly networked world, however, new threats have developed that we did not have to worry about 50 years ago.

There are a number of ways that we can break down the various threats. One way to categorize them is to look at those threats that come from outside of the organization versus those that are internal. Another is to look at the various levels of sophistication of the attacks, from those by "script kiddies" to "elite hackers." A third is to examine the level of organization of the various threats, from unstructured threats to highly structured threats. All of these are valid and, in fact, they overlap each other.

Viruses and Worms

While your organization may be exposed to viruses and worms as a result of your employees not following certain practices or procedures, generally you will not have to worry about your employees writing or releasing viruses and worms. It is important to draw a distinction between the writers of malware and those who release them. Debates over the ethics of writing viruses permeate the industry, but currently simply writing them is not considered a criminal activity. Like a baseball bat, it is not the bat that is evil, it is the inappropriate use of the bat (such as to smash a car's window) that falls into the category of criminal activity. (Some may argue that this is not a very good analogy since a baseball bat has a useful purpose—to play ball—but viruses *have* no useful purpose. In general, this is true but in some limited environments, such as in specialized computer science courses, the study and creation of viruses can be considered a useful learning experience.) By far, viruses and worms will be the most common problem that an organization faces since there are literally thousands of them that have been created. Fortunately, antivirus software and procedures can eliminate the largest portion of this threat. Viruses and worms are also generally non-discriminating threats that are released on the

Internet in a general fashion and aren't targeted at a specific organization. They are also typically highly visible once released, so they aren't the best tool to use in highly structured attacks where secrecy is vital. This is not to say that the technology used in virus and worm propagation won't be used by highly organized criminal groups, but their use for what these individuals are normally interested in accomplishing is limited. The same cannot be said for terrorist organizations that generally want to create a large impact and have it be highly visible.

Intruders

The act of deliberately accessing computer systems and networks without authorization is generally referred to as *hacking*. The term also applies to the act of exceeding ones authority in a system. This would include authorized users who attempt to gain access to files or obtain permissions that they have not been granted. While the act of breaking into computer systems and networks has been glorified in the media and movies, the physical act does not live up to the Hollywood hype. Intruders are, if nothing else, extremely patient since the process to gain access to a system takes persistence and dogged determination. The first attack may fail, so the intruders will need to try another angle, they will need to search for another possible vulnerability that may not have been patched. This second attempt may also be blocked so a third will be tried, and so on until either a new target is selected or the attackers eventually find a hole left unpatched. Generally, attacks by an individual or even small groups of attackers fall into the **unstructured threat** category. Attacks at this level are generally conducted over short periods of time (lasting at most a few months), do not involve a large number of individuals, have little financial backing, and are accomplished by insiders or outsiders who do not seek collusion with insiders.

Intruders, or those who are attempting to conduct an intrusion, definitely come in many different varieties and have varying degrees of sophistication. At the low end technically are what are generally referred to as **script kiddies**, individuals who do not have the technical expertise to develop scripts or discover new vulnerabilities in software but who have just enough understanding of computer systems to be able to download and run scripts that others have developed. These individuals are generally not as interested in attacking specific targets, but instead simply want to find any organization that may not have patched a newly discovered vulnerability for which the script kiddie has located a script to exploit. It is hard to estimate how many of the individuals performing activities such as probing networks or scanning individual systems are part of this group, but it is undoubtedly the fastest growing group and at least 85 to 90 percent of the "unfriendly" activity occurring on the Internet is probably carried out by these individuals.

At the next level are those people who are capable of writing scripts to exploit known vulnerabilities. These individuals are much more technically competent than script kiddies and they account for an estimated 8 to 12 percent of malicious Internet activity. At the top end of this spectrum are those highly technical individuals, often referred to as **elite hackers**, who not only have the ability to write scripts that exploit vulnerabilities but who also are capable of discovering new vulnerabilities. This group is the smallest of the lot, however, for at most only 1 to 2 percent of them are responsible for intrusive activity.

Insiders

It is generally acknowledged by security professionals that insiders are more dangerous in many respects than outside intruders. The reason for this is simple—insiders have the access and knowledge necessary to cause immediate damage to an organization. Most security is designed to protect against outside intruders and thus lies at the boundary between the organization and the rest of the world. Insiders may actually already have all the access they need to perpetrate criminal activity such as fraud. In addition to unprecedented access, insiders also frequently have knowledge of the security systems in place and will be better able to avoid detection.

Employees are not the only insiders that organizations need to be concerned with. There are often a number of other individuals who have physical access to facilities. Custodial crews will frequently have unescorted access throughout the facility, often when nobody else is around. Other individuals, such as contractors or partners, may not only have physical access to the organization's facilities but may also have access to computer systems and networks.

Criminal Organizations

As businesses became increasingly reliant upon computer systems and networks, and as the amount of financial transactions conducted via the Internet increased, it was inevitable that criminal organizations would eventually turn to the electronic world as a new target to exploit. Criminal activity on the Internet at its most basic is no different than criminal activity in the physical world. Fraud, extortion, theft, embezzlement, and forgery all take place in the electronic environment.

One difference between criminal groups and the "average" hacker is the level of organization that criminal elements may employ in their attack. Criminal groups may have more money to spend on accomplishing the criminal activity and are willing to spend extra time accomplishing the task provided the level of reward at the conclusion is great enough. With the tremendous amount of money that is exchanged via the Internet on a daily basis, the level of reward for a successful attack is high enough to interest criminal elements. Attacks by criminal organizations can fall into the **structured threat** category, which is characterized by a greater amount of planning, a longer period of time to conduct the activity, more financial backing to accomplish it, and possibly corruption of, or collusion with, insiders.

Terrorists and Information Warfare

As nations have increasingly become dependent on computer systems and networks, the possibility that these essential elements of society might become a target for organizations or nations determined to adversely affect another nation became a reality. Many nations today have developed to some extent the capability to conduct **information warfare**. There are several definitions for information warfare, but a simple one is that it is warfare conducted against the information and information processing equipment used by an adversary. In practice, this is a much more complicated subject since information may not only be the target of an adversary, it may also be used as a weapon. Whatever definition you use, information warfare falls into the **highly structured threat** category. This type of threat is characterized by a much longer period of preparation (years is not uncommon), tremendous financial backing, and a large and organized group of attackers. The threat may not only include attempts to subvert insiders but might also consist of attempts to plant individuals inside of a potential target in advance of a planned attack.

An interesting aspect of information warfare is the list of possible targets available. We have grown accustomed to the idea that, during war, military forces will target opposing military forces but will generally attempt to destroy as little civilian infrastructure as possible. In information warfare, military forces are certainly still a key target, but much has been written about other targets, such as the various infrastructures that a nation relies on for its daily existence. Water, electricity, oil and gas refineries and distribution, banking and finance and telecommunications—all fall into the category of *critical infrastructures* for a nation. **Critical infrastructures** are those whose loss would have severe repercussions on the nation. With countries relying so heavily on these infrastructures, it is inevitable that they would be viewed as valid targets during conflict. Given how dependent these infrastructures are on computer systems and networks, it is also inevitable that these same computer systems and networks may be targeted for a cyber attack in an information war.

Another interesting aspect of information warfare is the potential list of attackers. As mentioned, several countries are currently capable of conducting this type of warfare. Nations, however, are not the only ones that can conduct information, or cyber, warfare. Terrorist organizations can also accomplish this. Such groups fall into the category of highly structured threats since they too are willing to conduct long-term operations, have in some cases tremendous financial support, and often have a large following. Reports out of Afghanistan related stories of soldiers and intelligence officers finding laptop computers formerly owned by members of Al Qaeda that contained information about various critical infrastructures in the United States. This showed that terrorist organizations were not only considering targeting such infrastructures, but were doing so at an unexpected level of sophistication.

Security Trends

The biggest change that has occurred in security over the last 30 years has been the change in the computing environment from large mainframes to a highly interconnected network of much smaller systems (smaller is a relative term here since the computing power of desktop computers exceeds the power of many large mainframes of 30 years ago). What this has meant for security is a switch from an environment where everything was fairly contained and people operated in a closed environment to one in which access to a computer can occur from almost anywhere on the planet. This has, for obvious reasons, greatly complicated the job of the security professional.

The type of individual who attacks a computer system or network has also evolved over the last 30 years. There was, of course, the traditional intelligence service operator paid by a particular country to obtain secrets from other government computer systems. These people still exist. What has increased dramatically is the number of non-affiliated intruders. As discussed earlier, the rise of the "script kiddie" has greatly multiplied the number of individuals who probe organizations looking for vulnerabilities to exploit. This is actually the result of another recent trend: as the level of sophistication of attacks has increased, the level of knowledge necessary to exploit vulnerabilities has decreased.

This is due to the number of automated tools that have been created which allow even novice attackers to exploit highly technical and complex vulnerabilities. The resulting increase in network attacks has been reflected in a number of different studies conducted by various organizations in the industry.

One of the best-known security surveys is the joint survey conducted annually by the Computer Security Institute (CSI) and the FBI (this survey can be obtained from www.gocsi.com). The respondents, who normally number around 500, come from all walks of life: government, academia, and industry. Over the last several years (since 2000), the number of organizations that have reported unauthorized use of their computer systems has slowly been declining (from 70 percent in 2000 to 56 percent in 2003). At the same time, the number of organizations that have reported attacks over Internet connections has increased (from 59 percent in 2000 to 78 percent in 2003). Those citing independent hackers as a likely source of attacks have also increased (from 77 percent in 2000 to 82 percent in 2003). The two most frequent types of attacks—viruses and insider abuse—have remained constant.

One of the most interesting and oft-repeated statistics from the survey is the average loss experienced by organizations due to such incidents. With the exception of Denial-of-Service attacks and telecommunications fraud, all categories showed a steady increase from 2000 through 2002, but then sharply declined in 2003. The average loss as a result of theft of proprietary information, for example, hit a high of $6.57 million in 2002 but was only $2.70 million in 2003. Financial fraud plunged from $4.63 million in 2002 to $328,000 in 2003. While it is tempting to assume that this means we, as a community, are becoming more secure (and there is indeed some indication that organizations are doing a better job at securing their systems), the reality is that these figures reflect the difficulty in quantifying the actual state of Internet security and of producing accurate results. While we all like to use figures such as those from the CSI/FBI survey, the truth of the matter is that these numbers likely don't accurately portray the state of current security. They are, however, the only numbers we have.

Avenues of Attack

There are two general reasons a particular computer system is attacked: either it is specifically targeted by the attacker, or it is an opportunistic target. In the first case, the attacker has chosen the target not because of the hardware or software the organization is running but for another reason, perhaps a political reason. An example of this type of attack would be an individual in one country attacking a government system in another. Alternatively, the attacker may be targeting the organization as part of a **hacktivist** attack. An example, in this case, might be an attacker who defaces the web site of a company that sells fur coats because the attacker feels using animals this way is unethical. Perpetrating some sort of electronic fraud is another reason a specific system might be targeted. Whatever the reason, an attack of this nature is decided upon before the hardware and software of the organization is known.

The second type of attack, an attack against a target of opportunity, is conducted against a site that has hardware or software that is vulnerable to a specific exploit. The attackers, in this case, are not targeting the organization; they have instead learned of a vulnerability and are simply looking for an organization with this vulnerability that they can exploit. This is not to say that an attacker might not be targeting a given sector and looking for a target of opportunity in that sector, however. For example, an attacker may desire to obtain credit card or other personal information and may search for any exploitable company with credit card information in order to carry out the attack.

Targeted attacks are more difficult and take more time than attacks on a target of opportunity. The latter simply relies on the fact that with any piece of widely distributed software, there will almost always be somebody who has not patched the system as they should have.

The Steps in an Attack

The steps an attacker takes in attempting to penetrate a targeted network are similar to the ones that a security consultant performing a penetration test would take. The attacker will need to gather as much information about the organization as possible. There are numerous ways to do this, including studying the organization's own web site, looking for postings on newsgroups, or consulting resources such as the Securities and Exchange Commission's (SEC's) EDGAR web site (www.sec.gov/edgar.shtml). A number of different financial reports are available through the EDGAR web site that can provide information about an organization that is useful for an attack—particularly a social engineering attack. The type of information that the attacker wants includes IP addresses, phone numbers, names of individuals, and what networks the organization maintains.

Typically, the first step in the technical part of an attack is to determine what target systems are available and active. This is usually done with a **ping sweep**, which simply sends a "ping" (an ICMP echo request) to the target machine. If the machine responds, it is reachable. The next step is often to perform a **port scan**. This will help identify which ports are open, thus giving an indication of which services may be running on the target machine. Determining the operating system that is running on the target machine, as well as specific application programs, follows along with determining the services that are available. Various techniques can be used to send specifically formatted packets to the ports on a target system to view the response. Often this response provides clues as to which operating system and specific application is running on the target system. Once this is done, the attacker would have a list of possible target machines, the operating system running on them, and some specific applications or services to target.

Up until this point, the attacker has simply been gathering the information needed to take the next step: an actual attack on the target. Knowing the operating system and services on the target helps the attacker decide which tools to use in the attack.

Numerous web sites provide information on the vulnerabilities of specific application programs and operating systems. This information is valuable to administrators, since they need to know what problems exist and how to patch them. In addition to information about specific vulnerabilities, some sites may also provide tools that can be used to exploit the vulnerabilities. An attacker can search for known vulnerabilities and tools that exploit them, download the information and tools, and then use them against a site. If the administrator for the targeted system has not installed the correct patch, the attack may be successful; if the patch has been installed, the attacker will move on to the next possible vulnerability. If the administrator has installed all of the appropriate patches so that all known vulnerabilities have been addressed, the attacker may have to resort to a brute-force attack, which involves guessing a userid and password combination. Unfortunately, this type of attack, which could be easily prevented, sometimes proves successful.

This discussion of the steps in an attack is by no means complete. There are many different ways a system can be attacked. This, however, is the general process: gathering as much information about the target as possible (using both electronic and non-electronic means), gathering information about possible exploits based on the information about the system, and then systematically attempting to use each exploit. If the exploits don't work, other less system-specific attacks may be attempted.

Minimizing Possible Avenues of Attack

Understanding the steps an attacker will take enables you to limit the exposure of your system and minimize those avenues an attacker might possibly exploit.

The first step an administrator can take to reduce possible attacks is to ensure that all patches for the operating system and applications are installed. Many security problems that we read about, such as viruses and worms, exploit known vulnerabilities for which patches exist. The reason such malware caused so much damage in the past was that administrators did not take the appropriate actions to protect their systems.

The second step an administrator can take is to limit the services that are running on the system. As mentioned earlier, only using those services that are absolutely needed does two things: it limits the possible avenues of attack (those services with vulnerabilities that can be exploited), and it reduces the number of services the administrator has to worry about patching in the first place. This is one of the important first steps any administrator should take to secure a computer system.

Another strategy to minimize possible avenues of attack is to provide as little information on your organization and its computing resources as possible. Since the attacker is after information, don't make it easy to obtain.

Types of Attacks

There are a number of ways that a computer system or network can be attacked (this topic will be covered in greater detail in Chapter 15). If successful, the attack may produce one of the following: a loss of confidentiality where information is disclosed to individuals not authorized to see it, a loss of integrity where information is modified by individuals not authorized to change it, or a loss of availability where information or the systems processing it are not available for use by authorized users when they need them.

Chapter Review

Chapter Summary

After reading this chapter and completing the exercises, you should understand the following regarding security trends.

Security Problems

- Fifty years ago, few people had access to a computer system or network and securing them was a relatively easy matter.

- There are many different ways to attack computers and networks to take advantage of what has made shopping, banking, investment, and leisure pursuits a simple matter of "dragging and clicking" for many people.

- The different types of electronic crime fall into two main categories: crimes in which the computer was the target of the attack, and incidents in which the computer was a means of perpetrating a criminal act.

- There are a number of different threats to security, including viruses and worms, intruders, insiders, criminal organizations, terrorists, and information warfare conducted by foreign countries.

- The biggest change that has occurred in security over the last 30 years has been the change in the computing environment from large mainframes to a highly interconnected network of much smaller systems.

- One significant trend observed over the last several years has been the increase in the number of non-affiliated intruders as opposed to attacks by organized "hacking groups," criminal organizations, or nations.

Avenues of Attack

- There are two general reasons a particular computer system is attacked: it is specifically targeted by the attacker, or it is a target of opportunity.

- Targeted attacks are more difficult and take more time than attacks on a target of opportunity.

- The steps an attacker takes in attempting to penetrate a targeted network are similar to the ones that a security consultant performing a penetration test would take.

- A ping sweep simply sends a "ping" (an ICMP echo request) to the target machine.

- A port scan will help identify which ports are open, thus giving an indication of which services may be running on the targeted machine.

- Numerous web sites exist that provide information on vulnerabilities in specific application programs and operating systems.

- The first step an administrator can take to minimize possible attacks is to ensure that all patches for the operating system and applications are installed.

Key Terms

> Critical infrastructures *(9)*
> Elite hackers *(7)*
> Hacktivist *(10)*
> Highly structured threat *(8)*
> Information warfare *(8)*
> Ping sweep *(11)*
> Port scan *(11)*
> Script kiddies *(7)*
> Structured threat *(8)*
> Unstructured threat *(7)*

Key Terms Quiz

Use terms from the Key Terms list to complete the sentences that follow. Don't use the same term more than once. Not all terms will be used.

1. A(n) _____ is a threat characterized by a greater amount of planning, a longer period of time to conduct the activity, more financial backing to accomplish it, and the possible corruption of, or collusion with, insiders.

2. A hacker whose activities are motivated by a personal cause or position is known as a _____.

3. Infrastructures whose loss would have a severe detrimental impact on the nation are called _____.

4. _____ is warfare conducted against the information and information processing equipment used by an adversary.

5. A _____ simply sends a "ping" (an ICMP echo request) to the target machine.

6. A(n) _____ is a threat that is generally short-term in nature, does not involve a large group of individuals, does not have large financial backing, and does not generally include collusion with insiders.

7. _____ are the most technically competent individuals conducting intrusive activity on the Internet. They can not only exploit known vulnerabilities but are usually the ones responsible for finding those vulnerabilities.

8. A _____ helps identify which ports are open, thus giving an indication of which services may be running on the targeted machine.

9. _____ are individuals who do not have the technical expertise to develop scripts or discover new vulnerabilities in software but who have just enough understanding of computer systems to be able to download and run scripts that others have developed.

10. A(n) _____ is a threat characterized by a much longer period of preparation (years is not uncommon), tremendous financial backing, a large and organized group of attackers, and a large and organized group of attackers. It may include efforts to subvert insiders as well as plant individuals inside a potential target in advance of an attack.

Multiple-Choice Quiz

1. Which threats are characterized by possibly long periods of preparation (years is not uncommon), tremendous financial backing, a large and organized group of attackers, and attempts to subvert insiders or to plant individuals inside a potential target in advance of a planned attack?

   A. Unstructured threats

   B. Structured threats

   C. Highly structured threats

   D. Nation-state information warfare threats

2. Which of the following is an attempt to find and attack a site that has hardware or software that is vulnerable to a specific exploit?

   A. Target of opportunity attack

   B. Targeted attack

   C. Vulnerability scan attack

   D. Information warfare attack

3. Which of the following threats has not grown over the last decade as a result of increasing numbers of Internet users?

   A. Viruses

   B. Hackers

   C. Denial-of-Service attacks

   D. All of these have seen an increase over the last decade.

4. The rise of which of the following has greatly increased the number of individuals who probe organizations looking for vulnerabilities to exploit?

   A. Virus writers

   B. Script kiddies

   C. Hackers

   D. Elite hackers

5. Which of the following is generally viewed as the first Internet worm to have caused significant damage and to have "brought the Internet down"?

   A. Melissa

   B. The "Love Bug"

    C. The Morris Worm

    D. Code Red

6. Which of the following individuals convicted of various computer crimes was known for his ability to conduct successful social engineering attacks?

    A. Kevin Mitnick

    B. Vladamir Levin

    C. Timothy Lloyd

    D. David Smith

7. According to the CSI/FBI survey, which of the following is the only statistic to have shown a decrease in 2003?

    A. The number of organizations reporting the Internet as a point of attack.

    B. The number of organizations that have reported unauthorized use of their systems.

    C. The average loss as a result of theft of proprietary information.

    D. Both B and C

8. Which virus/worm was credited with reaching global proportions in less than ten minutes?

    A. Code Red

    B. The Morris Worm

    C. Melissa

    D. Slammer

9. The act of deliberately accessing computer systems and networks without authorization is generally known as:

    A. Computer intrusions

    B. Hacking

    C. Cracking

    D. Probing

10. What is the most common problem/threat an organization faces?

    A. Viruses/worms

    B. Script kiddies

    C. Hackers

    D. Hacktivists

11. Warfare conducted against the information and information processing equipment used by an adversary is known as:

    A. Hacking

    B. Cyber terrorism

    C. Information warfare

    D. Network warfare

12. An attacker who feels using animals to make fur coats is unethical and thus defaces the web site of a company that sells fur coats is an example of:

    A. Information warfare

    B. Hacktivisim

    C. Cyber crusading

    D. Elite hacking

13. Which of the following is not described as a critical infrastructure?

    A. Electricity (power)

    B. Banking and finance

    C. Telecommunications

    D. Retail stores

14. Criminal organizations would normally be classified as what type of threat?

    A. Unstructured

    B. Unstructured but hostile

    C. Structured

    D. Highly structured

15. Elite hackers don't account for more than what percentage of individuals conducting intrusive activity on the Internet?

    A. 1–2 percent

    B. 3–5 percent

    C. 7–10 percent

    D. 15–20 percent

Essay Questions

1. Reread the various examples of computer crimes at the beginning of this chapter. Categorize each as either a crime where the computer was either the target of the criminal activity or the computer was a tool in accomplishing the criminal activity.

2. Your boss has just heard about some "nefarious computer activities" called ping sweeps and port scans. He wants to know more about them and what the impact of these activities might be on your company. Write a brief description of what they are and include your assessment of whether this activity is something to worry about or not.

3. A friend of yours has just been hired by an organization as their security administrator. Your friend is a bit nervous about this new job and has come to you, knowing that you are taking a security class, to ask your advice on measures that can be taken that might help prevent an intrusion. What three things can you suggest that are simple but can tremendously help limit the possibility of an attack?

4. Discuss why insiders are considered such a threat to organizations?

5. Write a brief essay outlining what you learned from the security studies mentioned in the chapter.

Lab Projects

Lab Project 1.1

A number of different examples of computer crimes were discussed in this chapter. Similar activities seem to happen daily. Do a search on the Internet to see what other examples you can find. Try and obtain the most recent examples possible.

Lab Project 1.2

References to "script kiddies" were made frequently in this chapter. The implication was that it is easy today to perform certain types of activities because it is easy to find tools that allow you to perform them. *If* allowed at your school or by your ISP, perform a search of the Internet to see how easy it is to locate programs that will perform activities such as ping sweeps and port scans. What other types of security-related tools can you find?

General Security Concepts

Upon completion of this lesson, you will be able to:

- Define basic terminology associated with computer and information security
- Describe the basic approaches to computer and information security
- Describe various methods to implement access controls
- Identify and explain methods used to verify the identity and authenticity of an individual
- Describe some of the basic models of security used when implementing security in operating systems

In Chapter 1, we learned about some of the various threats that we, as security professionals, face on a daily basis. In this chapter, we start exploring the field of computer security.

Basic Security Terminology

The term **hacking** has been used frequently in the media. A *hacker* was once considered an individual who understood the technical aspects of computer operating systems and networks. Hackers were individuals you turned to when you had a problem and needed extreme technical expertise. Today, as a result of the media, the term is used more often to refer to individuals who attempt to gain unauthorized access to computer systems or networks. While some would prefer to use the terms *cracker* and *cracking* when referring to this nefarious type of activity, the terminology generally accepted by the public is that of hacker and hacking. A related term that may sometimes be seen is **phreaking**, which refers to the "hacking" of computers and systems used by the telephone company.

Security Basics

Computer security itself is a term that has many meanings and related terms. *Computer security* entails the methods used to ensure a system is secure. Subjects such as authentication and access controls must be addressed in broad terms of computer security. Seldom in today's world are computers not connected to other computers in networks. This then introduces the term *network security* to refer to the protection of the multiple computers and other devices that are connected together. Related to these two terms are two others: *information security* and *information assurance,* which place the focus of the security process not on the hardware and software being used but on the data that is processed by them. Assurance also introduces another concept, that of the availability of the systems and information when we want them.

Since the late 1990s, much has been seen in the media concerning computer and network security. Often the news is about a specific lapse in security, which has resulted in the penetration of a network or in the denial of service for a network. Over the last few years, the general public has become increasingly aware of its dependence on computers and networks and consequently has also become interested in the security of these same computers and networks.

As a result of this increased attention by the public, several new terms have become commonplace in conversations and print. Terms such as *hacking, virus, TCP/IP, encryption,* and *firewalls* are now frequently seen in mainstream news publications and have found their way into casual conversations. What was once the purview of scientists and engineers is now part of our everyday life.

With our increased daily dependence on computers and networks to conduct everything from making purchases at our local grocery store to driving our children to school (that new car you just bought is probably using a small computer to obtain peak engine performance), ensuring that computers and networks are secure has become of paramount importance. Medical information about each of us is probably stored in a computer somewhere. So is financial information and data relating to the types of purchases we make and store preferences (assuming you have and use a credit card to make purchases). Making sure that this information remains private is a growing concern to the general public, and it is one of the jobs of security to help with the protection of our privacy. Simply stated, computer and network security is now essential for us to function effectively and safely in today's highly automated environment.

The "CIA" of Security

Almost from its inception, the goal of computer security has been threefold: confidentiality, integrity, and availability—the "CIA" of security. The purpose of **confidentiality** is to ensure that only those individuals who have the authority to view a piece of information may do so. No unauthorized individual should ever be able to view data they are not entitled to. **Integrity** is a related concept but deals with the generation and modification of data. Only authorized individuals should ever be able to create or change (or delete) information. The goal of **availability** is to ensure that the data, or the system itself, is available for use when the authorized user wants it.

As a result of the increased use of networks for commerce, two additional security goals have been added to the original three in the CIA of security. **Authentication** deals with the desire to ensure that an individual is who they claim to be. The need for this in an online transaction is obvious. Related to this is **nonrepudiation**, which deals with the ability to verify that a message has been sent and received and that the sender can be identified and verified. The requirement for this capability in online transactions should also be readily apparent.

The Operational Model of Security

For many years, the focus of security was on prevention. If we could prevent somebody from gaining access to our computer systems and networks, then we assumed that we had obtained security. Protection was thus equated with prevention. While the basic premise of this is true, it fails to acknowledge the realities of the networked environment our systems are part of. No matter how well we seem to do in prevention technology, somebody always seems to find a way around our safeguards. When this happens, our system is left unprotected. What is needed is multiple prevention techniques and also technology to alert us when prevention has failed and to provide ways to address the problem. This results in a modification to our original security equation with the addition of two new elements—detection and response. Our security equation thus becomes:

$$\text{Protection} = \text{Prevention} + (\text{Detection} + \text{Response})$$

This is known as the **operational model of computer security**. Every security technique and technology falls into at least one of the three elements of the equation. Examples of the types of technology and techniques that represent each are depicted in Figure 2-1.

Security Principles

There are three ways an organization can choose to address the protection of its networks: ignore security issues, provide host security, and approach security at a network level. The last two, host and network security, have prevention as well as detection and response components.

If an organization decides to ignore security, it has chosen to utilize the minimal amount of security that is provided with its workstations, servers, and devices. No additional security measures will be implemented. Each "out of the box" system has certain security settings that can be configured, and they should be. To actually protect an entire network, however, requires work in addition to the few protection mechanisms that come with systems by default.

Host Security   **Host security** takes a granular view of security by focusing on protecting each computer and device individually instead of addressing protection of the network as a whole. When host security is used, each computer is relied upon to protect itself. If an organization decides to implement only host security and does not include network security, there is a high probability of introducing or overlooking vulnerabilities. Most environments are filled with different operating systems (Windows, UNIX, Linux, Macintosh), different versions of those operating systems, and different types of installed applications. Each operating system has security configurations that differ from other systems, and different versions of the same operating system may in fact have variations between them. Ensuring that every computer is "locked down" to the same degree as every other system in the environment can be overwhelming and often results in an unsuccessful and frustrating effort.

Protection =	Prevention	+	(Detection	+	Response)
	Access controls		Audit logs		Backups
	Firewalls		Intrusion detection systems		Incident response teams
	Encryption		Honeypots		Computer forensics

Figure 2-1   Sample technologies in the operational model of computer security

Host security is important and should always be addressed. Security, however, should not stop there, as host security is a complementary process to be combined with network security. If individual host computers have vulnerabilities embodied within them, then network security can provide another layer of protection that will hopefully stop any intruders getting that far into the environment. Topics covered in this book dealing with host security include: bastion hosts, host-based intrusion detection systems, antivirus software, and hardening of operating systems.

Network Security In some smaller environments, host security by itself may be an option, but as systems become connected into networks, security should include the actual network itself. In **network security**, an emphasis is placed on controlling access to internal computers from external entities. This control can be through devices such as routers, firewalls, authentication hardware and software, encryption, and intrusion detection systems (IDSs).

Network environments have a tendency to be unique entities because usually no two networks will have exactly the same number of computers, the same applications installed, the same number of users, the exact same configurations, or the same available servers. They will not perform the same functions or have the same overall architecture. Since networks have so many differences, there are many different ways that they can be protected and configured. This chapter covers some foundational approaches to network and host security. Each approach may be implemented in a myriad of ways.

Least Privilege

One of the most fundamental approaches to security is **least privilege**. This concept is applicable to many physical environments as well as network and host security. Least privilege means that a subject (which may be a user, application, or process) should have only the necessary rights and privileges to perform its task with no additional permissions. Limiting an object's privileges limits the amount of harm that can be caused, thus limiting an organization's exposure to damage. Users may have access to the files on their workstations and a select set of files on a file server, but no access to critical data that is held within the database. This rule helps an organization protect its most sensitive resources and helps ensure that whoever is interacting with these resources has a valid reason to do so.

Different operating systems and applications have different ways of implementing rights, permissions, and privileges. Before they are actually configured, an overall plan should be devised and standardized methods developed to ensure that a solid security baseline is actually implemented. For example, a company may want all of the Accounting employees, but no one else, to be able to access employee payroll and profit margin spreadsheets held on a server. The easiest way to implement this is to develop an Accounting group, put all Accounting employees in this group, and assign rights to the group instead of each individual person.

As another example, there may be a requirement to implement a hierarchy of administrators that perform different functions and require specific types of rights. Two people may be tasked with performing backups of individual workstations and servers; thus, they do not need administrative permissions with full access to all resources. Three people may be in charge of setting up new user accounts and password management, which means they do not need full, or perhaps any, access to the company's routers and switches. Once these lines are delineated, indicating what subjects require which rights and permissions, then it is much easier to configure settings to provide the least privileges for different subjects.

The concept of least privilege applies to more network security issues than just providing users with specific rights and permissions. When trust relationships are created, they should not be implemented in such a way that everyone trusts each other simply because it is easier. One domain should trust another for very specific reasons, and the implementers should have a full understanding of what the trust relationship allows between two domains. If one domain trusts another, do all of the users automatically become trusted, and can they thus easily access any and all resources on the other domain? Is this a good idea? Is there a more secure way of providing the same functionality? If a trusted relationship is implemented such that users in one group can access a plotter or printer that is available on only one domain, it might make sense to simply purchase another plotter so that other, more valuable or sensitive, resources are not accessible by the entire group.

Another issue that falls under the least privilege concept is the security context in which an application runs. All applications, scripts, and batch files run in the security context of a specific user on an operating system. They will execute with specific permissions as if they were a user. The application may be Microsoft Word and run in the space of a regular user, or it may be a diagnostic program that needs access to more sensitive system files and so must run under an administrative user account, or it may be a program that performs backups and so should operate within the security context of a backup operator. The crux of this issue is that programs should execute only in the security context that is needed for that program to perform its duties successfully. In many environments, people do not really understand how to make programs run under different security contexts or it just seems easier to have them all run under the administrator account. If attackers can compromise a program or service running under the administrative account, they have effectively elevated their access level and have much more control over the system and many more possibilities to cause damage.

Layered Security

A bank does not just protect the money that it stores only by using a vault. It has one or more security guards as a first defense to watch for suspicious activities and to secure the facility when the bank is closed. It may have monitoring systems that watch various activities that take place in the bank, whether involving customers or employees. The vault is usually located in the center of the facility, and thus there are layers of rooms or walls before arriving at the vault. There is access control, which ensures that the people entering the vault have to be given the authorization beforehand. And the systems, including manual switches, are connected directly to the police station in case a determined bank robber successfully penetrates any one of these layers of protection.

Networks should utilize the same type of **layered security** architecture. There is no 100 percent secure system, and there is nothing that is foolproof, so a single specific protection mechanism should never be solely relied upon. Every piece of software and every device can be compromised in some way, and every encryption algorithm can be broken, given enough time and resources. The goal of security is to make the effort of actually accomplishing a compromise more costly in time and effort than it is worth to a potential attacker.

As an example, consider the steps an intruder might have to take to access critical data held within a company's back-end database. The intruder will first need to penetrate the firewall and use packets and methods that will not be identified and detected by the intrusion detection system (more on these devices can be found in Chapter 8). The attacker will then have to circumvent an internal router performing packet filtering and possibly penetrate another firewall that is used to separate one internal network from another. From here, the intruder must break the access controls that are on the database, which means having to do a dictionary or brute-force attack to be able to authenticate to the database software. Once the intruder has gotten this far, the data still needs to be located within the database. This may in turn be complicated by the use of access control lists outlining who can actually view or modify the data. That is a lot of work.

This example illustrates the different layers of security many environments employ. It is important to implement several different layers because if intruders succeed at one layer, you want to be able to stop them at the next. The redundancy of different protection layers ensures that there is no one single point of failure pertaining to security. If a network used only a firewall to protect its assets, an attacker successfully able to penetrate this device would find the rest of the network open and vulnerable.

It is important that every environment have multiple layers of security. These layers may employ a variety of methods such as routers, firewalls, network segments, IDSs, encryption, authentication software, physical security, and traffic control. The layers need to work together in a coordinated manner so that one does not impede another's functionality and introduce a security hole. Security at each layer can be very complex, and putting different layers together can increase the complexity exponentially. Although having layers of protection in place is very important, it is also important to understand how these different layers interact either by working together or in some cases by working against each other.

One case of how different security methods can work against each other is exemplified when firewalls encounter encrypted network traffic. An organization may utilize encryption so that an outside customer communicating with a specific web server is assured that sensitive data being exchanged is protected. If this encrypted data is encapsulated within Secure Sockets Layer (SSL) packets and then is sent through a firewall, the firewall will not be able to read the payload information in the individual packets. This may enable the customer, or an outside attacker, to send malicious code or instructions through the SSL connection undetected. There are other mechanisms that can be introduced in these situations, such as designing web pages to accept information only in certain formats and having the web server parse through the data for malicious activity. The important piece is to understand the level of protection that each layer provides and how each level of protection can be affected by things that take place in other layers.

The layers usually are depicted starting at the top, with more general types of protection, and progressing downward through each layer, with increasing granularity at each layer as you get closer to the actual resource, as you can see in Figure 2-2. This is because the top-layer protection mechanism is responsible for looking at an enormous amount of traffic, and it would be overwhelming and cause too much of a performance degradation

Figure 2-2
Various layers
of security

if each aspect of the packet were inspected. Instead, each layer usually digs deeper into the packet and looks for specific items. Layers that are closer to the resource have to deal with only a fraction of the traffic that the top-layer security mechanism does, and thus it will not cause as much of a performance hit to look deeper and at more granular aspects of the traffic.

Diversity of Defense

Diversity of defense is a concept that complements the idea of various layers of security. It involves making different layers of security dissimilar so that even if attackers know how to get through a system making up one layer, they may not know how to get through a different type of layer that employs a different system for security.

If an environment has two firewalls that form a demilitarized zone (DMZ), for example, one firewall may be placed at the perimeter of the Internet and the DMZ. This firewall will analyze the traffic that is entering through that specific access point and will enforce certain types of restrictions. The other firewall may then be placed between the DMZ and the internal network. When applying the diversity of defense concept, you should set up these two firewalls to filter for different types of traffic and provide different types of restrictions. The first firewall, for example, may make sure that no FTP, SNMP, or Telnet traffic enters the network but allow SMTP, SSH, HTTP, and SSL traffic through. The second firewall may not allow SSL or SSH through and may interrogate SMTP and HTTP traffic to make sure that certain types of attacks are not part of that traffic.

Another type of diversity of defense is to use products from different vendors. Every product has its own security vulnerabilities that are usually known to experienced attackers in the community. A CheckPoint firewall has different security issues and settings than a Sidewinder firewall; thus different exploits can be used against them to crash them or compromise them in some fashion. Combining this type of diversity with the preceding example, you might utilize the CheckPoint firewall as the first line of defense. If attackers are able to penetrate it, they are less likely to get through the next firewall if it is one from another vendor, such as a Cisco PIX or Sidewinder firewall.

There is an obvious trade-off that must be considered before implementing diversity of security using different vendor products. Doing so usually also increases operational complexity, and security and complexity are seldom a good mix. When implementing products from more than one vendor, the staff has to know how to configure two different systems, the configuration settings will be totally different, the upgrades and patches will come out at different times and contain different changes, and the overall complexity of maintaining these systems may cause more headaches than security itself. This does not mean that you should not implement diversity of defense by installing products from different vendors; it just means that you should know the implications of this type of decision.

Security Through Obscurity

Another concept in security that should be discussed is the idea of *security through obscurity*. In this case, security is considered effective if the environment and protection mechanisms are confusing or supposedly not generally known. Security through obscurity uses the approach of protecting something by hiding it. Noncomputer examples of this concept include hiding your briefcase or purse if you leave it in the car so that it is not in plain view, hiding a house key under a doormat or in a planter, or pushing your favorite ice cream to the back of the freezer so that everyone else thinks it is all gone. The idea is that if something is out of sight, it is out of mind. This approach, however, does not provide actual protection of the object. Someone can still steal the purse by breaking into the car, lift the doormat and find the key, or dig through the items in the freezer to find your favorite ice cream. Security through obscurity may make someone work a little harder to accomplish a task, but it does not prevent anyone from eventually succeeding.

Similar approaches are seen in computer and network security when attempting to hide certain objects. A network administrator may, for instance, move a service from its default port to a different port so that others will not know how to access it as easily, or a firewall may be configured to hide specific information about the internal network in the hope that potential attackers will not obtain the information for use in an attack on the network.

In most security circles, security through obscurity is considered a poor approach, especially if it is the only approach to security. An organization can use security through obscurity measures to try to hide critical assets, but other security measures should also be employed to provide a higher level of protection. For example, if an administrator moves a service from its default port to a more obscure port, an attacker can still actually find this service; thus, a firewall should be used to restrict access to the service. Most people know that even if you do shove your ice cream to the back of the freezer, someone may eventually find it.

Keep It Simple

The terms security and complexity are often at odds with each other. This is because the more complex something is, the harder it is to understand, and you cannot truly secure something if you do not understand it. Another reason complexity is a problem within security is that it usually allows too many opportunities for something to go wrong. If an application has 4,000 lines of code, there are a lot fewer places for buffer overflows, for example, than in an application of two million lines of code.

As with any other type of technology or problem in life, when something goes wrong with security mechanisms, a troubleshooting process is used to identify the actual issue. If the mechanism is overly complex, identifying the root of the problem can be overwhelming if not nearly impossible. Security is already a very complex issue because there are so many variables involved, so many types of attacks and vulnerabilities, so many different types of resources to secure, and so many different ways of securing them. You want your security processes and tools to be as simple and elegant as possible. They should be simple to troubleshoot, simple to use, and simple to administer.

Another application of the principle of keeping things simple concerns the number of services that you allow your system to run. Default installations of computer operating systems often leave many services running. The keep-it-simple principle tells us to eliminate those that we don't need. This is also a good idea from a security standpoint because it results in fewer applications that can be exploited and fewer services that the administrator is responsible for securing. The general rule of thumb should be to always eliminate all nonessential services and protocols. This of course leads to the question, how do you determine whether a service or protocol is essential or not? Ideally, you should know what your computer system or network is being used for, and thus you should be able to identify those elements that are essential and activate only them. For a variety of reasons, this is not as easy as it sounds. Alternatively, a stringent security approach that one can take is to assume that no service is necessary (which is obviously absurd) and activate services and ports only as they are requested. Whatever approach is taken, there is a never-ending struggle to try to strike a balance between providing functionality and maintaining security.

Access Control

The term **access control** has been used to describe a variety of protection schemes. It is sometimes used to refer to all security features used to prevent unauthorized access to a computer system or network. In this sense, it may be confused with authentication. More properly, *access* is the ability of a subject (such as an individual or a process running on a computer system) to interact with an object (such as a file or hardware device). Authentication, on the other hand, deals with verifying the identity of a subject. To help understand the difference, consider the example of an individual attempting to log in to a computer system or network. *Authentication* is the process used to verify to the computer system or network that the individual is who they claim to be. The most common method to do this is through the use of a user ID and password. Once the individual has verified their identity, access controls regulate what the individual can actually do on the system. Just because a person is granted entry to the system, that does not mean that they should have access to all data the system contains.

To further illustrate, consider another example. When you go to your bank to make a withdrawal, the teller at the window will verify that you are indeed who you claim to be. This is usually done by asking you to provide some form of identification with your picture on it, such as your driver's license. You may also have to provide information such as your bank account number. Once the teller verifies your identity, you will have proved that you are a valid (authorized) customer of this bank. This does not, however, mean that you have the ability to view all information that the bank protects—such as your neighbor's balance. The teller will control what information, and funds, you may have access to and will grant you access only to that which you are authorized. In this example, your identification and bank account number serve as your method of authentication and the teller serves as the access control mechanism.

In computer systems and networks, there are several ways that access controls can be implemented. An *access control matrix* provides the simplest framework for illustrating the process. An example of an access control matrix is provided in Table 2-1. In this matrix, the system is keeping track of two processes, two files, and one hardware device. Process 1 can read both File 1 and File 2, but can write only to File 1. Process 1 cannot access Process 2, but Process 2 can execute Process 1. Both processes have the ability to write to the printer.

While simple to understand, the access control matrix is seldom used in computer systems because it is extremely costly in terms of storage space and processing. Imagine the size of an access control matrix for a large network with hundreds of users and thousands of files. The actual mechanics of how access controls are implemented in a system varies, though *Access Control Lists* (*ACLs*) are common. An ACL is nothing more than a list that contains the subjects that have access rights to a particular object. The list will identify not only the subject but the specific access that that subject has for the object. Typical types of access include read, write, and execute as indicated in our example access control matrix.

No matter what specific mechanism is used to implement access controls in a computer system or network, the controls should be based on a specific model of access. Several different models are discussed in security literature, including discretionary access control (DAC), mandatory access control (MAC), and role-based access control (RBAC).

Discretionary Access Control

Both **discretionary access control** and **mandatory access control** are terms originally used by the military to describe two different approaches to controlling what access an individual had on a system. As defined by the "Orange Book," a Department of Defense document that at one time was the standard for describing what constituted a trusted computing system, discretionary access controls are "a means of restricting access to objects based on the identity of subjects and/or groups to which they belong. The controls are discretionary in the sense that a subject with a certain access permission is capable of passing that permission (perhaps indirectly) on to any other subject." While this may appear to many to be typical "government-speak" and confusing, the principle is really rather simple. In systems that employ discretionary access controls, the owner

	Process 1	Process 2	File 1	File 2	Printer
Process 1	Read, write, execute		Read, write	Read	Write
Process 2	Execute	Read, write, execute	Read, write	Read, write	Write

Table 2-1   An Access Control Matrix

of an object can decide which other subjects may have access to the object and what specific access they may have. One common method to accomplish this is the permission bits used in UNIX-based systems. The owner of a file can specify what permissions (read/write/execute) members in the same group may have and also what permissions all others may have. Access control lists are another common mechanism used to implement discretionary access control.

Mandatory Access Control

A less frequently employed system for restricting access is mandatory access control. This system, generally used only in environments where different levels of security classifications exist, is much more restrictive of what a user is allowed to do. Again referring to the Orange Book, we can find a definition for mandatory access controls, which is "a means of restricting access to objects based on the sensitivity (as represented by a label) of the information contained in the objects and the formal authorization (i.e., clearance) of subjects to access information of such sensitivity." In this case, the owner or subject can't determine whether access is to be granted to another subject; it is the job of the operating system to decide. In MAC, the security mechanism controls access to all objects and individual subjects cannot change that access. The key here is the label attached to every subject and object. The label will identify the level of classification for that object and the level that the subject is entitled to. Think of military security classifications such as Secret and Top Secret. A file that has been identified as Top Secret (has a label indicating that it is Top Secret) may be viewed only by individuals with a Top Secret clearance. It is up to the access control mechanism to ensure that an individual with only a Secret clearance never gains access to a file labeled as Top Secret. Similarly, a user cleared for Top Secret access will not be allowed by the access control mechanism to change the classification of a file labeled as Top Secret to Secret or to send that Top Secret file to a user cleared only for Secret information. The complexity of such a mechanism can be further understood when you consider today's windowing environment. The access control mechanism will not allow a user to cut a portion of a Top Secret document and paste it into a window containing a document with only a Secret label. It is this separation of differing levels of classified information that results in this sort of mechanism being referred to as multilevel security. A final comment should be made: just because a subject has the appropriate level of clearance to view a document, that does not mean that they will be allowed to do so. The concept of "need to know," which is a discretionary access control concept, also exists in mandatory access control mechanisms.

Role-Based Access Control

Access control lists can be cumbersome and can take time to administer properly. Another access control mechanism that has been attracting increased attention is **role-based access control** (RBAC). In this scheme, instead of each user being assigned specific access permissions for the objects associated with the computer system or network, that user is assigned a set of roles that the user may perform. The roles are in turn assigned the access permissions necessary to perform the tasks associated with the role. Users will thus be granted permissions to objects in terms of the specific duties they must perform—not of a security classification associated with individual objects.

Authentication

Access controls define what actions a user can perform or what objects a user can have access to. These controls assume that the identity of the user has been verified. It is the job of authentication mechanisms to ensure that only valid users are admitted. Described another way, authentication is using some mechanism to prove that you are who you claim to be. There are three general methods used in authentication. In order to verify your identity, you can provide:

- Something you know
- Something you have
- Something about you (something that you are)

The most common authentication mechanism is to provide something that only you, the valid user, should know. The most frequently used example of this is the common user ID (or username) and password. In theory, since you are not supposed to share your password with anybody else, only you should know your password, and thus by providing it you are proving to the system that you are who you claim to be. In theory, this should be a fairly decent method to provide authentication. Unfortunately, for a variety of reasons, such as the fact that people have a tendency to choose very poor and easily guessed passwords, this technique to provide authentication is not as reliable as it should be. Other authentication mechanisms are consequently always being developed and deployed.

Another method to provide authentication involves the use of something that only valid users should have in their possession. A physical-world example of this would be a simple lock and key. Only those individuals with the correct key will be able to open the lock and thus provide admittance to your house, car, office, or whatever the lock was protecting. A similar method can be used to authenticate users for a computer system or network (though the key may be electronic and may reside on a smart card or similar device). The problem with this technology is that people will lose their keys (or cards), which means they can't log in to the system and somebody else who finds the key may then be able to access the system, even though they are not authorized. To address this problem, a combination of the something-you-know/something-you-have methods is often used so that the individual with the key may also be required to provide a password or passcode. The key is useless unless you know this code. An example of this is the ATM card most of us carry. The card is associated with a personal identification number (PIN), which only you should know. Knowing the PIN without having the card is useless, just as having the card without knowing the PIN will also not provide you access to your account.

The third general method to provide authentication involves something that is unique about you. We are used to this concept in our physical world, where people's fingerprints, or a sample of their DNA, can be used to identify them. This same concept can be used to provide authentication in the computer world. The field of authentication that uses something about you or something that you are is known as *biometrics*. A number of different mechanisms can be used to accomplish this type of authentication, such as a voice print, a retinal scan, or hand geometry. All of these methods obviously require some additional hardware in order to operate.

While these three approaches to authentication appear to be easy to understand and in most cases easy to implement, authentication is not to be taken lightly, since it is such an important component of security. Potential attackers are constantly searching for ways to get past the system's authentication mechanism, and there have been some fairly ingenious methods employed to do so. Consequently, security professionals are constantly devising new methods, building on these three basic approaches, to provide authentication mechanisms for computer systems and networks.

Kerberos

Developed as part of MIT's project Athena, Kerberos is a network authentication protocol designed for a client/server environment. Taking its name from the three-headed dog of Greek mythology, Kerberos is designed to work across the Internet, an inherently insecure environment. Kerberos uses strong encryption so that a client can prove its identity to a server and the server can in turn authenticate itself to the client. The basis for authentication in a Kerberos environment is something known as a *ticket*. Tickets are granted by the *authentication server*, which is an entity trusted by both the client and the server the client wishes to access. The client can then present this ticket to the server to provide proof of identity. Since the entire session can be encrypted, this will eliminate the inherently insecure transmission of items such as a password that can be intercepted on the network. Since the tickets are time-stamped, attempting to reuse them will not be successful. To illustrate how the Kerberos authentication service works, think about the common driver's license. You have received a license that you can present to other entities to prove you are who you claim to be. Because these other entities trust the state the license was issued in, they will accept your license as proof of your identity. The state the license was issued in is analogous to the Kerberos authentication service. It is the trusted entity both sides rely on to provide valid identifications. This analogy is not perfect, because we all probably have heard of individuals who obtained a phony driver's license, but it serves to illustrate the basic idea behind Kerberos.

CHAP

CHAP, the Challenge Handshake Authentication Protocol, is used to provide authentication across a point-to-point link using the Point-to-Point Protocol (PPP). In this protocol, authentication after the link has been established is not mandatory. CHAP is designed to provide authentication periodically through the use of a challenge/response system sometimes described as a three-way handshake, as illustrated in Figure 2-3. The initial challenge (a randomly generated number) is sent to the client. The client uses a one-way hashing function to calculate what the response should be and then sends this back. The server compares the response with what it calculated the response should be. If it matches, communication continues. If the two values don't match, then the connection is terminated. This mechanism relies on a shared secret between the two entities so that the correct values can be calculated.

Certificates

Certificates are a method to establish authenticity of specific objects such as an individual's public key (more on this specific subject in Chapter 5) or downloaded software. A *digital certificate* is generally seen as an attachment to a message and is used to verify

Figure 2-3 The CHAP challenge/response sequence

that the message did indeed come from the entity it claims to have come from. The digital certificate can also contain a key that can be used to encrypt further communication. For more information on this subject, refer to Chapter 10.

Tokens

A **token** is a hardware device that can be used in a challenge/response authentication process. In this way, it functions as both a something-you-have and something-you-know authentication mechanism. There have been several variations on this type of device, but they all work on the same basic principles. The device has an LCD screen and may or may not have a numeric keypad. Devices without a keypad will display a password (often just a sequence of numbers) that changes at a constant interval, usually about every 60 seconds. When an individual attempts to log in to a system, they enter their own user identification number and then the number that is showing on the LCD. The system knows which device they have and is synchronized with it so that it will know the number that should have been displayed. Since this number is constantly changing, a potential attacker who is able to see the sequence will not be able to use it later, since the code will have changed. Devices with a keypad work in a similar fashion (and may also be designed to function as a simple calculator). The individual who wants to log in to the system will first type their personal identification number into the calculator. They will then attempt to log in. The system will then provide a challenge; the user must enter that challenge into the calculator and press a special function key. The calculator will then determine the correct response and display it. The user provides the response to the system they are attempting to log in to, and the system verifies that this is the correct response. Since each user has a different PIN, two individuals receiving the same challenge will have different responses. The device can also use the date or time as a variable for the response calculation so that the same challenge at different times will yield different responses, even for the same individual.

Multifactor

Multifactor is a term used to describe the use of more than one authentication mechanism at the same time. An example of this is the hardware token, which requires both a personal identification number or password and the device itself to determine the correct response in order to authenticate to the system. This means that both the something-you-have and something-you-know mechanisms are used as factors in verifying authenticity of the user. Biometrics are also often used in conjunction with a personal identification number so that they too can be used as part of a multifactor authentication scheme, in this case, something you are as well as something you know. The purpose of multifactor authentication is to increase the level of security, since more than one mechanism would have to be spoofed in order for an unauthorized individual to gain access to a computer system or network. The most common example of multifactor security is the common ATM card most of us have in our wallets.

Mutual Authentication

Mutual authentication is a term used to describe a process in which each side of an electronic communication verifies the authenticity of the other. We are used to the idea of having to authenticate ourselves to our Internet service provider (ISP) before we access the Internet, generally through the use of a user identification/password pair, but how do we actually know that we are really communicating with our ISP and not some other system that has somehow inserted itself into our communication (a man-in-the-middle attack). Mutual authentication would provide a mechanism for each side of a client/ server relationship to verify the authenticity of the other to address this issue.

Security Models

An important issue when designing the software that will operate and control secure computer systems and networks is the security model that the system or network will be based upon. The security model will implement the security policy that has been chosen and enforce those characteristics deemed most important by the system designers. For example, if confidentiality is considered paramount, the model should make certain no data is disclosed to unauthorized individuals. A model enforcing confidentiality may allow unauthorized individuals to modify or delete data as this would not violate the tenets of the model since the true values for the data would still remain confidential. Of course, this model may not be appropriate for all environments. In some instances, the unauthorized modification of data may be considered a more serious issue than its unauthorized disclosure. In such cases, the model would be responsible for enforcing the integrity of the data instead of its confidentiality. Choosing the model to base the design on is critical if you want to ensure that the resulting system accurately enforces the security policy desired.

Confidentiality Models

Data confidentiality has generally been the chief concern of the military. For instance, the U.S. military encouraged the development of the **Bell-LaPadula security model** to address data confidentiality in computer operating systems. This model was especially useful in designing multilevel security systems that implemented the military's hierarchical security scheme which included levels of classification such as *Unclassified, Confidential, Secret,* and *Top Secret.* Similar classification schemes can be used in industry, where classifications might include *Publicly Releasable, Proprietary,* and *Company Confidential.*

The Bell-LaPadula security model employed both mandatory and discretionary access control mechanisms when implementing its two basic security principles. The first of these principles is called the **Simple Security Rule**, which stated that no subject (such as a user or a program) could read information from an object (such as a file) with a security classification higher than that possessed by the subject itself. This means that the system must prevent a user with only a Secret clearance, for example, from reading a document labeled Top Secret. This rule is often referred to as the "no-read-up" rule.

The second security principle enforced by the Bell-LaPadula security model is known as the ***-property** (pronounced "star property"). This principle stated that a subject could write to an object only if its security classification was less than or equal to the object's security classification. This means that a user with a Secret clearance could write to a file with a Secret or Top Secret classification but could not write to a file with only an Unclassified classification. This at first may appear to be a bit confusing since this principle would allow users to write to files that they were not allowed to view, thus they could actually destroy files that they didn't have the classification to see. This is true, but you have to recall that the Bell-LaPadula model is designed to enforce confidentiality, not integrity. Writing to a file that you don't have the clearance to view is not considered a confidentiality issue, it is an integrity issue.

Besides allowing a user to write to a file of equal or greater security classification, the *-property also doesn't allow a user to write to a file with a lower security classification. This too may also not be immediately understandable—after all, shouldn't a user with a Secret clearance, who can view a file marked Unclassified, be allowed to write to that file? The answer to this, from a security perspective, is "no." The reason again relates to wanting to avoid either accidental or deliberate security disclosures. The system is designed to make it impossible (hopefully) for data to be disclosed to those without the appropriate level to view it. Would it be possible for a user with a Top Secret clearance to either deliberately or accidentally write Top Secret information and place it in a file marked Secret? If so, a user with only a Secret security clearance could then access this file and view the Top Secret information. Thus, data would have been disclosed to an individual not authorized to view it. This is what the system should protect against and is the reason for what is known as the "no-write-down" rule.

Not all environments are more concerned with confidentiality than integrity. In a financial institution, for example, viewing somebody's bank balance is an issue, but a greater issue would be the ability to actually modify that balance. In environments where integrity is more important, a different model than the Bell-LaPadula security model is needed.

Integrity Models

The Bell-LaPadula model was developed in the early 1970s but was found to be insufficient for all environments. As an alternative, Biba studied the integrity issue and developed what is called the **Biba security model** in the late 1970s. Additional work was performed in the 1980s that led to the Clark-Wilson security model, which also places its emphasis on integrity rather than confidentiality.

The Biba Security Model

In the Biba model, instead of security classifications, *integrity levels* are used. A principle of integrity levels is that data with a higher integrity level is believed to be more accurate or reliable than data of a lower integrity level. Integrity levels indicate the level of "trust" that can be placed in information at the different levels. Integrity levels differ from security levels in another way—they limit the modification of information as opposed to the flow of information.

An initial attempt at implementing an integrity-based model was captured in what is referred to as the **Low-Water-Mark policy**. This policy in many ways is the opposite of the *-property in that it prevents subjects from writing to objects of a higher integrity level. The policy also contains a second rule that states the integrity level of a subject will be reduced if it reads an object of a lower integrity level. The reason for this is that if the subject then uses data from that object, the highest the integrity level can be for a new object created from it is the same level of integrity of the original object. In other words, the amount of trust you can place in data formed from data at a specific integrity level can not be higher than the level of trust you have in the subject creating the new data object, and the level of trust you have in the subject can only be as high as the level of trust you had in the original data. The final rule contained in the Low-Water-Mark policy states that a subject can only execute a program if the program's integrity level is equal to or less than the integrity level of the subject. This will ensure that data modified by a program will only have the level of trust (integrity level) that can be placed in the individual who executed the program.

While the Low-Water-Mark policy certainly will prevent unauthorized modification of data, it has the unfortunate side effect of eventually lowering the integrity levels of all subjects to the lowest level on the system (unless the subject always views files with the same level of integrity). This is because of the second rule, which lowers the integrity level of the subject after accessing an object of a lower integrity level. There is no way specified in the policy to ever raise the subject's integrity level back to its original value. A second policy, known as the **Ring policy**, addresses this issue by allowing any subject to read any object without regard to the object's level of integrity and without lowering the subject's integrity level. This, unfortunately, can lead to a situation where data created by a subject after reading data of a lower integrity level could end up having a higher level of trust placed upon it then it should.

The Biba security model implements a hybrid of the Ring and Low-Water-Mark policies. Biba's model in many respects is the opposite of the Bell-LaPadula model in that what it enforces are "no-read-down" and "no-write-up" policies. It also implements a third rule that prevents subjects from executing programs of a higher level. The Biba security model thus addresses the problems mentioned with both the Ring and Low-Water-Mark policies.

The Clark-Wilson Security Model

The **Clark-Wilson security model** takes an entirely different approach than the Biba and Bell-LaPadula models, using transactions as the basis for its rules. It defines two levels of integrity only: constrained data items (CDI) and unconstrained data items (UDI).

CID data is subject to integrity controls while UDI data is not. The model then defines two types of processes: integrity verification processes (IVP), which ensure that CDI data meet integrity constraints (to ensure the system is in a valid state) and transformation processes (TP), which change the state of data from one valid state to another. Data in this model can not be modified directly by a user, it must be changed by trusted transformation processes, access to which can be restricted (thus restricting the ability of a user to perform certain activities). It is useful to return to the banking account balance used earlier to describe the need for integrity-based models. In the Clark-Wilson model, the account balance would be a CDI because its integrity is a critical function for the bank. A client's color preference for their checkbook is not a critical function and would be considered a UDI. Since the integrity of account balances is of extreme importance, changes to a person's balance must be accomplished through the use of a TP. Ensuring that the balance is correct would be the duty of an IVP. Only certain employees of the bank should have the ability to modify an individual's account, so we can control this by limiting the number of individuals who have the authority to execute TPs that result in account modification. Certain very critical functions may actually be split into multiple TPs to enforce another important principle, *separation of duties*. This limits the authority any one individual has so that multiple individuals will be required for certain critical functions.

Chapter Review

Chapter Summary

After reading this chapter and completing the exercises, you should understand the following regarding the basics of security, security terminology, and security models.

Security Basics and Terminology

- Information assurance and information security place the security focus on the information and not the hardware or software used to process it.

- The original goal of computer and network security was to provide confidentiality, integrity, and availability—the "CIA" of security.

- As a result of the increased reliance on networks for commerce, authentication and nonrepudiation have been added to the original CIA of security.

- The operational model of computer security tells us that protection is provided by prevention, detection, and response.

- Host security focuses on protecting each computer and device individually instead of addressing protection of the network as a whole.

- Least privilege means that an object should have only the necessary rights and privileges to perform its task, with no additional permissions.

- Diversity of defense is a concept that complements the idea of various layers of security. It means to make the layers dissimilar so that if one layer is penetrated, the next layer can't also be penetrated using the same method.

- Access is the ability of a subject to interact with an object. Access controls are those devices and methods used to limit which subjects may interact with specific objects.

- Authentication mechanisms ensure that only valid users are provided access to the computer system or network.

- The three general methods used in authentication involve the users providing either something they know, something they have, or something unique about them (something they are).

- Multifactor is a term used to describe the use of more than one authentication mechanism at the same time.

- Mutual authentication is a term used to describe a process in which each side of an electronic communication verifies the authenticity of the other.

Security Models

- Security models enforce the chosen security policy.

- There are two basic categories of models: those that ensure confidentiality and those that ensure integrity.

- Bell-LaPadula is a confidentiality security model whose development was prompted by the demands of the U.S. military and its security clearance scheme.

- The Bell-LaPadula security model enforces "no-read-up" and "no-write-down" rules to avoid the deliberate or accidental disclosure of information to individuals not authorized to receive it.

- The Biba security model is an integrity-based model that, in many respects, implements the opposite of what the Bell-LaPadula model does—that is, "no-read-down" and "no-write-up" rules.

- The Clark-Wilson security model is an integrity-based model designed to limit the processes an individual may perform as well as require that critical data be modified only through specific transformation processes.

Key Terms

*-property *(34)*
Access controls *(27)*
Authentication *(20)*
Availability *(20)*
Bell-LaPadula security model *(33)*

Biba security model *(34)*
Certificates *(31)*
Clark-Wilson security model *(35)*
Confidentiality *(20)*
Discretionary access control *(28)*
Diversity of defense *(25)*
Hacker *(19)*
Host security *(21)*
Integrity *(20)*
Layered security *(23)*
Least privilege *(22)*
Low-Water-Mark policy *(35)*
Mandatory access control *(28)*
Multifactor *(32)*
Mutual authentication *(33)*
Network security *(22)*
Nonrepudiation *(20)*
Operational model of computer security *(21)*
Phreaking *(19)*
Ring policy *(35)*
Role-based access control (RBAC) *(29)*
Simple Security Rule *(34)*
Token *(32)*

Key Terms Quiz

Use terms from the Key Terms list to complete the sentences that follow. Don't use the same term more than once. Not all terms will be used.

1. _____ is a term used to describe a process in which each side of an electronic communication verifies the authenticity of the other.

2. The _____ security model is an integrity-based security model that bases its security on control of the processes that are allowed to modify critical data referred to as constrained data items.

3. The security principle used in the Bell-LaPadula security model that states that no subject can read from an object with a higher security classification is called _____.

4. The principle in which a subject has only the necessary rights and privileges to perform its task, with no additional permissions, is called _____.

5. _____ is the principle in security whose goal it is to ensure that data is only modified by individuals who are authorized to change it.

6. _____ is the term used to refer to the _____ of computers and systems used by the telephone company.

7. _____ is the process used to ensure that an individual is who they claim to be.

8. A hardware device that can be used in a challenge/response authentication process is called a(n) _____.

9. _____ is a means of restricting access to objects based on the sensitivity of the information contained in the objects, and the formal authorization of subjects to access information of such sensitivity.

10. _____ is a method to establish authenticity of specific objects such as an individual's public key or downloaded software.

Multiple-Choice Quiz

1. What is the most common form of authentication used?

   A. Smart card

   B. Tokens

   C. Username/password

   D. Retinal scan

2. The CIA of security includes…

   A. Confidentiality, integrity, authentication

   B. Confidentiality, integrity, availability

   C. Certificates, integrity, availability

   D. Confidentiality, inspection, authentication

3. The security principle used in the Bell-LaPadula security model that states that no subject can read from an object with a higher security classification is the…

   A. Simple Security Rule

   B. Ring policy

   C. Mandatory access control

   D. *-property

4. CHAP is the…

   A. Certificate Handling Application Program

   B. Controlling Hierarchical Access Protocol

   C. Confidentiality Handling Application Protocol

   D. Challenge Handshake Authentication Protocol

5. Which of the following is true about multifactor authentication?

    A. It incorporates both access-control and authentication mechanisms into a single device.

    B. It employs more than one method to verify authenticity.

    C. It allows for multiple users to utilize the same account but with different user IDs.

    D. It bases access decisions on the role of the user, as opposed to using the more common user ID/password combination.

6. The Bell-LaPadula security model is an example of a security model that is based on:

    A. The integrity of the data

    B. The availability of the data

    C. The confidentiality of the data

    D. The authenticity of the data

7. What was described in the chapter as being essential in order to implement mandatory access controls?

    A. Smart cards

    B. Certificates

    C. Security classifications and labels

    D. Mutual authentication mechanisms

8. In which access control mechanism does the operating system determine the access control permissions for subjects?

    A. Mandatory

    B. Role-based

    C. Discretionary

    D. Token-based

9. The problem with the Low-Water-Mark policy is that it...

    A. Is aimed at ensuring confidentiality and not integrity

    B. Could ultimately result in all subjects having the integrity level of the least trusted object on the system

    C. Could result in the unauthorized modification of data

    D. Does not adequately prevent users from viewing files they are not entitled to

10. What was the basis for authentication used in Kerberos?

    A. Ticket

    B. Token

C. Certificate

D. Biometrics

11. The alternative proposed by some to replace the term "hacker" (a reference to individuals who attempt to gain unauthorized access to computer systems or networks) is…

A. Lamer

B. Phreaker

C. Script kiddie

D. Cracker

12. The ability of a subject to interact with an object describes…

A. Availability

B. Access

C. Integrity

D. Role-based authentication

13. Information security places the focus of security efforts on:

A. The operating system and hardware it runs on

B. The application programs interacting with the user

C. The system (or security) administrators

D. The data the systems store and process

14. In role-based access control:

A. The user is responsible for providing both a password and a digital certificate in order to access the system or network.

B. A set of roles that the user may perform will be assigned to each user, thus controlling what the user can do and what information they may access.

C. The focus is on the confidentiality of the data the system protects and not its integrity.

D. Authentication and nonrepudiation are the central focus.

15. The security principle whose goal it is to ensure that information is only modified by those who have authority to change it is called…

A. Authenticity

B. Availability

C. Integrity

D. Confidentiality

Essay Quiz

1. Your boss has just received a sales pitch from a vendor pushing an operating system that implements mandatory access controls. Write a paragraph that will explain to him the differences between discretionary and mandatory access controls. Which one of these would you consider more restrictive, and why?

2. Your company has decided to increase the authentication security by requiring remote employees to use a security token as well as a password to log on to the network. The employees are grumbling about the new requirements because they don't want to have to carry around the token with them and don't understand why it's necessary. Write a brief memo to the staff to educate them on the general ways that authentication can be performed. Then explain why your company has decided to use security tokens in addition to passwords.

3. The new CEO for your company just retired from the military and wants to use some of the same computer systems and security software she used while with the military. Write an explanation for her to describe the reasons that confidentiality-based security models are not adequate for all environments. Provide at least two examples of environments where it is not sufficient.

4. Describe why the concept of "security through obscurity" is generally considered a bad principle to rely on. Provide some real-world examples of where you have seen this principle used.

5. Write a brief essay describing the principle of least privilege and how it can be employed to enhance security. Provide at least two examples of environments in which it can be used for security purposes.

Lab Projects

Lab Project 2.1

In an environment familiar to you (your school or where you work, for example) determine what different layers of security are employed. Discuss whether you think they are sufficient and whether the principle of diversity of defense has also been used.

Lab Project 2.2

Pick an operating system that enforces discretionary access controls and determine how it is implemented in that system.

Operational/ Organizational Security

Upon completion of this lesson, the learner will be able to:

- Describe the various operational aspects to security in an organization
- Describe physical security components that can used to protect computers and networks
- Explain how social engineering is used as a means to gain access to computers and networks and how an organization should deal with it
- Explain how the growing use of wireless cellular technology has impacted data transmission and how factors such as location affect our ability to secure it
- Describe how the use of shielding technology can prevent disclosure through electronic emanations
- Describe various fire suppression systems designed to limit the damage caused by fires

Recall from Chapter 2 the operational model of computer security. The model described the various components in computer and network security. Specifically, the operational model of computer security stated that:

Protection = Prevention + (Detection + Response)

Security Operations in Your Organization

Prevention technologies are designed to keep individuals from being able to gain access to systems or data they are not authorized to use. Originally, this was the sole approach to security. Eventually we learned that in an operational environment, prevention was extremely difficult and relying on prevention technologies alone was not sufficient. This led to the rise of technologies to detect and respond to events that occur when prevention failed. Together, these form the operational model for computer security.

Prevention technologies are static in the sense that they are put in place and generally left alone. This is not to say that they are not periodically updated as needed, but they are generally designed to serve in some way as a static barrier to intruders. Detection and response technologies, on the other hand, are dynamic in the sense that they acknowledge that security is an ongoing process. Systems and networks are constantly changing. They therefore need to be constantly monitored. Monitoring the operation of the various components that make up your security perimeter is an essential part of any organization's security program.

Policies, Procedures, Standards, and Guidelines

An important part of any organization's approach to implementing security are the policies, procedures, standards, and guidelines that are established to detail what users and administrators should be doing to maintain the security of the systems and network. Collectively, these documents provide the guidance needed to determine how security will be implemented in the organization. Given this guidance, the specific technology and security mechanisms required can be planned for.

Policies are high-level, broad statements of what the organization wants to accomplish. They are made by management when laying out the organization's position on some issue. **Standards** are mandatory elements regarding the implementation of a policy. They are accepted specifications providing specific details on how a policy is to be enforced. Some standards may be externally driven. Regulations for banking and financial institutions, for example, may require certain security measures be taken by law. Other standards may be set by the organization for its own goals. **Guidelines** are recommendations relating to a policy. The key term in this case is recommendation—guidelines are not mandatory steps. **Procedures** are the step-by-step instructions on how to implement policies in the organization. They describe exactly how employees are expected to act in a given situation or to accomplish a specific task.

Just as the network itself constantly changes, the policies, procedures, and guidelines should be living documents that are periodically evaluated and changed if necessary. The constant monitoring of the network and the periodic review of the relevant documents are part of the process that is the operational model. When applied to policies, this process results in what is known as the policy life cycle. This operational process roughly consists of four steps:

1. Plan (adjust)
2. Implement
3. Monitor
4. Evaluate

The first step is to plan for security in your organization. In this step, you develop the policies, procedures, and guidelines that will be implemented and design the security components that will protect your network. Once these are designed and developed, you can implement the plans. Part of the implementation of any policy, procedure, or guideline will be an instruction period where those who will be affected by the change or introduction of this new document will learn about its contents. Next, you monitor to ensure that both the hardware and the software as well as the policies, procedures, and guidelines are effective in securing your systems. Finally, you evaluate the effectiveness of the security measures you have in place. This step may include a vulnerability assessment and penetration test of your system to ensure the security is adequate. After evaluating your security posture, you begin again with step one, this time adjusting the security mechanisms you have in place, and then continue with this cyclical process.

The Security Perimeter

The discussion to this point has not included any mention of the specific technology used to enforce operational and organizational security or a description of the various

Figure 3-1

Basic diagram of an organization's network

components that constitute the organization's security perimeter. If the average administrator were asked to draw a diagram depicting the various components of their network, the diagram would probably look something like Figure 3-1.

This diagram includes the major components typically found in a network. There is some connection to the Internet. This connection will generally have some sort of protection attached to it such as a firewall. An intrusion detection system will also often be part of the security perimeter for the organization. This may be on the inside of the firewall, or the outside, or it may in fact be on both sides, the specific location depending on the company and what they are more concerned with preventing (i.e., the insider threat or external threats). Beyond this security perimeter is the corporate network. This is obviously a very simple depiction—an actual network may have numerous subnets and extranets—but the basic components are present. Unfortunately, if this were the diagram provided by the administrator to show the organization's basic network structure, the administrator would have missed a very important component. A more astute administrator would provide a diagram more like Figure 3-2.

Figure 3-2

A more complete diagram of an organization's network

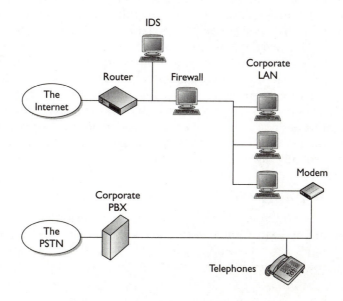

This diagram includes the other important network found in every organization, the telephone network that is connected to the public switched telephone network (PSTN), otherwise known as the phone company. The organization may or may not have any authorized modems, but the savvy administrator would realize that because the potential exists for unauthorized modems, the telephone network must be included as a possible source of access for the network. When considering the policies, procedures, and guidelines needed to implement security for the organization, both networks need to be considered.

While Figure 3-2 provides a more comprehensive view of the various components that need to be protected, it is still incomplete. Most experts will agree that the biggest danger to any organization does not come from external attacks but rather from the insider—a disgruntled employee or somebody else who may have physical access to the facility. Given physical access to an office, the knowledgeable attacker will quickly be able to find the information needed to gain access to the organization's computer systems and network. Consequently, every organization also needs security policies, procedures, and guidelines that cover physical security, and every security administrator should be concerned with these as well. While physical security will probably not fall under the purview of the security administrator, the operational state of the organization's physical security measures is just as important as many of the other network-centric measures.

Physical Security

Physical security consists of all mechanisms used to ensure that physical access to the computer systems and networks is restricted to only authorized users. Additional physical security mechanisms may be used to provide increased security for especially sensitive systems such as servers and devices such as routers, firewalls, and intrusion detection systems. When considering physical security, access from all six sides should be considered. Not only should the security of obvious points of entry be examined, such as doors and windows, but the walls themselves as well as the floor and ceiling should also be considered. Is there a false ceiling with tiles that can be easily removed? Do the walls extend to the actual ceiling or only to this false ceiling? Is there a raised floor? Do the walls extend to the actual floor, or do they stop at the raised floor? How are important systems situated? Do the monitors face away from windows, or could the activity of somebody at a system be monitored? Who has access to the facility? What type of access control is there, and are there any guards? Who is allowed unsupervised access to the facility? Is there an alarm system or security camera that covers the area? What procedures govern the monitoring of these and the response should unauthorized activity be detected? These are just some of the numerous questions that need to be asked when examining the physical security surrounding a system.

Access Controls

The purpose of physical access controls is the same as that of computer and network access controls—you want to restrict access to those who are authorized to have it. Similarly, physical access controls can be based on something the individual has, something they know, or something they are.

The most common physical access control device, which has been around in some form for centuries, is a lock. Combination locks represent an access control device that depends on something the individual knows (the combination). Locks with keys depend on something the individual has (the key). Each of these has certain advantages and disadvantages. Combinations don't require any extra hardware, but they must be remembered (which means individuals may write them down—a security vulnerability in itself) and are hard to control. Anybody who knows the combination may provide it to somebody else. Key locks are simple and easy to use, but the key may be lost, which means another has to be made or the lock rekeyed. Keys may also be copied and can be hard to control the dissemination of. Newer locks replace the traditional key with a card that must be passed through a reader or placed against it. The individual may also have to provide a personal access code, thus making this form of access both a something-you-know and something-you-have method. In addition to locks on doors, other common physical security devices include video surveillance and even simpler access control logs (sign-in logs). While sign-in logs don't provide an actual barrier, they do provide a record of access, and when used in conjunction with a guard who verifies an individual's identity, they can dissuade potential adversaries from attempting to gain access to a facility.

Another common access control mechanism is a human security guard. Many organizations employ a guard to provide an extra level of examination of individuals wanting to gain access. Other devices are limited to their designed function. A human guard can apply common sense to situations that might have been unexpected. Having security guards also addresses the common practice of piggybacking, where an individual follows another person closely to avoid having to go through the access control procedures. For example, if one employee enters the combination to a door and then opens it, another individual might follow quickly behind before the door closes to avoid having to enter the combination. A security guard checking each individual's identification would eliminate this problem.

Biometrics

Access controls that utilize something you know (e.g., combinations) or something you have (e.g., keys) are not the only methods to limit facility access to authorized individuals. A third approach is to utilize something unique about the individual, their fingerprints, for example, to identify them. Unlike the other two methods, the something you are, known as **biometrics**, does not rely on the individual to either remember something or to have something in their possession. Biometrics is a more sophisticated access control approach and is also more expensive. Other methods to accomplish biometrics include handwriting analysis, retinal scans, iris scans, voiceprints, hand geometry, and facial geometry.

Biometrics can be used to control access to computer systems and networks as well as to serve as a physical access control device. Used for physical access control, however, this approach allows for methods that are not generally used in biometric access control for computer systems and networks. Hand geometry, for example, requires a fairly large device. This can easily be placed outside of a door to control access to the room but would not be as convenient to control access to a computer system, since a reader would need to be placed with each computer or at least with groups of computers. In a mobile environment where laptops are being used, a device such as a hand geometry reader would be unrealistic.

To add an additional layer of security, biometrics are normally used in conjunction with another method. An individual might, for example, be required to also provide a personal access code or to pass a card through a reader, and thus the individual would also need something you have and something you know. While it may seem at first that nothing else should be needed besides a biometric access control, the biometric devices currently in use are not 100 percent accurate and have been known to allow access to individuals who were not authorized. This is the reason for the additional something-you-know or something-you-have method to supplement the biometric device.

It should be pointed out that all forms of authentication have weaknesses that can be exploited. It is for this reason that "strong authentication" or "two-factor authentication" is often used. These methods use two of the three different types of authentication (something you have, know, or are) to provide two levels of security. Which two are used in combination depends on a number of factors, including user acceptance, budget, and the exact level of security the organization is trying to obtain.

Physical Barriers

An even more common security feature than locks (using the term device to describe them is unusual) is a physical barrier. Physical barriers help implement the physical-world equivalent of layered security. The outermost layer of physical security should contain the more public activities. A guard at a gate in a fence, for example, would be visible by all who happen to pass by. As you progress through the layers, the barriers and security mechanisms should become less public to make it more difficult for observers to determine what mechanisms are in place. Signs are also an important element in security, as they announce to the public what areas are public and which are private. In addition to walls and fences, open space can also serve as a barrier. While this may at first seem to be an odd statement, consider the use of large areas of open space. For an intruder to cross this open space takes time—time in which they are vulnerable and their presence may be discovered. In today's environment in which terrorist attacks have become more common, areas that may be considered a possible target for terrorist activity should take additional precautions. In addition to open space, which is necessary to lessen the effect of explosions, concrete barriers that will stop vehicles from getting too close to facilities should also be used. It is not necessary for these to be unsightly concrete walls; many facilities have placed large, round concrete circles, filled them with dirt, and then planted flowers and other plants to construct a large, immovable planter.

Social Engineering

Social engineering is the process of convincing an authorized individual to provide confidential information or access to an unauthorized individual. Social engineering takes advantage of what continually turns out to be the weakest point in our security perimeter—the humans. Kevin Mitnick, a convicted cybercriminal turned security consultant, once stated "Don't rely on network safeguards and firewalls to protect your information. Look to your most vulnerable spot. You'll usually find that vulnerability lies in your people." In 2000 after being released from jail, Mitnick testified before Congress and spoke on several other occasions about social engineering and how effective it is. He stated that he "rarely had to resort to a technical attack" because of how easily information and access could be obtained through social engineering.

Individuals who are attempting to social-engineer some piece of information generally rely on two aspects of human nature. First, most people generally want to help somebody who is requesting help. Second, people generally want to avoid confrontation. The knowledgeable social engineer may call a help desk pretending to be a new employee needing help to log on to the organization's network. By doing so, valuable information may be obtained as to the type of system or network that is being employed. After making this call, a second call may be made that uses the information from the first call to provide background for the second call so that the next individual the attacker attempts to obtain information from will not suspect it is an unauthorized individual asking the questions. This works because people generally will assume that somebody is who they claim to be, especially if they have information that would be known by the individual they claim to be.

If the pleasant approach doesn't work, a more aggressive approach may be attempted. People will normally want to avoid unpleasant confrontations and will also not want to get into trouble with their superiors. An attacker, knowing this, may attempt to obtain information by threatening to go to the individual's supervisor or by claiming that they are working for somebody who is high up in the organization's management structure. Because employees want to avoid both a confrontation and a possible reprimand, they may provide the information requested even though they may realize that it is against the organization's policies or procedures.

The goal of social engineering is to gradually obtain the pieces of information necessary to make it to the next step. This is done repeatedly until the ultimate goal is reached. If social engineering is such an effective means of gaining unauthorized access to data and information, how can it be stopped? The most effective means is through the training and education of users, administrators, and security personnel. All employees should be instructed in the techniques that attackers might use and trained to recognize when a social engineering attack is being attempted. One important aspect of this training is for employees to recognize the type of information that should be protected and also how seemingly unimportant information may be combined with other pieces of information to potentially divulge sensitive information. This is known as *data aggregation.*

Environment

Environmental issues may not at first seem to be of a security concern, but when considering the availability of a computer system or network, they must be taken into consideration. Environmental issues include items such as heating, ventilation, and air conditioning (HVAC) systems, electrical power, and the "environments of nature." **HVAC** systems are used to maintain the comfort of an office environment. A few years back, they were also critical for the smooth operation of computer systems that had low tolerances for humidity and heat. Today's systems are much more tolerant, and the limiting factor is now often the human user. One interesting aspect of HVAC systems is that they themselves are often computer controlled and frequently provide remote access via telephone connections. These connections should be protected in a similar manner to computer modems, or else attackers may locate them and change the HVAC settings for an office or building.

Electrical power is obviously an essential requirement for computer systems and networks. Electrical power is subject to momentary surges and disruption. Surge protectors are needed to protect sensitive electronic equipment from fluctuations in voltage. **Uninterruptible power supplies** (UPSs) should be considered for critical systems so that a loss of power will not halt processing. The size of the batteries associated with a UPS will determine the amount of time that it can operate before it too loses power. Many sites ensure sufficient power to provide administrators the opportunity to cleanly bring the system or network down. For installations that require continual operations, even in the event of a power outage, electric generators may be purchased that can automatically start when a loss of power is detected. These systems may take a few seconds to start before they reach full operation, so a UPS should also be considered to smooth the transition between normal and backup power.

The frequency of natural disasters is a contributing factor that must be considered when making contingency processing plans for an installation. In an area that experiences frequent electric storms, for example, power surge protectors and UPSs are an absolute must. Frequent storms and floods may require devices that can sense water building up in a facility to warn of pending problems. Frequent hurricanes, earthquakes, and tornadoes in an area may require reinforced facilities to protect important processing equipment. All of these provide reasons for not only having an active program to ensure frequent backup of critical data, but off-site storage as well. Off-site storage limits the chance that a natural disaster affecting one area will result in the total loss of the organization's critical data. When considering backup and contingency plans, it is also important to consider a backup processing location in case a disaster not only destroys the data at the organization's primary site but all processing equipment as well.

Fire Suppression

According to the Fire Suppression Systems Association, 43 percent of businesses closed as a result of a fire never reopen. An additional 29 percent will fail within three years of the event. The ability to respond to a fire quickly and effectively is thus critical to the long-term success of any organization. Addressing potential fire hazards and vulnerabilities has long been a concern of organizations in their risk analysis process. The goal should obviously be never to have a fire, but in the event that one does occur, it is important that mechanisms are in place to limit the damage the fire can cause.

Water-Based Fire Suppression Systems

Water-based fire suppression systems have long been, and still are today, the primary tool to address and control structural fires. With the amount of electrical equipment found in today's office environment and since, for obvious reasons, this equipment does not react well to large applications of water, it is important to know what to do with equipment if it does become subjected to a water-based sprinkler system. The 1992 National Fire Protection Association Standard 75 on Electronic Computer/Data Processing Equipment outlines measures that can be taken to minimize the damage to electronic equipment exposed to water. This guidance includes these suggestions:

- Open cabinet doors, remove side panels and covers, and pull out chassis drawers to allow water to run out of equipment.
- Set up fans to move room-temperature air through the equipment for general drying. Move portable equipment to dry air-conditioned areas.
- Use compressed air at no higher than 50 psi to blow out trapped water.
- Use handheld dryers on lowest setting to dry connectors, backplane wirewraps, and printed circuit cards.

 CAUTION Keep the dryer well away from components and wires. Overheating of electrical components can cause permanent damage.

- Use cotton-tipped swabs for hard-to-reach places. Lightly dab the surfaces to remove residual moisture. Do not use cotton-tipped swabs on wirewrap terminals.
- Water-displacement aerosol sprays containing Freon-alcohol mixtures are effective as a first step in drying critical components. Follow up with professional restoration as soon as possible.

 NOTE The preceding list provides useful, albeit somewhat dated, guidance. Users will probably not see wirewrap terminals, and other compounds are now available to replace the Freon-alcohol mixture described. Overall, however, the guidance is still sound and provides a useful starting point to begin cleanup operations from.

Even if these guidelines are followed, damage to the systems may have already occurred. Since water is so destructive to electronic equipment, not only because of the immediate problems of electronic shorts to the system but also because of longer-term corrosive damage water can cause, alternative fire suppression methods have been sought. One of the more common alternative methods used was Halon-based systems.

Halon-Based Fire Suppression Systems
A fire needs fuel, oxygen, and high temperatures for the chemical combustion to occur. If you remove any of these, the fire will not continue. Halon interferes with the chemical combustion present in a fire. Even though Halon production was banned in 1994, a number of these systems still exist today. They were originally popular because Halon will mix quickly with the air in a room and will not cause harm to computer systems. Halon is also dangerous to humans, especially when subjected to extremely hot temperatures (such as might be found during a fire), when it can degrade into other toxic chemicals.

As a result of these dangers, and also because Halon has been linked with the issue of ozone depletion, Halon is no longer allowed to be used in new fire suppression systems. It is important to note that under the Environmental Protection Agency (EPA) rules that mandated no further production of Halon, existing systems were not required to be destroyed. Replacing the Halon in a discharged system, however, will be a problem, since only existing stockpiles of Halon may be used and the cost is becoming prohibitive. For this reason, many organizations are switching to alternative solutions. These alternatives are known as Clean Agent Fire Suppression Systems, since they not only provide fire suppression capabilities but also protect the contents of the room including people, documents, and electronic equipment. Examples of clean agents include carbon dioxide, Argon, Inergen, and FM200 (heptafluoropropane).

Clean-Agent Fire Suppression Systems

The use of Carbon Dioxide (CO_2) as a fire suppression agent has been known for a long time. The Bell Telephone Company used portable CO_2 extinguishers in the early part of the twentieth century. Carbon Dioxide extinguishers attack all three necessary elements for a fire to occur. CO_2 will displace oxygen so that the amount of oxygen remaining is insufficient to sustain the fire. It also provides some cooling in the fire zone and will also reduce the concentration of "gasified" fuel. Argon extinguishes fire by lowering the oxygen concentration below the 15 percent level required for combustible items to burn. Argon systems are designed to reduce the oxygen content to about 12.5 percent, which is below the 15 percent needed for the fire but is still above the 10 percent required by the EPA for human safety. INERGEN is composed of three gases: 52 percent nitrogen, 40 percent argon, and 8 percent carbon dioxide. In a manner similar to pure Argon systems, INERGEN systems reduce the level of oxygen to about 12.5 percent, which is sufficient for human safety but not sufficient to sustain a fire. Another chemical used to phase out Halon is FE-13, or trifluoromethane. This chemical was originally developed as a chemical refrigerant and works to suppress fires by raising the total heat capacity of the environment. FE-13 is gaseous and leaves behind no residue that would harm equipment and is considered safe to use in occupied areas.

Handheld Fire Extinguishers

Automatic fire suppression systems designed to discharge when a fire is detected are not the only systems you should be aware of. If a fire can be caught and contained before the automatic systems discharge, it can mean significant savings to the organization in terms of both time and equipment costs (including the recharging of the automatic system). Handheld extinguishers are common in offices, but the correct use of them must be understood or disaster can occur. There are four different types of fire, as shown in Table 3-1. Each type of fire has its own fuel source and method for extinguishing it. Type A systems, for example, are designed to extinguish fires with normal combustible material as the fire's source. Water can be used in an extinguisher of this sort, since it is effective against fires of this type. Water, as we've discussed, is not appropriate for fires involving wiring or electrical equipment. Using a type A extinguisher against an electrical fire will not only be ineffective but can result in additional damage. Some extinguishers are designed to be effective against more than one

Class of Fire	Type of Fire	Examples of Combustible Material	Examples of Suppression Methods
A	Common Combustibles	Wood, paper, cloth, plastics	Water or dry chemical
B	Combustible Liquids	Petroleum products, organic solvents	CO_2 or dry chemical
C	Electrical	Electrical wiring and equipment, power tools	CO_2 or dry chemical
D	Flammable Metals	Magnesium, titanium	Copper metal or sodium chloride

Table 3-1   Types of Fire and Suppression Methods

type of fire, such as the common ABC fire extinguishers. This is probably the best type of system to have in a data processing facility. All fire extinguishers should be easily accessible and should be clearly marked. Before anybody uses an extinguisher, they should know what type of extinguisher it is and what the source of the fire is. When in doubt, get out and let the fire department handle the situation.

Fire Detection Devices

Going hand-in-hand with fire suppression are fire detection devices (fire detectors). Detectors can be useful because some may be able to detect a fire in its very early stages before a fire suppression system is activated, and they can potentially sound a warning. This warning could provide employees the opportunity to address the fire before it becomes serious enough for the fire suppression equipment to kick in.

There are several different types of fire detectors. One type, of which there are two varieties, is activated by smoke. The two forms smoke detectors come in are ionization and photoelectric. A photoelectric detector is good for potentially providing advance warning of a smoldering fire. This type of device monitors an internal beam of light. If something degrades the light, for example by obstructing it, the detector assumes it is something like smoke and the alarm sounds. An ionization style of detector uses an ionization chamber and a small radioactive source to detect fast-burning fires. Shown in Figure 3-3, the chamber consists of two plates, one with a positive charge and one with a negative charge. Oxygen and nitrogen particles in the air become "ionized" (an ion is freed from the molecule). The freed ion, which will have a negative charge, will be attracted to the positive plate, and the remaining part of the molecule, now with a positive charge, will be attracted to the

Figure 3-3

An ionization chamber for an ionization type of smoke detector

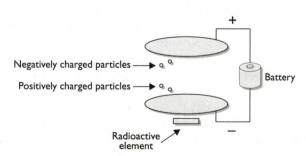

negative plate. This movement of particles creates a very small electric current that the device measures. Smoke will inhibit this process, and the resulting drop in current will be detected and an alarm sounded. Both of these devices are often referred to as smoke detectors, and combinations of both varieties are possible. For more information on smoke detectors, see http://home.howstuffworks.com/smoke2.htm.

Another type of fire detector is activated by heat. These devices come in two varieties. Fixed-temperature or fixed-point devices activate if the temperature in the area ever exceeds some predefined level. Rate-of-rise or rate-of-increase temperature devices activate when there is a sudden increase in local temperature that may indicate the beginning stages of a fire. Rate-of-rise sensors can provide an earlier warning but are also responsible for more false warnings.

A third type of detector is flame activated. This type of device relies on the flames from the fire to provide a change in the infrared energy that can be detected. Flame-activated devices are generally more expensive than the other two types but can frequently detect a fire sooner.

Wireless

When someone talks about wireless communication, they generally are referring to cellular phones. These devices have become ubiquitous in today's modern office environment. A cell phone network consists of the phones themselves, the cells with their accompanying base stations that they are used in, and the hardware and software that allow them to communicate. The base stations are made up of antennas, receivers, transmitters, and amplifiers. The base stations will communicate with those phones that are currently in the geographical area that is serviced by that station. As a person travels across town, they may exit and enter multiple cells. The stations must conduct a handoff to ensure continuous operation for the phone. As the individual moves toward the edge of a cell, a mobile switching center will notice the power of the signal beginning to drop. It will check to see if another cell has a stronger signal for your phone (cells frequently overlap) and if so, it can switch operation to this new cell and base station. All of this is done without the user ever knowing that they have moved from one cell to another.

Cellular telephones are a tremendous technology providing a great service to modern businesses and individuals. Cell phone technology is advancing, and more and more phones are being used for more than just voice communication. Phones can also provide messaging capability, some even provide Internet connectivity, and some can be used as digital cameras.

Wireless technology can also be used for networking. There are two main standards for wireless network technology. **Bluetooth** is designed as a short range (approximately 10 meters) Personal Area Network (PAN) cable replacement technology that may be built into a variety of devices such as mobile phones, PDAs, and laptop computers. The idea is to create low-cost wireless technology so that many different devices can communicate with each other. Bluetooth is also interesting because, unlike other wireless technology, it is designed so that devices can talk directly with each other without having to go through a central device (such as the base station described previously). This is known as peer-to-peer communication.

The other major wireless standard is the **IEEE 802.11** set of standards, which is well suited for the local area network environment. 802.11 networks can operate in either an ad hoc peer-to-peer fashion or an infrastructure mode, which is more common. In this mode, computers with 802.11 network cards will communicate with a wireless access point. This access point connects to the network so that the computers communicating with it are essentially also connected to the network.

In an office environment, wireless networks are tremendously useful, as they free the user to take their computer anywhere in the building (as long as an access point is nearby). If a new employee joins the company, wire cable does not need to be strung in order to connect them; instead, they simply need to be within transmission distance to an access point.

While wireless networks are very useful in today's modern office (and home), they are not without their security problems. Access points are generally placed throughout a building so that all employees can access the corporate network. The transmission and reception areas covered by access points are not easily controlled. Consequently, many publicly accessible areas might fall into the range of one of the organization's access points, and thus the corporate network may become vulnerable to attack. Wireless networks are designed to incorporate some security measures, but all too often the networks are set up without security enabled, and serious security flaws exist in the 802.11 design.

Electromagnetic Eavesdropping

In 1985, a paper by Wim van Eck of the Netherlands described what became known as the van Eck phenomenon. In the paper, van Eck described how eavesdropping on what was being displayed on monitors could be accomplished by picking up and then decoding the electromagnetic interference produced by the monitors. With the appropriate equipment, the exact image of what is being displayed can be re-created some distance away. While the original paper discussed emanations as they applied to video display units (monitors), the same phenomenon applies to other devices such as printers and computers as well.

This phenomenon had actually been known about for quite some time before van Eck published his paper. The U.S. Department of Defense used the term **TEMPEST** (Transient Electromagnetic Pulse Emanation Standard) as both a description for a program in the military to control these electronic emanations from electrical equipment and the actual process for controlling the emanations. One of the simplest ways to protect against equipment being monitored in this fashion is to put enough distance between the target and the attacker. The emanations can be picked up from only a limited distance. If the physical security for the facility is sufficient to put enough space between the equipment and publicly accessible areas that the signals cannot be picked up, then the organization doesn't have to take any additional measures to ensure security.

A natural question to ask is, how prevalent is this form of attack? The equipment needed to perform electromagnetic eavesdropping is not readily available, but it would not cost an inordinate amount of money to produce it. The cost could certainly be afforded by any large corporation, and industrial espionage using such a device is a possibility. While there are no public records of this sort of activity being conducted, it is reasonable to assume that it can and may be taking place in large corporations and the government, especially in foreign countries.

Shielding

Distance is not the only way to protect against eavesdropping on electronic emanations. Devices can be shielded so that their emanations are blocked. In fact, there are three basic ways to prevent these emanations from being picked up by an attacker:

- Put the equipment beyond the point that the emanations can be picked up.
- Provide shielding for the equipment itself.
- Provide a shielded enclosure (such as a room) to put the equipment in.

All of these solutions can be costly. Acquiring enough property to provide the necessary distance needed to protect against an eavesdropper may be possible if the facility is in the country with lots of available land surrounding it. If, however, the organization is in the middle of a city, then purchasing additional property may be prohibitive. Indeed, for smaller organizations that occupy only a few offices or floors in a large office building, it would be impossible to acquire enough space.

In this case, the organization may resort to purchasing shielded equipment. A "TEMPEST approved" computer will cost at least double what a normal computer would cost. Shielding a room (in what is known as a Faraday cage) is also an extremely expensive endeavor. The cost of shielding is so substantial that in most cases it probably cannot be justified. It may be a better idea to carefully select the location you put your most sensitive equipment—maybe it is possible to protect these computers by putting them in the center of your organization and leaving the less-sensitive equipment in the areas closest to public areas.

Location

On several occasions, the careful placement of equipment has come up as a possible means to provide security. It has been said that the three most important factors in the success of most businesses are location, location, and location. While the same is not exactly true of security (location is not the most important element in this case), it certainly can play a contributing role. In the case of a wireless network, the location one picks to place the wireless access points can make it easier or harder for an attacker to access the network from a publicly accessible area. For electromagnetic emanations, location is also a contributing factor. By placing the most sensitive equipment deep inside the organization, enough space may be obtained to protect the equipment from eavesdropping. Location also plays a significant role in physical security, since some facilities will be easier to protect than others, depending on their proximity to other buildings and roads.

Chapter Review

Chapter Summary

After reading this chapter and completing the exercises, you should understand the following regarding operational and organizational security.

Security Operations in Your Organization

- Prevention technologies are designed to keep individuals from being able to gain access to systems or data they are not authorized to use.

- Previously in operational environments, prevention was extremely difficult and relying on prevention technologies alone was not sufficient. This led to the rise of technologies to detect and respond to events that occur when prevention failed.

- An important part of any organization's approach to implementing security are the policies, procedures, standards, and guidelines that are established to detail what users and administrators should be doing to maintain the security of the systems and network.

Physical Security

- Physical security consists of all mechanisms used to ensure that physical access to the computer systems and networks is restricted to only authorized users.

- The purpose of physical access controls is the same as that of computer and network access controls—you want to restrict access to those who are authorized to have it.

Social Engineering

- Social engineering is the process of convincing an authorized individual to provide confidential information or access to an unauthorized individual.

- Social engineering takes advantage of what continually turns out to be the weakest point in our security perimeter—human beings.

Environment

- Environmental issues are important to security because they can affect the availability of a computer system or network.

- Problems with electrical power and fire are two of the more common environmental conditions that should be considered.

Wireless

- There are two main standards for wireless network technology: Bluetooth and 802.11.

- Wireless networks have many security issues including the transmission and reception areas covered by access points which are not easily controlled and can thus provide easy network access for intruders.

Electromagnetic Eavesdropping

- With the appropriate equipment, the exact image of what is being displayed on a computer monitor can be re-created some distance away allowing eavesdroppers to view what you are doing.

- Providing a lot of distance between the system you wish to protect and the closest place an eavesdropper could be is one way to protect against eavesdropping on electronic emanations. Devices can also be shielded so that their emanations are blocked.

Location

- The careful placement of equipment can provide security for known security problems exhibited by wireless devices and that arise due to electronic emanations.

Key Terms

Biometrics *(47)*
Bluetooth *(54)*
Guidelines *(44)*
HVAC *(49)*
IEEE 802.11) *(55)*
Physical security *(46)*
Policies *(44)*
Procedures *(44)*
Social engineering *(48)*
Standards *(44)*
TEMPEST *(55)*
Uninterruptible power supplies *(50)*

Key Terms Quiz

Use terms from the Key Terms list to complete the sentences that follow. Don't use the same term more than once. Not all terms will be used.

1. _____ are high-level statements made by management laying out the organization's position on some issue.

2. The process of convincing an authorized individual to provide confidential information or access to an unauthorized individual is known as _____.

3. _____ are devices designed to provide power to essential equipment for a period of time when normal power is lost.

4. Access control mechanisms in which a physical characteristic, such as a fingerprint or the geometry of an individual's hand, is used to uniquely identify users are called _____.

5. A _____ is an accepted specification providing specific details on how a policy is to be enforced.

6. _____ is a wireless technology designed as a short range (approximately ten meters) Personal Area Network (PAN) cable replacement technology that may be built into a variety of devices such as mobile phones, PDAs, and laptop computers.

7. The military program to control electronic emanations from electrical equipment is called _____.

8. _____ are step-by-step instructions that describe exactly how employees are expected to act in a given situation or to accomplish a specific task.

9. The set of standards for wireless networks which are well suited for the local area network environment and whose normal mode is to have computers with network cards communicating with a wireless access point is _____.

10. _____ are recommendations relating to a policy that are not mandatory steps.

Multiple-Choice Quiz

1. Which type of fire extinguisher can be used for combustible liquids?

   A. Type A

   B. Type AB

   C. Type C

   D. Type D

2. Social engineering attacks work so well because the individual who is the target of the attempted attack:

   A. Is usually too busy with other things to worry about security.

   B. Often either genuinely wants to help or is trying to avoid a confrontation, depending on the specific approach the attacker is taking.

   C. Was specifically chosen by the attacker because they are new to the organization and can't tell that the story they are being fed is bogus.

   D. Knows the attacker.

3. A security feature even more common than a lock is a...

   A. Physical barrier

   B. Card reader

   C. Hand geometry reader

   D. Security guard

4. During which step of the policy life cycle does training of users take place?

   A. Plan

   B. Implement

C. Monitor

D. Evaluate

5. Which of the following would NOT be considered a clean-agent fire suppression component?

A. Argon

B. CO_2

C. Halon

D. Inergen

6. Why is Halon being replaced as a fire suppression agent in computer and networking facilities?

A. Halon production has been banned and its use regulated because it is considered an ozone-depletion agent.

B. Halon will cause electrical shorts when discharged, thus ruining electronic equipment.

C. Halon is a corrosive agent and will destroy sensitive electronic equipment.

D. Halon was found to not be effective in combating fires caused by electrical equipment.

7. What technique can be used to protect against electromagnetic eavesdropping (known as the van Eck phenomenon)?

A. Provide sufficient distance between the potential target and the nearest location an attacker could be.

B. Put the equipment that you are trying to protect inside a shielded room.

C. Purchase "TEMPEST approved" equipment.

D. All of the above.

8. Which fire detection device relies on the temperature in an area rising above some predefined level to activate it?

A. Smoke detectors

B. Rate-of-rise fire detectors

C. Fixed-temperature fire detectors

D. Flame-activated fire detectors

9. When should a human security guard be used for physical access control?

A. When other electronic access control mechanisms will not be accepted by employees

B. To avoid issues such as piggybacking, which can occur with electronic access controls

C. When other access controls are too expensive to implement

D. When the organization wants to enhance its image

10. What device should be used only by organizations to protect sensitive equipment from fluctuations in voltage?

   A. A surge protector

   B. An uninterruptible power supply

   C. A backup power generator

   D. A redundant array of in-line batteries (RAIB)

11. Which of the following is one of the major reasons security problems exist with wireless?

   A. Implementing security for wireless devices is cost prohibitive.

   B. Users of wireless devices constitute such a varied cross-section of the public that it is impossible to provide technology that all can understand.

   C. The frequency spectrum in which wireless is broadcast is such that it does not permit effective encryption to take place.

   D. The fact that wireless transmissions can often be picked up in areas outside of your organization.

12. Which statement is most accurate when describing the prevalence of electromagnetic eavesdropping?

   A. It is so difficult that it is not likely to occur at any level.

   B. It requires technical equipment that only governments and large corporations would likely purchase or develop. It is therefore possible, but how extensive it is, is unknown.

   C. The equipment required to perform it is easy to assemble and inexpensive. Examples of this sort of activity have been seen at all levels of corporate and government organizations.

   D. It is extremely common; the equipment can be assembled by hobbyists who can easily re-create the signals from any organization that they can get close enough to.

13. Biometrics are access controls that employ…

   A. Something physically unique about the individual.

   B. Something physical that the user has (such as a key).

   C. Something that the user knows.

   D. The location of the user.

14. What common network access point is often forgotten when considering network electronic perimeter defenses?

   A. Web sites which provide the largest presence from an electronic commerce standpoint

   B. An organization's Internet service provider (ISP)

   C. The Public Switched Telephone Network accessible via modems

   D. Extranets connected to corporate partners

15. Which of the following is a step-by-step set of instructions that describe exactly how employees are expected to act in a given situation or to accomplish a specific task?

   A. Policy

   B. Procedure

   C. Guideline

   D. Standard

Essay Quiz

1. Describe the difference between fire suppression and fire detection systems.

2. What are the different classes of fires that can occur? Describe and provide examples of each one.

3. Discuss why an "insider" is potentially more dangerous than an external attacker.

4. Why is social engineering such a successful form of attack?

5. Outline the various components that make up (or should make up) an organization's security perimeter. Which of these can be found in your organization (or school)?

Lab Projects

Lab Project 3.1

Make a tour of your building on campus. Record the location and type of fire extinguishers that you find. Is the type of extinguisher you found appropriate for your location? Why? What other fire detection and/or fire suppressions systems did you find in the building?

Lab Project 3.2

Describe the four steps of the policy life cycle. Obtain a policy from your organization (such as an acceptable-use or Internet usage policy). How are users informed of this policy? How often is it reviewed? How would changes to it be suggested and who would make decisions on whether the changes were accepted?

The Role of People in Security

Upon completion of this lesson, you will be able to:
- Define basic terminology associated with Social Engineering
- Describe a number of poor security practices that may put an organization's information at risk
- Describe methods attackers may use to gain information about an organization
- List and describe ways in which users can aid instead of detract from security

The operational model of computer security discussed in the previous chapter acknowledges that absolute protection of computer systems and networks is not possible and that we need to be prepared to detect and respond to attacks that were able to circumvent our security mechanisms. Another very basic fact that should be recognized is that technology alone will not solve the security problem. No matter how advanced the technology is, it will ultimately be deployed in an environment where humans exist. It is the human element that causes what can be our biggest problem. It is hard to compensate for all of the possible ways that humans can deliberately or accidentally cause security problems or circumvent our security mechanisms. Despite all of the technology, despite all of the security procedures we have in place, and despite all of the security training we may provide, somebody will invariably not do what they are supposed to and will create a vulnerability in an organization's security posture. This chapter discusses the human element and the role that people play in security—both the user practices that can aid in securing an organization and the vulnerabilities or holes in security that users can introduce.

People—A Security Problem

The operational model of computer security acknowledges that prevention technology is not sufficient to protect our computer systems and networks. There are a number of explanations for this, some of them technical, but one of the biggest reasons that prevention technologies are not sufficient is that every network and computer system has at least one human user.

Poor Security Practices

A significant portion of human-created security problems result from poor security practices. These poor practices may be individual practices where the user is not following established security policies or processes, or they may be caused by a lack of security policies, procedures, or training within the user's organization.

Password Selection

For many years, computer intruders have relied on users selecting poor passwords to help them gain unauthorized access to a system or network. If attackers could obtain a list of the users' names, chances were good chance they could eventually access the system. Users pick passwords that are easy for them to remember and what easier password could there be than the same sequence of characters that they use for their user ID? If a system had an account with the username of *jdoe*, a reasonable first guess of the account's password would be *jdoe*. If this didn't work, then variations on the same would be tried: *doej, johndoe, johnd,* or *eodj*. All of which would be reasonable possibilities.

If variations on the username did not yield the correct password, all was not lost—more information was simply needed. Users also frequently pick names of family members, pets, or favorite sports team. If the user lived in San Antonio, TX, for example, a possible password might be *gospurs* in honor of their professional basketball team. If these didn't work, then hobbies of the user might be tried, or the name of their favorite make or model of car, or similar pieces of information. The key is that the user often picks something easy for them to remember, which means that the more you know about the user, the better your chance of discovering their password.

In an attempt to complicate the attacker's job, organizations have encouraged their users to mix upper- and lowercase characters and to include numbers and special characters in their password. While this does make it harder, the basic problem still remains: users will pick something that is easy for them to remember. Thus, our user in San Antonio may select the password *G0*Spurs*, capitalizing two of the letters, inserting a special character, and substituting the number zero for the letter O. This has made the password harder to crack, but there are a finite number of variations on the basic *gospurs* password so, while the attacker's job has been made more difficult, it is still possible to guess the password.

Organizations have also instituted additional policies and rules relating to password selection to further complicate an attacker's efforts. Organizations, for example, may require users to frequently change their password. This means that if an attacker is able to guess a password, it is only valid for a limited period of time before a new password is selected and the attacker is locked out. All is not lost for the attacker, however, since as we mentioned before, users will select passwords they can remember. For example, password changes often result in a new password that simply incorporates a number at the end of the old one. Thus, our San Antonio user might select *G0*Spurs1* as the new password and if so, the benefit in forcing password changes on a periodic, or even frequent, basis has been totally lost. It is a good bet that the next password chosen will be *G0*Spurs2*, followed by *G0Spurs3*, and so forth.

Another policy or rule governing password selection often adopted by organizations is that passwords should not be written down. This, of course, is difficult to enforce and thus users will frequently write them down, often as a result of what we can refer to as the password dilemma. The more difficult we make it for attackers to guess our passwords, and the more frequently we force password changes, the more difficult the passwords are for authorized users to remember and the more likely they are to write them down. Writing them down and putting them in a secure place is one thing, but all too often users will write them on a slip of paper and keep them in their calendar, wallet, or purse. Most security consultants generally agree that if they are given physical access to an office they will be able to find a password somewhere—the top drawer of a desk, inside of a desk calendar, attached to the underside of the keyboard, or even simply on a yellow "stickie" attached to the monitor.

With the proliferation of computers, networks, and users, the password dilemma has gotten worse. Today, the average Internet user probably has at least a half dozen different accounts and passwords to remember. Selecting a different password for each account, following the guidelines mentioned previously regarding character selection and frequency of changes, only aggravates the problem of remembering the passwords. This results in users all too frequently using the same password for all accounts. If a user does this, and then one of the accounts is broken, all other accounts are subsequently also vulnerable to attack.

As a final comment, good password selection and the protection of passwords also applies to another common feature of today's electronic world. Most people have at least one Personal Identification Number (PIN) associated with things such as their automated teller machine, or a security code to gain physical access to a room. Again, users will invariably select numbers that are easy to remember. Specific numbers, such as the individual's birth year, or their spouse's birth year, or the date of some other significant event are all common numbers to select. Other people will pick patterns that are easy to remember—2580, for example, uses all of the center numbers on a standard numeric pad on a telephone. Attackers know this, and guessing PINs follows the same sort of process that guessing a password does.

Piggybacking and Shoulder Surfing

People are often in a hurry and will frequently not follow good physical security practices and procedures. Attackers know this and may attempt to exploit this characteristic in human behavior. **Piggybacking** is the simple tactic of following closely behind a person who has just used their own access card or PIN to gain physical access to a room or building. An attacker can thus gain access to the facility without having to know the access code or having to acquire an access card. **Shoulder surfing** is a similar procedure in which attackers position themselves in such a way as to be able to observe the authorized user entering the correct access code. Both of these attack techniques can be easily countered by using simple procedures to ensure nobody follows you too closely or is in a position to observe your actions.

Dumpster Diving

As mentioned earlier, attackers need a certain amount of information before launching their attack. One common place to find this information, if the attacker is in the vicinity of the target, is to go through the target's trash in order to find little bits of information that could be useful. This process of going through a target's trash is known in the computer community as **dumpster diving**. If the attackers are very lucky, and the target's security procedures are very poor, they may actually find user IDs and passwords. As mentioned in the discussion on passwords, users sometimes write their password down. If, when the password is changed, they discard the paper the old password was written on without shredding it, the lucky dumpster diver can gain a valuable clue. Even if the attacker isn't lucky enough to obtain a password directly, employee names will undoubtedly be found and from that it's not hard to determine user IDs. Manuals from hardware or software that have been purchased may also provide clues as to what vulnerabilities exist on the target's computer systems and networks. Finally, as will be discussed shortly, the attacker may gather a variety of information which can be useful in a social engineering attack. With the cost of shredders being so small today, there is no excuse for not properly disposing of trash, no matter how small the organization.

Installing Unauthorized Hardware and Software

Organizations should have a policy that restricts the ability of normal users to install software and new hardware on their systems. A common example is communication software and a modem used to allow an individual to connect to their machine at work via a modem from their home. In this example, the user that does this sets up a **backdoor** into the network which can be used to circumvent all of the other security mechanisms in place. Backdoors are avenues that can be used to access a system while circumventing normal security mechanisms. Another common example of software that users often install on their systems is games. Unfortunately, not all games come in shrink-wrapped packages. Numerous small games can be downloaded from the Internet. The problem with this is that users don't always know where the software originally came from and what may be hidden inside it. Many individuals have unwittingly installed what seemed to be an innocuous game, only to have downloaded a piece of malicious code capable of many things, including opening a backdoor that allows attackers to connect to, and control, the system from across the Internet. Because of these potential hazards, many organizations do not allow their users to load software or install new hardware without the knowledge and assistance of administrators. Many also restrict what individuals can do via received e-mails. This helps prevent users from, say, unwittingly executing a hostile program that was sent as part of a worm or virus. Consequently, many organizations have their mail servers strip off executable attachments to e-mail so users can't accidentally cause a security problem.

Access by Non-Employees

As has been mentioned, if an attacker can gain physical access to a facility, chances are very good that enough information can be obtained to penetrate computer systems and networks. Many organizations require employees to wear identification badges when at work. This is an easy method to quickly spot who has permission to have physical access to the organization and who does not. While this method is easy to implement and can be a significant deterrent to unauthorized individuals, it also requires that employees actively challenge individuals who are not wearing the required identification badge. This is one area where organizations fail. Combine an attacker who slips in by piggybacking off of an authorized individual and an environment where employees have not been encouraged to challenge individuals without appropriate credentials and you have a situation where you might as well not have any badges in the first place. Organizations also frequently become complacent when faced with what appears to be a legitimate reason to access the facility, such as when an individual shows up with a warm pizza claiming it was ordered by an employee. It has often been stated by security consultants that it is amazing what you can obtain access to with a pizza box or a vase of flowers. If the organization doesn't enforce good password policies, a casual stroll through an office may yield passwords or other important information.

Another aspect that must be considered is personnel who have legitimate access to a facility but may not have the same regard for the intellectual property rights of the organization that their coworkers do. Physical access provides an easy opportunity for individuals to look for the occasional piece of critical information carelessly left out. With the proliferation of devices such as cell phones with built-in cameras, an individual could easily photograph information without it being obvious to employees. Contractors, consultants, and partners frequently not only have physical access to the facility but may also have network access. Other individuals that typically have unrestricted access to the facility when no one is around are nighttime custodial crewmembers and security guards. Such positions are often contracted out. As a result, hackers have been known to take temporary custodial jobs simply to gain access to facilities.

Social Engineering

Social engineering is a technique in which the attacker uses various deceptive practices to obtain information they would normally not be privileged to, or to convince the target of the attack to do something they normally wouldn't. Social engineering is very successful because of two general reasons. The first is the basic desire by many to be helpful. When somebody asks a question for which we know the answer, our normal response is not to be suspicious but rather to answer the question. The problem with this is that seemingly innocuous information can be used either directly in an attack or to build a bigger picture that can be used to create an aura of authenticity for the attacker. The more information an individual has about an organization, the easier it will be to convince others that he is part of the company and has a right to even sensitive information. This type of reasoning can be further broken down into one of three categories. The attacker may simply ask a question hoping to immediately obtain the desired information. For the most basic of information that is not considered sensitive, this generally will work. An example of this might be to call and ask who the IT manager is. If the attacker's desired information might be even slightly sensitive in nature, and possibly arouse suspicion, then another technique may be tried. The attacker may first attempt to engage the target in conversation and try to evoke sympathy so the target feels sorry for the individual and may more freely release the information. An example might be an attacker who calls and claims to be under some deadline from a supervisor who is upset for some reason. The target, feeling sorry for a fellow worker, may give up the information thinking that by doing so they are helping the attacker keep out of trouble. The attacker may also try another approach, appealing to the individual's ego. An example might be an individual who calls the IT department, claiming to have some sort of problem, and praising them for work they supposedly did to help another worker. After having somebody tell you how great you are and how much you helped somebody else, you will often be tempted to supply the same level of help to another individual.

The second reason that social engineering is successful is that individuals will normally seek to avoid confrontation and trouble. If the attacker attempts to intimidate the target, threatening to call the target's supervisor because of a lack of help, the target may give in and provide the information to avoid confrontation. This variation on the attack is often successful in organizations that have a strict hierarchical structure. In the military, for example, a lower ranking individual may be coerced into providing information from an individual claiming to be of higher rank or who claims to be working for another individual higher up in the chain of command.

A variation on social engineering uses means other than direct contact between the target and the attacker. An example of this type of attack might be a forged electronic mail or a bogus web site to obtain information from an individual or convince the individual to accomplish some action. Again, the goal in social engineering is to convince the target to provide information or accomplish some act that they normally would not do. An example of a slightly different attack that is generally still considered a social engineering attack is an attacker who replaces the blank deposit slips in a bank's lobby with ones containing his or her own account number but no name. When an unsuspecting customer uses one of the slips, a teller who is not observant may end up crediting the attacker's account with the deposit.

A final word on social engineering—up to this point, social engineering has been discussed in the context of an outsider attempting to gain information about the organization. This does not have to be the case. Insiders may also attempt to gain information they are not authorized to have. In may cases, the insider may be much more successful since they will already have a certain level of information regarding the organization and can therefore better spin a story that may be believable to other employees.

Stanley Mark Rifkin (1978)

An excellent example of social engineering occurred in 1978 when Stanley Mark Rifkin, from Carlsbad, California, stole $10.2 million from the Security Pacific Bank in Los Angeles. Details of the story vary as Rifkin has never publicly detailed his actions, but a number of facts are known. At the time of the attack, Rifkin was working as a computer consultant for the bank. While working there he learned details on how money could easily be transferred to accounts anywhere in the United States. The problem would be to actually obtain the money in the first place. In order to do this, he needed to have access to the electronic funds transfer (EFT) code used by the bank to transfer money to other banks. Using the excuse of checking on the computer equipment inside of the room from which the bank made its transfers, Rifkin was able to observe the code for the day. After leaving the room, he used this information to impersonate a bank officer and ordered the transfer of the $10.2 million. Since he had knowledge of the supposedly secret code, the transfer was made with little fanfare (this amount was well below any level that would trigger any suspicion). Earlier Rifkin had set up a bogus account in a New York bank using a false name and this money was now deposited into that account. He later transferred the money again to another account in Switzerland under a different name. He then used the money to purchase millions of dollars in diamonds which he then smuggled back into the United States. The crime might have gone undetected if he had not boasted of his exploits to an individual who was more than happy to turn him in. In 1979, Rifkin was sentenced to eight years in prison. At his trial, he attempted to convince the judge that he should be released so he could teach others how to protect their systems against the type of activity he perpetrated. The judge denied this request. The diamonds were ultimately turned over to the bank, which tried to recover their loss by selling them.

Reverse Social Engineering

A slightly different approach to social engineering is called **reverse social engineering**. In this technique, the attacker hopes to convince the target to initiate the contact. This obviously differs from the traditional approach where the target is the one that is contacted. The reason this attack may be successful is that, since the target is the one initiating the contact, attackers may not have to convince the target of their authenticity. The tricky part of this attack is, of course, convincing the target to make that initial contact. Possible methods to accomplish this might include sending out a spoofed e-mail claiming to be from a reputable source that provides another e-mail address or phone number to call for "tech support," or posting a notice or creating a bogus web site for a legitimate company that also claims to provide "tech support." This may be especially successful if accomplished in conjunction with the deployment of a new software or hardware platform. Another potential time to target an organization with this sort of attack is when there is a significant change in the organization itself. The sort of upheaval referred to here would occur if two companies merge or if a smaller company is acquired by a larger one. During these times, employees are not familiar with the new organization or its procedures and amidst the confusion it is easy to conduct either a social engineering or reverse social engineering attack.

People as a Security Tool

An interesting paradox when speaking of social engineering attacks is that people are not only the biggest problem and security risk but they are also the best tool in defending against a social engineering attack. The first step a company should take to fight potential social engineering attacks is to create the policies and procedures that establish the roles and responsibilities for not only security administrators but for all users. What is it that management expects, security-wise, from all employees? What is it that the organization is trying to protect, and what mechanisms are important for that protection?

Security Awareness

Probably the single most effective method to counter potential social engineering attacks, after establishment of the organization's security goals and policies, is an active security awareness program. The extent of the training will vary depending on the organization's environment and the level of threat, but initial employee training on social engineering at the time a person is hired is important, as well as periodic refresher training. Many government organizations have created security awareness posters to constantly remind individuals of this possible avenue of attack. Security newsletters, often in the form of e-mail, have also been used to remind employees of their security responsibilities.

An important element that should be stressed in training about social engineering is the type of information that the organization considers sensitive and which may be the target of a social engineering attack. There are undoubtedly signs that the organization could point to as indicative of an attacker attempting to gain access to sensitive corporate information. All employees should be aware of these indicators.

Individual User Responsibilities

Several times we've alluded to specific duties that users should be expected to perform. These vary between organizations and the type of business the organization is involved in, but there are certain very basic responsibilities that all users should adopt. These include:

- Locking the door to your office or workspace

- Not leaving sensitive information inside your car unprotected

- Securing storage media containing sensitive information in a secure storage device

- Shredding paper containing organizational information before discarding it

- Not divulging sensitive information to individuals (including other employees) that do not have an authorized need to know it

- Not discussing sensitive information with family members (the most common violation of this rule occurs in regards to human resources information as employees, especially supervisors, may complain to their spouse about other employees or problems that are occurring at work)

- Protecting laptops that contain sensitive or important organization information wherever the laptop may be stored or left (it's a good idea to ensure that sensitive information is encrypted on the laptop so that, should the equipment be lost or stolen, the information remains safe)

- Being aware of who is around you when discussing sensitive corporate information. Does everybody within earshot have the need to hear this information?

- Enforcing corporate access control procedures. Be alert to, and do not allow, piggybacking, shoulder surfing, or access without the proper credentials.

- Being aware of the correct procedures to report suspected or actual violations of security policies

- Establishing procedures to enforce good password security practices that all employees should follow. Passwords are such a critical element that they are frequently the ultimate target of a social engineering attack. Though such password procedures may seem too oppressive or strict, they are often the best line of defense.

As a final note on user responsibilities, corporate security officers must cultivate an environment of trust in their office, as well as an understanding of the importance of security. If users feel that security personnel are only there to make their life difficult or dredge up information that will result in an employee's termination, the atmosphere will quickly turn adversarial and be transformed into an "us versus them" situation. Security personnel need the help of all users and should strive to cultivate a team environment where users, when faced with a questionable situation, will not hesitate to call the security office. In situations like this, security offices should remember the old adage of "don't shoot the messenger."

Chapter Review

Chapter Summary

After reading this chapter and completing the exercises, you should understand the following regarding the role people can play in security.

People—A Security Problem

- No matter how advanced security technology is, it will ultimately be deployed in an environment where the human element may be its greatest weakness.

- A significant portion of employee-created security problems arise from poor security practices.

- For many years, computer intruders have relied on users selecting poor passwords to help them in their attempts to gain unauthorized access to a system or network.

- Attackers know that employees are frequently very busy and don't stop to think about security. They may attempt to exploit this work characteristic through piggybacking or shoulder surfing.

- One common way to find useful information (if the attacker is in the vicinity of the target) is to go through the target's trash looking for bits of information that could be useful to a penetration attempt.

- Organizations should have a policy that restricts the ability of normal users to install software and new hardware on their systems.

- Contractors, consultants, and partners may frequently not only have physical access to the facility but they may also have network access. Other groups that are given unrestricted, and unobserved, access to a facility are nighttime custodial crewmembers and security guards. Both are potential security problems.

- Social engineering is a technique in which the attacker uses various deceptive practices to obtain information which the attacker would normally not be privileged to, or to convince the target to do something they normally wouldn't.

- In reverse social engineering, the attacker hopes to convince the target to initiate contact.

People as a Security Tool

- An interesting paradox when speaking of social engineering attacks is that people are not only the biggest problem and security risk, but they are also the best line of defense against a social engineering attack.

- The single most effective method to counter potential social engineering attacks, after establishment of the organization's security goals and policies, is an active security awareness program.

Key Terms

Backdoor *(66)*
Dumpster diving *(66)*
Piggybacking *(65)*
Reverse social engineering *(69)*
Shoulder surfing *(65)*
Social engineering *(67)*

Key Terms Quiz

Use terms from the Key Terms list to complete the sentences that follow. Don't use the same term more than once. Not all terms will be used.

1. A _____ is an avenue that can be used to access a system while circumventing normal security mechanisms.

2. _____ is a procedure in which attackers position themselves in such a way as to be able to observe an authorized user entering the correct access code.

3. The process of going through a target's trash searching for information that can be used in an attack, or to gain knowledge about a system or network, is known as _____.

4. _____ is the simple tactic of following closely behind a person who has just used their access card or PIN to gain physical access to a room or building.

5. In _____, the attacker hopes to convince the target to initiate contact.

Multiple-Choice Quiz

1. Which of the following are considered good practices for password security?

   A. Using a combination of upper- and lower-case characters, a number, and a special character in the password itself

   B. Not writing the password down

   C. Changing the password on a regular basis

   D. All of the above

2. The password dilemma refers to the fact that:

   A. Passwords that are easy for users to remember are also easy for attackers to guess.

   B. The more difficult we make it for attackers to guess our passwords, and the more frequently we force password changes, the more difficult the passwords are for authorized users to remember and the more likely they are to write them down.

   C. Users will invariably attempt to select passwords that are words they can remember. This means they may select things closely associated with them, such as their spouse's or child's name, a beloved sports team, or a favorite model of car.

   D. Passwords assigned by administrators are usually better and more secure, but are often harder for users to remember.

3. The simple tactic of following closely behind a person who has just used their own access card or PIN to gain physical access to a room or building is called:

   A. Shoulder surfing

   B. Tagging-along

   C. Piggybacking

   D. Access drafting

4. The process of going through a target's trash in hopes of finding valuable information that might be used in a penetration attempt is known as:

   A. Dumpster diving

   B. Trash trolling

   C. Garbage gathering

   D. Refuse rolling

5. A mechanism that is used to circumvent a target's security mechanisms in order to gain unauthorized access to the network is known as a:

   A. Master-key code

   B. Secret door

   C. Backdoor

   D. Covert channel

6. Reverse social engineering involves…

   A. Contacting the target, eliciting some sensitive information, and convincing them that nothing out of the ordinary has occurred.

   B. Contacting the target in an attempt to obtain information that can be used in a second attempt with a different individual.

C. An individual lower in the chain of command convincing somebody at a higher level to divulge information that the attacker was not authorized to have.

D. An attacker attempting to somehow convince the target to initiate contact in order to avoid questions about authenticity.

7. The reason for not allowing users to install new hardware or software without the knowledge of security administrators is…

A. They may not complete the installation correctly and the administrator will have to do more work, taking them away from more important security tasks.

B. They may inadvertently install more than just the hardware or software; they may accidentally install a backdoor into the network.

C. They may not have paid for it and thus may be opening the organization up to civil penalties.

D. Unauthorized hardware and software are usually for leisure purposes and will distract employees from the job they were hired to perform.

8. Once an organization's security policies have been established, the single most effective method of countering potential social engineering attacks is…

A. An active security awareness program

B. A separate physical access control mechanism for each department in the organization

C. Frequent testing of both the organization's physical security procedures and employee telephone practices

D. Implementing access control cards and the wearing of security identification badges

9. Security administrators should be concerned about security guards and custodial crews because:

A. These individuals may not have had a thorough background investigation.

B. These individuals have access to facilities at times when nobody else is around to view their activities.

C. These individuals are frequently paid minimal salaries.

D. These individuals are frequently contracted and are not actually employees of the company.

10. In what ways are PINs similar to passwords? (Choose all that apply.)

A. Users will normally pick ones that are easy to remember, such as dates or specific patterns.

B. Attackers know common PINs and will try to use them or will attempt to learn more about the user in order to make an educated guess as to what the PIN might be.

C. Users may write them down to remember them.

D. All of the above

Essay Quiz

1. Explain the difference between social engineering and reverse social engineering.

2. Describe the process of piggybacking. Is this common attack technique possible in your work or school environment?

3. How might shoulder surfing be a threat in your school or work environment? What can be done to make this sort of activity more difficult?

4. For an environment familiar to you (such as work or school), describe the different non-employees that may have access to facilities that could contain sensitive information.

5. Describe some of the user security responsibilities that you feel are most important for users to remember.

Lab Projects

Lab Project 4.1

If possible at either your place of employment or school, attempt to determine how easy it would be to perform dumpster diving in order to gain access to information at the site. Are trash receptacles easy to gain access to? Are documents shredded before being discarded? Are areas where trash is stored easily accessible?

Lab Project 4.2

Perform a search on the Web for articles and stories of social engineering attacks or reverse social engineering attacks. How many were successful? How many failed and why? How could those that may have initially succeeded been prevented?

Cryptography

Upon completion of this lesson, you will be able to:
- Identify and describe the three types of cryptography
- List and describe current cryptographic algorithms
- Explain how cryptography is applied for security

Cryptography is the science of encrypting information. People's desire to hide information from each other extends well back into ancient times. Once people had determined that they could apply language to writing, they knew how to share information with others. The next step was to keep information from others. The easiest way for people to do this was to not teach others how to read and write the language. As that became ineffective, methods of shifting the letters around to make the text unreadable were attempted.

Spartans used a ribbon wrapped around a specific gauge cylinder and then wrote on the ribbon. When unwrapped, the ribbon appeared to hold a strange string of letters. The message could only be read when someone wrapped the ribbon back around the same gauge cylinder. This is an example of a **transposition cipher**, where the same letters are used but the order is changed.

The Romans typically used a different method known as a **shift cipher**. In this case, one letter of the alphabet is shifted a set number of places in the alphabet for another letter. A common modern-day example of this is the ROT13 cipher, where every letter is rotated 13 positions in the alphabet; *n* is written instead of *a*, *o* instead of *b*, etc.

These ciphers were simple to use and unfortunately also simple to break. This led to the need for more advanced transposition and substitution ciphers. As the systems became more complex, they were frequently automated by some mechanical or electro-mechanical device. A famous example of a modern encryption machine is the German Enigma machine from World War II. This machine used a complex series of substitutions to perform encryption, and interestingly enough gave rise to great amounts of research in computers.

Cryptanalysis, which is the process of analyzing available information to attempt to return the encrypted message to its original form, required advances in computer technology for the more complex encryption methods. The birth of the computer made it possible to easily execute more complex encryption algorithms, which is how encryption is performed today. Computer technology has also aided cryptanalysis, allowing new methods to be tried, such as linear and differential cryptanalysis. **Differential cryptanalysis** is done by comparing the input plaintext to the output ciphertext to try and determine the key. **Linear cryptanalysis** is similar in that it uses both plaintext and ciphertext, but it puts the plaintext through a simplified cipher to try and deduce what the key is likely to be in the full version of the cipher.

In this chapter, we will take a look at the most common algorithms in use today, both symmetric and asymmetric, as well as some of the things encryption is used to achieve on computer networks.

Algorithms

All current encryption schemes are based upon an **algorithm**, which is a step-by-step problem-solving procedure—a recursive computational procedure for solving a problem in a finite number of steps. The cryptographic algorithm, or what we commonly call the encryption algorithm or cipher, is made up of mathematical steps for encrypting and decrypting information. Figure 5-1 shows the process and will hopefully give better sense to the terms used in this chapter.

The best algorithms are always public algorithms that have been published for peer review by other cryptographic and mathematical experts. The actual steps for encrypting data can be published because of the design of the systems. They are designed to use a **key**, which is a special piece of data used in both the encryption and decryption processes. The algorithms that are used stay the same, but every implementation uses a different key, which ensures that even if someone knows the algorithm you are using, they cannot break your security. The classic example of this is the early shift cipher, known as Caesar's cipher.

Caesar's cipher uses an algorithm and a key, the algorithm specifying that you offset the alphabet either to the right (forwards) or to the left (backwards), and the key specifying how many letters the offset should be. For example, if the algorithm specified offsetting the alphabet to the right, and the key was three, the cipher would substitute for the real letter the letter three to the right in the alphabet. In this example, both the algorithm and key are simple, allowing for easy cryptanalysis of the cipher and easy recovery of the plaintext message.

The ease with which shift ciphers were broken led to the development of substitution ciphers. Substitution ciphers were very popular in Elizabethan England and are more complex than shift ciphers. They work on the principle of substituting a different letter for every letter: A becomes G, B becomes D, and so on. This system permits 26 possible values for every letter in the message, making the cipher many times more complex than a standard shift cipher. Simple analysis of the cipher could be performed to retrieve the

Figure 5-1

Diagram of the encryption and decryption process

key, however. By looking for common letters and patterns that would become words, you can determine which cipher letter corresponds to which plaintext letter and therefore you can determine this system's key value.

To correct this problem, more complexity had to be added to the system. The **Vigenère cipher** works as a polyalphabetic substitution cipher that depends on a password. This is done by setting up a substitution table like this one:

```
A B C D E F G H I J K L M N O P Q R S T U V W X Y Z
B C D E F G H I J K L M N O P Q R S T U V W X Y Z A
C D E F G H I J K L M N O P Q R S T U V W X Y Z A B
D E F G H I J K L M N O P Q R S T U V W X Y Z A B C
E F G H I J K L M N O P Q R S T U V W X Y Z A B C D
F G H I J K L M N O P Q R S T U V W X Y Z A B C D E
G H I J K L M N O P Q R S T U V W X Y Z A B C D E F
H I J K L M N O P Q R S T U V W X Y Z A B C D E F G
I J K L M N O P Q R S T U V W X Y Z A B C D E F G H
J K L M N O P Q R S T U V W X Y Z A B C D E F G H I
K L M N O P Q R S T U V W X Y Z A B C D E F G H I J
L M N O P Q R S T U V W X Y Z A B C D E F G H I J K
M N O P Q R S T U V W X Y Z A B C D E F G H I J K L
N O P Q R S T U V W X Y Z A B C D E F G H I J K L M
O P Q R S T U V W X Y Z A B C D E F G H I J K L M N
P Q R S T U V W X Y Z A B C D E F G H I J K L M N O
Q R S T U V W X Y Z A B C D E F G H I J K L M N O P
R S T U V W X Y Z A B C D E F G H I J K L M N O P Q
S T U V W X Y Z A B C D E F G H I J K L M N O P Q R
T U V W X Y Z A B C D E F G H I J K L M N O P Q R S
U V W X Y Z A B C D E F G H I J K L M N O P Q R S T
V W X Y Z A B C D E F G H I J K L M N O P Q R S T U
W X Y Z A B C D E F G H I J K L M N O P Q R S T U V
X Y Z A B C D E F G H I J K L M N O P Q R S T U V W
Y Z A B C D E F G H I J K L M N O P Q R S T U V W X
Z A B C D E F G H I J K L M N O P Q R S T U V W X Y
```

Then the password is matched up to the text it is meant to encipher. If the password is not long enough, the password is repeated until one character of the password is matched up with each character of the plaintext. For example, if the plaintext is "Sample Message" and the password is "password," the resulting match is

passwordpassw

samplemessage

The cipher letter is determined by use of the previous grid, matching the plaintext character's row with the password character's column, resulting in a single ciphertext character from where the two meet. Taking the preceding example, the first two letters are "p" and "s"; when plugged into the grid, they output a ciphertext character of "h." This process is repeated for every letter of the message.

In this example, the key in the encryption system is the password. It also illustrates that an algorithm can be simple and still have security. If someone knows what the table is, they can determine how the encryption was performed, but they still will not know the key to decrypting the message.

The more complex the key, the greater the security of the system. The Vigenère cipher system and systems like it make the algorithms rather simple but the key rather complex, with the best keys being very long and very random data. Key complexity is achieved by giving the key a large number of possible values. The **keyspace** is the size of every possible key value. When an algorithm lists a certain number of bits as a key, it is defining the keyspace. It is important to note that because keyspace is a numerical value, it is very important to ensure that comparisons are done using similar key types. Comparing a key made of 1 bit (2 possible values) and a key made of 1 letter (26 possible values) would not yield accurate results. Fortunately, the widespread use of computers have made almost all algorithms state their keyspace values in terms of bits.

It is easy to see how key complexity affects an algorithm when you look at some of the encryption algorithms that have been broken. DES (Data Encryption Standard) used a 56-bit key, allowing 72,000,000,000,000,000 possible values, but it has been broken by modern computers. The modern implementation of DES, Triple DES (commonly known as 3DES) uses a 128-bit key, or 340,000,000,000,000,000,000,000,000,000,000,000,000 possible values. You can see the difference in the possible values, and why 128 bits is generally accepted as the minimum to protect sensitive information.

When an algorithm is listed as being broken, it may be a result of the algorithm being faulty or having been based on poor math, but more likely the algorithm has been rendered obsolete by advancing technology. All encryption ciphers besides a "one-time pad" cipher are susceptible to a brute-force attack—attempting every possible key. With a very small key, such as a 2-bit key, trying every possible value is simple, as you only have four possibilities: 00, 01, 10, or 11. The 56-bit DES hs 72 quadrillion values, and while that seems like a lot, computers have advanced to the extent that they can attempt billions of keys every second. This makes brute forcing a key only a matter of time, so large keys are required to make brute-force attacks against the cipher take longer than the effective value of the information that is enciphered by them. One-time Pad ciphers are interesting because they have a key that is equal to the length of the message, and must use **completely** random data for the key. This allows the keyspace to be unlimited, therefore making a brute-force attack impossible.

Computers in cryptography and cryptanalysis have to handle all this data in a bit format. They would have difficulty in using the table shown earlier, so many encryption functions use a logical function to perform the encipherment. This function is typically **XOR**, which is the bitwise exclusive OR. XOR is used because

$$\text{If} \quad (P \text{ XOR } K) = C \quad \text{then} \quad (C \text{ XOR } K) = P$$

If P is the plaintext and K is the key, then C is the ciphertext, making a simple symmetric key cipher in the case where the sender and the receiver both have a shared secret (key) to encrypt and decrypt data. While symmetric encryption is the most common type of encryption, there are other types of encryption, such as public key or asymmetric encryption, and hashing or one-way functions. They all have situations that they are naturally suited for, and we will go over the way each type works and look at what they are commonly used for.

Hashing

Hashing functions are one of the most commonly used encryption methods. A **hash** is a special mathematical function that performs one-way encryption, meaning that once the algorithm is processed, there is no feasible way to take the ciphertext and retrieve the plaintext that was used to generate it. Also, ideally, there is no feasible way to generate two different plaintexts that compute to the same hash value. Figure 5-2 shows a generic hashing process.

Common uses of hashing functions are storing computer passwords and ensuring message integrity. The idea is that hashing can produce a unique value corresponding to the data entered, but the hash value is also reproducible by anyone else running the same algorithm against the data. So, you could hash a message to get a message authentication code (MAC), and the computational number of the message would show that no intermediary has modified the message. This process works because hashing methods are typically public, and anyone can hash data using the specified method. It is computationally simple to generate the hash, so it is simple to check the validity or integrity of something by matching the given hash to one that is locally generated.

A hash algorithm can be attacked with what is called a **collision attack**, where an attacker finds two different messages that hash to the same value. Two of the popular hash algorithms are Secure Hash Algorithm (SHA) and Message Digest of varying versions (MD2, MD4, MD5).

SHA

SHA was developed in 1993 by the National Institute of Standards and Technology (NIST) and the National Security Agency (NSA). It was designed as the algorithm to be used for secure hashing in the U.S. Digital Signature Standard (DSS). It is modeled on the MD4 algorithm and implements fixes in that algorithm discovered by the NSA. It creates message digests 160 bits long that then can be used by the Digital Signature Algorithm (DSA), which can then compute the signature of the message. This is computationally simpler, as the message digest is typically much smaller than the actual message. Smaller message = less work.

SHA works, as all hashing functions work, by applying a compression function to the data input. It accepts an input of up to 2^{64} bits or less and then compresses down to a hash of 160 bits. SHA works in block mode, separating the data into words first, and then grouping the words into blocks. The words are 32-bit strings converted to hex; grouped together as 16 words, they make up a 512-bit block. If the data that is input to SHA is not a multiple of 512, the message is padded with zeros and an integer describing the original length of the message.

Figure 5-2
How hashes work

Original message—plaintext   Padding   Message digest

Hash function

Once the message has been formatted for processing, the actual hash can be generated. The 512-bit blocks are taken in order $B_1, B_2, B_3, \ldots, B_n$ until the entire message has been processed. The computation uses 80 32-bit words labeled $W_0, W_1, W_2, \ldots, W_{79}$ being sent to two 5-word buffers. The first 5-word buffer's words are labeled A, B, C, D, E, and the second 5-word buffer has them labeled H_0, H_1, H_2, H_3, H_4. There is also a single-word buffer, TEMP. Before processing any blocks, the H_i are initialized as follows:

H_0 = 67452301

H_1 = EFCDAB89

H_2 = 98BADCFE

H_3 = 10325476

H_4 = C3D2E1F0

The first block now gets processed by dividing the first block into 16 words:

W_0 through W_{15}

For t = 16 through 79

$$W_t = S1(W_{t-3} \text{ XOR } W_{t-8} \text{ XOR } W_{t-14} \text{ XOR } W_{t-16})$$

Let $A = H_0 \; B = H_1 \; C = H_2 \; D = H_3 \; E = H_4$

For t = 0 through 79

Let $\text{TEMP} = S^5(A) + f_t(B,C,D) + E + W_t + K_t$;

$$E = D; \; D = C; \; C = S^{30}(B); \; B = A; \; A = \text{TEMP}$$

Let $H_0 = H_0 + A; \; H_1 = H_1 + B; \; H_2 = H_2 + C; \; H_3 = H_3 + D; \; H_4 = H_4 + E$

After this has been completed for all blocks, the entire message is now represented by the 160-bit string $H_0 \; H_1 \; H_2 \; H_3 \; H_4$.

SHA is one of the more secure hash functions, with no known successful attacks against it. Also, its output is 160 bits long versus the more common 128-bit result from MD5. This added security and resistance to attack in SHA requires more processing power.

Message Digest (MD)

Message Digest (MD) is the generic version of one of three algorithms, all designed to create a message digest or hash from data input into the algorithm. MD algorithms work in the same manner as SHA in that they use a secure method to compress the file and generate a computed output of a specified number of bits. They were all developed by Ronald L. Rivest of MIT.

MD2

Message Digest 2 was developed in 1989 and is in some ways an early version of the later MD5 algorithm. It takes a data input of any length and produces a hash output of 128 bits. It is different from MD4 and MD5 in that MD2 is optimized for 8-bit machines, whereas the other two are optimized for 32-bit machines. As with SHA, the input data is padded to become a multiple—in this case, a multiple of 16 bytes. After padding, a 16-byte checksum is appended to the message. The message is then processed in 16-byte blocks. After initialization, the algorithm invokes a compression function.

The compression function operates as shown here:

$$T = 0$$

For $J = 0$ through 17

For $k = 0$ through 47

$$T = Xk \text{ XOR } St$$

$$Xk = T$$

$$T = (T + J) \text{mod } 256$$

After the function has been run for every 16 bytes of the message, the output result is a 128-bit digest. The only known attack that is successful against MD2 is dependent on the checksum not being appended to the message before the hash function is run. Without a checksum, the algorithm can be vulnerable to a collision attack.

MD4

Message Digest 4 was developed in 1990 and is optimized for 32-bit computers. It is a fast algorithm, but it is not as secure. Like MD2, it takes a data input of some length and outputs a digest of 128 bits. The message is padded to become a multiple of 512, which is then concatenated with the representation of the message's original length.

As with SHA, it is then divided into blocks and also into 16 words of 32 bits. All blocks of the message are processed in three distinct rounds. The digest is then computed using a four-word buffer. The final four words left after compression are the 128-bit hash.

There is also an extended version of MD4 that computes the message in parallel and produces two 128-bit outputs—effectively a 256-bit hash. Even though a longer hash is produced, security has not been improved because of basic flaws in the algorithm. Dobbertin has shown how collisions in MD4 can be found in under a minute using just a PC. This vulnerability to collisions applies to 128-bit MD4 as well as 256-bit MD4. Most people are moving away from MD4 to MD5 or SHA.

MD5

Message Digest 5 was developed in 1991 and is structured after MD4 but with additional security to overcome the problems in MD4. Therefore, it is very similar to the MD4 algorithm, only slightly slower and more secure.

MD5 creates a 128-bit hash of a message of any length. Like MD4, it segments the message into 512-bit blocks and then into 16 32-bit words. First, the original message is padded to be 64 bits short of a multiple of 512 bits. Then, a 64-bit representation of the original length of the message is added to the padded value to bring the entire message up to a 512-bit multiple.

After padding is complete, four 32-bit variables, A, B, C, D, are initialized. A, B, C, D are copied into a, b, c, d, and then the main function begins. This has four rounds, each using a different nonlinear function 16 times. These functions operate on three of a, b, c, d, adding the result to the fourth variable; the fourth variable being a subblock of the text and a constant, then rotating the result of that addition to the right a variable number of bits, specified by the round of the algorithm. After adding the result of this operation to one of a, b, c, d, that sum replaces one of a, b, c, d. After the four rounds are completed, a, b, c, d are added to A, B, C, D, and the algorithm moves on to the next block. After all blocks are completed, A, B, C, D are concatenated to form the final output of 128 bits.

Currently, there are no true known attacks against MD5, but there has been cryptanalysis that displays weaknesses in the compression function. However, this weakness does not lend itself to an attack on MD5, itself. There are also methods to brute force hash functions for collisions, but the cost of hardware to perform the attack and the length of time required to produce the collision make the technique impractical. A custom machine to search for collisions was estimated to cost $10 million and require 24 days of run time by Paul C. van Oorschot and Michael J. Wiener in "Parallel Collision Search with Application to Hash Functions and Discrete Logarithms." The combination of these problems with MD5 has pushed people to adopt SHA for security reasons.

Hashing Summary

Hashing functions are very common, and they play an important role in the way information, such as passwords, is stored securely, and the way in which messages can be signed. By computing a digest of the message, less data needs to be signed by the more complex asymmetric encryption, and this still maintains assurances about message integrity. This is the primary purpose for which the protocols were designed, and their success will allow greater trust in electronic protocols and digital signatures.

Symmetric Encryption

Symmetric encryption is the older and more simple method of encrypting information. The basis of symmetric encryption is that both the sender and the receiver of the message have previously obtained the same key. This is, in fact, the basis for even the oldest ciphers—the Spartans needed the exact same size cylinder, making the cylinder the "key" to the message, and in shift ciphers both parties need to know the direction and amount of shift being performed. All symmetric algorithms are based upon this **shared secret** principle, including even the unbreakable one-time pad method. Figure 5-3 is a simple diagram showing the process that a symmetric algorithm goes through to provide encryption from plaintext to ciphertext. This ciphertext message is, presumably, transmitted to the message recipient who goes through the process to decrypt the message. Figure 5-3 shows the keys to the algorithm, which are the same value in the case of symmetric encryption.

Unlike hash functions, there is a cryptographic key involved in symmetric encryption, so there must be a mechanism for **key management**. Managing the cryptographic keys is very important in symmetric algorithms because the key unlocks the data you are trying to protect. However, the key also needs to be known or transmitted in a secret way to the other party that you wish to communicate with. This key management applies to all things that could happen to a key, securing it on the local computer, securing it on the remote one, protecting it from data corruption, protecting it from loss, as well as probably the most important step, protecting the key while it is transmitted between the two parties.

Later in the chapter, we will look at public key cryptography, which greatly eases the key management issue; for symmetric algorithms, the most important lesson is to store and send the key only by known secure means. We will also look at some of the more popular symmetric encryption algorithms in use today, such as DES, 3DES, AES, IDEA, and others, as well as their key lengths.

DES

DES stands for Data Encryption Standard. It was first developed over twenty years ago. In 1973, the National Bureau of Standards (NBS), now known as the National Institute of Standards and Technology (NIST), issued a request for proposals for a standard cryptographic algorithm. They received a promising response in an algorithm called Lucifer, originally developed by IBM. The NBS and the NSA worked together to analyze the algorithm's security, and eventually DES was adopted as a federal standard in 1976.

NBS specified that the DES standard had to be recertified every five years. While DES passed without a hitch in 1983, the NSA said it would not recertify it in 1987. However, since there was no alternative for many businesses, there were many complaints, and the NSA and NBS were forced to recertify it again. The algorithm was then recertified in 1993, but NIST is now looking at the Advanced Encryption Standard (AES) to replace DES.

DES is what is known as a **block cipher**, segmenting the input data into blocks of a specified size, typically padding the last block to make it a multiple of the block size required. In the case of DES, the block size is 64 bits, which means DES takes a 64-bit input and outputs 64 bits of ciphertext. This process is repeated for all 64-bit blocks in the message. DES uses a key length of 56 bits, and all security rests within the key. The same algorithm and key are used for both encryption and decryption.

Figure 5-3
Layout of a symmetric algorithm

Shared secret: Key   Shared secret: Key

Plaintext   Ciphertext   Plaintext

Encryption   Decryption

At the most basic level, DES performs a substitution and then a permutation (a form of transposition) on the input, based upon the key. This action is called a *round*, and DES performs this 16 times on every 64-bit block. It works in three stages:

1. The algorithm accepts plaintext, P, and performs an initial permutation, IP, on P producing P_0. The block is then broken into left and right halves, the left (L_0) being the first 32 bits of P_0 and the right (R_0) being the last 32 bits of P_0.

2. With L_0 and R_0, 16 rounds are performed until L_{16} and R_{16} are generated.

3. The inverse permutation, IP^{-1}, is applied to $L_{16}R_{16}$ to produce ciphertext C.

The second stage mentions executing 16 times, and these rounds are where the bulk of the encryption is performed. The individual rounds work with the following computation:

Where i represents the current round,

$$L_i = R_{i-1}$$

$$R_i = L_{i-1} \text{ XOR } f(R_{i-1}, K_i)$$

K_i represents the current round's 48-bit string derived from the 56-bit key, and f represents the diffusion function. This function operates as follows:

1. 48 bits are selected from the 56-bit key.

2. The right half is expanded from 32 bits to 48 bits via an expansion permutation.

3. Those 48 bits are combined via XOR with the 48-key bits.

4. This result is then sent through 8 S-boxes, producing 32 new bits, and then it is permuted again.

After all 16 rounds have been completed and the inverse permutation has been completed, the ciphertext is output as 64 bits. Then the algorithm picks up the next 64 bits and starts all over again. This is carried on until the entire message has been encrypted with DES. As mentioned before, the same algorithm and key are used to decrypt DES as to encrypt. The only difference is that the sequence of key permutations are used in reverse order.

Over the years that DES has been a cryptographic standard, there has been a lot of cryptanalysis, and while the algorithm has held up very well, there have been some concerns. Weak keys are keys that are less secure than the majority of keys allowed in the keyspace of the algorithm. In the case of DES, because of the way the initial key is modified to get the subkey, certain keys are weak keys. The weak keys are ones that equate in binary to having all ones or all zeros, or where one half is all ones and the other half is all zeros, like those shown in Figure 5-4.

There are also semi-weak keys, where two keys will encrypt plaintext to identical ciphertext, meaning that either key will decrypt the ciphertext. The total number of possibly weak keys is 64, which is very small compared with the 2^{56} possible keys in DES.

Binary Key

```
0000000 0000000
0000000 FFFFFFF
FFFFFFF 0000000
FFFFFFF FFFFFFF
```

There is also the question of 16 rounds. There have been multiple successful attacks against DES algorithms that use fewer rounds. Any DES with fewer than 16 rounds could be analyzed more efficiently with chosen plaintext than via a brute-force attack using differential cryptanalysis. With 16 rounds and not using a weak key, DES is reasonably secure, and amazingly has been for over 20 years. In 1999, there was a distributed effort consisting of a supercomputer and 100,000 PCs over the Internet to break a 56-bit DES key. By attempting over 240 billion keys per second, they were able to retrieve the key in less than a day. This demonstrates an incredible resistance to cracking a 20-year-old algorithm, but it also demonstrates that more stringent algorithms are needed to protect data today.

3DES

3DES (Triple DES) is a variant of DES. Depending on the specific variant, it uses either two or three keys instead of the single key that DES uses. It also spins through the DES algorithm three times via what's called **multiple encryption**.

Multiple encryption can be performed several different ways. The simplest method of multiple encryption is just to stack algorithms on top of each other—taking plaintext, encrypting it with DES, then encrypting the first ciphertext with a different key, then encrypting the second ciphertext with a third key. In reality, this technique is less effective than the technique that 3DES uses, which is to encrypt with one key, then decrypt with a second, and then encrypt with a third, as shown in Figure 5-5.

Figure 5-5
Diagram of 3DES

Triple DES (3DES)

This greatly increases the number of attempts needed to retrieve the key, and this is a significant enhancement of security. The additional security comes with a price, though. It can take up to three times as long to compute 3DES as it does to compute DES. However, the advances in memory and processing power in today's electronics should make this problem irrelevant in all devices except for very small low power handhelds.

The only weaknesses of 3DES are the ones that already exist in DES, and due to the use of different keys in the same algorithm, affecting a longer key length by adding the first keyspace to the second keyspace, and the greater resistance to brute forcing, 3DES has less actual weakness. 3DES is a good interim step before the new encryption standard, AES, is fully implemented to replace DES.

AES

Because of the advancement of technology and the progress being made in quickly retrieving DES keys, NIST put out a request for proposals for a new Advanced Encryption Standard (AES). It called for a block cipher using symmetric key cryptography and supporting key sizes of 128, 192, and 256 bits. After evaluation, the NIST had five finalists:

- **MARS**   IBM
- **RC6**   RSA
- **Rijndael**   John Daemen and Vincent Rijmen
- **Serpent**   Ross Anderson, Eli Biham, and Lars Knudsen
- **Twofish**   Bruce Schneier, John Kelsey, Doug Whiting, David Wagner, Chris Hall, and Niels Ferguson

In the fall of 2000, NIST picked Rijndael to be the new AES. It was chosen for its overall security as well as its good performance on limited capacity devices. Rijndael's design was influenced by Square, also written by John Daemen and Vincent Rijmen. Like Square, Rijndael is a block cipher separating data input in 128-bit blocks. Rijndael can also be configured to use blocks of 192 or 256 bits, but AES will standardize on 128-bit blocks. AES can have key sizes of 128, 192, and 256 bits, with the size of the key affecting the number of rounds used in the algorithm.

Like DES, AES works in three steps on every block of input data:

1. Add round key, performing an XOR of the block with a subkey.
2. Perform the number of normal rounds required by the key length.
3. Perform a regular round without the mix-column step found in the normal round.

After these steps have been performed, a 128-bit block of plaintext produces a 128-bit block of ciphertext. As mentioned in Step 2, AES performs multiple rounds. This is determined by the key size. A key size of 128 bits requires 9 rounds, 192-bit keys will require 11 rounds, and 256-bit keys use 13 rounds. There are four steps performed in every round:

- **Byte sub**   Each byte is replaced by its S-box substitute.
- **Shift row**   Bytes are arranged in a rectangle and shifted.
- **Mix column**   Matrix multiplication is performed based upon the arranged rectangle.
- **Add round key**   This round's subkey is cored in.

These steps are performed until the final round has been completed, and when the final step has been performed, the ciphertext is output.

This new algorithm is well thought-out and has suitable key length to provide security for many years to come. While there are currently no efficient attacks against AES, more time and analysis will tell if this standard can last as long as DES has.

CAST

CAST is an encryption algorithm similar to DES in its structure. It was designed by Carlisle Adams and Stafford Tavares. CAST uses a 64-bit block size for 64- and 128-bit key versions, and a 128-bit block size for the 256-bit key version. Like DES, it divides the plaintext block into a left half and a right half. The right half is then put through function f and then is XORed with the left half. This becomes the new right half, and the original right half becomes the new left half. This is repeated for eight rounds for a 64-bit key, and the left and right output is concatenated to form the ciphertext block.

As mentioned before, CAST supports longer key lengths than the original 64-bit one. Changes to the key length affect the number of rounds: CAST-128 specifies 16 rounds, and CAST-256 has 48 rounds. This algorithm in CAST-256 form was submitted for the AES standard but was not chosen. CAST has been through thorough analysis with only minor weaknesses discovered that are dependent on low numbers of rounds. There is currently no better way known to break high-round CAST than by brute forcing the key, meaning that with sufficient key length, CAST should be placed with other trusted algorithms.

RC

RC is a general term for several ciphers all designed by Ron Rivest—RC officially stands for Rivest Cipher. RC1, RC2, RC3, RC4, RC5, and RC6 are all ciphers in the series. RC1 and RC3 never made it to release, but RC2, RC4, RC5, and RC6 are all working algorithms.

RC2

RC2 was designed to be a DES replacement, and it is a variable-key-size block-mode cipher. The key size can be from 8 bits to 1,024 bits with the block size being fixed at 64 bits. RC2 breaks up the input blocks into four 16-bit words, and then puts them through 18 rounds of one of two operations. The two operations are mix and mash. The sequence in which the algorithms works is as follows:

1. Initialize the input block to words R_0 through R_3
2. Expand the key into K_0 through K_{63}

3. Initialize $j = 0$

4. Five mix rounds

5. One mash round

6. Six mix rounds

7. One mash round

8. Five mix rounds

This outputs 64 bits of ciphertext for 64 bits of plaintext. The individual operations are performed as follows, with "rol" in this description meaning to rotate the word left.

This is the mix operation:

$$Ri = R_i + K_j + (R_{i-1} \& R_{i-2}) + ((\sim R_{i-1}) \& R_{i-1})$$

$$j = j + 1$$

$$R_i = R_i \text{ rol } s_i$$

This is the Mash operation:

$$R_i = R_i + K[R_{i-1} \& 63]$$

According to RSA, RC2 is up to three times faster than DES. RSA maintained RC2 as a trade secret for a long time, with the source code eventually being illegally posted on the Internet. The ability of RC2 to accept different key lengths is one of the larger vulnerabilities in the algorithm. Any key length below 64 bits can be easily retrieved by modern computational power.

RC5

RC5 is a block cipher, written in 1994. It has multiple variable elements, numbers of rounds, key sizes, and block sizes. The algorithm starts by separating the input block into two words, A and B.

$$A = A + S_0$$

$$B = B + S_1$$

For $i = 1$ to r

$$A = ((A \text{ XOR } B) <<< B) + S_{2i}$$

$$B = ((B \text{ XOR } A) <<< A) + S_{2i+1}$$

A and B represent the ciphertext output. This algorithm is relatively new, but if configured to run enough rounds, RC5 seems to provide adequate security for current brute forcing technology. Rivest recommends using at least 12 rounds. With 12 rounds in the algorithm cryptanalysis in a linear fashion proves less effective than brute force against RC5, and differential analysis fails for 15 or more rounds. There is also a newer algorithm, RC6.

RC6

RC6 is based on the design of RC5. It uses a 128-bit block size, separated into four words of 32 bits each. It uses a round count of 20 to provide security, and it has three possible key sizes: 128, 192, and 256 bits. The four words are named A, B, C, D, and the algorithm works like this:

$$B = B + S_0$$

$$D = D + S_1$$

$$\text{For} \quad i = 1 - 20$$

$$[t = (B * (2B + 1)) <<< 5$$

$$u = (D * (2D + 1)) <<< 5$$

$$A = ((A \text{ XOR } t) <<< u) + S_{2i}$$

$$C = ((C \text{ XOR } u) <<< t) + S_{2i+1}$$

$$(A, B, C, D) = (B, C, D, A)]$$

$$A = A + S_{42}$$

$$C = C + S_{43}$$

The output of A, B, C, D after 20 rounds is the ciphertext.

RC6 is a modern algorithm that runs well on 32-bit computers. With a sufficient number of rounds, the algorithm makes both linear and differential cryptanalysis infeasible. The available key lengths make brute-force attacks extremely time-consuming. RC6 should provide adequate security for some time to come.

RC4

RC4 was created before RC5 and RC6, but it differs in operation. RC4 is a **stream cipher**, whereas all the symmetric ciphers we have looked at so far have been block-mode ciphers. A stream-mode cipher works by enciphering the plaintext in a stream, usually bit by bit. This makes stream ciphers faster than block-mode ciphers. Stream ciphers accomplish this by performing a bitwise XOR with the plaintext stream and a generated keystream.

RC4 operates in this manner. It was developed in 1987 and remained a trade secret of RSA until it was posted to the Internet in 1994. RC4 can use a key length of 8 to 2,048 bits, though the most common versions use 128-bit keys, or if subject to the old export restrictions, 40-bit keys. The key is used to initialize a 256-byte state table. This table is used to generate the pseudo-random stream that is XORed with the plaintext to generate the ciphertext.

The operation is performed as follows:

$$I = 0$$

$$j = 0$$

$$I = (I + 1) \bmod 256$$

$$j = (j + S_i) \bmod 256$$

Swap S_i and S_j

$$t = (S_i + S_j) \bmod 256$$

$$K = S_t$$

K is then XORed with the plaintext. Alternatively, K is XORed with the ciphertext to produce the plaintext.

The algorithm is fast, sometimes ten times faster than DES. The most vulnerable point of the encryption is the possibility of weak keys. One key in 256 can generate bytes closely correlated with key bytes.

Blowfish

Blowfish was designed in 1994 by Bruce Schneier. It is a block-mode cipher using 64-bit blocks and a variable key length from 32 to 448 bits. It was designed to run quickly on 32-bit microprocessors and is optimized for situations where there are few key changes. Encryption is done by separating the 64-bit input block into two 32-bit words, and then a function is executed every round. Blowfish has 16 rounds. Once the input has been split into left and right words, the following function is performed:

For $I = 1 - 16$

$$X_L = X_L \text{ XOR } P_i$$

$$X_R = F(X_L) \text{ XOR } X_R$$

Swap X_L and X_R

Then, swap X_L and X_R

$$X_R = X_R \text{ XOR } P_{17}$$

$$X_L = X_L \text{ XOR } P_{18}$$

The two words are then recombined to form the 64-bit output ciphertext.

The only successful cryptanalysis to date against Blowfish has been against variants that used reduced rounds. There does not seem to be a weakness in the full 16-round version.

IDEA

IDEA started out as PES, or Proposed Encryption Cipher, in 1990. It was modified to improve its resistance to differential cryptanalysis and its name was changed to IDEA (International Data Encryption Algorithm) in 1992. It is a block-mode cipher using a 64-bit block size and a 128-bit key. The input plaintext is split into four 16-bit segments, A, B, C, D. The process uses eight rounds with each round performing the following function:

$$A * S_1 = X_1$$

$$B + S_2 = X_2$$

$$C + S_3 = X_3$$

$$D * S_4 = X_4$$

$$X_1 \text{ XOR } X_3 = X_5$$

$$X_2 \text{ XOR } X_4 = X_6$$

$$X_5 * S_5 = X_7$$

$$X_6 + X_7 = X_8$$

$$X_8 * S_6 = X_9$$

$$X_7 + X_9 = X_{10}$$

$$X_1 \text{ XOR } X_9 = X_{11}$$

$$X_3 \text{ XOR } X_9 = X_{12}$$

$$X_2 \text{ XOR } X_{10} = X_{13}$$

$$X_4 \text{ XOR } X_{10} = X_{14}$$

$$X_{11} = A$$

$$X_{13} = B$$

$$X_{12} = C$$

$$X_{14} = D$$

Then the next round starts. After eight rounds are completed, four more steps are done:

$$X_{11} * S_{49} = C_1$$

$$X_{12} + S_{50} = C_2$$

$$X_{13} + S_{51} = C_3$$

$$X_{14} + S_{52} = C_4$$

The output of the last four steps is then concatenated to form the ciphertext.

This algorithm is new, but all current cryptanalysis on full, eight-round IDEA shows that the most efficient attack would be to brute force the key. The 128-bit key would prevent this attack being accomplished, given current computer technology. The only known issue is that IDEA is susceptible to a weak key—a key that is made of all zeros. This weak key is easy to check for, and the weakness is simple to mitigate.

Symmetric Encryption Summary

Symmetric algorithms are important because they are comparatively fast and have fewer computational requirements. Their main weakness is that two geographically distant parties need to have a key that matches exactly. In the past, keys could be much simpler and still be secure, but with today's computational power, simple keys can be brute forced very quickly. This means that larger and more complex keys must be used and exchanged. This exchange of keys is greatly facilitated by our next subject, asymmetric or public key cryptography.

Asymmetric Encryption

Asymmetric cryptography is in many ways completely different than symmetric cryptography. While both are used to keep data from being seen by unauthorized users, asymmetric cryptography uses two keys instead of one. It was invented by Whitfield Diffie and Martin Hellman in 1975. Asymmetric cryptography is more commonly known as public key cryptography. The system uses a pair of keys: a private one that is kept secret, and a public key that can be sent to anyone. The system's security relies upon resistance to deducing one key, given the other, and thus retrieving the plaintext from the ciphertext.

Public key systems typically work by using hard math problems. One of the more common methods is through the difficulty of factoring large numbers. These functions are often called **trapdoor functions**, as they are difficult to process without the key, but easy when you have the key—the trapdoor through the function. For example, given a prime number, say 293, and another prime, such as 307, it is an easy function to multiply them together to get 89,951. Given 89,951, it is not simple to find the factors 293 and 307 unless you know one of them already. Computers can easily multiply very large primes with hundreds or thousands of digits but cannot easily factor the product.

The strength of these functions is very important: because an attacker is likely to have access to the public key, they can run tests of known plaintext and produce ciphertext. This allows instant checking of guesses that are made about the keys of the algorithm. RSA, Diffie-Hellman, ECC, and ElGamal are all popular asymmetric protocols. We will look at all of them and their suitability for different functions.

RSA

RSA is one of the first public key cryptosystems ever invented. It can be used for both encryption and digital signatures. RSA is named after its inventors, Ron Rivest, Adi Shamir, and Leonard Adleman, and was first published in 1977.

This algorithm uses the product of two very large prime numbers and works on the principle of difficulty in factoring such large numbers. It's best to choose large prime numbers from 100 to 200 digits in length and that are equal in length. These two primes will be P and Q. Randomly choose an encryption key, E, so that E is greater than 1, E is less than $P * Q$, and E must be odd. E must also be relatively prime to $(P - 1)$ and $(Q - 1)$. Then compute the decryption key D:

$$D = E^{-1} \bmod ((P - 1)(Q - 1))$$

Now that the encryption key and decryption key have been generated, the two prime numbers can be discarded, but they should not be revealed. To encrypt a message, it should be divided into blocks less than the product of P and Q. Then,

$$C_i = M_i^E \bmod (P * Q)$$

C is the output block of ciphertext matching the block length of the input message, M. To decrypt a message take ciphertext, C, and use this function:

$$M_i = C_i^D \bmod (P * Q)$$

This use of the second key retrieves the plaintext of the message.

This is a simple function, but its security has withstood the test of over 20 years of analysis. Considering the effectiveness of RSA's security and the ability to have two keys, why are there symmetric encryption algorithms at all? The answer is speed. RSA in software can be 100 times slower than DES, and in hardware it can be even slower.

RSA can be used to do both regular encryption and digital signatures. Typically, RSA and the other public key systems are used in conjunction with symmetric key cryptography. Public key, the slower protocol, is used to exchange the private key, and then the communication uses the faster symmetric key protocol. This process is known as *electronic key exchange*.

Since the security of RSA is based upon the supposed difficulty of factoring large numbers, the main weaknesses are in the implementations of the protocol. Until recently, RSA was a patented algorithm, but it was a de facto standard for many years.

Diffie-Hellman

Diffie-Hellman was created in 1976 by Whitfield Diffie and Martin Hellman. This protocol is one of the most common encryption protocols in use today. It plays a role in the electronic key exchange method of the Secure Sockets Layer (SSL) protocol. It is also used by the SSH and IPsec protocols. This protocol is important because it enables the sharing of a secret key between two people who have not contacted each other before.

The protocol, like RSA, uses large prime numbers to work. Two users agree to two numbers, P and G, with P being a sufficiently large prime number, and G being the generator. Both users pick a secret number, a and b. Then both users compute their public number:

User 1 $X = Ga \bmod P$, with X being the public number

User 2 $Y = Gb \bmod P$, with Y being the public number

The users then exchange public numbers. User 1 knows P, G, a, X, Y.

User 1   Computes $Ka = Y^a \bmod P$

User 2   Computes $Kb = X^b \bmod P$

With $Ka = Kb = K$, now both users know the new shared secret K.

This is the basic algorithm, and though there have been methods to strengthen it, Diffie-Hellman is still in wide use. It remains very effective because of the nature of what it is protecting, which is just a temporary automatically generated secret key that is only good for a single communication session.

ElGamal

ElGamal can be used for both encryption and digital signatures. Taher ElGamal designed the system in the early 1980s. This system was never patented and is free for use. It is used as the U.S. government standard for digital signatures.

The system is based upon the difficulty of calculating discrete logarithms in a finite field. Three numbers are needed to generate a key pair. User 1 chooses a prime, P, and two random numbers, F and D. F and D should both be less than P. Then you can calculate the public key A:

$A = D^F \bmod P$

Then A, D, and P are shared with the second user, with F being the private key. To encrypt a message, M, a random key, k, is chosen that is relatively prime to $P - 1$. Then,

$C_1 = D^k \bmod P$

$C_2 = A^k M \bmod P$

C_1 and C_2 makes up the ciphertext. Decryption is done by

$$M = C_2/C_1^F \bmod P$$

ElGamal uses a different function for digital signatures. To sign a message, M, once again choose a random value k that is relatively prime to $P - 1$. Then,

$$C_1 = Dk \bmod P$$

$$C_2 = (M - C_1*F)/k \ (\bmod P - 1)$$

C_1 concatenated to C_2 is the digital signature.

ElGamal is an effective algorithm and has been in use for some time. It is used primarily for digital signatures. Like all asymmetric cryptography, it is slower than symmetric cryptography.

ECC

Elliptic curve cryptography (ECC) works on the basis of elliptic curves. An elliptic curve is a simple function that is drawn as a gently looping curve on the X,Y plane. They are defined by this equation:

$$y^2 = x^3 + ax^2 + b$$

Elliptic curves work because they have a special property—that you can add two points on the curve together and get a third point on the curve.

For cryptography, the elliptic curve works as a public key algorithm. Users agree on an elliptic curve and a fixed curve point. This information is not a shared secret, these points can be made public without compromising the security of the system. User 1 then chooses a secret random number, K_1, and then computes a public key based upon a point on the curve:

$$P_1 = K_1 * F$$

User 2 performs the same function and generates P2. Now user 1 can send user 2 a message by generating a shared secret:

$$S = K_1 * P_2$$

User 2 can generate the same shared secret independently:

$$S = K_2 * P_1$$

This is true because

$$K_1 * P_2 = K_1 * (K_2 * F) = (K_1 * K_2) * F = K_2 * (K_1 * F) = K_2 * P_1$$

The security of elliptic curve systems has been questioned, mostly because of lack of analysis. However, all public key systems rely on the difficulty of certain math problems. It would take a breakthrough in math for any of the mentioned systems to be weakened dramatically, but research has been done about the problems and has shown that the elliptic curve problem has been more resistant to incremental advances. Again, as with all cryptography algorithms, only time will tell how secure they really are.

Asymmetric Encryption Summary

Asymmetric encryption creates the possibility of digital signatures and also corrects the main weakness of symmetric cryptography. The ability to send messages securely without having to have had prior contact is growing to be one of the basic blocks of secure communication. Digital signatures will enable faster and more efficient exchange of all kinds of documents, including legal documents. With strong algorithms and good key lengths, security can be assured.

Usage

The use of cryptographic algorithms grows every day as more and more information becomes digitally encoded or put online. All of this data needs to be secured, and the best current way to do that has been encryption. We have looked at the algorithms; we will now consider some of the tasks they accomplish and things that they are best suited for. Security is typically defined as a product of five components: confidentiality, integrity, availability, authentication, and nonrepudiation. Encryption can address four of these five components with confidentiality, integrity, nonrepudiation, and authentication.

Confidentiality

Confidentiality is what is typically thought about when the term *security* comes up. Confidentiality is the ability to keep some piece of data a secret. In the digital world, confidentiality is something that encryption excels at providing.

There are two uses of confidentiality: on stored data and on transmitted data. In both cases, symmetric encryption is favored because of its speed and because some asymmetric algorithms can significantly increase the size of the object being encrypted. In the case of a stored item, there is typically no need to have a public key, as the item is being encrypted to protect it from others. In the case of transmitted data, the typical case is to use public key cryptography to exchange the secret key, and then to use symmetric cryptography to ensure the confidentiality of the data being sent.

Asymmetric cryptography does protect confidentiality, but its size and speed make it more efficient at protecting the confidentiality of small units, such as for electronic key exchange. In all cases, it is the strength of the algorithms and the length of the keys that ensure the secrecy of the data in question.

Integrity

Integrity is better known as *message integrity,* and it is a crucial component of message security. When a message is sent, both the sender and recipient need to know that the message was not altered in transmission. This is especially important when it comes to legal contracts—recipients need to know that the contracts have not been altered. The signers also have to have a way to validate that the contract they signed is not altered in the future.

This integrity is provided with one-way hash functions and digital signatures. The hash functions compute the message digests, and this guarantees the integrity of the message by allowing easy testing to determine whether any part of the message has been changed. The message now has a computed function (the hash value) to tell the users to resend the message if it was intercepted and interfered with.

This hash value is combined with asymmetric cryptography by taking the message's hash value and encrypting it with the user's private key. This lets anyone with the user's public key decrypt the hash and compare it to the locally computed hash, ensuring not only the integrity of the message but positively identifying the sender.

Nonrepudiation

An item of some confusion, nonrepudiation is actually fairly simple. It means that the sender cannot later deny that they sent the message. This is important in electronic exchanges of data because of the lack of face-to-face meetings. Nonrepudiation is based upon public key cryptography and the principle of only you knowing your private key. The presence of a message signed by you, using your private key, which nobody else should know, is an example of nonrepudiation. When a third party can check your signature using your public key, that disproves any claim that you were not the one who actually sent the message. Nonrepudiation is tied to asymmetric cryptography and cannot be implemented with symmetric algorithms.

Authentication

Authentication is simply being able to prove you are who you say you are. Authentication is similar to nonrepudiation, except that it is often used before communication begins, not after. Authentication is also typically used in both directions as part of a protocol.

Authentication can be done in a multitude of ways, the most basic being the use of a simple password. Every time you check your e-mail, you authenticate yourself to the server. This process can grow to need two or three identifying factors, like a password, a token, and a biometric.

Digital certificates are one form of such tokens. When you log in to a secure web site, one-way authentication occurs. You want to know that you are logging into the server that you mean to, so your browser checks the server's digital certificate. This is a token that is digitally signed by a trusted third party, assuring you that the sender is genuine.

This authentication is one way because the server does not need to know that you are who you say you are—it will authenticate your credit card later on. However, two-way authentication can work the same way, where you send your digital certificate signed by a third party, and the other entity you are communicating with sends theirs.

While symmetric encryption can be used as a simple manner of authentication (only the authorized should know the secret, after all), asymmetric encryption is better suited to show, via digital signatures and certificates, that you are who you say you are.

Digital Signatures

Digital signatures have been touted as being the key to truly paperless document flow, and they do have promise for improving the system. Digital signatures are based upon both hashing functions and asymmetric cryptography. Both encryption methods play an important role when signing digital documents.

Unprotected digital documents are very easy for anyone to change. If a document is edited after an individual signs it, it is important that this modification can be detected. To protect against document editing, hashing functions are used to create a digest of the message that is unique and easily reproducible by both parties. This ensures that the message integrity is complete.

Protection must also be provided that the intended party actually did sign the message, and that someone did not edit the message and the hash of the message. This is done by asymmetric encryption. The properties of asymmetric encryption allow anyone to use a person's public key to generate a message that can only be read by that person, as they are theoretically the only one with access to the private key. In the case of digital signatures, this process works exactly in reverse. When a user can decrypt the hash with the public key of the originator, that user knows that the hash was encrypted by the corresponding private key. This use of asymmetric encryption is a very good example of nonrepudiation, because only the signer would have access to the private key. This is how digital signatures work, by using integrity and nonrepudiation to prove not only that the people signed, but also what they signed.

Key Escrow

The impressive growth of the use of encryption technology has led to new issues in the handling of keys. Key escrow and key recovery are two issues in the use of asymmetric encryption that are often discussed.

Encryption became very good at hiding secrets, and with computer technology being affordable to everyone, criminals and other ill-willed people began using it to conceal communications and business dealings from law enforcement agencies. Government agencies, because they could not break the encryption, began asking for key escrow. **Key escrow**, in a simple form, is a system by which your private key is kept both by you and by the government. This allows people with a court order to retrieve your private key and have access to anything encrypted with your public key. Technically, this is typically done by encrypting the data with two keys, thereby giving the government access to your plaintext data. This has a tendency to negate the security provided by encryption, because the government will now have a huge complex infrastructure of systems to hold every escrowed key, and the security of those systems is less efficient than the security of your memorizing the key. These issues will affect the design and security of encryption technologies for the foreseeable future.

Chapter Review

Chapter Summary

After reading this chapter and completing the exercises, you should understand the following about cryptography.

Identify the Three Different Types of Cryptography

- Symmetric cryptography is based upon the concept of a shared secret or key.
- Asymmetric cryptography is based upon a key that can be made openly available to the public, yet still provide security.
- One-way, or hashing, cryptography takes data and enciphers it. However, there is no way to decipher it and no key.

Recognize the Current Cryptographic Algorithms

- Hashing
- SHA
- MD (Message Digest)
- MD2
- MD4
- MD5
- Symmetric
- DES (Data Encryption Standard)
- 3DES
- AES (Advanced Encryption Standard)
- CAST
- RC (Rivest Cipher)
- RC2
- RC4
- RC5
- RC6
- Blowfish
- IDEA
- Asymmetric

- RSA
- Diffie-Hellman
- ElGamal
- ECC

Show How Cryptography Is Used for Security

- Confidentiality is gained because encryption is very good at scrambling information to make it look like random noise, when in fact a key can decipher the message and return it to its original state.

- Integrity is gained because hashing algorithms are specifically designed to check integrity. They can reduce a message to a mathematical value that can be independently calculated, guaranteeing that any message alteration would change the mathematical value.

- Nonrepudiation is the property of not being able to claim that you did not send the data. This property is gained because of the properties of private keys.

- Authentication, or being able to prove you are you, is achieved through the private keys involved in digital signatures.

- Digital Signatures, combining multiple types of encryption, provide an authentication method verified by a third party, allowing you to use them as if you were actually signing the document with your regular signature.

Key Terms

Algorithm *(78)*
Block cipher *(85)*
Collision attack *(81)*
Cryptanalysis *(77)*
Cryptography *(77)*
Differential cryptanalysis *(77)*
Hash *(81)*
Key *(78)*
Key escrow *(100)*
Key management *(85)*
Keyspace *(80)*
Linear cryptanalysis *(78)*
Multiple encryption *(87)*
Shared secret *(84)*
Shift cipher *(77)*
Stream cipher *(91)*
Transposition cipher *(77)*
Trapdoor functions *(94)*
Vigenère cipher *(79)*
XOR *(80)*

Key Terms Quiz

Use terms from the Key Terms list to complete the sentences that follow. Don't use the same term more than once. Not all terms will be used.

1. The process of analyzing available information to return an encrypted message back to its original form is called _____.

2. A(n) _____ is a step-by-step problem-solving procedure.

3. A type of math problem that is difficult unless you know a specific value is called a(n) _____.

4. The results of one-way cryptographic functions are commonly called the _____.

5. _____ is the science of taking data and obscuring it so that it will be hidden from unauthorized users.

6. _____ refers to every possible value for a cryptographic key.

7. _____ is the function most commonly seen in cryptography, a "bitwise exclusive" or.

8. _____ is required for symmetric encryption.

9. A simple way to hide information, the _____ moves a letter a set number of places down the alphabet.

10. Attempts to find two sets of text that will generate the same hash is called a(n) _____.

Multiple-Choice Quiz

1. What is DES being replaced with?

   A. Diffie-Hellman

   B. AES

   C. RC6

   D. MD5

2. What kind of encryption uses the concept of public keys?

   A. Asymmetric

   B. Hash

   C. Linear cryptanalysis

   D. Authentication

3. How many bits are in a block of the SHA algorithm?

   A. 128

   B. 2048

    C. 512

    D. 56

4. If a message has a hash, how does the hash protect the message in transit?

    A. If the message is edited, the hash will no longer match.

    B. Hashing destroys the message so it cannot be read by anyone.

    C. Hashing encrypts the message so that only the private key holder can read it.

    D. The hash makes the message uneditable.

5. A secure encryption key is…

    A. Easy to remember

    B. Long and random

    C. Long and predictable

    D. Short

6. What does a hash function do?

    A. Creates a secure tunnel

    B. Breaks encryption by trying every possible key

    C. Multiplies two very large primes

    D. Creates a unique digest of a message

7. What is a shift cipher?

    A. A cipher with public and private keys

    B. A cipher that cannot be broken except by hand calculations

    C. One that uses the geometry of elliptical curves

    D. A cipher that shifts the letters in the alphabet by a numeric amount

8. A digital signature requires what types of encryption?

    A. Hashing and asymmetric

    B. Asymmetric and symmetric

    C. Hashing and symmetric

    D. ECC and asymmetric

9. What makes symmetric encryption superior to asymmetric for larger data sets?

    A. It's more secure.

    B. Speed

    C. Anyone with the public key could decrypt the data.

    D. It uses a hash.

10. How is 3DES different than many other types of encryption listed here?

    A. It only encrypts the hash.

    B. It hashes the message before encryption.

    C. It uses three keys and multiple encryption and/or decryption sets.

    D. It can display the key publicly.

11. What is typically necessary to perform cryptanalysis?

    A. The key

    B. Large amounts of plaintext and ciphertext

    C. A hash of the message

    D. Computers able to guess at key values faster than a billion times per second

12. What is a brute-force attack?

    A. Feeding certain plaintext into the algorithm to deduce the key

    B. Capturing ciphertext with known plaintext values to deduce the key

    C. Sending every key value at the algorithm to find the correct key

    D. Sending two large men to the key owner's house to retrieve the key

13. What cipher was chosen to be the new AES standard?

    A. IDEA

    B. RC6

    C. ECC

    D. Rijndael

14. When a message is sent, no matter what its format, why do we care about its integrity?

    A. To ensure proper formatting

    B. To show that the encryption keys are undamaged

    C. To show that a message has not been edited in transit

    D. To show that no one has viewed it

15. What is Diffie-Hellman most commonly used for?

    A. Symmetric encryption key exchange

    B. Signing digital contracts

    C. Securing e-mail

    D. Storing encrypted passwords

Essay Quiz

1. Describe how asymmetric encryption allows PKI to function.

2. Explain how symmetric encryption works to protect files.

3. Management brought in consultants at the beginning of the year, whose recommendations included implementation of a "paperless" office. Several

vendors to the company are also going paperless, but this has forced some changes to the process for contracts in the company. Since electronic documents could be altered after they have been signed, company counsel wants to ensure that a document that is sent is an exact duplicate of the original and that it has not been altered. Write a memo to counsel that explains clearly, without any technical jargon, how hash functions can provide this guarantee.

4. Explain why 3DES is stronger than regular DES.

5. Explain the concept of keyspace. How does it improve an algorithm's ability to protect data?

Lab Projects

Lab Project 5.1

View the public key that allows encryption to be performed for https connections. You will need a lab computer with a web browser installed to complete this project.
   Do the following:

1. Go to a web page that supports encrypted sessions. You can tell if the page supports encrypted sessions because a locked padlock icon will appear in the lower right-hand corner of your browser.

2. Depending on your browser, single- or double-click the locked padlock to bring up the certificate information.

3. Scroll down until you find the Field marked "Public Key."

4. Repeat the process with another site and compare the two public keys.

5. Convert the Hex notation the key comes in to binary, and verify the number of bits the key is supposed to have.

6. Document your results.

Lab Project 5.2

Test PGP to ensure that it is giving out different private key lengths.
   You will need the following materials:

• A lab computer with PGP installed on it

Then do the following:

1. Start PGPKeys.

2. Generate an RSA key with the smallest available bit strength.

3. Copy the key into a regular document.

4. Observe the length of seemingly random text.

5. Generate a Diffie-Hellman key with the largest possible bit strength.

6. Copy the key into a regular document.

7. Compare the length of the respective keys.

Public Key Infrastructure

Upon completion of this lesson, you will be able to:

- Explain the basics of public key infrastructures
- Describe the role of certificate authorities
- Describe the role of registration authorities
- Describe the purpose of certificate repositories
- Explain trust and certificate verification
- Be able to use digital certificates
- Compare and contrast centralized infrastructures and decentralized infrastructures
- List and describe means of ensuring private key protection
- Describe the role of public certificate authorities
- Describe the purpose of in-house certificate authorities
- Describe the purpose of outsourced certificate authorities
- Describe various trust models used when tying different PKIs together

Public key infrastructures (PKIs) are becoming a central security foundation for more and more companies. The technology was developed more than a decade ago, but only within the last few years has it really started to bloom and be integrated into diverse environments around the world. It can provide the underlying mechanisms that offer confidentiality, integrity, authentication, and nonrepudiation. It does this by offering an infrastructure that uses symmetric and asymmetric cryptographic technologies that can be used by e-mail clients, virtual private network products, web server components, and domain controllers to authenticate users for network participation and resource access. The important point here is that it offers an infrastructure or a framework that provides a foundation based on which different products and technologies can integrate with each other to supply various security services. The other approach, without PKIs, is to implement many different security solutions and hope for interoperability and equal levels of protection.

The Basics of Public Key Infrastructures

A PKI is a structure that provides all of the necessary components for different types of users and entities to be able to communicate securely and in a predictable manner. A PKI is made up of hardware, applications, policies, services, programming interfaces, cryptographic algorithms, protocols, users, and utilities. These components work together to allow communication to take place using public key cryptography and symmetric keys for digital signatures, data encryption, and integrity. (Please refer to Chapter 7 if you need a refresher on these concepts.) Many different applications and protocols can provide the same type of functionality, so why would anyone need to go through the trouble of constructing and implementing a PKI if applications and protocols can already do this? It all comes down to a level of trust.

If John and Diane want to communicate securely, John can generate his own public/private key pair and send his public key to Diane or place his public key in a directory that is available to everyone. If Diane receives John's public key, either from him or from a public directory, how does she know it really came from John? Maybe another individual is masquerading as John and replaced John's public key with her own, as shown in Figure 6-1. If this took place, Diane would believe that her messages could only be read by John and that the replies were actually from him. However, she would really be communicating with Katie. What is needed is a way to verify an individual's identity, to ensure that a person's public key is bound to their identity, and thus ensure that the previous scenario (and others) cannot take place.

In PKI environments, entities called *registration authorities* and *certificate authorities* will provide a service similar to that of the Department of Motor Vehicles (DMV). When

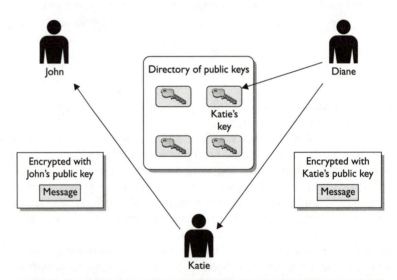

Figure 6-1 Without a PKI, individuals could spoof each other's identities.

Man-in-the-Middle Attack

1. Katie replaces John's public key with her key in the publicly accessible directory.
2. Diane extracts what she thinks is John's key, but it is in fact Katie's key.
3. Katie can now read messages Diane encrypts and sends to John.
4. After Katie decrypts and reads Diane's message, she encrypts it with John's public key and sends it on to him so he will not be the wiser.

John goes to register for a driver's license, he has to prove his identity to the DMV by providing his passport, birth certificate, or other identification documentation. If the DMV is satisfied with the proof John provides (and John passes a driving test), the DMV will create a driver's license that can then be used by John to prove his identity. If John is stopped by a police officer a few months later, the officer will ask for this license. The officer will not fully trust John, but the officer does trust the DMV and will be more willing to trust John and his identity claim if it matches what is stated on the license.

In the PKI context, while some variations exist in specific products, the registration authority will require proof of identity from the individual requesting a certificate and will validate this information. The registration authority will then advise the certificate authority to generate a certificate, which is analogous to a driver's license. The certificate authority will digitally sign the certificate using its private key. When Diane receives John's certificate and verifies that it was actually digitally signed by a certificate authority that she trusts, she will believe that the certificate is actually John's—not because she trusts John, but because she trusts the entity that is vouching for his identity (the certificate authority).

This is commonly referred to as a third-party trust model. Public keys are components of digital certificates, so when Diane verifies the certificate authority's digital signature, this verifies that the certificate is truly John's and that the public key the certificate contains is also John's. This is how John's identity is bound to his public key.

This process allows John to authenticate himself to Diane and communicate with her through encryption without prior communication or a preexisting relationship. Once Diane is convinced of the legitimacy of John's public key, she can use it to encrypt and decrypt messages between herself and John, as illustrated in Figure 6-2.

Figure 6-2
Public keys are components of digital certificates.

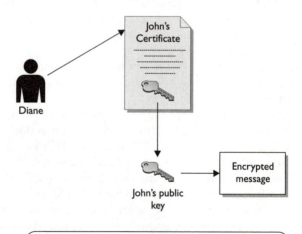

1. Diane validates the certificate.
2. Diane extracts John's public key.
3. Diane uses John's public key for encryption purposes.

There are several applications and protocols that can generate public/private key pairs and provide functionality similar to what a PKI provides, but there is no third party that the two communicating parties both trust. For two entities to choose to communicate this way without a third party vouching for each other's identity, they must choose to trust each other and the communication channel they are using. In many situations, it is impractical and dangerous to arbitrarily trust an individual you do not know, and this is when the components of a PKI must fall into place—to provide the necessary level of trust you cannot, or choose not to, provide on your own.

What does the "infrastructure" in "public key infrastructure" really mean? An infrastructure provides a sustaining groundwork for other things to be built upon. For example, network topology and data-link technologies (Ethernet, Token Ring, and the like) provide us with a foundation for a network, but without the operating systems, applications, and users, nothing very interesting can take place. On the other hand, without this network foundation (topology and data-link technologies) the operating systems, applications, and users could not communicate or participate in a network. So an infrastructure works at a low level to provide a predictable and uniform environment that allows other higher level technologies to work together through uniform access points. The environment that the infrastructure provides allows these higher level applications to communicate with each other and gives them the underlying tools to carry out their tasks.

Certificate Authorities

The **certificate authority (CA)** is the trusted authority for certifying individuals' identities and creating an electronic document indicating that individuals are who they say they are. That electronic document is referred to as a **digital certificate**, and it establishes an association between the subject's identity and a public key. The private key that is paired with the public key in the certificate is stored separately.

The CA is more than just a piece of software; it is actually made up of the software, hardware, procedures, policies, and people who are involved in validating individuals' identities and generating the certificates. This means that if one of these components is compromised, it can negatively affect the CA overall and can threaten the integrity of the certificates it produces.

Every CA should have a *certification practices statement (CPS)* that outlines how identities are verified, the steps the CA follows to generate, maintain, and transmit certificates, and why the CA can be trusted to fulfill its responsibilities. It describes how keys are secured, what data is placed within a digital certificate, and how revocations will be handled. If a company is going to use and depend upon a public CA, the company's security officers, administrators, and legal department should review the CA's entire CPS to ensure that it will properly meet the company's needs, and to make sure that the level of security claimed by the CA is high enough for their use and environment. A critical aspect of a PKI is the trust between the users and the CA, so the CPS should be reviewed and understood to ensure that this level of trust is warranted.

The **certificate server** is the actual service that issues certificates based on the data provided during the initial registration process. The server constructs and populates

How Do We Know We Can Actually Trust a CA?

This question is part of the continuing debate on how much security PKIs actually provide. Overall, people put a lot of faith in a CA. The companies that provide CA services understand this and also understand that their business is based on their reputation. If a CA was compromised or did not follow through on its various responsibilities, word would get out and they would quickly lose customers and business. CAs work to ensure the reputation of their product and services by implementing very secure facilities, methods, procedures, and personnel. But it is up to the company or individual to determine what degree of trust can actually be given and what level of risk is acceptable.

the digital certificate with the necessary information and combines the user's public key with the resulting certificate. The certificate is then digitally signed with CA's private key. (To learn more about how digital signatures are created and verified, review Chapter 10.)

Registration Authorities

The **registration authority** (RA) is the component that accepts a request for a digital certificate and performs the necessary steps of registering and authenticating the person requesting the certificate. The authentication requirements differ depending on the type of certificate being requested.

The types of certificates available can vary between different CAs, but there are usually at least three different types, and they are referred to as classes.

- **Class 1**   A Class 1 certificate is usually used to verify an individual's identity through e-mail. A person who receives a Class 1 certificate can use their public/private key pair to digitally sign e-mail and encrypt message contents.

- **Class 2**   A Class 2 certificate may be used for software signing. A software vendor would register for this type of certificate so they could digitally sign their software. This will provide integrity for the software after it is developed and released, and it will allow the receiver of the software to verify where the software actually came from.

- **Class 3**   A Class 3 certificate may be used by a company to set up its own certificate authority, which will allow it to carry out its own identification verification and generate certificates internally.

Each higher class of certificate can carry out more powerful and critical tasks than the one before it. This is why the different classes have different requirements for proof of identity. If you want to receive a Class 1 certificate, you may only be asked to provide your name, e-mail address, and physical address. For a Class 2 certification, you may need to give the RA more data, such as your driver's license, passport, and company information that can be verified. To obtain a Class 3 certificate, you will be asked to provide even more information and most likely will need to go to the RA's office for a face-to-face meeting. Each CA will outline the certification classes it provides and the identification requirements that must be met to acquire each type of certificate.

In most situations, when a user requests a Class 1 certificate, the registration process will require the user to enter specific information into a Web-based form. The web page will have a section that will step the user through creating a public/private key pair, which will allow the user to choose the size of the keys to be created. Once all the data is inserted into the form, the browser initiates the key generation process. It will often require random input values, which may be acquired through random mouse movements or keystrokes, or by extracting specific information from within the system itself. These random values are inserted into a cryptographic algorithm that is used to generate the keys, and the resulting keys are saved to a local key store. If the key store is being created for the first time, the application should request a password from the user that will be used to access and use the keys held within that particular key store.

Once these steps have been completed, the public key is attached to the certificate registration form and both are forwarded to the RA for processing. The RA is responsible only for the registration process and cannot actually generate a certificate. Once the RA is finished processing the request and verifying the individual's identity, the request will be sent to the CA. The certificate server (CS), which is a component of the CA, will generate the digital certificate, integrate the necessary data into the certificate fields (user identification information, public key, validity dates, proper use for the key and certificate, and so on), and send a copy of the certificate to the user. These steps are shown in Figure 6-3. The certificate may also be posted to a publicly accessible directory so that others can have access to it.

In the previous description, a web browser generated the cryptographic key pair, but other applications can have this capability, too. A user can also have more than one private/public key pair for different applications and for different purposes. In most implementations, different applications will create and maintain their own key store and not share it with other programs unless the different applications were created by the same vendor. If a user has two or more applications that were developed by the same software vendor, they might, but might not, share the same key pair and store.

The keys and certificates within the stores can be accessed through specific interfaces. If application A created its own key pair and key store, and application B knows how to make a request to this store's interface to use the keys and certificate, then it can use these items instead of having to generate its own. However, if applications A and B have created individual certificates and generated their own key pairs, they will most likely also have created their own key stores.

If an application creates a key store that can be accessed by other applications, it will provide a standardized interface, referred to as an application programming interface (API). In Netscape and UNIX systems, this interface is usually PKCS #11, and in

Figure 6-3   Steps for obtaining a digital certificate

Microsoft applications the interface is Crypto API (CAPI). As an example, Figure 6-4 shows that application A went through the process of registering a certificate and generating a key pair. It created a key store that provides an interface to allow other applications to communicate with it and use the items held within the store.

Figure 6-4
Some key stores
can be shared
by different
applications.

Sharing Stores

Different applications from the same vendor may share key stores. Microsoft applications keep a user's keys and certificates in a Registry entry within that particular user's profile. The applications save and retrieve them from this single location, or key store.

The local key store is just one location where these items can be held. Often, the digital certificate and public key are also stored in a certificate repository (as discussed in the "Certificate Repositories" section of this chapter) so that it is available to a subset of individuals.

Local Registration Authorities

A *local registration authority (LRA)* performs the same functions as an RA, but the LRA is closer to the end users. This component is usually implemented in companies that have their own internal PKI and have distributed sites. Each site has users that need RA services, so instead of requiring them to communicate with one central RA, each site can have their own LRA. This reduces the amount of traffic that would be created by several users making requests across WAN lines.

The LRA will perform identification, verification, and registration functions. It will then send the request, along with the user's public key, to a centralized CA so that the certificate can be generated. It acts as an interface between the users and the CA.

Certificate Repositories

Once the certificate is registered, identity proven, and a key pair generated, the certificate must be put somewhere. Public keys need to be available to whomever requires them to communicate within a PKI environment. These keys, and their corresponding certificates, are usually held in a publicly available repository. *Repository* is a general term that describes a centralized directory that can be accessed by a subset of individuals. The directories are usually LDAP-compliant, meaning that they can be accessed and searched via the Lightweight Directory Access Protocol (LDAP).

When an individual initializes communication with another person, the sender can send their certificate and public key to the receiver, which will allow the receiver to communicate with the sender using encryption or digital signatures (or both) without needing to track down the necessary public key in a certificate repository. This is equivalent to the sender saying, "If you would like to encrypt any future messages you send to me, or if you would like the ability to verify my digital signature, here are the necessary components." But if a person wants to encrypt the first message sent to the receiver, the sender will need to find the receiver's public key in a certificate repository. (For a refresher on how public and private keys come into play with encryption and digital signatures, please refer to Chapter 5.)

Since the certificates are to be available and used by the public, or by a wide range of people, special emphasis should be put into looking at the specific information included within the certificates. For example, some certificates allow the CA to insert an individual's address and phone number into specific fields within the certificate. This may be more information than a company wants to release about its employees. Similarly all certificates must contain a distinguished name, and this might give outsiders some insight into the naming conventions used by the company. Before these items are actually inserted into certificates and released, a company needs to ensure that it does not provide too much information and possibly open the door to a security compromise. The company can review the CA's CPS to find out exactly what type of data will and will not be included within the certificates the CA creates.

A **certificate repository** is a holding place for individuals' certificates and public keys that are participating in a particular PKI environment. The security requirements for repositories themselves are not as high as is needed for actual CAs and for the equipment and software used to carry out CA functions. Since each certificate is digitally signed by the CA, if a certificate stored in the certificate repository is modified, the recipient would be able to detect this change and not accept the certificate as valid.

Trust and Certificate Verification

We have explored the reason that we would need a PKI—we do not automatically trust individuals we do not know. Security is all about being suspicious and being safe, so we need a third party that we *do* trust to vouch for the other individual before confidence can be instilled and sensitive communication can take place. But what does it mean that we trust a CA, and how can we use this to our advantage?

Distinguished Names

A distinguished name is a label that follows the X.500 standard. This standard defines a naming convention that can be employed so that each subject within an organization has a unique name. An example is {Country = US, Organization = Real Secure, Organizational Unit = R&D, Location = Washington}.

CAs use distinguished names to identify the owners of specific certificates.

When a user chooses to trust a CA, they will download that CA's digital certificate and public key, which will be stored on their local computer. Most browsers have a list of CAs configured to be trusted by default, so when a user installs a new web browser several of the most well-known and most trusted CAs will be trusted without any change of settings. An example of this listing is shown in Figure 6-5.

In the Microsoft CAPI environment, the user can add and remove CAs from this list as needed. In production environments that require a higher degree of protection, this list will be pruned, and possibly the only CAs listed will be the company's internal CAs. This ensures that digitally signed software will only be automatically installed if it was signed by the company's CA. Other products, like Entrust, use centrally controlled policies to determine which CAs are to be trusted instead of expecting the user to make these critical decisions.

There are a number of steps involved in checking the validity of a message. Suppose Maynard receives a digitally signed message from Joyce, who he does not know or trust. Joyce has also included her digital certificate with her message, which has her public key embedded within it. Before Maynard can be sure of the authenticity of this message, he has some work to do. The steps are illustrated in Figure 6-6.

First, Maynard will see which CA signed Joyce's certificate and compare it to the list of CAs he has configured within his computer. He trusts the CAs in his list and no others. (If the certificate was signed by a CA he does not have in the list, he would not accept the certificate as being valid, and thus he could not be sure that this message was actually sent from Joyce or that the attached key was actually her public key.)

Figure 6-5
Browsers have a long list of CAs configured to be trusted by default.

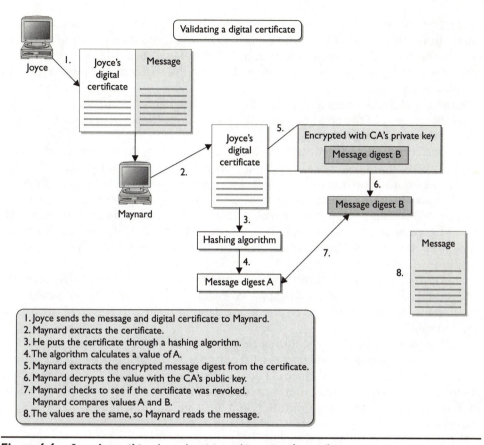

Figure 6-6 Steps for verifying the authenticity and integrity of a certificate

Maynard sees that the CA that signed Joyce's certificate is indeed in his list of trusted CAs, so he will pass Joyce's certificate through a hashing algorithm (such as MD5 or SHA1), which will result in a message digest—call the resulting message digest A.

Every certificate has a different encrypted message digest value embedded within it, which is the digital signature. The embedded message digest value is encrypted with the CA's private key, which is what digitally signing means—to encrypt a message digest with a private key. Maynard takes the CA's public key and decrypts the embedded digital signature value—call the decrypted digital signature value B.

If values A and B match, then Maynard can be assured that this CA did actually create the certificate, so he can now trust the origin of Joyce's certificate. But he is not done yet. Maynard needs to be sure that the issuing CA has not revoked this certificate.

The use of digital signatures allows certificates to be saved in public directories without the concern of them being accidentally or intentionally altered. If a user extracts a certificate from a repository and creates a message digest value that does not match the digital signature embedded within the certificate itself, that user will know that the certificate has been modified by someone other than the CA, and they will know not to accept the validity of the corresponding public key. Similarly, an attacker could not create a new message digest, encrypt it, and embed it within the certificate because they would not have access to the CA's private key.

Although Maynard trusts the CA that created this digital certificate for Joyce, and he trusts the integrity of the certificate (because the message digest values match), he still has a few steps to complete.

As stated earlier, the CA generates the certificate and inserts the requester's identification information within it. For a simple function, such as proving one's identity through e-mail, the information that the requester of the certificate has to provide is pretty minimal, but may include the user's e-mail address. Once Maynard goes through the previous steps, he will also compare the e-mail address the CA inserted in the certificate with the address that sent this message. If these values are the same, he can be assured that it came from the e-mail address that was provided during the registration process of this certificate.

The certificate also has start and stop dates, indicating a time during which the certificate is valid. If the start date hasn't happened yet, or the stop date has been passed, the certificate is not valid. Maynard reviews these dates to make sure the certificate is still deemed valid.

Another step Maynard may go through is to check whether this certificate has been revoked for any reason, so he will refer to a list of revoked certificates to see if Joyce's certificate is listed. The revocation list could be checked directly with the CA that issued the certificate or via a specialized online service that supports the Online Certificate Status Protocol (OCSP). (Certificate revocation and list distribution will be explained in the "Certificate Lifecycles" section later in this chapter.)

To recap, here are the steps for validating a certificate:

1. Compare the CA that digitally signed the certificate to a list of CAs that have already been loaded into the receiver's computer.

2. Calculate a message digest for the certificate.

3. Use the CA's public key to decrypt the digital signature and recover what is claimed to be the original message digest embedded within the certificate (validating the digital signature).

4. Compare the two resulting message digest values to ensure the integrity of the certificate.

5. Review the identification information within the certificate, such as the e-mail address.

6. Review the validity dates.

7. Check a revocation list to see if the certificate has been revoked.

Maynard now trusts that this certificate is legitimate and that it belongs to Joyce. Now what does he need to do? The certificate holds Joyce's public key, which he needs to validate the digital signature she appended to her message, so Maynard extracts Joyce's public key from her certificate, runs her message through a hashing algorithm, and calculates a message digest value of X. He then uses Joyce's public key to decrypt her digital signature (remember that a digital signature is just a message digest encrypted with a private key). This decryption process provides him with another message digest of value Y. Maynard compares values X and Y, and if they are the same, he is assured that the message has not been modified during transmission. Thus, he has confidence in the integrity of the message. But, how does Maynard know that the message actually came from Joyce? Because he can decrypt the digital signature using her public key. The public key can only decrypt something that was encrypted with the related private key, and only the owner of the private key is supposed to have access to it. Maynard can be sure that this message came from Joyce.

After all of this, he reads her message, which says, "Hi. How are you?" All of that work just for this message? Maynard's blood pressure would surely go through the roof if he had to do all of this work only to end up with short and not very useful messages. Fortunately, it all happens behind the scenes. Maynard didn't have to exert any energy. He simply replies, "Fine. How are you?"

Digital Certificates

A digital certificate binds an individual's identity to a public key, and it contains all the information a receiver needs to be assured of the identity of the public key owner. After an RA verifies an individual's identity, the CA generates the digital certificate, but how does the CA know what type of data to insert into the certificate? The certificates are created and formatted based on the **X.509** standard, which outlines the necessary fields of a certificate and the possible values that can be inserted into the fields. As of this writing, X.509 version 3 is the most current version of the standard. X.509 is a standard of the International Telecommunication Union (http://www.itu.int).

The different fields within a digital certificate are as follows:

Version number   Identifies the version of the X.509 standard that was followed to create the certificate. The version number indicates the format and fields that can be used.

Subject   Specifies the owner of the certificate.

Public key   Contains the public key being bound to the certified subject. The public key also identifies the algorithm that was used to create the private/public key pair.

Issuer   Identifies the CA that generated and digitally signed the certificate.

Serial number   Contains a unique number identifying this one specific certificate issued by a particular CA.

Validity   Specifies the dates through which the certificate is valid for use.

Certificate usage   Specifies the approved use of certificate, which dictates what the user can use this public key for.

Signature algorithm   Identifies the hashing algorithm and digital signature algorithm used to digitally sign the certificate.

Extensions   Allow additional data to be encoded into the certificate to expand the functionality of the certificate. Companies can customize the use of certificates within their environment by using these extensions. X.509 version 3 has extended the extension possibilities.

Figure 6-7 shows the actual values of these different certificate fields for a particular certificate in Internet Explorer. The version of this certificate is V3 (X.509 v3) and the serial number is also listed—this number is unique for each certificate that is created by a specific CA. The CA used the MD5 hashing algorithm to create the message digest value, and it then signed (or encrypted this value) with its private key using the RSA algorithm. The actual CA that issued the certificate is Root SGC Authority, and the Valid dates indicate how long this certificate is valid. The subject is MS SGC Authority, which is the entity that registered for this certificate and is the entity that is bound to the embedded public key. The actual public key is shown in the lower window and is represented in hexadecimal.

Figure 6-7

Fields within a digital certificate

The subject of a certificate is commonly a person, but it does not have to be. The subject can be a network device (router, web server, firewall, and so on), an application, a department, a company, or a person. Each has its own identity that needs to be verified and proven to another entity before secure, trusted communication can be initiated. If a network device is using a certificate for authentication, the certificate may contain the network address of that device. This means that if the certificate has a network address of 10.0.0.1, the receiver will compare this to the address from which it received the certificate to make sure a man-in-the-middle attack is not being attempted.

Certificate Attributes

There are four main types of certificates used:

- End-entity certificates
- CA certificates
- Cross-certification certificates
- Policy certificates

End-entity certificates are issued by a CA to a specific subject, such as Joyce, the Accounting department, or a firewall, as illustrated in Figure 6-8.

Figure 6-8
End-entity and
CA certificates

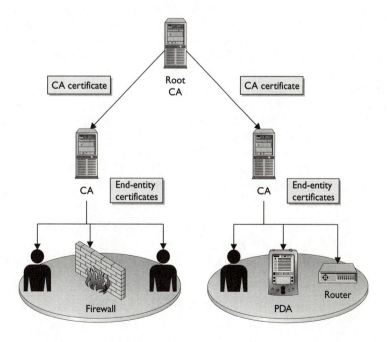

A **CA certificate** may be self-signed, in the case of a stand-alone or root CA, or it may be issued by a superior CA within a hierarchical model. In the model in Figure 6-8, the superior CA gives the authority and allows the subordinate CA to accept certificate requests and generate the individual certificates itself. This may be necessary when a company needs to have multiple internal CAs, and different departments within an organization need to have their own CA servicing their specific end-entities in their section. In these situations, a representative from each department requiring a CA registers with the higher trusted CA and requests a Certificate Authority certificate. (Public and private CAs are discussed in the "Public Certificate Authorities" and "In-House Certificate Authorities" sections later in this chapter, as are the different trust models that are available for companies.)

Cross-certificates, or *cross-certification certificates*, are used when independent CAs establish peer-to-peer trust relationships. Simply put, they are a mechanism through which one CA can issue a certificate allowing its users to trust another CA.

Within sophisticated CAs used for high-security applications, a mechanism is required to provide centrally controlled policy information to PKI clients. This is often done by placing the policy information in a *policy certificate*.

Certificate Extensions

Certificate extensions allow for further information to be inserted within the certificate, which can be used to provide more functionality in a PKI implementation. Certificate extensions can be standard or private. *Standard certificate extensions* are implemented for every PKI implementation. *Private certificate extensions* are defined for specific organizations (or domains within one organization), and they allow companies to further define different, specific uses for digital certificates to best fit their business needs.

There are several different extensions that can be implemented, one being key usage extensions. *Key usage extensions* dictate how the public key that is held within the certificate can be used. Remember that public keys can be used for different functions: symmetric key encryption, data encryption, verifying digital signatures, and more. The following are some key examples of certificate extension:

- **DigitalSignature**   The key is to be used to verify a digital signature.

- **KeyEncipherment**   The key is to be used to encrypt other keys used for secure key distribution.

- **DataEncipherment**   The key is to be used to encrypt data and cannot be used to encrypt other keys.

- **CRLSign**   The key is used to verify a CA signature on a revocation list.

- **KeyCertSign**   The key is used to verify CA signatures on certificates.

- **NonRepudiation**   The key is used when a nonrepudiation service is being provided.

A nonrepudiation service can be provided by a third-party notary. In this situation, the sender's digital signature is verified and then signed by the notary so that the sender cannot later deny signing and sending the message. This is basically the same function performed by a traditional notary using paper—validate the sender's identity and validate the time and date of an item being signed and sent. This is required when the receiver needs to *really* be sure of the sender's identity and wants to be legally protected against possible fraud or forgery.

If a company needs to be sure that accountable nonrepudiation services will be provided, a trusted time source needs to be used. This trusted time source can be a trusted third party, referred to as a time stamp authority. Using a trusted time source allows users to have a higher level of confidence as to *when* specific messages were digitally signed. For example, suppose Barry sends Ron a message and digitally signs it, and Ron later civilly sues Barry over a dispute. This digitally signed message may be submitted by Ron as evidence pertaining to an earlier agreement that Barry now is not fulfilling. If a trusted time source was not used in their PKI environment, Barry could claim that his private key had been compromised before that message was sent. If a trusted time source was implemented, then it could be shown that the message was signed *before* the date on which Barry claims his key was compromised. If a trusted time source is not used, no activity that was carried out within a PKI environment can be truly proven because it is so easy to change system and software time settings.

Critical and Non-Critical Extensions

Certificate extensions are considered either *critical* or *non-critical*, which is indicated by a specific flag within the certificate itself. When this flag is set to critical, it means that the extension *must* be understood and processed by the receiver. If the receiver is not configured to understand a particular extension marked as critical, and thus cannot process it properly, the certificate cannot be used for its proposed purpose. If the flag does not indicate that the extension is critical, then the certificate can be used for the intended purpose, even if the receiver does not process the appended extension.

So how does this work? When an extension is marked as critical, it means that the CA is certifying the key for only that specific purpose. If Joe receives a certificate with a DigitalSignature key usage extension and the critical flag is set, Joe can only use the public key within that certificate to validate digital signatures, and no more. If the extension was marked as non-critical, the key can be used for purposes outside of those listed in the extensions, so in this case it is up to Joe (and his applications) to decide how the key will be used.

Certificate Lifecycles

Keys and certificates should have lifetimes set, which will force the user to register for a new certificate after a certain amount of time. The proper length of these lifetimes is a trade-off. Shorter lifetimes limit the ability of attackers to crack them, but longer lifetimes lower system overhead. More sophisticated PKI implementations perform automated and often transparent key updates to avoid the time and expense of having users register for new certificates when old ones expire.

This means that the certificate and key pair has a lifecycle that must be managed. Certificate management involves administrating and managing each of these phases, including registration, certificate and key generation, renewal, and revocation.

Registration and Generation

A key pair (public and private keys) can be generated locally by an application and stored in a local key store on the user's workstation. The key pair may also be created by a central key-generation server, which will require secure transmission of the keys to the user. The key pair that is created on the centralized server can be stored on the user's workstation or on the user's smart card, which will allow for more flexibility and mobility.

In most modern PKI implementations, users have two key pairs. One key pair is often generated by a central server and used for encryption and key transfers. This allows the corporate PKI to retain a copy of the encryption key pair for recovery, if necessary. The second key pair, a digital signature key pair, is usually generated by the user to make sure that the user is the only one with a copy of the private key. Nonrepudiation can be challenged if there is any doubt about someone else obtaining a copy of an individual's signature private key. If the key pair was created on a centralized server, that could weaken the case that the individual was the only one who had a copy of their private key. If a copy of a user's signature private key is stored anywhere other than in their possession, or if there is a possibility of someone obtaining the user's key, then true nonrepudiation may not be provided.

The act of verifying that an individual indeed has the corresponding private key for a given public key is referred to as *proof of possession*. Not all public/private key pairs can be used for digital signatures, so asking the individual to sign a message and return it to prove that they have the necessary private key will not always work. If a key pair is used for encryption, the RA can send a challenge value to the individual, who, in turn, can use their private key to encrypt that value and return it to the RA. If the RA can successfully decrypt this value with the public key that was provided earlier, the RA can be confident that the individual has the necessary private key and can continue through the rest of the registration phase.

When the key pair is first generated, the administrator (or the individual user) chooses the algorithm that is to be used to generate the key pair and the key size. (Who actually chooses the algorithm type depends upon the configuration of the PKI implementation.) The specific algorithm will be chosen for its strength and interoperability with other algorithms that will most likely be used by other end-entities. The key size will depend upon the sensitivity of the data that is being protected. The RSA algorithm is the de facto standard for asymmetric key generation, and if the data you will be protecting with these keys is not considered sensitive, you may choose a key size of 128 bits. The estimated time necessary to break this cryptosystem is less than five minutes, if the hacker could dedicate at least 105 computers just to this task. If you choose a key size of 1,024 bits, the time estimated to break it would increase to three million years if the hacker has at least 114 computers dedicated to this task, with 170GB of memory, and that much time to kill.

So if it could take an attacker up to three million years to break the cryptosystem, why would you ever need to change the key pair? Surely the attackers won't have that type of time on their hands. Unfortunately, most encryption key compromises do not come from brute-force attacks but from improper key management processes, poor software implementations, and human error. A key can be shown in clear text or shared with another user, the key store may not be protected with a password, or a user may fall victim to a social engineering ploy. These types of attacks can be performed with the end goal of obtaining a cryptographic key, and they are usually much easier to carry out than a full brute-force attack on an algorithm.

Key regeneration and replacement is usually done to protect against these types of threats, although as computers increase in processing power and our knowledge of cryptography and new possible cryptanalysis attacks, key lifetimes may drastically decrease. As with everything within the security field, it is better to be safe than surprised later and sorry.

The PKI administrator usually configures the minimum required key size that users must use to have a key generated for the first time, and then for each renewal. In most applications, there is a drop-down list of possible algorithms to choose from, and possible key sizes. The key size should provide the necessary level of security for the current environment. The lifetime of the key should be long enough that continual renewal will not negatively affect productivity, but short enough to ensure that the key cannot be successfully compromised.

Renewal

The certificate itself has its own lifetime, which can be different than the key pair's lifetime. The certificate's lifetime is specified by the validity dates inserted into the digital certificate. These are beginning and ending dates indicating the time period during which the certificate is valid. The certificate cannot be used before the start date, and once the end date is met, the certificate is expired and a new certificate will need to be issued.

A renewal process is different than the registration phase in that the RA assumes that the individual has already successfully completed one registration round. If the certificate has not actually been revoked, the original keys and certificate can be used to provide the necessary authentication information and proof of identity for the renewal phase.

Approaches to Protection

Good key management and proper key replacement intervals protect keys from being compromised through human error. Choosing a large key size makes a brute-force attack more difficult.

The certificate may or may not need to change during the renewal process; it usually depends on why the renewal is taking place. If the certificate just expired and the keys will still be used for the same purpose, a new certificate can be generated with new validity dates. If, however, the key pair functionality needs to be expanded or restricted, new attributes and extensions may need to be integrated into the new certificate. These new functionalities may require more information to be gathered from the individual renewing the certificate, especially if the class changes or the new key uses allow for more powerful abilities.

This renewal process is required when the certificate has fulfilled its lifetime and its end validity date has been met. This is different than if a certificate is revoked.

Revocation

Certificates are revoked when the certificate's validity needs to be ended before its actual expiration date is met. There are several reasons why a certificate may need to be revoked: a user may have lost a laptop or a smart card that stored a private key, an improper software implementation may have been uncovered that directly affected the security of a private key, a user may have fallen victim to a social engineering attack and inadvertently given up a private key, data held within the certificate may no longer apply to the specified individual, or perhaps an employee left a company and should not be identified as a member of an in-house PKI any longer. In the last instance, the certificate, which was bound to the user's key pair, identified the user as an employee of the company, and the administrator would want to ensure that the key pair could not be used in the future to validate this person's affiliation with the company. Revoking the certificate does this.

If any of these things happen, a user's private key has been compromised or should no longer be mapped to the owner's identity. A different individual may have access to that user's private key and could use it to impersonate and authenticate as the original user. If the impersonator used the key to digitally sign a message, the receiver would verify the authenticity of the sender by verifying the signature by using the original user's public key, and the verification would go through perfectly—the receiver would believe it came from the proper sender and not the impersonator. If receivers could look at a list of certificates that have been revoked before verifying the digital signature, they could find out that the certificate had been revoked, and they would know not to trust the digital signature.

For example, if Joe stole Mike's laptop, which held, among other things, Mike's private key, Joe might be able to use it to impersonate Mike. Suppose Joe writes a message, digitally signs it with Mike's private key, and sends it to Stacy. Stacy communicates with Mike periodically and has his public key, so she uses it to verify the digital signature. It computes properly, so Stacy is assured that this message did indeed come from Mike, but in truth it did not. If, before validating any certificate or digital signature, Stacy could check a list of revoked certificates, she might not fall victim to Joe's false message.

The CA can provide this type of protection by maintaining a **certificate revocation list** (CRL), which is a list of serial numbers of certificates that have been revoked. The CRL also contains a statement indicating why the individual certificates were revoked and a date when the revocation took place. The list usually contains all certificates that have been revoked within the lifetime of the CA. Certificates that have expired are not the same as ones that have been revoked. If a certificate has expired, it means that its end validity date has been reached.

The CA is the entity that is responsible for the status of the certificates it generates, and it is who needs to be told of a revocation, and it must be the one to provide this information to others. The CA is responsible for maintaining the revocation list and posting it in a publicly available directory.

What if Stacy wants to get back at Joe for trying to trick her earlier, and she attempts to revoke Joe's certificate herself? If she is successful, then Joe's participation in the PKI can be negatively affected because others will not trust his public key. Although we might think Joe may deserve this, we need to have some system in place to make sure people cannot arbitrarily have others' certificates revoked, whether for revenge or for malicious purposes.

When a revocation request is submitted, the individual submitting the request must be authenticated. Otherwise, this could permit a type of denial of service attack, where someone has another person's certificate revoked. The authentication can involve an agreed upon password that was created during the registration process, but authentication should not be based on the individual proving that they have the corresponding private key, because it may have been stolen, and the CA would be authenticating an imposter.

The CRL's integrity needs to be protected to ensure that attackers cannot modify data pertaining to a revoked certification from the list. If this were allowed to take place, anyone who stole a private key could just delete that key from the CRL and continue to use the private key fraudulently. The integrity of the list also needs to be protected to ensure that bogus data is not added to it. Otherwise, anyone could add another person's certificate to the list and effectively revoke that person's certificate. The only entity that should be able to modify any information on the CRL is the CA.

The mechanism used to protect the integrity of a CRL is a digital signature. The CA's revocation service creates a digital signature for the CRL, as shown in Figure 6-9. To validate a certificate, the user goes to the directory where the CRL is posted, downloads the list, and verifies the CA's digital signature to ensure that the proper authority signed the list and to ensure that the list was not modified in an unauthorized manner. The user then looks through the list to see if the serial number of the certificate that they are trying to validate is listed. If the serial number is on the list, the private key should no longer be trusted, and the public key should no longer be used. This may sound like a cumbersome process, so it has been automated in several ways that are described in the next section.

Figure 6-9
The CA digitally signs the CRL to protect its integrity.

One concern is how up-to-date the CRL is—how often is it updated and does it actually reflect *all* the certificates currently revoked? The actual frequency with which the list is updated depends upon the CA and its certification practices statement (CPS). It is important that the list is updated in a timely manner so that anyone using the list has the most current information.

CRL Distribution

CRL files can be requested by individuals who need to verify and validate a newly received certificate, or the files can be periodically pushed down to all users participating within a specific PKI. This means the CRL can be pulled (downloaded) by individual users when needed, or the CRL can be pushed down (sent) to all users within the PKI on a timed interval.

The actual CRL file can grow substantially, and transmitting this file and requiring PKI client software on each workstation to save and maintain it can use a lot of resources, so the smaller the CRL is, the better. It is also possible to first push down the full CRL, and after that initial load, the following CRLs pushed down to the users are delta CRLs, meaning that they only contain the changes to the original or base CRL. This can greatly reduce the amount of bandwidth consumed when updating CRLs.

In implementations where the CRLs are not pushed down to individual systems, the users' PKI software needs to know where to look for the posted CRL that relates to the certificate it is trying to validate. The certificate itself may have an extension that points the validating user to the necessary *CRL distribution point*. The network administrator sets up the distribution points, and there may be just one point for a particular PKI or there may be more than one. The distribution point holds one or more lists containing the serial numbers of revoked certificates, and the user's PKI software scans the list for the serial number of the certificate the user is attempting to validate. If the serial number is not present, the user is assured that it has not been revoked. This approach helps point users to the right resource and also reduces the amount of information that needs to be scanned when checking that a certificate has not been revoked.

One last option for checking distributed CRLs is an online service. When a client needs to validate a certificate and ensure that it has not been revoked, they can communicate with an online service that will query the necessary CRLs available within the environment. This service can query the lists for the client instead of pushing down the full CRL to each and every system. So if Joe receives a certificate from Stacy, he can contact an online service and send it the serial number listed in the certificate Stacy sent. The online service would query the necessary revocation lists and respond to Joe indicating whether that serial number was listed as being revoked or not.

Online services are newer technologies, and there are different protocols being developed and used for these purposes. Figuring out how to get information from within the CRL to the different clients is one of the harder obstacles to be overcome in many PKI implementations. In many cases, clients do not even check with any lists, and they would never know if a certificate was revoked or not. This, of course, is not the optimal approach, and solutions and technologies to ensure that CRL data gets properly populated and reviewed is continually being improved upon.

One of the protocols used for online revocation services is *Online Certificate Status Protocol (OCSP)*. It is a request and response protocol that obtains the serial number of the certificate that is being validated and reviews revocation lists for the client. The protocol has a responder service that reports the status of the certificate back to the client, indicating whether it has been revoked, it is valid, or its status is unknown. This protocol and service saves the client from having to find the right lists, download, and process them.

Suspension

Instead of being revoked, a certificate may sometimes need to be *suspended*, meaning it is temporarily put on hold. If, for example, Bob is taking an extended vacation and wants to ensure that his certificate will not be compromised or used during that time, a suspension request can be made to the CA. The CRL would list this certificate and its serial number, and in the field that describes why a certificate was revoked, it would instead indicate a hold state. Once Bob returns to work, he can make a request to the CA to remove his certificate from the list.

Authority Revocation Lists

In some PKI implementations, a separate revocation list is maintained for CA keys that have been compromised or should no longer be trusted. This list is known as an *authority revocation list (ARL)*. In the event that a CA's private key is compromised or a cross certification is cancelled, the relevant certificate's serial number is included in the ARL. A client can review an ARL to make sure the CA's public key can still be trusted.

Another reason to suspend a certificate is if the administrator is suspicious that a private key may have been compromised. While the issue is under investigation, the certificate can be put on hold to ensure that it cannot be used.

Key Destruction

Key pairs and certificates have set lifetimes, meaning that they will expire at some specified time. It is important that the certificates and keys are properly destroyed when that time comes, wherever the keys are stored (on users' workstations, centralized key servers, USB token devices, smart cards, and so on).

The goal is to make sure that no one can gain access to a key after its lifetime has ended and use this key for malicious purposes. The attacker might use the key to digitally sign or encrypt a message with the hopes of tricking someone else about their identity (this would be an example of a man-in-the-middle attack). Also, if the attacker is performing some type of brute-force attack on your cryptosystem, trying to figure out specific keys that were used for encryption processes, obtaining an old key may give them more insight into how your cryptosystem generates keys. The less information you supply to potential hackers, the better.

The level of protection that is required within the environment will dictate the actual key destruction procedures that must be followed. In most environments, just allowing the applications that created the keys in the first place to delete the keys is enough. In environments that require higher levels of protection (such as government and military agencies), the media that holds the keys may need to go through a "zeroization" process. This means that a specialized tool is used to overwrite the media that held the cryptographic key, and the overwriting process that is usually carried out by this tool continually writes NULL values to the sectors until that media holds no remnants of the original key.

Note that in modern PKIs, encryption key pairs usually must be retained long after they expire so that users can decrypt information that was encrypted with the old keys. For example, if Bob encrypts a document using his current key and the keys are updated three months later, Bob's software must maintain a copy of the old key so he can still decrypt the document. In the PKI world, this issue is referred to as *key history maintenance*.

Centralized or Decentralized Infrastructures

Keys used for authentication and encryption within a PKI environment can be generated in a centralized or decentralized manner. In a *decentralized* approach, software on individual computers generates and stores cryptographic keys local to the systems themselves. In a *centralized* infrastructure, the keys are generated and stored on a central server, and the keys are transmitted to the individual systems as needed. There are several reasons to choose one type or the other.

If a company uses an asymmetric algorithm that is resource intensive to generate the public/private key pair, and if the key sizes that are needed are large (which is also resource intensive), then the individual computers may not have the necessary processing power to produce the keys in an acceptable fashion. In this situation, the company can choose a centralized approach where a very high-end server with powerful processing capabilities is used, probably along with a hardware-based random number generator.

To create cryptographic keys, the more randomness that is introduced, the better, because the resulting keys will be more indiscriminate and harder to brute force. The random number generator creates numbers that work as seed values, or starting values, for the algorithm to work from. The algorithm uses the seed value as a starting place to create a key, and if the algorithm used the same seed values over and over again, it would generate the same or similar keys over and over, which would make it easier for attackers to uncover the key. The more random the seed values, the better, which is why a random number generator is used.

Central key generation and storage has other benefits. For example, it is much easier to back the keys up and implement key recovery procedures, when compared to a decentralized approach. Implementing a key recovery procedure on each and every computer holding one or more key pairs is difficult, and many applications that generate their own key pairs do not usually interface well with a centralized archive system. This means that if a company chooses to allow their individual users to create and maintain their own key pairs on their separate workstations, no real key recovery procedure can be put in place. This puts the company at risk. If an employee leaves the organization or is unavailable for one reason or another, the company may not be able to access its own business information encrypted by that employee.

So a centralized approach seems like the best approach, right? Well, the centralized method has some drawbacks to consider, too. If the keys will be generated on a server, they need to be securely transmitted to the individual clients that require them. This can be harder than it sounds. A technology needs to be employed that will send the keys in an encrypted manner, ensure the keys' integrity, and make sure that only the intended user is actually receiving the key.

Also, the server that centrally stores the keys needs to be highly available and can provide a single point of failure, so some type of fault tolerance or redundancy mechanism may need to be put into place. If that one server goes down, no one could access their keys, which might prevent them from properly authenticating to the network, resources, and applications. Also, since all the keys are in one place, it is a prime target for an attacker—if the central key server is compromised, the whole environment is compromised.

Random Number Generators

In most cases, software- and hardware-based generators are actually considered *pseudo-random number generators* because they have a finite number of values to work from. They usually extract these values from their surroundings, which are predictable in nature—the values can come from the system's time or from CPU cycles. If the starting values are predictable, the numbers they generate cannot be truly random. An example of a true random number generator would be a system that collects radiation from a radioactive item. The elements that escape from the radioactive item do so in an unpredictable manner, and the results are used as seed values for key generation.

One other issue pertains to how the keys will actually be used. If a public/private key pair is being generated for digital signatures, and if the company wants to ensure that it can be used to provide *true* authenticity and nonrepudiation, the keys should not be generated at a centralized server. This would introduce doubt that only the one person had access to a specific private key.

If a company uses smart cards to hold users' private keys, the private key often has to be generated on the card itself and cannot be copied for archiving purposes. This is a disadvantage of the centralized approach. There are also some types of applications that have been developed to create their own public/private key pairs and do not allow other keys to be imported and used. This means the keys would have to be created locally by these applications, and keys from a central server could not be used. These are just some of the considerations that need to be evaluated before any decision is made and implementation begins.

Hardware Storage Devices

PKIs can be constructed in software without special cryptographic hardware, and this is perfectly suitable for many environments. But software can be vulnerable to viruses, hackers, and hacking. If a company requires a higher level of protection than a purely software-based solution can provide, there are several hardware-based solutions available.

In most situations, hardware key-storage solutions are only used for the most critical and sensitive keys, which are the root and possibly the intermediate CA private keys. If those keys are compromised, the whole security of the PKI is gravely threatened. If a person obtained a root CA private key, they could digitally sign any certificate, and that certificate would be quickly accepted by all entities within the environment. Such an attacker might be able to create a certificate that has extremely high privileges, perhaps allowing them to modify bank account information in a financial institution, and no alerts or warnings would be initiated because the ultimate supreme being (the root CA) signed it.

There are other hardware components that can be implemented within a PKI to hold users' private key information. These include smart cards, USB tokens, and Fortezza cards. These items can be used to securely hold a user's private key and can be inserted into a reader attached to a workstation or server when the user needs to present their private key for authentication purposes. These devices usually provide a higher level of protection compared to holding the keys in software because they are more tamper-proof in nature. These items are covered further in Chapter 7.

Private Key Protection

Although a PKI implementation can be complex, with many different components and options, there is a critical concept common to all PKIs that must be understood and enforced: the private key needs to stay private. A digital signature is created solely for the purpose of proving who sent a particular message by using a private key. This rests on the assumption that only one person has access to this private key. If an imposter obtains a person's private key, authenticity and nonrepudiation can no longer be claimed or proven.

When a private key is generated for the first time, it must be stored somewhere for future use. This storage area is referred to as a key store, and it is usually created by the application registering for a certificate, such as a web browser, smart card software, or other application. In most implementations, the application will prompt the user for a password, which will be used to create an encryption key that protects the key store. So if Cheryl used her web browser to register for a certificate, her private key would be generated and stored in the key store. Cheryl would then be prompted for a password, which the software would use to create a key that will encrypt the key store. When Cheryl needs to access this private key later that day, she will be prompted for the same password, which will decrypt the key store and allow her access to her private key.

Unfortunately, many applications do not require that a strong password must be chosen to protect the key store, and in some implementations the user can choose to not provide a password at all. The user still has a private key available, and it is bound to the user's identity, so what do we care if a password must be entered or not? If, for example, Cheryl decided to not use a password, another person could sit down at her computer, use her web browser and her private key and digitally sign a message. If Cliff received this message, he would think it came from Cheryl and not necessarily think that someone else could have sent it.

The moral to this story is that users should be required to provide some type of authentication information (password, smart card, PIN, or the like) before being able to use private keys. Otherwise, the keys could be used by other individuals or imposters, and authentication and nonrepudiation would be of no use.

A private key is a crucial component of any PKI implementation, so the key itself should contain the necessary characteristics and be protected at each stage of its life. The following list sums up the characteristics and requirements of proper private key use:

- The key size should provide the necessary level of protection for the environment.
- The lifetime of the key should correspond with how often it is used and the sensitivity of the data it is protecting.
- The key should be changed and not used past its allowed lifetime.
- Where appropriate, the key should be properly destroyed at the end of its lifetime.
- The key should never be exposed in clear text.
- No copies of the private key should be made if it is being used for digital signatures.
- The key should not be shared.
- The key should be stored securely.
- Authentication should be required before it can be used.

- The key should be transported securely.

- Software implementations that store and use the key should be evaluated to ensure they provide the necessary level of protection.

If digital signatures will be used for legal purposes, these points and others may need to be audited to ensure that true authenticity and nonrepudiation are provided.

Key Recovery

One individual may have one, two, or many key pairs that are tied to their identity. That is because users can have different needs and requirements for public/private key pairs. As mentioned earlier, certificates can have specific attributes and usage requirements dictating what their corresponding keys can and cannot be used for. For example, David can have one key pair he uses to encrypt and transmit symmetric keys. He can also have one key pair that allows him to encrypt data and another key pair to perform digital signatures. David can also have a digital signature key pair for his work-related activities and another pair for personal activities, as in e-mailing his friends. These key pairs need to be used only for their intended purposes, and this is enforced through certificate attributes and usage values.

If a company is going to perform and maintain a key recovery system, they will generally only back up the key pair used to encrypt data, not the key pairs that are used to generate digital signatures. The reason that a company archives keys is to ensure that if a person leaves the company, falls off a cliff, or for some reason is unavailable to decrypt important company information, the company can still get to its company-owned data. This is just a matter of the organization protecting itself. A company would not need to be able to recover a key pair that is used for digital signatures, since those keys are only to be used to prove the authenticity of the individual who sent a message. A company would not benefit from having access to those keys and really should not have access to them, since they are tied to one individual for a specific purpose.

CA Private Key

The most sensitive and critical public/private key pairs are those used by CAs to digitally sign certificates. These need to be highly protected because if they were compromised, the trust relationship between the CA and all of the end-entities would be threatened. In high security environments, these keys are often kept in a tamper-proof hardware encryption store, only accessible to individuals with a need to know.

There are two elements to backing up and restoring cryptographic keys: key archiving and key recovery. The **key archiving system** is a way of backing up keys and securely storing them in a repository; **key recovery** is the process of restoring lost keys to the users or the company.

If keys are backed up and stored in a centralized computer, this system must be tightly controlled, because if it were compromised, the attacker could then have access to all keys for the entire infrastructure. Also, it is usually not a good idea to have only one person who can recover all the keys within the environment, because that one person could use this power for evil purposes instead of just recovering keys when they are needed for legitimate purposes. In security systems, it is wise not to fully trust anyone.

Dual control can be used as part of a system to back up and archive data encryption keys. PKI systems can be configured to allow multiple individuals to be involved in any key recovery process. When a key recovery is required, at least two people can be required to authenticate by the key recovery software before the recovery procedure is performed. This enforces *separation of duties*, which means that one person cannot complete a critical task by themselves. Requiring two individuals to together recover a lost key is called **dual control**, which simply means that two people have to be present to carry out a specific task.

This approach to key recovery is referred to as the *"m of n" authentication*, where *n* number of people can be involved in the key recovery process, but at least *m* (which is a smaller number than *n*) *must* be involved before the task can be completed. The goal is to minimize fraudulent or improper use of access and permissions. A company would not require all possible individuals to be involved in the recovery process because getting all the people together at the same time could be impossible with meetings, vacations, sick time, and travel. At least some of all possible individuals must be available to participate, and this is the subset *m* of the number *n*.

All key recovery procedures should be highly audited. The audit logs should capture at least what keys were recovered, who was involved in the process, and the time and date. Keys are an integral piece of any encryption cryptosystem and are critical to a PKI environment, so you need to track who does what with them.

Key Escrow

Key recovery and *key escrow* are terms that are often used interchangeably, but they are terms that actually describe two different things. *You* should not use them interchangeably after you have read this section.

Key recovery is a process that allows for lost keys to be recovered. **Key escrow** is a process of giving keys to a third party so that they can decrypt and read sensitive information when this need arises. Key escrow almost always pertains to handing over encryption keys to the government so that they can use them to collect evidence during investigations.

There have been several movements, supported by parts of the U.S. government, that would require all or many people residing in the United States to hand over copies of the keys they use to encrypt communication channels. The movement behind the Clipper Chip is the most well-known effort to put this requirement and procedure in place. It was suggested that all American-made communication devices should have a hardware encryption chip within them. The chip could be used to encrypt data going back and forth between two individuals, but if a government agency uncovered a reason that they should be able to eavesdrop on this dialog, they would just need to obtain a court order. If the court order was approved, the law enforcement agent would take the order to two escrow agencies, each of which would have a piece of the key that was necessary to decrypt this communication information. The agent would obtain both pieces of the key and combine them, which would allow the agent to listen in on the encrypted communication outlined in the court order.

This was a standard that never saw the light of day because it seemed too "Big Brother" to many American citizens. But the idea was that the encryption keys would be escrowed to two agencies, meaning that each agency would hold one piece of the key. One agency could not hold the whole key, because they could then use this key to wiretap people's conversations illegally. Splitting up the key is an example of separation of duties, put into place to try and prevent fraudulent activities.

Public Certificate Authorities

An individual or company may decide to rely on a CA that is already established and being used by many other individuals and companies—this would be a *public CA*. A company, on the other hand, may decide that they need their own CA for internal use, which gives them more control over the certificate registration and generation process and allows them to configure items specifically for their own needs. This second type of CA is referred to as a *private CA* (or *in-house CA*).

A public CA is a company that specializes in verifying individual identities and creating and maintaining their certificates. These companies issue certificates that are not bound to specific companies or inter-company departments. Instead, their services are to be used by a larger and more diversified group of people and organizations. If a company uses a public CA, that means that it will be paying this other company for individual certificates and for the service of maintaining these certificates. Some examples of public CAs are VeriSign, Entrust, and Baltimore.

One advantage of using a public CA is that they are usually well known and easily accessible to many people. Most web browsers have a list of public CAs installed and configured by default, along with their corresponding root certificates. This means that if you install a web browser onto your computer, it is already configured to trust a list of CAs, even though you may have never heard of them before. So, if you receive a certificate from Bob, and his certificate was digitally signed by a CA listed in your browser, you will automatically trust the CA and can easily walk through the process of verifying Bob's certificate. This has raised some eyebrows among security professionals, since trust is installed by default, but the industry has deemed this is a necessary approach that provides users with transparency and increased functionality. Users can remove these CAs from their browser list if they want to have more control over who their system trusts and who it doesn't.

Earlier in the chapter, the different certificate classes and their uses were explained. There is no global standard defining these classes, the exact requirements for obtaining these different certificates, or their uses. There are standards in place, usually for a particular country or industry, but this means that public CAs can define their own certificate classifications. This is not necessarily a good thing for companies that depend upon public CAs, because it does not give enough control to the company over how the company should interpret certificate classifications and how they should be used.

This means another component needed to be carefully developed for companies that use and depend upon public CAs, and this component is referred to as the *certificate policy (CP)*. This policy allows the company to decide what certification classes are acceptable and how they will be used within the organization. This is different from the CPS, which is what explains how the CA verifies entities, generates certificates, and maintains these certificates. The CP is generated and owned by an individual company that uses an external CA, and it allows the company to enforce *its* security decisions and control how certificates are used with its applications.

In-House Certificate Authorities

A CA that is considered to be an in-house CA is implemented, maintained, and controlled by the company that implemented it. This type of CA can be used to create certificates for internal employees, devices, applications, partners, and customers. This approach allows the company to completely control how individuals are identified, what certification classifications are created, who can and cannot have access to the CA, and how the certifications can be used.

In-house CAs also provide more flexibility for companies, which often integrate them into current infrastructures and into applications for authentication, encryption, and nonrepudiation purposes. If the CA is going to be used over an extended period of time, this can be a cheaper method of generating and using certificates than having to purchase them through a public CA. However, when the decision between an in-house and public CA is made, various factors need to be identified and accounted for. Many companies have embarked upon implementing an in-house PKI environment, which they estimated would be implemented within x number of months and would cost approximately y amount in dollars. If the proper homework is not done, the current environment is not clearly understood, the intended purpose of the PKI is not completely hammered out, and there is not enough skilled staff supporting the project, time estimates can double or triple and the required funds and resources can become unacceptable. Several companies have started on a PKI implementation, only to quit halfway through, resulting in wasted time and money, with nothing to show for it except heaps of frustration and many ulcers.

In some situations, it is better for a company to use a public CA, since public CAs already have the necessary equipment, skills, and technologies. In other situations, companies may feel it is a better business decision to take on these efforts themselves. This is not always a strictly monetary decision—a specific level of security may be a requirement. Some companies do not feel that they can trust an outside authority to generate and maintain their users' and company's certificates. In this situation, the scale may tip towards an in-house CA.

Each company is different, with various goals, security requirements, functionality needs, budgetary restraints, and ideologies. The decision to use a private or in-house CA depends upon the expansiveness of the PKI within the organization, how integrated it will be with different business needs and goals, its interoperability with a company's current technologies, the number of individuals who will be participating, and how it will work with outside entities. This could be quite a large undertaking that ties up staff, resources, and funds, so a lot of strategic planning should be done, and a full understanding of what will and won't be gained from a PKI should be carried out before the first dollar is spent on the implementation.

Outsourced Certificate Authorities

The last available option for using PKI components within a company is to outsource different parts of it to a specific service provider. Usually, the more complex parts are outsourced, such as the CA, RA, CRL, and key recovery mechanisms. This is done if a company does not have the necessary skills to implement and carry out a full PKI environment.

An *outsourced CA* is different than a public CA in that it provides dedicated services, and possibly equipment, to an individual company. A public CA, in contrast, can be used by hundreds or thousands of companies—they don't maintain specific servers and infrastructures for individual companies.

Although outsourced services may be easier for the individual company to implement, several factors need to be reviewed before making this type of commitment. The company needs to determine what level of trust it is willing to give to the service provider and what level of risk it is willing to accept. Often, a PKI and its components serve as large security components within a company's enterprise, and allowing a third party to maintain the PKI may introduce too many risks and liabilities the company is not willing to undertake. The liabilities the service provider is willing to accept, security precautions and procedures the outsourced CAs provide, and the surrounding legal issues need to be examined before this type of agreement is made.

Some large vertical markets have their own outsourced PKI environments set up because they share similar needs and usually have the same requirements for certification types and uses. This allows several companies within the same market to split the costs of the necessary equipment, and it allows for industry-specific standards to be drawn up and followed. For example, although many medical facilities work differently and have different environments, they have a lot of the same functionality and security needs. If several of them came together, purchased the necessary equipment to provide CA, RA, and CRL functionality, employed one staff to maintain it, and each connected their different sites to the centralized components, they could save a lot of money and resources. In this case, not every facility would need to strategically plan their own full PKI, and they would not need to purchase redundant equipment or employ redundant staff members. Figure 6-10 illustrates how one outsourced service provider can offer different PKI components and services to different companies, and how companies within one vertical market can share the same resources.

Figure 6-10   A PKI service provider (represented by the four boxes) can offer different PKI components to companies.

A set of standards can be drawn up about how different facilities should integrate their own infrastructures and how they should integrate with the centralized PKI components. This also allows for less complicated intercommunication to take place between the different medical facilities, which will ease information-sharing attempts.

Tying Different PKIs Together

There are several reasons that more than one CA may be needed for a specific PKI to work properly, and there may be a requirement for different PKIs to intercommunicate. Here are some examples of where this may be required:

- A company wants to be able to communicate seamlessly with their suppliers, customers, or business partners via PKI.

- One department within a company may have higher security requirements than all other departments, and thus needs to configure and control their own CA.

- One department may need to have specially constructed certificates with unique fields and usages.

- Different parts of an organization want to control their own piece of the network and the CA that is encompassed within it.

- The number of certificates that need to be generated and maintained would overwhelm one CA, so multiple CAs may need to be deployed.

- The political culture of a company inhibits one department from being able to control elements of another department.

- Enterprises are partitioned geographically, and different sites need their own local CA.

These situations can add much more complexity to the overall infrastructure, intercommunication capabilities, and procedures for certificate generation and validation. To properly control this complexity from the beginning, these requirements need to be understood, addressed, and planned for. Then the necessary trust model needs to be chosen and molded for the company to build upon. Selecting the right trust model will give the company a solid foundation from the beginning, instead of trying to add structure to an inaccurate and inadequate plan later on.

Trust Models

There is more involved in the previously listed scenarios than just having more than one CA—each of the companies or each department of an enterprise can actually represent a trust domain itself. A *trust domain* is a construct of systems, personnel, applications, protocols, technologies, and policies that work together to provide a certain level of protection. All of these components can work together seamlessly within the same trust domain because they are known to the other components within the domain and are trusted to some degree. Different trust domains are usually managed by different groups of administrators, have different security policies, and restrict outsiders from privileged access.

Most trust domains (whether individual companies or departments) are not usually islands cut off from the world—they need to communicate with other less trusted domains. The trick is to figure out how much two different domains should trust each other, and how to implement and configure an infrastructure that would allow these two domains to communicate in a way that will not allow security compromises or breaches. This can be harder than it sounds.

In the non-digital world, it is hard to figure out who to trust, how to carry out legitimate business functions, and how to ensure that one is not being taken advantage of or lied to. Jump into the digital world and add protocols, services, encryption, CAs, RAs, CRLs, differing technologies and applications, and the business risks can become overwhelming and confusing. So start with a basic question: What is the criteria we will use to determine who we trust and to what degree?

One example of trust that we considered earlier in the chapter was the driver's license issued by the DMV. Suppose Bob is buying a lamp from Carol and he wants to pay by check. Since Carol does not know Bob, she does not know if she can trust him or have much faith in his check. But if Bob shows Carol his driver's license, she can compare the name to what is on the check, and she can choose to accept it. The *trust anchor* (the agreed-upon trusted third party) in this scenario is the DMV, since both Carol and Bob trust it more than they trust each other. Since Bob had to provide documentation to prove his identity to the DMV, and they trusted him enough to generate a license, and Carol trusts the DMV, she decides to trust Bob's check.

Consider another example of a trust anchor. If Joe and Stacy need to communicate through e-mail and would like to use encryption and digital signatures, they will not trust each other's certificate all by itself. But when they receive each other's certificate and see that they have been digitally signed by an entity they both do trust—the CA—then they have a deeper level of trust in each other. The trust anchor here is the CA. This is easy enough, but when we need to establish trust anchors between different CAs and PKI environments, it gets a little more complicated.

When two companies need to communicate using their individual PKIs, or if two departments within the same company each have their own CA, there are two separate trust domains to contend with. The users and devices from these different trust domains will need to communicate with each other, and they will need to exchange certificates and public keys. This means that trust anchors need to be identified, and a communication channel must be constructed and maintained.

A trust relationship must be established between two issuing authorities (CAs). This happens when one or both of the CAs issue a certificate for the other CA's public key, as shown in Figure 6-11. This means that each CA registers for a certificate and public key from the other CA. Each CA validates the other CA's identification information and generates a certificate containing a public key for that CA to use. This establishes a trust path between the two entities that can then be used when users need to verify other users' certificates that fall within the different trust domains. The trust path can be unidirectional or bidirectional, so either the two CAs trust each other (bidirectional) or only one trusts the other (unidirectional).

As illustrated in Figure 6-11, all the users and devices in trust domain 1 trust their own CA 1, which is their trust anchor. All users and devices in trust domain 2 have their own trust anchor, CA 2. The two CAs have exchanged certificates and trust each other, but they do not have a common trust anchor between them.

The trust models describe and outline the trust relationships between the different CAs and different environments, which will indicate where the trust paths reside. The trust models and paths need to be thought out before implementation to properly restrict and control access and to ensure that there are as few trust paths as possible. There are several different trust models: the hierarchical, peer-to-peer, and hybrid models will be discussed in the following sections.

1. Request identification information

2. Validate information

3. Generate a certificate

4. Vouch for each other's identity

CA 1

CA 2

Trust path

Trust domain 1

Trust domain 2

Figure 6-11   A trust relationship can be built between two trust domains to set up a communication channel.

Hierarchical Trust Model

The first type of trust model to look at is a basic hierarchical structure that contains a root CA, intermediate CAs, leaf CAs, and end-entities. The configuration is that of an inverted tree, as shown in Figure 6-12. The root CA is the ultimate trust anchor for all other entities in this infrastructure, and it generates certificates for the intermediate CAs, which in turn generate certificates for the leaf CAs, and the leaf CAs generate certificates for the end-entities (users, network devices, applications).

As shown in Figure 6-12, there are no bidirectional trusts—they are all unidirectional trusts, as indicated by the one-way arrows. Since no other entity can certify and generate certificates for the root CA, it creates a *self-signed certificate*. This means that the certificate's issuer and subject fields hold the same information, both representing the root CA, and the root CA's public key is what will be used to verify this certificate when that time comes. This root CA certificate and public key is distributed to all entities within this trust model.

Root CA

If the root CA's private key was ever compromised, all entities within the hierarchical trust model would be drastically affected, because this is their sole trust anchor. The root CA usually has a small amount of interaction with the intermediate CAs and end-entities, and can therefore be taken offline much of the time. This provides a greater degree of protection for the root CA, because when it is offline it is basically inaccessible.

Figure 6-12
The hierarchical trust model outlines trust paths.

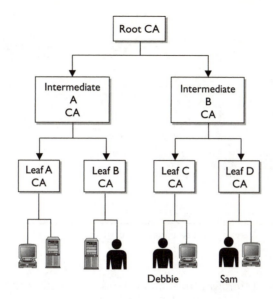

Walking the Certificate Path   When a user in one trust domain needs to communicate with another user in another trust domain, one user will need to validate the other's certificate. This sounds simple enough, but what it really means is that each certificate for each CA, all the way up to a shared trusted anchor, needs to be validated also. If Debbie needs to validate Sam's certificate, as shown in Figure 6-12, she actually also needs to validate the Leaf D CA and Intermediate B CA certificates, as well as Sam's.

So in Figure 6-12, we have a user, Sam, who digitally signs a message and sends it and his certificate to Debbie. Debbie needs to validate this certificate before she can trust Sam's digital signature. In Sam's certificate, there is an issuer field, which indicates that the certificate was issued by Leaf D CA. Debbie has to obtain Leaf D CA's digital certificate and public key to validate Sam's certificate. Remember that Debbie validates the certificate by verifying its digital signature. The digital signature was created by the certificate issuer using its private key, so Debbie needs to verify it using the issuer's public key.

Debbie tracks down Leaf D CA's certificate and public key, but now needs to verify this CA's certificate, so she looks at the issuer field, which indicates that Leaf D CA's certificate was issued by Intermediate B CA. Debbie now needs to get Intermediate B CA's certificate and public key.

Debbie's client software tracks this down and sees that the issuer for the Intermediate B CA is the Root CA, which she already has a certificate and public key for. So Debbie's client software had to follow the **certificate path**, meaning it had to continue to track down and collect certificates until it came upon a self-signed certificate. A self-signed certificate indicates that it was signed by a root CA, and Debbie's software has been configured to trust this entity as her trust anchor, so she can stop there. Figure 6-13 illustrates the steps Debbie's software had to carry out just to be able to verify Sam's certificate.

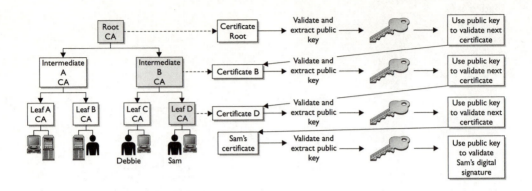

Figure 6-13 Verifying each certificate in a certificate path

This type of simplistic trust model works well within an enterprise that easily follows a hierarchical organizational chart, but many companies cannot use this type of trust model because different departments or offices may require their own trust anchors. These demands can be derived from direct business needs or from inter-organizational politics. This hierarchical model may also not be possible when two or more companies need to communicate with each other. Neither company will let the other's CA be the root CA, because they do not necessarily trust the other entity to that degree. In these situations, the CAs will need to work in a peer-to-peer relationship instead of in a hierarchical relationship.

Peer-to-Peer Model

In a *peer-to-peer* trust model, one CA is not subordinate to another CA, and there is no established trusted anchor between the CAs involved. The end-entities will look to their issuing CA as their trusted anchor, but the different CAs will not have an agreed-upon anchor.

Figure 6-14 illustrates this type of trust model. The two different CAs will certify the public key for each other, which creates a bidirectional trust. This is referred to as *cross certification,* since the CAs are not receiving their certificates and public keys from a superior CA, but instead they are creating them for each other.

One of the main drawbacks to this model is scalability. Each CA must certify every other CA that is participating, and a bidirectional trust path must be implemented, as shown in Figure 6-15. If there was one root CA certifying all the intermediate CAs, scalability would not be as much of an issue.

Figure 6-15 represents a fully connected *mesh architecture,* meaning that each CA is directly connected to and has a bidirectional trust relationship with every other CA. As you can see in this illustration, the complexity of this setup can become overwhelming.

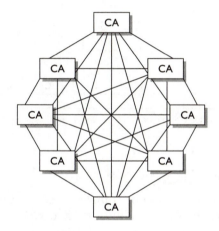

Hybrid Trust Model

Companies can be complex within themselves, and when the need arises to properly communicate with outside partners, suppliers, and customers in an authorized and secured manner, it can make sticking to either the hierarchical or **peer-to-peer trust model** difficult, if not impossible. In many implementations, the different model types have to be combined to provide the necessary communication lines and levels of trust. In a *hybrid* trust model, the two companies have their own internal hierarchical models and are connected through a peer-to-peer model using cross certification.

Another option in this hybrid configuration is to implement a *bridge CA*. Figure 6-16 illustrates the role that a bridge CA could play—it is responsible for issuing cross-certificates for all connected CAs and trust domains. The bridge is not considered a root or trust anchor, but just the entity that generates and maintains the cross certification for the connected environments.

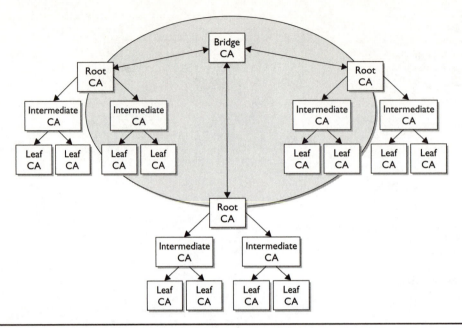

Figure 6-16   A bridge CA can control the cross-certification procedures.

Certificate Usage

Public key infrastructures can be complex beasts, as this chapter has shown. They have many different components that must work together seamlessly to provide the expected protection and functionality. The reason a PKI is implemented is to provide users and devices with the ability to communicate securely and to provide them with trust anchors, since they do not directly trust each other.

Certificate registration requests are validated by a registration authority (RA), and the certificate is then generated by a certificate authority (CA). The digital certificate binds an individual's identity to the public key that is within the certificate.

Certificates can expire, be revoked, or be suspended. When a user receives a certificate from another user, they must validate it, which means that the CA's digital signature that is embedded within the certificate itself must be validated. This may require the user to validate a whole string of certificates and digital signatures, referred to as a certificate path. This path must be followed until a self-signed trusted root certificate is reached.

Certificate authorities can be public, private (in-house), or outsourced, depending upon a company's needs. Internal PKIs can follow different trust models, which will dictate their trust paths and anchors.

PKIs have been waiting in the wings for several years—waiting for the time when they would finally be accepted and implemented. That time has come, and more and more companies are putting them into place. This also means more and more companies have experienced the pain of implementing such a complex framework into a preexisting working environment. All the aspects of a PKI must be understood before filling out the first purchase order, which also means determining exactly what a PKI will do for you and what it won't. In any security activity, understanding the reality of any protection mechanism is necessary, but this is especially true for a PKI because it can drastically affect the whole production environment in both good and bad ways.

Finally, it is important to understand that a majority of these authentication activities take place behind the scenes for the users—the technology and intelligence have been programmed into the software itself. So, in this chapter, when we said that users need to see if their system has been configured to trust a specific CA, or that they need to validate a digital signature or obtain a higher-level CA certificate, the user's client software is actually carrying out these tasks. A majority of what was discussed in this chapter happens transparently to the users.

Chapter Review

Chapter Summary

After reading this chapter and completing the exercises, you should understand the following about public key infrastructure.

- PKIs form the central management functionality used to enable encryption technologies.
- PKI solutions include Certificate Authorities (CA) and Registration Authorities (RA).
- RAs verify identities to be used on certificates.
- CAs create certificates for identified entities and maintain records of their issuance and revocation.
- Certificates are handled via a certificate server and client software.
- Three classes of certificates exist
  - Class 1   personal e-mail use
  - Class 2   software signing
  - Class 3   used to set up a CA
- There are three different architectures of CAs: hierarchical, peer-to-peer, and hybrid.

Key Terms

CA certificate *(122)*
Certificate authority *(110)*
Certificate path *(143)*
Certificate repository *(115)*
Certificate revocation list *(127)*
Certificate server *(110)*
Cross-certificate *(122)*
Digital certificate *(110)*
Dual control *(135)*
Hierarchical trust model *(142)*
Hybrid trust model *(145)*
Key archiving system *(135)*
Key escrow *(135)*
Key recovery *(135)*
Peer-to-peer model *(145)*
PKI *(107)*
Registration authority (RA) *(111)*
X.509 standard *(119)*

Key Terms Quiz

Use terms from the Key Terms list to complete the sentences that follow. Don't use the same term more than once. Not all terms will be used.

1. The _____ is the trusted authority for certifying individuals' identities and creating an electronic document indicating that individuals are who they say they are.

2. Requiring two individuals to recover a lost key together is called _____, which simply means that two people have to be present to carry out a specific task.

3. A _____ is a list of serial numbers of certificates that have been revoked.

4. The _____ is the actual service that issues certificates based on the data provided during the initial registration process.

5. The _____ outlines the necessary fields of a certificate and the possible values that can be inserted into the fields.

6. A _____ is a holding place for individuals' certificates and public keys that are participating in a particular PKI environment.

7. _____ are used when independent CAs establish peer-to-peer trust relationships.

8. A _____ is a structure that provides all of the necessary components for different types of users and entities to be able to communicate securely and in a predictable manner.

9. _____ is a process of giving keys to a third party so that others can decrypt and read sensitive information when this need arises.

10. In a _____ trust model, one CA is not subordinate to another CA, and there is no established trusted anchor between the CAs involved.

Multiple-Choice Quiz

1. In a *peer-to-peer* trust model…

    A. One CA is subordinate to another CA.

    B. There is an established trusted anchor between the CAs involved.

    C. One CA is not subordinate to another CA.

    D. The ruling of the senior CA is used to resolve ties.

2. A hierarchical trust model is characterized by…

    A. Numerous CAs in a peer-to-peer relationship.

    B. An inverted tree-type structure with a root node at the top.

    C. A mesh of interconnected CAs.

    D. A CA with recursive interconnects to itself.

3. Key escrow is…

    A. A government-backed scheme to enable government snooping.

    B. A way of "backing up" encryption keys.

    C. An unnecessary and archaic bureaucratic step that has been eliminated by software.

    D. A method to enable key reuse throughout an organization.

4. Certificate authorities (CAs) are…

    A. Private firms assigned by the Internet Society to enable encryption use across the Internet.

    B. Software programs to enable the use of certificates on end-user client machines.

    C. Government-regulated services that act as electronic identity brokers.

    D. The issuers of a certificate in a PKI scheme.

5. The length of time a private key needs to remain secure is…

    A. The length of time a certificate offers validity.

    B. Until a certificate has been revoked.

    C. As long as the material that has been encrypted needs to remain secure.

    D. Not applicable; once used, it is time invariant.

6. Certificates have what form of protection to enable continuing control by the owner?

    A. Use of a certificate revocation list as part of the validation process

    B. End dates for validity

    C. None. Once issued, there is no way for the owner to control a certificate.

    D. Certificates can be labeled on the certificate server as void, thus invalidating all copies.

7. A Class 1 digital certificate is commonly used for?

    A. Personal e-mail signing

    B. Personal web server ssl

    C. Code signing

    D. Denoting an entity as a CA

8. An item *not* found on a certificate is…

    A. Owner identity

    B. The issuing CA

    C. The expiration date

    D. The private key for the certificate holder

9. A firm wishing to customize a certificate…

    A. Must use a Class 3 certificate.

    B. Doesn't need to do anything; all certificates are expandable by the customer.

    C. Must use a Class 4 certificate (that is, a Class 3 certificate modified for internal use).

    D. Cannot do so; certificates are not structured to be expandable.

10. To obtain a certificate, a user must contact whom?

    A. Their ISP

    B. A registration authority (RA)

    C. A certificate authority (CA)

    D. The Internet Engineering Task force, via a X.509 request

11. The hybrid trust model is characterized by…

    A. A combination of hierarchical and peer-to-peer nodes

    B. A corporate intranet–based solution

C. A flat peer-to-peer network with a single common CA

D. Combining certificates from Microsoft and Netscape browsers into a cohesive environment

12. PKI adoption is hampered by...

A. Issues surrounding users remembering large keys or sets of keys

B. A lack of industry standardization

C. Government regulation of encryption

D. A lack of business understanding of its utility

13. What is a weakness of certificate revocation lists?

A. When establishing a connection to verify the certificate lineage, it may possibly force numerous CRL lookups.

B. Not all certificate types can be revoked.

C. End users must manually request updated checks on each use.

D. Not all CAs use CRLs.

14. PKI solutions are combinations of hardware and software to enable...

A. SSL web pages

B. Functional use of public key encryption technology

C. Proprietary LDAP information mechanisms to assist in Internet security

D. E-commerce vendors to track deadbeat customers

15. Which is not a trust model employed in PKIs?

A. The notary public trust model

B. The peer-to-peer trust model

C. The hybrid trust model

D. The hierarchical trust model

Essay Quiz

1. Describe the pros and cons of establishing a key escrow program for a small- to medium-sized business.

2. Why would a small- to medium-sized firm implement a PKI solution? What business benefits would ensue from such a course of action?

3. Describe the steps involved in verifying a certificate's validity.

4. Describe the different classes of digital certificates and their uses.

5. Compare and contrast the hierarchical trust model, peer-to-peer trust model, and hybrid trust model.

Lab Projects

Lab Project 6.1

Investigate the process of obtaining a personal certificate or digital ID for e-mail usage. What information is needed, what are the costs, and what protection is afforded based on the vendor?

Lab Project 6.2

Determine what certificates are registered with the browser instance on your computer.

Standards and Protocols

Upon completion of this lesson, you will be able to:

- List and explain various standards involved in establishing an interoperable Internet PKI
- Describe interoperability issues with PKI standards
- Describe how the common Internet protocols use and implement the PKI standards

One of the biggest growth industries in the 1990s was the commercial use of the Internet. While the early 2000s haven't seen explosive growth, due to other factors, none of the still steadily growing Internet commerce would be possible without the use of standards and protocols to provide a common, interoperable environment for securely exchanging information. Due to the wide distribution of users and businesses, the most practical solution to date has been the commercial implementation of **public key infrastructures** (PKIs).

This chapter examines the standards and protocols involved in secure Internet transactions and e-business using a PKI. Though you may only use a portion of the related standards and protocols on a daily basis, you should understand how they interact to provide the services that are critical for security: confidentiality, integrity, authentication, and nonrepudiation.

Chapter 6 introduced the algorithms and techniques used to implement a PKI, but as you probably noticed, there is a lot of room for interpretation. Various organizations have developed and implemented standards and protocols that have been accepted as the basis for secure interaction in a PKI environment. These standards fall into three general categories:

- **Standards that define the PKI**   These standards define the data and data structures exchanged and the means for managing that data to provide the functions of the PKI (**certificate** issuance, storage, revocation, registration, and management).

- **Standards that define the interface between applications and the underlying PKI**   These use the PKI to establish the services required by applications.

- **Standards that provide bits and pieces that glue everything together and may address not only the PKI structure and the methods and protocols** for using it, but that may also provide an overarching business process environment for PKI implementation (for example, ISO 17799 and the FIPS PUBS) These standards don't neatly fit in either of the previous two categories.

Figure 7-1 shows the relationships between these standards and protocols.

Figure 7-1 conveys the interdependence of the standards and protocols discussed in this chapter. The Internet PKI relies on three main standards for establishing interoperable PKI services: Public Key Infrastructure X.509 (PKIX), Public Key Cryptography Standards (PKCS), and **X.509**. There are other protocols and standards that help define the management and operation of the PKI and related services— **Internet Security Association and Key Management Protocol** (ISAKMP) and XML Key Management Specification (XKMS) are both key management protocols, while Certificate Management Protocol (CMP) is for managing certificates. **Wired Equivalent Privacy** (WEP) is used to encrypt wireless communications in an 802.11 environment to support some of the more application-oriented standards and protocols: **Secure/Multipurpose Internet Mail Extensions** (S/MIME) for e-mail; **Secure Sockets Layer** (SSL), **Transport Layer Security** (TLS), and **Wireless Transport Layer Security** (WTLS) for secure packet transmission; and **IP Security** (IPsec) and **Point-to-Point Tunneling Protocol** (PPTP) to support virtual private networks. ISO 17799, Common Criteria, and Federal Information Processing Standards Publications (FIPS) each address security at the business process, application, protocol, and PKI implementation levels. Finally, **Pretty Good Privacy** (PGP) provides an alternative method spanning the protocol and application levels.

We'll be examining each standard from the bottom up, starting with building an infrastructure through protocols and applications, detailing some of the inherent weaknesses of and potential attacks on a PKI as we go.

Figure 7-1
Relationships between PKI standards and protocols

Online banking and shopping — Business processes

E-mail, VPNs, EDI — Applications

S/MIME, SSL, TLS, WTLS, IPsec, PPTP — Standards/protocols that use PKI

ISAKMP, CMP, XKMS, X.509, PKIX, PKCS — PKI implementation level

PKIX/PKCS

Two main standards have evolved over time to implement PKI on a practical level on the Internet. Both are based on the X.509 certificate standard (discussed shortly in the "X.509" section) and establish complementary standards for implementing PKI. Public Key Infrastructure X.509 (PKIX) and Public Key Cryptography Standards (PKCS) intertwine to define the most commonly used set of standards.

PKIX was produced by the Internet Engineering Task Force (IETF) and defines standards for interactions and operations for four component types: the user (end-entity), **certificate authority** (CA), registration authority (RA), and the repository for certificates and **certificate revocation lists** (CRLs). PKCS defines many of the lower-level standards for message syntax, cryptographic algorithms, and the like. The PKCS set of standards is a product of RSA Security.

The PKIX working group was formed in 1995 to develop the standards necessary to support PKIs. At the time, the X.509 Public Key Certificate (PKC) format was proposed as the basis for a PKI. X.509 includes information regarding data formats and procedures used for CA-signed PKCs, but it doesn't specify values or formats for many of the fields within the PKC. X.509 v1 (version 1) was originally defined in 1988 as part of the X.500 Directory standard. After being co-opted by the Internet community for implementing certificates for secure Internet communications, it became apparent that there were several shortcomings. The current version, X.509 v3, was adopted in 1996. X.509 is very complex, allowing a great deal of flexibility in implementing certificate features. PKIX provides standards for extending and using X.509 v3 certificates and for managing them, enabling interoperability between PKIs following the standards.

PKIX uses the model in Figure 7-2 for representing the components and users of a PKI. The user, called an *end-entity*, is not part of the PKI, but they are either users of the PKI certificates, the subject of a certificate (an entity identified by it), or both. The certificate authority (CA) is responsible for issuing, storing, and revoking certificates—both Public Key Certificates (PKCs) and Attribute Certificates (ACs). The registration authority (RA) is responsible for management activities designated by the CA. The RA may, in

Figure 7-2
The PKIX model

fact, be a component of the CA rather than a separate component. The final component of the PKIX model is the repository, a system or group of distributed systems that provide certificates and certificate revocation lists to the end-entities.

PKIX Standards

Now that we have looked at how PKIX views the world, let's take a look at what PKIX does. Using X.509 v3, there are five major areas that the PKIX working group addresses:

- PKIX outlines certificate extensions and content not covered by X.509 v3 and the format of version 2 CRLs thus providing compatibility standards for sharing certificates and CRLs between CAs and end-entities in different PKIs. The PKIX profile of the X.509 v3 PKC describes the contents, required extensions, optional extensions, and extensions that need not be implemented. The PKIX profile suggests a range of values for many extensions. In addition, PKIX provides a profile for version 2 CRLs, allowing different PKIs to share revocation information. (For more information on PKIX see "Internet X.509 Public Key Infrastructure Certificate and CRL Profile" [RFC 3280].)

- PKIX provides certificate management message formats and protocols, defining the data structures, management messages, and management functions for PKIs. The working group also addresses the assumptions and restrictions of their protocols. This standard identifies the protocols necessary to support online interactions between entities in the PKIX model. The management protocols support functions for entity registration, initialization of the certificate (possibly key pair generation), issuance of the certificate, key pair update, certificate revocation, cross-certification (between CAs), and key pair recovery if available.

- PKIX outlines certificate policies and certification practices statements (CPSs), establishing the relationship between policies and CPSs. A policy is a set of rules that help determine the applicability of a certificate to an end-entity. For example, a certificate for handling routine information would probably have a policy on creation, storage, and management of key pairs quite different from a policy for certificates used in financial transactions, due to the sensitivity of the financial information. A CPS explains the practices used by a CA to issue certificates. In other words, the CPS is the method used to get the certificate, while the policy defines some characteristics of the certificate and how it will be handled and used.

- PKIX specifies operational protocols, defining the protocols for certificate handling. In particular, there are protocol definitions for using Lightweight Directory Access Protocol version 2 (LDAP v2), File Transfer Protocol (FTP), and Hypertext Transfer Protocol (HTTP) to retrieve certificates from repositories. These are the most common protocols for applications to use when retrieving certificates.

- PKIX includes time-stamping and data certification and validation services, which are areas of interest to the PKIX working group, and which will probably grow in use over time. A time stamp authority (TSA) certifies that a particular entity existed at a particular time. A Data Validation and Certification Server certifies the validity of signed documents, PKCs, and the possession or existence of data. These capabilities support nonrepudiation requirements and are considered building blocks for a nonrepudiation service.

PKCs are the most commonly used certificates, but the PKIX working group has been working on two other types of certificates: Attribute Certificates and Qualified Certificates.

An Attribute Certificate (AC) is used to grant permissions using rule-based, role-based, and rank-based access controls. ACs are used to implement a privilege management infrastructure (PMI). In a PMI, an entity (user, program, system, and so on) is typically identified as a client to a server using a PKC. There are then two possibilities: either the identified client pushes an AC to the server, or the server can query a trusted repository to retrieve the attributes of the client. This situation is modeled in Figure 7-3.

The client push of the AC has the effect of improving performance, but there is no independent verification by the server of the client's permissions. The alternative is to have the server pull the information from an AC issuer or a repository. This method is preferable from a security standpoint, because the server or server's domain determines the client's access rights. The pull method has the added benefit of requiring no changes to the client software.

The QC is based on the term used within the European Commission to identify certificates with specific legislative uses. This concept is generalized in the PKIX QC profile to indicate a certificate used to identify a specific individual (a single human rather than the *entity* of the PKC) with a high level of assurance in a nonrepudiation service.

Table 7-1 summarizes the Internet Requests For Comment (RFCs) that have been produced by the PKIX working group for each of these five areas.

There are other documents produced by the Internet Engineering Task Force PKIX working group, but the ones listed in Table 7-1 cover the major implementation details for PKIX. For a complete list of current and pending documents, see the Internet Draft for the PKIX working group roadmap.

Figure 7-3
The PKIX PMI model

Subject	RFCs
Certificate and CRL profiles	—RFC 3280 (replaces RFC 2459): Internet X.509 Public Key Infrastructure Certificate and CRL Profile —RFC 3039: Internet X.509 Public Key Infrastructure Qualified Certificates Profile —RFC 3280: Internet X.509 Public Key Infrastructure Certificate and Certificate Revocation List (CRL) Profile —RFC 3281: An Internet Attribute Certificate Profile for Authorization
Certificate management protocols	—RFC 2510: Internet X.509 Public Key Infrastructure Certificate Management Protocols —RFC 2511: Internet X.509 Certificate Request Message Format —RFC 2560: X.509 Internet Public Key Infrastructure Online Certificate Status Protocol—OCSP —RFC 2797: Certificate Management Messages over CMS
Certificate policies and CPSs	—RFC 2527: Internet X.509 Public Key Infrastructure Certificate Policy and Certification Practices Framework
Operational protocols	—RFC 2528: Internet X.509 Public Key Infrastructure Representation of Key Exchange Algorithm (KEA) Keys in Internet X.509 Public Key Infrastructure Certificates —RFC 2559: Internet X.509 Public Key Infrastructure Operational Protocols—LDAP v2 —RFC 2585: Internet X.509 Public Key Infrastructure Operational Protocols: FTP and HTTP —RFC 2587: Internet X.509 Public Key Infrastructure LDAP v2 Schema
Time-stamp and data validation	—RFC 2875: Diffie-Hellman Proof-of-Possession Algorithms —RFC 3029: Internet X.509 Public Key Infrastructure Data Validation and Certification Server Protocols —RFC 3161: Internet X.509 Public Key Infrastructure Time-Stamp Protocol (TSP)
Other PKIX topics	—RFC 3279: Algorithms and Identifiers for the Internet X.509 Public Key Infrastructure Certificate and Certificate Revocation List (CRL) Profile —RFC 3379: Delegated Path Validation and Delegated Path Discovery Protocol Requirements

Table 7-1   PKIX Subjects and Related RFCs

PKCS

RSA Laboratories created the Public Key Cryptography Standards (PKCS) to fill some of the gaps in the standards that existed in PKI implementation. Just as with the PKIX standards, PKI developers have adopted many of these standards as a basis for achieving interoperability between different certificate authorities. PKCS is composed of a set of (currently) 13 active standards, with 2 other standards that are no longer active. The standards are referred to as PKCS #1 through PKCS #15, as listed in Table 7-2. The standards combine to establish a common base for services required in a PKI.

Standard	Title and Description
PKCS #1	RSA Cryptography Standard: Definition of the RSA encryption standard.
PKCS #2	No longer active; it covered RSA encryption of message digests and was incorporated into PKCS #1.
PKCS #3	Diffie-Hellman Key Agreement Standard: Definition of the Diffie-Hellman key-agreement protocol.
PKCS #4	No longer active; it covered RSA key syntax and was incorporated into PKCS #1.
PKCS #5	Password-Based Cryptography Standard: Definition of a password-based encryption (PBE) method for generating a secret key.
PKCS #6	Extended-Certificate Syntax Standard: Definition of an extended certificate syntax that is being replaced by X.509 v3.
PKCS #7	Cryptographic Message Syntax Standard: Definition of the cryptographic message standard for encoded messages, regardless of encryption algorithm. Commonly replaced with PKIX Cryptographic Message Syntax.
PKCS #8	Private-Key Information Syntax Standard: Definition of a private key information format, used to store private key information.
PKCS #9	Selected Attribute Types: Definition of attribute types used in other PKCS standards.
PKCS #10	Certification Request Syntax Standard: Definition of a syntax for certification requests.
PKCS #11	Cryptographic Token Interface Standard: Definition of a technology-independent programming interface for cryptographic devices (such as smart cards).
PKCS #12	Personal Information Exchange Syntax Standard: Definition of a format for storage and transport of user private keys, certificates, and other personal information.
PKCS #13	Elliptic Curve Cryptography Standard: Description of methods for encrypting and signing messages using elliptic curve cryptography.
PKCS #14	A standard for pseudo-random number generation.
PKCS #15	Cryptographic Token Information Format Standard: Definition of a format for storing cryptographic information in cryptographic tokens.

Table 7-2   PKCS Standards

Though adopted early in the development of PKIs, some of these standards are being phased out. For example, PKCS #6 is being replaced by X.509 v3 (covered shortly in the "X.509" section) and PKCS #7 and PKCS #10 are used less, as their PKIX counterparts are being adopted.

Why You Need to Know

If you or your company are simply planning to use one of the existing certificate servers to support e-commerce, you may not need to know the specifics of these standards (except perhaps for your exam). However, if you plan to implement a private PKI to support secure services within your organization, you will need to understand what standards are out there and how the decision to use a particular PKI implementation (either home grown or commercial) may lead to incompatibilities with other certificate-issuing entities. Your business-to-business requirements must be taken into account when deciding how to implement a PKI within your organization.

X.509

So what is a certificate? In the late 1980s, the X.500 OSI Directory Standard was defined by ISO and the ITU. It was developed for implementing a network directory system, and part of this directory standard was the concept of authentication of entities within the directory. X.509 is the portion of the X.500 standard that addresses the structure of certificates used for authentication.

There have been several versions of the certificates, with version 3 being the current version (as this is being written). Each version has extended the contents of the certificates to include additional information necessary to use certificates in a PKI. The original ITU X.509 definition was published in 1988 and was formerly referred to as CCITT X.509 and is sometimes referred to as ISO/IEC/ITU 9594-8. The 1988 certificate format, version 1, was revised in 1993 as the ITU-T X.509 definition when two more fields were added to support directory access control. ITU-T is the Standards Section of the ITU created in 1992.

The 1993, version 2 specification was revised following lessons learned from implementing Internet Privacy Enhanced Mail (PEM). Version 3 added additional optional extensions for more subject identification information, key attribute information, policy information, and certification path constraints. In addition, version 3 allows additional extensions to be defined in standards or to be defined and registered by organizations or communities. Table 7-3 gives a description of the fields in a X.509 certificate.

Certificates are used to encapsulate the information needed to authenticate an entity. The X.509 specification defines a hierarchical certification structure that relies on a root certification authority that is *self-certifying* (meaning it issues its own certificate). All other certificates can be traced back to such a root through a *path*. A certificate authority issues a certificate to a uniquely identifiable entity (person, corporation, computer, and so on)—issuing a certificate to "John Smith" would cause some real problems if that were all the information you had when issuing the certificate. We are saved somewhat by the requirement that the CA determines what identifier is unique (the distinguished name), but when certificates and trust are extended between CAs, the unique identification becomes critical.

Field Name	Field Description
Certificate Signature	X.509 version used for this certificate: Version 1 = 0 Version 2 = 1 Version 3 = 2
Serial Number	A nonnegative integer assigned by the certificate issuer that must be unique to the certificate.

Signature Algorithm
  Algorithm
  Parameters (optional)
	The algorithm identifier for the algorithm used by the CA to sign the certificate. The optional "parameters" field is used to provide the cryptographic algorithm parameters used in generating the signature.

Issuer	Identification for the entity that signed and issued the certificate. This must be a distinguished name within the hierarchy of certificate authorities.

Validity
  Not valid before time
  Not valid after time
	Validity specifies a period of time during which the certificate is valid using a "not valid before" time and a "not valid after" time (expressed in UTC or in a generalized time).

Subject	The name for the certificate owner.
Subject Public Key Info	This field consists of an encryption algorithm identifier followed by a bit string for the public key.
Issuer Unique ID	Optional for versions 2 and 3—a unique bit-string identifier for the CA that issued the certificate.
Subject Unique ID	Optional for versions 2 and 3—a unique bit-string identifier for the subject of the certificate.

Extensions
  Extension ID
  Critical
  Extension Value
	Optional for version 3—the extension area consists of a sequence of extension fields containing an extension identifier, a Boolean field indicating whether the extension is critical, and an octet string representing the value of the extension. Extensions can be defined in standards or defined and registered by organizations or communities.

Thumbprint Algorithm
  Algorithm
  Parameters (optional)
	This field identifies the algorithm used by the CA to sign this certificate. This field must match the algorithm identified above.

Thumbprint	The signature is the bit-string hash value obtained when the CA signed the certificate. The signature certifies the contents of the certificate, binding the public key to the subject.

Certificate Contents (rows from Certificate Signature through Extensions)

Certificate Signature (rows Thumbprint Algorithm and Thumbprint)

Table 7-3   X.509 Certificate Fields

Some other extensions to the X.509 certificate have been proposed for use in implementing a PKI. For example, PKIX identified several extensions for use in the certificate policy framework (see RFC 2427). It is essential to ensure that your PKI ignores extensions that it is not prepared to handle.

SSL/TLS

Secure Sockets Layer (SSL) and Transport Layer Security (TLS) provide the most common means of interacting with a PKI and certificates. The older SSL protocol was introduced by Netscape as a means of providing secure connections for web transfers using encryption. These two protocols provide secure connections between the client and server for exchanging information. They also provide server authentication (and optionally, client authentication) and confidentiality of information transfers.

The IETF established the TLS Working Group in 1996 to develop a standard transport layer security protocol. The working group began with SSL version 3.0 as its basis and released RFC 2246, TLS Protocol Version 1.0, in 1999 as a proposed standard. The working group also published RFC 2712, "Addition of Kerberos Cipher Suites to Transport Layer Security (TLS)," as a proposed standard, and two RFCs on the use of TLS with HTTP. Like its predecessor, TLS is a protocol that ensures privacy between communicating applications and their users on the Internet. When a server and client communicate, TLS ensures that no third party may eavesdrop or tamper with any message.

TLS is composed of two parts: the TLS Record Protocol and the TLS Handshake Protocol. The TLS Record Protocol provides connection security by using supported encryption methods, such as the Data Encryption Standard (DES). The TLS Record Protocol can also be used without encryption. The TLS Handshake Protocol allows the server and client to authenticate each other and to negotiate a session encryption algorithm and cryptographic keys before data is exchanged (http://searchVB.techtarget.com/sDefinition/0,,sid8_gci211545,00.html).

Though TLS is based on SSL and is sometimes referred to as SSL, they are not interoperable. However, the TLS protocol does contain a mechanism that allows a TLS implementation to back down to SSL 3.0. The difference between the two is in the way they perform key expansion and message authentication computations. TLS uses the MD5 and SHA1 hashing algorithms XORed together to determine the session key. The most recent browser versions support TLS. Though SSL also uses both hashing algorithms, SSL is considered less secure because the way it uses them forces a reliance on MD5 rather than SHA1.

The TLS Record Protocol is a layered protocol. At each layer, messages may include fields for length, description, and content. The Record Protocol takes messages to be transmitted, fragments the data into manageable blocks, optionally compresses the data, applies a message authentication code (MAC) to the data, encrypts it, and transmits the result. Received data is decrypted, verified, decompressed, and reassembled, and then delivered to higher-level clients.

The TLS Handshake Protocol involves the following steps, which are summarized in Figure 7-4:

1. Exchange hello messages to agree on algorithms, exchange random values, and check for session resumption.

2. Exchange the necessary cryptographic parameters to allow the client and server to agree on a pre-master secret.

3. Exchange certificates and cryptographic information to allow the client and server to authenticate themselves.

4. Generate a master secret from the pre-master secret and exchanged random values.

5. Provide security parameters to the record layer.

6. Allow the client and server to verify that their peer has calculated the same security parameters and that the handshake occurred without tampering by an attacker.

Though it has been designed to minimize this risk, TLS still has potential vulnerabilities to a man-in-the-middle attack. A highly skilled and well-placed attacker can force TLS to operate at lower security levels. Regardless, through the use of validated and trusted certificates, a secure cipher suite can be selected for the exchange of data.

Once established, a TLS session remains active as long as data is being exchanged. If sufficient inactive time has elapsed for the secure connection to time out, it can be reinitiated.

Figure 7-4
TLS Handshake Protocol

ISAKMP

The Internet Security Association and Key Management Protocol (ISAKMP) provides a method for implementing a key exchange protocol and for negotiating a security policy. It defines procedures and packet formats to negotiate, establish, modify, and delete security associates. Because it is a framework, it doesn't define implementation-specific protocols, such as the key exchange protocol or hash functions. An example of ISAKMP is the Internet Key Exchange (IKE) protocol.

An important definition for understanding ISAKMP is the term *security association*. A security association (SA) is a relationship where two or more entities define how they will communicate securely. ISAKMP is intended to support security associations at all layers of the network stack. For this reason, it can be implemented on the transport level using TCP or UDP, or it can be implemented on IP directly.

Negotiation of a security association between servers occurs in two stages. First, the entities agree on how to secure negotiation messages (the ISAKMP SA). Once the entities have secured their negotiation traffic, they then determine the security associations for the protocols used for the remainder of their communications. Figure 7-5 shows the structure of the ISAKMP header. This header is used during both parts of the ISAKMP negotiation.

The initiator cookie is set by the entity requesting the SA, and the responder sets the responder cookie. The payload byte indicates the type of the first payload. Payload types include security associations, proposals, key transforms, key exchanges, vendor identities, and other things. The major and minor revision fields refer to the major version number and minor version number for the ISAKMP protocol. The exchange type helps determine the order of messages and payloads. The flag bits indicate options for the ISAKMP exchange, including whether the payload is encrypted, whether the initiator and responder have "committed" to the SA, and whether the packet is to be authenticated only (and is not encrypted). The final fields of the ISAKMP header indicate the

Bit position				
0 1 2 3 4 5 6 7 8 9 10 11 12 13 14 15 16 17 18 19 20 21 22 23 24 25 26 27 28 29 30 31				
Initiator cookie (8 bytes)				
Responder cookie (8 bytes)				
Payload (8 bits)	Major rev. (4 bits)	Minor rev. (4 bits)	Exchange type (8 bits)	Flags (8 bits)
Message identifier (4 bytes)				
Message length (4 bytes)				

Figure 7-5   ISAKMP header format

message identifier and a message length. Payloads encapsulated within ISAKMP use a generic header, and each payload has its own header format.

Once the ISAKMP SA is established, multiple protocol SAs can be established using the single ISAKMP SA. This feature is valuable due to the overhead associated with the two-stage negotiation. SAs are valid for specific periods of time, and once the time expires, the SA must be renegotiated. For more information on the ISAKMP protocol, see Internet RFC 2408. There are also many resources for specific implementations of ISAKMP within the IPsec protocol.

CMP

The PKIX Certificate Management Protocol (CMP) is specified in RFC 2510. This protocol defines the messages and operations required to provide certificate management services within the PKIX model. Though part of the IETF PKIX effort, CMP provides a framework that works well with other standards, such as PKCS #7 and PKCS #10. CMP provides for the following certificate operations:

- CA establishment, including creation of the initial CRL and export of the public key for the CA
- Certification of an end-entity, including the following:
  - Initial registration and certification of the end-entity (registration, certificate issuance, and placement of the certificate in a repository)
  - Updates to the key pair for end-entities, required periodically and when a key pair is compromised or keys cannot be recovered
  - End-entity certificate updates, required when a certificate expires
  - Periodic CA key pair update, similar to end-entity key pair updates
  - Cross-certification requests, placed by other CAs
  - Certificate and CRL publication, performed under the appropriate conditions of certificate issuance and certificate revocation
  - Key pair recovery, a service to restore key pair information for an end-entity; for example, if a certificate password is lost or the certificate file is lost
  - Revocation requests, supporting requests by authorized entities to revoke a certificate

CMP also defines mechanisms for performing these operations, either online or offline using files, e-mail, tokens, or web operations.

XKMS

The XML Key Management Specification defines services to manage PKI operations within the Extensible Markup Language (XML) environment. These services are provided for handling PKI keys and certificates automatically. Developed by the W3C, it is intended to simplify integration of PKIs and management of certificates in applications. As well as responding to problems of authentication and verification of electronic signatures, it also allows certificates to be managed, registered, or revoked.

XKMS services reside on a separate server that interacts with an established PKI. The services are accessible via a simple XML protocol. Developers can rely on the XKMS services, making it less complex to interface with the PKI. The services provide for retrieving key information (owner, key value, key issuer, and the like) and key registration and management (such as key registration and revocation).

Retrieval operations rely on the XML signature for the necessary information. There are three tiers of service based on the client requests and application requirements.

Tier 0 provides a means of retrieving key information by embedding references to the key within the XML signature. The signature contains an element called a RetrievalMethod that indicates ways to resolve the key. In this case, the client sends a request, using the retrieval method, to obtain the desired key information. For example, if the verification key contained a long chain of X.509 v3 certificates, a retrieval method could be included to avoid sending the certificates with the document. The client would use the retrieval method to obtain the chain of certificates. For tier 0, the server indicated in the retrieval method responds directly to the request for the key, possibly bypassing the XKMS server. The tier 0 process is shown in Figure 7-6.

With tier 1 operations, the client forwards the key information portions of the XML signature to the XKMS server, relying on the server to perform the retrieval of the desired key information. The desired information may be local to the XKMS server or it may reside on an external PKI system. The XKMS server provides no additional validation of the key information, such as checking to see if the certificate has been revoked and is still valid. Just as in tier 0, the client performs final validation of the document. Tier 1 is called the *locate service* because it locates the appropriate key information for the client, as shown in Figure 12-7.

Tier 2 is called the *validate service*, and it is illustrated in Figure 7-8. In this case, just as in tier 1, the client relies on the XKMS server to retrieve the relevant key information

Figure 7-6
Tier 0 XKMS
retrieval

Request for key info

Server response

Client

Server

Figure 7-7
XKMS tier 1
locate service

from the external PKI. The XKMS server also performs a data validation on a portion of the key information provided by the client for this purpose. This validation verifies the binding of the key information with the data indicated by the key information contained in the XML signature.

The primary difference between tier 1 and tier 2 is the level of involvement of the XKMS server. In tier 1, it may serve only as a relay or gateway between the client and the PKI. In tier 2, the XKMS server is actively involved in verifying the relation between the PKI information and the document containing the XML signature.

XKMS relies on the client or underlying communications mechanism to provide for the security of the communications with the XKMS server. The specification suggests using one of three methods for ensuring server authentication, response integrity, and relevance of the response to the request. The three methods are digitally signed correspondence, a transport layer security protocol (such as SSL, TLS, or WTLS), or a packet layer security protocol (such as IPsec). Obviously, digitally signed correspondence introduces its own issues regarding validation of the signature, which is the purpose of XKMS.

It is possible to define other tiers of service. Tiers 3 and 4, an *assertion service* and an *assertion status service*, respectively, are mentioned in the defining XKMS specification, but are not defined. The specification states they "could" be defined in other documents.

XKMS also provides services for key registration, key revocation, and key recovery. Authentication for these actions is based on a password or passphrase, which is provided when the keys are registered and when they must be recovered.

Figure 7-8
XKMS tier 2
validate service

S/MIME

The Secure/Multipurpose Internet Mail Extensions (S/MIME) message specification is an extension to the MIME standard that provides a way to send and receive signed and encrypted MIME data. RSA Security created the first version of the S/MIME standard, using the RSA encryption algorithm and the PKCS series of standards. The second version dates from 1998 but had a number of serious restrictions, including the restriction to 40-bit DES. The current version of the IETF standard is dated August 2002.

The changes in the S/MIME standard have been so frequent that the standard has become difficult to implement. Far from having a stable standard for several years that product manufacturers could have time to gain experience with, there have been changes to the encryption algorithms being used. Just as importantly, and not immediately clear from the IETF documents, the standard places reliance upon more than one other standard for it to function. Key amongst these is the format of a public key certificate as expressed in the X.509 standard.

The S/MIME v2 specifications outline a basic strategy to provide security services for electronic mail, but lack many security features required by the Department of Defense (DoD) for use by the military. In early 1996, the Internet Mail Consortium (IMC) was formed as a technical trade association pursuing cooperative use and enhancement of Internet electronic mail and messaging. An early goal of the IMC was to bring together the DoD (along with its vendor community) and commercial industry in order to devise a standard security protocol acceptable to both. Several existing security protocols were considered, including: MIME Object Security Services (MOSS), Pretty Good Privacy (PGP), and S/MIME v2. After examining these protocols, it was determined that none met the requirements of both the military and commercial communities. Instead of launching into a development of an entirely new set of specifications, however, the group decided that with certain enhancements the S/MIME set of specifications could be used. It was also decided that, since the discussion was about a common set of specifications to be used throughout the Internet community, it would be best if this resulting specification were brought under the control of the IETF.

Shortly after the decision was made to revise the S/MIME version 2 specifications, the DoD, its vendor community, and commercial industry met to begin development of the enhanced specifications. The new enhanced specifications would be known as S/MIME Version 3. It was quickly agreed upon by the participants that backward compatibility between the S/MIME v3 and v2 should be preserved, otherwise S/MIME v3-compatible applications would not be able to work with older S/MIME v2-compatible applications.

In order for different implementations of the new S/MIME v3 set of specifications to be interoperable, a minimum set of cryptographic algorithms were mandated. This minimum set must be implemented in an application for it to be considered S/MIME-compliant. Applications can implement additional cryptographic algorithms in order to meet their customer's needs, but the minimum set must also be present in the application for interoperability with other S/MIME applications. Thus, users are not forced to use S/MIME specified algorithms, they can choose their own, but if the application is to be considered S/MIME compliant, the standard algorithms must also be present.

IETF S/MIME v3 Specifications

Building upon the original work by the IMC organized group, the IETF has worked hard to enhance the S/MIME v3 specifications. The ultimate goal is to have the S/MIME v3 specifications receive recognition as an Internet standard. The current IETF S/MIME v3 set of specifications includes:

- Cryptographic Message Syntax (CMS)
- S/MIME version 3 message specification
- S/MIME version 3 certificate handling specification
- Enhanced security services (ESS) for S/MIME

The Cryptographic Message Syntax (CMS) defines a standard syntax for transmitting cryptographic information about contents of a protected message. Originally based on the PKCS #7 version 1.5 specification, the IETF S/MIME Working Group enhanced the specification to include optional security components. Just as the S/MIME version 3 provides backward compatibility with version 2, CMS provides backward compatibility with PKCS #7 so applications will be interoperable even if the new components are not implemented in a specific application.

Integrity, authentication, and nonrepudiation security features are provided by using digital signatures utilizing the SignedData syntax described by the CMS. CMS also describes what is known as the EnvelopedData syntax in order to provide confidentiality of the message's content through the use of encryption. The PKCS #7 specification supports key encryption algorithms, such as RSA. Algorithm independence is promoted through the addition of several fields to the EnvelopedData syntax in CMS, which is the major difference between the PKCS #7 and CMS specifications. The goal was to be able to support specific algorithms such as Diffie-Hellman and the Key Exchange Algorithm (KEA), which is implemented on the Fortezza Crypto Card developed for the DoD. One final significant change to the original specifications is the capability to include X.509 Attribute Certificates in the SignedData and EnvelopedData syntaxes for CMS.

CMS Triple Encapsulated Message

An interesting feature of CMS is the ability to nest security envelopes to provide a combination of security features. As an example, a CMS triple-encapsulated message can be created in which the original content and associated attributes are signed and encapsulated within the inner SignedData object. The inner SignedData is in turn encrypted and encapsulated within an EnvelopedData object. The resulting EnvelopedData object is then also signed and finally encapsulated within a second SignedData object, the outer SignedData object. Usually, the inner SignedData object is signed by the original user and the outer SignedData is signed by another entity such as a firewall or a mail list agent providing an additional level of security. It should be mentioned that this triple-encapsulation is not required of every CMS object. All that is required is a single SignedData object created by the user in order to sign a message or an EnvelopedData object if the user desired to encrypt a message.

PGP

Pretty Good Privacy (PGP) is a popular program that has been around for several years to encrypt and decrypt e-mail and files. It also provides the ability to digitally sign a message so the receiver can be certain of the sender's identity. Taken together, encrypting and signing a message, the receiver can be positive of who sent it and can be assured that it was not modified during transmission. Public domain versions of PGP have been available for years as well as inexpensive commercial versions. It is one of the most widely used programs and is frequently used by both individuals and businesses to ensure data and e-mail privacy. It was developed by Philip R. Zimmermann in 1991 and quickly became a de facto standard for e-mail security.

How It Works

PGP uses a variation of the standard public key encryption process. In public key encryption, the user (utilizing the encryption program) creates a pair of keys. One key is known as the public key and is designed to be given freely to others. The other key is called the private key and is designed to be known only by the creator. Individuals wishing to send a private message to the user will encrypt the message using the user's public key. The algorithm is designed such that only the private key can decrypt the message so only the user will be able to decrypt it. The method, known as public key or asymmetric encryption, is time-consuming. Symmetric encryption which uses only a single key is generally faster. It is because of this that PGP is designed the way it is. PGP uses a symmetric encryption algorithm to encrypt the message to be sent. It then encrypts the symmetric key used to encrypt this message with the public key of the intended recipient. Both the encrypted key and message is then sent. The receiver's version of PGP will first decrypt the symmetric key with the private key supplied by the recipient and then uses the resulting decrypted key to decrypt the rest of the message.

PGP can utilize two different public key algorithms—Rivest-Shamir-Adleman (RSA) or Diffie-Hellman. The RSA version uses the IDEA algorithm to generate a short symmetric key to be used to encrypt the message and RSA to encrypt the short IDEA key. The Diffie-Hellman version uses the CAST algorithm to encrypt the message and the Diffie-Hellman algorithm to encrypt the CAST key.

In order to generate a digital signature, PGP takes advantage of another property of public key encryption schemes. Normally, the sender will encrypt using the receiver's public key, and the message will be decrypted at the other end using the receiver's private key. The process can be reversed such that the sender encrypts with his own private key. The receiver then decrypts the message with the sender's public key. Since the sender is the only individual who has a key that will correctly be decrypted with the sender's public key, the receiver knows that the message was created by the sender who claims to have sent it. The way PGP accomplishes this task is to generate a hash value from the user's name and other signature information. This hash value is then encrypted with the sender's private key known only by the sender. The receiver uses the sender's public key, which is available to everyone, to decrypt the hash value. If the decrypted hash value matches the hash value sent as the digital signature for the message, then the receiver is assured that the message was sent by the sender who claims to have sent it.

Typically, versions of PGP will contain a user interface that works with common e-mail programs such as Outlook. If you want others to be able to send you an encrypted message, you will need to register your public key that was generated by your PGP program with a PGP public-key server. Alternatively, you will have to send your public key to all those who want to send you an encrypted message or post your key to some location they can download it from, such as your web page. Note that using a public-key server is the better method for all of the reasons of trust described in the discussions of PKIs found in Chapter 11. In order to help promote the use of public-key encryption, Network Associates maintains an LDAP/HTTP public-key server with hundreds of thousands of registered public keys.

Where Can You Use PGP?

For many years, the U.S. government raged a fight over the exportation of PGP technology and for many years its exportation was illegal. Today, however, PGP encrypted e-mail can be exchanged with most users outside the U.S. and many versions of PGP are available from numerous sites overseas. Of course, being able to exchange PGP encrypted e-mail requires the individuals on both sides of the communication to have valid versions of PGP. Interestingly, international versions of PGP are just as secure as domestic versions—a feature that is not true of other encryption products. It should be noted that the freeware versions of PGP are not licensed for commercial purposes.

HTTPS

Most web activity occurs using the Hypertext Transfer Protocol (HTTP), but it is also prone to interception. HTTPS uses the Secure Sockets Layer (SSL) to transfer information. Originally developed by Netscape Communications and implemented in their browser, HTTPS has since been incorporated into most common browsers. It uses the open standard SSL to encrypt data at the application layer. In addition, HTTPS uses the standard port 443 for TCP/IP communications rather than the standard port 80 used for HTTP. HTTPS makes use of the 40-bit RC4 encryption algorithm in most cases. A 128-bit version is also implemented.

IPSec

IPSec (Internet Protocol Security) is a collection of IP security features designed to introduce security at the network or packet-processing layer in network communication. Other approaches have attempted to incorporate security at higher levels of the TCP/IP protocol suite such as at the level where applications reside. IPsec is designed to be used to provide secure virtual private network capability over the Internet. In essence, what IPsec does is provide a secure version of the Internet Protocol by introducing authentication and encryption at the packet level. IPsec is optional for the current version of the IP protocol (IPv4) but is required for the next release (IPv6). Obviously, both ends of the communication need to use IPsec for the encryption/decryption process to occur.

IPsec provides two types of security service to ensure authentication and confidentiality for either the data alone (referred to as IPsec transport mode) or for both the data and header (referred to as tunnel mode). IPsec introduces several new protocols including the Authentication Header (AH), which basically provides authentication of the sender, and the Encapsulating Security Payload (ESP), which adds encryption of the data to ensure confidentiality. IPsec also provides for payload compression before encryption using IPcomp. Frequently, encryption negatively impacts the ability to fully compress data for transmission. By providing the ability to compress the data before encryption, IPsec addresses this issue.

CEP

Certificate Enrollment Protocol (CEP) was originally developed by VeriSign for Cisco Systems. It was designed to support certificate issuance, distribution, and revocation using existing technologies. Its use has grown in client and CA applications. The operations supported include CA and RA public key distribution, certificate enrollment, certificate revocation, certificate query, and CRL query.

One of the key goals of CEP was to use existing technology where possible. It uses both PKCS #7 (Cryptographic Message Syntax Standard) and PKCS #10 (Certification Request Syntax Standard) to define a common message syntax. It supports access to certificates and CRLs using either LDAP or the CEP-defined certificate query.

FIPS

The Federal Information Processing Standards Publications (FIPS PUBS or simply FIPS) describe various standards for data communication issues. These documents are issued by the U.S. government through the National Institute of Standards and Technology (NIST) who is tasked with their development. NIST develops these publications when there is a compelling government need for a standard for use in areas such as security or system interoperability when there is no recognized industry standard. There are three categories of FIPS PUBS currently maintained by NIST. These categories are

- Hardware and Software Standards/Guidelines
- Data standards/guidelines
- Computer security standards/guidelines

It is obviously this last category that we are most interested in. One way that these documents are used is to require products sold to the U.S. government to comply with one (or more) of the FIPS standards. The standards can be obtained from http://www.itl.nist.gov/fipspubs.

Common Criteria (CC)

The Common Criteria (CC) are the result of an effort to develop a joint set of security processes and standards that could be used by the international community. The major contributors to the CC are the governments of the U.S., Canada, France, Germany, the Netherlands, and the United Kingdom. The CC also provides a listing of laboratories that apply the criteria in the testing of security products. Products that are evaluated by one of the approved laboratories receive an Evaluation Assurance Level of EAL1 through EAL7 (EAL7 is the highest level) with EAL4, for example, designed for environments requiring a moderate to high level of independently assured security, and EAL1 being designed for environments in which some confidence in the correct operation of the system is required but where the threats to the system are not seen as serious. The Common Criteria also provide a listing of products by function that have performed at a specific Evaluation Assurance Level.

WTLS

The Wireless Transport Layer Security (WTLS) protocol is based on the Transport Layer Security (TLS) protocol. WTLS provides reliability and security for wireless communications using the **Wireless Application Protocol** (WAP). WTLS is necessary due to the limited memory and processing capabilities of WAP-enabled phones.

WTLS can be implemented in one of three classes. Class 1 is called anonymous authentication but is not designed for practical use. Class 2 is called server authentication and is the most common model. The clients and server may authenticate using different means. Class 3 is server and client authentication. In Class 3 authentication, the client and server's WTLS certificates are authenticated. Class 3 is the strongest form of authentication and encryption.

WEP

The Wired Equivalent Privacy (WEP) algorithm is part of the 802.11 standard and is used to protect wireless communications from interception. A secondary function is to prevent access to a wireless network from unauthorized access. WEP relies on a secret key that is shared between a mobile station and an access point. In most installations, a single key is used by all of the mobile stations and access points.

WEP Security Issues

In modern corporate environments, it is not uncommon to have wireless networks created in which systems with 802.11 network interface cards communicate with wireless access points which connect the computer to the corporation's network. WEP is an optional security protocol specified in the 802.11 standard designed to address the security needs in this wireless environment. It uses a 24-bit initialization vector as a seed value to begin the security association. This, in itself, is a potential security problem as there are only just over sixteen million possible vectors with 24 bits. At the speeds modern networks operate, it does not take long before initialization vectors will repeat. The secret key is only 40 to 64 bits in length, another problem since it does not take too long to brute-force break encryption schemes utilizing key lengths this short. Some vendors are providing 128-bit WEP 2 keys in their products to overcome the short encryption key length. In addition, the WEP keys are static. It is up to the system administrator to manually change WEP keys. One final problem with WEP is that many wireless network implementations do not even come with WEP enabled.

ISO 17799

ISO 17799 is a very popular and detailed standard for creating and implementing security policies. ISO 17799 is based on Version 2 of the British Standard 7799 (BS7799) published in May 1999. With the increased emphasis placed on security in both the government and industry over the last few years, many organizations are now training their audit personnel to evaluate their organization against the ISO 17799 standard. The standard is divided into ten sections, each containing more detailed statements describing what is involved for that topic. The ten major sections, as originally detailed in BS7799, are

- Business continuity planning
- System access control
- System development and maintenance
- Physical and environmental security
- Compliance
- Personnel security
- Security organization
- Computer and network management
- Asset classification and control
- Security policy

Chapter Review

Chapter Summary

After reading this chapter and completing the exercises, you should understand the following about standards and protocols.

Establishing an Interoperable Internet PKI

- Chapter 6 discussed the various components of a public key infrastructure (PKI). This chapter continued the discussion of the many different standards and protocols that have been implemented to support PKI.

Interoperability Is Crucial

- Standards and protocols are important because they define the basis for how communication will take place.

- The use of standards and protocols provides a common, interoperable environment for securely exchanging information.

- Without these standards and protocols, two entities may independently develop their own method to implement the various components for a PKI, and the two will not be compatible.

- On the Internet, not being compatible and not being able to communicate is not an option.

Protocols that Use and Implement the PKI Standards

- Three main standards have evolved over time to implement PKI on the Internet.

- Two of them are based on a third standard, the X.509 standard, and establish complementary standards for implementing PKI. These two standards are Public Key Infrastructure X.509 (PKIX) and Public Key Cryptography Standards (PKCS).

- PKIX defines standards for interactions and operations for four component types: the user (end-entity), certificate authority (CA), registration authority (RA), and the repository for certificates and certificate revocation lists (CRLs).

- PKCS defines many of the lower-level standards for message syntax, cryptographic algorithms, and the like.

- There are other protocols and standards that help define the management and operation of the PKI and related services, such as ISAKMP, XKMS, and CMP.

- WEP is used to encrypt wireless communications in an 802.11 environment and S/MIME for e-mail.

- SSL, TLS, and WTLS are used for secure packet transmission.
- IPSec and PPTP are used to support virtual private networks.
- The Common Criteria establishes a series of criteria from which security products can be evaluated.
- The ISO 17799 standard provides a point from which security policies and practices can be developed in ten areas.
- Various types of publications are available from NIST such as those found in the FIPS series.

Key Terms

Certificate *(153)*
Certificate Authority *(155)*
Certificate Revocation Lists *(155)*
Internet Security Association
and Key Management Protocol (ISAKMP) *(154)*
IPSec *(154)*
Point-to-Point Tunneling Protocol *(154)*
Pretty Good Privacy (PGP) *(154)*
Public key infrastructure *(153)*
Secure/Multipurpose Internet Mail Extensions (S/MIME) *(154)*
Secure Sockets Layer (SSL) *(154)*
Transport Layer Security *(154)*
Wired Equivalent Privacy (WEP) *(154)*
Wireless Application Protocol (WAP) *(173)*
Wireless Transport Layer Security (WTLS) *(154)*
X.509 *(154)*

Key Terms Quiz

Use terms from the Key Terms list to complete the sentences that follow. Don't use the same term more than once. Not all terms will be used.

1. _____ is a protocol used to secure IP packets during transmission across a network. It offers authentication, integrity, and confidentiality services. It uses Authentication Headers (AHs) and Encapsulating Security Payload (ESP) to accomplish this functionality.

2. An encryption capability designed to encrypt above the transport layer, enabling secure sessions between hosts is called the _____.

3. _____ is an entity that is responsible for issuing and revoking certificates. This term is also applied to server software that provides these services.

4. A digitally signed object that lists all of the current but revoked certificates issued by a given certificate authority is called the _____. It allows users to verify whether a certificate is currently valid even if the expiration date hasn't passed.

5. _____ is a format that has been adopted to standardize digital certificates.

6. Infrastructure for binding a public key to a known user through a trusted intermediary, typically a certificate authority, is called the _____.

7. The _____ is a protocol framework that defines the mechanics of implementing a key exchange protocol and negotiation of a security policy.

8. The encryption protocol that is used on Wireless Application Protocol (WAP) networks is called the _____.

9. A protocol for transmitting data to small handheld devices like cellular phones is the _____.

10. _____ is a popular encryption program that has the ability to encrypt and digitally sign e-mail and files.

Multiple-Choice Quiz

1. Which organization created PKCS?

   A. OSI

   B. ISO

   C. RSA

   D. IEEE

2. Which of the following is not part of a public key infrastructure?

   A. A substitution cipher

   B. The certificate revocation list (CRL)

   C. The certificate authority (CA)

   D. Certificates

3. Which of the following is used to grant permissions using rule-based, role-based, and rank-based access controls?

   A. A qualified certificate

   B. A control certificate

   C. An attribute certificate

   D. An optional certificate

4. Which of the following is subject to reuse of its initialization vector?

   A. Certificate Enrollment Protocol (CEP)

   B. Wireless Transport Layer Security (WTLS)

   C. Wireless Access Protocol (WAP)

   D. Wired Equivalency Protocol (WEP)

5. Transport Layer Security consists of which two protocols?

   A. The TLS Record Protocol and TLS Handshake Protocol

   B. The TLS Record Protocol and TLS Certificate Protocol

   C. The TLS Certificate Protocol and TLS Handshake Protocol

   D. The TLS Key Protocol and TLS Handshake Protocol

6. Which of the following provides connection security by using common encryption methods?

   A. The TLS Certificate Protocol

   B. The TLS Handshake Protocol

   C. The TLS Key Protocol

   D. The TLS Record Protocol and TLS Handshake Protocol

7. Which of the following provides a method for implementing a key exchange protocol?

   A. EISA

   B. ISAKMP

   C. ISA

   D. ISAKEY

8. Which of the following is a detailed standard for creating and implementing security policies?

   A. PKIX

   B. ISO 17799

   C. FIPS

   D. X.509

9. A relationship where two or more entities define how they will communicate securely is known as what?

   A. A three-way handshake

   B. A security association

   C. A three-way agreement

   D. A security agreement

10. The entity requesting an SA sets what?

   A. The session number

   B. The session ID

   C. The initiator cookie

   D. The process ID

11. What protocol is used to establish a CA?

    A. The Internet Key Exchange Protocol

    B. The Secure Sockets Layer Protocol

    C. The Public Key Infrastructure Protocol

    D. The Certificate Management Protocol

12. What is the purpose of XKMS?

    A. Extends session associations over many transport protocols

    B. Encapsulates session associations over TCP/IP

    C. Defines services to manage heterogeneous PKI operations via XML

    D. Designed to replace SSL

13. Which of the following is a secure e-mail standard?

    A. POP3

    B. IMAP

    C. SMTP

    D. S/MIME

14. Which of the following is a joint set of security processes and standards used by approved laboratories to award an Evaluation Assurance Level (EAL) from EAL1 to EAL7?

    A. Common Criteria

    B. FIPS

    C. ISO 17700

    D. IEEE X.509

15. Secure Sockets Layer uses what port to communicate?

    A. 53

    B. 80

    C. 143

    D. 443

Essay Quiz

1. You are the Information Security Officer at a medium-sized company (1,500 employees). The CIO has asked you to explain why you recommend using commercial PKI rather than implementing such a capability in-house with the software developers you already have. Write three succinct sentences that would get your point across and address three key issues.

2. You're still the Information Security Officer and you're still in the office with the CIO. Even though the Wired Equivalency Protocol (WEP) has some known shortcomings/vulnerabilities, explain to your CIO what you can do with WEP to make your wireless network more secure.

3. Imagine you are a web developer for a small locally owned business. Explain when using HTTP would be satisfactory and why, and when you should use HTTPS and why.

4. Explain in your own words how, by applying both asymmetric and symmetric encryption, your browser uses SSL to protect the privacy of the information passing between your browser and a web server.

5. It is well understood that asymmetric encryption consumes more computing resources than symmetric encryption. Explain how PGP uses both asymmetric and symmetric encryption to be both secure and efficient.

Lab Projects

Note that for these lab projects, it would be best to have a partner so that you can each have your own pair of public/private keys to confirm the operation of PGP.

Lab Project 7.1

Visit www.pgp.com/products/freeware.html and download PGP Freeware. Install it and create yourself a public/private key pair. Create a document using a word processor and encrypt it using the receiver's public key. Send it to a partner (or yourself) and then decrypt it using the corresponding private key.

Lab Project 7.2

Create another document different from the one used in Lab Project 7.1. This time use your private key to digitally sign the document and send it to a partner (or yourself) who can then use the public key to confirm that it really is from the indicated sender.

The Impact of Physical Security on Network Security

Upon completion of this chapter, you will be able to:
- Describe how physical security directly affects computer and network security
- Discuss how steps can be taken to help mitigate risks

Physical security is an important topic for everyone. Almost everyone in this country locks the doors to their home when they leave. This is the primary function of physical security for their homes. Other people choose to set up some kind of burglar alarm system in addition to their locked doors. This could be for several reasons, but probably the commonest is that they feel they have something significant to protect. Businesses have the responsibility of attempting to secure their profitability, which is made up of a number of things. They need to secure their employees, product inventory, trade secrets, and strategy information. All of these assets affect the profitability of a company and its future survival. Therefore, companies perform many activities to attempt to provide security. More recently, companies have also put a large amount of effort into network security. In this chapter, we will learn about how these two efforts are linked, as well as learn several methods by which companies can minimize their exposure to physical security events that can diminish their network security.

The Problem

The problem that faces professionals charged with securing a company's network can be stated rather simply. Physical access negates all other security measures. No matter how impenetrable the firewall and Intrusion Detection System, if an attacker can find a way to walk up and touch the server, then he can probably break into it. The more remarkable thing is that physical access to a number of machines is not that difficult. Consider that most security measures are, from necessity, directed at protecting a company from the Internet. This fact results in a lot of companies allowing any kind of traffic on the local area network. So an attacker attempting to gain access to a server, who can't manage to get into it over the Internet, may be able to gain access to the receptionist's machine, and by quickly compromising it, can use it as a remotely controlled zombie to attack what he is really after.

Physical access allows an attacker to do a number of interesting things, the most basic of which is probably to simply plug into an open Ethernet jack. The advent of handheld devices with the capability to run operating systems with full networking support has made this attack even more feasible. Originally, the attacker would have to be in a secluded area with dedicated access to the Ethernet for a time. This would allow an attacker to sit with a laptop and run a variety of tools against the network. Being internally based typically puts them behind the firewall and intrusion detection system. However, PDAs can assist this by having a small device that could be placed onto the network and act as a wireless bridge. This allows an attacker to use a laptop to remotely attack a network from outside the building. If power is available near the Ethernet jack, this attack can also be done with an off-the-shelf access point. The only difficulty is finding an Ethernet jack that isn't covered by furniture or some other obstruction.

Another simple attack that can be used when an attacker has physical access is called a **bootdisk**. Before there were bootable CD-ROMs in computers, a boot floppy had to be used to start the system and prepare the hard drives to load the operating system. Since most machines still have floppy drives, boot floppies can still be used. These floppies can contain a number of different programs, but the most typical ones would be NTFSdos or a floppy-based Linux distribution. This enables the floppies to perform a number of tasks including the mounting of the hard drives and performing at least read operations. Once an attacker is able to read the drive, the password file can be copied off the machine for offline password cracking attacks. If write access to the drive is obtained, the attacker could alter the password file, or place a remote control program to be automatically executed upon the next boot, guaranteeing continued access to the machine. Bootable CD-ROMs are a danger for the same reason, perhaps even more so, since they can contain a bootable version of an entire operating system complete with drivers for most devices. This gives an attacker a greater array of tools than could be loaded onto a floppy disk. An example is that an attacker would most likely not have access just to the disk, but an operational network interface, allowing them to send the drive data over the Internet if properly connected. These bootable operating systems could also be custom built to contain any tool that runs under Linux, allowing an attacker to have a standard bootable attack image. The use of bootdisks also leads us into the next area of concern, making an image of the hard drive for later investigation. This is because some form of bootable media is often used to load the imaging software.

Drive imaging is the process of taking the entire contents of a hard drive and copying them to a single file on a different media. This process is often used by people who perform forensic investigations of computers. Typically, a bootable media is used to start the computer and load the drive imaging software. This software is designed to make a bit-by-bit copy of the hard drive to a file on another media, usually another hard drive or a CD-R/DVD-R burnable media. This is done in investigations to make an exact copy that can be observed and played with, while keeping the original exactly as it was for evidence purposes. From an attacker's perspective, this kind of software is useful because it pulls ALL information from a computer while still leaving the machine in its original state. The information contains everything that was on this computer, any locally stored documents, locally stored e-mails, and every other piece of information that the machine contained. This potentially could be very valuable if the machine held sensitive information about the company. Physical access is the commonest way of imaging a drive, and the biggest benefit for the attacker is that it leaves absolutely no trace of the crime.

An even simpler version of the drive imaging attack is to steal the computer outright. Most times, stealing a computer is typically done for monetary gain, the thief later selling his prize. What we're concerned with here is the theft of a computer in order to obtain the data it holds. While physical thievery is not a very technical attack, it is often carried in conjunction with a bit of social engineering—for example, appearing to be a legitimate computer repair person may allow an attacker to walk out of the building with anything they want. For anyone who discounts this type of attack, take the following incident. In Australia, two individuals entered a government computer room and managed to walk off with two large servers. They not only escaped with two valuable computers but also the data they contained.

Many of the things mentioned so far, like computer theft, can be used to perform a Denial-of-Service (DoS) attack. Physical access to the computers can be much more effective than a network-based DoS. The theft of a computer, using a bootdisk to simply erase all data on the drives, or simply unplugging computers are all effective for Denial-of-Service attacks. Depending on the company's quality and frequency of backing up critical systems, the DoS might have lasting effects.

As mentioned before, physical access can negate almost all the security that the network attempts to provide. Considering this, it is important to determine the level of physical access that attackers might obtain. Of special consideration in this are persons with authorized access but who are not authorized users of the systems. Cleaning personnel and others have authorized access to many areas, but do not have authorized system access. An attacker could pose as one of these individuals, or attempt to gain access to the facilities through them.

Physical Security Safeguards

While it is difficult, if not impossible, to be totally secure, there are many steps that can be taken to mitigate the risk to information systems from a physical threat. Thus, we'll next discuss policies and procedures, as well as access control methods. Following this, we will explore various authentication methods and how they help protect against physical threats.

Policies and Procedures

Policies vary in their effectiveness depending on the culture of an organization, so all of the items mentioned here should be followed up by functional procedures that are designed to implement them. **Policies and procedures** in this area relate to two distinct areas: those that affect the computers themselves, and those that affect users.

To mitigate the risk to computers, physical security needs to be extended to the computers themselves. To combat the threat of bootdisks, the simplest answer is to remove or disable floppy drives from all desktops that do not require them. The advance of hard drive capacity has pushed the average file size beyond what floppies can typically hold. Local area networks with constant Internet connectivity has made network services more the focus of how files are moved and distributed. These two factors have reduced floppy usage to the point where many manufacturers are making floppy drives a paid option. It should also make the transition to an office without floppy drives fairly painless.

The second boot device to consider is the CD-ROM/DVD-ROM. This is another device that, more than likely, can be removed or disabled from a number of machines. The CD-ROM not only can be used as a boot device, but can also be exploited via the **auto-run** feature that some operating systems support. If auto-run is programmed maliciously, it could run an executable that installs malicious code to allow an attacker to later gain control of the machine remotely. Disabling auto-run is an easy task to accomplish and should be done to improve security. Some users will undoubtedly insist on having one in their machines, but if possible they should be removed from every machine. If removal is not feasible, particularly on machines that require CD-ROM use, **BIOS passwords** should be set. Setting a password on the BIOS should delay or prevent an attacker from resetting the boot sequence to boot from a device other than the hard drive. These passwords should be unique to the machine, and if possible, complex, using multiple upper- and lowercase characters as well as numerics. Considering how often they will be used, it is probably best to list them all in an encrypted file so that a master passphrase will give access to them.

As mentioned before, floppy drives are being eliminated from manufacturers' machines because of their limited usefulness, but new devices are being adopted in their place, such as **USB devices**. USB ports have greatly expanded the ability of users to connect devices and have them autorecognize and work, usually without needing additional drivers or software. This has spawned a legion of devices, from MP3 players to CD-burners. The most interesting of these, for security purposes, is the USB hard drives and USB drive keys. USB drive keys, which are basically flash memory with a USB interface in a device about the size of your thumb, provide a way to easily move files from computer to computer. When plugged into a USB interface, these devices automount and behave like another drive attached to the computer. For security purposes, their small size and relatively large capacity, coupled with instant read-write capability, presents problems. They allow an individual with malicious intent to easily conceal the removal of files or data from the building. It also presents a number of problems because of the possibility of bringing files into the office. An attacker could use them to bring malicious code in an attempt to load it onto a machine, though the attacker would need at least user access to run or copy the files over. Even well-intentioned users could accidentally introduce malicious code to these devices by using them on an infected home machine and then bringing them to the office. If these USB devices are allowed, aggressive virus scanning should be implemented. The devices can be disallowed, though, either by disabling the USB devices if running Operating systems, such as Windows 2000 or XP, or by unloading and disabling the entire USB driver if running an OS that does not support disabling of the device. Either option prevents all USB devices from working. This is probably the most effective solution for users that would not be authorized for these devices; however, users that must have authorization for them need to be educated about the dangers of their use.

As mentioned earlier, the final type of physical attack is outright theft of the machine. This attack can be mitigated in a number of ways, but the most effective method is to lock up those machines that contain important data. Insurance can cover the loss of the physical equipment, but can do little to get the business up and running again quickly.

Therefore, special access controls for server rooms, as well as simply locking the racks up when maintenance is not being performed, are good ways to secure an area. From a data standpoint, try and keep mission-critical or high-value information from being stored anywhere other than on a server. This can mitigate the risk of a desktop or laptop being stolen for the data it contains. All of these things can improve the physical security of the computers themselves, but most of these measures can be defeated if the users are not involved in the security program.

Users are sometimes mentioned as the weakest link in the security chain, and that can also apply to physical security. Fortunately, in physical security, users are often one of the beneficiaries of the security itself. Part of what a security department protects is its information assets, but it also protects the people of the organization. The main principle here is that users need to be aware of security issues and they also need to be involved in security enforcement. A company culture of security will go a long way to assist this. If users in the office see a strange person, they should challenge their presence—this is especially true if visitor badges are required. A policy of having a visible badge with the employee's photo on it also assists everyone in recognizing persons that may not belong.

Users should also be briefed on the proper departments or personnel to contact when they suspect a security violation. Users are also the only ones who can perform one of the most simple, yet important security tasks, locking a workstation immediately when they step away from it. While a locking screensaver is a good policy, most people cannot be productive with it set to less than 15 minutes. An attacker only needs to be lucky enough to catch a machine that has been left alone for five minutes.

While security guards are not users, they need to be educated about proper network security as well as physical security involving users. They are a company's eyes and ears for suspicious activity, so the network security department needs to train them to see suspicious network activity as well. Multiple extensions ringing in sequence during the night, computers rebooting all at once, or strange people parked in the parking lot with laptop computers are all indicators of a network attack that might be missed. It is also important to know about the people in the organization. New hires should have a background check performed before being given access to network resources. This policy should also apply to all personnel that will have unescorted physical access to your facility. People that are responsible for cleaning your work environment are still in that environment, and you should make certain they are who they claim to be.

All of these items make good policies, though some may or may not work in a particular organization. However, the physical security of computers as well as the procedures that affect the users of those computers are two areas where good data security needs to be maintained.

Access Controls

Access controls means exactly what it sounds like, physical barriers. The design and construction of all sizes and types have been covered much more appropriately in other texts. However, we will explore a few important points to help safeguard the information infrastructure, especially where it meets with the physical access control system, and talk about layered access systems, as well as electronic door control systems. We will also discuss Closed Circuit Television Systems (CCTV), and the implications of the different CCTV system types.

Layered access is an important topic in security. It is often mentioned when people talk about network security perimeters, but today we are going to relate it to the concept of physical security perimeters. To help prevent an attacker from gaining access to important assets, several perimeters should be put around those assets. Servers should be placed in a separate secure area, ideally with a separate authentication mechanism. For example, if an organization has an electronic door control system using **contactless access cards**, a combination of that card as well as a separate PIN code would be needed to open the door to the server room. Access to the server room should be limited to staff with a legitimate need to work on the servers. To layer the protection, the area surrounding the server room should also be limited to just the people that work in that area.

Many organizations use electronic access control systems to control the opening of doors. Having a centralized system that can instantly grant or refuse access based upon a token that is given to the user is a good idea. This kind of system also logs user access providing non-repudiation of a specific user's presence. The one caution that must be given about these kinds of systems is that they usually work with a software package that runs on a computer, and as such this computer should not be attached to the company network. While attaching it to the network can allow easy administration, the last thing you want an attacker to have control of is the system that allows physical access to your facility. With this control, an attacker could input the ID of a badge that they own, allowing full legitimate access to an area the system controls.

Closed circuit television systems are similar to the door control systems—they can be very effective, but care should be given to how they are implemented. Many IP-based CCTV systems are coming onto the market. These add useful functionality, such as being able to check on the building from the Internet. This makes the cameras subject to any normal IP-based network attack as well. The last thing that anyone would want would be a Denial-of-Service attack launched at the CCTV system just as a break-in was planned. If CCTV cameras are going to be IP-based, they should be placed on their own, physically separate, network that can only be accessed by security personnel. The same goes for any IP-based camera infrastructure. Time-lapse tape recorders are slowly being replaced with digital video recorders. While the advance in technology is significant, be careful if and when these devices become IP enabled since they, too, will become a security issue, just like everything else that touches the network.

We have talked here about some of the access control methods, and some of the issues that they can present. These issues are especially prevalent when physical access control devices are connected to network resources. No access controls, network or physical, would work without some form of authentication.

Authentication

Authentication is the process by which a user proves that they are who they say they are. Authentication is performed to allow or deny access to a physical space. The heart of any access control system is to allow access to the authorized and make sure access is denied to the unauthorized. Authentication is required because many companies have gotten so large that not every employee knows every other employee. Electronic access control systems spawned from the need to have more logging and control than the older method of metallic keys. Most of these electronic systems currently use a token-based card that if passed near a reader, and if you have permission from the computer, will unlock the door strike and let you into the area. Newer technology is attempting to make the authentication process easier and more secure. In this section, we will discuss how tokens, and even biometrics, are being used for authentication. We will also look into how multiple-factor authentication can be used for physical access.

Access tokens are the traditional form of physical access authentication. Your house key, in essence, is a physical access token to allow you into your home. Keys have worked as token authentication for over a hundred years, but they have several limitations. Keys are paired exclusively with a lock or a set of locks, and they are not easily changed. It is easy to add an authorized user by giving them a copy of the key, but it is much harder to give that user selective access unless that specified area is already set up as a separate key. It is also very difficult to take access away from a single key or key holder, usually requiring a rekey of the whole system.

In many cases, physical access authentication has moved to contactless radio frequency cards and readers. When passed near a card reader, the card sends out a code via radio. The reader picks up this code and transmits it to the control panel. The control panel checks the code against the reader it is being read from and the type of access the card has in its database. The advantages of this kind of token-based system include the fact that any card can be deleted from the system without affecting any other card or the rest of the system. Also, all doors connected to the system can be segmented in any form or fashion to create multiple access areas, with different permissions for each one. The tokens themselves can also be grouped in multiple ways to provide different access levels to the different groups of people.

Newer technologies are adding capabilities to the standard token-based systems. The advent of **smart cards** (cards that contain integrated circuits) has enabled cryptographic types of authentication. The primary drawback of this kind of token-based authentication is that the token is what is actually being authenticated. Therefore, the theft of the token could allow anyone who possessed the token access to what the system protects. The risk of the theft of the token can be offset through the use of multiple-factor authentication. One of the other ways that people have tried to avoid this risk is to change to a biometric-based authentication system.

Biometrics use the measurement of certain biological factors to identify one specific person from others. These factors are based upon parts of the human body that are unique. The most well-known of these unique biological factors is the fingerprint. However, there are many others—for instance, the retina of the eye, the iris of the eye, the geometry of the hand, and the geometry of the face. When these things are used for authentication, a computer takes the image of the factor and reduces it to a numeric value. Then, when the user comes to an area, they get re-scanned by the reader, and the computer compares the numeric value being read to the one stored in the database. Since these factors are unique, then theoretically only the actual authorized persons can open the door.

In the real world, however, the theory behind biometrics breaks down. Tokens that have a digital code work very well because everything remains in the digital realm. A computer checks your code, like 123, against the database; if the computer finds 123 and it has access, the computer opens the door. Biometrics, however, take an analog signal, like a fingerprint or a face, and attempt to digitize it, and then match it against the digits that are in the database. The problem with an analog is that it may not encode the exact same way twice. For example, what if you came to work with a bandage on your chin—would the face-based biometrics grant you access or deny it?

The engineers that have designed these systems understood that, if a system was set to exact checking, an encoded biometric might never grant access since it might never scan the exact same biometric twice. Since they understood this problem, most systems have tried to allow a certain amount of error in the scan while not allowing too much. This leads us to the concept of false positives and false negatives. A **false positive** is when a biometric is scanned and allows access to someone who is not authorized. An example of this would be two people who have very similar fingerprints—and the computer thinks they are the same person. A **false negative** is when the system denies access to someone who is authorized. An example would be the guy at the hand geometry scanner who forgot to wear a ring he usually wears. For biometric authentication to work properly, and also be trusted, it must minimize the existence of both false positives and false negatives. To do that, a balance between exacting and error must be created so that the machines will allow a little physical variance—but not too much.

The other concern with biometrics is that if someone is able to steal the uniqueness factor that the machine scans—your fingerprint from a glass, for example—and is able to reproduce that factor in a substance that fools the scanner, that person now has your access. This idea is compounded by the fact that it is impossible for you to change your fingerprint if it gets stolen. It is easy to replace a lost or stolen token, and delete the missing one from the system, but it is much more difficult to replace a human hand. Another problem with biometrics is that parts of the human body can change. A human face can change, through scarring, weight loss, or surgery. A fingerprint can be changed through damage to the fingers. Eye retinas can be affected by some types of diabetes or pregnancy. All of these changes force the biometric system to allow a higher tolerance for variance in the biometric being read. This has lead the way for high-security installations to move towards our next topic, multifactor authentication.

Multiple-factor authentication is simply the combination of two or more types of authentication. There are three broad categories of authentication: what you are (for example, biometrics), what you have (for instance, tokens), and what you know (passwords and other information). Two-factor authentication combines any two of these before granting access. An example would be a card reader that then turns on a fingerprint scanner—if your fingerprint matches the one on file for the card, you are granted access. Three-factor authentication would combine all three types, such as a smart card reader that asks for a PIN number before enabling a retina scanner. If all three correspond to a valid user and each other in the computer database, then access is granted.

Multiple-factor authentication methods greatly enhance security by making it very difficult for an attacker to obtain all the correct materials for authentication. They also protect against the risk of stolen tokens, as the attacker also needs to have the correct biometric, password, or both. More importantly, it enhances the security of biometric systems. Multifactor authentication does this by protecting against a stolen biometric. Changing the token makes the biometric useless unless the attacker can steal the new token. It also reduces false positives by trying to match the supplied biometric with only the one that is associated with the supplied token. This prevents the computer from seeking a match using the entire database of biometrics. Using multiple factors is one of the best ways to ensure proper authentication and access control.

Chapter Review

Chapter Summary

After reading this chapter and completing the exercises, you should understand the following facts about how physical security impacts network security.

How Physical Security Directly Affects Computer and Network Security

- Physical access defeats all network security protections.
- Bootdisks allow file system access.
- Drive imaging is simple to accomplish with access.
- Access to the internal network is simple with physical access.
- Theft of hardware can be an attack in and of itself.

Steps that Can Be Taken to Help Mitigate Risks

- Removal of floppy drives when they are unnecessary can help mitigate bootdisk attacks.
- Removal of CD-ROM devices also makes physical access attacks more difficult.
- BIOS passwords should be used to protect the boot sequence.
- USB devices are a threat and, if possible, USB drivers should be removed.
- All users need security training.
- Background checks of new hires help ensure security.
- Access controls should have layered areas and electronic access control systems.
- Electronic physical security systems need to be protected from network-based attacks.
- Authentication systems should use multiple factors when feasible.

Key Terms

Access control *(185)*
Access tokens *(187)*
Auto-run *(184)*
Biometrics *(187)*
BIOS passwords *(184)*
Bootdisk *(182)*
Closed circuit television systems (CCTV) *(186)*
Contactless access card *(186)*
Drive imaging *(182)*

False negatives *(188)*
False positives *(188)*
Layered access *(186)*
Multiple-factor authentication *(188)*
Policies and procedures *(183)*
Smart card *(187)*
USB devices *(184)*

Key Terms Quiz

Use terms from the Key Terms list to complete the sentences that follow. Don't use the same term more than once. Not all terms will be used.

1. When users are forced to provide ID at the entrance doors, and then another type of ID at the doors to their office, they are passing through _____.

2. _____ is the function that executes a program when a CD-ROM is inserted into a computer

3. _____ happens when an authorized user is refused access.

4. Removable media from which a computer can be booted is called a _____.

5. _____ is how a complete, bit-by-bit copy of a hard drive is made, typically onto another hard drive.

6. Items carried by the user to allow them to be authenticated are called _____.

7. _____ is the measurement of unique biological properties, like the fingerprint.

8. _____ is a card with an integrated circuit allowing information storage.

9. _____ are systems where the camera and monitor are directly linked.

10. Written guidelines for employees are called _____.

Multiple-Choice Quiz

1. Which of the following is a biometric used for authentication?

   A. Waistline

   B. Hair color

   C. Eye retina

   D. Fingernail dimensions

2. Why is a floppy drive a threat to security?

   A. It allows a bootdisk to be used.

    B. It provides the ability to remove the operating system.

    C. It transmits the location of the computer back to the administrators.

    D. It forces the user to use floppies to store data.

3. How does multiple-factor authentication improve security?

    A. It denies access to the attacker multiple times.

    B. By using a combination of authentications, it is more difficult to gain access by pretending to be an authorized user.

    C. By using biometrics, no other person can authenticate.

    D. It restricts users to smaller spaces.

4. Why is access to an Ethernet jack a risk?

    A. Wireless traffic can find its way onto the local area network.

    B. An attacker can use it to create a door card entry for himself.

    C. It allows access to the internal network.

    D. A special plug can be used to short out the entire Ethernet system.

5. When a biometric device has a false positive, it has…

    A. Generated a positive charge to the system that needs to be compensated for.

    B. Allowed access to a person that is not authorized.

    C. Denied access to a person that is authorized

    D. Failed, forcing the door it controls to be propped open.

6. The traditional type of access token was a…

    A. Smart card

    B. Handwriting sample

    C. PDA

    D. Key

7. The feature that could allow a CD to load malicious code is called…

    A. An MBR or master boot record

    B. Auto-run

    C. A CD-key

    D. A false negative

8. An IP-based CCTV system needs to be implemented carefully because…

    A. The network cables are more easily cut.

    B. They don't record images, they just supply them to web pages.

    C. They could be remotely attacked via the network.

    D. Camera resolutions are lower.

9. What is the commonest threat to token-based access controls?

    A. Loss or theft of the token

    B. Demagnetization of the strip

    C. A system crash

    D. Forgetting the password

10. Whom should a company perform background checks on?

    A. System administrators only

    B. Contract personnel only

    C. All individuals who have unescorted physical access

    D. Background checks are not needed outside of the military

11. A perfect bit-by-bit copy of a drive is called a...

    A. Drive-copy

    B. Drive-picture

    C. Drive-partition

    D. Drive-image

12. Which one is not a unique biometric?

    A. Eye retina

    B. Hand geometry

    C. Shoulder-to-waist geometry

    D. Fingerprint

13. Why should security guards get cross-training in network security?

    A. They are the only people in the building at night.

    B. They are the eyes and ears of the corporation when it comes to security.

    C. They have the authority to detain violators.

    D. They are more qualified to know what a security threat is.

14. Probably the simplest physical attack is...

    A. Accessing an Ethernet jack to attack the network.

    B. Using an imitation to fool a biometric authenticator.

    C. Installing a virus on the CCTV system.

    D. Outright theft of the computers.

15. Why is physical security so important to maintain good network security?

    A. Because physical access defeats almost all network security measures

    B. Because the majority of attacks are performed by company insiders

C. Because the attacker can now steal all the biometric identities

D. Because encryption is not involved

Essay Quiz

1. Explain why physical security is important.

2. Your corporation has traditionally had a physical security department manned with security guards, but a network security department has grown out of the IT department in recent years. These groups have very little coordination and communication. Explain to management why this should change and how you would accomplish the change.

3. Explain why biometrics is proving to be a popular replacement for token-based authentication.

4. Management has decided to rewrite the policies and procedures for physical security. Considering physical security's impact on network security, write a memo to management giving several recommendations that would get users more involved with security.

5. The CEO of your company read an article about the new biometric technologies that are being sold for physical access authentication. Since the company has had problems with lost access cards in the past, he wants you to give recommendations for a new access control system that uses biometrics. Write a few paragraphs describing how biometrics could be best used for your company.

Lab Projects

Lab Project 8.1

Create a bootdisk for Windows 2000 computers, allowing you to view and copy files. You will need the following materials:

- A computer with a version of Windows 2000 installed

- An empty formatted floppy disk

Then do the following:

1. Download a bootdisk image. A good site for this is www.bootdisk.com/.

2. Place the floppy disk in the drive.

3. Run the executable. This will load the boot image onto the floppy disk.

4. Download the free copy of NTFSdos from Sysinternals at www.sysinternals.com/ntw2k/freeware/NTFSDOS.shtml.

5. Install the program onto your bootdisk.

6. Reboot the machine, allowing the bootdisk to start the machine in DOS.

7. Run NTFSdos.

8. Verify full read access to the NTFS drive volumes, and then copy a file to the boot floppy.

9. Place the floppy in another machine, or boot this machine back into windows 2000, and then verify the existence of the copied file.

Lab Project 8.2

Research several different biometric systems and then write a recommendation to management as to which product to implement, how to implement it, and why.

You will need the following materials:

• A computer with an Internet connection

Then do the following:

1. Find information on at least five current biometric factors that are being used for authentication.

2. Determine each factor's strengths and weaknesses as they relate to false positives, false negatives, and each factor's susceptibility to being forged.

3. Choose a biometric factor that you deem best.

4. Determine the best way to implement that biometric to control access.

5. Write a convincing recommendation that includes policies and procedures for the type of access the biometric is going to grant, as well as the theoretical employee groups it would allow access to.

Network Fundamentals

Upon completion of this chapter, you will be able to:

- Learn the basic network architectures
- Discover basic network protocols
- Examine routing and address translation

The term "**network**" has different meanings depending on the context and usage. A network can be a group of friends and associates, a series of interconnected tunnels, or, from a computer-oriented perspective, a collection of interconnected devices. For the purposes of this discussion, we'll focus on the more widely accepted definition of a network to mean any series of interconnected information systems and devices. Networks are all around us, and they enable the computers we use to interact—exchanging information on everything from credit-card transactions to the latest news and weather. Essentially, the Internet itself is one giant network consisting of interconnected PCs, servers, routers, and switches.

By the simplest definition in the data world, a network is a means to connect two or more computers together for the purposes of sharing information. Network sizes and shapes vary drastically—from two personal computers connected with a crossover cable or wireless router to the Internet, encircling the globe and linking together untold numbers of individual, distributed systems. Though data networks vary widely in size and scope, they are generally defined in terms of their architecture, topology, and protocol.

Network Architectures

Every network has an architecture—whether by design or accident. Defining or describing a specific network's architecture involves the network's physical configuration, logical operation, structure, procedures, data formats, protocols, and other components. For the sake of simplicity and categorization, people tend to divide network architectures into two main categories: LANs and WANs. **LANs**, or local area networks, are typically smaller in terms of size and geographic coverage and consist of two or more connected devices. Home networks and most small office networks can be classified as LANs. **WANs**, or wide area networks, tend to be larger, covering more geographic area and consist of two or more systems in geographically separated areas connected by any of a variety of methods such as leased lines, radio waves, satellite relays, microwaves, or even dial-up connections. With the advent of wireless networking, optical, and cellular technology, the lines between LAN and WAN sometimes blur, merging seamlessly into a single network entity. For example, most corporations have multiple LANs within each office location which all connect to a WAN that provides intercompany connectivity. Figure 9-1 shows an example of a corporate network. Each office location will typically have one or more LANs, which are connected to the other offices and the company headquarters through a corporate WAN.

As networks grew, diversified, and multiplied, the line between LAN and WAN started to blur. To better describe emerging, specialized network structures, new terms were added to better classify networks based on size and use:

- **CAN** Campus Area Network (also referred to as a Campus Wide Area Network)—a network connecting any number of buildings in an office or university complex.

- **Intranet** A "private" network only accessible to authorized users. Many large corporations host an intranet to facilitate information sharing within their organization.

- **Internet** "The global network" connecting hundreds of millions of systems and users.

- **MAN** Metropolitan Area Network—a network designed for a specific geographic locality such as a town or a city.

- **SAN** Storage Area Network, a high speed network connecting a variety of storage devices such as tape systems, RAID arrays, optical drives, file servers, and others.

- **VLAN** Virtual local area network—a logical network allowing systems on different physical networks to interact as if they were connected to the same physical network.

- **Client-Server** A network where powerful, dedicated systems called *servers* provide resources to individual workstations or *clients*.

- **Peer-to-Peer** A network where every system is treated as an equal, such as a home network.

Figure 9-1
Example of
a corporate
network with
interconnected
LANs and WANs

Figure 9-2
Star topology

Network Topology

One major component of every network's architecture is the network's **topology**—how the network is physically or logically arranged. Again, terms to classify a network's topology were developed, often reflecting the physical layout of the network. The main classes of network topologies are star, ring, bus, and mixed.

- **Star**   Network components are connected to a central point. (See Figure 9-2.)
- **Bus**   Network components are connected to the same cable, often called "the bus" or "the backbone." (See Figure 9-3.)
- **Ring**   Network components are connected to each other in a closed loop with each device directly connected to two other devices. (See Figure 9-4.)

Larger networks, such as those inside an office complex may use more than one topology at the same time. For example, an office complex may have a large ring topology that interconnects all the buildings in the complex. Each building may have a large bus topology to interconnect star topologies located on each floor of the building. This is called a mixed topology. (See Figure 9-5.)

Figure 9-3
Bus topology

Figure 9-4
Ring topology

With recent advances in technology, these topology definitions often break down. While a network consisting of five computers connected to the same coaxial cable is easily classified as a bus topology, what about those same computers connected to a hub or switch using cat-5 cables? With a hub, each computer is connected to a central node, much like a star topology, but the hub is a shared medium, much like a bus topology. With a switch, each computer has its own exclusive connection to the switch like a star topology, but has to share the switch's communications backbone with all the other computers, much like a bus topology. To avoid this type of confusion, many people use topology definitions to only apply to the physical layout of the network, focusing on how the devices are connected to the network. If we apply this line of thinking to our example, the five-computer network becomes a star topology whether we use a hub or a switch.

Figure 9-5   Mixed topology

Network Protocols

How do all these interconnected devices communicate? What makes a PC in China able to view web pages on a server in Brazil? When engineers first started to connect computers together via networks, they quickly realized they needed a commonly accepted method for communicating—a protocol. A **protocol** is an agreed upon format for exchanging or transmitting data between systems. A protocol defines a number of agreed upon parameters, such as the data compression method, the type of error checking to use, and mechanisms for systems to signal when they have finished either receiving or transmitting data. There are a wide variety of protocols, each designed with certain benefits and uses in mind. Some of the more common protocols are

- **AppleTalk**   The communications protocol developed by Apple to connect Macintosh computers and printers.

- **Asynchronous Transfer Mode (ATM)**   A protocol based on transferring data in fixed size packets. The fixed packet sizes help ensure that no single data type monopolizes the available bandwidth.

- **DECnet**   Protocol developed by Digital Equipment Corporation that's used to connect PDP and VAX systems.

- **Ethernet**   The LAN protocol developed jointly by Xerox, DEC, and Intel—the most widely implemented LAN standard.

- **Fiber Distributed Data Interface (FDDI)**   The protocol for sending digital data over fiber-optic cabling.

- **Internet Protocols (IP)**   The protocols for managing and transmitting data between packet-switched computer networks originally developed for the Department of Defense. Most users are familiar with Internet Protocols such as e-mail, File Transfer Protocol (FTP), Telnet, and HyperText Transfer Protocol (HTTP).

- **Internetwork Packet Exchange (IPX)**   The networking protocol used by Novell NetWare operating systems.

- **Netware**   The LAN protocol developed by Novell Corporation.

- **Signaling System 7 (SS7)**   The telecommunications protocol used between PBXes to handle tasks such as call setup, routing, and teardown.

- **Systems Network Architecture (SNA)**   A set of network protocols developed by IBM, originally used to connect IBM's mainframe systems.

- **Token Ring**   A LAN protocol developed by IBM where systems must possess the network "token" before transmitting data.

- **Transmission Control Protocol/Internet Protocol (TCP/IP)**   The collection of communications protocols used to connect hosts on the Internet. TCP/IP is by far the most commonly used network protocol and is a combination of the TCP and IP protocol.

- **X.25** A protocol developed by the Comité Consultatif International Téléphonique et Télégraphique (CCITT) for use in packet-switched networks. The CCITT was a subgroup within the ITU before the CCITT was disbanded in 1992.

In most cases, communications protocols were developed around the Open System Interconnection (OSI) model. The OSI model, or OSI Reference Model, is an ISO standard for worldwide communications—defining a framework for implementing protocols in seven distinct layers. Within the OSI model, control is passed from one layer to another (top-down) before it exits one system and enters another system where control is passed bottom-up to complete the communications cycle. It is important to note that most protocols only loosely follow the OSI model; several protocols combine one or more layers into a single function. The OSI model also provides a certain level of abstraction and isolation for each layer, which only need to know how to interact with the layer above and below it. The Application layer, for example, only needs to know how to communicate with the Presentation layer—it does not need to talk directly to the physical layer. Figure 9-6 shows the different layers of the OSI model.

Packets

Networks are built to share information and resources, but like everything else, networks and the protocols they use have limits and rules that must be followed for effective communication. For example, large chunks of data must typically be broken up into smaller, more manageable chunks before they are transmitted from one computer to

Figure 9-6
The OSI model

7	Application Layer	Program level communication.
6	Presentation Layer	Performs data conversion functions when needed.
5	Session Layer	Establishes and maintains communications channels.
4	Transport Layer	Handles end-to-end transmission and integrity of transmission and integrity of transmitted data.
3	Network Layer	Routes data from one system to another.
2	Data Link Layer	Handles the physical passing of data from one system to another.
1	Physical Layer	Manages the transmission and reception of data on the network media.

another. Breaking the data up has advantages—you can more effectively share bandwidth with other systems and you don't have to retransmit the entire dataset if there is a problem in transmission. When data is broken up into smaller pieces for transmission, the smaller pieces are typically called **packets**. Each protocol has its own definition of a packet—dictating how much data can be carried, what information is stored where, how the packet should be interpreted by another system, and so on. A standard packet structure is a crucial element in a protocol definition. Without a standard packet structure, systems would not be able to interpret the information coming to them from other systems. To better understand packet structure, let's examine the packet structure defined by the **IP protocol**. IP packets, often called **datagrams**, have two main sections: the header and the data section (sometimes called the payload). The header section contains all of the information needed to describe the packet:

- What kind of packet it is (protocol version number)
- How large the header of the packet is (packet header length)
- How to process this packet (type of service telling the network whether or not to use options such as minimize delay, maximize throughput, maximize reliability, and minimize cost)
- How large the entire packet is (overall length of packet—since this is a 16-bit field, the maximum size of an IP packet is 65,535 bytes, but in practice most packets are around 1500 bytes)
- A unique identifier so this packet can be distinguished from other packets
- Whether or not this packet is part of a longer data stream and should be handled relative to other packets
- A description of where this packet fits into the data stream as compared to other packets (the fragment offset)
- A checksum of the packet header (to minimize the potential for data corruption during transmission)
- Where the packet is from (Source IP address such as 10.10.10.5)
- Where the packet is going (Destination IP address such as 10.10.10.10)
- Option flags that govern security and handling restrictions, whether or not to record the route this packet has taken, whether or not to record timestamps, and so on
- The data this packet carries

Figure 9-7 shows the logical layout of an IP packet.

As you can see, this standard packet definition allows systems to communicate. Without this type of "common language," the global connectivity we enjoy today would be impossible—the IP protocol is the primary means for transmitting information across the Internet.

Figure 9-7
Logical layout
of an IP packet

4-bit version	4-bit header length	8-bit type of services (TOS)	16-bit total length (in bytes)	
16-bit identification			3-bit flags	13-bit fragment offset
8-bit time to live (TTL)		8-bit protocol	16-bit header checksum	
32-bit source IP address				
32-bit destination IP address				
Options (if used)				
Data Payload				

TCP vs. UDP

Protocols are typically developed to enable a certain type of communication or solve a specific problem. Over the years, this approach has lead to the development of many different protocols, each critical to the function or process it supports. However, there are two protocols that have grown so much in popularity and use that without them, the Internet as we know it would cease to exist. These two protocols, the **Transmission Control Protocol (TCP)** and **User Datagram Protocol (UDP)** are protocols that run on top of the IP network protocol. As separate protocols, they each have their own packet definitions, capabilities, and advantages, but the most important difference between TCP and UDP is the concept of "guaranteed" reliability and delivery.

UDP is known as a "connectionless" protocol since it has very few error recovery services and no guarantee of packet delivery. With UDP, packets are created and sent on their way. The sender has no idea if the packets were successfully received or whether or not they were received in order. In that respect, UDP packets are much like postcards—you address them and drop them in the mailbox, not really knowing if, when, or how the postcards reach your intended audience. Even packet loss and corruption is relatively rare on modern networks. UDP is considered to be an unreliable protocol and is often only used for network services that are not greatly affected by the occasional lost or dropped packet. Time synchronization requests, name lookups, and streaming audio are good examples of network services based on the UDP protocol. UDP also happens to be a fairly "efficient" protocol in terms of content delivery versus overhead. With the UDP protocol, more time and space is dedicated to content, or data, delivery than other protocols such as TCP. This makes UDP a good candidate for streaming protocols, since more of the available bandwidth and resources are used for data delivery than with other protocols.

TCP is a "connection oriented" protocol and was specifically designed to allow for a reliable connection between two hosts exchanging data. TCP was also designed to ensure packets are processed in the same order they were sent. As part of the TCP protocol, each packet has a sequence number to show where that packet fits into the overall conversation. With the sequence numbers, packets can arrive in any order and at different times and the receiving system will still know the correct order for processing them. The sequence numbers also let the receiving system know if packets are missing—receiving packets 1, 2, 4, and 7 tells us that packets 3, 5, and 6 are missing and needed as part of this conversation. The receiving system can then request retransmission of packets from the sender to fill in any gaps.

The "guaranteed and reliable" aspect of the TCP protocol makes it very popular for many network applications and services such as HTTP, FTP, and Telnet. As part of the connection, the TCP protocol requires that systems follow a specific pattern when establishing communications. This pattern, often called the **"three-way handshake"** (shown in Figure 9-8), is a sequence of very specific steps:

1. The originating host (usually called the client) sends a SYN (synchronize) packet to the destination host (usually called the server). The SYN packet tells the server what port the client wants to connect to and the initial packet sequence number of the client.

2. The server sends a SYN/ACK packet back to the client. This SYN/ACK (synchronize/acknowledge) tells the client "I received your request" and also contains the server's initial packet sequence number.

3. The client responds to the server with an ACK packet to complete the connection establishment process.

ICMP

While TCP and UDP are arguably the most common protocols, the **Internet Control Message Protocol (ICMP)** is probably the third most commonly used protocol. During the development of large networks, it was quickly discovered that there needed to be some mechanism for managing the overall infrastructure—handling connection status, traffic flow, availability, and errors. This mechanism is the ICMP protocol. ICMP is a control and information protocol and is used by network devices to determine things like a remote network's availability, length of time to reach a remote network, and the best route for packets to take when traveling to that remote network. ICMP can also be used to handle the flow of traffic, telling other network devices to "slow down" transmission speeds if packets are coming in too fast. ICMP, like UDP, is a connectionless protocol. ICMP was designed to carry small messages quickly with minimal overhead or impact to bandwidth. ICMP packets are sent using the same header structure as IP packets with the Protocol Field set to "1" to indicate it is an ICMP packet. Each packet also contains a "type" which indicates what type of ICMP message it is as well as a "code" field which tells us what the message really means. For example, an ICMP packet with a type of 3 and a code of 1 would tell us this is a "Destination Unreachable" message and, more specifically, a "Host Unreachable" message—usually indicating that we are unable to communicate with the intended destination.

Figure 9-8
TCP's three-way handshake

Unfortunately, the ICMP protocol has been greatly abused by attackers over the last few years to execute **Denial-of-Service (DoS)** attacks. As ICMP packets are very small and connectionless, thousands and thousands of ICMP packets can be generated by a single system in a very short period of time. Attackers developed methods to trick many systems into generating thousands of ICMP packets with a common destination—the attacker's target. This creates a literal flood of traffic that the target, and in most cases the network the target sits on, is incapable of dealing with. The ICMP flood drowns out any other legitimate traffic and prevents the target from accomplishing its normal duties—denying access to the service the target normally provides. This has lead to many organizations blocking all external ICMP traffic at the perimeter of their organization.

Packet Delivery

Protocols are designed to help information get from one place to another, but in order to deliver a packet we have to know where it is going. Packet delivery can be divided into two sections: local and remote packet delivery. Local delivery applies to packets being sent out on a local network while remote delivery applies to packets being delivered to a remote system, such as across the Internet. Ultimately, packets may follow a local delivery, remote delivery, local delivery pattern before reaching their intended destination. The biggest difference in local versus remote delivery is how packets are addressed. Network systems have addresses, not unlike office numbers or street addresses, and before a packet can be successfully delivered, the sender needs to know the address of the destination system. These addresses are usually called MAC addresses for local packet delivery and IP addresses for remote packet delivery.

Local Packet Delivery

Packets delivered on a local network, such as an office LAN, are usually sent using the destination system's hardware address, or **Media Access Control (MAC)** address. Each network card or network device is supposed to have a unique hardware address so it can be specifically addressed for network traffic. MAC addresses are assigned to a device or network card by the manufacturer, and each manufacturer is assigned a specific block of MAC addresses to prevent two devices from sharing the same MAC address. MAC addresses are usually expressed as six pairs of hexadecimal digits such as 00:07:e9:7c:c8:aa. In order for a system to send data to another system on the local network, it must first find out the destination system's MAC address.

Maintaining a list of every local system's MAC address is both costly and time-consuming and while a system may store MAC addresses temporarily for convenience, in many cases, the sender must find the destination MAC address before sending any packets. To find another system's MAC address, the **Address Resolution Protocol (ARP)** is used. Essentially, this is the computer's way of finding out "who owns the blue convertible with license number 123JAK." In most cases, systems know the IP address they wish to send to, but not the MAC address. Using an ARP request, the sending system will send out a query: Who is 10.1.1.140? This broadcast query is examined by every system on the local network, but only the system whose IP address is 10.1.1.140 will respond. That system will send back a response that says "I'm 10.1.1.140 and my MAC address is 00:07:e9:7c:c8:aa." The sending system will then format the packet for delivery and drop it on the network media, stamped with the MAC address of the destination workstation.

Remote Packet Delivery

While local packet delivery is usually accomplished with MAC addresses, remote packet delivery is usually accomplished using **Internet Protocol (IP)** addresses. IP addresses are 32-bit numbers that we usually see expressed as a group of four numbers (such as 10.1.1.132). In order to send a packet to a specific system on the other side of the world, you have to know the remote system's IP address. Storing large numbers of IP addresses on every PC is far too costly and most humans are not good at remembering collections of numbers. However, humans are good at remembering names and so the **Domain Name System (DNS)** protocol was created.

DNS translates names into IP addresses. When you enter the name of your favorite web site into the location bar of your web browser and press ENTER, the computer has to figure out what IP address belongs to that name. Your computer takes the entered name and sends a query to a local DNS server. Essentially, your computer asks the DNS server "What IP address goes with www.myfavoritesite.com?" The DNS server, whose main purpose in life is to handle DNS queries, looks in its local records to see if it knows the answer. If it doesn't, the DNS server queries another higher-level domain server. That server checks its records and queries the server above it and so on until a match is found. That name-to-IP address matching is passed back down to your computer so it can create the web request, stamp it with the right destination IP address, and send it.

Before sending the packet, your system will first determine if the destination IP address is on a local or remote network. In most cases, it will be a remote network and your system will not know how to reach that remote network. Again, it would not be practical for your system to know how to directly reach every other system on the Internet, so your system will forward the packet to a network gateway. Network gateways, usually called routers, are devices that are used to interconnect networks and move packets from one network to another. That process of moving packets from one network to another is called **routing** and is critical to the flow of information across the Internet. To accomplish this task, routers use forwarding tables to determine where a packet should go. When a packet reaches a router, it will look at the destination address to determine where to send the packet. If the router's forwarding tables know where the packet should go, the router will send the packet out along the appropriate route. If the router does not know where the destination network is, it will forward the packet to its defined gateway, which will repeat the same process. Eventually, after traversing various networks and being passed through various routers, our packet will come to the router serving the network with the web site we are trying to reach. This router will determine the appropriate MAC address of the destination system and forward the packet accordingly.

Subnetting

In the last section, we mentioned that IP addresses are 32-bit numbers. Of those 32-bits, some are used for the network portion of the address, and some are used for the host portion of the address. The network portion is typically called the **subnet** and the process of dividing that 32-bit space into networks is called **subnetting**. Subnetting tells you how much of the 32-bit space will be used for the network portion of the address and how much will be used for the host portion of the address. As you can guess, where and how you divide the 32-bits determines how many networks and how many host addresses you may have. To interpret the 32-bit space correctly, we must use a **subnet mask**, which tells us exactly how much of the space is the network portion and how much is the host portion. Let's look at an example using the IP address 10.10.10.101 with a subnet mask of 255.255.255.0.

Subnet Mask: 255.255.255.0

IP Address: 10.10.10.101

First, you must convert the address and subnet mask to their binary representations:

Subnet Mask: 11111111.11111111.11111111.00000000

IP Address: 00001010. 00001010. 00001010.01100101

Then, you perform a bitwise AND operation to get the subnet address. The bitwise AND operation examines each set of matching bits from the binary representation of the subnet mask and the binary representation of the IP address. For each set where both the mask and address bits are 1, the result of the AND operation is a 1. Otherwise, if either bit is a 0, the result is a 0. So, for our example we get

Subnet Address: 00001010. 00001010. 00001010.00000000

which in decimal is 10.10.10.0, the subnet address of our IP network address.

The subnet address and mask together tell us that the first three parts of our address are network-related, which means that the last part of our address is the host portion. In our example, the network portion of the address is 10.10.10 and the host portion is 101.

Subnets are usually divided into one of three classes:

- **Class A addresses** Supports 16 million hosts on each of 27 networks
  Subnets: 0.0.0.0 to 126.255.255.255 (127.0.0.0 to 127.255.255.255 is reserved for loopback and is not included in the class A range)

- **Class B addresses** Supports 65,000 hosts on each of 16,000 networks
  Subnets: 128.0.0.0 to 191.255.255.255

- **Class C addresses** Supports 254 hosts on each of 2,000,000 networks
  Subnets: 192.0.0.0 to 223.255.255.255
  Everything above 224.0.0.0 is reserved for either multicasting or future use.

In addition, certain subnets are reserved for private use and are not routed across public networks.

- 10.0.0.0 to 10.255.255.255

- 172.16.0.0 to 172.31.255.255

- 192.168.0.0 to 192.168.255.255

Finally, when determining the valid hosts that can be placed on a particular subnet, you have to keep in mind that the "all 0s" address of the host portion is reserved for the network address and the "all 1s" address of the host portion is reserved for the broadcast address of that particular subnet. Again from our earlier example:

Subnet Network Address: 10.10.10.0
                                          00001010. 00001010. 00001010.00000000

Broadcast Address: 10.10.10.255
                                          00001010. 00001010. 00001010.11111111

In their forwarding tables, routers maintain lists of networks and the accompanying subnet mask. With these two pieces, the router can examine the destination address of each packet and then forward the packet on to the appropriate destination.

IP Address Assignment

When an administrator sets up a network, they usually assign IP addresses to systems in one of two ways: statically or through DHCP. A static IP address assignment is fairly simple; the administrator decides what IP address to assign to a server or PC and that IP address stays assigned to that system until the administrator decides to change it. The other popular method is through **Dynamic Host Configuration Protocol (DHCP)**. Under DHCP, when a system boots up or is connected to the network, it will send out a query looking for a DHCP server. If a DHCP server is available on the network, it will answer the new system and temporarily assign the new system an IP address from a pool of dedicated, available addresses. DHCP is an "as available" protocol—if the server has already allocated all the available IP addresses in the DHCP pool, the new system will not receive an IP address and will not be able to connect to the network. Another key feature of DHCP is the ability to limit how long a system may keep its DHCP-assigned IP address. DHCP addresses have a limited lifespan and once that time period expires, the system using that IP address must either renew use of that address or request another address from the DCHP server. The requesting system may end up with the same IP address, or it may be assigned a completely new address depending on how the DHCP server is configured, as well as the current demand for available addresses. DHCP is very popular in large user environments where the cost of assigning and tracking IP addresses among hundreds or thousands of user systems is extremely high.

Network Address Translation

If you're thinking that a 32-bit address space that's chopped up and subnetted isn't enough to handle all the systems in the world, you're right. While IP address blocks are assigned to organizations such as companies and universities, there usually aren't enough Internet-visible IP addresses to assign every system on the planet a unique, Internet-routable IP address. To compensate for this lack of available IP address space, we use **Network Address Translation (NAT)**. NAT translates private (non-routable) IP addresses into public (routable) IP addresses.

From our discussions earlier in this chapter, you may remember that certain IP address blocks are reserved for "private use," and you'd probably agree that not every system in an organization needs a direct, Internet-routable IP address. Actually, for security reasons, it's much better if most of an organization's systems are hidden from direct Internet access. Most organizations build their internal networks using the private IP address ranges (such as 10.1.1.XXX) to prevent outsiders from directly accessing those internal networks. However, in many cases those systems still need to be able to reach the Internet. This is accomplished by using a NAT device (typically, a firewall or router) that translates the many internal IP addresses into one or a small handful of public IP addresses.

For example, consider a fictitious company, Acme.com. Acme has several thousand internal systems using private IP addresses in the 10.X.X.X range. To allow those IPs to communicate with the outside world, Acme leases an Internet connection and a few public IP addresses, and an NAT-capable device. Acme administrators configure all their internal hosts to use the NAT device as their external gateway. When internal hosts need to send packets outside the company, they send them to the NAT device. The NAT device will remove the internal address and stamp the outbound packets with the NAT device's public, routable address and send them on their way. When response packets are received from outside sources, the device performs NAT in reverse, stripping off the external, public IP address and stamping the packet with the correct internal, private IP address before sending it on into the private Acme.com network. Figure 9-9 illustrates this NAT process.

In Figure 9-9, we see an example of NAT being performed. An internal workstation (10.1.1.121) wants to visit the CNN web site at www.cnn.com. When the packet reaches

Figure 9-9 Logical depiction of NAT

the NAT device, the device translates the 10.1.1.123 source address to the globally routable 63.69.110.110 address, the IP address of the device's externally visible interface. When the CNN web site responds, it will respond to the device's address just as if the NAT device had originally requested the information. The NAT device must then remember which internal workstation requested the information and route the packet to the appropriate destination.

Chapter Review

Chapter Summary

After reading this chapter and completing the exercises, you should understand the following about networks.

Understand the Basic Network Architectures

- There are two broad categories of networks: LANs and WANs.
- The physical arrangement of a network is typically called the network's topology.
- There are four main types of network topologies: Ring, Bus, Star, and Mixed.

Understand Basic Network Protocols

- Protocols, an agreed upon format for exchanging or transmitting data between systems, enable computers to communicate.
- When data is transmitted over a network, it is usually broken up into smaller pieces called packets.
- Most protocols define the types and format for packets used in that protocol.
- The TCP protocol is connection-oriented, requires the three-way handshake to initiate a connection, and provides guaranteed and reliable data delivery.
- The UDP protocol is connectionless, lightweight, and provides no error checking or delivery guarantee.
- Each network device has a unique hardware address known as a MAC address. The MAC address is used for packet delivery on local networks.
- Network devices are also typically assigned a 32-bit number known as an IP address.
- The Domain Name System (DNS) translates names, like www.cnn.com, into IP addresses.

Explain Routing and Address Translation

- The process of moving packets from one end device to another through different networks is called routing.

- Subnetting allows you to divide the 32-bit IP address space into a network portion and a host portion.
- The DHCP protocol allows network devices to be automatically configured on a network and be temporarily assigned an IP address.
- Network Address Translation (NAT) converts private, internal IP addresses to public, routable IP addresses and vice versa.

Key Terms

Address Resolution Protocol (ARP) *(204)*
Bus topology *(197)*
Datagram *(201)*
Denial-of-Service (DoS) attack *(204)*
Dynamic Host Configuration Protocol (DHCP) *(207)*
Domain Name System (DNS) *(205)*
Internet Control Message Protocol (ICMP) *(203)*
Internet Protocol (IP) *(205)*
Local Area Network (LAN) *(195)*
Media Access Control (MAC) address *(204)*
Network Address Translation (NAT) *(208)*
Network *(195)*
Packet *(201)*
Protocol *(199)*
Ring topology *(197)*
Routing *(205)*
Star topology *(197)*
Subnet *(206)*
Subnetting *(206)*
Subnet mask *(206)*
Three-way handshake *(203)*
Transmission Control Protocol (TCP) *(202)*
Topology *(197)*
User Datagram Protocol (UDP) *(202)*
Wide area network (WAN) *(195)*

Key Terms Quiz

Use terms from the Key Terms list to complete the sentences that follow. Don't use the same term more than once. Not all terms will be used.

1. A _____ is a group of two or more devices linked together to share data.

2. Packets in an IP network are sometimes called _____.

3. Moving packets from source to destination across multiple networks is called _____.

4. The _____ is the hardware address used to uniquely identify each device on a network.

5. The prefix portion of an IP address used to describe the network portion of the IP address is called the _____.

6. The shape or arrangement of a network, such as bus, star, ring, or mixed is known as the _____ of the network.

7. A small, typically local network covering a relatively small area such as a single floor of an office building is called a _____.

8. A _____ is an agreed-upon format for exchanging information between systems.

9. The packet exchange sequence (SYN, SYN/ACK, ACK) that initiates a TCP connection is called the _____.

10. _____ is the protocol that allows the use of private, internal IP addresses for internal traffic and public IP addresses for external traffic.

Multiple-Choice Quiz

1. Which of the following topologies connects all the network devices to a central point?

    A. Mixed

    B. Ring

    C. Bus

    D. Star

2. In this chapter, what does WAN stand for?

    A. Wide area node

    B. Wide alternate network

    C. Wide area network

    D. Wide automated network

3. What is Layer 1 of the OSI model called?

    A. The physical layer

    B. The network layer

    C. The initial layer

    D. The presentation layer

4. The UDP protocol…

    A. Provides excellent error checking algorithms

    B. Is a connectionless protocol

    C. Guarantees delivery of packets

    D. Requires a permanent connection between source and destination

5. The process that dynamically assigns an IP address to a network device is called:

    A. NAT

    B. DNS

    C. DHCP

    D. Routing

6. What is the three-way handshake sequence used to initiate TCP connections?

    A. ACK, SYN/ACK, ACK

    B. SYN, SYN/ACK, ACK

    C. SYN, SYN, ACK/ACK

    D. ACK, SYN/ACK, SYN

7. For transmission, large amounts of data are normally broken up into smaller pieces known as:

    A. UDPs

    B. ICMPs

    C. Packets

    D. Subnets

8. Which of the following is a control and information protocol used by network devices to determine things like a remote network's availability and length of time to reach a remote network?

    A. UDP

    B. NAT

    C. TCP

    D. ICMP

9. What is the name of the protocol that translates names into IP addresses?

    A. TCP

    B. DNS

    C. ICMP

    D. DHCP

10. Dividing the 32-bit IP address space into networks is called what?

    A. Translating

    B. Network configuration

    C. Subnetting

    D. Address translation

11. Which protocol translates private (non-routable) IP addresses into public (routable) IP addresses?

    A. NAT

    B. DHCP

    C. DNS

    D. ICMP

12. The TCP protocol…

    A. Is connectionless

    B. Provides no error checking

    C. Allows for packets to be processed in the order they were sent

    D. Has no overhead

13. What is the most widely used network protocol?

    A. SS7

    B. Token Ring

    C. Ethernet

    D. SNA

14. Which of the following would be a valid MAC address?

    A. 00:07:e9

    B. 00:07:e9:7c:c8

    C. 00:07:e9:7c:c8:aa

    D. 00:07:e9:7c:c8:aa:ba

15. What is DHCP an acronym for?

    A. Dynamic Host Configuration Protocol

    B. Dynamic Host Control Protocol

    C. Data Hyper Compression Protocol

    D. Datagram High Correction Process

Essay Quiz

1. A developer in your company is building a new application and has asked you if it should use TCP- or UDP-based communications. Provide her with a brief discussion of the advantages and disadvantages of each protocol.

2. Your boss wants to know if DHCP is appropriate for both server and PC environments. Provide her with your opinion and be sure to include a discussion of how DCHP works.

3. Describe the three basic types of network topologies and provide a sample diagram of each type.

4. Describe the three-way handshake process used to initiate TCP connections.

5. Your boss wants to know how subnetting works. Provide her with a brief description and be sure to include an example to illustrate how subnetting works.

Lab Projects

Lab Project 9.1

A client of yours only has five external, routable IP addresses but they have over 50 systems that they want to be able to reach the Internet for web surfing, e-mail, and so on. Design a network solution for them that addresses their immediate needs but will still let them grow in the future.

Lab Project 9.2

Your boss wants you to learn how to use the "arp" and "nslookup" commands. Find a Windows 2000 or XP machine and open a command/DOS prompt. Type in **arp** and press ENTER to see the options for the arp command. Use the arp command to find the MAC address of your system and at least five other systems on your network. When you are finished with arp, type in **nslookup** and press ENTER. At the prompt, type in the name of your favorite web site, such as www.cnn.com. The nslookup command will return the IP addresses that match that domain name. Find the IP addresses of at least five different web sites.

Infrastructure Security

Upon completion of this chapter, you will be able to:

- List and describe various types of network devices used to construct networks
- List and describe the types of media used to carry network signals
- List and describe various types of storage media used to store information
- Describe how the use of security zones and various other topologies provide network-based security
- Define basic terminology for a series of network functions related to information security

Infrastructure security begins with the actual design of the infrastructure itself. The proper use of the right components not only improves performance but also improves security. Today, a computing environment is not isolated from its network components. The network components are part of the overall computing environment and have become an essential aspect of a total computing environment. From routers, switches, and cables that connect the devices, to the firewalls and gateways that manage communication, from the network design to the protocols employed—all of these items have essential roles, from both performance and security standpoints. In the CIA of security, the A for availability is often overlooked. Yet it is this concept, availability, that has moved computing into this networked framework, and again it is this concept that has a significant role in security. A failure in security can easily lead to a failure in availability, and hence a failure of the system to meet user needs. Security failures can occur in two ways. First, a failure can allow unauthorized users access to resources and data they are not authorized to use, compromising information security. Second, a failure can prevent an authorized user from access to resources and data they are authorized to use. This second failure is often overlooked, but it can be as serious as the first. The primary goal of network infrastructure security is to allow all authorized use and deny all unauthorized use of resources.

Devices

A complete network computer solution in today's business environment consists of more than just client computers and servers. Devices are needed to connect the clients and servers together and to regulate the traffic between them. Devices are also needed to expand this network beyond simple client computers and servers to include yet other devices such as wireless and handheld systems. Devices come in many forms and with many functions, from hubs and switches, to routers, wireless access points, and special-purpose devices such as VPN devices. Each of these devices has a specific network function, and each has a role in maintaining network infrastructure security.

Workstations

Workstations are the device that most users are familiar with. These are the client computers in the client/server model. The workstation is the machine that sits on a user's desktop and is used every day for tasks from e-mail, to spreadsheets, to application programs, even games. If a workstation is connected to a network, it is an important part of the security solution for the network. The list of threats to security from a workstation is large, but much can be done in a few simple steps to provide protection from many of these threats. Although safety is a relative term, the following basic steps should increase workstation security immensely:

- Remove unnecessary protocols such as Telnet, NetBIOS, IPX.
- Remove modems unless needed and authorized.
- Remove all shares that are not necessary.
- Rename the administrator account, securing it with a strong password.
- Remove or disable unnecessary user accounts.
- Install an antivirus program and keep it up-to-date.
- If the floppy drive is not needed, remove or disconnect it.
- If there is no corporate firewall between machine and Internet, install a firewall.
- Keep the OS patched and up-to-date.

Antivirus Software for Workstations

Antivirus packages are available from a wide range of vendors. Running a network of computers without this basic level of protection will be an exercise in futility. Even if a virus attack is rare, the time and money spent cleaning it up will more than equal the cost of protection. Even more important, once connected by networks, computers can spread a virus between machines with even greater ease than simple floppy disk transfer. One unprotected machine can lead to problems throughout a network as other machines have to use their antivirus software to attempt to clean up a spreading infection. Even secure networks can fall prey to virus and worm contamination; there are even cases of infection from commercial packages. As important as antivirus software is, it is even more important to keep the virus definitions for the software up-to-date. Out-of-date definitions can lead to a false sense of security, and many of the most potent virus and worm attacks are the newest ones being developed. The risk associated with a new virus is actually higher than for many of the old ones, which have been eradicated to a great extent by antivirus software.

Workstations are the primary mode of entry for a virus into a network. A virus is a piece of software that must be introduced to the network and then executed on a machine. There are a lot of methods for introducing a virus to a network, but the two most common are transfer of an infected file from another machine and e-mail. A lot of work has gone into software to clean e-mail while in transit and at the mail server. But transferred files are a different matter altogether. People bring files from home, from friends, from places unknown and then execute them on a PC for a variety of purposes. It doesn't matter if it is a funny executable, a game, or even an authorized work application—the virus doesn't care what the original file is, it just uses it to gain access. Even sharing of legitimate work applications can introduce a virus.

The form of transfer is not an issue either; floppy, CD, or FTP, it really doesn't matter. When the transferred file is executed, the virus is propagated. Simple removal of floppy disks does not adequately protect against this threat; nor does training, for users will eventually justify a transfer. The only real defense is an antivirus program that monitors all file movements.

Personal firewalls are another necessity if a machine has an unprotected interface to the Internet. These are seen less often in commercial networks, as it is more cost effective to connect through a firewall server. With the advent of broadband connections for homes and small offices, this needed device is frequently missed. This can result in penetration of a PC from an outside hacker or a worm infection. Worst of all, the workstation may become part of a larger attack against another network, unknowingly joining forces with other compromised machines in a distributed denial of service attack.

The practice of disabling or removing unnecessary devices and software from workstations is also a sensible precaution. If there is no need for a particular service, device, or account, disabling or removing it will prevent unauthorized use by others. Having a standard image of a workstation and duplicating it across a bunch of identical workstations will reduce the workload for maintaining these requirements and reduce total cost of operations. Proper security at the workstation level can increase availability of network resources to users, enabling the business to operate as effectively as possible.

Servers

Servers are the computers in a network that host applications and data for everyone to share. Servers come in many sizes, from small single-CPU boxes that can be less powerful than a workstation to multiple-CPU monsters up to and including mainframes. The operating systems used by servers range from Windows Server to UNIX to MVS and other mainframe operating systems. The OS on a server tends to be more robust than a workstation system and is designed to service multiple users over a network at the same time. Servers can host a variety of applications, including web servers, databases, e-mail servers, file servers, print servers, and application servers for middleware applications.

TIP The specific security needs for a server can vary depending on the server's specific use, but as a minimum:

- Remove unnecessary protocols/services such as Telnet, NetBIOS, IPX, FTP.
- Remove all shares that are not necessary.
- Rename the administrator account, securing it with a strong password.
- Remove unnecessary user accounts.
- Keep the OS patched and up-to-date.
- Control physical access to servers.

The key management issue behind running a secure server setup is to identify the specific needs of a server for its proper operation and enable only items necessary for those functions. Keeping all other services and users off the system improves system throughput and increases security. Once a server has been built and is ready to place into operation, the recording of MD5 checksums on all of its crucial files will provide valuable information later in case of a question concerning possible system integrity after a detected intrusion.

Antivirus Software for Servers

The need for antivirus protection on servers depends a great deal upon the use of the server. Some types of servers, such as e-mail servers, can require extensive antivirus protection because of the services they provide. Other servers (domain controllers and remote access servers, for example) may not require any antivirus software, as they do not allow users to place files on them. File servers will need protection, as will certain types of application servers. There is no general rule, so each server and its role in the network will need to be examined for applicability of antivirus software.

Network Interface Cards (NICs)

To connect a server or workstation to a network, a device known as a **network interface card** (NIC) is used. A NIC is a card with a connector port for a particular type of network connection, either Ethernet or Token Ring. The most common network type in use for local area networks is the Ethernet protocol, and the most common connector is the RJ-45 connector. Figure 10-1 shows a RJ-45 connector (lower) compared to a standard phone connector (upper). Additional types of connectors include coax cable connectors, frequently used with cable modems, from the wall to the cable modem.

The purpose of a NIC is to provide lower-level protocol functionality from the OSI model. As the NIC defines the type of physical layer connection, different NICs are used for different physical protocols. NICs come as single-port and multiport NICs. Most workstations use only a single-port NIC, for only a single network connection is needed. For servers, multiport NICs are used to increase the number of network connections, increasing the data throughput to and from the network.

Figure 10-1   Comparison of RJ-45 (lower) and phone connectors (upper)

Hubs

Hubs are pieces of networking equipment that connect devices using the same protocol at the physical layer of the OSI model. The purpose for a hub is to allow multiple machines in an area to be connected together in a star configuration with the hub as the center of the star. This can save significant amounts of cable and is an efficient method of configuring an Ethernet backbone. Hubs are characterized as having all connections share a single collision domain. Hubs are basically simple signal conditioners that connect multiple devices to a common signal. This is equivalent to a party line, and as network traffic increases, it can become limited by collisions. What hubs lose in traffic management ability, they make up for in cost, with small, eight-port hubs being available for as little as $10. The collision issue has made hubs obsolete in newer, higher-performance networks, with low-cost switches and switched Ethernet keeping costs low and usable bandwidth high.

Bridges

Bridges are pieces of networking equipment that connect devices using the same protocol at the physical layer of the OSI model. Bridges can reduce collisions by separating pieces of a network into two separate collision domains, but this only cuts the collision problem in half. Although this is useful, a better solution is to use switches for network connections.

Switches

Switches form the basis for connections in most Ethernet-based local area networks. Although hubs and bridges still exist, in today's high-performance network environment switches have replaced hubs and bridges. A switch has separate collision domains for each port. This means for a particular port, there are two collision domains; one from the port to the client on the downstream side and one from the switch to the network upstream. When full duplex is employed, collisions are virtually eliminated from the two nodes, host and client. This also acts as a security factor in that a sniffer can see only limited traffic, as opposed to a hub-based system, where a single sniffer can see all of the traffic to and from connected devices.

As switches have replaced lower-level network equipment such as hubs and bridges, they are also moving into the network layer of the OSI model. Switches originally operated at the data-link layer, with routing occurring at the network layer. New breeds of switches can now switch at the network layer, bringing switching speed to network layer path optimization. For intranets, switches have become what routers are on the Internet—the device of choice for connecting machines.

Switches can also perform a variety of security functions. Switches work by moving packets from inbound connections to outbound connections. While moving the packets, it is possible to inspect the packet headers and enforce access control lists. Access control lists (ACLs) act as a series of rules governing whether a packet is allowed or blocked from a connection. This is the very function that a firewall uses for its determination, and this same functionality is what allows an 802.1x device to act as an edge device.

 NOTE ACLs can be a significant effort to establish and maintain. Creating them is a straightforward task, but judicious use of this capability will yield security benefits with a limited amount of maintenance. This can be very important in security zones such as a DMZ and at edge devices, blocking undesired outside contact while allowing known inside traffic.

Virtual Local Area Networks

The other security feature that can be enabled in switches is the concept of virtual local area networks (VLANs). Cisco defines a VLAN as a "broadcast domain within a switched network," meaning that information is carried in broadcast mode only to devices within a VLAN. Switches that allow multiple VLANs to be defined enable broadcast messages to be segregated into the specific VLANs. If each floor of an office were to have a single switch and you had accounting functions on two floors, engineering functions on two floors, and sales functions on two floors, then separate VLANs for accounting, engineering, and sales would allow separate broadcast domains for each of these groups, even ones that spanned floors. This increases network segregation, increasing throughput and increasing security.

Unused switch ports can be preconfigured into empty VLANs that do not connect to the rest of the network. This significantly increases security against unauthorized network connections. If a building is wired with network connections in all rooms, including multiple connections for convenience and future expansion, then these unused ports become open to the network. One solution is to disconnect the connection at the switch, but this merely moves the network opening into the switch room. The better solution is to disconnect it and disable the port in the switch. One method for doing this is to connect all unused ports into a VLAN that isolates them from the rest of the network.

One of the security concerns with switches is that, like routers, they are intelligent network devices and are therefore subject to hijacking by hackers. Should a hijacker break into a switch and change its parameters, it would be possible to eavesdrop on specific or all communications, virtually undetected. Switches are commonly administered using the Simple Network Management Protocol (SNMP), which has a serious weakness in that it involves sending passwords across the network in the clear. A hacker armed with a sniffer that observes maintenance on a switch can capture the administrative password. This gives the hacker the ability to later come back to the switch and configure it as an administrator. An additional problem is that switches are shipped with default passwords, and if not changed when set up, they offer an unlocked door to a hacker.

 CAUTION   To secure a switch, it is important to disable all access protocols other than a secure serial line, or a secure protocol such as Secure Shell (SSH). Using only secure methods to access a switch will limit the exposure to hackers and malicious users. Maintaining secure network switches is even more important than securing individual boxes, for the span of control to intercept data is much wider on a switch, especially if reprogrammed by a hacker.

Routers

Routers are network traffic management devices used to connect different network segments together. Routers operate at the network layer of the OSI model, routing traffic using the network address (typically an IP address) utilizing routing protocols to determine optimal routing paths across a network. Routers form the backbone of the Internet, moving traffic from network to network, inspecting packets from every communication as they move traffic in optimal paths.

Routers operate by examining each packet, looking at the destination address, and using algorithms and tables to determine where to send the packet next. This process of examining the header to determine the next hop can be done in quick fashion. It is also possible to examine the source address and determine whether or not to allow a packet to pass. This allows routers equipped with ACLs to drop packets according to rules. This can be a cumbersome process to set up and maintain, and as the list grows in size, routing efficiency can be decreased. It is also possible to configure some routers to act as quasi–application gateways, performing stateful packet inspection and using contents as well as IP addresses to determine whether or not to permit a packet to pass. This can tremendously increase the time for a router to pass traffic and can significantly decrease router throughput. Configuring ACLs and other aspects of setting up routers for this type of use are beyond the scope of this book.

One serious operational security concern of routers is over the access to a router and control of its internal functions. Like a switch, a router can be accessed using SNMP and programmed remotely. Because of the geographic separation of routers, this can become a necessity, for many routers in the world of the Internet can be hundreds of miles apart, in separate locked structures. Physical control over a router is absolutely necessary, for any device, be it server, switch, or router, if physically accessed by a hacker should be considered compromised, and thus such access must be prevented. As with switches, it is important to ensure that the administrative password is never passed in the clear, only secure mechanisms are used to access the router, and all of the default passwords are reset to strong passwords.

Routers come from numerous vendors and can come in sizes big and small. A typical small home office router for use with cable modem/DSL service is shown in Figure 10-2. Larger routers can handle traffic of up to tens of gigabytes per second per channel, using fiber optic inputs and moving tens of thousands of concurrent Internet connections across the network. These routers can cost hundreds of thousands of dollars and form an essential part of e-commerce infrastructure enabling large enterprises such as Amazon and eBay to serve multiple customers concurrently.

Firewalls

A *firewall* is a network device—hardware, software, or a combination—whose purpose is to enforce a security policy across its connections. It is much like a wall that has a window: the wall serves to keep things out, except those permitted through the window (see Figure 10-3). A security policy acts like the glass in the window; it permits some things to pass, light, while blocking others, air. The heart of a firewall is the security policy that it enforces.

Security policies are a series of rules that define what traffic is permissible and what traffic is to be blocked or denied. These are not universal rules, and there are many different sets of rules for a single company with multiple connections. A web server connected to the Internet may be configured only to allow traffic on port 80 for HTTP, and have all other ports blocked. An e-mail server may have only necessary ports for e-mail open, with others blocked. A key to security policies for firewalls is the same as has been seen for other security policies—the principle of least access. Only allow the necessary access for a function; block or deny all unneeded functionality. How a firm deploys its firewalls determines what is needed for security policies for each firewall.

As will be discussed later, the security topology will determine what network devices are employed at what points in a network. At a minimum, the corporate connection to the Internet should pass through a firewall. This firewall should block all network traffic except that specifically authorized by the security policy. This is actually easy to do: blocking communications on a port is simple, just tell the firewall to close the port. The issue comes in deciding what services are needed and by whom, and thus which ports should be open and which should be closed. This is what makes a security policy useful. The perfect security policy is one that the end user never sees and one that never allows

Figure 10-2   A small home office router for cable modem/DSL use

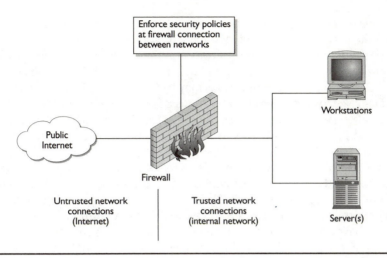

Figure 10-3   Firewall usage

even a single unauthorized packet to enter the network. As with any other perfect item, it will be rare to find the perfect security policy for a firewall.

In order to develop a complete and comprehensive security policy, it is first necessary to have a complete and comprehensive understanding of your network resources and their uses. Once you know what your network will be used for, you will have an idea of what to permit. Also, once you understand what you need to protect, you will have an idea of what to block. Firewalls are designed to block attacks before they get to a target machine. Common targets are web servers, e-mail servers, DNS servers, FTP services, and databases. Each of these has separate functionality, and each of these has separate vulnerabilities. Once you have decided who should receive what type of traffic and what types should be blocked, you can administer this through the firewall.

How Do Firewalls Work?

Firewalls are there to enforce the established security policies. They can do this through a variety of mechanisms, including:

- Network Address Translation (NAT)
- Basic packet filtering
- Stateful packet filtering
- ACLs
- Application layer proxies

One of the most basic security functions provided by a firewall is Network Address Translation (NAT). This service allows you to mask significant amounts of information from outside of the network. This allows an outside entity to communicate with an entity inside the firewall without truly knowing its address.

Basic packet filtering, the next most common firewall technique, involves looking at packets, their protocols and destinations, and checking that information against the security policy. Telnet and FTP connections may be prohibited from being established to a mail or database server, but they may be allowed for the respective service servers. This is a fairly simple method of filtering based on information in each packet header, like IP addresses and TCP/UDP ports. This will not detect and catch all undesired packets, but it is fast and efficient.

To look at all packets, determining the need for each and its data, requires stateful packet filtering. Advanced firewalls employ stateful packet filtering to prevent several types of undesired communications. Should a packet come from outside the network, in an attempt to pretend that it is a response to a message from inside the network, the firewall will have no record of its being requested and can discard it, blocking access. As many communications will be transferred to high ports (above 1023), stateful monitoring will enable the system to determine which sets of high communications are permissible and which should be blocked. The disadvantage to stateful monitoring is that it takes significant resources and processing to do this type of monitoring and this reduces efficiency and requires more robust and expensive hardware. However, this type of monitoring is essential in today's comprehensive networks and given the variety of remotely accessible services.

As they are in routers, switches, servers, and other network devices, ACLs are a cornerstone of security in firewalls. Just as you must protect the device from physical access, ACLs do the same task for electronic access. Firewalls can extend the concept of ACLs by enforcing them as well at a packet level when packet-level stateful filtering is performed. This can add an extra layer of protection, making it more difficult for an outside hacker to breach a firewall.

Some high-security firewalls also employ application layer proxies. As the name implies, packets are not allowed to traverse the firewall, but data instead flows up to an application that in turn decides what to do with it. For example, an SMTP proxy may accept inbound mail from the Internet and forward it to the internal corporate mail server. While proxies provide a high level of security by making it very difficult for an attacker to manipulate the actual packets arriving at the destination, and while they provide the opportunity for an application to interpret the data prior to forwarding it to the destination, they generally are not capable of the same throughput as stateful packet inspection firewalls. The trade-off between performance and speed is a common one and must be evaluated with respect to security needs and performance requirements.

Wireless

Wireless devices bring additional security concerns. There is, by definition, no physical connection to a wireless device. Using radio waves or infrared to carry data allows anyone within range access to the data. This means that unless you take specific precautions, you have no control over who can see your data. Placing a wireless device behind a firewall does not do any good, for the firewall stops only physically connected traffic from getting to the device. Outside traffic can come literally from the parking lot directly to the wireless device.

The point of entry from a wireless device to a wired network is performed at a device called a *wireless access point*. Wireless access points can support multiple concurrent devices accessing network resources through the network node they provide. A typical wireless access point can be seen here.

A typical wireless access point

For notebooks and PCs, a PCMCIA adapter for wireless networks is available from several vendors. The following illustration shows one vendor's card—note the extended length used as an antenna. Not all cards have the same configuration, although they all perform the same function, to enable a wireless network connection. Wireless access points and cards must be matched by protocol for proper operation.

A typical PCMCIA wireless network card

NOTE To prevent unauthorized wireless access to the network, configuration of remote access protocols to a wireless access point is common. Forcing authentication and verifying authorization is a seamless method of performing basic network security for connections in this fashion. These protocols are covered in Chapter 3.

Some wireless devices, such as those intended for operation on IEEE 802.11 wireless LANs, include security features such as the Wired Equivalent Privacy (WEP) protocol. This is designed to prevent wireless sniffing of network traffic over the wireless portion of the network. WEP is described in Chapter 3.

Modems

Modems were once a slow method of remote connection that was used to connect client workstations to remote services over standard telephone lines. Modem is a shortened form of modulator/demodulator, covering the functions actually performed by the device as it converts analog signals to digital and vice versa. To connect a digital computer signal to the analog telephone line required one of these devices. Today, the use of the term modem has expanded to cover devices connected to special digital telephone lines—DSL modems—and to cable television lines—cable modems. Although these devices are not actually modems in the true sense of the word, the term has stuck through marketing efforts directed to consumers. DSL and cable modems offer broadband high-speed connections and the opportunity for continuous connections to the Internet. Along with these new desirable characteristics come some undesirable ones as well. Although they both provide the same type of service, there are some differences between cable and DSL modems. A **digital subscriber line** (DSL) modem provides a direct digital connection between a subscriber's computer and an Internet connection at the local telephone company's switching station. This private connection offers a degree of security, as it does not involve others sharing the circuit. Cable modems are set up in shared arrangements that theoretically would allow a neighbor to sniff a user's cable modem traffic.

Cable modems were designed to share a party line in the terminal signal area, and the cable modem standard, the **Data Over Cable Service Interface Specification** (DOCSIS), was designed to accommodate this concept. DOCSIS includes built-in support for security protocols, including authentication and packet filtering. Although this does not guarantee privacy, it prevents ordinary subscribers from seeing others' traffic without specialized hardware.

Both cable and DSL services are designed for a continuous connection, which brings up the question of IP address life for a client. Although some services originally used a static IP arrangement, virtually all have now adopted the **Dynamic Host Configuration Protocol** (DHCP) to manage their address space. A static IP has an advantage of being the same and enabling convenient DNS connections for outside users. As cable and DSL services are primarily designed for client services as opposed to host services, this is not a relevant issue. A security issue of a static IP is that it is a stationary target for hackers. The move to DHCP has not significantly lessened this threat, however, for the typical IP lease on a cable modem DHCP is for days. This is still relatively stationary, and some form of firewall protection needs to be employed by the user.

Cable/DSL Security

The modem equipment provided by the subscription service converts the cable or DSL signal into a standard Ethernet signal that can then be connected to a network interface card (NIC) on the client device. This is still just a direct network connection, without any security device separating the two devices. The most common security device used in cable/DSL connections is a firewall. The firewall needs to be installed between the cable/DSL modem and client computers. Two common methods exist for this in the marketplace. The first is software on each client device. Numerous software companies offer Internet firewall packages, which can cost under $50. Another solution is the use of a cable/DSL router with a built-in firewall. These are also relatively inexpensive, in the $100 range, and can be combined with software for an additional level of protection. Another advantage to the router solution is that most such routers allow multiple clients to easily share a common Internet connection; most can also be enabled with other networking protocols such as VPN. A typical small home office cable modem/DSL router is shown in earlier Figure 10-2. The bottom line is simple: Even if you connect only occasionally and you disconnect between uses, you need a firewall between the client and the Internet connection. Most commercial firewalls for cable/DSL systems come preconfigured for Internet use and require virtually no maintenance other than keeping the system up-to-date.

RAS

Remote Access Service (RAS) is a portion of the Windows OS that allows the connection between a client and a server via a dial-up telephone connection. Although slower than cable/DSL connections, this is still a common method for connecting to a remote network. When a user dials into the computer system, authentication and authorization are performed through a series of remote access protocols, described in Chapter 3. For even greater security, a callback system can be employed, where the server calls back to the client at a set telephone number for the data exchange.

RAS can also mean Remote Access Server, a term for a server designed to permit remote users access to a network and to regulate their access. A variety of protocols and methods exist to perform this function; they are described in detail in Chapter 3. Once connected to the RAS server, a client has all the benefits of a direct network connection. The RAS server treats its connected clients as extensions of the network. For security purposes, a RAS server should be placed in the DMZ and considered insecure. Additional security checks can be performed at the inner DMZ firewall before access to the internal network is granted.

Telecom/PBX

Private branch exchanges (PBXs) are an extension of the public telephone network into a business. Although typically considered a separate entity from data systems, they are frequently interconnected and have security requirements as part of this interconnection as well as of their own. PBXs are computer-based switching equipment designed to connect telephones into the local phone system. Basically digital switching systems, they can be compromised from the outside and used by phone hackers (phreakers) to make phone calls at the business' expense. Although this type of hacking has decreased with lower-cost long distance, it has not gone away, and as several firms learn every year, voice mail boxes and PBXs can be compromised and the long-distance bills can get very high, very fast.

Another problem with PBXs arises when they are interconnected to the data systems, either by corporate connection or by rogue modems in the hands of users. In either case, a path exists for connection to outside data networks and the Internet. Just as a firewall is needed for security on data connections, one is needed for these connections as well. Telecommunications firewalls are a distinct type of firewall designed to protect both the PBX and the data connections. The functionality of a telecommunications firewall is the same as that of a data firewall; it is there to enforce security policies. Telecommunication security policies can be enforced even to cover hours of phone use to prevent unauthorized long-distance usage through the implementation of access codes and/or restricted service hours.

VPN

A virtual private network (VPN) is a construct used to provide a secure communication channel between users across public networks such as the Internet. As described in Chapter 3, a variety of techniques can be employed to instantiate a VPN connection. The use of encryption technologies allows either the data in a packet to be encrypted or the entire packet to be encrypted. If the data is encrypted, the packets can still be sniffed and observed between source and destination, but the encryption protects the contents from inspection. If the entire packet is encrypted, it is then placed into another packet and sent via tunnel across the public network. Tunneling can protect even the identity of the communicating parties.

The most common implementation of VPN is via IPSec, a protocol for IP security devised for IPv6. This protocol series was back-fitted into the current IP protocol, IPv4, and can be implemented in hardware, software, or a combination of both.

IDS

Intrusion detection systems (IDSs) are systems designed to detect, log, and respond to unauthorized network or host use, both in real time and after the fact. IDSs are available from a wide selection of vendors and are an essential part of network security. These systems are implemented in software, but in large systems, dedicated hardware is required as well. IDSs can be broken into two categories, network-based systems and host-based systems, and there are two primary methods of detection, signature-based and anomaly-based.

Network-based IDS solutions are connected to a segment of the network where they examine all of the passing packets. Using signatures of known attacks, a network IDS can observe misuse as it is initiated and, if operating as a firewall, has the ability to stop it before it occurs. This approach represents an ideal solution but is hampered by two facts. First, seldom is all traffic passed over a single segment in a network. The same segmentation used to increase network bandwidth by separating signals across lines impairs an IDS by hiding a portion of the traffic from its view. The second issue is that not all attacks can be classified according to a signature that can be observed at a packet level. Although an IDS functioning this way can take care of many attacks, it will miss some.

To address the network connectivity and segmentation issue, it is common to place the IDS sensor just outside, or just inside the firewall at the port of entry into the network from the Internet, as shown by the leftmost dashed line in Figure 10-4. This seems like a solution to the segmentation problem except for two additional issues. Large networks can have multiple Internet connections for bandwidth and reliability, and many remote access protocols employ encryption technology that would hide the contents of packets from IDS inspection. To solve this problem, multiple network-based IDS sensors must be deployed at critical points inside a network and then the results combined.

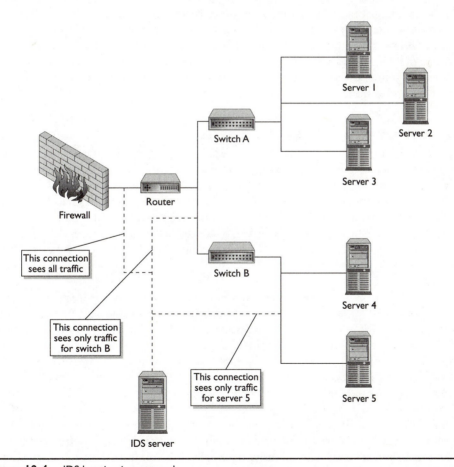

Figure 10-4   IDS location in a network

Host-based IDS solutions provide another method for looking at multiple points in a network. A host-based IDS works by collecting information from all of the servers on the network. Each server has an agent that collects specific performance and usage parameters, such as disk usage, network traffic, and CPU utilization and sends these to the IDS for analysis. The host-based IDS then looks at the collected information and can spot specific trends that have been shown to correlate with unauthorized use. Alerts to unusual activity can then be sent to a network monitoring center for investigation. The main drawback of this type of implementation is simple scaling. Host-based IDSs work very well in smaller networks, but in large commercial networks with hundreds of active servers, the ability to monitor all the traffic becomes an issue.

The other method of analyzing traffic or user behavior, the anomaly method, works by analyzing statistical patterns of usage of a network. Under normal conditions, a pattern of typical network usage is developed and then the system can alert operators to patterns that substantially deviate from this norm. Although this method is great in theory, the problem lies in execution. Anomaly detection works well in detecting large-scale changes and can do so rapidly, even for changes never seen before, the weakness of signatures. But as the level of difference is dialed down to provide finer-grain determination, normal statistical differences such as user behavior, employee movement between machines, and other normal random behavior forces false alarms. Too many false alarms render the system unusable, so research into solving this problem is underway at many locations.

Network Monitoring/Diagnostic

The computer network itself can be considered a large computer system, with performance and operating issues. Just as a computer needs management, monitoring, and fault resolution, so do networks. The **Simple Network Management Protocol** (SNMP) was developed to perform this function across networks. The idea is to enable a central monitoring and control center to maintain, configure, and repair network devices, such as switches and routers, as well as other network services such as firewalls, IDSs, and remote access servers. SNMP has some security limitations, and many vendors have developed software solutions that sit on top of SNMP, providing better security and better management tool suites.

The concept of a **network operations center** (NOC) comes from the old phone company network days, when central monitoring centers monitored the health of the telephone network and provided interfaces for maintenance and management. This same concept works well with computer networks, and companies with midsize and larger networks employ the same philosophy. The NOC allows operators to observe and interact with the network, using the self-reporting and in some cases self-healing nature of network devices to ensure efficient network operation. Although generally a boring operation under normal conditions, when things start to go wrong, as in the case of a virus or worm attack, the center can become a busy and stressful place as operators attempt to return the system to full efficiency while not interrupting existing traffic.

As networks can literally be spread out globally, it is not feasible to have a person go to each device for control functions. Software enables controllers at NOCs to measure the actual performance of network devices and make changes to the configuration and operation of devices. The ability to make remote connections with this level of functionality is both a blessing and a security issue. Although this allows efficient network operations management, it also is an opportunity for unauthorized entry into a network. For this reason, a variety of security controls are used, from secondary networks to VPNs and advanced authentication methods with respect to network control connections.

Network monitoring is an ongoing concern for any significant network. In addition to monitoring traffic flow and efficiency, monitoring of security is necessary. Intrusion detection systems act merely as alarms, indicating the possibility of a breach associated with a specific set of activities. These indications still need to be investigated and an appropriate response initiated by security personnel. Simple items such as port scans may be ignored by policy, but an actual unauthorized entry into a network router, for instance, would require NOC personnel to take specific actions to limit the potential damage to the system. The coordination of system changes, dynamic network traffic levels, potential security incidents, and maintenance activities is a daunting task requiring numerous personnel working together in any significant network. Software has been developed to help manage the information flow required to support these tasks. Such software can enable remote administration of devices in a standard fashion so that the control systems can be devised in a hardware vendor–neutral configuration.

SNMP is the main standard embraced by vendors to permit interoperability. Although SNMP has received a lot of security-related attention of late due to various security holes in its implementation, it is still an important part of a security solution associated with network infrastructure. Many useful tools have security issues; the key is to understand the limitations and to use the tools within correct boundaries to limit the risk associated with the vulnerabilities. Blind use of any technology will result in increased risk, and SNMP is no exception. Proper planning, setup, and deployment can limit exposure to vulnerabilities. Continuous auditing and maintenance of systems with the latest patches is a necessary part of operations and is essential to maintaining a secure posture.

Mobile Devices

Mobile devices such as personal digital assistants (PDAs) and mobile phones are the latest devices to join the corporate network. These devices can perform significant business functions, and in the future, more of them will enter the corporate network and more work will be performed with them. These devices add several challenges for network administrators. When they synchronize their data with that on a workstation or server, the opportunity exists for viruses and malicious code to be introduced to the network. This can be a major security gap, as a user may access separate e-mail accounts, one personal, without antivirus protection, the other corporate. Whenever data is moved from one network to another via the PDA, the opportunity to put a virus onto the workstation exists. Although the virus may not affect the PDA or phone, these devices can act as a transmission vector. Currently, at least one vendor offers antivirus protection for PDAs, and similar protection for phones is not far away.

Media

The base of communications between devices is the physical layer of the OSI model. This is the domain of the actual connection between devices, whether by wire, fiber, or RF waves. The physical layer separates the definitions and protocols required to physically transmit the signal between boxes from higher-level protocols that deal with the details of the data itself. There are four common methods of connecting equipment at the physical layer:

- Coaxial cable
- Twisted-pair cable
- Fiber optics
- Wireless

Coax

Coaxial cable is very familiar to many households as a method of connecting televisions to VCRs or to satellite or cable services. It is used in these arenas because of its high bandwidth and shielding capabilities. Compared to standard twisted-pair lines such as telephone lines, coax is much less prone to outside interference. It is also much more expensive to run, both from a cost per foot measure and from a cable dimension measure. Coax costs much more per foot than standard twisted pair and carries only a single circuit for a large wire diameter.

A coax connector

An original design specification for Ethernet connections, coax was used from machine to machine in early Ethernet implementations. The connectors were easy to use and ensured good connections, and the limited distance of most office LANs did not carry a large cost penalty. The original ThickNet specification for Ethernet called for up to 100 connections over 500 meters at 10 Mbps.

Today, almost all of this older Ethernet specification has been replaced by faster, cheaper twisted-pair alternatives and the only place one is likely to see coax in a data network is from the cable box to the cable modem.

UTP/STP

Twisted-pair wires have all but completely replaced coaxial cables in Ethernet networks. Twisted-pair wires use the same technology used by the phone company for the movement of electrical signals. Single pairs of twisted wires reduce electrical crosstalk and electromagnetic interference. Multiple groups of twisted pairs can then be bundled together in common groups and easily wired between devices.

Twisted pairs come in two types, shielded and unshielded. Shielded twisted-pair (STP) has a foil shield around the pairs to provide extra shielding from electromagnetic interference. Unshielded twisted-pair (UTP) relies on the twist to eliminate interference. UTP has a cost advantage over STP and is usually sufficient for connections except in very noisy electrical areas.

A typical 8-wire UTP line

A typical 8-wire STP line

A bundle of UTP wires

Twisted-pair lines are categorized by the level of data transmission they can support. There are three current categories in use:

- Category 3 (Cat 3) minimum for voice and 10Mbps Ethernet
- Category 5 (Cat 5) for 100Mbps Fast Ethernet
- Category 6 (Cat 6) for Gigabit Ethernet

The standard method for connecting twisted-pair cables is via an 8-pin connector called an RJ-45 connector. This looks like a standard phone jack connector but is slightly larger. One nice aspect of twisted-pair cabling is its ease of splicing and changing of connectors. Many a network administrator has made Ethernet cables from stock Cat 5 wire, two connectors and a crimping tool. This ease of connection is also a security issue, as twisted-pair cables are very easy to splice into and rogue connections for sniffing could be made without detection in cable runs. Both coax and fiber are much more difficult to splice, with both of these needing a tap to connect, and taps are easier to detect.

Fiber

Fiber optic cable uses beams of laser light to connect devices over a thin glass wire. The biggest advantage to fiber is its bandwidth, with transmission capabilities into the terabits per second range. Fiber optic cable is what is used to make high-speed connections between servers and is the backbone medium of the Internet and large networks. For all of its speed characteristics, fiber has one major drawback—cost.

The cost of using fiber is a two-edged sword. It is cheaper when measured by bandwidth to use fiber than competing wired technologies. The length of runs of fiber can be much longer, and the data capacity of fiber is much higher. But connections to a fiber are difficult and expensive and fiber is impossible to splice. Making the precise connection on the end of a fiber optic line is a highly skilled job and is done by specially trained professionals who maintain a level of proficiency. Once the connector is fitted on the end, several forms of connectors and blocks are used, as shown in the images that follow.

A typical fiber optic fiber and terminator

Another type of fiber terminator

A connector block for fiber optic lines

Splicing fiber optic is nearly impossible; the solution is to add connectors and connect through a repeater. This adds to the security of fiber in that unauthorized connections are all but impossible to make. The high cost of connections to fiber and the higher cost of fiber per foot also make fiber less attractive for the final mile in public networks where users are connected to the public switching systems. For this reason, cable companies use coax and DSL providers use twisted pairs to handle the last-mile scenario.

Unguided Media

Electromagnetic waves have been transmitted to convey signals literally since the inception of radio. Unguided media is a phrase used to cover all transmission media not guided by wire, fiber, or other constraints; it includes radio frequency (RF), infrared (IR), and microwave methods. Unguided media have one attribute in common, that they are unguided and as such can travel to many machines simultaneously. Transmission patterns may be modulated by antennas, but the target machine can be one of many in a reception zone. As such, security principles are even more critical, as they must assume that an unauthorized user has access to the signal.

Infrared

Infrared (IR) is a band of electromagnetic energy just beyond the red end of the visible spectrum. IR has been used in remote control devices for years and has the property that it cannot penetrate walls but instead bounces off them. IR made its debut in computer networking as a wireless method to connect to printers. Now there are wireless keyboards, wireless mice, PDAs exchanging data via IR—it seems to be everywhere. IR can also be used to connect devices in a network configuration, but a drawback is that it is slow compared to other wireless technologies. It also suffers from not being able to penetrate solid objects, so stack a few items in front of the transceiver and the signal is lost.

RF/Microwave

The use of radio frequency (RF) waves to carry communication signals goes back to the beginning of the twentieth century. Radio frequency (RF) waves are a common method of communicating in a wireless world. RF waves use a variety of frequency bands, each with special characteristics. The term microwave is used to describe a specific portion of the RF spectrum that is used for communication as well as other tasks such as cooking.

Point-to-point microwave links have been installed by many network providers to carry communications over long distances and rough terrain. Microwave communications of telephone conversations were the basis for forming the telecommunication company MCI. Many different frequencies are used in the microwave bands for many different purposes. Today, home users can use wireless networking throughout their house and enable laptops to surf the Web while walking between rooms. Corporate users are experiencing the same phenomenon, with wireless networking enabling corporate users to check e-mail on laptops while riding a shuttle bus on a business campus. These wireless solutions carry the information via microwaves; they are covered in detail in Chapter 3.

One key feature of microwave communications is that microwave RF energy can penetrate reasonable amounts of building structure. This allows one to connect network devices in separate rooms and can remove the constraints on equipment location imposed by fixed wiring. Another key feature is broadcast capability. By its nature, RF energy is unguided and can be received by multiple users simultaneously. Microwaves allow multiple users access in a limited area, and microwave systems are seeing application as the last mile of the Internet in dense metropolitan areas. Point-to-multipoint microwave devices can deliver data communication to all the business users in a downtown metropolitan area through rooftop antennas, reducing the need for expensive building-to-building cables. Just as microwaves carry cell phone and other data communications, the same technologies offer a method to bridge the last-mile solution. The "last mile" problem is the connection of individual consumers to a backbone, an expensive proposition because of the sheer number of connections and unshared line at this point in a network. Again, cost is an issue, as transceiving equipment is expensive, but in densely populated areas, such as apartments and office buildings in metropolitan areas, the user density can help defray individual costs. Speed on commercial microwave links can exceed 10 Gbps, so speed is not a problem for connecting multiple users, or for high-bandwidth applications.

Security Concerns for Transmission Media

The primary security concern for a system administrator has to be preventing physical access to a server by an unauthorized individual. Such access will almost always spell disaster, for with direct access and the correct tools, any system can be broken into. One of the next major concerns should be preventing unfettered access to a network connection. Access to switches and routers is almost as bad as direct access to a server, and access to network connections would rank third in terms of worst-case scenarios. To prevent such access is costly, yet the cost of replacing a server because of theft is also costly.

Physical Security

A balanced approach is the most sensible approach when addressing physical security, and this applies to transmission media as well. Keeping network switch rooms secure and cable runs secure seems obvious, but cases of using janitorial closets for this vital business purpose abound. One of the keys to mounting a successful attack on a network is information. Usernames, passwords, server locations—all of these can be obtained if someone has the ability to observe network traffic, in a process called sniffing. A sniffer can record all the network traffic, and this data can be mined for accounts, passwords, and traffic content, all of which may be useful to an unauthorized user. Many common scenarios exist when unauthorized entry to a network occurs, including:

- Insertion of a node and functionality that is not authorized on the network, such as a sniffer device or unauthorized wireless access point
- Modifying firewall security policies
- Modifying ACLs for firewalls, switches, or routers
- Modifying network devices to echo traffic to an external node

One starting point for many intrusions is the first scenario, insertion of an unauthorized sniffer into the network, with the fruits of its labors driving the remaining unauthorized activities. The best first effort is to physically secure the actual network equipment to prevent this type of intrusion.

Network devices and transmission media become targets because they are dispersed through an organization and physical security of many dispersed items can be difficult to manage. This work is not glamorous and has been likened to guarding plumbing. The difference is that in the case of network infrastructure, unauthorized physical access strikes at one of the most vulnerable points and, in many cases, is next to impossible to detect. Locked doors and equipment racks are easy to implement, yet this step is frequently overlooked. Raised floors, cable runs, closets—there are many places to hide an unauthorized device. Add to this the fact that a large percentage of unauthorized users have a direct connection to the target of the unauthorized use—they are employees, students, or the like. Twisted pair and coax make it easy to tap into a network without signaling one's presence. A person with talent can make such a tap without interrupting network traffic.

Although limiting physical access is difficult, it is essential. The least level of skill is still more than sufficient to accomplish unauthorized entry into a network if physical access to the network signals is allowed. This is one factor driving many organizations to use fiber optics, for these are much more difficult to tap. Although many tricks can be employed with switches and VLANs to increase security, it is still essential to prevent unauthorized contact with the network equipment.

Wireless networks make the intruder's task even easier, as they take the network to the users, authorized or not. A new technique, called War-Driving, involves using a laptop and software to find wireless networks from outside the premises. A typical use of War-Driving is to locate a wireless network with poor (or no) security and obtain free Internet access, but the other uses can be more devastating. Methods for securing even the relatively weak WEP protocol are not difficult; they are just typically not followed. A simple solution is to place a firewall between the wireless access point and the rest of the network and authenticate users before allowing entry, even if the encryption setup matches the WEP setup. Home users can do the same thing to prevent neighbors from "sharing" their Internet connections. To ensure that unauthorized traffic does not enter your network through a wireless access point, you must either use a firewall with an authentication system or establish a VPN.

Removable Media

One task common to all computer users is storage of data. Sometimes this storage occurs on a file server; sometimes it is on movable media, allowing it to be transported between machines. Moving storage media represents a security risk from a couple of different angles, the first being the potential loss of control over the data on the moving media. Second is the risk of introducing unwanted items, such as a virus or a worm, when the media are attached back to a network. There are methods of combating both of these issues, through policies and software. The key is to ensure they are occurring. To describe media-specific issues, it is easiest to divide the media into three categories: magnetic, optical, and electronic.

Magnetic Media

Magnetic media store data through the rearrangement of magnetic particles on a nonmagnetic substrate. Common forms include hard drives, floppy disks, Zip disks, and magnetic tape. Although the specific format may differ, the basic concept is the same. All of these devices share some common characteristics. Each has sensitivity to external magnetic fields. Attach a floppy disk to the refrigerator door with a magnet if you wish to test the sensitivity. They are also affected by high temperatures as in fires, and by exposure to water.

Hard Drives

Hard drives used to be large machines in mainframes. Now they can be found small enough to attach to PDAs and small handheld devices. The concepts remain the same among all of them: a spinning patter rotates the magnetic media beneath heads that read the patterns in the oxide coating. As drives have gotten smaller and rotation speeds increased, the capacities have also grown. Today, gigabytes can be stored in a device slightly larger than a bottle cap. Portable hard drives in the 20–120GB range are now available and affordable, some for less than $300.

External Portable 80GB hard drive with USB connection

Diskettes

Floppy disks were the industry's first attempt at portable magnetic media. The movable medium was placed in a protective sleeve, and the drive remained in the machine. Capacities up to 1.4MB were achieved, but the fragility of the device as the size increased, as well as competing media, has rendered floppies almost obsolete. A better floppy, the Zip disk from Iomega Corporation, improved on the floppy with a stronger case and higher capacity (100MB and 250MB); it has become a common backup and file transfer medium. But even the increased size of 250MB is not large enough for some multimedia files, and recordable optical (CD-R) drives have arrived to fill the gap; they will be discussed shortly in this chapter.

Comparison of Zip disk (left) and 3.5-inch floppy (right)

Tape

Magnetic tape has had a place in computer centers since the beginning of computing. The primary use has been bulk offline storage and backup. Tape functions well in this role because of its low cost. The disadvantage of tape is its nature as a serial access medium, making it a slow medium to work with for large quantities of data. Several types of magnetic tape are in use today, ranging from quarter inch to digital linear tape (DLT) and digital audio tape (DAT). These cartridges can hold upward of 60GB of compressed data. Tapes are still a major concern from a security perspective, as they are still used to back up many types of computer systems. The security concern is over the physical protection afforded the tapes, for if they were stolen, then an unauthorized user could establish a network and recover your data on his system, where he has access to it all. Offsite storage is needed for proper disaster recovery protection, but secure offsite storage and transport is what is really needed. This important issue is frequently overlooked in many facilities.

A magnetic tape used for backups

Optical Media

Optical media are characterized by the use of a laser to read data stored on a physical device. Rather than a magnetic head picking up magnetic marks on a disk, a laser picks up deformities embedded in the media that contain the information. As with magnetic media, optical media can be read/write, although the read-only version is still more common.

CD-R/DVD

The compact disc (CD) took the music industry by storm, and then it took the computer industry by storm as well. A digital record, a standard CD holds over 640MB of data. A newer form, the digital video disc (DVD), can hold almost 4GB of data. These new devices operate as optical storage, with little marks burned in them to represent 1's and 0's on a microscopic scale. The most common type of CD is the read-only version, where the data is written to the disc once and only to read afterward. This has become a popular method for distributing computer software, although recently higher-capacity DVDs have begun to replace CDs for program distribution.

A DVD (left) and a CD-R (right)

A second-generation device, the recordable compact disc (CD-R), allows users to create their own CDs using a burner device in their PC and special software. This has enabled users to back up data, make their own audio CDs, and use CDs as high-capacity diskettes. Their relatively low cost (less than 50 cents each in bulk) has made it economical to use them only once. CDs have a thin layer of aluminum inside the plastic, upon which bumps are burned by the laser when recorded. CD-Rs use a reflective layer, such as gold, upon which a dye is placed that changes upon impact by the recording laser. A newer type, CD-RW, has a different dye that allows discs to be erased and reused. The cost of the media increases from CD to CD-R to CD-RW.

DVDs may in the future occupy the same role that CDs have in the recent past, except that they hold over seven times the data of a CD. This makes full-length movie recording possible on a single disc. The increased capacity comes from finer tolerances and the fact that DVDs can hold data on both sides. Formats for burners to allow home burning of DVDs are still in their infancy, with a couple of competing formats available. They have raised digital rights management issues as well, to prevent the copying of digital media such as movies.

Electronic Media

The latest form of removable media is electronic memory. Electronic circuits of static memory, which can retain data even without power, fill a niche where high density and small size are needed. Primarily used in audio devices and digital cameras, these electronic media come in a variety of vendor-specific types, such as Smart Cards, Smart Media, Flash Cards, Memory Sticks, and CompactFlash devices. Several recent photo-quality color printers have been released with ports to accept the cards directly, so that a computer is not required for printing. Computer readers are also available to permit storing data from the card onto hard drives and other media in a computer. The size of storage on these devices ranges from 16MB to 2GB, with higher capacities on the horizon.

Smart Media card

Smart Media USB reader

Although they are primarily used for photos and music, there is nothing to prevent these devices from moving any digital data from one machine to another. To a machine, equipped with a connector port, these look like any other file storage location. Being able to hold 256MB on a chip the size of a postage stamp and 1/8-inch thick brings a lot of uses to mind. Cost is still fairly high, with a 256MB card costing $75, but it wasn't so many years ago we would have gladly paid that for a hard drive with the same capacity but a significantly larger footprint.

These devices can be connected to a system through a special reader or directly via a USB port. In newer PC systems, a USB boot device is being used to replace the older floppy drive. These devices are small, can hold a significant amount of data, up to 2GB at time of writing, and are easy to move from machine to machine. Another novel interface is a mouse that has a slot for a memory stick. This dual-purpose device conserves space, conserves USB ports, and is intuitively easy to use. You put the memory stick in the mouse and use the mouse normally. When you are finished, you take the stick with you. The mouse works with or without the memory stick; it is just a convenient device to use for a portal.

Security Topologies

Networks are different than single servers; networks exist as connections of multiple devices. A key characteristic of a network is its layout, or topology. A proper network topology takes security into consideration and assists in "building security" into the network. **Security-related topologies** include separating portions of the network by use and function, strategically designing in points to monitor for IDS systems, building in redundancy, and adding fault-tolerant aspects.

Security Zones

The first aspect of security is a layered defense. Just as a castle has a moat, an outside wall, an inside wall, and even a keep, so too does a modern secure network have its different layers. Different zones are designed to provide layers of defense, with the outermost layers providing basic protection and the innermost layers providing the highest level of protection. A constant issue is that accessibility tends to be inversely related to level of protection, so it is harder to provide complete protection and unfettered access at the same time. Trade-offs between access and security are handled through zones, with successive zones guarded by firewalls enforcing ever increasingly strict security policies. The outermost zone is the Internet, a free area, beyond any specific controls. Between the inner secure corporate network and the Internet is an area where machines are considered at risk. This zone has come to be called the **DMZ**, after its military counterpart, the demilitarized zone, where neither side has any specific controls. Once inside the inner secure network, separate branches are frequently carved out to provide specific functionality; under this heading, we will discuss intranets, extranets, and virtual LANs.

DMZ

The demilitarized zone, or DMZ, is a military term for ground separating two opposing forces, by agreement and for the purpose of acting as a buffer between the two sides. A DMZ in a computer network is used in exactly the same way; it acts as a buffer zone between the Internet, where no controls exist, and the inner secure network, where an organization has security policies in place (see Figure 10-5). To demarcate the zones and enforce separation, a firewall is used on each side of the DMZ. The area between these firewalls is accessible from either the inner, secure, network or the Internet. Figure 10-5 illustrates these zones as caused by firewall placement. The firewalls are specifically designed to prevent access across the DMZ directly, from the Internet to the inner, secure, network.

Figure 10-5 The DMZ and zones of trust

Special attention should be paid to the security settings of network devices placed in the DMZ, and they should be considered at all times to be compromised to unauthorized use. A common industry term, *hardened operating system,* applies to machines where special attention is paid to locking down the functionality to preserve security. This approach needs to be applied to the machines in the DMZ, and although it limits functionality, it enables them to work properly in this less-secure environment.

Many types of servers belong in this area, including web servers that are serving content to Internet users, as well as remote access servers and external e-mail servers. In general, any server directly accessed from the outside, untrusted Internet zone needs to be in the DMZ. Other servers should not be placed in the DMZ. Domain name servers for your inner, trusted, network should not be accessible from the outside, nor should the database servers that house corporate databases. Application servers, file servers, print servers—all of the standard servers used in the trusted network should be behind both firewalls. And not just the servers, but the routers and switches that connect these machines together.

The idea behind the use of the DMZ topology is to force a user to make at least one hop in the DMZ before accessing information inside the trusted network. If the outside user makes a request for a resource from the trusted network, say a data element from a database via a web page, then this request needs to follow the following scenario:

1. A user from the untrusted network (the Internet) requests data via a web page from a web server in the DMZ.

2. The web server in the DMZ requests the data from the application server, which can be in the DMZ or in the inner, trusted network.

3. The application server requests the data from the database server in the trusted network.

4. The database server returns the data to the requesting application server.

5. The application server returns the data to the requesting web server.

6. The web server returns the data to the requesting user from the untrusted network.

This separation accomplishes two specific, independent tasks. First, the user is separated from the request for data on a secure network. By having intermediaries do the requesting, this layered approach allows significant security levels to be enforced. Users do not have direct access or control over their requests, and this filtering process can put controls in place. Second, scalability is more easily realized. The multiple-server solution can be made to be very scalable to literally millions of users, without slowing down any particular layer.

Internet

The **Internet** is the name given to the worldwide connection of networks. This network can be used to transport e-mail, files, financial records, remote access—you name it, and the Internet carries it today from one network to another. A formal way of looking at the Internet is not as a single network, but as a series of interconnected networks that allow protocols to operate to enable data to flow across it. This means that even if your network doesn't have direct contact with a resource, as long as a neighbor, or a neighbor's neighbor, etc., can get there, so can you. This large mesh allows users almost infinite ability to communicate between systems.

Because everything and everyone can access this interconnected mesh and it is outside of your control and ability to enforce security policies, the Internet should be considered to be untrusted. A firewall should exist at any connection between your trusted network and the Internet. This is not to imply that the Internet is a bad thing—it is a great resource for all networks and adds significant functionality to our computing environments. It is just not an area where you can use your own security policies and trust content or identities.

The term World Wide Web (WWW) is frequently used synonymously with the term Internet, but it actually is just one set of services available via the Internet. WWW is more specifically the Hypertext Transfer Protocol (HTTP)–based services that are made available over the Internet. This can include a variety of actual services and content, including text files, pictures, streaming audio and video, even viruses and worms.

Intranet

Intranet is a term used to describe a network that has the same functionality as the Internet for users but lies completely inside the trusted area of a network and is under the security control of the system and network administrators. Typically referred to as *campus* or *corporate* networks, intranets are used everyday in companies around the world. An intranet allows a developer and a user the full set of protocols, HTTP, FTP, instant messaging, etc., that is offered on the Internet, but with the added advantage of trust from the network. Content on web servers on intranets by definition is not available over the Internet to untrusted users. This layer of security offers a significant amount of control and regulation, allowing users to fulfill business functionality while ensuring security.

Should information need to be made available to outside users, two methods exist. Duplication onto machines in the DMZ can place the material in a position to be made available for other users. Proper security checks and controls can be made prior to duplicating the material to ensure security policies concerning specific data availability are being followed. The other method to extend distribution is through the use of extranets, which are the publishing of material to trusted partners.

Should users inside the intranet require access to information from the Internet, then a proxy server can be used to mask the requestor's location. This helps secure the intranet from outside mapping of its actual topology. All Internet requests go to the proxy server. If a request passes filtering requirements, the proxy server, assuming it is also a cache server, looks in its local cache of previously downloaded web pages. If it finds the page in its cache, it returns the page to the requestor without needing to send the request to the Internet. If the page is not in the cache, the proxy server, acting as a client on behalf of the user, uses one of its own IP addresses to request the page from the Internet. When the page is returned, the proxy server relates it to the original request and forwards it on to the user. This masks the user's IP address from the Internet. Proxy servers can perform several functions for a firm; for example, they can monitor traffic requests, eliminating improper requests, i.e., inappropriate content for work. They can also act as a cache server, cutting down on outside network requests for the same object. Finally, proxy servers protect the identity of internal IP addresses, although this function can also be done through a router or firewall using NAT.

Extranet

An **extranet** is an extension of a selected portion of a company's intranet to external partners. This allows a business to share information with customers, suppliers, partners, and other trusted groups while using a common set of Internet protocols to facilitate operations. Extranets can use public networks to extend their reach beyond a company's own internal network, and some form of security, typically VPN, is used to secure this channel. The use of the term extranet implies both privacy and security. Privacy is required for many communications, and security is needed to prevent unauthorized use and events from occurring. Both of these functions can be achieved through the use of technologies described in this chapter and other chapters in this book. Proper firewall management, remote access, encryption, authentication, secure tunnels across public networks—these are all methods used to ensure privacy and security for extranets.

VLANs

A local area network (LAN) is a set of devices with similar functionality and similar communication needs, typically collocated and operated off a single switch. This is the lowest level of a network hierarchy and defines the domain for certain protocols at the data-link layer for communication. **Virtual local area networks** (VLANs) are a method of using a single switch and dividing it into multiple broadcast domains and/or multiple network segments. This is a very powerful technique that allows significant network flexibility, scalability, and performance. VLANs are implemented at a switch level and are often combined with a technique known as trunking.

Trunking

Trunking is the process of spanning a single VLAN across multiple switches. A trunk- based connection between switches allows packets from a single VLAN to travel between switches, as shown in Figure 10-6. Two trunks exist in Figure 10-6: VLAN 10 is implemented with one trunk, and VLAN 20 is implemented by the other. Hosts on different VLANs cannot communicate using trunks and are switched across the switch network. Trunks enable network administrators to set up VLANs across multiple switches with minimal effort. With a combination of trunks and VLANs, network administrators can subnet a network by user functionality without respect to host location on the network or recabling machines.

Security Implications

VLANs have several security implications. First and foremost is the ability to divide a single network into multiple subnets based on functionality. This would permit engineering and accounting to share a switch because of proximity and yet have separate

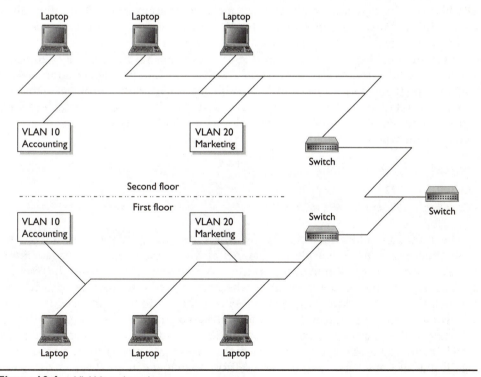

Figure 10-6   VLANs and trunks

traffic domains. The physical placement of equipment and cables is logically and programmatically separated so adjacent ports on a switch can reference separate subnets. This prevents unauthorized use of physically close devices through separate subnets, but the same equipment. VLANs also allow a network administrator to define a VLAN that has no users and map all of the unused ports to this VLAN. Then if an unauthorized user should gain access to the equipment, they will be unable to use unused ports, as those ports will be securely defined to nothing.

 CAUTION   Trunks and VLANs also have security implications that need to be heeded so that firewalls and other segmentation devices are not breached through their use. They also require understanding of their use to prevent an unauthorized user from reconfiguring them to gain undetected access to secure portions of a network.

NAT

Network Address Translation (NAT) is a method for using two sets of IP addresses for resources, one for internal use and a different one for external (Internet) use. NAT was developed as a solution to the rapid depletion of IP addresses in the IPv4 address space; it has since became an Internet standard (see RFC 1631 for details). NAT is used to translate between the two addressing schemes and is typically performed at a firewall or router. This permits enterprises to use the nonroutable private IP address space internally and reduce the number of external IP addresses used across the Internet.

There are three sets of IP addresses that are defined as nonroutable. By definition, nonroutable addresses will not be routed across the Internet. These addresses are routable internally and routers can be set to route them, but the routers across the Internet are set to discard packets sent to these addresses. This approach enables a separation of internal and external traffic and allows these addresses to be reused by anyone and everyone who wishes to do so. The three address spaces are

Class A	10.0.0.0 – 10.255.255.255
Class B	172.16.0.0 – 172.31.255.255
Class C	192.168.0.0 – 192.168.255.255

The use of these addresses inside a network is unrestricted, and they function like any other IP addresses. When outside, i.e., Internet-provided resources are needed for one of these addresses, NAT is required to produce a valid external IP address for the resource. NAT operates by translating the address when traffic passes the NAT device, such as a firewall. The external addresses used are not mappable 1:1 to the internal addresses, for this would defeat the purpose of reuse and address space conservation. Typically, a pool of external IP addresses is used by the NAT device, with the device keeping track of which internal address is using which external address at any given time. This provides a significant layer of security, as it makes it difficult to map the internal network structure behind a firewall and directly address it from the outside. NAT is one of the methods for enforcing perimeter security by forcing users to access resources through defined pathways such as firewalls and gateway servers.

To accomplish NAT, several different techniques are used. *Static* NAT is where there is a 1:1 binding of external address to internal address; it is needed for services where external sources reference internal sources, such as web servers or e-mail servers. For DMZ resources that reference outside resources, addresses can be shared, through dynamic NAT. In *dynamic* NAT, a table is constructed and used by the edge device to manage the translation. As the address translation can change over time, the table changes as well. Even finer-grained control can be obtained through port address translation (PAT), where actual TCP/UDP ports are translated as well. This will enable a single external IP address to serve two internal IP addresses through the use of ports. Resources that need long-running NAT, but only specific ports, for instance, a web server on port 80 or e-mail on port 25, can share a single external IP, conserving resources.

Tunneling

Tunneling is a method of packaging packets so that they can traverse a network in a secure, confidential manner. Tunneling involves encapsulating packets within packets, enabling dissimilar protocols to coexist in a single communication stream, as in IP traffic routed over an ATM network. Tunneling also can provide significant measures of security and confidentiality through encryption and encapsulation methods. The best example of this is the VPN method, where a virtual private network is established over a public network through the use of a tunnel, as shown in Figure 10-7, connecting a firm's Boston office to its NYC office.

Assume a company has multiple locations and decides to use the public Internet to connect the networks at these locations. To make these connections secure from outside unauthorized use, the company can employ a VPN connection between the different networks. On each network, an edge device, usually a router, connects to another edge device on the other network. Then using IPSec protocols, these routers establish a secure, encrypted path between them. This securely encrypted set of packets cannot be read by outside routers; only the addresses of the edge routers are visible. This arrangement thus acts as a tunnel across the public Internet and establishes a private connection, secure from outside snooping or use.

Because of ease of use, low-cost hardware, and strong security, tunnels and the Internet are a combination that will see more use in the future. IPSec, VPN, and tunnels will become a major set of tools for users requiring secure network connections across public segments of networks.

Figure 10-7   Tunneling across a public network

Chapter Review

Chapter Summary

After reading this chapter and completing the exercises, you should understand the following about infrastructure security.

Network Components

- Networks are comprised of many different pieces of hardware including workstations, servers, hubs, bridges, routers, and wireless access points.

- Different security efforts have been applied to different aspects of the network, the two working together to provide a comprehensive security solution.

- Information storage media exist in a variety of forms and can contribute to overall security if some basic steps are taken to manage data storage on the storage media.

- Forms of external storage media range from small USB devices that are read/write capable, to CDs/DVDs which are read-only to external hard drives and tape drives, with storage capacities into the GBs.

Transmission Media

- Transmission media connecting network elements can be divided into two classes, guided and unguided.

- Guided media are characterized by physical connections between machines, as in fiber optic connections, twisted pair copper wire connections, and coaxial cable connections.

- Unguided media include wireless, IR, and satellite links and result in new security challenges since signals can be intercepted by unauthorized parties.

Security Design

- Physical security, the prevention of unauthorized access to actual equipment, transmission lines, and data is particularly challenging with wireless transmissions and the plethora of small data storage devices that can be easily connected to the network via workstations.

- The basis for the design of security into a network and its components comes from security policies and a strong understanding of the network resources and data that is being secured.

- Security zones and security topologies provide order with respect to the wide range of data availability and security concerns, including Internet, DMZ, intranet, and extranet functionality.

- The commonest topology when connecting an internal network to the Internet involves a set of two firewalls, with a DMZ area between them and no direct connections allowed across both firewalls.

Key Terms

Bridge *(219)*
DHCP (Dynamic Host Configuration Protocol) *(226)*
DMZ (demilitarized zone) *(243)*
DOCSIS (Data Over Cable Service Interface Specification) *(226)*
DSL (digital subscriber line) *(226)*
Extranet *(246)*
Hub *(219)*
Internet *(245)*
Intranet *(245)*
Modem (modulator-demodulator) *(226)*
NAT (Network Address Translation) *(248)*
Network interface card (NIC) *(218)*
Network operations center (NOC) *(230)*
Router *(221)*
Security topology *(243)*
Server *(217)*
SNMP (Simple Network Management Protocol) *(230)*
Switch *(219)*
VLAN *(246)*
Workstation *(216)*

Key Terms Quiz

1. A _____ is a piece of networking hardware designed to connect devices at the data link or OSI layer 2 level.

2. _____ is a protocol to standardize the elements necessary for network management functionality.

3. _____ is a method of packaging packets so that they can traverse a network in a secure, confidential manner.

4. The _____ is the hardware element used to connect a workstation or server to a network.

5. _____ is the use of two different IP addresses for one resource: one for internal use and the other for external use.

6. _____ is a method of using a single switch and dividing it into multiple broadcast domains and/or multiple network segments.

7. _____ is the term used to describe the portion of a network where a company's intranet is extended to include trusted customers/vendors/partners.

8. The area between the Internet and a company's internal trusted network is referred to as a _____.

9. _____ is a broadband method of Internet access over PSTN infrastructure.

10. _____ is a method of dynamically assigning IP addresses to devices from a pool of available IP addresses at system startup.

Multiple-Choice Quiz

1. Which of the following is an example of guided media?

   A. Satellite

   B. Microwave

   C. Fiber optic

   D. Infrared

2. UTP cables are terminated for Ethernet using what type of connector?

   A. A BNC plug

   B. An Ethernet connector

   C. A standard phone jack connector

   D. An RJ-45 connector

3. How many physical channels does a coaxial cable carry?

   A. Two

   B. Four

   C. One

   D. None of the above

4. Which of the following is associated with NAT?

   A. Routers and firewalls

   B. SNMP

   C. Switches

   D. Hubs

5. Which of the following does a VLAN utilize?

   A. Trunking

   B. Hubs

   C. Routers

   D. NAT

6. The purpose of twisting the wires in twisted-pair circuits is to…

   A. Increase physical strength for pulling

    B. Increase usable bandwidth

    C. Reduce crosstalk

    D. Allow easier tracing

7. NAT is used to…

    A. Provide for separation between public and private address spaces and addressing, thus masking internal IP addresses

    B. Simplify internal address architectures

    C. Prevent external connections to internal resources

    D. Increase internal bandwidth

8. The purpose of a DMZ in a network is to…

    A. Provide easy connections to the Internet without an interfering firewall

    B. Allow server farms to be divided into similar functioning entities

    C. Provide a place to lure and capture hackers

    D. Act as a buffer between untrusted and trusted networks

9. What security advantage does guided media have over unguided media?

    A. Higher bandwidth

    B. Control over physical access

    C. Stronger protocols

    D. Use of encryption

10. What is the highest bandwidth media?

    A. STP

    B. UTP

    C. Infrared

    D. Fiber optic

11. Which of the following is IDS associated with?

    A. IPSec

    B. Unauthorized access prevention

    C. VPN

    D. Unauthorized access detection

12. What are network operations centers used for?

    A. They are used as house application servers.

    B. They are used to remotely monitor network operations.

    C. They are used to centralize antivirus efforts.

    D. They are used to lower costs by utilizing higher capacity servers.

13. Microwave communications are limited by...

    A. Speed—the maximum for microwave circuits is 1Gbps

    B. Cost—microwaves take a lot of energy to generate

    C. Line of sight—microwaves don't propagate over the horizon

    D. Lack of standard operation protocols for widespread use

14. Antivirus measures include solutions aimed at...

    A. Application servers

    B. Hubs

    C. Bridges

    D. UTP connections

15. What is a primary security concern surrounding transmission channels?

    A. Accessibility by sniffers

    B. Bandwidth

    C. Error rate

    D. Protocol usage

Essay Quiz

1. Your company, ABC Plastics, is a firm that buys plastic resin from manufacturers and sells it to small users. To be competitive, your firm needs to conduct business via the Internet, and along these lines has decided to connect its internal network, consisting of an e-mail server, a file server, and a database server to the Internet. To facilitate B2B transaction processing, a web server and application server are being added to the network. The company understands the critical nature associated with this change and has initiated a project under your direction to design the new environment. Describe the security topology you would recommend in this instance. Include an explanation of where each server should be located in the network and the rationale behind the placement decision.

2. You are the new IT person in a small startup firm. The current network setup consists of several desktops and a few servers connected together. The company is not currently using antivirus software, and with the impending connection of the network to the Internet, you have convinced management of the need to take this action. Describe the deployment of an antivirus solution across the enterprise. What elements are needed at what points for complete coverage?

3. Describe the use of VLANs to improve network performance. How can they be used to increase security of unused, but wired, connections?

4. Compare and contrast different external storage media for workstations and servers. What are three advantages and three disadvantages of two different examples of external media?

5. Compare and contrast guided and unguided media. Give examples of each with their particular strengths and weaknesses.

Lab Projects

Lab Project 10.1

Design a network for a medium-sized company with connections to the Internet. Include provisions for a web server, external e-mail server, an extranet, and a secure internal database server. Show where firewalls would be placed and antivirus solutions anchored. Give example IP addresses demonstrating NAT.

Lab Project 10.2

Show how a VLAN can be configured to connect sales, engineering, and management on three floors of a building where offices are mixed on each floor. Include security aspects and guidance for expansion to include accounting at a later date.

Remote Access

Upon completion of this chapter, you will be able to:
- Describe various methods and protocols for remote access to networks
- Define and describe authentication, authorization, and accounting (AAA) protocols
- Describe various wireless protocols and the security implications in their use
- Define virtual private networks (VPNs) and describe their security aspects
- Define Internet Protocol Security (IPSec) and describe its use in securing communications

Remote access enables users outside a network to have network access and privileges as if they were inside the network. Being *outside* a network means that the user is using a machine that is not physically connected to the network in question and must therefore establish a connection through a remote means, such as dialing in, connecting via the Internet, or connecting through a wireless connection. A user accessing resources from the Internet through their ISP is also connecting remotely to the resources via the Internet.

To achieve these network connections, a variety of methods are used, varying depending upon network type, the hardware and software employed, and any security requirements. Microsoft Windows has a specific server component, the Remote Access Service, which is designed to facilitate the management of remote access connections through dial-up modems. Cisco has implemented a variety of remote access methods through its networking hardware and software. UNIX systems have built-in methods, as well.

The Remote Access Process

The process of connecting by remote access involves two elements: a temporary network connection and a series of protocols to negotiate privileges and commands. The temporary network connection can be via a dial-up service, the Internet, wireless access, or any other method of connecting to a network. Once the connection is made, the primary issue is identifying the user and establishing proper privileges for that user. This is done using a combination of protocols and the operating system on the host machine.

The three steps in the establishment of proper privileges are authentication, authorization, and accounting (AAA). *Authentication* is the matching of user-supplied credentials to previously stored credentials on a host machine, and it is usually done with an account name and password. Once the user is authenticated, the authorization step takes place. *Authorization* is the granting of specific permissions based on the privileges held by the account. Does the user have permission to use the network at this time, or is their use restricted? Does the user have access to specific applications, such as mail and FTP, or are some of these restricted? These checks are carried out as part of authorization, and in many cases, this is a function of the operating system in conjunction with its established security policies. A last function, *accounting*, is the collection of billing and other detail records. Network access is often a billable function, and a log of how much time, bandwidth, file transfer space, or other resources were used needs to be maintained. Other accounting functions include keeping detailed security logs to maintain an audit trail of tasks being performed. All of these standard functions are part of normal and necessary overhead in maintaining a computer system, and the protocols used in remote access provide the necessary input for these functions.

The primary role of the protocols is one of network connectivity, of which security plays an integral role. When defining security, the terms *confidentiality*, *integrity*, and *availability* are commonly used. All of these have a role in remote access, but availability is used specifically to mean authorized access. Confidentiality, integrity, and availability are major pieces of the foundation of security and they are well supported by properly implemented remote access protocols.

By using encryption, remote access protocols can establish a secure network connection, through which the operating system on the host machine can authenticate and authorize a user according to previously established privilege levels. The authorization phase can keep unauthorized users out, but after that, the encryption of the communications channel becomes very important in preventing others from breaking in on an authorized session and hijacking the authorized user's credentials. As more and more networks rely on the Internet for connecting remote users, the need for and importance of remote access protocols and security will continue to grow. When a user dials in to the Internet through their ISP, this is similarly a case of remote access—the user is establishing a connection to their ISP's network, and the same security issues apply. The issue of *authentication*, the matching of user-supplied credentials to previously stored credentials on a host machine, is usually done with an account name and password. Once the user is authenticated, then the authorization step takes place.

There are many different remote access protocols in use today, and more will be put into service in the future. Some are designed around specific methods of connection; others have specific functionality designed into them for special purposes. Some are private, some are based on common security mechanisms, and some have proprietary algorithms. This is important from a conceptual point of view, but in terms of functionality, these protocols are designed to do many of the same functions.

Identification

Identification is the process of ascribing a computer ID to a specific user, computer, or network device. User identification enables authentication and authorization, and these form the basis for accountability. This enables you to trace activities to individual users or computer processes so that they can be held responsible for their actions. Identification usually takes the form of logon ID or userID. A required characteristic of such IDs is that they must be unique. For accountability purposes they should not be shared, and for security purposes they should not be descriptive of job function.

Authentication

Authentication is the process of binding a specific ID to a specific computer connection. Historically, there have been three categories of things used to identify a user. Originally published by the U.S. Government in one of the Rainbow series of manuals on computer security, they are

- What users know (such as a password)
- What users have (such as tokens)
- What users are (this can involve static biometrics such as fingerprints)

Today, because of technological advances, a new category has emerged, patterned after subconscious behavior:

- What users do (this can involve dynamic biometrics such as a voice print)

These methods can be used individually or in combination. The most common method is using a userID and password. For greater security, you can add an element from a separate group, such as a smart card token, something a user has in their possession. A common example is a bankcard and PIN. Although a 4-digit PIN (something you know) does not offer much security, when coupled with possession of the correct bankcard (something you have), together they form a reasonable level of security.

Authorization

Authorization is the process of permitting or denying access to a specific resource. Once identity is confirmed via authentication, specific actions can be authorized or denied. Many types of authorization schemes are used, but the purpose is the same: determine whether a given user who has been identified has permissions for a particular object or resource being requested. This functionality is frequently part of the operating system and is transparent to users.

The separation of tasks, from identification to authentication to authorization, has several advantages. There are many methods to perform each task, and on many systems several methods are concurrently present for each task. Separation of these tasks into individual elements allows combinations of implementations to all work together.

Authentication is a process of verifying properly presented credentials; the source of the credentials is not a relevant item. You can authenticate users and computer processes

(ID carried by script); the concept of authentication and implementation is identical. Different forms of authorization can be implemented, based on the resource being requested, such as database access or router admin access.

Any system or resource, be it hardware (router, workstation) or a software component (database system) that requires authorization can use its own authorization method once authentication for a connection has been resolved for it. This makes for efficient and consistent application of these principles.

Telnet

Telnet is the standard terminal-emulation protocol within the TCP/IP protocol series, and it is defined in RFC 854. Telnet allows users to log in remotely and access resources as if the user had a local terminal connection. Telnet is an old protocol and has little security. Information is passed in the clear over the TCP/IP connection, including account names and passwords.

Telnet makes its connection using TCP port 23. (A list of remote access networking port assignments is provided in Table 11-2 in the Connection Summary section.) As Telnet is implemented on most products using TCP/IP, it is important to control access to Telnet on machines and routers when setting them up. Failure to control access by using firewalls, access lists, and other security methods, or even by disabling the telnet daemon, is equivalent to leaving an open door for unauthorized users on a system.

SSH

Secure Shell (SSH) is a protocol series designed to facilitate secure network functions across an insecure network. SSH provides direct support for secure remote login, secure file transfer, and secure forwarding of TCP/IP and X Window System traffic.

SSH has its origins all the way back in the beginning of the UNIX operating system. An original component of UNIX was telnet, which allowed users to connect between systems. Telnet, although still in existence and in use today, had some drawbacks, such as passing information in the clear across the network, making it easy for anyone to obtain sensitive information, such as userIDs and passwords by sniffing. Some enterprising Berkeley students subsequently developed the **r-** commands, such as **rlogin**, to permit access based on the user and source system, as opposed to passing passwords. This was not perfect either, however, for when a login was required, it was still passed in the clear. This led to the development of Secure Shell (SSH), a protocol series designed to eliminate all of the insecurities associated with telnet, **r-** commands, and other means of remote access.

SSH opens a secure transport between machines by using an SSH daemon on each end. These daemons initiate contact over TCP port 22 and then communicate over higher ports in a secure mode. One of the strengths of SSH is its support for many different encryption protocols. SSH 1.0 started with RSA algorithms, but at the time they were still under patent, and this led to SSH 2.0 with extended support for 3DES and other encryption methods. Today, SSH can be used with a wide range of encryption protocols, including RSA, 3DES, Blowfish, IDEA, CAST128, AES256, and others.

The SSH protocol has facilities to automatically encrypt data, provide authentication, and compress data in transit. It can support strong encryption, cryptographic host authentication, and integrity protection. The authentication services are host-based and not user-based. If user authentication is desired in a system, it must be done separately at a higher level in the OSI model. The protocol is designed to be flexible and simple and it is specifically designed to minimize the number of round-trips between systems. The key exchange, public key, symmetric key, message authentication, and hash algorithms are all negotiated at connection time. Individual data-packet integrity is assured through the use of a message authentication code that is computed from a shared secret, the contents of the packet, and the packet sequence number.

The SSH protocol consists of three major components:

- **Transport layer protocol**   Provides server authentication, confidentiality, integrity, and compression.
- **User authentication protocol**   Authenticates the client to the server.
- **Connection protocol**   Provides multiplexing of the encrypted tunnel into several logical channels.

SSH is very popular in the UNIX environment, and it is actively used as a method of establishing virtual private networks (VPNs) across public networks. As all communications between the two machines are encrypted at the OSI application layer by the two SSH daemons, this leads to the ability to build very secure solutions, and even solutions that defy the ability of outside services to monitor. As SSH is a standard protocol series with connection parameters established via TCP port 22, different vendors can build differing solutions that still can interoperate. As such, if SSH is enabled on a UNIX platform, it is a built-in method of establishing secure communications with that system.

Although Windows server implementations of SSH exist, this has not been a popular protocol in the Windows environment from a server perspective. The development of a wide array of commercial SSH clients for the Windows platform indicates the marketplace strength of interconnection from desktop PCs to UNIX-based servers utilizing this protocol.

L2TP and PPTP

Layer Two Tunneling Protocol (L2TP) and **Point-to-Point Tunneling Protocol** (PPTP) are both OSI layer two tunneling protocols, and PPTP is probably the most common implementation of tunneling today. Tunneling is the encapsulation of one packet within another, which allows you to hide the original packet from view, or to change the nature of the network transport. This can be done for both security and practical reasons.

From a practical perspective, assume that you are using the TCP/IP protocol to communicate between two machines. Your message may pass over an Asynchronous Transfer Mode (ATM) network as it moves from source to destination. As the ATM protocol can neither read nor understand TCP/IP packets, something must be done to make them passable. By taking a packet and encapsulating it as the payload in a separate protocol, so it can be carried across a section of a network, a tunnel is created. At each end of the tunnel, called the tunnel endpoints, the payload packet is read and understood. As it goes into the tunnel, you can envision your packet being placed in an envelope with the address of the appropriate tunnel endpoint on the envelope. When the envelope arrives at the tunnel endpoint, the original message (the tunnel packet's payload) is re-created, read, and sent to its appropriate next stop. The material being tunneled is only read and understood at the tunnel endpoints; it is not relevant to intermediate tunnel points because it is only a payload.

If you encrypt the original packet, intermediate points in the tunneled journey cannot read the original packet, thus ensuring message security. Additional use of cryptological tools can provide authenticity information and other protections; this will be described in the "IPSec" section of this chapter.

Point-to-Point Protocol (PPP) is a widely used protocol for establishing dial-in connections over serial lines or ISDN services. PPP has several authentication mechanisms, including Password Authentication Protocol (PAP), **Challenge Handshake Authentication Protocol** (CHAP), and the Extensible Authentication Protocol (EAP). These protocols are used to authenticate the peer device, not a user of the system. PPP is a standardized Internet encapsulation of IP traffic over point-to-point links, such as serial lines. The authentication process is performed only when the link is established.

PPTP

Microsoft led a consortium of networking companies to extend the PPP protocol to enable the creation of virtual private networks (VPNs). The result was the PPTP protocol. PPTP is a network protocol that enables the secure transfer of data from a remote PC to a server by creating a VPN across a TCP/IP network. This remote network connection can also span a public switched telephone network (PSTN) and is thus an economical way of connecting remote dial-in users to a corporate data network. The incorporation of the PPTP protocol into the Microsoft Windows product line provides a built-in secure method of remote connection using the operating system, and this has given PPTP a large marketplace footprint.

For most PPTP implementations, there are three computers involved: the PPTP client, the network access server (NAS), and a PPTP server, as shown in Figure 11-1. The connection between the remote client and the network is established in stages, as illustrated in Figure 11-2. First the client makes a PPP connection to a NAS, typically an ISP.

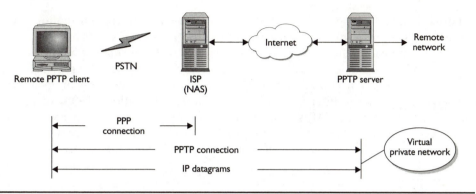

Figure 11-1   PPTP communication diagram

Once the PPP connection is established, a second connection is made over the PPP connection to the PPTP server. This second connection creates the VPN connection between the remote client and the PPTP server. This connection acts as a tunnel for future data transfers.

As mentioned earlier in this chapter, tunneling is the process of sending packets as data within other packets across a section of a network. This encapsulation enables a network to carry a packet type that it cannot ordinarily route, and it also provides the opportunity to secure the contents of the first packet through encryption. PPTP establishes

Figure 11-2   PPTP message encapsulation during transmission

a tunnel from the remote PPTP client to the PPTP server and enables encryption within this tunnel. This provides a secure method of transport. To do this and still enable routing, an intermediate addressing scheme, Generic Routing Encapsulation (GRE), is used.

To establish the connection, PPTP uses communications across TCP port 1723 (see Table 11-2 in the Connection Summary section), so this port must remain open across the network firewalls for PPTP to be initiated. Although PPTP allows the use of any PPP authentication scheme, CHAP is used when encryption is specified to provide an appropriate level of security. For the encryption methodology, Microsoft chose the RSA RC4 cipher, either with a 40-bit or 128-bit session key length, and this is operating-system driven.

L2TP

L2TP is also an Internet standard and came from the Layer Two Forwarding (L2F) protocol, a Cisco initiative designed to address issues with PPTP. Whereas PPTP is designed around PPP and IP networks, L2F, and hence L2TP, is designed for use across all kinds of networks including ATM and frame relay. Additionally, where PPTP is designed to be implemented in software at the client device, L2TP was conceived as a hardware implementation using a router or a special purpose appliance.

L2TP works in much the same way as PPTP, but it opens several items up for expansion. For instance, in L2TP, routers can be enabled to concentrate VPN traffic over higher bandwidth lines, creating hierarchical networks of VPN traffic that can be more efficiently managed across an enterprise. L2TP also has the ability to use IPSec and DES as encryption protocols, providing a higher level of data security. L2TP is also designed to work with established AAA services, such as RADIUS and TACACS+ (explained in the "RADIUS" and "TACACS+" sections of this chapter) to aid in user authentication, authorization, and accounting.

L2TP is established via User Datagram Protocol (UDP) port 1701, so this is an essential port to leave open across firewalls supporting L2TP traffic. This port is registered with the Internet Assigned Numbers Authority (IANA), as is 1723 for PPTP (see Table 11-2 in the Connection Summary section). Microsoft supports L2TP in Windows 2000 and above, but because of the computing power required, most implementations will use specialized hardware (such as a Cisco router).

IEEE 802.11

The IEEE 802.11 protocol series covers the use of microwave communications media in networks, and 802.16 is the protocol series for wireless metropolitan area networks (MANs). 802.11 is designed for wireless LANs, and the remainder of this discussion will focus on the 802.11 series, because it has become widespread in use.

This is not a single protocol, but an entire series of them, with 802.11b, 802.11a, and 802.11g being common wireless protocols that allow wireless connectivity to a

LAN and ad hoc peer-to-peer wireless networking. Products for these protocols have become very common, and they are available from a variety of vendors, often for under $100. These devices are beginning to find their use in corporate networks, metropolitan hot spots, and even home networks. The advantage of wireless communication is simple to understand—the requirement for a physical wire and various boxes is eliminated. This provides tremendous ease of setup for a network engineer from a cabling point of view, because there are no cables to connect. This pays off again if a corporation moves employees between desks, because again there are no wires to move when moving PCs. For laptop users, this means machines and devices can be mobile and remain connected to the network.

The lack of a physical cable does not change security requirements—the wireless solution has to face a tougher standard. Offering wireless connectivity is equivalent to giving an outsider a network drop, and it must be assumed that an intruder is connected at all times.

The actual communication method for 802.11 devices is via either direct-sequence spread spectrum (DSSS) or frequency-hopping spread spectrum (FHSS). These methods employ a range of frequencies to mitigate noise and propagation problems. These methods also prevent casual eavesdropping, as the frequency on which the data moves is always moving in time. This only affects casual eavesdropping, though, because a wireless access device is specifically designed to locate and track a signal from an access point. Frequency hopping has very little effect, from a security point of view.

For security purposes, the 802.11 standards contain an optional protocol called Wired Equivalent Privacy (WEP). This is an encryption method that is optional, so not all vendors support this option, nor do all network administrators enable this option. The default WEP method is a 40-bit form of the RC4 stream-cipher encryption algorithm, although many vendors offer a 128-bit version, as well. The WEP method uses a static shared secret key between devices, with a variable initialization vector.

The particular implementation of the initialization vector in WEP has been shown to have a fault that can allow an outsider to break the key in a 40-bit system after a few hours of studying traffic on a Pentium 4 class machine. The problem lies not with the RC4 algorithm, but with the initialization vector, which is repeated after a certain amount of time, and the way RC4 is used within WEP. Someone watching the pattern can find the repeated sequences and then break the shared secret key. This is one of the factors leading to the adoption of a new WEP method that does not cycle keys in the same manner as the current version. The weak initialization vector problem is not significantly improved upon by using a longer key. Even with a 128-bit key, the initialization vector stays the same length, and initialization vector collisions will therefore occur in the same relatively short period of time.

The current WEP method requires all clients that use the same access point to use the same key for session initiation. This introduces a key management issue and also adds concerns about eavesdropping between clients on the same access point. For this reason, many installations of wireless LANs also use other security protocols, such as layer three

Table 11-1	Protocol	Frequency	Maximum Network Speed
Comparison of 802.11 Protocol Parameters	802.11a	5 GHz	54 Mbps
	802.11b	2.4 GHz	11 Mbps
	802.11g	2.4 GHz	54 Mbps

tunneling, as in VPNs. Also, newer wireless access points have functionality built in to use access control lists against MAC addresses to filter LAN connections, but this adds significant management overhead in larger installations.

From a hardware point of view, a wireless network consists of two pieces: a wireless access point connected to a network, and a wireless network interface card on a client machine. The access point can be shared among multiple users, and users can move between access points. Each wireless access point has a usable range of up to about 200 feet, depending upon the antenna configuration, the building's configuration and interference sources. Transmission speed is dependent upon the range, with distant users running at slower speeds. The actual connection speed depends upon the protocol and signal strength, with Table 11-1 giving the standard values.

VPN

Virtual private networks (VPNs) are secure "virtual" networks built on top of physical networks. Their security lies in the encryption of packet contents between the endpoints that define the VPN network. The physical network upon which a VPN is built is typically a public network, such as the Internet. Because the packet contents between VPN endpoints are encrypted, to an outside observer on the public network, the communication is secure, and depending on how the VPN is set up, security may even extend to the two communicating parties machines.

Virtual private networking is not a protocol per se, but rather a method of using protocols to achieve a specific objective, secure communications, as shown in Figure 11-3. A user wishing to have a secure communication channel with a server across a public

Figure 11-3   VPN service over an Internet connection

network can set up two intermediary devices, VPN endpoints, to accomplish this task. The user can communicate with his endpoint, and the server can communicate with its endpoint. The two endpoints then communicate across the public network. VPN endpoints can be software solutions, routers, or specific servers set up for specific functionality. This implies that VPN services are set up in advance and are not something negotiated on the fly.

A typical use of VPN services is a user accessing a corporate data network from a home PC across the Internet. The employee will install VPN software from work on their home PC. This software is already configured to communicate with the corporate network's VPN endpoint; it knows the location, the protocols that will be used, and so on. When the home user wishes to connect to the corporate network, they connect to the Internet and then start the VPN software. The user can then log in to the corporate network by using an appropriate authentication and authorization methodology. The sole purpose of the VPN connection is to provide a private connection between the machines. Identification, authorization, and all other standard functions are done with the standard mechanisms for the established system.

VPNs can use many different protocols to offer a secure method of communicating between endpoints. Common methods of encryption on VPNs include PPTP, IPSec, SSH, and L2TP, all of which are discussed in this chapter. The key is that both endpoints know the protocol and share a secret. All of this necessary information is established when the VPN is set up. At the time of use, the VPN only acts as a private tunnel between the two points, and does not constitute a complete security solution.

IPSec

IPSec, short for IP Security, is a set of protocols developed by the Internet Engineering Task Force (IETF) to securely exchange packets at the network layer of the OSI model (RFC 2401–2412). Although these protocols only work in conjunction with IP networks, once an IPSec connection is established, it is possible to tunnel across other networks at lower levels of the OSI model. The set of security services provided by IPSec occurs at the network layer of the OSI model, so higher layer protocols, such as TCP, UDP, ICMP, BGP, and the like, are unaffected by the implementation of IPSec services.

The IPSec protocol series has a sweeping array of services it is designed to provide, including, but not limited to, access control, connectionless integrity, traffic-flow confidentiality, rejection of replayed packets, data security (encryption), and data-origin authentication. IPSec has two defined methods—transport and tunneling—and these two methods provide different levels of security. IPSec also has three modes of connection: host to server, server to server, and host to host.

The transport method encrypts only the data portion of a packet, thus enabling an outsider to see source and destination IP addresses. This protects the data being transmitted, but allows knowledge of the transmission itself. Protection of the data portion of a packet is referred to as *content protection*.

Tunneling provides encryption of source and destination IP addresses, as well as of the data itself. This provides the greatest security, but it can only be done between IPSec servers (or routers) because the final destination needs to be known for delivery. Protection of the header information is known as *context protection*.

It is possible to use both methods at the same time, such as using transport within one's own network to reach an IPSec server, which then tunnels to the target server's network, connecting to an IPSec server there, and then using the transport method from the target network's IPSec server to the target host.

IPSec Configurations

There are four basic configurations for machine-to-machine connections using IPSec. The simplest is a host-to-host connection between two machines, as shown in Figure 11-4. In this case, the Internet is not a part of the security association between the machines. A security association is a formal manner of describing the necessary and sufficient portions of the IPSec protocol series to achieve a specific level of protection. As many options exist, both communicating parties must agree on the use of the protocols that are available, and this agreement is referred to as a security association.

The next level of implementation places two security devices in the stream, relieving the hosts of the calculation and encapsulation duties. These two gateways have a security association between them, but the network is assumed to be secure from each machine to its gateway, and no IPSec is performed in this hop. Figure 11-5 shows the two gateways with a tunnel across the Internet, although either tunnel or transport mode may be actually used.

A third case combines the first two. A separate security association exists between the gateway devices, but additionally, a security association exists between hosts. This could be considered a tunnel inside a tunnel, as shown in Figure 11-6.

A common situation is where a remote user connects through the Internet to an organization's network. The network has a security gateway through which it secures traffic to and from its servers and authorized users. In this case, illustrated in Figure 11-7, the user establishes a security association with the security gateway and then a separate association with the desired server, if required. This can be done using software on a remote laptop and hardware at the organization's network.

Windows has the ability to act as an IPSec server, as do routers and other servers. The primary issue is CPU usage, and where the computing power should be implanted. This consideration has led to the rise of IPSec appliances, hardware devices that perform the IPSec function specifically for a series of communications. Depending on the number of connections, network bandwidth, and so on, these devices can run as little as $150 (for small office or home office use) or as much as tens of thousands of dollars for large implementations.

IPSec Security

IPSec uses two protocols to provide traffic security:

- Authentication Header (AH)
- Encapsulating Security Payload (ESP)

Figure 11-4   Host-to-host IPSec connection

Figure 11-5   IPSec between machines using gateway security devices

Figure 11-6   Separate IPSec tunnels—gateway to gateway and host to host

Figure 11-7   Remote connection across the Internet using IPSec

For key management and exchange, three protocols exist:

* **Internet Security Association** and Key Management Protocol (ISAKMP)
* Oakley
* Secure Key Exchange Mechanism for Internet (SKEMI)

These key management protocols can be collectively referred to as Internet Key Management Protocol (IKMP) or **Internet Key Exchange** (IKE).

IPSec does not define specific security algorithms, nor does it require specific methods of implementation. IPSec is an open framework that allows vendors to implement existing industry-standard algorithms suited for specific tasks. This flexibility is key in IPSec's ability to offer a wide range of security functions. IPSec allows several security technologies to be combined into a comprehensive solution for network-based confidentiality, integrity, and authentication. IPSec uses

* Diffie-Hellman key exchange between peers on a public network
* Public key signing of Diffie-Hellman key exchanges to guarantee identity and avoid man-in-the-middle attacks
* Bulk encryption algorithms, such as IDEA and 3DES, for encrypting data
* Keyed hash algorithms, such as HMAC, and traditional hash algorithms, such as MD5 and SHA-1, for packet-level authentication
* Digital certificates to act as digital ID cards between parties

To provide traffic security, two header extensions have been defined for IP datagrams. The **Authentication Header** (AH), when added to an IP datagram, ensures the integrity of the data and also the authenticity of the data's origin. By protecting the non-changing elements in the IP header, the AH protects the IP address, which enables data-origin authentication. The **Encapsulating Security Payload** (ESP) provides security services for the higher-level protocol portion of the packet only, not the IP header.

AH and ESP can be used separately or in combination, depending on the level and types of security desired. Both also work with the transport and tunnel modes of IPSec protocols. In transport mode, the two communication endpoints are providing security primarily for the upper layer protocols. The cryptographic endpoints, where encryption and decryption occurs, are located at the source and destination of the communication channel. For AH in transport mode, the original IP header is exposed, but its contents are protected via the AH block in the packet, as illustrated in Figure 11-8. For ESP in transport mode, the data contents are protected by encryption, as illustrated in Figure 11-9.

Tunneling, as described previously, is a means of encapsulating packets inside a protocol that is understood only at the entry and exit points of the tunnel. This provides security during transport in the tunnel, because outside observers cannot decipher packet contents, or even the identity of the communicating parties. IPSec has a tunnel mode that can be used from server to server across a public network. Although

Figure 11-8
IPSec use of
AH in transport
mode

Authentication Header in Transport Mode

Figure 11-8
IPSec use of
AH in transport
mode

the tunnel endpoints are referred to as servers, these devices can be routers, appliances, or servers. In tunnel mode, the tunnel endpoints merely encapsulate the entire packet with new IP headers to indicate the endpoints, and they encrypt the contents of this new packet. The true source and destination information is contained in the inner IP header, which is encrypted in the tunnel. The outer IP header contains the addresses of the endpoints of the tunnel.

As described earlier, AH and ESP can be employed in tunnel mode. When AH is employed in tunnel mode, portions of the outer IP header are given the same header protection that occurs in transport mode, with the entire inner packet receiving protection. This is illustrated in Figure 11-10. ESP affords the same encryption protection to the contents of the tunneled packet, which is the entire packet from the initial sender, as illustrated in Figure 11-11. Together, in tunnel mode, AH and ESP can provide complete protection across the packet, as shown in Figure 11-12. The specific combination of AH and ESP is referred to as a security association in IPSec.

In IP version 4 (IPv4), IPSec is an add-on, and its acceptance is vendor driven. It is not a part of the original IP protocol—one of the short-sighted design flaws of the original IP protocol. In the next version of the IP protocol suite, IPv6, IPSec is integrated into the IP protocol and is native on all packets. Its use is still optional, but its inclusion in the protocol suite will guarantee interoperability across vendor solutions when they are compliant with IPv6 standards. This is one of the major reasons firms will move to IPv6; the increased security will become a driving force behind the adoption of the new protocol series.

Figure 11-9
IPSec use of
ESP in transport
mode

Encapsulating Security Payload in Transport Mode

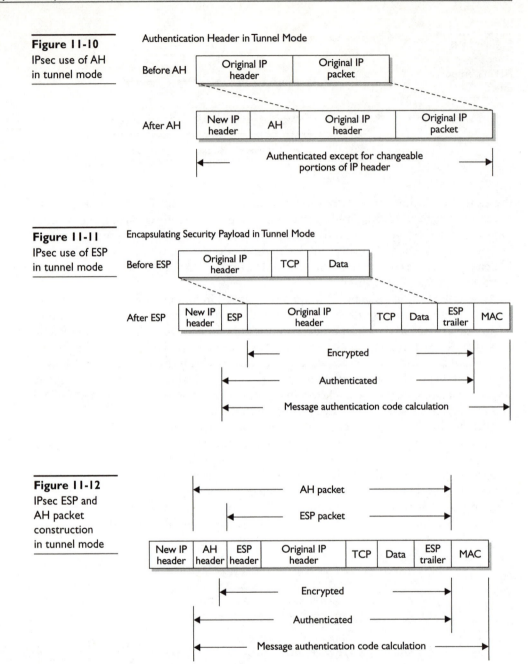

Figure 11-10 IPsec use of AH in tunnel mode

Authentication Header in Tunnel Mode

Before AH

| Original IP header | Original IP packet |

After AH

| New IP header | AH | Original IP header | Original IP packet |

Authenticated except for changeable portions of IP header

Figure 11-11 IPsec use of ESP in tunnel mode

Encapsulating Security Payload in Tunnel Mode

Before ESP

| Original IP header | TCP | Data |

After ESP

| New IP header | ESP | Original IP header | TCP | Data | ESP trailer | MAC |

Encrypted

Authenticated

Message authentication code calculation

Figure 11-12 IPsec ESP and AH packet construction in tunnel mode

AH packet

ESP packet

| New IP header | AH header | ESP header | Original IP header | TCP | Data | ESP trailer | MAC |

Encrypted

Authenticated

Message authentication code calculation

IPSec uses cryptographic keys in its security process and has both manual and automatic distribution of keys as part of the protocol series. Manual key distribution is included, but is only practical in small static environments and does not scale to enterprise-level implementations. The default method of key management is automated and is typically referred to as IKE (Internet Key Exchange). IKE authenticates each peer involved in IPSec and negotiates the security policy, including the exchange of session keys. IKE creates a secure tunnel between peers and then negotiates the security association for IPSec across this channel. This is done in two phases: the first develops the channel, and the second the security association.

IEEE 802.1x

The **IEEE 802.1x** standard is for a protocol to support communications between a user and an authorization device, such as an edge router. This protocol describes methods to authenticate a user prior to granting access to an authentication server, such as a RADIUS server. 802.1x acts through an intermediate device, such as an edge switch, enabling ports to carry normal traffic if the connection is properly authenticated. This prevents unauthorized clients from accessing the publicly available ports on a switch, keeping unauthorized users out of a LAN. Until a client has successfully authenticated itself to the device, only Extensible Authentication Protocol over LAN (EAPOL) traffic is passed by the switch.

EAPOL is an encapsulated method of passing EAP messages over 802 frames. EAP is a general protocol that can support multiple methods of authentication, including one-time passwords, Kerberos, public keys, and security device methods such as smart cards. Once a client successfully authenticates itself to the 802.1x device, the switch opens ports for normal traffic. At this point, the client can communicate with the system's AAA method, such as a RADIUS server, and authenticate itself to the network.

RADIUS

Remote Authentication Dial-In User Service (RADIUS) is a protocol that was developed originally by Livingston Enterprises (acquired by Lucent) as an AAA protocol. It was submitted to the IETF as a series of RFCs: RFC 2058 (RADIUS specification), RFC 2059 (RADIUS accounting standard), and updated RFCs 2865–2869 are now standard protocols. The IETF AAA Working Group has proposed extensions to RADIUS (RFC 2882) and a replacement protocol DIAMETER (Internet Draft DIAMETER Base Protocol).

RADIUS is designed as a connectionless protocol utilizing UDP as its transport level protocol. Connection type issues, such as timeouts, are handled by the RADIUS application instead of the transport layer. RADIUS utilizes UDP ports 1812 for authentication and authorization and 1813 for accounting functions (see Table 11-2 in the Connection Summary section).

RADIUS is a client/server protocol. The RADIUS client is typically a NAS, and the RADIUS server is a process or daemon running on a UNIX or Windows NT machine. This is important to note, for if the user's machine (the PC) is not the RADIUS client (the NAS), then communications between the PC and the NAS are typically not encrypted and are passed in the clear. Communications between a RADIUS client and RADIUS server are encrypted using a shared secret that is manually configured into each entity and not shared over a connection. Hence, communications between a RADIUS client (typically a NAS) and a RADIUS server are secure, but the communications between a user (typically a PC) and the RADIUS client are subject to compromise.

RADIUS Authentication

The RADIUS protocol is designed to allow a RADIUS server to support a wide variety of methods to authenticate a user. When the server is given a username and password, it can support PPP, PAP, CHAP, UNIX login, and other mechanisms, depending on what was established when the server was set up. A user login authentication consists of a query (Access-Request) from the RADIUS client and a corresponding response (Access-Accept or Access-Reject) from the RADIUS server, as you will see in Figure 11-13.

The Access-Request message contains the username, encrypted password, NAS IP address, and port. The message also contains information concerning the type of session the user wishes to initiate. Once the RADIUS server receives this information, it searches its database for a match on the username. If a match is not found, either a default profile is loaded or an Access-Reject reply is sent. If the entry is found, or the default profile is used, the next phase involves authorization, for in RADIUS, these steps are performed in sequence.

RADIUS Authorization

In the RADIUS protocol, the authentication and authorization steps are performed together in response to a single Access-Request message, although they are sequential steps (see Figure 11-13). Once an identity has been established, either known or default, the authorization process determines what parameters are returned to the client. Typical authorization parameters include the service type allowed (shell or framed), the protocols allowed, the IP address to assign to the user (static or dynamic), the access list to apply or static route to place in the NAS routing table. These parameters are all defined in the configuration information on the RADIUS client and server during setup. Using this information, the RADIUS server returns an Access-Accept message with these parameters to the RADIUS client.

RADIUS Accounting

The RADIUS accounting function is performed independently of RADIUS authentication and authorization. The accounting function uses a separate UDP port, 1813 (see Table 11-2 in the Connection Summary section). The primary functionality of RADIUS accounting was established to support Internet service providers in their user account-

Figure 11-13 RADIUS communication sequence

ing, and it supports typical accounting functions for time billing and security logging. The RADIUS accounting functions are designed to allow data to be transmitted at the beginning and end of a session, and it can indicate resource utilization, such as time, bandwidth, and so on.

When RADIUS was first designed in the mid-1990s, the role of ISP NASs was relatively simple. Allowing and denying access to a network and timing usage were the major concerns. Today, the Internet and its access methods have changed dramatically, and so have the AAA requirements. As individual firms extended RADIUS to meet these needs, interoperability became an issue, and a new AAA protocol called DIAMETER, designed to address these issues in a comprehensive fashion, has been proposed and is entering the final stages of the Internet Draft/RFC process.

DIAMETER

DIAMETER is a proposed name for the new AAA protocol suite, designated by the IETF to replace the aging RADIUS protocol. DIAMETER operates in much the same way as RADIUS, in a client/server configuration, but it improves upon RADIUS, resolving discovered weaknesses. DIAMETER is a TCP-based service and has more extensive capabilities in authentication, authorization, and accounting. DIAMETER is also designed for all types of remote access, not just modem pools. As more and more users adopt broadband and other connection methods, these newer services require more options to properly determine permissible usage and to account for and log the usage. DIAMETER is designed with these needs in mind.

DIAMETER also has an improved method of encrypting message exchanges to prohibit replay and man-in-the-middle attacks. Taken all together, DIAMETER, with its enhanced functionality and security, built on the proven design of the old RADIUS standard, will prove to be the replacement of RADIUS in the next few years.

TACACS+

The **Terminal Access Controller Access Control System+** (TACACS+) protocol is the current generation of the TACACS family. Originally, TACACS was developed by BBN Planet Corporation for MILNET, an early military network, but it has been enhanced by Cisco and expanded twice. The original BBN TACACS system provided a combination process of authentication and authorization. Cisco extended this to Extended Terminal Access Controller Access Control System (XTACACS), which provided for separate authentication, authorization, and accounting processes. The current generation, TACACS+, has extended attribute control and accounting processes.

One of the fundamental design aspects is the separation of authentication, authorization, and accounting in this protocol. Although there is a straightforward lineage of these protocols from the original TACACS, TACACS+ is a major revision and is not backward compatible with previous versions of the protocol series.

TACACS+ uses TCP as its transport protocol, typically operating over TCP port 49. This port is used for the login process and is reserved in the assigned numbers RFC, RFC 3232, manifested in a database from IANA. In the IANA specification, both UDP and TCP port 49 are reserved for TACACS login host protocol (see Table 11-2 in the Connection Summary section).

TACACS+ is a client/server protocol, with the client typically being a NAS and the server being a daemon process on a UNIX, Linux, or Windows NT server. This is important to note, for if the user's machine (usually a PC) is not the client (usually a NAS), then communications between PC and NAS are typically not encrypted and are passed in the clear. Communications between a TACACS+ client and TACACS+ server are encrypted using a shared secret that is manually configured into each entity and is not shared over a connection. Hence, communications between a TACACS+ client (typically a NAS) and a TACACS+ server are secure, but the communications between a user (typically a PC) and the TACACS+ client are subject to compromise.

TACACS+ Authentication

TACACS+ allows for arbitrary length and content in the authentication exchange sequence, enabling many different authentication mechanisms to be used with TACACS+ clients. Authentication is optional and is determined as a site-configurable option. When authentication is used, common forms include PPP PAP, PPP CHAP, PPP EAP, token cards, and Kerberos. The authentication process is performed using three different packet types: START, CONTINUE, and REPLY. START and CONTINUE packets originate from the client and are directed to the TACACS+ server. The REPLY packet is used to communicate from the TACACS+ server to the client.

The authentication process is illustrated in Figure 11-14, and it begins with a START message from the client to the server. This message may be in response to an initiation from a PC connected to the TACACS+ client. The START message describes the type of authentication being requested (simple plaintext password, PAP, CHAP, etc.). This START message may also contain additional authentication data, such as username and password. A START message is also sent as a response to a restart request from the server in a REPLY message. A START message always has its sequence number set to 1.

When a TACACS+ server receives a START message, it sends a REPLY message. This REPLY message will indicate whether the authentication is complete or needs to be continued. If the process needs to be continued, the REPLY message also specifies what additional information is needed. The response from a client to a REPLY message requesting additional data is a CONTINUE message. This process continues until the server has all the information needed, and the authentication process concludes with a success or failure.

TACACS+ Authorization

Authorization is defined as the action associated with determining permission associated with a user action. This generally occurs after authentication, as shown in Figure 11-14, but this is not a firm requirement. A default state of "unknown user" exists before a user is authenticated, and permissions can be determined for an unknown user. As with authentication, authorization is an optional process and may or may not be part of a site- specific operation. When it is used in conjunction with authentication, the authorization process follows the authentication process and uses the confirmed user identity as input in the decision process.

The authorization process is performed using two message types: REQUEST and RESPONSE. The authorization process is performed using an authorization session consisting of a single pair of REQUEST and RESPONSE messages. The client issues an authorization REQUEST message containing a fixed set of fields that enumerate the authenticity of the user or process requesting permission and a variable set of fields enumerating the services or options for which authorization is being requested.

Figure 11-14 TACACS+ communication sequence

The RESPONSE message in TACACS+ is not a simple yes or no; it may also include qualifying information, such as a user time limit or IP restrictions. These limitations have important uses, such as enforcing time limits on shell access, or IP access list restrictions for specific user accounts.

TACACS+ Accounting

As with the two previous services, accounting is also an optional function of TACACS+. When utilized, it typically follows the other services. Accounting in TACACS+ is defined as the process of recording what a user or process has done. Accounting can serve two important purposes:

- It may be used to account for services being utilized, possibly for billing purposes.
- It may be used for generating security audit trails.

TACACS+ accounting records contain several pieces of information to support these tasks. The accounting process has the information revealed in the authorization and authentication processes, so it can record specific requests by user or process. To support this functionality, TACACS+ has three types of accounting records: START, STOP, and UPDATE. Note that these are record types, not message types as earlier discussed.

START records indicate the time and user or process that began an authorized process. STOP records enumerate the same information concerning the stop times for specific actions. UPDATE records act as intermediary notices that a particular task is still being performed. Together these three message types allow the creation of records that delineate the activity of a user or process on a system.

Vulnerabilities

The primary vulnerability associated with all of these methods of remote access is the passing of critical data in the clear. Plaintext passing of passwords provides no security if the password is sniffed, and sniffers are easy to use on a network. Even plaintext passing of usernames gives away data that can be correlated and possibly used. This is one of the fundamental flaws with telnet, and is why SSH was developed. This is also one of the flaws with RADIUS and TACACS+, as they have a segment unprotected. There are methods for overcoming these limitations, although they require discipline and understanding in setting up a system.

The strength of the encryption algorithm is also a concern. Should a specific algorithm or method prove to be vulnerable (such as WEP), services that rely solely on it are also vulnerable. To get around this dependency, many of the protocols allow numerous encryption methods, so that should one prove vulnerable, a shift to another restores security.

As with any software implementation, there always exists the possibility that a bug opens the system to attack. Bugs have been corrected in most software packages to close holes that left systems vulnerable, and remote access software is no exception. This is not a Microsoft-only phenomenon, as one might believe from the popular press. Critical flaws have been found in almost every product, from open system implementations such as OpenSSH to proprietary systems such as Cisco's IOS. The important issue is not the presence of software bugs, for as software continues to become more complex, this is an unavoidable issue. The true key is vendor responsiveness to fixing the bugs once they are discovered, and the major players, such as Cisco and Microsoft, have been very responsive in this area.

Connection Summary

There are many methods for achieving security under remote access conditions, and the number is growing as new protocols are developed to meet the ever-increasing use of remote access. From the beginnings of Telnet, to IPv6 with built-in IPSec, the options are many, but the task is basically the same. Perform the functions of authentication, authorization, and accounting while providing message and data security from outside intervention. (See Table 11-2.)

Some of the remote access solutions have a hardware component (such as L2F and RADIUS), some have software (SSH and PPTP), and some can have both (VPN and IPSec), depending upon the vendor's implementation and system requirements. The choice of a remote access solution will depend upon several factors, including security requirements, the type of network, the type of clients, required access methods, scalability, existing authentication mechanisms, and cost. Each system has its strengths and weaknesses, and when properly employed, each can be used effectively within its own limitations. There is no best solution at the present time, but as the Internet advances and IPv6 is adopted, IPSec will move up the list into a prime spot and provide a significant number of these required services as part of the TCP/IPv6 protocol suite.

TCP Port Number	UDP Port Number	Keyword	Protocol
20		FTP-Data	File Transfer (Default Data)
21		FTP	File Transfer Control
22		SSH	Secure Shell Login
23		TELNET	Telnet
25		SMTP	Simple Mail Transfer
37	37	TIME	Time
49	49	TACACS+	TACACS+ login
53	53	DNS	Domain Name Server
65	65	TACACS+	TACACS+ database service
88	88	Kerberos	Kerberos
500	500	ISAKMP	ISAKMP protocol
512		rexec	
513		rlogin	UNIX rlogin
	513	rwho	UNIX Broadcast Naming Svc
514		rsh	UNIX rsh and rep
	514	SYSLOG	UNIX system logs
614	614	SSHELL	SSL Shell
	1701	L2TP	L2TP
1723	1723	PPTP	PPTP
1812	1812	RADIUS	RADIUS authorization
1813	1813	RADIUS-actg	RADIUS accounting

Table 11-2   Common TCP/UDP Remote Access Networking Port Assignments

Chapter Review

Chapter Summary

Remote Access Protocols

- A wide variety of protocols and options exist for remote access including SSH, Telnet, RADIUS, TACACS+, PTPP, L2TP, and others.

- Understand the role of security with respect to remote access and the primary methods to support secure remote access.

- RADIUS and TACAS+ are both authentication, authorization, and accounting (AAA) protocols used for remote access administration.

Wireless Access

- Wireless protocols and the security implications in their use for remote access create a challenge for security.

- WEP provides for a specific level of security in order to offer relatively safe remote connections.

- Flaws in WEP leave it vulnerable to specific technical attacks.

VPN/IPsec

- Virtual private networks (VPN) and Internet Protocol Security (IPSec) offer methods for ensuring confidentiality and integrity during remote connections.

- Tunneling is a means of encapsulating packets inside a protocol that is understood only at the entry and exit points of the tunnel to provide a secure network connection across a public section of a TCP/IP network.

- PTPP is a tunneling protocol, popular with Microsoft Windows, that implements tunnels in software.

- IPSec is the most comprehensive architecture of VPN implementation.

Key Terms

802.1x *(273)*
Authentication Header (AH) *(270)*
Challenge Handshake Authentication Protocol (CHAP) *(262)*
DIAMETER *(276)*
Encapsulating Security Payload (EAPOL) *(273)*
ESP *(270)*
Internet Key Exchange (IKE) *(270)*
IPSec *(267)*

L2TP *(261)*
PTPP *(261)*
RADIUS *(273)*
Internet Security Association *(270)*
Secure Shell (SSH) *(260)*
TACACS+ *(276)*
Virtual Private Networks (VPN) *(266)*

Key Terms Quiz

Use terms from the Key Terms list to complete the sentences that follow. Don't use the same term more than once. Not all terms will be used.

1. _____ provides direct support for secure remote login, secure file transfer, and secure forwarding of TCP/IP and X Window System traffic.

2. _____ is the most common implementation of OSI Layer 2 tunneling today.

3. _____ is a connectionless AAA protocol utilizing UDP for its transport layer protocol.

4. _____ are virtual networks that are constructed over existing physical networks using tunneling mechanisms.

5. _____ and _____ are used in IPSec to protect elements of the packet header and data segments respectively.

6. Password Authentication Protocol (PAP), _____ , and the Extensible Authentication Protocol (EAP) are used to authenticate the peer device, not a user of the system.

7. The default method of key exchange for IPSec is commonly referred to as _____.

8. _____ is a tunneling protocol designed to be implemented in hardware rather than software.

9. _____ is an encapsulated method of passing EAP messages over 802 frames.

10. The _____ standard is for a protocol to support communications between a user and an authorization device, such as an edge router to authenticate a user prior to granting access to an authentication server.

Multiple-Choice Quiz

1. Authentication is the process of...

   A. Verifying the correctness of data being transmitted

   B. Determining specific user access based on identity

    C. Verifying a user's identity

    D. Implementing a lattice-based access control

2. IPSec uses _____ to implement data confidentiality

    A. Tunneling

    B. Proprietary protocols

    C. EAPOL

    D. IKE

3. PTPP is used to...

    A. Authenticate a user connection to a remote device

    B. Create a VPN over a TCP/IP network

    C. Communicate AAA information over a network

    D. Validate wireless connections via a WEP

4. VPNs create security through...

    A. Encryption technology

    B. Proprietary protocols

    C. User authentication

    D. SSH

5. TACACS+ is used to...

    A. Establish VPNs

    B. Implement key exchange for IPSec

    C. Remotely authenticate users

    D. Implement data encryption protocols for security

6. Secure Shell provides for...

    A. Secure remote access channels

    B. Implementing a VPN connection

    C. An open source method of implementing encryption technology

    D. AAA functions in an enterprise

7. What does RADIUS use for its transport layer protocol?

    A. UDP

    B. IP

    C. TCP

    D. EAP

8. Remote connections between a PC client and a server can be secured using…

   A. IEEE 802.1x

   B. PPTP

   C. RADIUS

   D. WEP

9. Which protocol is used to communicate over a serial interface channel between computers?

   A. CHAP

   B. IPSec

   C. SSH

   D. PPP

10. A firewall will not block which protocols?

    A. RADIUS

    B. PPTP

    C. TACACS+

    D. SSH

11. Secure Shell uses which port to establish secure communications?

    A. TCP port 80

    B. UDP port 22

    C. TCP port 22

    D. TCP port 110

12. Context protection is delivered via what?

    A. EAPOL

    B. IPSec AH

    C. IPSec ESP

    D. RADIUS

13. Firewalls affect PPTP in what fashion?

    A. In no fashion; PPTP is immune to firewalls.

    B. By blocking TCP port 1723, a firewall can block the establishment of PPTP.

    C. By blocking UDP port 1723, a firewall can block the establishment of PPTP.

    D. Firewalls block PPTP with no recourse.

14. Which of the following is not used to establish a VPN?

    A. SSH

    B. IPSec

C. PTPP

D. TACACS+

15. Encryption provides confidentiality with which service?

A. FTP

B. Telnet

C. RADIUS

D. PPTP

Essay Questions

1. Describe how tunneling works and what are the implications for data communications?

2. Describe how IPSec can provide functions of data integrity and confidentiality.

3. What role does WEP play in wireless remote access and data protection? Why?

4. You have been asked by your boss to develop a corporate security policy for your small firm of 75 users, with respect to use of SSH. Assume that all data transfers require confidentiality due to the nature of your business. Describe the role of SSH in your enterprise and what its relationship is to remote access and security.

5. You have been placed in charge of a project to add remote access to your internal network. Develop a white paper that describes the steps in managing remote access functionality in a small firm.

Lab Projects

Lab Project 11.1

You are the system administrator for a medium-sized local business. Executives and managers want to have remote access to their business applications from home, as well as on the road. Since these applications harbor sensitive company data, how will you propose securing these connections in a simple fashion? Describe the technology you would employ and what resources it would need.

Lab Project 11.2

Your college has decided to implement wireless access to the backbone campus network for students. What technologies could you employ to restrict access to current students, faculty, and staff? What protocols and systems would be employed and what roles would they play in the solution?

Wireless and Instant Messaging

Upon completion of this chapter, you will be able to:
- Describe the security implications of wireless networks
- Describe the security implications of instant messaging

Wireless and instant messaging are two topics of great importance to computer and network security. Wireless network applications are very important to understand because the risks inherent in broadcasting a network signal across public airwaves are tantamount to posting all your company's passwords by the front door of your building. Instant messaging is another important application to people who control security, as currently, it can be hard to suppress these applications. When they are installed on any networked machine, they can allow not only unencrypted chat traffic to and from the Internet-based messaging servers, but also file transfer capabilities.

Wireless

Wireless networking is the transmission of packetized data by means of a physical topology not using direct physical links. We will narrow this definition to apply to networks that use radio waves to carry the signals, over either public or private bands. While there are proprietary applications that use point-to-point technology with narrowband radios and highly directional antennas, this technology is not common enough to produce any significant research into its vulnerabilities, and anything that was developed would have little usefulness. So we will focus on point-to-multipoint systems, the two most common of which are the **Wireless Application Protocol** (WAP) and **IEEE 802.11**. The Wireless Application Protocol is a system developed to send data to small handheld devices such as cellular phones, wireless e-mail handhelds, and PDAs. The 802.11 protocol has been standardized by the IEEE for wireless local area networks. It has three versions currently in production, 802.11b, 802.11a, and the most recent, 802.11g.

The 802.11b standard was the first to market, 802.11a followed, and at the time of writing, 802.11g products are just becoming available. The security world ignored wireless for a long time, and then within the space of a few months, it seemed like everyone was attempting to breach the security of wireless networks and transmissions. One reason that wireless suddenly found itself vulnerable is because wireless targets are so abundant and so unsecured, simply because they are not necessarily attached to crucial infrastructure. The dramatic proliferation of these inexpensive products has made the security ramifications of the protocol astonishing. No matter what the system, wireless security is a very important topic as more and more applications are designed to use wireless to send data. Wireless is particularly problematic from a security standpoint because there is no control over the physical layer of the traffic. In most wired local area networks, the administrators have physical control over the network and can control to some degree who can actually connect to the physical medium. This prevents large amounts of unauthorized traffic and makes snooping around and just listening to the traffic difficult. Wireless does away with the physical limitations. If an attacker can get close enough to the signal's source as it is being broadcast, he can at the very least listen to the radios talking and capture all the packets for examination. Attackers can also try to modify the traffic being sent, or to send their own traffic to disrupt the system. In this chapter, you will learn of the different types of attacks that wireless networks face.

 TIP Any wireless transmission is subject to interception and should be treated as such. Bluetooth, while not specifically covered in this chapter, can also be a security risk.

WAP and WTLS

Small and inexpensive products have made the wireless market grow by leaps and bounds, as traditional wireless devices such as cellular phones and pagers are replaced by wireless e-mail devices and PDAs. The newer generations of handheld cellular phones also have these features built in. All these new devices have generated a demand for additional services. The Wireless Application Protocol was designed to fulfill these needs. It uses a private-band, point-to-multipoint signal to deliver packet data to small wireless devices. To avoid broadcasting the data in the clear over the airwaves, the designers derived a lightweight encryption protocol called **Wireless Transport Layer Security** (WLTS) from the current Transport Layer Security protocol in use across the Internet. This new protocol was designed to meet the three fundamental requirements for security: confidentiality, integrity, and authentication. To have security in any network-based protocol, you must have these three things, and WAP is no different. So it's time to see how WTLS implements these three necessary attributes.

Confidentiality

Confidentiality is easy enough in theory: make sure that no one can read the packets that you are sending and receiving but you and the party you are intending to talk to. Confidentiality can be assured in several ways, but because wireless affords no control over the physical medium that the packets are traveling over, there is no way to stop another party from listening in. This is especially true with WAP, as the central aggregation point for the network is the cellular provider's tower. So given that anyone can listen in, the best way to ensure data confidentiality is through the use of data encryption. Encryption is explained in detail later in the book; the simplest explanation is that the data plaintext is encrypted and then sent over the airwaves as ciphertext. The originator and the recipient both have keys to decrypt the data and reproduce the plaintext. This method of ensuring confidentiality is very common, and if the encryption is well designed and implemented, then it is very hard for unauthorized users to take captured ciphertext and reproduce the plaintext that created it. WTLS uses a modified version of the TLS protocol, formerly known as SSL. The WTLS protocol supports several popular bulk encryption algorithms, including DES, Triple DES (more commonly referred to as 3DES), RC5, and IDEA. They can support 40- and 56-bit keys in the case of DES and 3DES, and 40-, 56-, and 128-bit keys in the case of RC5 and IDEA. These algorithms depend on the client and the server having a shared secret. To establish what this shared secret is, WTLS must carry out a key exchange, exactly as TLS does every time you log into a secure web site. WTLS supports several key exchange methods: Diffie-Hellman, Elliptic Curve Diffie-Hellman, and RSA. Both the algorithm used to encrypt the session and the method of key exchange in WTLS are decided during the WTLS handshake.

Integrity

Integrity means reliable information. When you are sending data to and receiving it from a specific place, you want assurances that what you sent is what was received. This is typically accomplished not by making the information completely invulnerable to replacement or substitution, but by giving indications if the information has been tampered with. Typically, this is done by generating a checksum of the message with a one- way hash function. When the receiver gets the data, it hashes it as well and compares the two sums; if they match, then the data was unaltered. WTLS implements integrity through the use of *message authentication codes (MACs)*. A MAC algorithm generates a one-way hash of the compressed WTLS data. WTLS supports the MD5 and SHA MAC algorithms. The MAC algorithm is also decided during the WTLS handshake.

Authentication

Authentication is the process by which each end of the data flow proves that they are who they say they are. This is necessary to prevent information flow to an unintended or unauthorized person. Authentication is typically accomplished by the sending party sending something that proves the sender is who they say they are. The sender will also want assurances that the party they are contacting is whom they mean to send data to. Authentication can be performed in several ways, including digital certificates, tokens, or simple passwords. A popular way to perform authentication over the Internet is the use of digital certificates, cryptographic messages issued by a trusted third party. The key provided can then be used to encrypt a private shared key to enable ciphered communication. Authentication in WTLS is done with digital certificates; the types of certificates supported by WTLS include the native WTLS type, X509, and X9.68. Authentication is optional in the WTLS protocol; if the client and the server choose to use authentication, then the process begins immediately after the hello exchange. The server will send its certificate and the client will then provide its certificate, if possible, to the server. Once the certificates are processed, authentication is complete.

Security Issues with WTLS

As WTLS implements the three parts of security into the protocol, it also has to allow for the unique requirements of the devices that are using the protocol. The TLS protocol that WTLS is based on is designed around Internet-based computers, machines that have relatively high processing power, large amounts of memory, and sufficient bandwidth available for Internet applications. The PDAs and other devices that WTLS must accommodate are limited in all these respects. Thus WTLS has to be able to cope with small amounts of memory and limited processor capacity, as well as long round-trip times that TLS could not handle well. These requirements are the primary reasons that WTLS has security issues. As the protocol is designed around more capable servers than devices, the specification can allow connections with little to no security. Clients with low memory or CPU capabilities cannot support encryption, and choosing null or weak encryption greatly reduces confidentiality. Authentication is also optional in the protocol, and omitting authentication reduces security by leaving the connection vulnerable to a man-in-the-middle-type attack. In addition to the general flaws in the protocol's implementation, there are several known security vulnerabilities, including those to the chosen plaintext attack, the PKCS #1 attack, and the alert message truncation attack.

The chosen plaintext attack works on the principle of predictable initialization vectors (IVs). By the nature of the transport medium that it is using, WAP, WTLS needs to support unreliable transport. This forces the IV to be based upon data already known to the client, and WTLS uses a linear IV computation. Because the IV is based upon the sequence number of the packet and several packets are sent unencrypted, entropy is severely decreased. This lack of entropy in the encrypted data reduces confidentiality.

Now consider the PKCS #1 attack. PKCS, used in conjunction with RSA encryption, gives a standard for formatting the padding used to generate a correctly formatted block size. When the client receives the block, it will reply to the sender as to the validity of the block. An attacker takes advantage of this by attempting to send multiple guesses at the padding to force a padding error. In vulnerable implementations, WTLS will return error messages providing an oracle decrypting RSA with roughly 2^{20} chosen ciphertext queries.

Alert messages in WTLS are sometimes sent in plaintext and are not authenticated. This fact could allow an attacker to overwrite an encrypted packet from the actual sender with a plaintext alert message, leading to possible disruption of the connection through, for instance, a truncation attack.

 TIP WAP is a point-to-multipoint protocol, but can face disruptions or attacks because it aggregates at well-known points: the cellular antenna towers.

There has also been some concern over the so-called "**WAP GAP**." This concern involves confidentiality of information where the two different networks meet, the WAP gateway. WTLS acts as the security protocol for the WAP network, and TLS is the standard for the Internet, so the WAP gateway has to perform translation from one encryption standard to the other. This translation forces all messages to be seen by the WAP gateway in plaintext. This is a weak point in the network design, but from an attacker's perspective it is a much harder target than the WTLS protocol itself. Threats to the WAP gateway can be minimized through careful infrastructure design, such as secure physical location and allowing only outbound traffic from the gateway. There is still a risk of compromise, and an attacker would find a WAP gateway an especially appealing target, as plaintext messages are processed through it from all wireless devices, not just a single user. The solution for this is to have end-to-end security layered over anything underlying, in effect creating a VPN from the endpoint to the mobile device, or to standardize on a full implementation of TLS for end-to-end encryption and strong authentication. Neither of these solutions are currently possible with the majority of mobile devices, but one of them may be a viable solution in the future.

WAP in Sum

As with any wireless protocol, extra care should be taken to ensure that the security of the protocol is not compromised. WAP's biggest weakness is its lack of control over the physical medium of data transmission. The limited nature of the devices also hampers the ability of the security protocols to operate as intended, compromising any real security to be had on WAP networks. However, even wireless implementations intended for full-power computers don't always provide security, as you will see in the next section.

802.11

The 802.11b protocol was an IEEE standard that was ratified in late 1999, launching a range of products that would open the way to a whole new genre of attacks for the attackers and a new series of headaches for security administrators everywhere. This was a new standard for sending packetized data traffic over radio waves in the unlicensed **2.4 GHz band**. As the products matured and became easy to use and affordable, security experts started to deconstruct the limited security that had been built into the standard. The 802.11a protocol is another standard for wireless networking, but it works only to improve the speed of the network and does not have security updates. At the time of writing, 802.11g has just started to appear on the market. This technology has been focused on making traffic in the 2.4 GHz band run at the data rates supported by the 802.11a's 5 GHz band. While the 802.11g standard does support a longer WEP key, this does not solve the problems with WEP. What this means is that for security purposes, 802.11b and 802.11g are virtually identical. Now, several new IEEE standards for wireless networks are also being worked on, but only one of them deals with increasing the security in 802.11. We will go over the 802.11b and 802.11a protocols and then discuss the security problems involved with them as well as some proposed solutions.

 TIP The best place for current 802.11 standards and upcoming draft standard information is in the RFCs. You can find them at www.ietf.org/rfc.html.

The 802.11b protocol provides for multiple-rate Ethernet over 2.4 GHz spread-spectrum wireless. It provides transfer rates of 1 Mbps, 2 Mbps, 5.5 Mbps, and 11 Mbps and typically uses **direct-sequence spread spectrum** (DSSS). The most common layout is a point-to-multipoint environment with the available bandwidth being shared by all users. Typical range is roughly 100 yards indoors and 300 yards outdoors line of sight.

The 802.11a protocol is newer, with products only recently becoming available. It operates in the 5 GHz spectrum using orthogonal frequency division multiplexing (OFDM). Supporting rates of up to 54 Mbps, it is the faster brother of 802.11b. Although it is faster, the higher frequency used by 802.11a shortens the usable range of the devices. The 802.11g draft uses portions of both of the other standards: it uses the 2.4 GHz band for greater range but uses the OFDM transmission method to achieve the faster 54 Mbps data rates.

All these protocols operate in bands that are "unlicensed" by the FCC. This means that people operating this equipment do not have to be certified by the FCC, but it also means that the devices could possibly share the band with other devices, such as cordless phones, CCTV wireless transceivers, and other similar equipment. This other equipment can cause interference with the 802.11 equipment, possibly causing speed degradation. The 802.11 protocol designers knew that there were going to be some security concerns and attempted to build provisions into the 802.11 protocol that would ensure adequate security. The 802.11 standard includes attempts at rudimentary authentication and confidentiality controls. Authentication is handled in its most basic form by the 802.11 access point forcing the clients to perform a handshake when attempting to "associate" to the AP. Association is the process needed before the AP will allow the client to talk across the AP to the network. Association occurs only if the client has all the correct parameters needed in the handshake, among them the *service set identifier (SSID)*. This SSID setting should limit access to only the authorized users of the wireless network.

The designers of the standard also attempted to maintain confidentiality by introducing **Wired Equivalent Privacy** (WEP). WEP uses the **RC4 stream cipher** to encrypt the data as it is transmitted through the air. This encryption is synchronous and based upon a key shared by the AP and all the clients using the AP. WEP comes in both 40- and 104-bit key strengths, typically advertised as 60 and 128 bit. The 802.11a and 802.11g products typically have support for 152-bit WEP, but this greater key length does not affect the weaknesses. To understand what security problems 802.11 has, you must first look at some of the reasons it got to be as prominent a technology as it is.

Wireless networks came along in 2000 and became very popular. For the first time, it was possible to have almost full-speed network connections without having to be tied down to an Ethernet cable. The technology quickly took off, allowing prices to drop into the consumer range. Once the market shifted to focus on customers who were not necessarily technologists, the products also became very easy to install and operate. Default settings were designed to get the novice users up and running without having to alter anything substantial, and products were billed to be plug-in and work. These developments further enlarged the market for the low-cost, easy-to-use wireless access points. Then attackers realized that instead of attacking machines over the Internet, they could drive around and seek out these APs. Having physical control of an information asset is critical to its security. Physical access to a machine will enable an attacker to bypass *any* security measure that has been placed on that machine.

Typically, access to actual Ethernet segments is protected by physical security measures. This structure allows security administrators to plan for only internal threats to the network and gives them a clear idea of the types and number of machines connected to it. Wireless networking takes the keys to the kingdom and tosses them literally out the window and into the parking lot. A typical wireless installation broadcasts the network right through the physical controls that are in place. An attacker can now drive up and have the same access as by plugging into an Ethernet jack inside the building—in fact better access, because 802.11 is a shared medium, allowing sniffers to view all packets being sent to or from the AP and all clients. These access points were also typically behind any security measures the companies had in place, such as firewalls and IDSs. This kind of access into the internal network has caused a large stir among computer security professionals, and eventually, the media. War-driving, war-flying, war-walking, war-chalking—all of these terms have been splayed across security article after security article. However, wireless is a popular target for several reasons, as mentioned before: the access gained from wireless, the lack of default security, and the wide proliferation of devices.

There are also other reasons. The first of these is anonymity: an attacker can probe your building for wireless access from the street. Then he can log packets to and from the AP without giving any indication that an attempted intrusion is taking place. The attacker will announce his presence only if he attempts to associate to the access point. Even then, an attempted association is recorded only by the MAC address of the wireless card associating to it, and most APs do not have alerting functionality for when users associate to it. This fact gives administrators a very limited view of who is gaining access to their network, if they are even paying attention at all. It gives attackers the ability to seek out and compromise wireless networks with relative impunity.

The second reason is the low cost of the equipment needed. A single wireless access card costing less than a hundred dollars can give access to any unsecured access point within driving range. The final reason for the popularity of attacking wireless is the relative ease compared to other target hosts. Windows-based tools for locating and sniffing wireless-based networks have turned anyone who can download files from the Internet and has a wireless card into a potential attacker.

The most common tools for an attacker to use are reception-based programs that will listen to the beacon frames put out by other wireless devices and programs that will promiscuously capture all traffic. The most widely used of these programs is called Netstumbler by Marius Milner, shown in Figure 12-1. This program listens for the beacon

Figure 12-1   Netstumbler on a Windows PC

frames of access points that are within range of the card attached to the Netstumbler computer. When it receives them, it logs all available information about the access point for later analysis. If the computer has a GPS unit attached to it, the program also logs the access point's coordinates. This information can be used to return to the access point, or to plot maps of access points in a city. This is a Windows-based application, but there are programs that work on the same principle for Mac, BSD, Linux, and other operating systems.

Once an attacker has located a network, and assuming that they cannot directly connect and start active scanning and penetration of the network, they will use the best attack tool there is: a network sniffer. The network sniffer, when combined with a wireless network card it can support, is a powerful attack tool, as the shared medium of a wireless network exposes all packets to interception and logging. Popular wireless sniffers are Ethereal and WildPackets AiroPeek. Regular sniffers used on wireline Ethernet have also been updated to include support for wireless, with a popular example being Sniffer Pro 4.0, shown in Figure 12-2.

Specialized sniffer tools have come out recently, designed with a single objective, to crack WEP keys. Wired Equivalent Privacy is the encryption protocol that 802.11 uses to attempt to ensure confidentiality of wireless communications. Unfortunately, it has turned out to have several problems. These weaknesses are specifically targeted for attack by the specialized sniffer programs. They work by exploiting weak initialization vectors in the encryption algorithm. To exploit this weakness, you need a certain number of ciphertext packets; once you have captured enough packets, however, the program can very quickly decipher the encryption key being used. WEPCrack was the first available program to use this flaw to crack the WEP keys; however, WEPCrack depends on a

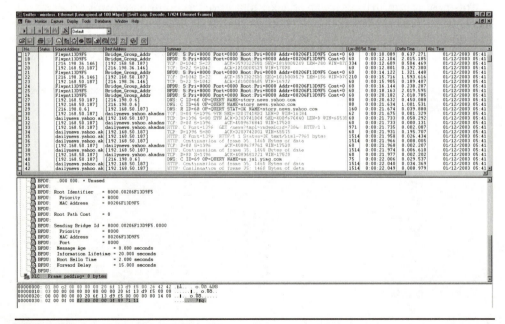

Figure 12-2   Sniffer Pro on a Windows PC

dump of actual network packets from another sniffer program. AirSnort is a stand-alone program that captures its own packets; once it has captured enough ciphertext, it will provide the WEP key of the network.

All of these tools are used by the wireless attacker to compromise the network. They are also typically used by security professionals when doing a wireless site survey of an organization. The site survey has a simple purpose: to minimize the available wireless signal being sent beyond the physical controls of the organization. By using the sniffer and finding access point beacons, a security official can determine which access points are transmitting into uncontrolled areas. The access point can then be tuned, either by relocation or through the use of directional antennas, to minimize radiation beyond an organization's walls. A proper site survey is an important step in securing a wireless network because the other default tools for securing wireless are so ineffective.

802.11b has primarily two tools for security, one designed solely for authentication, and the other for authentication and confidentiality. The authentication function is known as the **service set identifier** (SSID). This is a unique 32-character identifier attached to the header of the packet. As this is, hopefully, a unique identifier, only people who know the identifier will be able to complete association to the access point. While this is a good idea in theory, the SSID is sent in plaintext in the packets, so in practice SSID has little security significance—any sniffer can determine the SSID, and some operating systems, Windows XP, for instance, will display a list of SSIDs active in the area and prompt the user to choose which one to connect to. This weakness is magnified by most access points' default setting, to transmit **beacon frames**. The beacon frame's purpose is to announce the wireless network's presence and capabilities so that WLAN cards can attempt to associate to it. This can be disabled in software for many access points, especially the more sophisticated ones. From a security perspective, the beacon frame is damaging because it contains the SSID, and this beacon frame is transmitted at a set interval. (The default interval is ten times a second.) Since a default access point without any other traffic is sending out its SSID in plaintext ten times a second, you can see why the SSID does not provide true authentication. Scanning programs like Netstumbler work by capturing the beacon frames and thereby the SSIDs of all access points.

WEP is the 802.11 protocol's method for ensuring confidentiality and authentication. WEP encrypts the data traveling across the network with an RC4 stream cipher, attempting to ensure confidentiality. This is a synchronous method of encryption, ensuring some method of authentication. The system depends on the client and the access point having a shared secret "key," ensuring that only authorized people with the proper key have access to the wireless network. WEP supports two key lengths, 40 and 104 bits, though these are more typically referred to as 64 and 128 bits. In 802.11a and 802.11g, manufacturers have extended this to 152-bit WEP keys. This is because in all cases, 24 bits of the overall key length are for the **initialization vector**.

The IV is the primary reason for the weaknesses in WEP. This IV is sent in the plaintext part of the message, and because the total keyspace is approximately 16 million keys, the same key will be reused. Once the key has been repeated, an attacker has two ciphertexts encrypted with the same key stream. This allows the attacker to examine the ciphertext and retrieve the key. This attack can be improved by examining only packets that have weak IVs, reducing the amount of packets needed to crack the key. Using only weak IV packets, the number of required captured packets is reduced to around four or five million, taking only a few hours on a fairly busy access point. For a point of reference, this means that equipment with an advertised WEP key of 128 bits can be cracked in under a day, whereas to crack a normal 128-bit key would take roughly 2,000,000,000,000,000,000 years on a computer able to attempt one trillion keys a second. As mentioned before, AirSnort is a modified sniffing program that takes advantage of this weakness to retrieve the WEP keys. The biggest weakness of the WEP protocol is that the IV problem exists regardless of key length, because the IV always remains at 24 bits. Most access points also have the capability to lock access in to only known MAC addresses, providing a limited authentication capability. Given sniffers' capacity to grab all active MAC addresses on the network, this capability is not very effective. An attacker simply configures their wireless cards to a known good MAC address.

After the limited security functions of a wireless network are broken, it behaves exactly like a regular Ethernet network and is subject to the exact same vulnerabilities. The host machines that are on or attached to the wireless network are vulnerable just as if they and the attacker were physically connected. Being on the network opens all machines up to vulnerability scanners, Trojan horse programs, virus and worm programs, and traffic interception via sniffer programs. Any unpatched vulnerability on any machine accessible from the wireless segment is now open to compromise.

Knowing all of these things, you can do several things to maximize the security of the wireless network. Even though WEP can be easily broken, employ it to defeat curious passers-by. Enable MAC address limiting on the access point, although this is also a security measure that will defeat only a casual attacker. If possible, disable beacon frames on the access point; this will help to keep your wireless off the majority of access point maps and defeat people that are not attempting a targeted attack against the organization. The most important tool that can be used to ensure that the 802.11 system does not get compromised is a good site survey. Making sure that wireless is not detectable casually will thwart the majority of attempts, as many attackers are seeking only the most simple of targets.

Note that 802.11 security is in the process of being improved. While future standards are attempting to replace WEP with an Advanced Encryption Standard–based protocol, most of the current work is being done on improving authentication. Since the current security and authentication methods are so weak, vendors have been turning to anything to improve the situation. One of the first things that they came up with was 802.1x, which is an authentication protocol designed for regular wired Ethernet networks. It is part of the IETF Extensible Authentication Protocol and uses its authentication framework. It is intended to provide strong authentication of both the client and the server, and then provide a key management structure for the underlying encryption mechanisms.

WEP was designed to provide some measure of confidentiality on an 802.11 network similar to what is found on a wired network, but that has not been the case. Accordingly, new standards are being developed to improve upon WEP. The 802.11i standard is to be the new IEEE standard for security in wireless networks. It will specify the use of 802.1x to provide authentication, and the use of AES as the encryption protocol. The 802.11i standard specifies the use of the Temporal Key Integrity Protocol (TKIP) and the Counter Mode with CBC-MAC Protocol (in full, the Counter Mode with Cipher Block Chaining–Message Authentication Codes Protocol, or simply CCMP). These two protocols have different functions, but they both serve to enhance security. TKIP works by using a shared secret combined with the card's MAC address to generate a new key, which is then mixed with the initialization vector to make per-packet keys that then encrypt a single packet using the same RC4 cipher that traditional WEP uses. This overcomes the WEP key weakness, as a key is used on only one packet. The other advantage to this method is that it can be retrofitted to current hardware with only a software change, unlike AES and **802.1X**. CCMP is actually the mode that the AES cipher is used in to provide message integrity. Unlike TKIP, CCMP requires new hardware to perform the AES encryption. This should correct the weaknesses of the WEP protocol.

 TIP Cisco is currently shipping products that support LEAP, their implementation of the TKIP protocol. LEAP enabled products can be configured to be much more secure than other products that do not support dynamic WEP keys.

The 802.1X protocol can support a wide variety of authentication methods and also fits well into existing authentication systems such as RADIUS and LDAP. This allows 802.1X to interoperate well with other systems such as VPNs and dial-up RAS. Unlike other authentication methods such as the Point-to-Point Protocol over Ethernet (PPPoE), 802.1X does not use encapsulation, so the network overhead is much lower. Unfortunately, the protocol is just a framework for providing implementation, so there are no specifics guaranteeing strong authentication or key management. Implementations of the protocol vary from vendor to vendor in method of implementation and strength of security, especially when it comes to the difficult test of wireless security. There are four common ways of implementing 802.1X: EAP-TLS, EAP-TTLS, EAP-MD5, and EAP–Cisco Wireless, or LEAP.

EAP-TLS relies on Transport Layer Security, an attempt to standardize the SSL structure to pass credentials. The standard, developed by Microsoft, uses X.509 certificates and offers dynamic WEP key generation. This means that the organization must have the ability to support PKI in the form of X.509 digital certificates. Also, per-user per-session dynamically generated WEP keys help prevent anyone from cracking the WEP keys in use, as each user individually has their own WEP key. Even if a user were logged onto the access point and transmitted enough traffic to allow cracking of the WEP key, access would be gained to only that user's traffic. No other user's data would be compromised, and the attacker could not use the WEP key to connect to the access point. This standard authenticates the client to the access point, but it also authenticates the access point to the client, helping to avoid man-in-the-middle attacks. The main problem with the EAP-TLS protocol is that it is designed to work with only Microsoft's Active Directory and Certificate Services; it will not take certificates from other certificate issuers. Thus a mixed environment would have implementation problems.

EAP-TTLS (the acronym stands for EAP–Tunneled TLS Protocol) is a variant of the EAP-TLS protocol. EAP-TTLS works much the same way as EAP-TLS, with the server authenticating to the client with a certificate, but the protocol tunnels the client side of the authentication, allowing the use of legacy authentication protocols such as PAP, CHAP, MS-CHAP, or MS-CHAP-V2. This makes the protocol more versatile while still supporting the enhanced security features such as dynamic WEP key assignment.

EAP-MD5, while it does improve the authentication of the client to the access point, does little else to improve the security of your access point. The protocol works by using the MD5 encryption protocol to hash a user's username and password. The problems with this protocol are that it provides no way for the access point to authenticate with the client, and that it does not provide for dynamic WEP key assignment. In the wireless environment, without strong two-way authentication it is very easy for an attacker to perform a man-in-the-middle-type attack. Normally, these type of attacks are difficult to perform, requiring a traffic redirect of some kind, but wireless changes all those rules. By setting up a rogue access point, an attacker can attempt to get clients to connect to it as if it were authorized and then simply authenticate to the real access point, a simple way to have access to the network and the client's credentials. The problem of not dynamically generating WEP keys is that it simply opens up the network to the same lack of confidentiality that a normal access point is vulnerable to. An attacker only has to wait for enough traffic to crack the WEP key, and can then observe all traffic passing through the network.

LEAP is a protocol developed by Cisco to improve wireless security; it was then rolled into the EAP standard. LEAP works much like EAP-MD5 in that the access point accepts the username-password combination and forwards them to the RADIUS server. LEAP differs from EAP-MD5 in that it requires two-way authentication, causing the access point to authenticate to the client as well as the client to the access point. It also generates per-user per-session WEP keys, helping to defeat attackers sniffing the network. One of the drawbacks to using LEAP is that it operates only on Cisco equipment, though other vendors are sure to provide interoperability.

In summation, 802.1x is a very versatile protocol and can add a great deal of security to 802.11 networks.

Because the security of wireless LANs has been ineffective, many users have simply switched to a layered security approach. That is, they have moved their access points to untrustworthy portions of the network and have forced all clients to authenticate through the firewall to a third-party VPN system. The additional security comes at a price of putting more load on the firewall and VPN infrastructure and possibly adding cumbersome software to the users' devices. While wireless can be set up in a very secure manner in this fashion, it can also be set up poorly. Some systems lack strong authentication of both endpoints, leading to possibilities of a man-in-the-middle-type attack. Also, even though the data is tunneled through, IP addresses are still sent in the clear, giving an attacker information about what and where your VPN endpoint is. While VPNs may be the best stopgap measure currently, they need to be properly configured and carefully maintained if they are exposed on wireless LANs. True security will be much improved once the lower layers of encryption are fixed for wireless access points.

802.11 has enjoyed tremendous growth because of its ease of use and popularity, but that growth is threatened by many organizational rules prohibiting its use due to security measures. As you have seen here, the current state of wireless security is very poor, making attacking wireless a popular activity. With the addition of strong authentication and better encryption protocols, wireless should become both convenient and safe.

Instant Messaging

Instant messaging is another technology that has seen widespread acceptance in recent years. With the growth of the Internet threatening to pull customers away from America Online, one of the largest dial-up providers in the U.S., that company had to look at new ways of providing content. One of the things that it started was AIM, or **AOL Instant Messenger**. Conceived as a way to find people of like interests online, it was modeled after earlier chat programs. With GUI features and enhanced ease of use, it quickly became popular enough for AOL to release to regular users of the Internet as well. With several competing programs, AIM was now feeding the tremendous growth of the instant messaging segment. The programs had to appeal to a wide variety of users, so ease of use was paramount, and security was not a priority. Now that people are used to instant messaging applications, they see the benefit of using them not only for personal chatting on the Internet, but also for legitimate business use. When people install these applications, they unwittingly expose the corporate network to security breaches. Several of the security problems inhere in the nature of the programs themselves, while others are a function of the implementation.

Instant messaging programs are designed to attach to a server, or network of servers, and allow you to talk with other people on the same network of servers in near real time. The nature of this type of communication opens several holes in a system's security. First, the program has to attach to a server, typically announcing the IP address of the originating client. This is not a problem in most applications, but IM identifies a specific user associated with the IP address, making attacks more likely. Also associated with this fact is that for other users to be able to send you messages, the program is forced to announce your presence on the server. So now a user is displaying that their computer is on, and is possibly broadcasting the source IP address to anyone who is looking. This problem is compounded by the tendency for people to run these programs in the background so that they don't miss any messages.

The popular IM clients were not implemented with security in mind. All support sending files as attachments, few currently support encryption, and they do not have a virus scanner built into the file sharing utility. File sharing in any form must be a carefully handled application to prevent the spread of viruses and other malicious code. Chat programs produce security risks because the sharing is done ad hoc between end users, administrators have no control over the quality of the files being sent, and there is no monitoring of the original sources of those files. The only authentication for the files is the human interaction between the two users in question. This kind of vulnerability coupled with a social engineering attack can produce dramatic enough results for CERT to issue an incident note (CERT Incident Note IN-2002-03 Social Engineering Attacks via IRC and Instant Messaging). This personal type of authentication was abused, tricking people into downloading and executing backdoor or Trojan horse programs. A user can also be persuaded autonomously to download and run a file via IM. Several worms exist that attempt, via IM, to get users to download and run the payload. Goner, running via ICQ, asks users to download a screen saver. Choke, spreading via MSN, attempts to get users to download a game; if the game is downloaded, the worm will then attempt to spread to any user the infected user chats with. These worms and ones like it all depend on user interaction to run the payload. This file sharing mechanism bypasses all the server-side virus protection that is part of most organizations' e-mail infrastructure.

One of the largest problems with IM programs is the lack of support for encryption. AIM, ICQ, MSN Messenger, and Yahoo Messenger all currently do not support encryption of the text messages traveling between users. This flaw was not a significant concern while these programs were still primarily used for personal communication, but with businesses moving to adopt the systems, people are not aware of the infrastructure difference between IM and e-mail. Intracompany e-mail never leaves the company's network, but an intracompany instant message typically will do so unless the organization purchases a product and operates an internal IM server. This can and does expose large amounts of confidential business information to anyone who is physically in a spot to monitor and has the desire to capture the traffic.

 TIP It is useful to remember that plaintext messages flow in both directions, if a company chooses to set up an internal IM server, then remote users should be using VPN technology to access the IM server.

If you think about how often client information is sent in e-mail between two people at a company, you start to see the danger that sending it via IM creates. IM is an application that is typically installed by the end user, without the knowledge of the administrator. These types of rogue applications have always been a danger to a network's security, but administrators have typically been able to control these types of applications by eliminating the applications' ports through the firewall.

Some instant messaging applications have even been programmed for use as rogue apps. In the event that they can't reach a server on the default ports, they begin to scan all ports looking for one that is allowed out of the firewall. As these applications can connect on any port, including common ones such as 23 Telnet and 80 HTTP, they are very hard to control. These types of security risks go above and beyond the routine security holes generated in IM software that arise as in any other piece of software, through coding errors.

IM applications work only in a networked environment and therefore are forced to accept traffic as well as send it, giving attackers a way to exploit flaws in the code of the program. AIM has had two buffer overflow problems, allowing a remote attacker to gain control of the user's computer. These flaws, which since have been patched, are just the beginning—with the proliferation of these applications, many more bugs are out there waiting to be exploited.

Several things can be done to improve the security of IM now, and new programs will have improved security features. The first thing businesses that use instant messaging should do is to use a local server. Keeping messages within the perimeter of the organization goes a long way to ensuring that confidential information does not get out. Microsoft Exchange can act as an internal IM server, routing employee-to-employee IMs within the organization. Trillian is a new chat client program that works with multiple chat networks; its most significant feature is that it can encrypt the chat messages, on AIM and ICQ networks, that the client sends to the server. While this does not help with file sharing problems, it will provide confidentiality in one direction. To have confidentiality across the entire chat session, both users must be using Trillian. Trillian and other tools exist to provide confidentiality, but to protect the method of file exchange the clients will have to be changed to integrate a virus scanner. These solutions and others should be applied widely to ensure that IM will be done securely.

Instant messaging is an application that can increase productivity by saving communication time, but it's not without risks. The protocol sends messages in plaintext and thus fails to preserve their confidentiality. It also allows for sharing of files between clients, allowing a backdoor access method for files. There are some methods to minimize security risks, but more development has to be done before IM is ready to be implemented in a secure fashion.

Chapter Review

Chapter Summary

After reading this chapter and completing the exercises, you should understand the following about wireless and wireless security.

Identify the Different Wireless Systems in Use Today

- Wireless Application Protocol or WAP is used on small, handheld devices like cell phones for out-of-the-office connectivity.

- 802.11, the standard for wireless local area networks, and the different specifications of the standard, such as 802.11b, 802.11a, and 802.11g.

Identify WAP and Its Security Implications

- WAP is the data protocol used by many cellular phones to deliver e-mail and lightweight web services.

- Designers created WTLS as a method to ensure privacy of the data because it was being broadcast.

- WTLS has a number of inherent security problems, such as weak encryption necessitated by the low computing power of the devices and the network transition that must occur at the cellular provider's network, or the WAP GAP.

Understand 802.11's Security Issues and Possible Solutions

- 802.11 does not allow physical control of the transport mechanism.

- Transmission of all network data wirelessly transmits frames to all wireless machines, not just a single client, similar to Ethernet hub devices.

- Poor authentication. The SSID is broadcast to anyone listening.

- Flawed implementation of the RC4 encryption algorithm makes even encrypted traffic subject to interception and decryption.

Describe Instant Messaging Systems and Their Security Issues

- AOL Instant Messenger, ICQ, and MSN Messenger are all different versions of instant messaging programs.

- They all send messages in the clear, without a native encryption built into the default clients.

- All the clients need to attach to a server in order to communicate. Therefore, when attached to the server, they announce the source IP of a particular user.

- Instant messaging can also transfer files. This activity typically bypasses any security built into the network, especially mail server virus protections.

Key Terms

2.4GHz band *(291)*
802.1X *(297)*
AOL Instant Messenger *(299)*
Authentication *(289)*
Beacon frames *(295)*
Confidentiality *(288)*
Direct-sequence spread spectrum (DSSS) *(291)*
IEEE 802.11 *(287)*
initialization vector *(295)*
Integrity *(289)*
RC4 stream cipher *(292)*
Service set identifier (SSID) *(295)*
WAP GAP *(290)*
Wired Equivalent Privacy (WEP) *(292)*
Wireless application protocol (WAP) *(287)*
Wireless Transport Layer Security (WTLS) *(288)*

Key Term Quiz

Use terms from the Key Terms list to complete the sentences that follow. Don't use the same term more than once. Not all terms will be used.

1. The reliability that information has not been altered in transit is referred to as
   _____.

2. The _____ is a term used to describe the network transition from a provider's network to the Internet.

3. An 802.11 access point transmits _____ by default to announce the AP's availability.

4. WAP uses the _____ protocol to attempt to ensure confidentiality of data.

5. The 32-character identifier attached to the header of a packet used for authentication to an 802.11 access point is the _____.

6. The main weakness of WEP is its 24-bit _____.

7. _____ is a new standard for strong Ethernet authentication.

8. _____ is an unlicensed band that is used for wireless local area networks.

9. _____ is the protocol used to send data to small handheld devices like cellular phones.

10. The default encryption protocol used by 802.11 is called _____.

Multiple-Choice Quiz

1. WTLS ensures integrity through what device?

   A. Public key encryption

   B. Message authentication codes

   C. Source IP

   D. Digital signatures

2. Why is 802.11 wireless more of a security problem than any other type of network?

   A. It has more readily readable frames.

   B. It provides access to the physical layer of Ethernet without needing physical access to the building.

   C. Wireless is the only network that allows sniffing of the traffic.

   D. It draws too much power and the other servers reboot.

3. How do WAP endpoints choose which security parameters of WTLS to use for a session?

   A. Security is an on or off option, there are no other parameters.

   B. The user codes them through DTMF tones.

   C. The cell tower dictates them.

   D. The WTLS handshake determines what parameters to use.

4. What instant messaging client currently supports encryption?

   A. Yahoo

   B. MSN

   C. Trillian

   D. AIM

5. What protocol is WTLS trying to secure?

   A. WAP

   B. TDMA

   C. GSM

   D. 802.11

6. While the SSID provides some measure of authentication, why is it not very effective?

   A. It is dictated by the manufacturer of the access point.

   B. It is encrypted.

   C. It is broadcast in every beacon frame.

   D. SSID is not an authentication function.

7. The 802.1X protocol is a new protocol for Ethernet _____.

   A. Authentication

   B. Speed

   C. Wireless

   D. Cabling

8. WTLS must have support for short key lengths, limiting the amount of security the protocol can provide. What is the cause?

   A. Security is not necessary in WAP.

   B. The algorithm doesn't gain any security with longer keys.

   C. Longer keys cannot be used with the WAP protocol.

   D. WTLS has to support devices with low processor power and limited RAM.

9. Why are instant messaging protocols dangerous for file transfer?

   A. They bypass server-based virus protections.

   B. File sharing is never dangerous.

   C. They allow everyone you chat with to view all your files.

   D. You'll end up receiving many spam files.

10. How do some instant messaging programs cause problems for intrusion detection systems?

   A. They cause the IDS system to shut down.

   B. They force the IDS system to decode your conversations.

   C. They run on regular Windows PCs.

   D. They can scan for open ports, trying to find a server.

11. Why should wireless have strong two-way authentication?

    A. So that only the executives can use the wireless system.

    B. Because wireless is especially susceptible to a man-in-the-middle attack.

    C. Because you want to know when you are being attacked.

    D. Strong authentication is needed so that all virus definitions are checked on the client computer.

12. The popularity of looking for and attacking wireless networks has increased greatly in the last few years. What has caused this?

    A. It's more prestigious.

    B. There are more people attacking networks now.

    C. It's easy.

    D. Most of the access points come from a single vendor.

13. What two key lengths do most implementations of WEP support?

    A. 64 and 56

    B. 104 and 40

    C. 512 and 256

    D. 1024 and 2048

14. WEP has used an implementation of which of the following encryption algorithms?

    A. SHA

    B. ElGamal

    C. RC4

    D. Triple-DES

15. One of the best ways to help control access to a wireless network is?

    A. Samba

    B. SSID

    C. Site surveys

    D. Policies and procedures

Essay Quiz

1. You have been asked to write a security policy regarding wireless-based e-mail for your corporation. Go over the details of why you would or would not allow sensitive information to be sent over this medium.

2. Management is considering rolling out 802.11 wireless and would like your input on what to choose. Describe the different.802.11 protocols and what has made them so popular, concluding with your recommendation to the management team.

3. The security team wants more information about possible wireless solutions. They feel that it is secure because encryption can be used at 128 bits. You need to make clear to them what the primary weakness in the WEP protocol is and how can it be exploited.

4. The IT department has decided to get better logging of the Ethernet system by rolling out an 802.1X implementation. Use a few sentences to describe how 802.1X can help the 802.11 protocol.

5. The marketing department wants to start using IM instead of e-mail, they claim to be able to increase productivity, but the CIO has doubts about the security of IM. Describe how you would secure an instant messaging implementation in the organization.

Lab Projects

Lab Project 12.1

Set up NetStumbler or Kismet on a computer, and then use it to find wireless access points.

You will need the following:

- A laptop with Windows or Linux installed
- A compatible wireless 802.11 network adapter

Then do the following:

1. Download NetStumbler from http://www.netstumbler.com/ or Kismet from http://www.kismetwireless.net/.

2. For NetStumbler, run the windows installer. For Kismet, un-tar the source and perform a "./configure" then "make" then "make install."

3. Start the program and make sure that it sees your wireless adapter.

4. Take the laptop on your normal commute with NetStumbler/Kismet running.

5. Log any access points you detect.

Lab Project 12.2

Set up a wireless network and then test the security provided by the default configuration.

You will need the following materials:

- An 802.11 access point and a computer using a wireless adapter, or two computers with wireless adapters
- A lab computer with a wireless network adapter and a wireless sniffer program loaded

Then do the following:

1. Set the access point to its default factory settings and make the first computer associate with it; confirm that you can get data to that PC. If using two PCs, set up an ad-hoc network between the two computers. Make sure they can see each other and share files.

2. Start the wireless sniffer on the other PC. Make no attempt to associate to either the access point or the ad-hoc network.

3. Verify that you are receiving all the packets on the network.

4. Check for both network MAC addresses in the sniff trace.

5. Make sure that you are able to capture the SSID of the network from the existing packets and beacon frames.

6. If you are using an access point, enhance security by turning on MAC address locking and turning off beacon frames.

7. Use the sniffer to check to see if the same information, MAC and SSID, are still being sent between the two hosts.

8. Turn on WEP and watch the changes in the sniffer data as the wireless traffic becomes encrypted.

9. Document your results.

Lab Project 12.3

Prove that instant messaging software behaves like a port scanner when it cannot find an IM server.

You will need the following materials:

- A lab computer with an instant messaging program installed
- A lab computer with a sniffer program loaded
- A regular Ethernet hub from which to monitor the traffic

Then do the following:

1. Plug both computers into the hub and make sure that they are not connected to the Internet.

2. Start the sniffer software. Ensure that you can see traffic from both machines.

3. Start the IM software on the other computer.

4. Watch the IM software scan through a series of ports looking for a valid outbound connection.

5. Document this behavior.

Intrusion Detection Systems

Upon completion of this chapter, you will be able to:
- Explain host-based intrusion detection systems
- Explain network-based intrusion detection systems
- Describe honeypots and explain what they are used for
- Describe how to conduct incident response operations

Network security can be fairly easily compared to physical security—the more you wish to protect something and restrict access to it, the more security you need. In the world of physical security, you have locks, walls, gates, guards, motion sensors, pressure plates, etc. As you add more protective devices, you are adding "layers" of security that an intruder would have to overcome or breach to obtain access to whatever you are protecting. Correspondingly, in the network and data security arenas you have protective layers in the form of passwords, firewalls, access lists, file permissions, and intrusion detection systems. Most organizations have their own approach to network security, choosing the "layers" that make sense for them after they weigh risks, potential for loss, cost, and manpower requirements.

The foundation for a layered network security approach usually starts with a well-secured system regardless of the system's function (whether it's a user PC or a corporate e-mail server). A well-secured system is one with up-to-date application and operating system patches, well-chosen passwords, the minimum number of services running, and restricted access to available services. On top of that foundation, you can add layers of protective measures such as antivirus products, firewalls, sniffers, and intrusion detection systems.

Some of the more complicated and interesting types of network/data security devices are intrusion detection systems. **Intrusion detection systems** (IDSs) are to the network world what burglar alarms are to the physical world. The main purpose of an intrusion detection system is to identify suspicious or malicious activity, note activity that deviates from normal behavior, catalog and classify the activity, and if possible, respond to the activity. In this chapter, you will look at the history of IDS, various types of intrusion detection systems, how they work, benefits and weaknesses of specific types, and what the future may hold for these systems. You'll also look at some complementary topics to intrusion detection systems: honeypots and incident response.

History of Intrusion Detection Systems

Like much of the network technology we see today, intrusion detection systems grew from a need to solve specific problems. Like the Internet itself, the IDS concept came from Department of Defense–sponsored research. In the early 1970s, the U.S. government and military became increasingly aware of the need to protect the electronic networks that were becoming critical to daily operations. In 1972, James Anderson published a paper for the United States Air Force outlining the growing number of computer security problems and the immediate need to secure Air Force systems (James P. Anderson, "Computer Security Technology Planning Study Volume 2," October 1972, http://seclab.cs.ucdavis.edu/projects/history/papers/ande72.pdf). Anderson continued his research and in 1980 published a follow-up paper outlining methods to improve security auditing and surveillance methods (James P. Anderson, "Computer Security Threat Monitoring and Surveillance," 15 April 1980, http://seclab .cs.ucdavis.edu/projects/history/papers/ande80.pdf). In this paper, Anderson pioneered the concept of using system **audit files** to detect unauthorized access and misuse. He also suggested the use of automated detection systems, which paved the way for misuse detection on mainframe systems in use at the time.

While Anderson's work got the efforts started, the concept of a real-time, rule-based IDS didn't really exist until Dorothy Denning and Peter Neumann developed the first real-time IDS model, called "The Intrusion Detection Expert System (IDES)," from their research between 1984 and 1986. In 1987, Denning published "An Intrusion-Detection Model," a paper that laid out the model on which most modern intrusion detection systems are based, which appears in *IEEE Transactions on Software Engineering*, Vol. SE-13, No. 2 (February 1987): 222–232.

With a model and definitions in place, the U.S. government continued to fund research that led to projects such as Discovery, Haystack, Multics Intrusion Detection and Alerting System (MIDAS), and Network Audit Director and Intrusion Reporter (NADIR). Finally, in 1989, Haystack Labs released "Stalker," the first commercial intrusion detection system. Stalker was host-based and worked by comparing audit data to known patterns of suspicious activity. While the military and government embraced the concept, the commercial world was very slow to adopt IDS products and it was several years before other commercial products began to emerge.

In the early to mid-1990s, computer systems continued to grow and companies were starting to realize the importance of intrusion detection systems; however, the solutions available were host-based and required a great deal of time and money to manage and operate effectively. Focus began to shift away from host-based systems, and network-based intrusion detection systems began to emerge. In 1995, WheelGroup was formed in San Antonio, Texas, to develop the first commercial, network-based intrusion detection product, called NetRanger. NetRanger was designed to monitor network links and the traffic moving across the links to identify misuse as well as suspicious and malicious activity. NetRanger's release was quickly followed by Internet Security Systems'

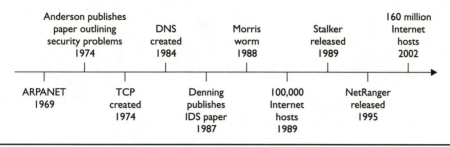

Figure 13-1   History of the Internet and IDS

RealSecure in 1996. Several other players followed suit and released their own IDS products, but it wasn't until the networking giant Cisco Systems acquired WheelGroup in February 1998 that intrusion detection systems were recognized as a vital part of any network security infrastructure. Figure 13-1 offers a timeline for these developments.

IDS Overview

As we mentioned before, an IDS is somewhat like a burglar alarm. An IDS watches the activity going on around it and tries to identify undesirable activity. Intrusion detection systems are typically divided into two main categories, depending on how they monitor activity: host-based and network-based.

- A **host-base IDS** examines activity on an individual system, such as a mail server, web server, or individual PC. It is concerned only with an individual system and usually has no visibility into the activity on the network or systems around it.

- A **network-based IDS** examines activity on the network itself. It has visibility only into the traffic crossing the network link it is monitoring and typically has no idea of what is happening on individual systems.

Whether or not it is network- or host-based, an intrusion detection system will typically consist of several specialized components working together, as illustrated in Figure 13-2. These components are often logical and software-based rather than physical and will vary slightly from vendor to vendor and product to product. Typically, an IDS will have the following logical components:

- **Traffic collector**   This component collects activity/events for the IDS to examine. On a host-based IDS, this could be log files, audit logs, or traffic coming to or leaving a specific system. On a network-based IDS, this is typically a mechanism for copying traffic off the network link—basically functioning as a sniffer.

Figure 13-2   Logical depiction of IDS components

- **Analysis engine**   This component examines the collected network traffic and compares it to known patterns of suspicious or malicious activity stored in the signature database. The analysis engine is the "brains" of the IDS.

- **Signature database**   The signature database is a collection of patterns and definitions of known suspicious or malicious activity.

- **User interface and reporting**   This is the component that interfaces with the human element, providing alerts when appropriate and giving the user a means to interact with and operate the IDS.

Most IDSs can be "tuned" to fit a particular environment. Certain **signatures** can be turned off, telling the IDS not to look for certain types of traffic. For example, if you are operating in a pure UNIX environment, you may not wish to see Windows-based alarms, as they will not affect your systems. Additionally, the severity of the alarm levels can be adjusted depending on how concerned you are over certain types of traffic. Some IDSs will also allow the user to "exclude" certain patterns of activity from specific hosts. In other words, you can tell the IDS to ignore the fact that some systems generate traffic that looks like malicious activity, because it really isn't.

Host-Based Intrusion Detection Systems

As we mentioned in our history of intrusion detection systems, the first IDSs were host-based and designed to only examine activity on a specific host. A host-based IDS (HIDS) is a system that examines log files, audit trails, and network traffic coming in to or leaving a specific host. Host-based IDSs can operate in real time, looking for activity as it occurs, or batch mode, looking for activity on a periodic basis. Host-based systems are typically self-contained, but many of the newer commercial products have been designed to report to and be managed by a central system. Host-based systems also take local system resources to operate. In other words, a host-based IDS will use up some of the memory and CPU cycles of the system it is protecting. Early versions of host-based IDSs ran in batch mode, looking for suspicious activity on an hourly or daily basis, and typically only looked for specific events in the system's log files. As processor speeds increased, later versions of host-based IDSs began to look through the log files in real time and even added the ability to examine the data traffic the host was generating and receiving.

Most host-based intrusion detection systems focus on the log files or audit trails generated by the local operating system. On UNIX systems, the examined logs usually include those created by syslog such as messages, kernel logs, and error logs. On Windows systems, the examined logs are typically the three event logs: Application, System, and Security. Some host-based IDSs have the ability to cover specific applications, such as FTP or web services, by examining the logs produced by those specific applications or examining the traffic from the services themselves. Within the log files, the IDS is looking for certain activities that typify hostile actions or misuse such as:

- Logins at odd hours

- Login authentication failures

- Adding new user accounts

- Modification or access of critical system files

- Modification or removal of binary files (executables)

- Starting or stopping processes

- Privilege escalation

- Use of certain programs

In general, most host-based intrusion detection systems will operate in a very similar fashion. (Figure 13-3 shows the logical layout of a host-based IDS.) By considering the function and activity of each component, you can gain some insight into how they operate.

Figure 13-3   Host-based IDS components

As on any IDS, the *traffic collector* on a host-based IDS pulls in the information the other components, such as the analysis engine, need to examine. For most host-based systems, the traffic collector pulls data from information the local system has already generated, such as error messages, log files, and system files. The traffic collector is responsible for reading those files, selecting which items are of interest, and forwarding them to the analysis engine. On some host-based systems, the traffic collector will also examine specific attributes of critical files such as file size, date modified, or checksum.

 NOTE   Critical files are those that are vital to the system's operation or overall functionality. They may be program (or binary) files, files containing user accounts and passwords, or even scripts to start or stop system processes. Any unexpected modifications to these files could mean the system has been compromised or modified by an attacker. By monitoring these files, the IDS can warn users of potentially malicious activity.

The *analysis engine* is perhaps the most important component of the IDS, as it must decide what activity is "okay" and what activity is "bad." The analysis engine is a sophisticated decision and pattern matching mechanism—it looks at the information given to it by the traffic collector and tries to match it against known patterns of activity stored in the signature database. If the activity matches a known pattern, the analysis engine can react, usually by issuing an alert or alarm. An analysis engine may also be capable of remembering how the activity it is looking at right now compares to traffic it has already seen or may see in the near future so that it can match more complicated, multistep malicious activity patterns. An analysis engine must also be capable of examining traffic patterns as quickly as possible, as the longer it takes to match a malicious pattern, the less time the IDS or human operator has to react to malicious traffic. Most IDS vendors will build a "**decision tree**" into their analysis engines to expedite pattern matching.

The *signature database* is a collection of predefined activity patterns that have already been identified and categorized—activity patterns that typically indicate suspicious or malicious activity. When the analysis engine has a traffic pattern to examine, it will compare that pattern to the appropriate signatures in the database. The signature database can contain anywhere from a few to a few thousand signatures, depending on the vendor, type of IDS, space available on the system to store signatures, etc.

The *user interface* is the visible component of the intrusion detection system—this is the part that humans interact with. The user interface varies widely depending on the product and vendor and could be anything from a detailed graphical interface to a simple command line. Regardless of the type and complexity, the interface is provided to allow the user to interact with the system: changing parameters, receiving alarms, tuning signatures and response patterns, etc.

To better understand how a host-based IDS operates, take a look at examples from a UNIX system and a Windows system.

On a UNIX system, the host-based IDS is most likely going to be examining any of a number of system logs—basically large text files containing entries about what is

Decision Tree

In computer systems, a "tree" is a data structure where each element in the structure is attached to one or more structures directly beneath it (the connections are called "branches"). Structures on the end of a branch without any elements below them are called "leaves." Trees are most often drawn inverted, with the "root" at the top and all subsequent elements branching down from the root. Trees where each element has no more than two elements below it are called "binary" trees.

In intrusion detection systems, a decision tree is used to help the analysis engine quickly examine traffic patterns. The decision tree helps the analysis engine eliminate signatures that don't apply to the particular traffic being examined so that the fewest number of comparisons can be made. For example, in the following illustration, the sample IDS decision tree shown may contain a section dividing the traffic into three sections based upon origin of the traffic (a log entry for events taken from the system logs, file changes for modifications to critical files, or user actions for something a user has done). When the analysis engine looks at the traffic pattern and starts down the decision tree, it must decide which path to follow. If it is a log entry, the analysis engine can then concentrate on only the signatures that apply to log entries; it does not need to worry about signatures that apply to file changes or user actions. This type of decision tree allows the analysis engine to function much faster, as it does not have to compare traffic to every signature in the database, just the signatures that apply to that particular type of traffic.

happening on the system. For our example, we'll use the following lines from the "messages" log on a Red Hat 8.0 system:

```
Jan 5 18:20:39 jeep su(pam_unix)[32478]: session opened for user bob by (uid=0)
Jan 5 18:20:47 jeep su(pam_unix)[32516]: authentication failure;
   logname= uid=502 euid=0 tty= ruser=bob rhost= user=root
Jan 5 18:20:53 jeep su(pam_unix)[32517]: authentication failure; logname= id=5
```

```
02 euid=0 tty= ruser=bob rhost= user=root
Jan 5 18:21:06 jeep su(pam_unix)[32519]: authentication failure; logname= uid=5
02 euid=0 tty= ruser=bob rhost= user=root
```

In the first line, you see a session being opened by a user named "bob." This usually indicates that whoever owns the account "bob" has logged into the system. On the next three lines, you see authentication failures as Bob tries to become "root"—the superuser account that can do anything on the system. In this case, "bob" tries three times to become root and fails on each try. This pattern of activity could mean a number of different things—"bob" could be an admin and have forgotten the password for the root account, "bob" could be an admin and someone changed the root password without telling him, "bob" could be a user attempting to guess the root password, or an attacker could have compromised Bob's account and is now trying to compromise the root account on the system. In any case, our host-based IDS will work through its decision tree to see if an "authentication failure" in the message log is something it needs to examine. In this instance, when the IDS examines these lines in the log, it will note the fact that three of the lines in the log match one of the patterns it has been told to look for (as determined by information from the decision tree and the signature database) and it will react accordingly, usually by generating an alarm or alert of some type that appears on the user interface or in an e-mail, page, or other form of message.

On a Windows system, the host-based IDS is most likely going to be examining the application logs generated by the operating system. These three logs (application, system, and security) are similar to the logs on a UNIX system, though the Windows logs are not stored as text files and typically require a utility or application to read them. For our example, we will be using the security log from a Windows 2000 Professional system.

```
Failure Audit  1/5/2003  6:47:29 PM  Security  Logon/Logoff          529  SYSTEM
Failure Audit  1/5/2003  6:47:27 PM  Security  Logon/Logoff          529  SYSTEM
Failure Audit  1/5/2003  6:47:26 PM  Security  Logon/Logoff          529  SYSTEM
Success Audit  1/5/2003  6:47:13 PM  Security  Privilege Use         578  Administrator
Success Audit  1/5/2003  6:47:12 PM  Security  Privilege Use         577  Administrator
Success Audit  1/5/2003  6:47:12 PM  Security  Privilege Use         577  Administrator
Success Audit  1/5/2003  6:47:06 PM  Security  Account Management    643  SYSTEM
Success Audit  1/5/2003  6:46:59 PM  Security  Account Management    643  SYSTEM
```

In the first three lines of our security log, you see a "Failure" audit entry for the "Logon/Logoff" process. This indicates someone has tried to log in to the system three times and has failed each time (much like our UNIX example). You don't see the name of the account until you expand the log entry within the Windows event viewer tool, but for this example, let's assume it was the "Administrator" account—the Windows equivalent of the root account. Here again, you see three login failures—if our host-based IDS has been programmed to look for failed login attempts, then it will generate alerts when it examines these log entries.

Advantages of Host-Based IDSs

Host-based IDSs have certain advantages that make them a good choice for certain situations:

- **They can be very operating system–specific and have more detailed signatures** A host-based IDS can be very specifically designed to run on a certain operating system or to protect certain applications. This narrow focus lets developers concentrate on only the things that affect the specific environment they are trying to protect. With this type of focus, the developers can avoid generic alarms and develop much more specific, detailed signatures to more accurately identify malicious traffic.

- **They can reduce false positive rates** When running on a specific system, the IDS process is much more likely to be able to determine whether or not the activity being examined is malicious or not. By more accurately identifying which activity is "bad," the IDS will generate fewer "false positives" (alarms generated when the traffic matches a pattern but is not actually malicious).

- **They can examine data after it has been decrypted** With security concerns constantly on the rise, many developers are starting to encrypt their network communications. When designed and implemented in the right manner, a host-based IDS will be able to examine traffic that is unreadable to a network-based IDS. This particular ability is becoming more important each day as more and more web sites start to encrypt all of their traffic.

- **They can be very application specific** On a host level, the IDS can be designed, modified, or tuned to work very well on specific applications without having to analyze or even hold signatures for other applications that are not running on that particular system. Signatures can be built for specific versions of web server software, FTP servers, mail servers, or any other application housed on that host.

- **They can determine whether or not an alarm may impact that specific system** The ability to determine whether or not a particular activity or pattern will really affect the system being protected assists greatly in reducing the number of generated alarms. As the IDS resides on the system, it can verify things such as patch levels, presence of certain files, and system state when it analyzes traffic. By knowing what state the system is in, the IDS can more accurately determine if an activity is potentially harmful to the system.

Disadvantages of Host-Based IDSs

Host-based IDSs also have certain disadvantages that must be weighed into the decision to deploy this type of technology:

- **The IDS must have a process on every system you want to watch** In order to watch a host, you must have an IDS process or application on every host you want to watch. To cover 100 systems, you will need to deploy 100 host-based IDSs to watch those systems.

- **The IDS can have a high cost of ownership and maintenance**   Depending on the specific vendor and application, a host-based IDS can be fairly costly in terms of time and manpower to maintain. Unless there is some type of central console that allows you to maintain remote processes, administrators must maintain each IDS process individually. Even with a central console, with a host-based IDS there will be a high number of processes to maintain, software to update, and parameters to tune.

- **The IDS uses local system resources**   In order to function, the host-based IDS must use CPU cycles and memory from the system it is trying to protect. Whatever resources the IDS uses are no longer available for the system to perform its other functions. This becomes extremely important on applications such as high-volume web servers where fewer resources usually means fewer visitors served and the need for more systems to handle expected traffic.

- **The IDS has a very focused view and cannot relate to activity around it**   The host-based IDS has a very limited view of the world, as it can only see activity on the host it is protecting. It has little to no visibility into traffic around it on the network or events taking place on other hosts. Consequently, a host-based IDS can tell you only if the system it is running on is under attack.

- **The IDS, if logged locally, could be compromised or disabled**   When an IDS generates alarms, it will typically store the alarm information in a file or database of some sort. If the host-based IDS stores its generated alarm traffic on the local system, an attacker that is successful in breaking into the system may have the capability to modify or delete those alarms. This makes it difficult for security personnel to discover the intruder and conduct any type of postincident investigation. A capable intruder may even be able to turn off the IDS process completely.

Active vs. Passive Host-Based IDSs

Most intrusion detection systems can be distinguished by how they examine the activity around them and whether or not they interact with that activity. This is certainly true for host-based IDSs. On a **passive** system, the IDS is exactly that—"passive." It simply watches the activity, analyzes it, and generates alarms. It does not interact with the activity itself in any way, and it does not modify the defensive posture of the system to react to the traffic. A passive IDS is very similar to a simple motion sensor—it generates an alarm when it matches a pattern much as the motion sensor generates an alarm when it sees movement. An **active** IDS will contain all the same components and capabilities of the passive IDS with one critical exception—the active IDS can *react* to the activity it is analyzing. These reactions can range from something simple, such as running a script to turn a process on or off, to something as complex as modifying file permissions, terminating the offending processes, logging off specific users, and reconfiguring local capabilities to prevent specific users from logging in for the next 12 hours.

Network-Based Intrusion Detection Systems

Network-based intrusion detection systems came along a few years after host-based systems. After running host-based systems for a while, many organizations grew tired of the time, energy, and expense involved with managing the first generation of these systems. The desire for a "better way" grew along with the amount of interconnectivity between systems and consequently the amount of malicious activity seen coming across the networks themselves. This fueled development of a new breed of IDS designed to focus on the source for a great deal of the malicious traffic—the network itself. The network IDS integrated very well into the concept of "perimeter security." More and more companies began to operate their computer security like a castle or military base with attention and effort focused on securing and controlling the means in and out—the idea being that if you could restrict and control access at the perimeter, you didn't have to worry as much about activity inside the organization. Even though the idea of a security perimeter is somewhat flawed (many security incidents originate inside the perimeter), it caught on very quickly, as it was easy to understand and devices such as firewalls, bastion hosts, and routers were available to define and secure that perimeter. The best way to secure the perimeter from outside attack is to reject all traffic from external entities, but as it is impossible and impractical to do so, security personnel needed a way to let traffic in but still be able to determine whether or not the traffic was malicious. This is the problem that network-based intrusion detection system developers were trying to solve.

A network-based IDS, as the name suggests, focuses on network traffic—the bits and bytes traveling along the cables and wires that interconnect the systems. A network IDS (NIDS) must examine the network traffic as it passes by and be able to analyze traffic according to protocol, type, amount, source, destination, content, traffic already seen, etc. This analysis must happen quickly, and the IDS must be able to handle traffic at whatever speed the network operates on to be effective. Network-based IDSs are typically deployed so that they can monitor traffic in and out of an organization's major links: connections to the Internet, remote offices, partners, etc. Like host-based systems, network-based IDSs look for certain activities that typify hostile actions or misuse such as:

- Denial of service attacks
- Port scans or sweeps
- Malicious content in the data payload of a packet or packets
- Vulnerability scanning
- Trojans, viruses, or worms
- Tunneling
- Brute-force attacks

In general, most network-based intrusion detection systems will operate in a fairly similar fashion. Figure 13-4 shows the logical layout of a network-based IDS and by

Figure 13-4   Network IDS components

considering the function and activity of each component you can gain some insight into how they operate.

As you can see, the logical components of a network-based intrusion detection system are very similar to those of the host-based system. In the simplest form, a network-based IDS has the same major components: traffic collector, analysis engine, reports, and a user interface.

In a network-based IDS, the *traffic collector* is specifically designed to pull traffic from the network. This component usually behaves in much the same way as a network traffic sniffer—it simply pulls every packet it can see off the network it is connected to. In a network-based IDS, the traffic collector will logically attach itself to a network interface card (NIC) and instruct the NIC to accept every packet it can. A NIC that accepts and processes every packet regardless of the packet's origin and destination is said to be in "promiscuous" mode.

The *analysis engine* in a network-based IDS has the same function as its host-based counterpart, with some substantial differences. The network analysis engine must be capable of collecting packets and examining them individually or, if necessary, reassembling them into an entire traffic session. The patterns and signatures being matched are far more complicated than host-based signatures, so the analysis engine must be capable of remembering what traffic preceded the traffic currently being analyzed so that it can determine whether or not that traffic fits into a larger pattern of malicious activity. Additionally, the network-based analysis engine must be able to keep up with the flow of traffic on the network, rebuilding network sessions and matching patterns in real time.

The network-based IDS *signature database* is usually much larger as well. When examining network patterns, the IDS must be able to recognize traffic targeted at many different applications and operating systems as well as traffic from a wide variety of threats (worms, assessment tools, attack tools, etc.). Some of the signatures themselves can be quite large, as the IDS must look at network traffic occurring in a specific order over a period of time in order to match a particular malicious pattern.

With the lessons learned from the early host-based systems, the network-based IDS developers modified the logical component design somewhat to distribute the user interface and reporting functions. As many companies had more than one network link, they would need an IDS capable of handling multiple links in many different locations. The early IDS vendors solved this dilemma by dividing the components and assigning them to separate entities. The traffic collection, analysis engine, and signature database were bundled into a single entity usually called a "sensor" or "appliance." The sensors would report to and be controlled by a central system or master console. This central system, shown in Figure 13-5, consolidated alarms and provided the user interface and reporting functions that allowed users in one location to manage, maintain, and monitor sensors deployed in a variety of remote locations.

By creating separate entities designed to work together, the network IDS developers were able to build a more capable and flexible system. With encrypted communications, network sensors could be placed around both local and remote perimeters and still be monitored and managed securely from a central location. Placement of the sensors very quickly became an issue for most security personnel, as the sensors obviously had to have visibility of the network traffic in order to analyze it. Because most organizations with network-based IDSs also had firewalls, location of the IDS relative to the firewall had to be considered as well. Placed before the firewall, as shown in Figure 13-6, the IDS will see all traffic coming in from the Internet, including attacks against the firewall itself. This includes traffic that the firewall stops and does not permit into the corporate network. With this type of deployment, the network IDS sensor will generate a large number of alarms (including alarms for traffic that the firewall would stop) that tends to overwhelm the human operators managing the system.

Placed after the firewall, as shown in Figure 13-7, the network IDS sensor sees and analyzes the traffic that is being passed through the firewall and into the corporate network. While this does not allow the IDS to see attacks against the firewall, it generally results in far fewer alarms and is the most popular placement for network IDS sensors.

Figure 13-5   Distributed network IDS components

Figure 13-6 IDS sensor placed in front of firewall

As you already know, network-based intrusion detection systems examine the network traffic for suspicious or malicious activity. Here are two examples to illustrate the operation of a network IDS:

- **Port scan** A port scan is a reconnaissance activity a potential attacker will use to find out information about the systems they wish to attack. Using any of a number of tools, the attacker will attempt to connect to various services (Web, FTP, SMTP, etc.) to see if they exist on the intended target. In normal network traffic, a single user might connect to the FTP service provided on a single system. During a port scan, an attacker may attempt to connect to the FTP service on every system. As the attacker's traffic passes by the IDS, this pattern of attempting to connect to different services on different systems will be noticed. When the IDS compares the activity to its signature database, it will very likely match this traffic against the port scanning signature and generate an alarm.

Figure 13-7 IDS sensor placed behind firewall

- **Ping of death**   Toward the end of 1996, it was discovered that certain operating systems, such as Windows, could be crashed by sending a very large ICMP echo request packet to that system. The vulnerable operating systems did not handle the packet correctly and would subsequently reboot or lock up after receiving the packets. This is a fairly simple traffic pattern for a network IDS to identify, as it simply has to look for ICMP packets over a certain size.

Advantages of a Network-Based IDS

A network-based IDS has certain advantages that make it a good choice for certain situations:

- **It takes fewer systems to provide IDS coverage**   With a few well-placed network IDS sensors, you can monitor all the network traffic going in and out of your organization. Fewer sensors usually equates to less overhead and maintenance, meaning you can protect the same number of systems at a lower cost.

- **Deployment, maintenance, and upgrade costs are usually lower**   The fewer systems that have to be managed and maintained to provide IDS coverage, the lower the cost to operate the IDS will be. Upgrading and maintaining a few sensors is usually much cheaper than upgrading and maintaining hundreds of host-based processes.

- **A network-based IDS has visibility into all network traffic and can correlate attacks among multiple systems**   Well-placed network IDS sensors can see the "big picture" when it comes to network-based attacks. The network sensors can tell you if attacks are widespread and unorganized or focused and concentrated on specific systems.

Disadvantages of a Network-Based IDS

A network-based IDS has certain disadvantages:

- **It is ineffective when traffic is encrypted**   When network traffic is encrypted from application to application or system to system, a network-based IDS sensor will not be able to examine that traffic. With the increasing popularity of encrypted traffic, this is becoming a bigger problem for effective IDS operations.

- **It can't see traffic that does not cross it**   The IDS sensor can examine only traffic crossing the network link it is monitoring. With most IDS sensors being placed on perimeter links, traffic traversing the internal network is never seen.

- **It must be able to handle high volumes of traffic**   As network speeds continue to increase, the network sensors must be able to keep pace and examine the traffic as quickly as it can pass the network. When network-based intrusion detection systems were introduced, 10 Mbps networks were the norm. Now 100Mbps and even 1 Gbps networks are commonplace. This increase in traffic speeds means IDS sensors must be faster and more powerful than ever before.

- **It doesn't know about activity on the hosts themselves** As the name suggests, network-based intrusion detection systems focus on network traffic. Activity that occurs on the hosts themselves will not be seen by a network IDS.

Active vs. Passive Network-Based IDSs

Most network-based intrusion detection systems can be distinguished by how they examine the traffic and whether or not they interact with that traffic. On a *passive* system, the IDS is exactly that—"passive." It simply watches the traffic, analyzes it, and generates alarms. It does not interact with the traffic itself in any way, and it does not modify the defensive posture of the system to react to the traffic. A passive IDS is very similar to a simple motion sensor—it generates an alarm when it matches a pattern much as the motion sensor generates an alarm when it sees movement. An *active* IDS will contain all the same components and capabilities of the passive IDS with one critical addition—the active IDS can *react* to the traffic it is analyzing. These reactions can range from something simple, such as sending a TCP reset message to interrupt a potential attack and disconnect a session, to something complex such as dynamically modifying firewall rules to reject all traffic from specific source IP addresses for the next 24 hours.

The most common defensive capability for an active IDS is to send a TCP reset message. Within the TCP protocol, the reset message (RST) essentially tells both sides of the connection to drop the session and stop communicating immediately. While this mechanism was originally developed to cover situations like systems accidentally receiving communications intended for other systems, the reset message works fairly well for intrusion detection systems. There is one serious drawback—a reset message affects only the current session. There is nothing to prevent the attacker from coming back and trying again and again. Despite the "temporariness" of this solution, sending a reset message is usually the only defensive measure implemented on IDS deployments, as the fear of blocking legitimate traffic and disrupting business processes, even for a few moments, often outweighs the perceived benefit of discouraging potential intruders.

Signatures

As you have probably deduced from our discussion so far, one of the critical elements of any good intrusion detection system is the signature set—that set of patterns the IDS uses to determine whether or not activity is potentially hostile. Signatures can be very simple or remarkably complicated, depending on the activity they are trying to highlight. In general, signatures can be divided into two main groups, depending on what the signature is looking for.

Content-based signatures are generally the simplest. They are designed to look at the content of such things as network packets or log entries. Content-based signatures are typically easy to build and look for something simple such as a certain string of characters or a certain flag set in a TCP packet. Here are some example content-based signatures:

- *Matching the characters "/etc/passwd" in a telnet session.* On a UNIX system, the names of valid user accounts (and sometimes the passwords for those user accounts) are stored in a file called "passwd" located in the "etc" directory.

- *Matching a TCP packet with the synchronize, reset, and urgent flags all set.* This combination of flags is impossible to generate under normal conditions, and the presence of all of these flags in the same packet would indicate this packet was likely "created" by a potential attacker for a specific purpose.

- *Matching the characters "to: decode" in the header of an e-mail message.* On certain older versions of sendmail, sending an e-mail message to "decode" would cause the system to execute the contents of the e-mail.

Context-based signatures are generally more complicated, as they are designed to match large patterns of activity and examine how certain types of activity fit into the other activities going on around them. Context signatures generally address the question "How does this event compare to other events that have already happened or might happen in the near future?" Context signatures are more difficult to analyze and take more resources to match, as the IDS must be able to "remember" past events to match certain context signatures. Some example context-based signatures:

- *Match a potential intruder scanning for open web servers on a specific network.* A potential intruder may use a port scanner to look for any systems accepting connections on port 80. To match this signature, the IDS must analyze all attempted connections to port 80 and then be able to determine which connection attempts are coming from the same source but are going to different destinations.

- *Identify a Nessus scan.* Nessus is an open-source vulnerability scanner that allows security administrators (and potential attackers) to quickly examine systems for vulnerabilities. Depending on the tests chosen, Nessus will typically perform the tests in a certain order, one after the other. To be able to determine the presence of a Nessus scan, the IDS must know which tests Nessus runs as well as the typical order the tests are run in.

- *Identify a ping flood attack.* A single ICMP packet on its own is generally regarded as harmless, certainly not worthy of an IDS signature. Yet, thousands of ICMP packets coming to a single system in a short period of time can have a devastating effect on the receiving system. By flooding a system with thousands of valid ICMP packets, an attacker can keep a target system so busy it doesn't have time to do anything else—a very effective denial of service attack. To identify a ping flood, the IDS must recognize each ICMP packet and keep track of how many ICMP packets different systems have received in the recent past.

To function, the IDS must have a decent signature base with examples of known, undesirable activity that it can use when analyzing traffic or events. Any time an IDS matches current events against a signature, the IDS could be considered successful, as it has correctly matched the current event against a known signature and reacted accordingly (usually with an alarm or alert of some type).

False Positives and Negatives

Viewed in its simplest form, an IDS is really just taking activity (be it host-based or network-based) and matching it against a predefined set of patterns. When it matches activity to a specific pattern, there is no way for the IDS to know the true intent behind that activity—whether or not it is benign or hostile—and therefore the IDS can react only as it has been programmed to do. In most cases, this means generating an alert that must then be analyzed by a human who tries to determine the intent of the traffic from whatever information they have available. When an IDS matches a pattern and generates an alarm for benign traffic, meaning the traffic was not hostile and not a threat, this is called a **false positive**. In other words, the IDS matched a pattern and raised an alarm when it didn't really need to. Again, keep in mind that the IDS can only match patterns and has no capability to determine intent behind the activity, so in some ways this is an unfair label. Technically, the IDS is functioning correctly by matching the pattern, but from a human standpoint this is not information the analyst needed to see, as it does not constitute a threat and does not require intervention.

An IDS is also limited by its signature set—it can match only activity for which it has stored patterns. Hostile activity that does not match an IDS signature and therefore goes undetected is called a **false negative**. In this case, the IDS is not generating any alarms, even though it should be, giving a false sense of security.

IDS Models

In addition to being divided along the host and network lines, intrusion detection systems are often classified according to the detection model they use: anomaly or misuse. For an IDS, a model is a method for examining behavior so that the IDS can determine if that behavior is "not normal" or in violation of established policies.

An **anomaly** detection model is the more complicated of the two. In this model, the intrusion detection system must know what "normal" behavior on the host or network being protected really is. Once the "normal" behavior baseline is established, the IDS can then go to work identifying deviations from the norm, which are further scrutinized to determine if that activity is malicious. Building the profile of normal activity is usually done by the IDS, with some input from security administrators, and can take anywhere from days to months. The IDS must be flexible and capable enough to account for things such as new systems, new users, movement of information resources, etc., but be sensitive enough to detect a single user illegally switching from one account to another at 3 A.M. on a Saturday. Anomaly detection was developed to make the system capable of dealing with variations in traffic and better able to determine which activity patterns were malicious. A perfectly functioning anomaly-based system would be able to ignore patterns from legitimate hosts and users but still identify those patterns as suspicious should they come from a potential attacker. Unfortunately, most anomaly-based systems suffer from extremely high false positives, especially during the "break-in" period while the IDS is learning the network. On the other hand, an anomaly-based system is not restricted to a specific signature set and is far more likely to identify a new exploit or attack tool that would go unnoticed by a traditional intrusion detection system.

A **misuse** detection model is a little simpler to implement, and therefore the more popular of the two models. In a misuse model, the IDS looks for suspicious activity or activity that violates specific policies and then reacts as it has been programmed. This reaction may be an alarm, e-mail, router reconfiguration, or TCP reset message. Technically, this is the more efficient model, as it takes fewer resources to operate, does not need to learn what "normal" behavior is, and will generate an alarm whenever a pattern is successfully matched. However, the misuse model's greatest weakness is its reliance on a predefined signature base—any activity, malicious or otherwise, that the misuse-based IDS does not have a signature for will go undetected. Despite that drawback and because it is easier and cheaper to implement, most commercial IDS products are based on the misuse detection model.

Preventative Intrusion Detection Systems

While current intrusion detection systems do a fairly decent job of alerting the user to suspicious or malicious activity, they don't really provide too many capabilities to prevent the attacker from damaging your information systems. As many security personnel and system administrators have found out, there's less value in knowing what happened after the fact than there is in preventing the damage from occurring in the first place. This is the philosophy behind a new movement in intrusion detection systems—systems designed to both identify malicious activity and prevent it from having any impact on your network and information systems. This new breed of IDS, called a **preventative IDS**, is rapidly gaining in popularity, and several commercial vendors are already offering products with this type of capability.

The concept behind a preventative IDS is simple: identify bad traffic and make sure it doesn't do any harm. In many ways, a preventative IDS is similar to an antivirus product. An antivirus product may spot an infected e-mail attachment coming into the mail server and will quarantine the incoming message, preventing the message from being opened and the virus from being executed. In the same fashion, a preventative IDS may see an attacker attempting to execute a buffer overflow on a local system and will intercept the attacker's system call to prevent it from executing. To be effective, a preventative IDS will typically be some type of hybrid system, having both network-based and host-based portions. The host-based portion serves as a security wrapper for the protected system, filtering such things as system calls, user input, and program executions. Activity that matches a known, malicious pattern, such as a buffer overflow, is caught by the host wrapper and stopped before the attack is allowed to execute and affect the local system. The network-based portion operates in a similar manner, filtering network traffic for things like scans, network-based attacks, and denial of service attacks. Like its host counterpart, the preventative network IDS catches the malicious activity and prevents it from reaching the intended target.

In many ways, preventative intrusion detection systems are the wave of the future. Traditional misuse model–based IDSs are continually playing catch-up to increasingly sophisticated attackers. Additionally, most IDSs are limited to a detection role much like a burglar alarm—they can tell you when certain things have happened, but they have a limited ability to prevent things from happening. Even when the ability to prevent malicious activity is available, as by sending a TCP reset or reconfiguring firewall rulesets, it is often not used, as the potential for accidentally blocking legitimate traffic is extremely high. By contrast, a preventative IDS will still have the ability to detect and identify malicious activity, but it will also have the capability to prevent that activity from damaging or disabling critical information assets. This promise of a "better way" to perform security operations is attracting a large audience whose interest ensures preventative intrusion detection systems will receive some serious attention from commercial security companies in the very near future.

IDS Products and Vendors

There are quite a few intrusion detection products available on the market today, with prices ranging from free to very expensive. Table 13-1 provides a list of some of the IDS products and vendors currently available.

Honeypots

As is often the case, one of the best tools available to information security personnel has always been knowledge. To properly secure and defend a network and the information systems on that network, security personnel need to know what they are up against. What types of attacks are being used? What are the tools and techniques that are popular right now? How effective is a certain technique? What sort of impact does this specific tool have on my network? Often this sort of information is passed through white papers, conferences, mailing lists, or even word of mouth. In some cases, the tool developers themselves provide much of the information in the interest of promoting better security for everyone. Information is also gathered through examination and forensic analysis, often after a major incident has already occurred and information systems are

Name	Product	Where to Find More Information
Cisco Systems, Inc.	Cisco IDS	www.cisco.com
Computer Associates	eTrust	www.ca.com
Enterasys Network	Dragon	www.enterasys.com
Internet Security Systems, Inc.	RealSecure	www.iss.net
Intrusion, Inc.	SecureNet, SecureHost	www.intrusion.com
Intruvert Networks	IntruShield	www.intruvert.com
iPolicy Networks	ipEnforcer	www.ipolicynetworks.com
NetScreen	NetScreen IDP	www.netscreen.com
NFR Security, Inc.	NFR	www.nfr.com
Snort	Snort (free, open source)	www.snort.org
Symantec Corporation	Intruder Alert	www.symantec.com
TippingPoint Technologies	UnityOne	www.tippingpoint.com
Tripwire, Inc.	Tripwire	www.tripwiresecurity.com

Table 13-1 List of IDS Vendors and Products

already damaged. One of the most effective techniques for collecting this type of information is to observe activity first-hand—watching an attacker as they probe, navigate, and exploit their way through a network. To accomplish this without exposing critical information systems, security researchers often use something called a "honeypot."

A **honeypot** or **honeynet** is sometimes called a digital sandbox. In essence, a honeypot is an artificial environment where attackers can be contained and observed without putting real systems at risk. A good honeypot gives the appearance of a real network, application servers, users systems, network traffic, etc., but in most cases is made up of one or a few systems running specialized software to simulate the user and network traffic common to most targeted networks. Figure 13-8 illustrates a simple honeypot layout where a single system is placed on the network to deliberately attract attention from potential attackers.

Figure 13-8 shows the security researcher's view of the honeypot, while Figure 13-9 shows the attacker's view. The security administrator knows that, in this case, the honeypot really only consists of a single system running software designed to react to probes, reconnaissance attempts, and exploits as if it were an entire network of systems. When the attacker connects to the honeypot, they are presented with an entire "virtual" network of servers and PCs running a variety of applications. In most cases, the honeypot will appear to be running versions of applications that are known to be vulnerable to specific exploits. All this is designed to provide the attacker with an enticing and, hopefully, irresistible target.

Anytime an attacker has been lured into probing or attacking the virtual network, the honeypot records the activity for later analysis: what the attacker does, which systems and applications they concentrate on, what tools are run, how long they stay, etc. All this information is collected and analyzed in the hopes that it will allow security personnel to better understand and protect against the threats to their systems.

There are many honeypots in use, specializing in everything from wireless to denial of service attacks; most are being run by research, government, or law enforcement organizations. Why aren't more businesses running honeypots? Quite simply, the time and cost are prohibitive. Honeypots take quite a bit of time and effort to manage and maintain and even more effort to sort, analyze, and classify the traffic the honeypot collects.

Figure 13-8   Logical depiction of a honeypot

Attacker

Virtual network created by
the honeypot

Figure 13-9 Virtual network created by the honeypot

Unless they are developing security tools, most companies focus their limited security efforts on preventing attacks, and in many cases, companies aren't even that concerned with detecting attacks as long as the attacks are blocked, are unsuccessful, and don't affect business operations. So for now, honeypots will probably continue to be specialized research tools that you aren't likely to find in most companies' security deployments.

Incident Response

If you spend any time at all in the fields of network security or system administration, you will likely be involved in some sort of **incident response** or recovery effort. An "incident" can be anything from a hardware failure to a full-scale security breach, and while each one is handled in a slightly different manner, there are some similarities we will discuss in this section. Essentially, incident response is how an organization reacts to an unusual negative situation. Incident response covers the technical and administrative aspects of dealing with incidents and can range in formality from a simple "call Superman" approach to a formal, detailed step-by-step response plan including procedures and tools that covers every situation imaginable. Some companies have a full-scale response team, while others have that proverbial "go to" person that handles everything on their own. Entire books have been written about this topic, and while we won't attempt to cover it in anywhere close to that amount of detail, we will cover a few fundamental concepts that should be included in any incident response approach.

Regardless of your particular organization's approach, it is always a good idea to start with an incident response plan. Ideally, your incident response plan is a well-thought-out set of documents that include all the necessary processes and pieces of information to deal with specific incidents. The idea is to sit down ahead of time and plan out how you need to react to and deal with different kinds of incidents. Make your response procedures as specific as you can—the less you leave to chance, the less likely you are to make a mistake when handling an incident. When building your response procedures, think about topics such as:

- What immediate steps need to be taken?
- Does the security posture need to be modified? When? How?
- Who needs to be notified of this event? When? How?
- What impact does this have on business operations?
- What tools will be used to investigate this incident? Who will use them and how?
- Which is more important, system recovery or evidence collection?
- Will forensic activity occur? What evidence will be collected, and how will it be preserved?
- At what point do you contact law enforcement? Who makes that call, and whom do you call?
- What other resources are available?
- Where are things like replacement hardware and software located?
- Do system images or backups exist to aid in recovery?
- How do you contact hardware, software, or security vendors if you need to?
- Will this incident become public knowledge? Is a press release needed?

These questions are just examples—not every incident is the same, and while you can't plan for everything, you do need to plan for everything you can. The biggest advantage to prebuilt incident response plans is that they provide a framework and offer guidance during what is usually a frantic and tense situation. By following a plan, organizations can usually recover faster and with less impact than by "winging it" when something happens.

Another key factor you have to consider when responding to an incident, particularly an intrusion or security breach, is the involvement of law enforcement. If you have any notion of attempting to track down and prosecute the intruder, you will need to involve law enforcement as quickly as possible. Start with your local police department and the FBI; you may also want to engage one of the many consulting firms that specialize in incident response and computer forensics. Keep in mind that there are specific guidelines for handling and preserving digital evidence and in many cases, the steps necessary to preserve evidence are contrary to business recovery efforts. For example, if your main e-commerce web server is attacked, business recovery would want the system up and online as soon as possible. To properly examine and preserve evidence, though, you may not be able to return that system to operation for days or months. These conflicting priorities make it difficult for many companies, particularly smaller ones, to properly investigate and respond to incidents.

Computer incidents are increasing at such a high rate that some insurance firms are now offering "incident insurance" to protect your organization in the event of a serious computer-related incident. As with most insurance policies, premium reductions are granted for proactive measures like installing firewalls and intrusion detection systems.

While insurance may protect you from immediate monetary losses, your organization may sustain more permanent long-term damage such as a loss of public confidence as a result of the incident—particularly damaging if you are a financial or retail organization.

Chapter Review

Chapter Summary

After reading this chapter and completing the exercises, you should understand the following facts about intrusion detection systems, honeypots, and incident response.

Intrusion Detection Systems

- Intrusion detection systems are mechanisms for detecting unexpected or unauthorized activity on computer systems.
- Intrusion detection systems can be host-based or network-based.
- Signatures are pre-defined patterns used to spot malicious or suspicious traffic. They may be either content- or context-based.
- Anomaly-based IDSs look for activities that do not match "normal" patterns.
- Misuse-based IDSs match suspicious or malicious patterns using signatures.
- Some IDSs include prevention capabilities that automatically block suspicious or malicious traffic before it reaches its intended destination.

Honeypots

- Honeypots are based on the concept of luring attackers away from legitimate systems by presenting more tempting or interesting systems that, in most cases, appear to be easy targets.
- Security personnel monitor traffic in and out of a honeypot to better identify potential attackers along with their tools and capabilities.
- Honeypots create virtual servers and services that offer inviting targets for potential attackers.

Incident Response

- Incident response is the formalized response of reacting to a situation such as a security breach or system outage.
- While many incident response systems are based on threats from potential attackers, incident response can be used to deal with other situations such as virus outbreaks, hardware outages, and loss of network connectivity.
- Incident response requires procedures that outline steps to take for notification, analysis, and remediation.

Key Terms

Active IDS *(318)*
Anomaly detection model *(326)*
Audit files *(310)*
Content-based signatures *(324)*
Context-based signatures *(325)*
Decision tree *(314)*
False negative *(326)*
False positive *(326)*
Honeypot/honeynet *(329)*
Host-based IDS *(311)*
Incident response *(330)*
Intrusion detection system *(309)*
Misuse detection model *(327)*
Network-based IDS *(311)*
Passive IDS *(318)*
Preventative IDS *(327)*
Signature *(312)*

Key Terms Quiz

Use the Key Terms list to complete the sentences that follow. Don't use the same term more than once. Not all terms will be used.

1. A _____ is a type of IDS that is not very effective against encrypted traffic.

2. A pre-defined pattern of activity used by an IDS is called a _____.

3. When an IDS matches a pattern, but the activity is not malicious, this is called a _____.

4. A _____ is a type of IDS that runs on a single system looking for suspicious or malicious traffic.

5. An IDS that can disrupt or prevent malicious traffic is called a _____.

6. _____ is the formalized response of reacting to a situation such as a security breach or system outage.

7. To create virtual targets for potential attackers, you might use a _____.

8. An IDS that examines traffic looking for activity that does not appear "normal" is based on the _____.

9. Detecting a ping flood on a network-based IDS would require a _____ signature.

10. _____ are typically divided into two main categories, depending on how they monitor activity: host-based and network-based.

Multiple-Choice Quiz

1. The foundation for a layered security approach usually starts with:

   A. A honeypot

   B. A host-based IDS

   C. A well-secured system

   D. A network-based IDS

2. Preventative intrusion detection systems:

   A. Are far more expensive and effective than other types

   B. Can only monitor activity on the host itself

   C. Were the first types of IDSs

   D. Are designed to stop malicious activity from occurring

3. An IDS is most like:

   A. A dead-bolt

   B. A burglar alarm

   C. A pressure sensor

   D. An electric gate

4. What are the main types of IDS signatures? (Choose only one answer.)

   A. Active and reactive

   B. Context-based and content-based

   C. Active and passive

   D. Network-based and file-based

5. What does a host-based IDS examine?

   A. Feeds from network capture devices such as sniffers

   B. Honeypot activity

   C. Firewall activity records

   D. Activity on the local host

6. What was the first network-based IDS product?

   A. IDES

   B. Stalker

   C. RealSecure

   D. NetRanger

7. Detecting and responding to malicious traffic on a network segment requires:

   A. An active host-based IDS

    B. A passive host-based IDS

    C. An active network-based IDS

    D. A passive network-based IDS

8. What are the two main types of intrusion detection systems?

    A. Signature-based and event-based

    B. Network-based and host-based

    C. Active and reactive

    D. Intelligent and passive

9. Honeypots are primarily used to:

    A. Collect evidence for law enforcement

    B. Research behavior of attackers using virtual targets

    C. Process events from firewalls and routers

    D. Attract customers to e-commerce sites

10. Incident response:

    A. Is only done for hardware failures

    B. Details how a company will continue to conduct business after a natural disaster such as a fire and flood

    C. Involves a detailed, formal response plan

    D. Is used by law enforcement for evidence collection

11. Which of the following is true for host-based IDSs?

    A. They are not application-specific.

    B. They cannot determine whether or not an alarm really applies to the local system.

    C. They use local system resources.

    D. They are not operating system–specific.

12. The analysis engine of an IDS…

    A. Contains stored patterns of malicious behavior

    B. Collects packets from the network, local processes, and log files

    C. Examines the collected network traffic and compares it to known patterns of suspicious or malicious activity

    D. Provides the human interface into the IDS

13. Which of the following is a context-based signature?

    A. Matching the characters "/etc/passwd" in a Telnet session

    B. Identifying a Nessus scan

    C. Matching a TCP packet with the synchronize, reset, and urgent flags all set

    D. Matching the characters "to: decode" in the header of an e-mail message

14. Incident Response plans should be developed…

    A. When critical hardware or software components fail

    B. Only for situations involving loss of network connectivity

    C. As a formal, detailed step-by-step response plan including procedures and tools

    D. As a joint venture between your organization and local authorities

15. A port scan is…

    A. An attack involving large ICMP packets

    B. A method for breaking into web servers

    C. A reconnaissance activity

    D. Only effective against firewalls and routers

Essay Quiz

1. Your company is trying to determine what type of IDS to implement. Write a brief comparison of host- and network-based intrusion detection systems. Include advantages and disadvantages of each.

2. Discuss how you would create your own content-based signature. Include a specific description of the patterns you would look for and why. Discuss why this signature would be important and what activity you are trying to detect.

3. Develop an incident response plan for a specific situation such as a network outage or power failure. Be sure to include the personnel involved, specific steps to take, and any tools (software or hardware) that may be required.

Lab Projects

Lab Project 13.1

You've just been asked to deploy an IDS at your company. The company has 500 desktops, 20 servers, and two connections to the Internet. Describe which type of IDS you would deploy and why. Create network diagrams to show placement of components. Describe how the system would be installed, maintained, and monitored.

Lab Project 13.2

Download and install Back Officer Friendly from NFR Security, Inc. on a Windows-based lab system (www.nfr.com/resource/backOfficer.php). This free utility serves as a very basic host-based IDS and honeypot. Once the software is installed, configure it to listen for incoming connections on FTP, SMTP, Telnet, and so forth. Then have a friend try to connect to various ports on your lab system. (HINT: From the Windows command line, you can type: **telnet <target IP address> <port number>**. For example: **telnet 192.168.50.50 25** will make a connection to port 25 on the specified IP address.) For more interesting results, install and run Back Officer Friendly on a PC connected to the Internet via a DSL or cable modem.

14

Security Baselines

Upon completion of this chapter, you will be able to:
- Describe ways of hardening various operating systems
- Describe methods for hardening network devices
- Describe issues related to hardening various applications

Computers are such an integral part of everything we do now that it is difficult imagining life without them. Operating systems, network devices, and applications all work together on millions of computers to process, transmit, and store the billions of pieces of information exchanged every day. Everything from cars to credit cards require computers to operate.

The many uses for systems and operating systems require flexible components, allowing users to design, configure, and implement the systems they need. Yet, it is this very flexibility that causes some of the biggest weaknesses in computer systems. Computer and operating system developers often build and deliver systems in "default" modes that do little to secure the system from external attacks. From the view of the developer, this is the most efficient mode of delivery, as there is no way they could anticipate what every user in every situation will need. From the user's view, however, this means a good deal of effort must be put into protecting and securing the system before it is ever put into service. The process of securing and preparing a system for the production environment is called **hardening**. Unfortunately, many users don't understand the steps necessary to effectively secure their systems, resulting in hundreds of compromised systems every day.

Overview Baselines

To effectively and consistently secure systems, one must take a structured and logical approach. This starts with an examination of the system's intended functions and capabilities to determine what processes and applications will be housed on the system. As a best practice, anything that is not required for operations should be removed or disabled on the system. Then all the appropriate patches, hotfixes, and settings are applied to protect and secure the systems.

This process of establishing a system's security state is called **baselining**, and the resulting product is a security *baseline* that allows the system to run safely and securely.

Once the process has been completed for a particular hardware and software combination, any like systems can be configured with the same baseline and achieve the same level and depth of security and protection. Uniform baselines are critical in large-scale operations, as it is far too costly to maintain separate configurations and security levels for hundreds or thousands of systems.

Password Selection

Password selection is one of those critical activities that is often neglected as part of a good security baseline. The heart of the problem is this—most systems today are only protected by a simple userID and password. If an attacker guesses the right userID and password combination, then they are in, and have completely bypassed all the other steps taken to secure the system. Worse still, on a system supporting multiple users, the attacker only has to guess one correct userID and password combination to gain access.

This basic security challenge exists for every other topic we will examine in this chapter, from operating systems to applications. Selecting a good password for all user accounts is critical to protecting information systems. So how does one select a good password? One that is still relatively easy to remember but still difficult to "guess?" Unfortunately, there is no magic answer to cover all situations, but there are some basic guidelines and principles to help ensure good password selection.

Password Policy Guidelines

The username and password challenge is arguably the most popular security mechanism in use today. Unfortunately, it's also the most poorly configured, neglected, and easily circumvented. The first step in addressing the password issue is to create an effective and manageable **password policy** that both system administrators and users can work with. In creating a policy, you should examine your business and security needs carefully. What level of risk is acceptable? How secure does the system need to be? How often should users change their passwords? Should you ever lock accounts? What guidelines should users use when selecting passwords? Your list of questions will vary greatly, but the key is to spend time identifying your concerns and addressing them specifically in your password policy.

Once you have created your password policy, spread the word. Make sure every user gets a copy. Post it on your company intranet. Have new users read a copy of the policy before creating an account for them. Periodically send out e-mail reminders highlighting items in the password policy. Make announcements at company gatherings. The method is not important—the goal is simply to ensure that every single user understands what the policy is.

Once you have taught everyone what the policy is, you have to enforce it to make it effective. Set a minimum number of characters for passwords, and never accept a shorter password. Implement password aging and prompt users to change passwords on a regular basis. Do not accept passwords based on dictionary words. Do not allow users to use the same password over and over. Many operating systems have built-in utilities or add-ons that allow administrators to enforce good password selection, force password aging, and prevent password reuse. Here are some useful references for different operating systems:

- **Microsoft Windows NT 4.0, Service Pack 2**   Introduced PASSFILT.DLL, which forces users to follow specific conventions when creating new passwords: http://support.microsoft.com/support/kb/articles/q161/9/90.asp

- **Linux**

  - **Npasswd**   A replacement for passwd that provides intelligent password screening to help users select a more secure password: www.utexas.edu/cc/unix/software/npasswd/

  - **PAM (Pluggable Authentication Modules)**   Provides a common authentication scheme that can be used for a variety of applications. Go to www.redhat.com and search for "PAM."

- **Solaris**

  - **PAM (Pluggable Authentication Modules)**   The Solaris implementation of a common authentication scheme: www.sun.com/solaris/pam/.

Take the time to audit your own password files by running some of the more popular password cracking utilities against them. In a large organization with many user accounts (over a thousand), this will take some time and computing power, but it is well worth the effort. Perform these audits as often as you can—monthly, every other month, or every quarter. If you find accounts with easily cracked passwords, have the users review your password policy and change the passwords immediately. Remember, there are many publicly available password cracking tools, and any account you crack easily can be cracked by someone else. Here are some of the more popular password cracking utilities:

- **LC4 (formerly L0phtCrack) for Windows 2000 and NT**   www.atstake.com/research/lc/

- **John the Ripper (UNIX and DOS)**   www.openwall.com/

- **Crack (UNIX)**   packetstormsecurity.nl/Crackers/crack/

Selecting a Password

There are many different methods of selecting a password, ranging from random generation to one-time use. Each method has its own advantages and weaknesses, but typically when security increases, usability tends to decrease. For example, random generation tends to produce secure passwords composed of random letters (no dictionary words, and a mix of upper- and lowercase letters with usually one or two numbers) that are very difficult to guess and will defeat most password cracking utilities. Unfortunately, randomly generated passwords tend to be difficult to remember, and users often write such passwords down, usually in a location close to the machine, thus defeating the purpose of the password. The best compromise between security and usability lies in teaching users how to select their own secure password based on an easy-to-remember **passphrase**.

A password based on a passphrase can be formed in many ways: taking the first letter of each word in a sentence; taking the first letter from the first word, second letter from the second word, and so on; combining words; or replacing letters with other characters. Here are some passphrase examples and the resulting passwords:

- Use the first letter of each word in the following sentence:
  Sentence   I love to drive my 1969 Mustang!
  Password   Iltdm69M!
- Combining words and replacing letters with characters:
  Sentence   Bad to the Bone
  Password   Bad2theB1

Passphrases can be almost anything—lines from your favorite movie, lyrics from your favorite song, or something you make up on the spot. Use any method you choose, but the end result should be a difficult-to-guess, easy-to-remember password.

Components of a Good Password

By using the passphrase method, users should be able to create their own easy-to-remember passwords. However, since a password is meant to protect access and resources from intruders, it should not be easy for someone else to guess or obtain using password cracking utilities, such as John the Ripper, L0phtCrack, or Crack. To make a password more difficult to guess or obtain, make sure your new password meets the following guidelines:

- Should be at least eight characters long (some operating systems require longer passwords by default)
- Should have at least three of the following four elements:
  - One or more uppercase letters (A – Z)
  - One or more lowercase letters (a – z)
  - One or more numerals (0 – 9)
  - One or more special characters or punctuation marks (!@#$%^&*,.:;?)
- Should not consist of dictionary words
- Should never be the same as the user's login name or contain the login name
- Should not consist of the user's first or last name, family member's names, birth dates, pet names, or any other item that is easily identified with the user

Password Aging

Given enough time and computing power, virtually any password can be cracked by simply testing all possible passwords. It is therefore necessary to have users change their passwords on a regular basis. Additionally, since any password can be cracked eventually, it is necessary to prevent users from "recycling" passwords (using the same password over and over). Many operating systems have options allowing system administrators to enforce password aging and prevent password reuse. Consider using the following guidelines:

- Have users change their passwords every 60 to 90 days (very secure facilities may want to change passwords every 30 to 45 days)

- Have the system "remember" the user's last five to ten passwords, and do not allow the user to use those passwords again

Operating System and Network Operating System Hardening

The **operating system** (OS) of a computer is the basic software that handles things such as input, output, display, memory management, and all the other highly detailed tasks required to support the user environment and associated applications. Most users are familiar with the Microsoft family of operating systems: Windows 95, Windows 98, Windows NT, Windows 2000, Windows ME, and Windows XP. Indeed, the vast majority of home and business PCs run some version of a Microsoft operating system. Other users may be familiar with Mac OS, Solaris, or one of the many varieties of the UNIX operating system.

A **network operating system** (NOS) is an operating system that includes additional functions and capabilities to assist in connecting computers and devices, such as printers, to a local area network. Some of the more common network operating systems include Novell's Netware and SpartaCom's LANtastic. For most modern operating systems, including Windows 2000, Solaris, and Linux, the terms *operating system* and *network operating system* are used interchangeably as they perform all the basic function and provide enhanced capabilities for connecting to LANs.

Operating system developers and manufacturers all share a common problem. There is no possible way they can anticipate the many different configurations and variations that the user community will require from their products. So, rather than spending countless hours and funds attempting to meet every need, manufacturers provide a "default" installation for their products that usually contains the base operating system and some more commonly desirable options, such as drivers, utilities, and enhancements. As the operating system could be used for any of a variety of purposes, and could be placed in any number of logical locations (local LAN, DMZ, WAN, and so on), the manufacturer typically does little to nothing with security. The manufacturer may provide some recommendations or simplified tools and settings to facilitate securing the system, but in general, the end users are responsible for securing their own systems. Generally this involves removing unnecessary applications and utilities, disabling unneeded services, setting appropriate permissions on files, and updating the operating system and application code to the latest version.

This process of securing an operating system is called *hardening*, and it is intended to make the system more resistant to attack, much like armor or steel is hardened to make it less susceptible to breakage or damage. Each operating system has its own approach to security, and while the process of hardening is generally the same, different steps must be taken to secure each operating system.

Hardening Microsoft Operating Systems

When we talk about securing or hardening Windows operating systems, we generally only discuss the Windows NT, Windows 2000, or Windows XP family of operating systems. Older Microsoft operating systems, such as Windows 3.11, Windows 95, Windows 98, and Windows ME were designed with very little in the way of security capabilities, and not much can be done to harden those particular operating systems. For the purposes of this discussion, we will focus on hardening the Windows 2000 and Windows XP operating systems, as they are the most popular choices for business servers and desktops.

General Steps for Securing Windows Operating Systems

The following is a general guide for securing Windows operating systems such as Windows 2000 or XP Professional. It is by no means an exhaustive list, but can help you address some of the more critical areas of Windows security.

1. *Disable all unnecessary services.* In general, Windows systems will serve one main purpose (web server, mail server, DNS server, domain/login server, and so on). Once you have determined what the main purpose of the system will be, disable any service not absolutely necessary to support that purpose.

2. *Restrict permissions on files and access to the Registry.* While this step may take some time, restricting who can read, write, and execute certain files can provide some much-needed security. Additionally, the Windows Registry must be protected to ensure that entries are not modified or deleted.

3. *Remove unnecessary programs.* Any application or utility not needed should be removed. This reduces the chances of an attacker exploiting a weakness or enabling unneeded services.

4. *Apply the latest patches and fixes.* Ensure that the operating system and all applications have the latest vendor-supplied patches applied.

5. *Remove unnecessary user accounts and ensure password guidelines are in place.* Default accounts such as "guest" should be disabled or removed. Password guidelines should be enabled and enforced to ensure that users choose appropriate passwords.

Hardening Windows 2000

When Microsoft introduced Windows 2000 in February of 2000, many users were thrilled at the additional stability and security promised by this new operating system. While Windows 2000 did deliver on some fronts, like many previous Microsoft products there were some significant vulnerabilities discovered, and these vulnerabilities were used by attackers to disable, disrupt, or modify hundreds of thousands of systems over the last two years. A large number of these vulnerabilities came from default settings or applications that were never addressed by the end users when they installed the operating system and attached their computer to the Internet. Windows 2000 security can be significantly improved, and there are a number of guides out there to assist you in securing your Windows system. In this chapter, we will examine the steps recommended by Microsoft's own security team.

NOTE Microsoft updates their online content on a fairly frequent basis. Should the Microsoft checklist be updated from the material available in this text, please use the suggested checklist from Microsoft.

The first step, though it is not covered in Microsoft's own checklist, is rather obvious but extremely important. You must determine which version of the operating system you are securing (Professional, Server, or Advanced Server) and what purpose the system will serve (user desktop, web server, file server, and so on). We will assume we are working on a Windows 2000 Server system destined to be a file server (web servers are a special case, and we will discuss them in the "Web Servers" section later in this chapter). There are six recommended steps in the Windows security checklist on Microsoft's TechNet (http://www.microsoft.com/technet/treeview/default.asp?url=/technet/security/tools/ChkList/wsrvSec.asp

NOTE Step 7 applies to web servers only, so we will not include that step in this particular discussion.

1. Install the latest Windows 2000 service pack, following the recommended steps in the "Microsoft Windows 2000 Service Pack Installation and Deployment Guide." Visit the Windows Update site to receive any additional updates released after the latest service pack.

2. Configure Window's "Automatic Updates" service to check the Microsoft site and inform you when new security fixes become available. As an option, the automatic update service can be configured to download and install updates without manual intervention.

3. Keep up with the latest security patches using Microsoft's Security Bulletins Search.

4. Follow the guidelines in the "Microsoft Windows 2000 Server Baseline Security Checklist" and update your antivirus tools and signature files against viruses. Check Microsoft's virus alerts regularly.

5. Read "Securing Windows 2000 Server," "Security Operations Guide for Windows 2000 Server" and the "Security Administration Operations Guide"—all available from Microsoft.com.

6. Use the "Baseline Security Analyzer" tool to scan and evaluate the security of your system.

Step 1 recommends installing the latest Windows 2000 service pack and critical updates using the Windows Update site. *Service packs* are Microsoft's way of bundling updates, fixes, and new functions into a large, self-installing package. Service packs can be found on Microsoft's main download page and vary in size from less than 1MB to over 100MB. Installing a service pack is usually quite simple and consists of downloading an executable file from Microsoft and running it. While this may seem to be an easy and agreeable process, service packs themselves have introduced new functions and vulnerabilities, disabled old functions, and caused third-party applications to fail. Even so, to secure your Windows systems, you must make sure you update them with the latest service pack—in this case, the good outweighs the bad. Critical updates are small, but important updates, that are provided on an individual basis as they become available. Eventually, critical updates get rolled up into the next service pack.

Step 2 recommends configuring the "Automatic Updates" service that is installed automatically with Service Pack 3. Once configured, the service automatically checks the Windows Update site for any new security fixes. This utility can be configured to download and install security updates without manual intervention.

Step 3 urges you to keep up with the latest security patches using the Security Bulletins Search. Microsoft provides security bulletins to alert its user community to problems, issues, or vulnerabilities with Microsoft's products. The security bulletins usually identify the problem, the affected software and versions, and how the problem can be addressed.

Step 4 recommends following the "Microsoft Windows 2000 Server Baseline Security Checklist." This is a 17-step checklist that we will examine in more detail in the next section. Step 4 also recommends keeping your antivirus software and associated signature files updated.

Step 5 instructs us to read three documents available from Microsoft that detail best practices for securing, running, and maintaining Windows 2000 servers.

Step 6 recommends use of the "Baseline Security Analyzer." This free tool from Microsoft can scan and evaluate the security state of your Windows system to ensure the latest patches and fixes are in place, user accounts are secured, and appropriate permissions have been applied to files and directories.

Microsoft Windows 2000 Server Baseline Security Checklist   To assist its end-user community, Microsoft has provided a baseline security checklist specifically for Windows 2000 servers. This checklist applies to both the Windows 2000 Server and Advanced Server operating systems and outlines the steps to achieve a minimum baseline of security. The following list reviews each step to better understand what each step requires and the benefit it provides.

- *Verify that all disk partitions are formatted with NTFS.* NTFS is the NT file system, a Microsoft-developed file system that provides features, such as enhanced security and reliability, that its previous file systems lacked. NTFS allows you to set access permissions using an **Access Control List** on files and directories, so you can control what users or groups of users can read the contents of a particular file, or modify it. Microsoft's permissions consist of *none, read, write, execute, delete, change permissions,* and *take ownership,* and they can be applied to both files and directories in various combinations.

   In most cases, the choice to format a particular disk partition as NTFS occurs during installation, but you can convert a partition from FAT or FAT32 to NTFS by using the Disk Management tools provided with Windows 2000, as shown in Figure 14-1. In this example, you can see that the first partition (C:) is NTFS, but the second (OTHER HALF) is FAT32. You could apply ACLs to the files and directories in the first partition, but not the second. Anyone with access to this system would be able to read, write, modify, and delete files on the FAT32 partition.

- *Verify that the Administrator account has a strong password.* The Administrator account is a special account under the Windows 2000 operating system. This is the "superuser" account that has the ability to control virtually everything on that

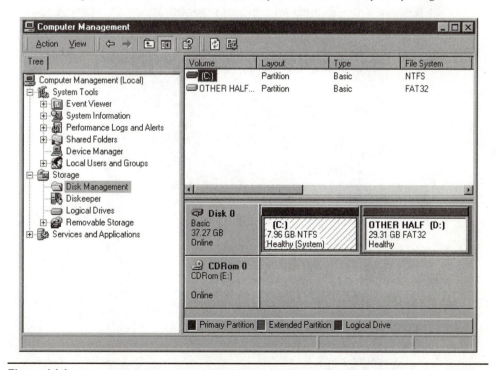

Figure 14-1   Viewing disk partitions with the Windows 2000 Disk Management utility

system, much like the "root" account on UNIX systems. As such, the Administrator account is a frequent target, as attackers attempt to guess or otherwise obtain the password for this account. In general, a password should be selected with care, and this is even more important for an account with this level of privilege. Good passwords typically consist of eight or more characters, at least one change in case, one number, and one special character.

- *Disable unnecessary services.* Any service not absolutely required to support the intended function of the server should be disabled or removed from the system completely. For example, a dedicated web server should not have SMTP or FTP services running on it, and there's usually no legitimate reason for file and print sharing to be enabled on a publicly viewable system. Additionally, there are often components of services that should be removed. For example, within IIS there are often data-access components and sample files that are placed on the system during installation. Like any component not vital to the operation of the system, sample files and unnecessary functions, plug-ins, and expansion packs should be removed.

- *Disable or delete unnecessary accounts.* Removing or disabling unnecessary accounts is a standard best practice for any system, but is particularly applicable for servers. User accounts on public systems should be limited to only those absolutely necessary. On a Windows 2000 system, use the Users and Passwords tool (see the following illustration) to view and remove accounts from the system. To remove an unnecessary account, simply highlight the account and click Remove. For additional security, some organizations will also rename the Administrator account or create an equivalent account under a different name.

- *Protect files and directories.* Certain Windows operating systems (such as 2000 and XP) have the ability to restrict access to files and directories through the use of Access Control Lists (ACLs). An ACL is a list of permissions that controls who may write, modify, delete, or access a specific file or directory. A default, "clean" installation of Windows 2000 places restrictive permissions on certain system files and directories that prevent the average user from tampering with or removing those system files. An upgraded version of Windows 2000 (from Windows 98 or NT) will not have the same default permissions in place, so to secure the system, an administrator must enable those permissions and protect the system files. It is important to note that file and directory permissions can only be implemented on NTFS disk partitions—FAT and FAT32 partitions do not support ACLs for files and directories. The next illustration shows the ACLs placed on the WINNT directory in a default Windows 2000 install. By right-clicking any file or directory on an NTFS partition, selecting Properties, and clicking the Security tab, you can see the permissions associated with each group or user account for that particular file or directory. For more specific information on what each permission setting means, see Table 14-1.

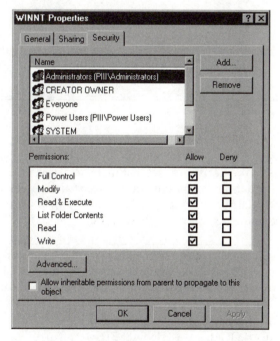

- *Make sure the Guest account is disabled.* In a default installation of Windows 2000, the Guest account is disabled, meaning that it is no longer accessible for use on that system. Older versions of Windows NT and older systems that have been upgraded to Windows 2000 may not have the Guest account disabled. To ensure that the Guest account (or any other account) is disabled, use the Users and Passwords tool found in the Control Panel.

Permissions	Full Control	Modify	Read & Execute	List Folder Contents (folders only)	Read	Write
Traverse Folder/Execute File	x	x	x	x		
List Folder/Read Data	x	x	x	x	x	
Read Attributes	x	x	x	x	x	
Read Extended Attributes	x	x	x	x	x	
Create Files/Write Data	x	x				x
Create Folders/ Append Data	x	x				x
Write Attributes	x	x				x
Write Extended Attributes	x	x				x
Delete Subfolders and Files	x					
Delete	x	x				
Read Permissions	x	x	x	x	x	x
Change Permissions	x					
Take Ownership	x					
Synchronize	x	x	x	x	x	x

Table 14-1   Permissions on Windows 2000

- *Protect the Registry from anonymous access.* By default, Windows does not restrict remote access to the Registry, a fact that many attackers take advantage of when collecting information (such as user accounts, shared drives, resources, and so on) from potential Windows targets. To restrict network access to the Registry, Microsoft recommends following these steps:

 NOTE   Editing the registry incorrectly can lead to an unstable Windows system. If you are not familiar with the tools and techniques required to complete these steps, contact your local system administrator or a qualified professional.

1. Add the following key to the Registry using regedit:
   Hive   HKEY_LOCAL_MACHINE \SYSTEM
   Key   \CurrentControlSet\Control\SecurePipeServers
   Value Name   \winreg

2. Select winreg (the key you just created), click the Security menu, and then click Permissions.

3. Set the Administrators permission to Full Control, make sure no other users or groups are listed, and then click OK.

- *Apply appropriate Registry ACLs.* In a default installation of Windows 2000, the Registry has secure ACLs enabled by default. Unfortunately, this is not the case for systems upgraded to Windows 2000. To enable the appropriate Registry ACLs, refer to Microsoft's TechNet web site (www.microsoft.com/technet) for more information, and search for a white paper entitled "Default Access Control Settings in Windows 2000."

- *Restrict access to public local security authority (LSA) information.* The LSA within Windows handles specific aspects of security administration on the local computer, including access to the system itself, and permissions checking for files and folders. To prevent potential attackers from extracting information from your system anonymously, create the following Registry key using regedit:

Hive   HKEY_LOCAL_MACHINE\SYSTEM
Key   CurrentControlSet\Control\LSA
Value Name   RestrictAnonymous
Type   REG_DWORD
Value   1

For additional security, you can also use the Local Security Policy Setting tool to restrict anonymous connections, as shown in the following illustration. Select Administrative Tools from the Control Panel, then select Local Security Policy, Local Policies, Security Options, and Additional Restrictions for Anonymous Connections. In the drop-down box, select None, Do Not Allow Enumeration Of SAM Accounts And Shares, or No Access Without Explicit Anonymous Permissions. The most secure setting is the latter, which will help prevent potential attackers from anonymously gathering information from your Windows systems.

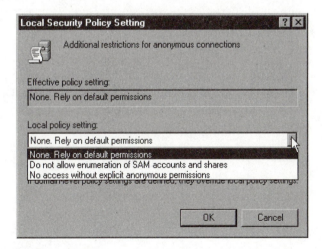

- *Set stronger password policies.* Password policies are extremely important to the security of any system. More often than not, the only thing that stands between an attacker and access to the system is a simple userID and password pair. You can always educate a user on how to select a good password, but it often helps to have the system itself enforce good password selection. Within Windows 2000, you can enable certain features regarding password selection by using the Password Policy Tool found by selecting Administrative Tools from the Control Panel. Then select Local Security Policy, Account Policies, and Password Policies. This will open the Local Security Settings window shown here.

In the preceding illustration, there are six options for local password policies. Enforce Password History allows you to specify the number of previous passwords that the system should remember and prevent users from reusing. Maximum Password Age specifies how long a user may maintain the same password before being forced to select a new one. Minimum Password Age specifies the minimum number of days that must pass after a successful password change before a user is allowed to change their password again. Minimum Password Length specifies the minimum number of characters the user must include in an acceptable password. For example, if the minimum password length were set at 4, then the user's password must be at least four characters long. Passwords Must Meet Complexity Requirements specifies additional restrictions on password selection. When this option is enabled, all passwords must be at least six characters long (regardless of the minimum password length setting), the password cannot contain the username or any part of the user's full name, and the password must contain at least one character from three of the four classes of characters identified in the following table:

Character Class	Examples
Uppercase letters	A, B, C, ... Z
Lowercase letters	a, b, c, ... z
Numerals	0, 1, 2, ... 9
Non-alphanumeric ("special characters")	Punctuation marks and other symbols

Storing passwords using reversible encryption is essentially the same as storing a cleartext version of the password as it makes the password easy to access for third-party applications. In most environments, this option should never be enabled.

- *Set the account lockout policy.* To protect against brute-force password-guessing attacks, Windows 2000 includes an account lockout feature that will disable an account after a specified number of login failures. For example, the administrator may choose to enable account lockout after three unsuccessful login attempts. The account lockout policies shown in the following illustration give the administrator three distinct capabilities. Account Lockout Duration tells the system how long to leave an account locked once the account lockout threshold has been reached (this can be anywhere from minutes to hours to until the administrator manually unlocks the account). Account Lockout Threshold tells the system how many unsuccessful login attempts to allow before locking a user account. Reset Account Lockout Counter After tells the system how long to wait after the last unsuccessful login attempt before clearing out the unsuccessful-login-attempt counter.

NOTE It is highly recommended that you enable reset options and account lockout durations if you choose to enable an account lockout threshold. If each account must be manually unlocked by an administrator once it is locked, then a large-scale, brute-force attack will cause a great deal of additional effort for your system administrators.

- *Configure the Administrator account.* While in actual practice this is rarely done, for additional security, the built-in Administrator account can be modified and hidden to make it less obvious to potential attackers. For added security, the Administrator account can be renamed to something obscure that does not indicate that this is the administrator level account (do not use names such as "admin" or "root"). Once the Administrator account has been renamed, you can create a dummy account called "Administrator" but ensure that it has no privileges of any kind. This gives you the ability to still look for password-guessing attacks against the dummy Administrator account in the event logs, but it does not risk the actual administration account. By disabling the Administrator account, attackers won't be able to use the account in any way, even if they are able to guess the password assigned to the account. If you are really concerned about security, you can enable account lockout features on the admin account you created, but be warned that this could cause problems if the entire system comes under a brute-force attack and every account on the system becomes locked.

- *Revoke the Debug programs user right.* By default, Windows 2000 grants administrators the "Debug programs" user right. If abused, this capability allows administrators (or a virus, Trojan, or malicious piece of code accidentally run by the administrator) to obtain sensitive information from system memory, such as hashed passwords. Unless absolutely required, this right should be removed from all administrator accounts.

- *Remove all unnecessary file shares.* In any operating system, information that does not absolutely have to be shared should not be. In Windows this means removing sharing on every file and folder unless it is absolutely necessary. Be aware that Windows creates hidden administrative shares for certain resources by default (a hidden share is created for each drive on the system as well as the WINNT directory). Hidden shares are marked with a dollar sign ($) in front of the name. For example, $C is the admin share for the C drive on a Windows 2000 system. The admin shares function much like other shared files and folders—anyone accessing the $C share would be accessing the C drive as if it were one large, shared folder. You can disable these admin shares after installation, but doing so may cause many Microsoft or third-party administration tools to fail. If you do wish to disable the admin shares, you can do so by following these steps:

1. Start the Registry Editor (Regedt32.exe).
2. Locate and then click the following key in the Registry: HKEY_LOCAL_MACHINE\SYSTEM\CurrentControlSet\Services\ LanmanServer\Parameters\AutoShareServer
3. Change the value of the AutoShareServer key to 0 (zero).

NOTE A setting of 0 prevents the administrative shares, such as C$, D$, and Admin$, from being created automatically.

4. Quit the Registry Editor.

CAUTION Editing of the Registry should only be performed by qualified individuals. Alterations to the system Registry can cause the system to become unstable or even nonfunctional.

- *Set appropriate ACLs on all necessary file shares.* By default, any newly created file shares on an NTFS file system will give Full Control access to all users. To prevent unauthorized access and manipulation of these files, administrators must modify permissions by right-clicking on the shared folder or file and selecting Properties then clicking the Security tab. In the Security tab, the administrator can manually assign or remove permissions for the appropriate users or groups.

- *Enable security event auditing.* By default, Windows 2000 does not perform logging of security events such as successful or failed logons. The Audit Policy section found under the Local Policies section of the Local Security Settings tool allows administrators to record the success or failure of certain actions. Microsoft recommends carefully selecting which events to log as logging too many events creates extremely large log files. Microsoft recommends enabling only Success and Failure auditing for the Audit account logon events policy.

- *Set log on warning message.* Windows 2000 provides administrators with the ability to display a message to any users attempting to log in to the system. By displaying a message indicating that system use is restricted to authorized users as well as information regarding monitoring and the prosecution of unauthorized access attempts, organizations can enhance their ability to perform forensic and legal actions.

- *Install antivirus software and updates.* With damage estimates for recent virus outbreaks and their associated cleanup efforts in the billions of dollars, installing antivirus software is a critical best practice for maintaining a functional and secure system. Installing antivirus software is merely the first step though. The antivirus signatures must be kept up-to-date as new viruses, worms, and Trojans are discovered every day. Most antivirus software programs contain utilities that will automatically update antivirus signatures for you at preset intervals. In general, antivirus signatures should be updated at least once a week.

- *Automate patch deployment.* With the release of Service Pack 3, Microsoft added a capability called "Automatic Updates." By enabling this utility, administrators can have systems automatically check Microsoft for new security updates and, if desired, download and install those updates automatically.

- *Scan system with the Baseline Security Analyzer.* To help address the complexity of keeping Windows systems up-to-date, Microsoft introduced a free utility that can be used to scan the local system, identify potential vulnerabilities and missing updates, and assist the user in addressing any discovered issues. At a minimum this utility should be run on any newly installed Windows system.

- *Install the latest service pack.* Keeping operating system and application software up-to-date is also critical for maintaining the security and functionality of your systems. Microsoft releases major revisions to its operating systems called *service packs*, which contain a large collection of modifications and corrections to eliminate bugs, vulnerabilities, or misconfigurations in previous versions of the code. Service packs are usually numbered, inclusive of previous updates (Service Pack 3 contains the fixes from Service Packs 1 and 2), and they can be found on the Microsoft web site in the download section. In general, service packs are quite large and can be ordered in CD format if your Internet connection does not support downloading 20MB to 100MB files.

- *Install the appropriate post-service-pack security hotfixes.* New service packs are not released for each discovered vulnerability—this would simply be too much effort for an organization like Microsoft. Instead, Microsoft will release *hotfixes* designed to correct specific vulnerabilities. These hotfixes are eventually collected into a service pack over time, but in order to maintain security on your system, you must install the latest service pack and then any appropriate hotfixes. Fortunately, Microsoft has made this task a little easier through the Windows Update function found in Internet Explorer. From an Internet Explorer window, select Tools and then Windows Update. This will launch the Windows Update utility, shown in Figure 14-2, which will scan your system and provide a list of appropriate updates and hotfixes for your system. Running this Windows Update tool each week will help ensure that your system is kept up-to-date.

- *Remove File And Printer Sharing protocol.* On certain systems, such as web servers or any other system maintained in your DMZ, you should consider removing or disabling the File And Printer Sharing For Microsoft Networks protocol from all network interfaces. This prevents administrators from accidentally sharing out directories and files on publicly visible systems and will help prevent certain types of reconnaissance and network-based attacks.

Figure 14-2   Microsoft's Windows Update site

In addition to the Windows 2000 hardening checklist, Microsoft has provided some additional tools to help you keep your Windows systems up-to-date. The Microsoft Security Baseline Analyzer (MSBA) is an automated tool that scans your Windows systems and does the following:

- Checks to ensure the latest security patches and service packs have been installed

- Checks to ensure the strong passwords requirements are enabled

- Scans Internet Information Server and SQL Server for common security-related misconfigurations

- Checks for misconfigured security zone settings in Microsoft Office, Outlook, and Internet Explorer

The MSBA is available from Microsoft's TechNet (www.microsoft.com/technet/default .asp) by selecting Security, Tools and Checklists, and MBSA (www.microsoft.com/ technet/treeview/default.asp?url=/technet/security/tools/Tools/mbsaqa.asp).

In addition to the MSBA, the Internet Information Server (IIS) Lockdown Tool is available to help secure IIS servers from attack (we will discuss this tool in the "Microsoft's Internet Information Server" section later in this chapter). If you don't wish to run the fully implemented version of the MSBA, you can run HFNetChk—a command-line tool that will scan your system to ensure it is up-to-date with the latest security fixes and service packs.

As you can see, the Microsoft checklist for securing Windows 2000 systems contains many different steps, all designed to help secure the system by examining a specific area. This checklist is designed to help you create a secure baseline for your Windows 2000 systems by following the same basic tenets as any other operating system baselining process: remove unnecessary components and services, restrict and limit access to files and directories, and apply the latest patches. After following the checklist and making the appropriate choices for your specific environment, you should end up with your own secure Windows baseline.

One item the Microsoft checklist does not adequately cover is logging. Logging, or auditing, is the process of recording events or actions that take place. More specifically in this case, the recording of events or actions that take place on the system itself—events such as logins, program executions, file or directory modifications, and so on. Recording these events makes it possible for security personnel and administrators to determine what has happened on the system and whether or not the security of the system has been compromised in any way. The logging facilities within Windows are fairly simple and essentially consist of turning logging on or off for certain events. Logged events within Windows are placed into one of three event logs: Application Log, Security Log, or System Log. The event logs can be accessed through the Event Viewer provided with Windows, as shown in the following illustration, or through any of a number of third-party tools.

Determining your logging and auditing requirements is an important part of the overall baselining process. You must decide which events to record, what the records will be used for, when and how to examine the records, and how long to maintain these records. Setting up logging should be a part of every security baseline checklist or process, and it is typically done just after the system is installed and configured, but before the system has been placed on the network or into production.

Removing or disabling programs or services in Windows is usually relatively simple. Many applications contain their own uninstaller, which is designed to remove the application from the system. Others rely on the built-in Windows Add/Remove Programs utility found in the Control Panel and shown in the following illustration. Removing an application is a simple process: select the application you want to remove by clicking it, and then click the Remove button. In most cases, this works quite well, but there are many cases where files and directories get left behind and require manual intervention to completely remove them from the system.

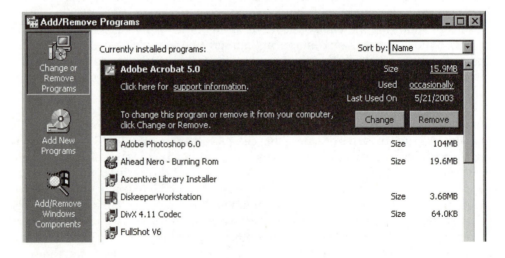

Removing or disabling services is fairly simple, as Microsoft has provided a Services utility under the Administrative Tools section of the Control Panel. By using this utility, shown in Figure 14-3, administrators can examine those services that are running on their system, how the services are started, and when they are started. Administrators can also use this utility to stop or start specific services, as well as disable services that should not be running on the system.

Hardening UNIX- or Linux-Based Operating Systems

As a general rule, any operating system can be made relatively secure, but by default UNIX operating systems tend to be more secure than default installations of Windows operating systems. However, that does not mean that UNIX systems are *completely* secure by default and don't need any additional security configuration. UNIX systems, like Windows systems, need to be carefully examined, modified, and baselined to provide secure operations.

Depending on the skill and knowledge of the system administrator, securing UNIX systems can be more challenging than securing Windows systems because the operating system is so powerful and flexible and so much control is placed in the hands of the administrator. Unlike Windows, there is no single manufacturer to provide specific guidelines and step-by-step checklists for securing UNIX systems. Instead, there are many general and version-specific guidelines that must be adapted and applied to your specific version of UNIX to complete the baselining process. This section examines some of the common guidelines for a sampling of the more popular versions of UNIX.

Figure 14-3   Starting or stopping services with the Windows Services utility

General UNIX Baselines

General UNIX baselining is the same as for Windows operating systems: disable unnecessary services, restrict permissions on files and directories, remove unnecessary software, apply patches, remove unnecessary users, and apply password guidelines. Some versions of UNIX provide GUI-based tools for these tasks, while others require administrators to manually edit configuration files. In most cases, anything that can be accomplished through a GUI interface can be accomplished from the command line or by manually editing configuration files.

Like Windows systems, UNIX systems are easiest to secure and baseline if they are providing a single service or performing a single function, such as acting as an SMTP or web server. Prior to performing any installing or baselining, the purpose of the system should be defined and all required capabilities and functions should be identified. One nice advantage of UNIX systems is that you typically have complete control over what does or does not get installed on the system. During the installation process, you can select which services and applications are placed on your system, giving administrators a good opportunity to simply not install services and applications that will not be required. However, this assumes that the administrator knows and understands the purpose of this system, which is not always the case. In other cases, the function of the system, itself, may have changed.

Regardless of the installation decisions, the administrator may sometimes need to remove applications or components that are no longer needed. With UNIX systems, there is typically no "add/remove program" wizard as there is with Windows, but you will often encounter package managers that enable administrators to remove unneeded components and applications automatically. On some UNIX versions, though, you must manually delete the files associated with the applications or services you wish to remove.

Services on a UNIX system can be controlled through a number of different mechanisms. As the root user, an administrator can start and stop services manually from the command line. The operating system can also stop and start services automatically through configuration files (usually contained in the /etc directory). Unlike Windows, UNIX systems can also have different **run levels**, where the system can be configured to bring up different services depending on the run level selected.

On a running UNIX system, you can see which processes, applications, and services are running by using the process status or **ps** command, as shown in Figure 14-4. To stop a running service, an administrator can identify the service by its unique **process identifier** or *PID* and then use the **kill** command to stop the service. For example, if you wanted to stop the klogd service in Figure 14-4, you would use the command **kill 743**. To prevent this service from starting again when the system is rebooted, you would have to modify the appropriate run levels to remove this service or modify the configuration files that control this service.

Accounts on a UNIX system can also be controlled via GUIs in some cases and command-line interfaces in others. On most popular UNIX versions, the user information can be found in the passwd file located in the /etc directory. By manually editing this file, you can add, delete, or modify user accounts on the system. By examining this file, an administrator can see which user accounts exist on the system and then determine

```
C:\WINNT\System32\telnet.exe                                                        _ □ ×
UID        PID  PPID  C STIME TTY           TIME CMD
root         1     0  0 May13 ?        00:00:04 init
root         2     1  0 May13 ?        00:00:00 [keventd]
root         3     1  0 May13 ?        00:00:00 [kapmd]
root         4     1  0 May13 ?        00:00:00 [ksoftirqd_CPU0]
root         5     1  0 May13 ?        00:00:24 [kswapd]
root         6     1  0 May13 ?        00:00:05 [bdflush]
root         7     1  0 May13 ?        00:00:00 [kupdated]
root         8     1  0 May13 ?        00:00:00 [mdrecoveryd]
root        16     1  0 May13 ?        00:00:04 [kjournald]
root        95     1  0 May13 ?        00:00:00 [khubd]
root       223     1  0 May13 ?        00:00:00 [kjournald]
root       224     1  0 May13 ?        00:00:13 [kjournald]
root       225     1  0 May13 ?        00:00:00 [kjournald]
root       739     1  0 May13 ?        00:00:01 syslogd -m 0
root       744     1  0 May13 ?        00:00:00 klogd -x
rpc        764     1  0 May13 ?        00:00:00 portmap
rpcuser    792     1  0 May13 ?        00:00:00 rpc.statd
root       904     1  0 May13 ?        00:00:00 /usr/sbin/apmd -p 10 -w 5 -W -P
root       959     1  0 May13 ?        00:00:00 /usr/sbin/sshd
root       992     1  0 May13 ?        00:00:00 xinetd -stayalive -reuse -pidfil
root      1020     1  0 May13 ?        00:00:00 sendmail: accepting connections
root      1039     1  0 May13 ?        00:00:00 gpm -t ps/2 -m /dev/mouse
--More--
```

Figure 14-4   Running the **ps** command on a UNIX system

which accounts to remove or disable. On most UNIX systems, if you remove the user account from the passwd file, you must manually remove any files that belong to that user, including their home directories.

How you patch a UNIX system depends a great deal on the UNIX version in use and the patch being applied. In some cases, a patch will consist of a series of manual steps requiring the administrator to replace files, change permissions, and alter directories. In other cases, the patches are executable scripts or utilities that perform the patch actions automatically. Some UNIX versions, such as Red Hat and Solaris, have built-in utilities that handle the patching process. In those cases, the administrator downloads a specifically formatted file that the patching utility then processes to perform any modifications or updates that need to be made.

To better illustrate UNIX baselines, we will examine two popular UNIX-based operating systems: Solaris and Red Hat Linux.

Solaris   The Solaris operating system is developed and distributed by Sun Microsystems and has been an extremely popular choice in high-performance and high-availability environments. As a commercial operating system, Solaris is typically bundled with a hardware platform from Sun, but it can be purchased separately and is even available for Intel-based processor platforms (Solaris x86). For more secure environments, a specially hardened version called Trusted Solaris is available, though this is typically only used by the government, military, and banking communities.

Baselining a Solaris system is fairly simple. Once the system's purpose is defined, installation is typically done through a graphical interface that allows the administrator to select which applications and services should be loaded on the system. On a running Solaris system, patches and services can be added or removed using the **pkgadd** command, which adds binary packages, and the **pkgrm** command, which removes binary packages.

The binary packages themselves are unusable in the format in which they are downloaded or delivered on removable media. The pkg utilities take care of interpreting the package's software control files to determine where to either install or remove files or directories. Any package handled by the Solaris system is stored in a package information database, so administrators can easily obtain a list of currently installed software. Software can also be installed or removed using the Admintool shown in Figure 14-5.

Obtaining a list of running services on a Solaris system is much the same as on all UNIX systems. You can use the **ps** command to view running processes, and you can examine the Internet servers configuration file, called inetd.conf in Solaris. The inetd.conf file, located in the /etc directory, contains a list of services controlled by the Internet services daemon, simply called **inetd**. On Solaris, and many other UNIX variants, inetd listens for incoming connections on the TCP and UDP ports associated with each of the services listed in its configuration file, inetd.conf. When a connection request is received, inetd will launch the program or process associated with that service, if necessary, and pass the connection request to the appropriate service. To prevent unwanted services from running and processing requests, administrators can edit inetd.conf and either comment out or remove the lines for the services they wish to disable.

In addition to disabling or removing unnecessary network services, Solaris allows administrators to use local security mechanisms called **tcp wrappers** that provide additional layers of security for network services. TCP wrappers are essentially filters that compare incoming connection requests to lists of authorized and unauthorized connections. If a connection is authorized, then it is permitted to reach the network service it is attempting to contact. If a connection is unauthorized, it is dropped by the TCP wrappers. These functions are controlled by two files: hosts.allow and hosts.deny. The hosts.allow file contains a list of IP addresses or subnets that are allowed to connect to a specific service, such as "10.0.0.0: FTP," which would allow any address in the 10.X.X.X network to connect to the FTP service on the local machine. In more secure installations, the hosts.allow file is populated, and the entry "ALL: ALL" is placed in the hosts.deny

Figure 14-5
The Solaris Admintool is used to add or remove software

file. This type of configuration will reject any inbound connections to the local system unless they are specifically authorized by the hosts.allow file.

Securing access to files and directories in Solaris is done in the same manner as in most UNIX variants. Each file and directory has a list of associated permissions for the owner of the file or directory, the group owner of the file or directory, and anyone else (often called the "world"). The permissions are listed in owner-group-world order and consist of three values for each grouping: read, write, and execute. The logical representation looks like this: rwx rwx rwx. Read (r) allows for viewing of the file or listing of the directory. Write (w) allows for modification of the file or directory. Execute (x) allows the file, usually an executable or script, to be run. If you want a file to have read, write, and execute permissions for the owner, read and write permissions for the group, and no permissions for the world, the permissions could be logically represented as shown here.

Owner	Group	World
rwx	**rw-**	**---**

In Solaris, you can use the **chmod** command to modify the permissions associated with a file or directory. Similarly the **chown** command allows you to modify the ownership of a file or directory, and **chgrp** allows you to change the group ownership of a file or directory. To adequately secure a Solaris system, you should ensure that all configuration and system files have appropriately restrictive permissions—you don't want any user on the system to be able to modify inted.conf without appropriate access. To assist you in securing files and directories, there are many different resources available on Sun's web site, as well as on security-related web sites.

A crucial step in baselining a Solaris system is to ensure that all the latest patches and fixes are in place. Patches for Solaris systems are typically distributed from Sun and are available from Sun's web site but can also be obtained on CD, floppy, or tape in some cases. Once obtained, patches must be processed, and Solaris provides several tools to assist administrators in managing and maintaining patches: **patchadd**, **patchrm**, **smpatch**, and **pkgparam**. The **patchadd** command can be used to add patches to the system as well as obtain information about what patches are currently installed on the system. The **patchrm** command can be used to remove installed patches from the system. The **smpatch** command is used to process signed patches. The **pkgparam** command shows patches installed for a specific software package. In addition to the command-line tools, Solaris provides a GUI-based management console, called the Solaris Management Console, that provides the same level of functionality. The Solaris Management Console is shown in Figure 14-6.

In spite of the security efforts identified so far, a Solaris system can still be easily compromised if the user base is not effectively managed and maintained. The keys to protecting accounts and system access are to remove or disable unused accounts and to ensure that all accounts are secured with a good, strong password. In Solaris, user accounts are maintained in the passwd file, and groups are maintained in the groups file, both of which are located in the /etc directory. There are three main methods for maintaining users and groups on a Solaris system: manually editing the required configuration files,

Figure 14-6   Solaris Management Console

using command line interface tools such as **useradd**, and using the management console. Each method can be used interchangeably, offering a level of flexibility not found on Windows systems. Removing unused user accounts can be accomplished through any of these methods—the end result is the same.

The second step to effectively managing your user base is to ensure that users select good passwords. On Solaris systems, passwords are generally stored in a separate file called shadow. This file contains the encrypted password for each account on the system, and it must therefore be guarded and protected appropriately. An administrator can use any of a number of popular password cracking programs to check the user passwords to ensure that they are not easily guessed or based on a simple dictionary word. Additionally, Solaris already imposes some restrictions on what is considered a "suitable" password for users. In most implementations, a password must be at least six characters long, must contain at least two letters and one number or symbol, must not be the same as the login ID, and must be different than the previous password. If these are not strict enough guidelines, the administrator can alter these parameters by using the **passwd** command and the appropriate option flag or by modifying the parameters in /etc/default/passwd. Solaris also supports PAM (Pluggable Authentication Modules), a mechanism for providing interoperation and secure access to a variety of services on different platforms.

Linux Linux is a rather unique operating system. It is UNIX-based, very powerful, open source, can be obtained for free, and is available in many different "distributions" from several vendors. Linux was initially conceived and written by Linus Torvalds in 1991. His concept of creating a lightweight, flexible, and free operating system gave rise to an entirely new operating system that is very popular and is installed on millions of computers around the world. Due to its open nature, the entire source-code base for the operating system is available to anyone who wants to examine it, modify it, or recompile it for their own specific uses. Linux is a favored operating system among security professionals, system administrators, and other highly technical users who enjoy the flexibility and power that Linux provides.

While most versions of Linux can be obtained for free simply by downloading them from the Internet (including major commercial distributions), you can also purchase commercial versions of the Linux operating system from vendors, such as Red Hat, Slackware, SuSE, and Debian, who have built a business out of providing custom versions of Linux along with support and training. Red Hat is arguably the most popular of these commercial Linux distributions, and we will use it as the example for the rest of this section. Regardless of which Linux version you prefer, baselining a Linux system follows the same guidelines as any other UNIX system: disable unnecessary services, restrict permissions on files and directories, remove unnecessary software, apply patches, remove unnecessary users, and apply password guidelines.

Services under Linux are normally controlled by their own configuration files or by xinetd, the extended Internet services daemon. Instead of starting all Internet services, such as FTP servers, at system startup, Linux uses xinetd to listen for incoming connections. Xinetd listens to all the appropriate ports (those that match the services in its configuration files), and when a connection request comes in, xinetd starts the appropriate server and hands over the connection request. This "master process" approach makes it fairly simple to disable unwanted services—all the configuration information for each server is located in /etc/xinetd.d with a configuration file for each process, as shown in Figure 14-7.

```
[root@Jeep xinetd.d]# ls -la
total 64
drwxr-xr-x    2 root     root         4096 Feb 16 17:54
drwxr-xr-x   62 root     root         4096 Apr  5 15:18
-rw-r--r--    1 root     root          563 Nov 19 11:00 chargen
-rw-r--r--    1 root     root          580 Nov 19 11:00 chargen-udp
-rw-r--r--    1 root     root          419 Nov 19 11:00 daytime
-rw-r--r--    1 root     root          438 Nov 19 11:00 daytime-udp
-rw-r--r--    1 root     root          341 Nov 19 11:00 echo
-rw-r--r--    1 root     root          360 Nov 19 11:00 echo-udp
-rw-r--r--    1 root     root          312 Nov 19 11:00 servers
-rw-r--r--    1 root     root          314 Nov 19 11:00 services
-rw-r--r--    1 root     root          392 Apr  7  2002 sgi_fam
-rw-r--r--    1 root     root          363 Nov 20 11:24 swat
-rw-r--r--    1 root     root          304 Feb 16 16:54 telnet
-rw-r--r--    1 root     root          497 Nov 19 11:00 time
-rw-r--r--    1 root     root          518 Nov 19 11:00 time-udp
-rw-r--r--    1 root     root          329 Feb 16 16:55 wu-ftpd
[root@Jeep xinetd.d]# _
```

Figure 14-7   Listing of server configuration files for xinetd

```
[root@Jeep xinetd.d]# more telnet
# default: on
# description: The telnet server serves telnet sessions; it uses \
#              unencrypted username/password pairs for authentication.
service telnet
{
        flags           = REUSE
        socket_type     = stream
        wait            = no
        user            = root
        server          = /usr/sbin/in.telnetd
        log_on_failure  += USERID
        disable         = no
}

[root@Jeep xinetd.d]#
```

Figure 14-8   Telnet service configuration file under Red Hat Linux

Inside each configuration file are the options to be used when starting the service, the location where the server binary is located, and the disable flag. By changing the value of the disable flag to "yes," you can disable any process controlled by xinetd. Figure 14-8 shows the configuration file for the telnet service on a Red Hat Linux system. Services in Red Hat Linux can also be configured via a GUI-based utility, as shown in Figure 14-9. Regardless of the method chosen, the end result should the same—all unnecessary services should be removed or disabled.

Permissions under Linux are the same as for other UNIX-based operating systems. There are permissions for owner, group, and others (or world). Permissions are based on the same read-write-execute principle and can be adjusted using the **chmod** command.

Figure 14-9

Red Hat Linux's GUI-based service configuration

Individual and group ownership information can be changed using **chown** and **chgrp**, respectively. As with other baselining exercises, permissions should be as restrictive as functionally possible, giving read-only access when possible and write or execute access when necessary.

Adding and removing software under Linux is typically done through a package manager. In Red Hat Linux, the package manager is called Red Hat Package Manager, or rpm for short. Using rpm, you can add, modify, update, or remove software packages from your system. Using the **rpm -qa** command will give you a list of all the software packages installed on your Red Hat system. You can remove any packages you do not wish to leave installed using the **rpm -e** command. As with most things under Linux, there is a GUI-based utility to accomplish this same task. The GUI-based Package Management utility is shown in Figure 14-10.

Patching and keeping a Red Hat Linux system up-to-date is a fairly simple exercise, as well. Red Hat has provided an Update Agent that, once configured, will examine your system, obtain the list of available updates from Red Hat, and, if desired, install those updates on your system. Like any other operating system, it is important to maintain the patch level of your Red Hat system. For more information on the Red Hat Update Agent, see the "Updates (aka Hotfixes, Service Packs, and Patches)" section later in this chapter.

Managing and maintaining user accounts under Linux can be accomplished with either the command line or a GUI interface. Unlike certain other operating systems, there's really only one default account for Linux systems—the root or superuser account. The root account has complete and total control over the system and should therefore be protected with an exceptionally strong password. Many administrators will configure their systems to prevent anyone from logging in directly as root; instead, they

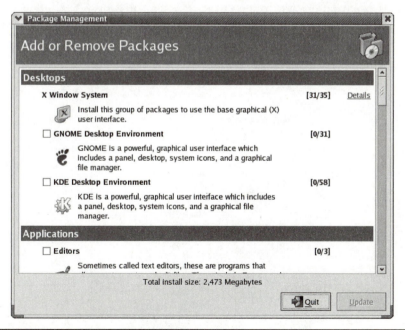

Figure 14-10   Red Hat Package Management utility

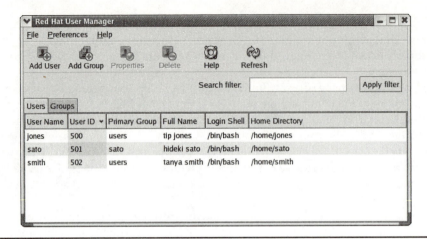

Figure 14-11 Managing user accounts with the Red Hat User Manager

must log in with their own personal accounts and switch to the root account using the **su** command. Adding user accounts can be done with the **useradd** command, and unwanted user accounts can be removed using the **userdel** command. Additionally, you can manually edit /etc/passwd to add or remove user accounts. User accounts can also be managed via a GUI interface, as shown in Figure 14-11.

For increased local security, Red Hat also provides a built-in firewall function that can be managed either via the command line or through a GUI interface, as shown in the following illustration. To protect network access to the local system, administrators can control which ports external users may connect to, such as mail, FTP, or web. Administrators may choose a security level, from high, medium, off, and a customized option, where they can individually select which ports on which interfaces external users may connect to.

In addition to the built-in firewall functions, administrators may also use TCP wrappers like those discussed earlier in the Solaris section of this chapter. By specifying host and port combinations in /etc/hosts.allow, administrators can allow certain hosts to connect on certain ports. The firewall function and hosts.allow must work together if both functions are used on the same system. The connection must be allowed by both utilities or it will be dropped.

Mac OS X

Apple's latest version of its operating system is essentially a new variant of the UNIX operating system. While this brings a new level of power, flexibility, and stability to Mac users everywhere, it also brings a new level of security concerns. Traditionally, the Mac OS was largely ignored by the hacker community—the deployment was relatively small, largely being restricted to individual users or departments, and harder to obtain information on. With the migration to a UNIX-based OS, Mac users should anticipate a sharp increase in unwanted attention and scrutiny from potential attackers.

Because it is a UNIX-based operating system, the same rough guidelines for all UNIX systems apply to Mac OS X. As with Solaris, Linux, and all the other UNIX variants, each workstation can become an instant server by installing the right application or enabling a specific service. As with other UNIX variants, it is important with Mac OS X to disable unnecessary services, such as web, mail, FTP, and so on, unless they are going to be properly configured and secured. Mac OS X services can be manually controlled by editing the appropriate files, as with other UNIX variants, but one of Apple's strengths (or weaknesses, depending on how you look at it) is providing user interfaces that greatly simplify tasks for their user base. For example, within Mac OS X, Apple has provided Services, Firewall, and Internet tabs under the Sharing window. As Figure 14-12 shows, certain services can be turned on or off simply by clicking the box next to the appropriate service.

Figure 14-12
Turning services on and off in the Services tab in Mac OS X

Figure 14-13
Turning the firewall settings on and off in the Firewall tab in Mac OS X

The Firewall tab similarly provides users with the ability to restrict incoming connections to the system, again by simply clicking on the box next to the service you wish to allow to reach your computer, as shown in Figure 14-13.

For Mac OS X users, the task of identifying and disabling unwanted services is relatively simple compared to some other operating systems. Apple has conveniently located the services and the firewall functions together and has reduced the administration tasks to just selecting the appropriate check boxes.

File permissions in Mac OS X are nearly identical to any other UNIX variant and are based on separate read, write, and execute permissions for owner, group, and world. While these permissions can be adjusted manually using a command line interface, with the standard **chown**, **chmod**, and **chgrp** commands, Apple again provides some nice interface capabilities for viewing and managing file and directory permissions. By selecting the properties of any given file or folder, the user can view and modify the permissions for that file or folder, as shown in Figure 14-14. Note that the GUI interface follows the same user-group-world pattern of permissions as other UNIX variants, though Apple uses the term *others* as opposed to *world*.

This GUI interface allows users to quickly and effectively restrict access to sensitive files and directories. By default, Mac OS X limits a user's ability to access or modify certain areas of the file system, including those areas containing system binaries. However, these restrictions can be circumvented by a user with the appropriate permissions or by certain third-party applications.

Removing unwanted or unnecessary programs in Mac OS X is usually done through the program's own uninstaller utility or by simply using the Finder to locate and then delete the folder containing the program and associated utilities. Like Windows, Mac OS X

Figure 14-14
Setting file
permissions
in Mac OS X

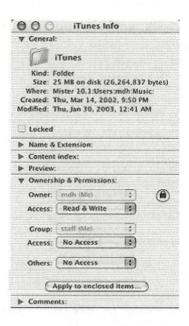

maps certain file extensions to specific programs, so deleting a program that handles specific extension types may require administrators to clear up associated extensions.

Like most UNIX-based operating systems, Mac OS X is a multiuser platform. As part of the baselining effort, the active user accounts should be examined to ensure they have the right level of access, permissions, group memberships, and so on. In addition, any accounts that are not used should be removed from the system completely. To access the user accounts under Mac OS X, select the Users icons under System Preferences—this should display the Users window, as shown here.

As can be seen in the preceding illustration, adding, editing, and deleting users is simply a matter of selecting the user account and clicking the correct button on the right side of the window. Mac OS X also permits administrators to lock accounts so they can only be modified by users with administrative-level privileges. Those who are familiar with UNIX operating systems may notice something odd about Mac OS X—there is no root account enabled by default. The root account does exist and can be enabled, but for "security reasons," it is not enabled by default.

Updates (a.k.a. Hotfixes, Service Packs, and Patches)

Operating systems are large and complex mixes of interrelated software modules written by dozens or even thousands of separate individuals. With the push toward GUI-based functionality and enhanced capabilities that has occurred over the past several years, operating systems have continued to grow and expand. Windows 2000 contains approximately 29 million lines of code, and though it may be the largest in that respect, other modern operating systems are not far behind. As operating systems continue to grow and introduce new functions, the potential for problems with the code grows as well. It is almost impossible for an operating system vendor to test their product on every possible platform under every possible circumstance, so functionality and security issues do arise after an operating system has been released.

To the average user or system administrator, this means a fairly constant stream of updates designed to correct problems, replace sections of code, or even add new features to an installed operating system. Vendors typically follow a hierarchy for software updates:

- **Hotfix** This is a term given to a (usually) small software update designed to address a specific problem, such as a buffer overflow in an application that exposes the system to attacks. Hotfixes are typically developed in reaction to a discovered problem and are produced and then released rather quickly.

- **Patch** This term is usually applied to a more formal, larger software update that may address several or many software problems. Patches often contain enhancements or additional capabilities as well as fixes for known bugs. Patches are usually developed over a longer period of time.

- **Service pack** This term is usually given to a large collection of patches and hotfixes that are rolled into a single, rather large package. Service packs are designed to bring a system up to the latest known, good level all at once, rather than requiring the user or system administrator to download dozens or hundreds of updates separately.

Every operating system, from Linux to Solaris to Windows, requires software updates, and each operating system has different methods of assisting users in keeping their systems up-to-date. Microsoft, for example, typically makes updates available for download from their web site. While most administrators or technically proficient users may prefer to identify and download updates individually, Microsoft recognizes that nontechnical users prefer a simpler approach, which they built into their Internet Explorer browser. By selecting Windows Update from the Tools menu in Internet Explorer (shown previously in Figure 14-2), users will be taken to the Microsoft web site. By selecting Scan For Updates, users can allow their systems to be examined for needed or required updates. The web site will identify which updates the user's system needs and will provide the user with the option to download and install the required updates. While this typically requires admin or power-user level access, it does simplify the update process for most users.

In addition to a web-based update utility, Microsoft also provides an automated update functionality that will, once configured, locate any required updates, download them to your system, and even install the updates if that is your preference. Figure 14-15 shows the Automatic Updates window, which can be found in the Control Panel. Note that both the web-based updates and automatic updates require active Internet connections to retrieve information and updates from Microsoft.

Microsoft is not alone in providing utilities to assist users in keeping their systems up-to-date and secure. The latest versions of Red Hat Linux contain a utility called the Red Hat Update Agent, which does essentially the same thing. By registering your system and user profile with Red Hat, you can obtain a customized list of updates for your specific system. By customizing your system profile, as shown in Figure 14-16, you can even tell the Red Hat Update Agent to look for updates on specific packages only.

Once the profile has been built, the Update Agent contacts the Red Hat update server to obtain information on available updates for the packages selected in the profile. Once a list of updates is obtained, the Update Agent allows the user to select which updates to download and install, as shown in Figure 14-17. This gives the user the ability to selectively download and install updates at their convenience. Again, an active Internet connection is required to use the Red Hat Update Agent.

Regardless of the method used to update the operating system, it is critically important to keep systems up-to-date. New security advisories come out every day, and while a buffer overflow may be a "potential" problem today, it will almost certainly become a "definite" problem in the near future. Much like the steps taken to baseline and initially secure an operating system, keeping every system patched and up-to-date is critical to protecting the system and the information it contains.

Figure 14-15

Setting up Microsoft's Automatic Updates utility in Windows 2000

Figure 14-16
Registering a
system with the
Red Hat Update
Agent

Network Hardening

While considering the baseline security of systems, attention must be given to the role the network connection plays in the overall security profile. The tremendous growth of the Internet and the affordability of multiple personal computers and Ethernet networking have caused almost every computer to be attached to some kind of network, and once computers are attached to a network, they are open to access from any other user on that

Figure 14-17
Selecting from
available updates
in the Red Hat
Update Agent

network. Proper controls over network access must be established. On computers, this is done by controlling the services that are running and the ports that are opened for network access. In addition to servers and workstations, however, network devices must also be examined: routers, switches, and modems, as well as other various components.

Today's network infrastructure components are similar to other computing devices on the network—they have dedicated hardware that runs an operating system, typically with one or more open ports for direct connection to the operating system, as well as ports supporting various network services. Any flaws in the coding of the operating system can be exploited to gain access as with any "regular" computer. These network devices should be configured with very strict parameters to maintain network security. Like normal computer operating systems that need to be patched and updated, the software that runs network infrastructure components needs to be updated regularly, as well. Finally, an outer layer of security should be added by implementing appropriate firewall rules and router access control lists.

Software Updates

Maintaining current vendor patch levels for your software is one of the most important things you can do to maintain security. This is also true for the infrastructure that runs the network. While some equipment is unmanaged and typically has no network presence and few security risks, any managed equipment that is responding on network ports will have some software or firmware controlling it. This software or firmware needs to be updated on a regular basis.

The most common device that connects people to the Internet is the network router. There are dozens of brands of routers, but the market is dominated by Cisco Systems. Their popular Internetwork Operating System (IOS) runs on over 70 of Cisco's devices and is installed countless times at countless locations. This popularity has fueled research into vulnerabilities in the code, and over the past few years quite a few vulnerabilities have been reported. These vulnerabilities can take many forms as routers send and receive several different kinds of traffic, from the standard Telnet remote terminal, to routing information in the form of Routing Information Protocol (RIP) or Open Shortest Path First (OSPF) packets, to Simple Network Management Protocol (SNMP) packets. This highlights the need to update the IOS software on a regular basis.

Cisco's IOS also runs on many of their Ethernet switching products. Like routers, these too have capabilities for receiving and processing protocols like Telnet and SNMP. Smaller network components do not usually run large software suites and typically have smaller software loaded on internal Non-Volatile RAM (NVRAM). While the update process for this kind of software is typically called a **firmware update**, this does not change the security implications of keeping it up-to-date. In the case of a corporate network with several devices, someone must take ownership of updating the devices, and updates must be performed regularly according to security and administration policies.

Device Configuration

As important as it is to keep software up-to-date, properly configuring network devices is equally, if not more, important. Many network devices, such as routers and switches, now have advanced remote management capabilities and can have multiple open ports accepting network connections. Proper configuration is necessary to keep these devices secure. Choosing a good password is very important in maintaining external and internal security, and closing or limiting access to any open ports is also a good step for securing the devices. On the more advanced devices, care must also be taken about what services the device is running, just like with a computer.

In many cases, a network device's primary protection method is a password. Good passwords are one of the most effective security tools, because a good password can be resistant to several forms of attack. This resistance makes an attacker use simple brute forcing methods, taking tremendous amounts of time and generating a large amount of network traffic, both increasing the likelihood of the attacker's efforts being detected. Unfortunately, good passwords are often hard to remember, so weaker passwords are usually used.

To recognize the impact on security a bad password can have, consider the fact that a typical brute forcing program can try every word in the unabridged English dictionary in under a day, but it would take several thousand years to attempt to brute force an eight-character password. This is based upon using not only the standard 26-character alphabet, but also adding capitalization for 26 more characters, numeric digits for 10 more, and special characters, adding another 32 different characters. This totals 95 different characters that can be used, giving 6,704,780,954,517,120 or six quadrillion different possibilities for a one- to eight-character password. This is in stark contrast to the estimated two million words in the English language, or the 217 billion possibilities provided by simple lowercase alphabetic characters.

The best kinds of passwords are ones that bear no resemblance to actual words, such as "AvhB42^&nFh." However, although such passwords provide greater security, they are difficult to remember, leading users to use passwords that are based upon regular dictionary words. While this is a concern for any password on any system, it is of greater concern on network infrastructure equipment because many pieces of network equipment require only password authentication for access—there is typically no username.

One of the password-related issues that many administrators overlook is SNMP. SNMP was developed in 1988 and has been implemented on a huge variety of network devices. Its wide implementation is directly related to its simplicity and extensibility. Since every manufacturer can add objects to the Management Information Base (MIB), they can add functionality without interfering with any other manufacturer's portion of the MIB tree. This feature of the protocol lets manufacturers make SNMP very powerful for configuration and monitoring purposes. The downside is that many devices have SNMP turned on by default. Network administrators not using SNMP will often forget to disable SNMP or will forget to change the well-known default passwords—typically "public" for read-only access and "private" for read/write access. With the SNMP service active and using a default password, an attacker can retrieve a great deal of interesting information from a network device, as well as altering any SNMP-capable settings. If SNMP is employed, well thought-out passwords should be used, as well as a schedule for password updates.

Keep in mind that SNMP passwords are often passed in the clear, so it should never be treated as a trusted protocol. The SNMP service should also be limited to only connections from the management station's IP address. If SNMP is not used, the service should be disabled, if possible. Otherwise the ports for SNMP should not be accessible from anywhere on the external or internal network.

As with any system, security is largely dependent on proper configuration of the system itself. A router can be secured with proper configuration just as easily as it can be left unsecured through poor configuration. Good passwords and knowledge of what services the devices are running is important to maintaining the security of those devices.

Ports and Services

A part of configuration that deserves its own section is the configuration of ports and services. For any networked machine, you need to take care to establish which ports and services are running and then conduct regular audits to ensure that only the authorized ports and services are open.

The advent and growth of networks permit almost any machine to be electronically connected to any other machine. This is a danger, as many machines are designed around a principle of trusting any other system on their local network. This causes problems because many machines have default configurations that offer a wide variety of services to the network, resulting in a large number of open ports. The overarching rule of security, here, is to give an attacker as little information or opportunity as possible, whether the attacker is inside or outside your network. While not all ports can be dangerous, they might provide information, so it is best to only have ports open that are necessary to run the services that the machine provides. By limiting the number of open ports, you reduce not only the possible avenues an attacker can use to compromise a machine, but also the amount of information that they can retrieve about the system. Table 14-2 shows an example output from a very popular port scanning program called "nmap." This tool checks remote systems for open services and reports back which services are "open" and accepting connections and which ports are "closed" and not accepting connections. In this example, nmap has scanned for open services on 1,013 different ports—any port not listed in Table 14-2 is "closed."

Table 14-2 shows interesting ports on localhost (127.0.0.1). The 1013 ports scanned but not shown are in state: Closed.

NOTE Nmap typically lists open services as "number/protocol," as shown in Table 14-2. The service name is a "best guess" by nmap based on the service typically running on that specific port.

There are also many ports left open by default on Windows systems, such as 135 epmap, 139 netbios-ssn, and 445 microsoft-ds.

Typically most servers are only used to provide one or two services, the most prevalent service on Internet servers being web and secure web, or 80/tcp and 443/tcp, respectively. Having web servers that also run telnet, SMTP, or POP3 provides multiple paths for an attacker who is attempting to compromise the system. It also requires more administration, as every service that is running needs to have its patch level kept up-to-date to ensure security. Figure 14-18 shows the output of a **netstat –a** command on a workstation running Windows 2000 Professional.

Port	State	Service
21/tcp	open	ftp
22/tcp	open	ssh
23/tcp	open	telnet
25/tcp	open	smtp
80/tcp	open	http
110/tcp	open	pop
111/tcp	open	pop
113/tcp	open	ident
143/tcp	open	imap2
512/tcp	open	exec
513/tcp	open	login
514/tcp	open	shell
587/tcp	open	unknown
783/tcp	open	unknown
940/tcp	open	unknown
946/tcp	open	unknown
7256/tcp	open	smtp-stats

Table 14-2 Open Ports and Services on a Typical UNIX Machine

TIP To list open, or listening, ports on most machines, use the command **netstat -l** or **netstat -a** (shown in Figure 14-18).

Figure 14-18   Output from netstat—a command on Windows 2000

Once the running services are known, the best thing to do is to shut off the unused ones. This is done by editing the inetd.conf file found in /etc on most UNIX systems, or by erasing the software that is providing the service (such as by completely removing Sendmail from the system). In Windows NT or 2000, the service must be stopped and set to "disable" in the Services Control Panel. Netstat can be rerun multiple times while editing the configuration files to ensure that all unnecessary services are shut down.

Any networked computer is typically going to have open ports and services, but many networked devices are being delivered with advanced remote management capabilities and have their own open ports and services. The most common are remote terminal services, such as telnet 23/tcp, SSH 22/tcp, embedded web services on HTTP 80/tcp or HTTPS 443/tcp, and SNMP services on 161/udp. These types of services are harder to disable on network equipment, but is sometimes possible. In Cisco's IOS, the command **no snmp-server** in config mode will disable the server service and close the port. Contact the vendor of your network equipment for information on disabling unnecessary services or limiting access to network services.

Some equipment will simply not allow you to disable the running service, but there is almost always another way to restrict access. Quite often, the most effective method is to perform filtering on the equipment itself, in the form of Access Control Lists.

Traffic Filtering

Filtering is one of the most common tools used in security. If something is trying to get in that you don't want to get in, you filter it. This is accomplished in a variety of ways, but they all consist of the same basic elements—rules that accept traffic and rules that deny traffic. These rules are typically arranged into sequential lists that the device steps through, one by one, as it receives traffic and attempts to find a match between rule and traffic. If this methodology looks familiar, that's because it is also how many brands of firewalls handle network traffic. While routers and other network devices typically make poor firewalls, they do have filtering capabilities that can be used to help secure the network as well as the routers and network devices themselves.

Filtering, while always following the same basic principle, is accomplished in many ways on different types of equipment. One of the most common places to do at least rudimentary filtering for your network is at the border routers. In Cisco's IOS, these filters are referred to as *access control lists (ACLs)*. Routers were originally built for the forwarding of traffic between networks, and current ones are optimized for that task. Traffic filtering was later added as a convenience, so ACLs can assist in the control of traffic across the network, but they will not make a router into a true firewall.

Access lists, like the majority of filtering rules, work on the principle of pattern matching. Every packet that the router accepts is examined for a match between the packet and the rules in the ACL. The ACL rules are processed in sequential order, meaning that the packet is compared against the first rule, then the second, then the third, and so on, until a match is found or the packet has been compared to every rule. At very high data rates, or for very long lists of rules, this can become computationally intensive. This large drain on resources is the primary reason to avoid using a router as a firewall, but using ACLs to drop known rogue traffic at the borders to the network makes good sense.

A typical access-list entry would be something like this:

```
Access-List 201 deny icmp any 192.168.1.0 255.255.255.0
```

This will drop Internet Control Message Protocol (ICMP) traffic from anywhere to the 192.168.1.0 network. These ACL entries must follow a specific syntax. The first component is an access-list name, in this case, 201. The next part of the rule is the action that the rule will take—"permit" or "deny" if the traffic matches this particular rule. The type of traffic that the rule applies to is next, and while it is ICMP in this case, it can be set to any particular type of traffic you wish to allow or deny. The next required component is the source address and mask. This can be as specific as a single address, a list of addresses, or it can be set to all 0's or a wildcard to signify all addresses. In this case, "any" is used as an abbreviation of the all 0's address. The last component is the destination address and mask. This follows the same format as the source address and mask, and it can also be a single address, a list of addresses, or all addresses.

While Cisco dominates the router market, other manufacturers do produce similar products. These products generally follow a similar format for their filtering rules, possibly with different syntax; however, they generally have statements involving traffic type, source, destination, and the action to be performed on the traffic. The versatility of ACLs allows a lot of filtering power, but filtering on a router should primarily be used to drop large blocks of the Internet that are known to not have contact with your organization, or to drop entire types of traffic from the entire Internet. This allows the firewall to handle the more complex rules for traffic filtering.

The next piece of equipment that should handle traffic after it passes through the router is the firewall. This is where the most complex filtering is performed, but it is typically still done with ACL-like statements. However, while the configuration is similar, extra care must be taken with firewalls, as they typically bridge public networks and private ones—if an attacker breaches the firewall, they will have a great deal of access to all the networks that the firewall is in contact with.

Firewalls should have all their open ports and services restricted to a very limited number of source addresses, typically the authorized control stations. Once traffic has been allowed inside the firewall, it can also be filtered on the host itself, as both Windows 2000 and most variants of UNIX support traffic filtering natively. Almost any other operating system can have traffic filtering added as an application. Windows 2000 provides traffic filtering on a per-port basis, and many versions of UNIX support traffic filtering to the point that they are well suited to be firewalls. IPFW, ipchains, and iptables are all programs that implement the same filtering concept, which is once again based upon access control statements formed into lists. Ipchains and iptables both have multiple lists allowing further specialization of inbound and outbound traffic on each interface. The statements that make up the lists follow the same format of list, action, type of traffic, source, and destination.

There is also the capability in many UNIX flavors to do filtering within certain applications. Tcpwrapper is a program that sits between inetd (the UNIX Internet superserver described in the Solaris and Linux sections of this chapter) and the individual services.

When a request comes in, inetd starts tcpwrapper, and it will allow authorized connections to the associated daemon when that specific service, such as FTP or Telnet, is needed by an authorized connection. Some newer versions of inetd now contain tcpwrapper-like functionality.

Filtering rules for tcpwrapper are typically contained in two separate files: /etc/hosts.allow and /etc/hosts.deny. These files enumerate the hosts allowed to connect to certain services, as well as those that are denied access to certain services. These files are processed from top to bottom until a matching rule is found, but they work on only source address and service. The rules in the files are formatted as "SERVICE:SOURCE," so an example hosts.allow might read as follows:

```
telnetd: ALL
ftpd: 192.168.1
sendmail: localhost
```

Any traffic that matches a rule in the hosts.allow file is allowed to connect to the system. The hosts.deny file has the same format, but it denies traffic that matches its rules. This functionality can be very useful for protecting not only against external threats, but also against internal threats, because you are locking down services to only the machines authorized to make use of them. TCP wrappers checks hosts.allow first and then hosts.deny—any traffic permitted by hosts.allow will be allowed in regardless of any rules contained in hosts.deny. This allows administrators to specify connections in hosts.allow and then place a generic "deny all" statement in hosts.deny to reject anything not specifically allowed in the hosts.allow file.

Network hardening is, on first glance, a fairly simple task. Disallow any traffic that is unauthorized by filtering it at all possible junctures in the network, and keep all software up-to-date on any devices that have contact with the network. Actually accomplishing that task is much more complex and maintenance oriented. The tools for controlling traffic are ACLs, traffic filters like tcpwrapper, and closing all unnecessary ports by properly configuring them. Vendor patches and firmware updates should be installed regularly. As always, any open services should be configured with maximum authentication and good passwords. Taking these steps will not completely solve the problem of security, but will ensure that an attack is as difficult as it can be.

Application Hardening

Perhaps as important as operating system and network hardening is application hardening—securing an application against local and Internet-based attacks. Hardening applications is fairly similar to hardening operating systems—you remove the functions or components you don't need, restrict access where you can, and make sure the application is kept up-to-date with patches. In most cases, the last step in that list is the most important for maintaining application security. After all, you need to make applications accessible to users or they serve no purpose. As most problems with applications tend to be buffer overflows in legitimate user input fields, patching the application is often the only way to secure it from attack.

Application Patches

As obvious as this seems, application patches are most likely going to come from the vendor that sells the application. After all, who else has access to the source code? In some cases, such as with Microsoft's Internet Information Server, this is the same company that sold the operating system that the application runs on. In other cases, such as Apache, the vendor is operating-system independent and provides an application with versions for many different operating systems.

Application patches are likely to come in three varieties: hotfixes, patches, and upgrades. As for operating systems, *hotfixes* are usually small sections of code designed to fix a specific problem. For example, a hotfix may be released to address a buffer overflow in the login routine for an application. *Patches* are usually collections of fixes, they tend to be much larger, and they are usually released on a periodic basis or whenever enough problems have been addressed to warrant a patch release. *Upgrades* are another popular method of patching applications, and they tend to be received with a more positive spin than patches. Even the term *upgrade* has a positive connotation—you are moving up to a better, more functional, and more secure application. For this reason, many vendors will release "upgrades" that consist mainly of fixes rather than new or enhanced functionality.

Application patches can come in a variety of forms. They can be downloaded from the vendor's web site or FTP site, or they can be received on a CD. In many cases, a patch is a small binary application that, when run, automatically replaces defective application binaries with updated ones. The patch may also change settings or modify configuration files. In other cases, the patch will be a zipped archive of files with a set of instructions that require the user or administrator to manually replace defective applications with the updated ones. Some advanced applications will have automatic update routines that update the application automatically in much the same fashion as an operating system.

Web Servers

Without a doubt, the most common Internet server-side application in use is the web server. Web servers are designed to provide content and functionality to remote users through a standard web browser. Web servers are used to deliver news, sell just about every product ever created, conduct auctions, and show pictures of someone's wedding. Due to their popularity and prolific use, web servers have become extremely popular targets for attackers. Web sites are defaced, and the original content is replaced with something the owner did not intend to display. E-commerce sites are attacked, and credit card numbers and user information is stolen.

Vendors have made setting up a web server remarkably easy, and this is one of the reasons for their enormous popularity. Unfortunately, vendors don't always provide good security configurations as part of the default installation. Fortunately, hardening a web server is not that difficult, as will be illustrated with examples of the two most popular web servers: IIS and Apache.

Microsoft's Internet Information Server

Microsoft's Internet Information Server (IIS) is one of the most popular web server applications in use today. IIS comes as a standard package with the Windows 2000 Server and Advanced Server operating systems and can be loaded at install time or added to the configuration of a running system. Due to its widespread use, IIS is a very popular target, and new vulnerabilities and exploits are released on an almost weekly or even daily basis.

The first step in securing an IIS server is to remove all sample files. To assist users in setting up their new web servers, Microsoft provides a number of sample files that users can examine and use as references when constructing their web sites. Unfortunately, these sample applications tend to be full of vulnerabilities and holes and should therefore never be present on a production web server. To remove IIS sample applications, remove the virtual and physical directories where the samples exist. For more information on the location of the sample files, refer to the following table:

Sample Name	Virtual Directory	Location
IIS Samples	\IISSamples	C:\Inetpub\IISsamples
IIS Documentation	IISHelp	C:\Winnt\Help\IISHelp
Data Access	\MSADC	C:\Program files\Common files\System\MSadc

Next, you should set up the appropriate permissions for the web server's files and directories. In IIS, you can do this using access control lists (ACLs), which are essentially the same file permissions that were discussed in the context of operating system hardening. As web servers are usually designed to give the public at large access, the key is to limit the user's ability to browse or navigate outside the intended path. This will typically involve removing permissions for the "everyone" group from certain files and directories. In most cases, you should never allow the "everyone" group to have write and execute privileges to the same directory. For that matter, in most cases you will not want to allow users to have write permissions for any of the web server's directories. Microsoft has provided some suggested ACL settings that are outlined in the following table:

File Type	ACL
CGI (exe, dll, cmd, pl)	Everyone (execute) Administrators (full control) System (full control)
Script files (asp)	Everyone (execute) Administrators (full control) System (full control)
Include files (inc, shtm, shtml)	Everyone (execute) Administrators (full control) System (full control)
Static content (txt, gif, jpg, html)	Everyone (read-only) Administrators (full control) System (full control)

Patching is also an extremely important part of the process of securing an IIS server. Since IIS is almost an integral part of the Windows Server operating system, the service packs for the operating system often contain patches and fixes for IIS. Microsoft also releases security bulletins to address each specific vulnerability that is discovered. Within each security bulletin there are links to the patch or hotfix that will mitigate or remove the reported vulnerability or manual steps an administrator can perform until a formal patch is released.

IIS is such a popular target that it is often very difficult for an administrator to keep pace with all the discovered vulnerabilities and patches required to keep it up-to-date and secure from attack. To ease the burden somewhat, Microsoft has developed two tools specifically designed to help secure IIS servers: the URLScan and IIS LockDown tools. URLScan is a monitoring utility and preprocessor that examines all incoming URLs and rejects any requests for files, directories, or services outside the intended scope of the web site. The IIS LockDown tool asks the administrator a series of questions to determine which features are needed. Based on the answers, IIS LockDown can deny write permissions for anonymous accounts, disable WebDAV, remove dynamic script type associations, restore default security settings, and back up the IIS Metabase and ACLs.

Apache

The Apache HTTP server from the Apache Software Foundation is the most popular web server in use today. Its Internet presence is greater than all the other web server versions combined. In 1995, a group of individuals known as the Apache Group joined to develop the Apache HTTP server. By 1999, the web server software and associated projects had become so popular that the organization grew into the Apache Software Foundation, a non-profit corporation. According to the Apache.org web site, "The Apache HTTP Server Project is an effort to develop and maintain an open-source HTTP server for modern operating systems including UNIX and Windows NT. The goal of this project is to provide a secure, efficient and extensible server that provides HTTP services in sync with the current HTTP standards." This statement highlights two of the keys to Apache's popularity—the software is open source, and it is available for virtually every popular operating system.

The first step in securing an Apache web server is to secure the host operating system. Due to the fact that Apache is available for most popular operating systems, outlining the possible security issues here could be a large task and would depend heavily on the operating system chosen. For the sake of brevity, we'll just say that a secure host operating system is one that is patched, has strong passwords for all user accounts, has no unnecessary services or software, has strong file and directory permissions, and has auditing enabled.

Once the host operating system has been taken care of, you will need to create an unprivileged account that will run the Apache server. This account, typically called "httpd" or "apache," is given the minimum permissions necessary to run the server software. Additional security measures include locking the account so it can never be used to log in to the system and assigning it to a special group where it is the only member. What you essentially end up creating is a user account that is only able to run the web server software and nothing more—this is fairly close to the ideal for Internet-visible services. By running the Apache software under an unprivileged account, you reduce the risk of potential compromise.

How you install the Apache software depends on whether you choose a precompiled binary or choose to compile it from the source code yourself. Regardless of the method you choose for installation, it is essential that you delete unneeded files and directories immediately after installation. Any source code files, samples, cgi-bin scripts, HTML pages, or documentation files that you don't absolutely need should be removed from the system. Like IIS, some of Apache's vulnerabilities have been in sample files and scripts that should not be placed on a production web server.

Locking down file and directory permissions is also important when securing an Apache server. In most cases, you are going to restrict access to web server configuration files to highly privileged users only, such as the root user. Files used for development or for maintaining the site itself are usually restricted to the web server development or maintenance team. The unprivileged user that was created to run the server is typically given read access to the web site content, and in some cases read and execute permission on any scripts required to support web site functionality. By restricting permissions and access to files and directories in this manner, you can help prevent web site visitors from wandering off the intended path or gaining access to files they should not see.

Patching an Apache server is just as critical as patching or maintaining any other application. New vulnerabilities are discovered on a frequent basis, and in some cases the only defense is to either disable functionality or implement the patch to correct the issue. There are no specific tools available to ensure that your version of Apache is up-to-date , so the best defense is to regularly visit the main Apache web site at www.apache.org for more information.

Mail Servers

Electronic mail is such an integral part of business and, for many of us, our daily lives that it is hard to imagine getting by without it. It has literally changed the way the world communicates and is so popular that there are millions of mail servers spread across the Internet sending billions of messages each day. As with so many things, increased popularity, use, and presence on the Internet also bring an increase in attention from potential attackers. Mail servers have become very popular targets, which makes securing them a constant challenge for administrators.

Securing a mail server typically means removing or disabling unwanted functionality and ensuring the software is patched. Earlier versions of mail server packages often contained bugs or even backdoors, such as the **wiz** command that gave potential attackers complete access to the host system. As mail server software matured, attacks started to focus on three areas: reconnaissance, relaying, and buffer overflows.

Reconnaissance or **information discovery** on a mail server is rather simple. The attacker's goal is to pull information from the system without having to authenticate or provide any information in return. Reconnaissance usually involves an attacker attempting to discover the names and addresses of valid user accounts, which are used for other purposes later. The two most common techniques use the **vrfy** and **expn** commands. When an attacker connects to a mail server, usually by telnetting to port 25 on the target system, the attacker can then enter commands and interact with the mail server itself. The **vrfy** command was initially designed to allow servers to verify e-mail addresses. For example, **vrfy jones** may yield a result of "jones@sample.com". This tells the attacker that the account "jones" does exist and gives the correct e-mail address for that account. The **expn** command expands an alias list into the full list of e-mail addresses belonging to that list. For example, **expn all-users** would provide a list of every e-mail address belonging to the mailing list called "all-users," if that mailing list existed. As you can see, while neither of these commands causes any direct harm, they do provide some useful information. For that reason, most administrators disable the **vrfy** and **expn** functions on their mail servers.

Relaying occurs when a mail server handles a message and neither the sender nor the recipient is a local user. Essentially, an attacker can take advantage of the mail server to send out e-mail on their behalf, even though they are not a legitimate user of that system. Spammers—those parties responsible for filling your e-mail inbox with unwanted junk messages promising to make you rich beyond your wildest dreams—actively seek out open mail relays so they can take advantage of someone else's resources to do their dirty work. Attackers also seek out open relays and leverage them to launch e-mail attacks, flooding a recipient with so many messages that their mailbox fills up or their mail server crashes. Preventing your mail server from becoming an open relay usually involves ensuring only authenticated users are allowed to send outgoing mail. Many mail server software packages, such as Sendmail, now provide relay-prevention capabilities as part of the default install. In most cases, you can also specify which systems, by system and domain name or IP address, are allowed to send mail through the server.

Buffer overflows continue to be the greatest danger to mail server security. A buffer overflow is a rather simple attack—you find a place where the server is accepting input, and you provide more input than the server is expecting to receive. Depending on the "extra" input provided and the software being attacked, a buffer overflow can do anything from crashing the server to giving the attacker remote access to the system. These continue to be extremely popular attacks, and the most effective way to prevent them is to ensure your mail server software is kept patched and up-to-date.

Microsoft's Exchange

Microsoft's mail server implementation is called Exchange, and, like other Microsoft products, it has had its share of vulnerabilities. By default, **vrfy** and **expn** are disabled in later versions of Exchange, but they can be enabled if required by modifying certain Registry settings. Service packs and patches for later versions of Exchange also provide anti-relay capabilities that can be configured through the Routing tab of the Internet Mail Service Properties.

Microsoft also provides a tool called the Baseline Security Analyzer, designed to scan Exchange, along with other applications and the operating system itself, to ensure that the software is up-to-date and patched appropriately. Running this tool on a regular basis will help ensure your Exchange system is patched against the latest vulnerabilities.

Microsoft also offers several useful guides, such as "Security Operations Guide for Exchange 2000 Server," to assist administrators in securing Exchange servers.

Sendmail

Sendmail was the initial mail server software, and it is still extremely popular. It is available as a completely free, open source product or as a fully licensed commercial product.

By default, recent versions of Sendmail disable the **expn** and **vrfy** functions, but they can be disabled in earlier versions by adding **PrivacyOptions=noexpn novrfy** to the sendmail.cf configuration file. Relaying is also restricted by default in recent versions, though an administrator can allow relaying for specific IPs or domains by modifying the relay-domains configuration file. Buffer overflows have been a frequent problem for

Sendmail—as usual, the best defense is to ensure your Sendmail software is patched and up-to-date. For more information on Sendmail, refer to www.sendmail.org.

FTP Servers

The File Transfer Protocol (FTP) allows users to access remotely stored files, and the applications that provide FTP services are very popular. Users can typically download files from FTP sites and, in certain cases, may even be allowed to upload files to the server. FTP is most commonly used as a distribution method for application updates, device drivers, free software—anything that needs to be made available to a large group of people.

FTP servers are typically configured as read-only services, meaning that you can download files from the server but cannot upload files or modify anything on the server itself. The most interesting dilemma concerning FTP servers is the use of anonymous access. In many cases, this is exactly what the system has been designed to do—permit thousands of remote users to anonymously download files and information. So in some cases, anonymous is the expected condition, assuming all related security precautions have been taken. Anonymous access to FTP servers only becomes a problem when the administrator does not mean to provide anonymous access or does not properly secure the FTP service. This typically involves setting the appropriate permissions, having the FTP process run by a nonprivileged user, and not allowing users to upload or modify files. Some FTP servers are meant as an upload and download service for authorized users only—in those cases, anonymous access should be completely removed.

Like many other Internet services, buffer overflows have been a consistent problem for FTP servers. Ensuring your FTP server software is up-to-date and patched is the best defense against buffer overflows. If you are not providing anonymous FTP services, you may also wish to restrict which external IP addresses are allowed to connect to the FTP service.

DNS Servers

Domain Name Service (DNS) is an integral part of making the Internet work. Human beings are not good at remembering long strings or numbers like IP addresses, but we are pretty good at remembering names like cnn.com, yahoo.com, or amazon.com. To navigate the Internet, your computer will need to know the IP address of your destination system, and DNS provides the translation from name to IP address that makes it all possible. DNS services are built as a hierarchical structure with many systems, called nameservers, working together to resolve names into IP addresses. When you request a name resolution, your system queries a local nameserver. If the nameserver does not know how to perform the translation (doesn't know the name-to-IP address translation), it asks the next nameserver up in that chain. This continues until the answer is found and is passed back down to your system. At the top of the DNS tree are 13 root nameservers that provide the definitive answers for all DNS queries.

The most popular DNS server implementation is Berkeley Internet Name Domain (BIND). BIND is an open-source, free server package that can be downloaded and run on a variety of operating systems. The two most common types of attacks against DNS servers are reconnaissance attacks and buffer overflows.

Reconnaissance attacks against DNS servers usually consist of an attacker attempting a zone transfer. A *zone transfer* occurs whenever a DNS server provides all the information it knows about an entire zone, which usually corresponds to an entire domain name. This information typically consists of all the names and IP addresses of systems in that zone—a very useful set of information for a potential attacker. Zone transfers also have a legitimate use, as they can be used to update zone information between nameservers. To protect against zone transfers, some organizations employ a split DNS architecture by using one nameserver to handle internal name queries and another server to handle external name queries. The two nameservers are never connected and never share information—the internal server is only visible from inside the network, and the external server knows nothing about the internal organization. Other organizations block all inbound connections on TCP port 53—the port used for zone transfers. You can also specify on your nameserver which external systems are allowed to execute zone transfers.

Buffer overflows are best defeated by ensuring the DNS software is patched and up-to-date. BIND, due to its popularity and widespread use, has been an extremely popular target in the last few years, and new vulnerabilities are introduced on a fairly regular basis. For the latest version and patches, see the main BIND web site at www.isc.org/products/BIND.

File and Print Services

Securing file and print services really boils down to a matter of permissions and ensuring legitimate users have access while unauthorized users do not. Network print services should be configured so that they receive print jobs from authorized, authenticated users. Users should, in most cases, be allowed to stop, pause, or delete their own print jobs. Only administrators should be able to control or modify the entire print queue or the printer itself.

In a similar manner, securing file services is usually a matter of permissions. Users should be given full control over their own files, read access to public resources that should not be modified, and possibly read and write access to group folders. In most cases, file services are extensions of the operating system itself, but there are some specialized file-service applications, such as Network File System (NFS), that are specifically designed to provide network access to stored data and files. NFS, a service that has a long history of security problems, has made advancements in recent versions, including better authentication methods, encryption, and PKI support.

Active Directory

The old adage "the network is the system" comes much closer to reality with systems like Microsoft's Active Directory services. Active Directory allows single login access to multiple applications, data sources, and systems, and includes advanced encryption capabilities, such as Kerberos and PKI.

Active Directory is built around a database, called a *schema*, containing information about network objects, such as domains, servers, workstations, printers, groups, and users. Each object is placed into a domain, which can then be used to control which users may access which objects. Each domain has its own security policies, administrative control, privileges, and relationships to other domains.

Domains are organized into a hierarchical structure called a forest, with the forest root domain being at the top of the tree. Branching off the main domain are trees containing parent and child domains. Every child domain has a two-way trust with its parent, which, by virtue of design, extends to every other child domain under that parent. Under this concept, when a user authenticates successfully into one child domain, all the other child domains under the same parent will accept the authentication as well, due to the two-way trust system. While the other child domains may accept the authentication information, access to resources is still controlled by the access controls for each specific child domain. So while a child domain may recognize you as an authenticated user from another child domain, it may not grant you access to its resources, due to local access controls.

Another key feature of Active Directory is delegation—the ability to selectively push administrative control to users in each domain. While enterprise-level administrative accounts only exist in the root domain, local admin accounts can exist in child domains. This means that you can have a high level admin in the central office grant local authority to add users, configure printers, and so on, to local admins in remote offices. This type of selective, localized administrative control can be very useful in large, distributed organizations.

Each object in Active Directory also has an access control list to determine who can view the object, what attributes they can read, and what actions each user can perform on the object. Access controls can be inherited or passed down from a parent to a child. For example, administrators can set permissions on a specific folder and specify that every subfolder or file in that folder receive the same permissions.

Active Directory also maintains a global catalog that contains a subset of information on all the objects in the Active Directory database. The global catalog is used for many functions within Active Directory, including user identification and e-mail addresses. The global catalog must be available and queryable for Active Directory to function properly. To update and query Active Directory, Microsoft uses the Lightweight Directory Access Protocol (LDAP). Every object in Active Directory has a unique name for use in LDAP queries and updates. Unfortunately, LDAP is not, by default, an encrypted protocol, meaning that anyone on the network could intercept and examine LDAP queries and updates.

The key to securing Active Directory is carefully planning and using appropriate permissions. While the granular control and enhanced capabilities of Active Directory could lead to more secure systems, its complexity can also lead to administrators overwriting each other's changes or accidentally granting access to unauthorized individuals. Microsoft provides some very good Active Directory resources on its web site.

Chapter Review

Chapter Summary

Security Baselines

- The process of establishing a system's security state is called *baselining*, and the resulting product is a security *baseline* that allows the system to run safely and securely.

- Security baselines are critical to protecting information systems, particularly those allowing connections from external users.
- Hardening is the process by which operating systems, network resources, and applications are secured against possible attacks.

Password Selection

- The first step in addressing the password issue is to create an effective and manageable *password policy* that both system administrators and users can work with.
- There are many tools available to help enforce the selection of strong, hard-to-guess passwords.
- Selecting passwords based on "passphrases" can be an easy and effective method of selecting a good password.
- Users should change their passwords every 60 to 90 days and should not be allowed to reuse old passwords.

Operating System and Network Operating System Hardening

- Securing operating systems consists of removing or disabling unnecessary services, restricting permissions on files and directories, removing unnecessary software (or not installing it in the first place), applying the latest patches, removing unnecessary user accounts, and ensuring strong password guidelines are in place.
- There are many good resources, such as Microsoft's security checklists, that can assist system administrators in securing their systems.
- Hardening Microsoft, UNIX, and Mac OS operating systems follow the same basic guidelines, but each OS has specific steps and guidelines that must be followed to ensure that a particular OS is secure.
- Ensuring systems are patched in a timely manner is critical to maintaining a secure state.

Network Hardening

- Securing network resources consists of disabling unnecessary functions, restricting access to ports and services, ensuring strong passwords are used, and ensuring the code on the network devices is patched and up-to-date.
- Controlling the types and amount of traffic allowed to move through network devices can help ensure effective, secure operations.

Application Hardening

- Securing applications depends heavily on the application involved, but typically consists of removing samples and default materials, preventing reconnaissance attempts, and ensuring the software is patched and up-to-date.
- Application patches should be tested before they are placed on a production system.

Key Terms

Access Control List *(345)*
Baselining *(337)*
Buffer overflow *(384)*
Firmware update *(373)*
Hardening *(337)*
Hotfix *(370)*
inetd *(360)*
Network operating system *(341)*
Operating system *(341)*
Password policy *(338)*
Passphrase *(340)*
Patch *(370)*
Process identifier *(358)*
Run level *(358)*
Service pack *(370)*
TCP wrappers *(360)*
Relaying *(384)*

Key Terms Quiz

Use terms from the Key Terms list to complete the sentences that follow. Don't use the same term more than once. Not all terms will be used.

1. _____ is the process of establishing a system's security state.

2. Securing and preparing a system for the production environment is called _____.

3. A _____ is a small software update designed to address a specific problem.

4. The basic software on a computer that handles input and output is called the _____.

5. _____ occurs when a mail server handles a message and neither the sender nor the recipient is a local user.

6. _____ is the master services daemon used by many UNIX operating systems.

7. A _____ is a bundled set of software updates, fixes, and additional functions contained in a self-installing package.

8. In most UNIX operating systems, each running program is given a unique number called a _____.

9. An _____ is associated with a file or directory to identify what level of access each user has to that file or directory.

10. When a user or process supplies more data than was expected, a _____ may occur.

Multiple-Choice Quiz

1. A small software update designed to address an urgent or specific problem is called a…

   A. Hotfix

   B. Service pack

   C. Patch

   D. None of the above

2. In a UNIX operating system, the master services daemon is called…

   A. Firmware

   B. An Access Control List

   C. inetd

   D. netstat

3. TCP wrappers do what?

   A. Help secure the system by restricting network connections

   B. Help prioritize network traffic for optimal throughput

   C. Encrypt outgoing network traffic

   D. Strip out excess input to defeat buffer overflow attacks

4. File permissions under UNIX consist of what three types?

   A. Modify, read, and execute

   B. Read, write, and execute

   C. Full control, read-only, and run

   D. Write, read, and open

5. The combination of hardware and software running on most routers, switches, and network devices is called…

   A. inetd

   B. A network operating system

   C. An operating system

   D. Firmware

6. Picking the first letter of each word in a sentence to create a password is a…

   A. Baseline

   B. Password policy

   C. Wrapper

   D. Passphrase

7. Which of the following would make the best password?

    A. Snorkel1

    B. TommyJones

    C. Inlk9

    D. Iltdm69m!

8. Users should change their passwords:

    A. Once a year

    B. Every six months

    C. Every 120 to 180 days

    D. Every 60 to 90 days

9. Microsoft's way of bundling updates, fixes, and new functions into a large, self-installing package is called a...

    A. Service pack

    B. Hotfix

    C. Upgrade

    D. Firmware update

10. Applying the latest patches is important for maintaining the security of:

    A. Applications only

    B. Operating systems and applications

    C. Firmware only

    D. Buffer overflows

11. To stop a particular service or program running on a UNIX operating system, you might use the _____ command.

    A. Netstat

    B. Ps

    C. Kill

    D. Inetd

12. Updating the software loaded on non-volatile RAM is called:

    A. A buffer overflow

    B. A firmware update

    C. A hotfix

    D. A service pack

13. What command expands an alias list into the full list of e-mail addresses belonging to that list?

    A. Ps

    B. Vrfy

    C. Expn

    D. ACL

14. An attack conducted by supplying more data than is expected is called:

    A. A buffer overflow

    B. Relaying

    C. Smurfing

    D. Access list trashing

15. Under Microsoft's operating systems, what does LDAP stand for?

    A. Long Directory Access Project

    B. Lightweight Directory Access Protocol

    C. Large Data Access Project

    D. Limited Data Accessibility Program

Essay Quiz

1. Create a password policy for your organization or a fictional organization. Be sure to include specifications such as password length and aging, as well as plans for educating users about the password policy and password security.

2. Explain the difference between a "hotfix" and a "service pack" and why they are so important.

3. A new administrator needs some help creating a security baseline. Create a checklist/template that covers the basic steps in creating a security baseline to assist them and explain why each step is important.

4. Describe how a buffer overflow works and explain why they are a threat to security.

5. Allowing "guest" or "anonymous" access to resources is generally considered to be a poor security practice. Explain why this is the case and cite examples of where guest or anonymous access would be harmful.

Lab Projects

Lab Project 14.1

Find a lab system running Linux with at least one open service such as FTP, Telnet, or SMTP. From another lab system, connect to the Linux system and observe your results. Configure TCP wrappers on the Linux system to reject all connection attempts from the other lab system. Now try to reconnect and observe your results. Document your steps and explain how TCP wrappers work.

Lab Project 14.2

A user is questioning your organization's password policy. The user claims that a six-character password consisting of letters only is just as secure as your organization's policy which requires eight characters or more, at least one letter, and at least one special character. To prove your case to the user, calculate the possible combinations in the following examples:

- A six-character password consisting only of lowercase letters

- A six-character password consisting of only upper- and lowercase letters

- An eight-character password consisting only of lowercase letters

- An eight-character password consisting of only upper- and lowercase letters

- An eight-character password consisting of upper- and lowercase letters and at least one numeric digit (0–9)

- A ten-character password consisting of upper- and lowercase letters and at least one numeric digit (0–9)

Attacks and Malware

Upon completion of this chapter, you will be able to:

- Describe various types of computer and network attacks, including Denial-of-Service, spoofing, hijacking, and password guessing
- Describe the different types of malicious software that exist, including viruses, worms, Trojan horses, and logic bombs
- Explain how social engineering can be used as a means to gain access to computers and networks
- Explain the importance of auditing and what should be audited

While hackers and viruses receive the most attention in the news (due to the volume of these forms of attack), they are not the only methods for attacking computer systems and networks. This chapter addresses the many different ways computers and networks come under attack on a daily basis. Each type of attack threatens at least one of the three security requirements mentioned in Chapter 1—confidentiality, integrity, and availability (the CIA of security). Attacks are thus attempts by unauthorized individuals to access or modify information, to deceive the system so that an unauthorized individual can take over an authorized session, or to disrupt service to authorized users.

Attacking Computer Systems and Networks

From a high-level standpoint, attacks on computer systems and networks can be grouped into two broad categories: attacks on specific software (such as an application or the operating system itself) and attacks on a specific protocol or service. Attacks on a specific application or operating system are generally possible because of either an oversight in the code (and possibly in the testing of that code) or because of a flaw or bug in the code (again indicating a lack of thorough testing). Attacks on specific protocols or services are attempts to either take advantage of a specific feature of the protocol or service or to use the protocol or service in a manner for which it was not intended. In addition, the target of an attacker can be of two types: targets of opportunity where the attacker is attempting to find any machine that is susceptible to a specific vulnerability, and defined targets where the attacker wants to gain access to a very specific target and must attempt to find a vulnerability that exists in that target. The remainder of this section discusses the various forms of attacks that security professionals need to be aware of.

Denial-of-Service Attacks

Denial-of-Service (DOS) attacks can exploit a known vulnerability in a specific application or operating system, or they may attack features (or weaknesses) in specific protocols or services. In this form of attack, the attacker is attempting to deny authorized users access either to specific information or to the computer system or network itself.

The purpose of such an attack can be to simply prevent access to the target system, or the attack can be used in conjunction with other actions in order to gain unauthorized access to a computer or network. For example, a SYN flooding attack may be used to temporarily prevent service to a system in order to take advantage of a trusted relationship that exists between that system and another.

SYN flooding is an example of a DOS attack that takes advantage of the way TCP/IP networks were designed to function, and it can be used to illustrate the basic principles of any DOS attack. SYN flooding utilizes the TCP three-way handshake that is used to establish a connection between two systems. Under normal circumstances, the first system sends a SYN packet to the system it wishes to communicate with. The second system will respond with a SYN/ACK if it is able to accept the request. When the initial system receives the SYN/ACK from the second system, it responds with an ACK packet, and communication can then proceed. This process is shown in Figure 15-1.

 NOTE A SYN/ACK is really a combination of the SYN packet sent to the first system, combined with an ACK packet acknowledging the first system's SYN packet.

In a SYN flooding attack, the attacker sends fake communication requests to the targeted system. Each of these requests will be answered by the target system, which then waits for the third part of the handshake. Since the requests are fake (a nonexistent IP address is used in the requests, so the target system is responding to a system that doesn't exist), the target will wait for responses that will never come, as shown in Figure 15-2. The target system will drop these connections after a specific time-out period, but if the attacker sends requests faster than the time-out period eliminates them, the system will quickly be filled with requests. The number of connections a system can support is finite, so when more requests come in than can be processed, the system will soon be reserving all its connections for fake requests. At this point, any further requests are simply dropped (ignored), and legitimate users who want to connect to the target system will not be able to. Use of the system has thus been denied to them.

Another simple DOS attack is the famous ping-of-death (POD), and it illustrates the other type of attack—one targeted at a specific application or operating system, as opposed to SYN flooding, which targets a protocol. In the POD attack, the attacker sends

Figure 15-1   The TCP three-way handshake

Figure 15-2   A SYN flooding DOS attack

an Internet Control Message Protocol (ICMP) "ping" packet equal to, or exceeding 64KB (which is to say, greater than 64 * 1024 = 65,536 bytes). This type of packet should not occur naturally (there is no reason for a ping packet to be larger than 64KB). Certain systems were not able to handle this size of packet, and the system would hang or crash.

DOS attacks are conducted using a single attacking system. A Denial-of-Service attack employing multiple attacking systems is known as a distributed Denial-of-Service (DDOS) attack. The goal of a DDOS attack is the same: to deny the use of or access to a specific service or system. DDOS attacks were made famous in 2000 with the highly publicized attacks on eBay, CNN, Amazon, and Yahoo.

In a DDOS attack, the method used to deny service is simply to overwhelm the target with traffic from many different systems. A network of attack agents (sometimes called zombies) is created by the attacker, and upon receiving the attack command from the attacker, the attack agents commence sending a specific type of traffic against the target. If the attack network is large enough, even ordinary web traffic can quickly overwhelm the largest of sites, such as the ones targeted in 2000.

Creating a DDOS network is not a simple task. The attack agents are not willing agents—they are systems that have been compromised and on which the DDOS attack software has been installed. In order to compromise these agents, the attacker has to have gained unauthorized access to the system or tricked authorized users to run a program that installed the attack software. The creation of the attack network may in fact be a multistep process in which the attacker first compromises a few systems that are then used as handlers or masters, and which in turn compromise other systems. Once the network has been created, the agents wait for an attack message that will include data on the specific target before launching the attack. One important aspect of a DDOS attack that should be mentioned is that with just a few messages to the agents, the attacker can have a flood of messages sent against the targeted system. Figure 15-3 illustrates a DDOS network with agents and handlers.

How can you stop or mitigate the effects of a DOS or DDOS attack? One important precaution is to ensure that you have applied the latest patches and upgrades to your systems and the applications running on them. Once a vulnerability is discovered, it does not take long before multiple exploits are written to take advantage of it. Generally, you will have a small window of opportunity in which to patch your system between the time a vulnerability is discovered and the time exploits become widely available.

Figure 15-3   Distributed denial of service attacks

Another approach involves changing the timeout option for TCP connections so that attacks such as the SYN flooding attack, described previously, are harder to perform because unused connections are dropped more quickly.

For DDOS attacks, much has been written about distributing your own workload across several systems so that any attack against your system would have to target several hosts in order to be completely successful. While this is true, if large enough DDOS networks are created (with tens of thousands of zombies, for example) any network, no matter how much the load is distributed, can be successfully attacked. This approach also involves an additional cost to your organization in order to establish this distributed environment. Addressing the problem in this manner is actually an attempt to mitigate the effect of the attack, as opposed to preventing or stopping an attack.

In order to prevent a DDOS attack, you have to either be able to intercept or block the attack messages or keep the DDOS network from being established in the first place. Tools have been developed that will scan your systems, searching for sleeping zombies waiting for an attack signal. The problem with this type of prevention approach, however, is that it is not something you can do to prevent an attack on your network—it is something you can do to keep your network from being used to attack other networks or systems. You have to rely on the rest of the community to test their own systems in order to prevent attacks on yours.

A final option you should consider that will address several forms of DOS and DDOS attacks is to block ICMP packets at your border, since many attacks rely on ICMP. Careful consideration should be given to this approach, because it will also prevent the use of some possibly useful troubleshooting tools.

Backdoors and Trapdoors

Backdoors were originally (and sometimes still are) nothing more than methods used by software developers to ensure that they could gain access to an application even if something were to happen in the future to prevent normal access methods. An example would be a hard-coded password that could be used to gain access to the program in the event that administrators forgot their own system password. The obvious problem with this sort of backdoor (also sometimes referred to as a *trapdoor*) is that, since it is hard-coded, it cannot be removed. Should an attacker learn of the backdoor, all systems running that software would be vulnerable to attack.

The term *backdoor* is also, and more commonly, used to refer to programs that attackers install after gaining unauthorized access to a system to ensure that they can continue to have unrestricted access to the system, even if their initial access method is discovered and blocked. Backdoors can also be installed by authorized individuals inadvertently, should they run software that contains a Trojan horse (more on these later in this chapter). Common backdoors include NetBus and Back Orifice. Both of these, if running on your system, will allow an attacker remote access to your system—access that allows them to perform any function on your system. A variation on the backdoor is the *rootkit*, and they are established not to gain root access but rather to ensure continued root access. Rootkits are generally installed at a lower level, closer to the actual kernel level of the operating system.

Sniffing

The group of protocols that make up the TCP/IP suite was designed to work in a friendly environment where everybody who connected to the network used the protocols as they were designed. The abuse of this friendly assumption is illustrated by network-traffic sniffing programs, sometimes referred to as *sniffers*.

A network **sniffer** is a software or hardware device that is used to observe traffic as it passes through a network on shared broadcast media. The device can be used to view all traffic, or it can target a specific protocol, service, or even string of characters (for example, looking for logins). Normally, the network device that connects a computer to a network is designed to ignore all traffic that is not destined for that computer. Network sniffers ignore this friendly agreement and observe all traffic on the network, whether destined for that computer or others, as shown in Figure 15-4. A network card that is listening to all network traffic and not just its own is said to be in "promiscuous mode." Some network sniffers are designed not just to observe all traffic but to modify traffic as well.

Network sniffers can be used by network administrators for monitoring network performance. They can be used to perform traffic analysis, for example, in order to determine what type of traffic is most commonly carried on the network and to determine which segments are most active. They can also be used for network bandwidth analysis and to troubleshoot certain problems (such as duplicate MAC addresses).

Network sniffers can also be used by attackers to gather information that can be used in penetration attempts. Information such as an authorized user's username and password can be viewed and recorded for later use. The contents of e-mail messages can also be viewed as the messages travel across the network. It should be obvious that administrators and security professionals will not want unauthorized network sniffers on their networks because of the security and privacy concerns they introduce. Fortunately, in order for network sniffers to be most effective, they need to be on the internal network, which generally means that the chances for outsiders to use them against you is extremely limited.

Figure 15-4
Network sniffers
listen to all
network traffic

Spoofing

Spoofing is nothing more than making data look like it has come from a different source. This is possible in TCP/IP because of the friendly assumptions behind the protocols. When the protocols were developed, it was assumed that individuals who had access to the network layer would be privileged users who could be trusted.

When a packet is sent from one system to another, it includes not only the destination IP address and port but the source IP address as well. You are supposed to fill in the source with your own address, but there is nothing that stops you from filling in another system's address. This is one of the several forms of spoofing.

Spoofing E-mail

E-mail spoofing is where you send a message with a From address different than your own. This can be easily accomplished, and there are several different ways to do it and programs that can assist you in doing so. A very simple method often used to demonstrate how simple it is to spoof an e-mail address is to telnet to port 25 (the port associated with e-mail) on a system. From there, you can fill in any address for the From and To sections of the message, whether or not the addresses are yours and whether they actually exist or not.

There are some simple ways to determine that an e-mail message was probably not sent by the source it claims to have been sent from, but most users do not question their e-mail and will accept where it appears to have come from. A variation on e-mail spoofing, though it is not technically spoofing, is for the attacker to acquire a URL close to the one they want to spoof so that e-mail sent from their system appears to have come from the official site unless you read the address carefully. For example, if attackers wanted to spoof XYZ Corporation, which owned XYZ.com, the attackers might gain access to the URL XYZ.Corp.com. An individual receiving a message from the spoofed corporation site would not normally suspect it to be a spoof but would take it to be official. This same method can be, and has been, used to spoof web sites. The most famous example of this is probably www.whitehouse.com. The www.whitehouse.gov site is the official site for the White House. The www.whitehouse.com URL takes you to a pornographic site. In this case, nobody is likely to take the pornographic site to be the official government site, and it was not intended to be taken that way. If, however, the attackers made their spoofed site appear similar to the official one, they could easily convince many viewers that they were at the official site.

IP Address Spoofing

The way the IP protocol is designed to work is to have the originators of any IP packet include their own IP address in the "From" portion of the packet. While this is the intent, there is nothing that prevents a system from inserting a different address in the "From" portion of the packet. This is known as IP Address Spoofing. An IP address may be spoofed for several reasons. In a specific DOS attack known as a *smurf* attack, the attacker sends a spoofed packet to the broadcast address for a network, which distributes the packet to all systems on that network. In the smurf attack, the packet sent by the attacker to the broadcast address is an echo request with the From address forged so that it appears that another system (the target system) has made the echo request. The normal response of a system to an echo request is an echo reply, and it is used in the ping utility to let a user know if a remote system is reachable and is responding. In the smurf attack, the request is sent to all systems on the network, so all will respond with an echo reply to the target system, as shown in Figure 15-5. The attacker has sent one packet and has been able to generate as many as 254 responses aimed at the target. Should the attacker send several of these spoofed requests, or send them to several different networks, the target can quickly become overwhelmed with the volume of echo replies it receives.

Figure 15-5

Spoofing used in a smurf DOS attack

Spoofing and Trusted Relationships

Spoofing can also take advantage of a trusted relationship between two systems. If two systems are configured to accept the authentication accomplished by each other, an individual logged on to one system might not be forced to go through an authentication process again to access the other system. An attacker can take advantage of this arrangement by sending a packet to one system that appears to have come from a trusted system. Since the trusted relationship is in place, the targeted system may perform the requested task without authentication.

Since a reply will often be sent once a packet is received, the system that is being impersonated could interfere with the attack, since it would receive an acknowledgment for a request it never made. The attacker will often initially launch a DOS attack (such as a SYN flooding attack) to temporarily take out the spoofed system for the period of time that the attacker is exploiting the trusted relationship. Once the attack is completed, the DOS attack on the spoofed system would be terminated and possibly, apart from having a temporarily nonresponsive system, the administrators for the systems may never notice that the attack occurred. Figure 15-6 illustrates a spoofing attack that includes a SYN flooding attack.

Because of this type of attack, administrators are encouraged to strictly limit any trusted relationships between hosts. Firewalls should also be configured to discard any packets from outside of the firewall that have From addresses indicating they originated from inside the network (a situation that should not occur normally and that indicates spoofing is being attempted).

Spoofing and Sequence Numbers

How complicated the spoofing is depends heavily on several factors, including whether the traffic is encrypted and where the attacker is located in relationship to the target. Spoofing attacks from inside a network, for example, are much easier to perform than attacks from outside of the network because the inside attacker can observe the traffic to and from the target and can do a better job of formulating the necessary packets.

Formulating the packets is more complicated for external attackers because there is a sequence number associated with TCP packets. A sequence number is a 32-bit number established by the host that is incremented for each packet sent. Packets are not guaranteed to be received in order, and the sequence number can be used to help reorder packets as they are received and to refer to packets that may have been lost in transmission.

In the TCP three-way handshake discussed previously, two sets of sequence numbers are created, as shown in Figure 15-7. The first system chooses a sequence number to

Figure 15-6

Spoofing to take advantage of a trusted relationship

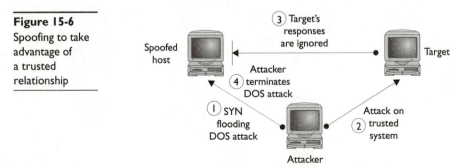

Figure 15-7

Three-way
handshake
with sequence
numbers

 Host 1

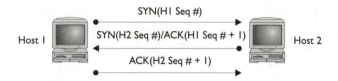

SYN(H1 Seq #)

SYN(H2 Seq #)/ACK(H1 Seq # + 1)

ACK(H2 Seq # + 1)

Host 2

send with the original SYN packet that it sends. The system receiving this SYN packet acknowledges with a SYN/ACK. It sends back the first sequence number plus one (that is, it increments the sequence number sent to it by one). It then also creates its own sequence number and sends that along with it. The original system receives the SYN/ACK with the new sequence number. It increments the sequence number by one and uses it in an ACK package it responds with.

The difference in the difficulty of attempting a spoofing attack from inside a network and from outside involves determining the sequence number. If the attacker is inside of the network and can observe the traffic the target host responds with, the attacker can easily see the sequence number the system creates and can respond with the correct sequence number. If the attacker is external to the network, the sequence number the target system generates will not be observed, making it hard for the attacker to provide the final ACK with the correct sequence number. What the attacker has to do is guess what the sequence number might be.

Predicting sequence numbers is possible, because sequence numbers are somewhat predictable. Sequence numbers for each session are not started from the same number, so that different packets from different concurrent connections will not have the same sequence numbers. Instead, the sequence number for each new connection is incremented by some large number to keep them from being the same. The sequence number may also be incremented by some large number every second (or some other time period). What an external attacker has to do is determine what the values used for these increments are. The attacker can do this by attempting connections at various time intervals in order to observe how the sequence numbers are incremented. Once the pattern is determined, the attacker can attempt a legitimate connection to determine the current value, and then immediately attempt the spoofed connection. The spoofed connection sequence number should be the legitimate connection incremented by the determined value or values.

Sequence numbers are also important in session hijacking, which will be discussed in the "TCP/IP Hijacking" section of this chapter.

Man-in-the-Middle Attacks

A **man-in-the-middle attack**, as the name implies, generally occurs when attackers are able to place themselves in the middle of two other hosts that are communicating in order to view and/or modify the traffic. Ideally, this is done by ensuring that all communication going to or from the target host is routed through the attacker's host (which may be accomplished if the attacker can compromise the router for the target host). The attacker can then observe all traffic before relaying it and can actually modify or block traffic. To the target host, it appears that communication is occurring normally, since all expected replies are received. Figure 15-8 illustrates this type of attack.

Figure 15-8
A man-in-the-middle attack

Communication appears to be direct

Host 2

Host 1

Attacker relays messages to
destination host

Communication
actually sent to attacker

Attacker

The amount of information that can be obtained in a man-in-the-middle attack will obviously be limited if the communication is encrypted. Even in this case, however, sensitive information may still be obtained, since knowing what communication is being conducted, and between which individuals, may in fact provide information that is valuable in certain circumstances.

Man-in-the-Middle Attacks on Encrypted Traffic

The term "man-in-the-middle attack" is sometimes used to refer to a more specific type of attack—one in which the encrypted traffic issue is addressed. Public and private key encryption will be discussed in much greater detail in Chapter 10, but for now it should be understood that public key encryption requires the use of two keys: your public key, which anybody can use to encrypt or "lock" your message, and your private key, which only you know and which is used to "unlock" or decrypt a message locked with your public key.

If you wanted to communicate securely with your friend Bob, you might ask him for his public key so you could encrypt your messages to him. You, in turn, would supply Bob with your public key. An attacker can conduct a man-in-the-middle attack by intercepting your request for Bob's public key and the sending of your public key to him. The attacker would replace your public key with the attacker's public key, and would send it on to Bob. The attacker's public key would also be sent to you by the attacker instead of Bob's public key. Now when either you or Bob encrypt a message, it will be encrypted using the attacker's public key. The attacker can now intercept it, decrypt it, and then send it on by re-encrypting it with the appropriate key for either you or Bob. Each of you thinks you are transmitting messages securely, but in reality your communication has been compromised. Well-designed cryptographic products use techniques such as mutual authentication to avoid this problem.

Replay Attacks

A **replay attack** is exactly what it sounds like: it is an attack where the attacker captures a portion of a communication between two parties and retransmits it at a later time. For example, an attacker might replay a series of commands and codes used in a financial transaction in order to cause the transaction to be conducted multiple times. Generally, replay attacks are associated with attempts to circumvent authentication mechanisms, such as the capturing and reuse of a certificate or ticket.

The best way to prevent replay attacks is with encryption, cryptographic authentication, and time stamps. If a portion of the certificate or ticket includes a date/time stamp or an expiration date/time, and this portion is also encrypted as part of the ticket or certificate, replaying it at a later time will prove useless, since it will be rejected as having expired.

TCP/IP Hijacking

TCP/IP hijacking and *session hijacking* are terms used to refer to the process of taking control of an already existing session between a client and a server. The advantage to an attacker of hijacking over attempting to penetrate a computer system or network is that the attacker doesn't have to circumvent any authentication mechanisms, since the user has already authenticated and established the session. Once the user has completed the authentication sequence, the attacker can then usurp the session and carry on as if the attacker, and not the user, had authenticated with the system. In order to prevent the user from noticing anything unusual, the attacker may decide to attack the user's system and perform a Denial-of-Service attack on it, taking it down so that the user, and the system, will not notice the extra traffic that is taking place.

Hijack attacks generally are used against web and telnet sessions. The previous discussion on sequence numbers as they applied to spoofing also applies to session hijacking, since the hijacker will need to provide the correct sequence number to continue the appropriated sessions.

Attacks on Encryption

Cryptography is the art of "secret writing," and encryption is the process of transforming *plaintext* into an unreadable format known as *ciphertext* using a specific technique or algorithm. Most encryption techniques use some form of key in the encryption process. The key is used in a mathematical process to scramble the original message to arrive at the unreadable ciphertext. Another key (sometimes the same one and sometimes a different one) is used to decrypt or unscramble the ciphertext to re-create the original plaintext. The length of the key often directly relates to the strength of the encryption.

Cryptanalysis is the process of attempting to break a cryptographic system—it is an attack on the specific method used to encrypt the plaintext. There are various ways cryptographic systems can be compromised. Encryption will be discussed in greater detail in Chapter 10 of this book.

Weak Keys

Certain encryption algorithms may have specific keys that yield poor, or easily decrypted, ciphertext. Imagine an encryption algorithm that consisted solely of a single XOR function (an exclusive OR function where two bits are compared and a 1 is returned if either of the original bits, but not both, is a 1), where the key was repeatedly used to XOR with the plaintext. A key where all bits are 0's, for example, would result in ciphertext that is the same as the original plaintext. This would obviously be a weak key for this encryption algorithm. In fact, any key with long strings of 0's would yield portions of the ciphertext that were the same as the plaintext. In this simple example, there would be many keys that could be considered weak.

Encryption algorithms used in computer systems and networks are much more complicated than a simple, single XOR function, but some algorithms have still been found to have weak keys that make cryptanalysis easier.

Exhaustive Search of Key Space

Even if the specific algorithm used to encrypt a message is complicated and has not been shown to have weak keys, the key length will still play a significant role in how easy it is to attack the method of encryption. Generally speaking, the longer a key is, the harder it will be to attack. Thus, a 40-bit encryption scheme will be easier to attack using a brute-force technique (which tests all possible keys, one by one) than a 256-bit method will be. This is easily demonstrated by imagining a scheme that employed a 2-bit key. Even if the resulting ciphertext were completely unreadable, performing a brute-force attack until one key is found that can decrypt the ciphertext would not take long, since there are only four possible keys. Every bit that is added to the length of a key doubles the number of keys that have to be tested in a brute-force attack on the encryption. It is easy to understand why a scheme utilizing a 40-bit key would be much easier to attack than a scheme that utilized a 256-bit key.

Indirect Attacks

One of the most common ways of attacking an encryption system is to find weaknesses in mechanisms surrounding the cryptography. Examples include poor random number generators, unprotected key exchanges, keys stored on hard drives without sufficient protection, and other general programmatic errors, such as buffer overflows. In attacks that target these types of weaknesses, it is not the cryptographic algorithm itself that is being attacked, but rather the implementation of that algorithm in the real world.

Password Guessing

The most common form of authentication is the user ID and password combination. While it is not inherently a poor mechanism for authentication, the user ID and password combination can be attacked in several ways. All too often, these attacks will yield favorable results for the attacker not as a result of a weakness in the scheme but usually due to the user not following good password procedures.

Poor Password Choices

The least technical of the various password-attack techniques consists of the attacker simply attempting to guess the password of an authorized user of the system or network. It is surprising how often this simple method works, and the reason it does is because people are notorious for picking poor passwords. The problem the users face is that they need to select a password that they can remember. In order to do this, many select simple things, such as their birthday, their mother's maiden name, the name of their spouse or one of their children, or even simply their user ID itself. All it takes is for the attacker to obtain a valid user ID (often a simple matter, because organizations tend to use an individual's names in some combination—first letter of their first name combined with their last name, for example) and a little bit of information about the user before guessing can begin. Organizations sometimes make it even easier for attackers to obtain this sort of information by posting the names of their "management team" and other individuals, sometimes with short biographies, on their web sites.

Even if the person doesn't use some personal detail as their password, the attacker may still get lucky, since many people pick a common word for their password. Attackers can obtain lists of common passwords—there are a number of them on the

Internet. Words such as "password" and "secret" have often been used as passwords. Names of favorite sports teams also often find their way onto lists of commonly used passwords.

Dictionary Attack

Another method of determining passwords is to use a password-cracking program. There are a number of both commercial and public-domain password cracking programs available. The programs use a variety of methods to crack passwords, including using variations on the user ID. These programs often also use a dictionary of words—the words can be used by themselves, or two or more smaller ones may be combined to form a single possible password.

The programs often permit the attacker to create various rules that tell the program how to combine words to form new possible passwords. Users commonly substitute certain numbers for specific letters. If the user wanted to use the word *secret* for a password, for example, the letter *e* may be replaced with the number *3* yielding *s3cr3t*. This password will not be found in the dictionary, so a pure dictionary attack will not crack it. At the same time, the password is still easy for the user to remember. If a rule were created that tried all words in the dictionary and then tried the same words substituting the number *3* for the letter *e*, the password would be cracked.

Rules can also be defined so that the cracking program will substitute special characters for other characters, or combine words together. The ability of the attacker to crack passwords is directly related to the method the user employed to create the password in the first place, as well as the dictionary and rules used.

Brute-Force Attack

If the user has selected a password that will not be found in a dictionary, even if various numbers or special characters are substituted for other letters, the only way the password can be cracked is to attempt a brute-force attack. This entails the password cracking program attempting all possible password combinations.

The length of the password and the size of the set of possible characters in the password will greatly affect the time a brute-force attack will take. A few years ago, this method of attack was very unreliable, since it took considerable time to generate all possible combinations. With the increase in computer speed, however, the time it takes to generate password combinations makes it much more feasible to launch brute-force attacks against certain computer systems and networks. A brute-force attack on a password can take place at two levels. It can be an attack on a system where the attacker is attempting to guess the password at a login prompt, or it can be an attack against the list of passwords contained in a password file. The first attack can be made more difficult by locking the account after a few failed login attempts. The second attack can be thwarted by securely maintaining your password file so that others may not obtain a copy of it.

Birthday Attack

The birthday attack is a special type of brute-force attack. It gets its name from something known as the *birthday paradox,* which states that in a group of at least 23 people, the chance that there will be two individuals with the same birthday is greater than 50 percent. Mathematically, we can use the equation $1.2k^{1/2}$ (with k equaling the size of the set of possible values), and in the birthday paradox, k would be equal to 365 (the number of possible birthdays). This same phenomenon applies to passwords, with k just being quite a bit larger.

Software Exploitation

An attack that takes advantage of bugs or weaknesses in software is referred to as **software exploitation**. These weaknesses can be the result of poor design, poor testing, or poor coding practices. They may also result from what are sometimes called "features." An example of this might be a debugging feature, which when used during debugging might allow unauthenticated individuals to execute programs on a system. If this feature is left in when the final version of the software is shipped, it creates a weakness that is just waiting to be exploited.

One common weakness that has been exploited on a number of occasions is buffer overflows. A buffer overflow occurs when a program is provided more data for input than it was designed to handle. For example, what would happen if a program that asks for a 7–10 character phone number instead receives a string of 150 characters? Many programs will provide some error checking to ensure that this will not cause a problem. Some programs, however, do not handle this error, and the extra characters continue to fill memory, overwriting other portions of the program. This can result in a number of problems, including causing the program to abort or the system to crash. Under certain circumstances, the program may execute a command now supplied by the attacker.

Wardialing and WarDriving

Wardialing is the term used to describe an attacker's attempt to discover unprotected modem connections to computer systems and networks. The term's origin comes from the 1983 movie *WarGames*, in which the star has his machine systematically call a sequence of phone numbers in an attempt to find a computer connected to a modem. In the case of the movie, the intent was to find a machine with games the attacker could play, though obviously an attacker could have other purposes once access is obtained.

Wardialing is surprisingly successful, mostly because of rogue modems. These are unauthorized modems attached to computers on a network by authorized users. Generally, the reason for attaching the modem is not malicious—the individual may simply want to be able to go home and then connect to the organization's network in order to continue working. The problem is that if a user can connect, so can an attacker. If the authorized user has not implemented any security protection, access could be totally open. This is often the case. Most organizations have a strict policy against connecting unauthorized modems, but it is hard to enforce. Recently, new technology has been developed to address this common backdoor into corporate networks. Telephone firewalls have been created, which block any unauthorized modem connections into an organization. These devices make it impossible for an unauthorized modem connection to be established and can also enforce strict access policies on any authorized modems.

Another avenue of attack on computer systems and networks that has seen a tremendous increase over the last few years is due to the use of wireless networks. Wireless networks have some obvious advantages—they free employees from the cable connection to a port on their wall, allowing them to wander throughout the building with their machine and still be connected. An employee could, for example, leave their desk with their laptop and move to a conference room where they could then make a presentation, all without ever having to disconnect their machine from the wall or find a connection in the conference room.

The problem with wireless networks is that it is hard to limit access to them. Since there is no physical connection, the distance that a user can go and still remain connected is a function of the wireless network itself and where the various components of the network are placed. In order to ensure access throughout a facility, stations are often placed at numerous locations, some of which may actually provide access to areas outside of the organization in order to ensure that the farthest offices in the organization can be reached. Frequently, access extends into adjacent offices or even into the parking lot or street. Attackers can locate these access areas that fall outside of the organization and attempt to gain unauthorized access.

The term **WarDriving** has been used to refer to the activity where attackers wander throughout an area (often in a car) toting a computer with wireless capability as they search for wireless networks they can access. There are security measures that can limit an attacker's ability to succeed at this activity, but, just as in wardialing, the individuals who set up the wireless networks don't always activate these security mechanisms.

Social Engineering

Social engineering (covered extensively in Chapter 4) relies on lies and misrepresentation, which an attacker uses to trick an authorized user into providing information or access that the attacker would not normally be entitled to. The attacker might, for example, contact a system administrator pretending to be an authorized user in order to have a password reset. Another common ploy is to pose as a representative from a vendor needing temporary access in order to perform some emergency maintenance. Social engineering also applies to physical access. Simple techniques include impersonating pizza or flower delivery personnel in order to gain physical access to a facility.

Attackers know that, due to poor security practices, if they can gain physical access to an office, the chances are good that, given a little unsupervised time, a user ID and password pair might be found on a notepad or sticky note. Unsupervised access may not even be required, depending on how poor the security practices of the organization are. One of the authors of this book was once considering opening an account at a bank near his home. As he sat down at the desk across from the bank employee taking his information, the author noticed one of the infamous little yellow notes attached to the computer monitor the employee was using. The note read "password for July is julyjuly." It probably isn't too hard to guess what August's password might be. Unfortunately, this is all too often the state of security practices in most organizations. With that in mind, it is easy to see how social engineering might work and might provide all the information needed to gain unauthorized access to a system or network.

Malware

The term **Malware** (also known as *malicious code*) refers to software that has been designed for some nefarious purpose. Such software may be designed to cause damage to a system, such as by deleting all files, or it may be designed to create a backdoor in the system in order to grant access to unauthorized individuals. Generally, the installation of malicious code is done so that it is not obvious to the authorized users. There are several different types of malicious software, such as viruses, Trojan horse, logic bombs, and worms, and they differ in the ways they are installed and their purposes.

Viruses

The best-known type of malicious code is the **virus**. Much has been written about viruses as a result of several high-profile security events that involved them. A virus is a piece of malicious code that replicates by attaching itself to another piece of executable code. When the other executable code is run, the virus also executes and has the opportunity to infect other files and perform any other nefarious actions it was designed to do. The specific way that a virus infects other files, and the type of files it infects, depends on the type of virus. The first viruses were of two types—boot sector or program viruses.

Boot Sector Virus A boot sector virus infects the boot sector portion of either a floppy disk or a hard drive (just a few years ago, not all computers had hard drives, and many booted from a floppy). When a computer is first turned on, a small portion of the operating system is initially loaded from hardware. This small operating system then attempts to load the rest of the operating system from a specific location (sector) on either the floppy or the hard drive. A boot sector virus infects this portion of the drive.

An example of this type of virus was the Stoned virus, which moved the true Master Boot Record (MBR) from the first to the seventh sector of the first cylinder, and replaced the original MBR with itself. When the system was then turned on, the virus was first executed, which had a one in seven chance of displaying a message stating the computer was "stoned"; otherwise, it would not announce itself and would instead attempt to infect other boot sectors. This virus was rather tame in comparison to other viruses of its time, which often were designed to delete the entire hard drive after a period of time in which they would attempt to spread.

Program Virus A second type of virus is the program virus, which attaches itself to executable files—typically files ending in .exe or .com on Windows-based systems. The virus is attached in such a way that it is executed before the program. Most program viruses also hide a nefarious purpose, such as deleting the hard drive, which is triggered by a specific event, such as a date or after a certain number of other files were infected. Like other types of viruses, program viruses are often not detected until after they execute their malicious payload. One method that has been used to detect this sort of virus before it has an opportunity to damage a system is to calculate checksums for commonly used programs or utilities. Should the checksum for an executable ever change, it is quite likely that this is due to a virus infection.

Macro Virus In the late '90s, another type of virus appeared that now accounts for the majority of viruses. As systems became more powerful, as well as the operating systems that managed them, the boot sector virus, which once accounted for most reported infections, became less common. Systems no longer commonly booted from floppies, which were the main method for boot sector viruses to spread. Instead, the proliferation of software that included macro-programming languages resulted in a new breed of virus—the macro virus.

The Concept virus was the first known example of this new breed. It appeared to be created to demonstrate the possibility of attaching a virus to a document file, something that had been thought to be impossible before the introduction of software that included powerful macro language capabilities. By this time, however, Microsoft Word documents could include segments of code written in a derivative of Visual Basic. Further development of other applications that allowed macro capability, and enhanced versions of the original macro language, had the side effect of allowing the proliferation of viruses that took advantage of this capability.

This type of virus is so common today that it is considered a security best practice to advise users to never open a document attached to an e-mail if it seems at all suspicious. Many organizations now routinely have their mail servers eliminate any attachments containing Visual Basic macros.

Avoiding Virus Infection Always being cautious about executing programs or opening documents given to you is a good security practice. "If you don't know where it came from or where it has been, don't open or run it" should be the basic guideline for all computer users.

Another security best practice for protecting against virus infection is to install and run an antivirus program. Since these programs are designed to protect against known viruses, it is also important to maintain an up-to-date listing of virus signatures for your antivirus software. Antivirus software vendors provide this, and administrators should stay on top of the latest updates to the list of known viruses.

Two advances in virus writing have made it more difficult for antivirus software to detect viruses. These advances are the introduction of *stealth virus* techniques and *polymorphic viruses*. A stealthy virus employs techniques to help evade being detected by antivirus software that uses checksums or other techniques. Polymorphic viruses also attempt to evade detection, but they do so by changing the virus itself (the virus "evolves"). Because the virus changes, signatures for that virus may no longer be valid, and the virus may escape detection by antivirus software.

Virus Hoaxes Viruses have caused so much damage in the last few years that many Internet users have become extremely cautious anytime a rumor of a new virus is heard. Many users will not connect to the Internet when they hear about a virus outbreak, just to be sure they don't get infected themselves. This has given rise to virus hoaxes, in which word is spread about a new virus and the extreme danger it poses. It may warn users to not read certain files or connect to the Internet.

A good example of a virus hoax was the Good Times virus warning, which has been copied repeatedly and can still be seen in various forms today. It caused widespread panic as users read about this extremely dangerous virus, which could actually cause the processor to overheat (from being put into an "nth complexity infinite binary loop") and be destroyed. Many folks saw through this hoax, but many less experienced users did not, and they passed the warning along to all of their friends.

Hoaxes can actually be even more destructive than just wasting time and bandwidth. Some hoaxes warning of a dangerous virus have included instructions to delete certain files if found on the user's system. Unfortunately for those who follow the advice, the files may actually be part of the operating system, and deleting them could keep the system from booting properly. This suggests another good piece of security advice: make sure of the authenticity and accuracy of any virus report before following somebody's advice. Antivirus software vendors are a good source of factual data for this sort of threat as well (see http://www.symantec.com/avcenter/hoax.html or http://vil.mcafee.com/hoax.asp for examples of hoaxes).

Trojan Horses

A **Trojan horse**, or simply *Trojan*, is a piece of software that appears to do one thing (and may, in fact, actually do that thing) but that hides some other functionality. The analogy to the famous story of antiquity is very accurate. In the original case, the object appeared to be a large wooden horse, and in fact it was. At the same time, it hid something much more sinister and dangerous to the occupants of the city. As long as the horse was left outside the city walls, it could cause no damage to the inhabitants. It had to be taken in by the inhabitants, and it was inside that the hidden purpose was activated. A computer Trojan works in much the same way. Unlike a virus, which reproduces by attaching itself to other files or programs, a Trojan is a stand-alone program that must be copied and installed by the user—it must be "brought inside" the system by an authorized user. The challenge for the attacker is enticing the user to copy and run the program. This generally means that the program must be disguised as something that the user would want to run—a special utility or game, for example. Once it has been copied and is "inside" the system, the Trojan will perform its hidden purpose with the user often still unaware of its true nature.

A good example of a Trojan is Back Orifice (BO), originally created in 1999 and now in several versions. BO can be attached to a number of types of programs. Once it is, and once an infected file is run, BO will create a way for unauthorized individuals to take over the system remotely, as if they were sitting at the console. BO is designed to work with Windows-based systems.

The single best method to prevent the introduction of a Trojan to your system is to never run software if you are unsure of its origin, security, and integrity. A virus-checking program may also be useful in detecting and preventing the installation of known Trojans.

Logic Bombs

Logic bombs, unlike viruses and Trojans, are a type of malicious software that is deliberately installed, generally by an authorized user. A logic bomb is a piece of code that sits dormant for a period of time until some event invokes its often malicious payload. An example of a logic bomb might be a program that is set to automatically load and run, and that periodically checks an organization's payroll or personnel database for a specific employee. If the employee is not found, the malicious payload executes, deleting vital corporate files.

If the trigger is some event, such as not finding a specific name in the personnel file, the code is referred to as a *logic bomb*. If the event is a specific date or time, the program will often be referred to as a *time bomb*. In one famous example of a time bomb, a disgruntled employee left a time bomb in place just prior to being fired from his job. Two weeks later, thousands of client records were deleted. Police were able to eventually track the malicious code to the disgruntled ex-employee, who was prosecuted for his actions. He had hoped that the two weeks that had passed since his dismissal would have caused investigators to assume he could not have been the individual who had caused the deletion of the records.

Logic bombs are difficult to detect because they are often installed by authorized users and, in particular, have been installed by administrators who are also often responsible for security. This demonstrates the need for a separation of duties and a periodic review of all programs and services that are running. It also illustrates the need to maintain an active backup program so that if your organization loses critical files to this sort of malicious code, you only lose transactions since the most recent backup and don't permanently lose the data.

Worms

Originally, it was easy to distinguish between a **worm** and a virus. Recently, with the introduction of new breeds of sophisticated malicious code, the distinction has blurred. Worms are pieces of code that attempt to penetrate networks and computer systems. Once a penetration occurs, the worm will create a new copy of itself on the penetrated system. Reproduction of a worm thus does not rely on the attachment of the virus to another piece of code or to a file, which is the definition of a virus.

The blurring of the distinction between viruses and worms has come about because of the attachment of malicious code to e-mail. Viruses were generally thought of as a system-based problem, and worms were network-based. If the malicious code is sent throughout a network, it may subsequently be called a worm. The important distinction, however, is whether the code has to attach itself to something else (a virus), or if it can "survive" on its own (a worm).

The Morris Worm

The most famous example of a worm was the Morris worm in 1988. Also sometimes referred to as the Internet worm, because of its effect on the early Internet, the worm was able to insert itself into so many systems connected to the Internet that it has been repeatedly credited with "bringing the Internet to its knees" for several days. It was this worm that provided the impetus for the creation of what was once the Computer Emergency Response Team Coordination Center though is now simply the CERT Coordination Center (CERT/CC) located at Carnegie Mellon University.

The Morris worm was created by a graduate student named Robert Morris. It utilized several known vulnerabilities to gain access to a new system, and it also relied on password guessing to obtain access to accounts. Once a system had been penetrated, a small bootstrap program was inserted into the new system and executed. This program then downloaded the rest of the worm to the new system. The worm had some stealth characteristics to make it harder to determine what it was doing, and it suffered from one major miscalculation. The worm would not be loaded if a copy of it was already found on the new system, but it was designed to periodically ignore this check, reportedly to ensure that the worm could not be easily eliminated. The problem with this plan was that interconnected systems were constantly being reinfected. Eventually, the systems were running so many copies of the worm that the system response time ground to a stop. It took a concerted effort by many individuals before the worm was eliminated. While the Morris worm carried no malicious payload, it is entirely possible for worms to do so.

Code-Red

Much was learned from the Morris Worm, and many new safeguards and procedures were implemented to try and keep from having a similar incident occur. Today, however, the level of connectivity far surpasses what constituted as the Internet in Morris' day, and the sophistication of the average user has also decreased. Coupled with what seems to be a constant discovery of new vulnerabilities in operating systems and application programs, the current environment still provides a breeding ground for new virus and worm outbreaks. With all of our virus protection software, and with the introduction of technology such as firewalls and intrusion detection systems since Morris' time, one might wonder if a new outbreak of a worm could have the same devastating impact on the Internet such as that seen in the Morris incident. The outbreak of the Code-Red worm in July, 2001 effectively answered this question.

On July 19, 2001, over 350,000 computers connected to the Internet were infected by the Code-Red worm. This infection took only 14 hours to occur. The cost estimate for how much damage the worm caused (including variations of the worm released at later dates) exceeds $2.5 billion. There are a couple of interesting points to consider when examining the Code-Red worm, most of which are just as applicable today as they were in 2001 when the worm hit. First of all, the vulnerability exploited by the Code-Red worm was not revealed as a result of the attack. The vulnerability it exploited had been known for a month. The worm took advantage of a buffer-overflow condition in Microsoft's IIS web servers. Microsoft released a patch for this vulnerability along with an announcement of the problem itself on June 18, 2001, and a little less than a month later, on July 12, the first version of the Code-Red worm was released, which took advantage of this vulnerability. The initial version of the worm did little damage as it spread slowly across the Internet, but the worm itself is memory-resident, so simply turning off the computer would not eliminate the worm. Unfortunately, unless the system was patched, a user was likely to become reinfected soon after rebooting and reconnecting to the Internet.

The worm itself didn't carry a malicious payload designed to destroy data on the infected system. On some systems, the message "Hacked by Chinese" was added to the top-level page for the infected host's web site. If the date was between the 1st and 19th of the month, upon infecting a system the worm would generate a random list of IP addresses and attempt to infect them. The first version of the worm used the same seed for the random number generator so each system actually generated the same list of random IP addresses. Thus, this first version of the worm spent much time attempting to reinfect the same machines and, as a consequence, spread very slowly. If the date was between the 20th and the 28th of the month, the worm attempted to launch a Denial-of-Service attack against a web site owned by the White House. After the 28th, the worm remained dormant until the 1st of the following month. All of this changed when the second version of the worm was released on July 19th.

The only change between the first and second versions of the worm was a fix to the seed for the random number generator. The second version of the worm did not use the same seed for each infection. Instead, new seeds were utilized, thus causing a different list of random IP addresses to be created. This small change had a devastating affect on the Internet. No longer were infected systems trying to reinfect the same list of systems. Now each new virus was attempting to infect their own list of IP addresses, resulting in a much wider coverage of the Internet. This resulted in the more than 350,000 machines becoming infected in a 14-hour period on July 19th. Additional problems were seen with this second version since numerous routers, switches, and other networked devices not susceptible to infection were sometimes still unable to handle the data being sent to them, causing many to crash or reboot. Additional versions of the worm were discovered the next month. The date the second version was released played a large part in keeping the number of infected machines from being even greater. Since the worm was released on the 19th, when the date changed to the 20th, the machines stopped trying to infect other machines and instead started to launch their DoS attack. This provided a period of several days for systems to be rebooted and patched before the worms attempted to infect systems again. This programmed lull played a major part in being able to address this worm.

Slammer

The rapid spread of the Code-Red worm startled many users of the Internet who didn't realize a worm could spread so quickly. If the speed of the Code-Red infection surprised some people, the speed that another worm spread totally amazed everybody else. On Saturday, January 25, 2003, the Slammer virus was released. It exploited a buffer overflow vulnerability in computers running Microsoft's SQL Server or Microsoft SQL Server Desktop Engine. Like the vulnerability in Code-Red, this vulnerability was not new and in fact had been discovered in July, 2002; Microsoft had released a patch for the vulnerability before it was even announced. By the next day, the worm had infected at least 120,000 hosts, had caused network outages, and disrupted airline flights, elections, and ATM services. At its peak, Slammer-infected hosts were generating a reported 1 terabit of worm-related traffic EVERY SECOND.

The truly amazing and frightening aspect of the Slammer worm was its rate of infection. The worm doubled its number of infected hosts every 8 seconds. It is estimated that it took less than 10 minutes to reach global proportions and infect 90 percent of the possible hosts it could infect. This was a dynamic difference when compared to the Code-Red rate, which doubled its number of infected hosts about every 35 minutes. Once a machine was infected (and it took a single packet to infect a machine), the host would start randomly selecting targets and sending packets to them to attempt infection at a rate of 25,000 per second. Like Code-Red, Slammer did not contain a malicious payload. The problems it caused were as a result of the massively overloaded networks, which could not sustain the traffic generated by the thousands of infected hosts. It is interesting to note that this damage was caused with only one out of every thousand systems being vulnerable. One can only imagine the damage and even greater rates of infection had the worm exploited a vulnerability that affected a larger percentage of hosts.

The worm sent its single packet to a specific UDP port—1434—which provided an immediate fix for networks. The response to Slammer was rapid (though not as rapid as the infection itself). Administrators quickly blocked all traffic to UDP port 1434, effectively blocking the spread to new machines. Once again, we can only imagine what the effect would have been had the worm been spread using a more common, and Internet-essential, port such as TCP port 80 (used for HTTP traffic).

Protection Against Worms

How you protect a system against worms depends on the type of worm. Those attached and propagated through e-mail can be avoided by following the same guidelines about not opening files and not running attachments unless you are absolutely sure of their origin and integrity. Protecting against the Morris type of Internet worm involves securing systems and networks against penetration in the same way you would protect your systems against human attackers. Install patches, eliminate unused and unnecessary services, enforce good password security, and utilize firewalls and intrusion detection systems.

Mobile Code

Mobile code is segments of code sent from another host that is executed on your system. The commonest example of mobile code is web applets written in JAVA. The possible problem with mobile code should be apparent: Can you trust code sent by another system to run on your system? How do you know what the code will do, and that it will only do what the user/system you received it from claims it will do. The threats to your system from hostile mobile code include disclosure of information and modification or damage to information. Safe execution of mobile code will require controlled access to resources. In an ideal environment, this access should really be negotiated for each piece of mobile code received.

Auditing

Auditing, in the financial community, is done to verify the accuracy and integrity of financial records. There have been many standards established in the financial community about how to correctly record and report a company's financial status. In the computer security world, auditing serves a similar function. It is a process of assessing the security state of an organization compared against an established standard. Ensuring that employees are following established procedures and guidelines is one of the methods we can use to address the numerous possible attacks that have been discussed in this chapter.

The important element in auditing is the standard used to evaluate personnel and procedures. Organizations from different communities may have widely different standards, and any audit will need to consider the appropriate elements for the specific community. Audits differ from security or vulnerability assessments in that assessments measure the security posture of the organization but may do so without any mandated standards to compare them against. In a security assessment, generally agreed-upon security "best practices" may be used, but they may lack the regulatory teeth that standards often provide. Penetration tests may also be encountered—these are tests conducted against an organization to see if any holes in the organization's security can be found. The goal of the penetration test is just that, to penetrate the security rather than measuring it against some standard. Penetration tests are often viewed as *white-hat hacking* in that the methods used often mirror those that an attacker might use.

It is important to conduct some form of security audit or assessment on a regular basis. Your organization may spend quite a bit on security, and it is important to measure how effective the efforts have been. In certain communities, audits may be regulated on a periodic basis with very specific standards that must be measured against. Even if your organization is not part of such a community, periodic assessments are important.

There are many things that may be evaluated during an assessment, but at a minimum, the security perimeter (with all of its components, including host-based security) should be examined, as well as the organization's policies, procedures, and guidelines governing security. Employee training is another aspect that should be examined, since employees are the targets of social engineering and password-guessing attacks.

Security audits, assessments, and penetration tests are a big business, and there are a number of organizations that can perform them. The cost of these varies widely depending on the extent of the test you desire, the background of the company you are contracting with, and the size of the organization to be tested.

Chapter Review

Chapter Summary

After reading this chapter and completing the exercises, you should understand the following regarding malware and attacks on computer systems and networks.

Attacks on Computer Systems and Networks

- Attacks on computer systems and networks can be grouped into two broad categories: attacks on specific software and attacks on a specific protocol or service.

- The target of an attacker can be of two types: targets of opportunity and defined targets. There are a number of different types of attacks, including Denial-of-Service attacks, the installation of backdoors, sniffing, spoofing, man-in-the-middle and replay attacks, TCP/IP session hijacking, wardialing and WarDriving, and attacks on encryption.

- In a Denial-of-Service attack, the attacker is attempting to deny authorized users access either to specific information or to the computer system or network itself.

- The term backdoor is commonly used to refer to programs that attackers install after gaining unauthorized access to a system to ensure that they can continue having unrestricted access to the system.

- Network sniffers are software or hardware devices used to observe traffic as it passes through a network on shared broadcast media.

- Spoofing is a type of attack in which data is made to look like it has come from a different source.

- A man-in-the-middle attack is a type of attack that generally occurs when attackers are able to place themselves in the middle of two other hosts that are communicating, thus allowing the attacker to view and/or modify the traffic.

- Replay attacks are attacks in which the attacker captures a portion of network traffic between two parties and retransmits it at a later time.

- TCP/IP hijacking, also called *session hijacking,* refers to attacks designed to take control of an already existing session between a client and a server.

- All too often attempts at password guessing yield favorable results for the attacker, not as a result of a weakness in the scheme, but usually because the user is not following good password procedures.

Malware

- Malware, also known as *malicious code,* refers to software that has been designed for some nefarious purpose. Malware includes viruses, worms, Trojan horses, logic bombs, and hostile mobile code.

- A virus is a piece of malicious code that replicates by attaching itself to another piece of executable code.

- A Trojan horse, or simply *Trojan,* is a piece of software that appears to do one thing (and may, in fact, actually do that thing) but which hides some other functionality.

- Logic bombs, unlike viruses and Trojans, are a type of malicious software that is deliberately installed, generally by an authorized user. A logic bomb is a piece of code that sits dormant for a period of time until some event invokes its payload.

- Worms are pieces of code that attempt to propagate through penetration of networks and computer systems.

Key Terms

Backdoor *(398)*
Denial-of-Service attack *(396)*
Logic bomb *(412)*
Malware *(409)*
Man-in-the-middle attack *(403)*
Replay attack *(404)*
Sniffers *(399)*
Software exploitation *(408)*
Spoofing *(400)*
TCP/IP hijacking *(405)*
Trojan horse *(412)*
Virus *(410)*
Wardialing *(408)*
WarDriving *(409)*
Worm *(413)*

Key Terms Quiz

Use terms from the Key Terms list to complete the sentences that follow. Don't use the same term more than once. Not all terms will be used.

1. A piece of code that sits dormant for a period of time until some event invokes its payload is known as a _____.

2. A _____ is a software or hardware device used to observe traffic as it passes through a network on shared broadcast media.

3. An attack that takes advantage of bugs or weaknesses in software is called

_____.

4. _____ is a type of attack in which data is made to look like it has come from a different source.

5. _____ the term used to describe an attacker's attempt to discover unprotected modem connections to computer systems and networks.

6. An attack in which the attacker is attempting to deny authorized users access either to specific information or to the computer system or network itself is known as a _____ attack.

7. A _____ is a piece of code that attempts to propagate through penetration of networks and computer systems.

8. Attacks designed to take control of an already existing session between a client and a server are called _____ or _____.

9. _____ is the term commonly used to refer to programs that attackers install after gaining unauthorized access to a system to ensure that they can continue to have unrestricted access to that system.

10. A _____ is a piece of malicious code that replicates by attaching itself to another piece of executable code.

Multiple-Choice Quiz

1. A SYN flood is an example of what type of attack?

   A. Malicious code

   B. Denial-of-Service

   C. Man-in-the-middle

   D. Spoofing

2. An attack in which attackers place themselves in the middle of two other hosts that are communicating in order to view and/or modify the traffic is known as...

   A. A man-in-the-middle attack

   B. A Denial-of-Service attack

   C. A sniffing attack

   D. A backdoor attack

3. Which attack takes advantage of a trusted relationship that exists between two systems?

   A. Spoofing

   B. Password guessing

   C. Sniffing

   D. Brute force

4. In what type of attack does an attacker resend the series of commands and codes used in a financial transaction in order to cause the transaction to be conducted multiple times?

   A. Spoofing

   B. Man-in-the-middle

   C. Replay

   D. Backdoor

5. The trick in both spoofing and TCP/IP hijacking is in trying to...

   A. Provide the correct authentication token

   B. Find two systems between which a trusted relationship exists

   C. Guess a password or brute force a password to gain initial access to the system or network

   D. Maintain the correct sequence numbers for the response packets

6. The most ominous aspect of the Slammer worm was the fact that...

   A. It exploited a vulnerability that had previously not been known

   B. It spread so quickly, affecting 90 percent of vulnerable systems in less than 10 minutes

   C. It affected multiple platforms and multiple operating systems as it utilized a segment of mobile code

   D. It contained a malicious payload that was not detected until over a week after the initial attack

7. The ability of an attacker to crack passwords is directly related to the method the user employed to create the password in the first place, as well as...

   A. The length of the password

   B. The size of the character set used in generating the password

   C. The speed of the machine cracking the password

   D. The dictionary and rules used by the cracking program

8. A piece of malicious code that must attach itself to another file in order to replicate is known as...

    A. A worm

    B. A virus

    C. A logic bomb

    D. A Trojan

9. A piece of code that attempts to propagate through penetration of networks and computer systems is known as…

    A. A worm

    B. A virus

    C. A logic bomb

    D. A Trojan

10. An attack in which the attackers attempt to lie and misrepresent themselves in order to gain access to information that can be useful in an attack is known as what?

    A. Social science

    B. White-hat hacking

    C. Social engineering

    D. Social manipulation

11. A virus that attempts to avoid detection by periodically modifying portions of itself would be what type of virus?

    A. A stealth virus

    B. A delayed propagation virus

    C. A polymorphic virus

    D. An evasive code virus

12. The best way to minimize possible avenues of attack for your system is to…

    A. Install a firewall and check the logs daily

    B. Monitor your intrusion detection system for possible attacks

    C. Limit the information that can be obtained on your organization and the services that are run by your Internet-visible systems

    D. Ensure that all patches have been applied for the services that are offered by your system

13. A wardialing attack is an attempt to exploit what technology?

    A. Fiber-optic networks whose cables often run along roads and bridges

    B. Cellular telephones

    C. Modems and public switched telephone networks (PSTNs)

    D. Wireless networks

14. How can you protect against worms of the type that Robert Morris unleashed on the Internet?

    A. Follow the same procedures as you would to secure your system from a human attacker

    B. Install antivirus software

    C. Ensure that no executable attachments to e-mails are executed unless their integrity has been verified

    D. Monitor for changes to utilities and other system software

15. Malicious code that is set to execute its payload on a specific date or at a specific time is known as…

    A. A logic bomb

    B. A Trojan horse

    C. A virus

    D. A time bomb

Essay Quiz

1. Outline the differences between viruses and worms?

2. What is social engineering? Describe how it might be used to gain unauthorized access to a computer system or network.

3. What are the implications of the speed at which the Slammer virus spread?

4. Describe the type of information that attackers might try to obtain if they were able to install a sniffer on a network.

5. Outline the steps in spoofing a system across the Internet.

Lab Projects

Lab Project 15.1

If allowed to do so in your lab, download and install a sniffer and observe the traffic that can be seen on your network. Access a web site and observe the traffic that is sent from your system to the web server.

Lab Project 15.2

E-mail spoofing is a simple matter if you can telnet to port 25 on a system running sendmail. If allowed in your lab, attempt to access this port and send a message to yourself or a friend that is obviously spoofed. Make sure that the "acceptable use policy" for your school and other local rules will allow you to perform this lab before you attempt it.

E-mail

Upon completion of this chapter, you will be able to:

- List various security issues associated with e-mail
- Describe some of the security practices for e-mail
- List and describe software used to improve e-mail confidentiality

E-mail is the most popular application on the Internet. It is also by far the most popular application on intracompany networks. Roughly 12 million e-mails were sent each day in 2001, giving a rough total of 4.38 billion e-mails sent in that year. In 2000, there were 569 million e-mail boxes in the world.

Security of E-mail Transmissions

Considering the old statistics, it is easy to see that e-mail needs to have security. E-mail started with mailbox programs on early time-sharing machines, allowing researchers to leave messages for others using the same machine. The first inter-machine e-mail was sent in 1972, and a new era in person-to-person communication was launched. E-mail proliferated, but it remained unsecured, only partly because most e-mail is sent in plaintext, providing no privacy in its default form.

Viruses started as simple self-replicating programs that spread via the transfer of floppy disks, but e-mail gave virus files a passport to travel. Sending themselves to every user that they possibly can, they have achieved record-breaking infection rates. **Trojan horse programs** are also often sent through the mail, with computer owners as accomplices, compromising hundreds of machines every day.

There is also the strange nature of **e-mail hoaxes**, those Internet-based urban legends that are spread through e-mail, with users forwarding them in seemingly endless loops around the globe. And, of course, there are the ubiquitous **spam** e-mails, which, despite the remarkable advance of every other technology, people still haven't found a good way to block.

Securing e-mail is something that must be done by the users themselves, because they are the ones who will actually be sending and receiving the messages. However, security administrators can give users the tools they need to fight the problems. **S/MIME** and **PGP** are two very popular methods of encrypting e-mail. Server-based and desktop-based virus protection can help against malicious code, and spam filters attempt to block all **unsolicited commercial e-mail**. E-mail users need to be educated about security, though, because the popularity and functionality of e-mail is only going to increase.

Malicious Code

Viruses and worms are popular programs because they make themselves popular. When viruses were constrained to only one computer, they attempted to spread by attaching themselves to every executable program that they could find. This worked out very well for the viruses because they could piggyback onto a floppy disk with a program that was being transferred to another computer.

The advent of computer networks was a computer virus writer's dream, allowing viruses to attempt to infect every network share that the computer was attached to. This extended the virus's reach from a set of machines that might share a floppy disk to every machine on the network. Because the e-mail protocol permits users to attach files to e-mail messages, viruses can travel by e-mail from one local network to another, anywhere on the Internet. This changes the nature of virus programs, as they once were localized, but now can spread virtually everywhere. This changes the virus from having a local reach to a global one.

Viruses spread by e-mail further and faster than ever before, but viruses also evolved. This evolution started with viruses that were scripted to send themselves to other users, and this type of virus was known as a **worm**. A worm uses its code to automate the infection process. For example, when the worm program is executed, the code may seek out the user's e-mail address book and mail itself to as many people as the worm's programming dictates. This method of transmission depends on the user actually executing the worm file. Some worms use multiple methods of attack, not only sending multiple infected e-mails, but also scanning hosts on the Internet, looking for a specific vulnerability. Upon finding the vulnerability, the worm infects the remote host and starts the process all over again.

Viruses and worms are a danger not only to the individual user's machine, but also to network security because they can introduce malicious traffic to other machines. This can cause not only loss of data, but sometimes can send data out to other users. The Sircam worm attached random files from the infected user's hard drive to the e-mails the worm sent out.

Worms can also carry Trojan horse payloads, just as any e-mail message can. A Trojan horse is a program that seems to be one thing while actually having a more sinister hidden purpose. For example, an executable game program or an executable self-playing movie could be a Trojan. These programs will run and do what they claim, but they typically also install some other program, such as a remote control package like SubSeven or Back Orifice. These programs allow an attacker to remotely control an infected machine. Once control is achieved, the attacker can use the machine to perform a number of tasks, such as using it in distributed denial of service (DDOS) attacks, using it as a launching point to compromise other machines, or simply using it as a remote place to store some extra files.

While the distribution of malicious code in e-mail is tied to the files that are attached to the e-mail messages, in the past a user actually had to execute the attached file. The original system of e-mail used plain text to send messages, but the advent of the Web changed this. Hypertext Markup Language (better known as HTML) was created to allow plain text to represent complex page designs in a standardized way. HTML was soon adopted by e-mail programs so users could use different fonts and colors and embed pictures in their e-mails. E-mail programs then grew more advanced and, like web browsers, were designed to automatically open files attached to e-mails. When active content was designed for the Web, in the form of Java and ActiveX scripts, these scripts were interpreted and run by the e-mail programs, and that's when the trouble began. Some e-mail programs, most notably Microsoft Outlook, have what's known as a preview pane, which allows users to read e-mails without opening them in the full screen. Unfortunately, this preview still activates all the content in the e-mail message, and because Outlook supports VB scripting, it was vulnerable to e-mail worms. A user doesn't need to actually run the program or even open the e-mail to activate the worm—they just need to preview the e-mail in the preview pane. This form of automatic execution was the primary reason for the spread of the ILOVEYOU worm.

Viruses are a security threat, and one of the most common transfer methods is through e-mail. The solution to this problem comes in two parts: user education and virus scanning.

Although the great majority of users are now aware of viruses and the damage they can cause, further education may be needed to instruct them on the specific things that need to be addressed when the virus comes through the e-mail. These specific things can vary from organization to organization and from e-mail software to e-mail software. Some useful examples of good practices include examining all e-mails for a known source as well as a known destination, especially if the e-mails have attachments. Strange files or unexpected attachments should always be checked before execution. Users also need to know that some viruses can be executed simply by opening the e-mail or viewing it in the preview pane. Education and proper administration is also useful in configuring the e-mail software to be as virus resistant as possible; turning off scripting support and the preview pane are good examples.

The other protection is to have well-thought-out virus scanning procedures. If possible, perform virus scanning on every e-mail as it comes into the corporation's server. Some users will also attempt to retrieve e-mail off-site from their normal ISP account, which can bypass the server-based virus protection, so every machine should also be protected with a host-based virus protection program that scans all files on a regular basis and performs checks of files upon their execution. While these steps will not eliminate the security risks of malicious code in e-mail, it will limit infection and help to keep the problem to manageable levels.

Hoax E-mails

An interesting offshoot of e-mail viruses is the phenomenon of e-mail hoaxes. If you've had an Internet e-mail address for more than a couple of months, you've probably received at least one of these. The Neiman-Marcus cookie recipe that is sent to you because someone was charged $250, the "famous" commencement speech by Kurt Vonnegut, and the young dying boy whose last wish was to make it into the record books by receiving the most get well cards ever—these are the most famous of the e-mail hoaxes, though there are many others.

E-mail hoaxes are mostly a nuisance, but they do cost everyone, not only in the time wasted by receiving and reading the e-mail, but also in the Internet bandwidth and server processing time they take up. E-mail hoaxes are basically global urban legends, perpetually traveling from one e-mail account to the next, and most have a common theme of some story you must tell ten people about right away or some virus that everyone should beware of. Hoaxes are similar to chain letters, but instead of promising a reward, the story in the e-mail is typically what produces the action. Whether it's a call for sympathy from a dying boy, or an overly expensive recipe sent to the masses in the name of justice, all hoaxes prompt action of some sort, and this call for action is probably what keeps them going. Hoaxes have been circling the Internet for many, many years, and many web sites are dedicated to debunking them.

The power of the e-mail hoax is actually quite amazing. The Neiman-Marcus story, in which someone gets charged $250 for a chocolate chip cookie recipe, thinking that she is only being charged $2.50, used to have a fatal flaw: Neiman-Marcus did not sell chocolate chip cookies (but they do now simply because of the hoax). The Kurt Vonnegut hoax was convincing enough to fool his wife, and the dying boy, who is now 20, still receives cards in the mail. The power of these hoaxes probably means that they will never be stopped, though they might be slowed down. The most important thing to do in this case is educate e-mail users. Show them a hoax before you put them online, and teach them how to search the Internet for hoax information. Users need to apply the same common sense on the Internet that they would in real life: If it sounds too outlandish to be true, it probably isn't.

Unsolicited Commercial E-mail (Spam)

Spam is something that every Internet user has received, usually on a daily basis. Spam is the common term for unsolicited commercial e-mail. These commercial e-mails got the name spam when the Internet was much smaller and commercial interests were rather rare. The term *spam* comes from a skit on Monty Python's Flying Circus where two people are in a restaurant that only serves spam. This concept of the repetition of unwanted things is the key to spam.

The first spam e-mail was sent in 1978 by a DEC employee. However, the first spam that really captured everyone's attention was in 1994 when two lawyers posted a commercial message to every Usenet newsgroup. This was the origin of using the Internet to send one message to as many recipients as possible via an automated program. Commercial e-mail programs have taken over, resulting in the variety of spam that most users receive in their mailboxes every day. In 2000, America Online estimated that nearly 30 percent of e-mail sent to its systems is spam, accounting for nearly 24 million messages a day.[*] The worst thing about spam is its apparent popularity—Jupiter Communications estimates that by 2005, every user will receive 1,600 spam e-mails a year.[*]

The appeal to the people generating the spam is the extremely low cost per advertising impression. The senders of spam e-mail can generally send the messages for less than a cent apiece. This is much less expensive than more traditional direct mail or print advertisements, and this low cost will ensure the continued growth of spam e-mail unless something is done about it. The amount of spam being transmitted has been large enough to trigger state and federal legislators to consider action, but no effective laws have been passed yet. This has forced most people to seek out technical solutions to the spam problem.

The first thing to be done is educate users about spam. A good way for users to fight spam is to be cautious about where on the Internet they post their e-mail address.

However, you can't keep e-mail addresses secret just to avoid spam, so one of the steps that the majority of system administrators running Internet e-mail servers have taken to reduce spam, and which is also a good e-mail security principle, is to shut down **mail relaying**. Port scanning occurs across all hosts all the time, typically with a single host scanning large subnets for a single port, and some of these people could be attempting to send spam e-mail. When they scan for TCP port 25, they are looking for open **SMTP** servers, and once they find a host that is an open relay, they can use that host to send as many commercial e-mails as possible. The reason that they look for an open relay is that spammers typically do not want the e-mails traced back to them.

Since it may not be possible to close all mail relays, and because some spammers will mail from their own mail servers, software must be used to combat spam at the recipient's end. There are two main places to filter spam: at the host itself, or at the server. Filtering spam at the host level is usually done with basic pattern matching, focusing on the sender, subject, or text of the e-mail. This is a fairly effective system, but it uses an inordinate amount of bandwidth and processing power on the host computer. These problems can be solved by filtering spam at the mail server level.

There is a benefit to the server-based approach, because there are other methods of filtering spam at the server: pattern matching is still used, but some mail software can also use the **Realtime Blackhole List**. This list is maintained in real time specifically for blocking spam mail. Started in 1997, this service is so popular that many programs include support for it by default, such as Sendmail, Postfix, and Eudora Internet Mail Server. This blacklist is effective because it is run by a not-for-profit organization devoted to reducing spam. As such, they have the most community participation and product support from multiple vendors, which helps them have a larger, more complete black-hole list. There are also commercial packages that block spam at the server level using both methods mentioned previously, maintaining their own blacklists and pattern-matching algorithms.

---

[*] Adam S. Marlin, "Spammers, Keep Out," *The Standard* (June 12, 2000): www.thestandard.com/article/0,1902,15586,00.html

These methods will take care of 90 percent of the junk mail clogging the networks, but they cannot stop it entirely. To truly combat spam, all network administrators will have to work together to eliminate it. One of the current better ideas is to block port TCP 25 from all hosts except for designated mail servers. This would stop spammers using remote open relays and prevent many users from running unauthorized e-mail servers of their own. This is a controversial measure and probably will not come to pass.

Because of the low cost of generating spam, until serious action is taken, or spam is somehow made unprofitable, spam will remain with us.

Mail Encryption

The e-mail concerns discussed so far in this chapter are all global issues involving security, but there is a more important security problem with e-mail—the lack of confidentiality or as it is sometimes referred to, privacy. E-mail has always been a plaintext protocol. When many people first got onto the Internet, there was a standard lecture about not sending anything through e-mail that you wouldn't want posted on a public bulletin board. Part of the reason for this was that e-mail is sent with the clear text of the message exposed to anyone who is sniffing the network. Any attacker at a choke point in the network could read all e-mail passing through that network segment. There are tools that solve this problem by encrypting the e-mail's content. The first method of mail **encryption** is called S/MIME and the second is called PGP.

S/MIME stands for Secure/Multipurpose Internet Mail Extensions, which means it is a secure implementation of the MIME (Multipurpose Internet Mail Extensions) protocol specification. MIME was created to allow Internet e-mail to support new and more creative features. The original e-mail RFC only specified text e-mail, so any non-text data had to be handled by a new specification—MIME. MIME handles audio files, images, applications, and multipart e-mails. This allows e-mail to handle multiple types of content in an e-mail, including file transfers. Every time you send a file as an e-mail attachment, you are using MIME. S/MIME takes this content and specifies a framework for encrypting the message as a MIME attachment.

S/MIME was developed by RSA Data Security and uses the X.509 format for certificates. The specification supports both 40-bit RC2 and 3DES for symmetric encryption. The protocol can affect the message in one of two ways: the host mail program can encode the message with S/MIME, or the server can act as the processing agent, encrypting all messages between hosts.

The host-based operation starts when the user clicks Send—the mail agent will then encode the message using the generated symmetric key. Then the symmetric key is encoded with the remote user's public key or the local user's private key. This enables the remote user to decode the symmetric key and then decrypt the actual content of the message. Of course, all of this is handled by the user's mail program, requiring the user simply to tell the program to decode the message. If the message is signed by the sender, it will be signed with the sender's public key, guaranteeing the source of the message. The reason that both symmetric and asymmetric encryption are used in the mail is to increase the speed of encryption and decryption. As encryption is based on difficult mathematical problems, it takes time to encrypt and decrypt. To speed this up, the more difficult process, asymmetric encryption, is used to only encrypt a relatively small amount of data, the symmetric key. The symmetric key is then used to encrypt the rest of the message.

The S/MIME process of encrypting e-mails provides integrity, privacy, and, if the message is signed, authentication. Several popular e-mail programs support S/MIME, including the popular Microsoft products, Outlook and Outlook Express. They both manage S/MIME keys and functions through the Security screen, as shown in Figure 16-1. This figure shows the different settings that can be used to encrypt messages and use X.509 digital certificates. This allows interoperability with web certificates, and trusted authorities are available to issue the certificates. Trusted authorities are needed to ensure the senders are who they claim to be, an important part of authentication. In Outlook Express the window is more simplistic (see Figure 16-2), but the same functions of key management and secure e-mail operation are available.

While S/MIME is a good and versatile protocol for securing e-mail, there are a few potential problems with its implementation. S/MIME allows the user to select low strength (40-bit) encryption, which means a user can send a message that is thought to be secure but that can be more easily decoded than messages sent with 3DES encryption. Also, as with any protocol, there can be bugs in the software itself. Just because an application is designed for security does not mean that it, itself, is secure. In October of 2002, a buffer overrun was found in Outlook Express's S/MIME error handling. Apart from potential flaws, S/MIME is a tremendous leap in security over regular e-mail.

Figure 16-1
S/MIME Options
in Outlook

Figure 16-2
S/MIME Options
in Outlook
Express

Pretty Good Privacy (PGP) implements e-mail security in a similar fashion to S/MIME but using completely different protocols. The basic framework is the same. Again, the user sends the e-mail, and the mail agent applies encryption as specified in the mail program's programming. The content is encrypted with the generated symmetric key, and that key is encrypted with the public key of the recipient of the e-mail, or with the private key of the sender. The sender can also choose to sign the mail with their private key, allowing the recipient to authenticate the sender. Currently, PGP supports Public Key Infrastructure (PKI) provided by multiple vendors, including X.509 certificates, LDAP key sources such as Microsoft's Active Directory, and Novell's NDS.

In Figure 16-3, we see how PGP managed keys locally in its own software. This is where a user stores not only local keys, but also any keys that were gotten from other people. There is a free key server for storing PGP public keys. PGP can generate its own keys using either Diffie-Hellman or RSA, and it can then transmit the public keys to the PGP LDAP server so other PGP users can search for and locate your public key in order to communicate with you. This key server is convenient as each person using PGP for communications does not have to implement a server to handle key management. For the actual encryption of the e-mail content itself, PGP supports IDEA, 3DES, and CAST for symmetric encryption. PGP provides pretty good security against brute-force attacks by using a 3DES key length of 168 bits, an IDEA key length of 128 bits, and a CAST key length of 128 bits. All of these algorithms are difficult to brute force with existing hard-

Figure 16-3
PGP key
management

ware, requiring well over a million years to break the code. While this is not a promise of future security against brute-force attacks, the security is reasonable today.

PGP has plug-ins for many popular e-mail programs, including Outlook, Outlook Express, and Qualcomm's Eudora. These plug-ins handle the encryption and decryption behind the scenes, and all that the user must do is enter the encryption key's passphrase to ensure that they are the owner of the key. In Figure 16-4, you can see the string of encrypted text that makes up the MIME attachment. This text includes the encrypted content of the message and the encrypted symmetric key. Also, you can see that the program does not decrypt the message upon receipt; it waits until instructed to decrypt it. PGP also stores encrypted messages in the encrypted format, as does S/MIME. This is important, as it provides end-to-end security for the message.

Like S/MIME, the PGP protocol is not problem free. Diligence must be applied to keep the software up-to-date and fully patched, because vulnerabilities are occasionally found. For example, a buffer overflow was found in the way PGP was handled in Outlook, causing the overwriting of heap memory and leading to possible malicious code execution. There is also a lot of discussion about the way PGP handles key recovery, or key escrow. PGP uses what's called Additional Decryption Key (ADK), which is basically an additional public key stacked upon the original public key. This, in theory, would give the proper organization a private key that would be used to retrieve the secret messages. In practice, the ADK is not always controlled by a properly authorized organization, and the danger exists for someone to add an ADK and then distribute it to the world. This creates a situation where other users will be sending messages that they believe can only be read by the first party, but that can be read by the third party who modified the key. These are just examples of the current vulnerabilities in the product, showing that PGP is just a tool, not the ultimate answer to security.

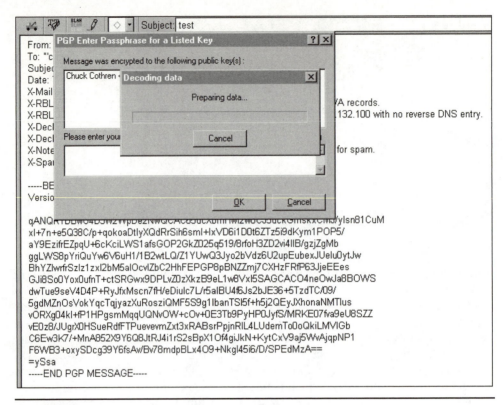

Figure 16-4 Decoding a PGP-encoded message in Eudora

Chapter Review

Chapter Summary

After reading this chapter and completing the exercises, you should understand the following facts about e-mail.

Identify the Security Issues with E-mail

- Malicious code is code that performs something harmful to the computer it runs on. Malicious code is often sent through e-mail.

- Viruses are pieces of malicious code that require user action to spread.

- Trojan programs deceive the user into thinking that a program is something innocuous, when it is actually a piece of malicious code.

- Worms are pieces of malicious code that use automated methods to spread.

- Spam, or unsolicited commercial e-mail, is e-mail that is sent to you without you requesting it, attempting to sell you something. The electronic equivalent of a telemarketing call.

- Hoax e-mails are e-mails that travel from user to user because of the compelling story contained in them.

Describe the Security Practices Associated with E-mail

- How to protect your e-mail system from virus code
  - Don't execute any attachment from an unknown source.
  - Use antivirus programs that run on the server to filter all e-mails.
  - Use client-side antivirus programs to catch any viruses that might come from web-based e-mail accounts.
- Keep all software up-to-date to help prevent worm propagation.
- Server-side filtering software and the application of spam blackhole lists help limit the amount of unsolicited mail.
- E-mail encryption is a great way to protect the privacy of communication since e-mail is a cleartext medium.

Name Software that Improves Security in E-mail

- PGP, or Pretty Good Privacy
- S/MIME, or Secure/Multipurpose Internet Mail Extensions
- Antivirus software

Key Terms

E-mail hoax *(423)*
Encryption *(428)*
Mail relaying *(427)*
PGP *(423)*
Realtime Blackhole List *(427)*
S/MIME *(423)*
SMTP *(427)*
Spam *(423)*
Trojan horse program *(423)*
Unsolicited commercial e-mail *(424)*
Virus *(423)*
Worm *(424)*

Key Terms Quiz

Use terms from the Key Terms list to complete the sentences that follow. Don't use the same term more than once. Not all terms will be used.

1. A large source of spam is e-mail servers configured for _____.

2. A _____ is a list of servers that are blocked because they have been known to send spam.

3. The process of concealing information in an e-mail to protect privacy is called _____.

4. Programs that look like a normal application but contain malicious code are _____.

5. _____ are malicious code programs that need user intervention to spread.

6. Spam is the popular term for _____.

7. _____ are false e-mails that tell a compelling story, and typically prompt the user to forward them to other users.

8. _____ and _____ are two popular e-mail encryption programs.

9. A _____ is a malicious code program that automates the infection process.

10. The most prevalent protocol that e-mail is sent by is _____.

Multiple-Choice Quiz

1. What is a Trojan horse program?

    A. A program that encrypts e-mail for security

    B. A program that appears legitimate but is actually malicious code

    C. A program that only runs on a single computer

    D. A program that self-compiles before it runs

2. What is one of the popular Trojan horse payloads?

    A. A word processor

    B. A web server

    C. Remote control programs

    D. Music sharing programs

3. What is end-to-end security?

    A. When e-mail messages are stored in encrypted format before and after they have been decrypted.

    B. When e-mail messages remain encrypted, no matter how many e-mail servers they pass through.

C. When e-mail messages are sent through special secure servers.

D. When e-mail is sent directly from the local host to the remote host, bypassing servers entirely.

4. Why is HTML e-mail dangerous?

A. It can't be read by some e-mail clients.

B. It sends the content of your e-mails to web pages.

C. It can allow launching of malicious code from the preview pane.

D. It is the only way spam can be sent.

5. Why is an open e-mail relay bad?

A. It allows anyone to remotely control the server.

B. It makes the e-mail server reboot once a day.

C. No e-mail will go through.

D. It will allow anyone to send spam through the server.

6. What is one of the largest reasons spam is prevalent today?

A. E-mail relays are left open.

B. Regular mail is too slow.

C. Spam is popular among recipients.

D. Spam is sent from the government.

7. Why do PGP and S/MIME need public key cryptography?

A. Public keys are necessary to determine if the e-mail is encrypted.

B. The public key is necessary to encrypt the symmetric key.

C. The public key unlocks the password to the e-mail.

D. The public key is useless and just gives a false sense of privacy.

8. What symmetric encryption protocols does S/MIME support?

A. AES and RC4

B. IDEA and 3DES

C. 3DES and RC2

D. RC4 and IDEA

9. Why is S/MIME sometimes considered unsecured?

A. It doesn't actually encrypt the e-mail.

B. It can send unsigned e-mails.

C. It uses inferior Triple DES encryption.

D. It can be used with only 40-bit ciphers.

10. What symmetric encryption protocols does PGP not support?

    A. IDEA

    B. CAST

    C. Triple DES

    D. Diffie-Hellman

11. What makes spam so popular as an advertising medium?

    A. Its low cost per impression

    B. Its high rate of return

    C. Its ability to canvass multiple countries

    D. Its quality of workmanship

12. What is spam?

    A. Unsolicited commercial e-mail

    B. A Usenet archive

    C. A computer virus

    D. An encryption algorithm

13. How does the Realtime Blackhole List help fight spam?

    A. It is a universal Internet receptacle for spam.

    B. It maintains current signatures of all available spam for download.

    C. It takes all spam and returns it to the sender.

    D. It maintains a list of spam sources that e-mail servers can check messages against.

14. How many bits are needed in a symmetric encryption algorithm to give decent protection from brute-force attacks?

    A. 24 bits

    B. 40 bits

    C. 56 bits

    D. 128 bits

15. What makes e-mail hoaxes popular enough to keep the same story floating around for years?

    A. They are written by award-winning authors.

    B. The story prompts action on the reader's part.

    C. The story will only give good luck if the user forwards it on.

    D. The hoax e-mail forwards itself.

Essay Quiz

1. You are working as a security administrator and you start to impose more restrictions on the e-mail system, such as disallowing the transmission of executable attachments and forcing users to log into the company's VPN system before checking their e-mail. Other users of the system don't understand why the company's e-mail doesn't allow a functionality that their home e-mail does, and so they begin to complain. Draft a memo to all users explaining the security risks present in e-mail, and why these steps are necessary to protect your company's information.

2. Why is it problematic to send confidential information over e-mail? What is a solution to this problem?

3. You realize that a new e-mail game has been making the rounds at your company, and you are concerned that it is a Trojan horse program. Describe a few of the steps that can be used to prevent malicious code from infecting systems.

4. What elements are almost always present in an effective hoax e-mail?

5. The IT department is debating several different e-mail packages, and they ask you to present the security implications of automated malicious code. Write a few sentences on how worms propagate through e-mail, and why Microsoft Outlook is such a popular target for them.

Lab Projects

Lab Project 16.1

You have been asked to help secure e-mail for the university. To accomplish this, everyone must use an e-mail encryption program, so you decide on PGP. Download PGP and install it, sending yourself an encrypted test e-mail.

You will need a lab computer with Windows installed, as well as Outlook, Outlook Express, or Eudora.

Then do the following:

1. Download PGP from http://web.mit.edu/network/pgp.html.

2. Run the Installer program.

3. Generate a private key using PGPkeys.

4. Send a signed and encrypted e-mail to yourself using your public key. Upon reception of the e-mail, verify decryption with your private key.

Lab Project 16.2

Find at least ten pieces of spam mail from any account, whether it be home, work, school, or something else. Using the e-mail headers, and any web site that might provide information, attempt to trace the spam mail back to its original source.

You will need the following materials:

- Ten separate spam mails
- An Internet connection

Then do the following:

1. Collect the e-mails and view the e-mail header information in your e-mail program.
2. Find the "Received:" field in the headers and write down as many DNS names or IP addresses you can. Also look for common details in the header elements of the different messages, such as the same e-mail servers and spammers.
3. Using the Internet, research the physical locations of the IP addresses.
4. Report the different locations where your spam e-mail originated. What did you learn about tracing e-mail and spam?

Web Components

Upon completion of this chapter, you will be able to:

- Describe the protocols used with web components, including SSL/TLS protocol suite, LDAP, and FTP
- Describe web applications, such as Web Services and plug-ins, and explain their associated security issues
- Describe and explain secure file transfer options
- Explain how directory services can be used to aid in data retrieval
- Describe how scripting and other Internet functions can cause security concerns
- Describe how using cookies maintains parameters between web pages

The World Wide Web was invented by Tim Berners-Lee to give physicists a convenient method of exchanging information. What began in 1990 as a physics tool in the European Laboratory for Particle Physics (CERN) has grown into a complex system that is used by millions of computer users for tasks from e-commerce, to e-mail, chatting, games, and even the original intended use—file and information sharing. Before the World Wide Web, there were plenty of methods to perform these tasks, and they were already widespread in use. File Transfer Protocol (FTP) was used to move files, and Telnet allowed access to other machines. What was missing was the common architecture brought by Berners-Lee. First, a common addressing scheme, built around the concept of a **Uniform Resource Locator** (URL). Second was the concept of linking documents to other documents by URLs through the **Hypertext Markup Language** (HTML).

Although these elements may seem minor, they formed a base that spread like wildfire. Berners-Lee developed two programs to demonstrate the usefulness of his vision: a web server to serve documents to users, and a web browser to retrieve documents for users. Both of these were key elements and contributed to the spread of this new technological innovation. The success of these components led to network after network being connected together in a "network of networks" known today as the Internet. Much of this interconnection was developed and funded through grants from the U.S. government to further technological and economic growth.

What enabled the Web's explosive growth into the PC market were the application programs, called browsers, that were developed to use these common elements and allow users ease of access to the new world of connected resources. Browsers became graphically based, and as more users began to use them, a market for more services via this new World Wide Web channel was born. Out of this market, standards emerged to provide the required levels of security necessary as the user base and functionality of the World Wide Web expanded.

The commercialization of browsers began with a program called Mosaic. Mosaic was developed at the National Center for Supercomputing Applications (NCSA) at the University of Illinois at Urbana-Champaign. A team headed by Marc Andreessen developed Mosaic for their own use, but a businessman, Jim Clark, from Silicon Valley realized the commercial potential and formed a company called Mosaic Communications to realize that potential. Andreessen and his team joined Clark, and the firm became Netscape Communications. Netscape was an early innovator and inventor of many of the protocols that drive the important elements of the Web today. Microsoft joined the browser world with its Internet Explorer and eventually became the leader in terms of market share.

Current Web Components and Concerns

The usefulness of the World Wide Web is due not just to browsers, but also to web components that enable services for end users through their browser interfaces. These web components use a wide range of protocols and services to deliver the desired content to end users. From a security perspective, these components offer end users an easy to use, secure method of conducting data transfers over the Internet. Many protocols have been developed to deliver this content, although for most users, the browser handles the details of these methods and protocols.

From a systems point of view, many security concerns have arisen, but they can be grouped in three main tasks:

- Securing a server that delivers content to users over the Web
- Securing the transport of information between users and servers over the Web
- Securing the user's computer from attack over a web connection

This chapter will present the components used on the Web to request and deliver information securely over the Internet.

Protocols

When two people communicate, several things must happen for the communication to be effective. They must use a language that both parties understand, and they must correctly use the language, i.e., structure and syntax, to express their thoughts. The mode of communication is a separate entity entirely, for the previous statements are important in both spoken and written forms of communication. The same requirements are present with respect to computer communications, and they are addressed through protocols. Protocols refer to agreed upon sets of rules that allow different vendors to produce hardware and software that can interoperate with pieces developed by other vendors. Because of the worldwide nature of the Internet, protocols are very important and form the basis by which all the separate parts can work together. The specific instantiation of protocols is done through hardware and software components. The majority of this chapter will concentrate on protocols related to the Internet as instantiated by software components.

Encryption (SSL and TLS)

Secure Sockets Layer (SSL) is a general-purpose protocol developed by Netscape for managing the encryption of information being transmitted over the Internet. It began as a competitive feature to drive sales of Netscape's web server product, which could then send information securely to end users. This early vision of securing the transmission channel between the web server and the browser became an Internet standard. Today, SSL is almost ubiquitous with respect to e-commerce—all browsers support it as do web servers, and virtually all sensitive financial traffic from e-commerce web sites use this method to protect information in transit between web servers and browsers.

The Internet Engineering Task Force (IETF) embraced SSL in 1996 through a series of RFCs and named the group **Transport Layer Security (TLS)**. Starting with SSL 3.0, in 1999 the IETF issued RFC 2246, "TLS Protocol Version 1.0," followed by RFC 2712, which added Kerberos authentication, and then RFCs 2817 and 2818, which extended TLS to HTTP version 1.1 (HTTP/1.1). Although SSL has been through several versions, TLS begins with an equivalency to SSL 3.0, so today SSL and TLS are essentially the same protocol although not interchangeable.

SSL/TLS is a series of functions that exist in the OSI model between the application layer and the TCP/IP implementation in the transport and network layers. The goal of TCP is to send an unauthenticated error-free stream of information between two computers. SSL/TLS adds message integrity and authentication functionality to TCP through the use of cryptographic methods. As cryptographic methods are an ever-evolving field, and for them to be used both parties must agree on an implementation method, SSL/TLS has embraced an open, extensible, and adaptable method to allow flexibility and strength. When two programs initiate an SSL/TLS connection, one of the first tasks is to compare available protocols and agree on an appropriate common cryptographic protocol for use in this particular communication. As SSL/TLS can use separate algorithms and methods for encryption, authentication, and data integrity, each of these is negotiated and determined depending upon need at the beginning of a communication. Currently the browsers from Netscape and Microsoft allow fairly extensive SSL/TLS setup options as illustrated in Figure 17-1, Figure 17-2, and Figure 17-3.

How SSL/TLS Works

SSL/TLS uses a wide range of cryptographic protocols. To effectively use these protocols between a client and a server, an agreement must be reached on which protocol to use. The SSL handshake process is used to accomplish this task. The handshake process begins

Figure 17-1
SSI and TLS options in Microsoft Internet Explorer

with a client request for a secure connection, and a server's response. The questions that must be asked and answered are which protocol and which cryptographic algorithm will be used. For the client and server to communicate, both sides have to agree on a commonly held protocol (SSL v1, v2, v3, or TLS v1). Commonly available cryptographic algorithms include Diffie-Hellman and RSA. The handshake begins with the

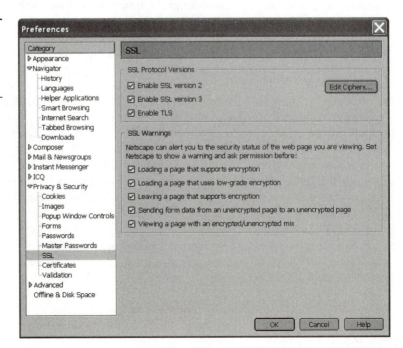

Figure 17-2
SSI and TLS options in Netscape Communicator

Figure 17-3
Cryptographic protocol options in Netscape Communicator

exchange to agree on parameters. The next step is to exchange certificates and keys as necessary to enable authentication. Authentication was a one-way process for SSL v1 and v2, with only the server providing authentication. In SSL v3/TLS, mutual authentication of both client and server is possible. The certificate exchange is via X.509 certificates, and public key cryptography is used to establish authentication. Once authentication is established, the channel is secured with symmetric key cryptographic methods and hashes, typically RC4 or 3DES for symmetric key and MD5 or SHA-1 for the hash functions.

At this point, the authenticity of the server and possibly the client has been established, and the channel is protected by encryption against eavesdropping. All of this work requires CPU time, hence SSL/TLS connections require significantly more overhead than unprotected connections. Establishing connections is particularly time-consuming, so even stateless web connections are held in a stateful fashion when secured via SSL/TLS, to avoid repeating the handshake process for each request. This makes some web server functionality more difficult, such as implementing web farms, and it requires either an SSL/TLS appliance before the web server to maintain state, or the SSL/TLS state information must be maintained in a directory type service accessible by all of the web farm servers. Either method requires additional infrastructure and equipment. However, to enable secure e-commerce and other private data transactions over the Internet, this is a cost-effective method to establish a specific level of necessary security.

The use of certificates is a way to have a third party act as notary in the electronic world. A certificate is merely a standard set of formatted data that represents the authenticity of the public key associated with the signer. Microsoft is, in theory, the only firm that can offer a signed certificate saying they are in fact Microsoft. A certificate can be trusted as a notary to a signature. You would only trust a notary as far as you can verify their ability to vouch for something. A person using a notary assumes the notary is honest, and states have regulations and notaries have insurance to protect against fraud. The same idea is true with certificates, although the legal system has not caught up to the electronic age, nor has the business of liability insurance. Still, certificates provide a method of proving who someone is, provided you trust the issuer. If the issuer is a third party of stature, such as VeriSign or AT&T, then you may have something to rest your faith upon. If the issuer is a large firm such as Microsoft, then again you can probably trust them since you are downloading their code. If the issuer is Bob's Certificate Shack, well, unless you know Bob, there may be cause for concern. Again, certificates do not vouch for code security, only that who is signing them is actually the person they say they are.

The use of certificates could present a lot of data and complication to a user. Fortunately, browsers have incorporated much of this desired functionality into a seamless operation. Once you have decided to always accept code from XYZ Corporation, subsequent certificate checks are handled by the browser. The ability to manipulate certificate settings is under the Options menus in both Microsoft Internet Explorer and Netscape Communicator, as shown in Figure 17-4, Figure 17-5, and Figure 17-6.

SSL/TLS is specifically designed to provide protection from man-in-the-middle attacks. By authenticating the server end of the connection, SSL/TLS prevents the initial hijacking of a session. By encrypting all of the conversations between the client and the server, SSL/TLS prevents eavesdropping. Even with all of this, though, SSL/TLS is not a complete security solution and it can be defeated. Once a communication is in the SSL/TLS channel, it is very difficult to defeat the protocol. Before data enters the secured channel, however, defeat is possible. A Trojan program that copies keystrokes and echoes them to another TCP/IP address in parallel with the intended communication can defeat SSL/TLS, provided that the Trojan program copies the data prior to SSL/TLS encapsulation. This type of attack has occurred and has been used to steal passwords and other sensitive material from users, performing the theft as the user actually types in the data.

Figure 17-4

Certificate options in Microsoft Internet Explorer

Figure 17-5
Certificate
management
options dialog
in Microsoft
Internet Explorer

The Web (HTTP and HTTPS)

The Hypertext Transfer Protocol (HTTP) is the protocol designated for the transfer of hypertext-linked data over the Internet, from web servers to browsers. When a user types a URL such as http://www.example.com into a browser, the http:// portion indicates that the desired method of data transfer is via the Hypertext Transfer Protocol. Although this was initially just for HTML pages, today many protocols deliver content over this connection protocol. HTTP traffic takes place over TCP port 80 by default, and this port is typically left open on firewalls because of this protocol.

Figure 17-6
Certificate
management
options dialog
in Netscape
Communicator

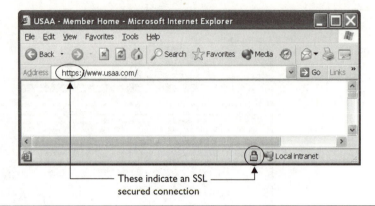

These indicate an SSL
secured connection

Figure 17-7   HTTPS connection in Microsoft Internet Explorer

One of the primary drivers behind the development of SSL/TLS was the desire to hide the complexities of cryptography from end users. When using an SSL/TLS-enabled browser, this can be done simply by requesting a secure connection from a web server instead of nonsecure connection. With respect to HTTP connections, this is as simple as using https:// in place of http://.

When a browser is SSL/TLS-aware, the entry of an SSL/TLS-based protocol will cause the browser to perform the necessary negotiations with the web server to establish the required level of security. Once these negotiations have been completed and the session is secured by a session key, then a closed padlock icon is displayed in the lower right of the screen (in Internet Explorer and Communicator) to indicate that the session is secure. Figure 17-7 shows a secure connection in Microsoft Internet Explorer, while Figure 17-8 illustrates the same thing in Netscape Communicator. As the tiny padlock can be easily missed, when in doubt, the best solution is to look at the URL. If the protocol is https: your connection is secure; if it is http:, then the connection is carried by plaintext for anyone to see.

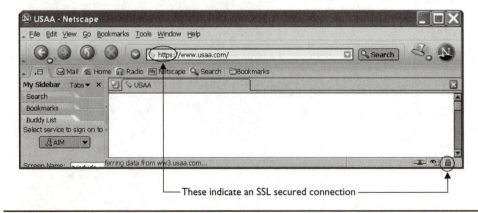

These indicate an SSL secured connection

Figure 17-8   HTTPS connection in Netscape Communicator

The objective of enabling cryptographic methods in this fashion is to make it easy for end users to use these protocols. SSL/TLS is designed to be protocol agnostic. Although designed to run on top of TCP/IP, it can operate on top of other lower-level protocols, such as X.25. SSL/TLS requires a reliable lower-level protocol, so it is not designed and cannot properly function on top of a non-reliable protocol such as the IP User Datagram Protocol (UDP). Even with this limitation, SSL/TLS has been used to secure many common TCP/IP-based services, as shown in Table 17-1.

Web Services

Web Services is a widely used industry term with various marketing definitions depending upon what is being marketed, and to whom. Although the term has become abused, its underlying core is an application program accessible using open protocols. With a distributed computing lineage, Web Services have been defined through industry standardization around a series of specifications, including XML Schema and Web Services Description Language (WDSL). As envisioned by the driving forces of firms such as IBM, Microsoft, and others, Web Services represent state-of-the-art distributed component technology. Web Services have an industry association, Web Services Interoperability Organization (WS-I), www.ws-i.org, specifically founded to ensure a successful firm-independent Web Services–world. By standardizing across many firms in the industry, Web Services are attempting to eliminate interoperability issues that have stalled other distributed application technologies. By focusing on core standards and inter- operability, and avoiding language and platform specific issues, Web Services is becoming an industry-wide standard that is the leader of distributed computing solutions.

A Web Service can be as simple as a remote procedure invoked on a remote computer via common data formats and protocols. A common method of invoking a Web Service is via a Simple Object Access Protocol (SOAP) request over an HTTP connection. This type of mechanism uses open standards such as XML, HTTP, and Universal Description, Discovery, and Integration (UDDI). A set of extensions to SOAP to address security issues, Web Services Security Language (WS_Security), has been proposed by IBM and Microsoft. In simple terms, a Web Service can be seen as an application that is accessed via a standard set of remote procedure calls implemented over HTTP, where the content will be passed using XML over SOAP. Having everything defined as a set of open standards makes this solution very attractive to developers.

The deployment of Web Services is still in its infancy, so the effectiveness of the security mechanisms being built into the standards is yet unknown. Web Services have several weaknesses, such as:

- HTTP/Web server vulnerabilities
- SOAP Structure vulnerabilities
- WSDL vulnerabilities
- Application layer vulnerabilities

As Web Services communicate over HTTP and through web servers, any vulnerability of the web server can manifest itself as a vulnerability to the web service. This is not truly a vulnerability of the web service, per se, but of the supporting infrastructure. The fact that SOAP and WDSL are both defined standards does not mean that all users will conform to this defined structure. Departures from the defined standard can result in weakness, such as when Denial-of-Service attacks are carried out against the structure using malformed messages aimed at structural issues. Defense against these types of attacks will ultimately rest with the standards community.

The greatest risk is associated with the actual Web Service code itself. A direct attack against the application code such as a buffer overflow attack, SQL injection, or parameter/data manipulation is still a significant security issue. Because Web Services are designed to increase distributed code and usage, control over users of Web Services lessen and it is far from safe to assume every usage will be with properly conformed messages for a particular Web Service. This places a responsibility on the Web Services application programmer to develop secure code. Assuming standards, encryption, and infrastructure (such as authentication and authorization) will take care of all security issues is misguided and incorrect and will lead to security issues.

SOAP

Simple Object Access Protocol (SOAP) began as a method of invoking remote procedures over the Internet. It is actually much more complicated than that: SOAP forms a framework for generalized XML messaging between applications in a language-neutral and platform-independent fashion. The S in SOAP stands for Simple, and as such it is valued highly and the entire framework was built to ensure continued simplicity. The basic SOAP framework is devoid of many features, such as routing and security. These are taken care of in the extensible nature of the basic framework. Layered extensions allow for the addition of these services in a cohesive and controlled fashion. The addition of security has been proposed through WS-Security and comprises a complete set of security functions for SOAP messages used in Web Services.

XML

Extensible Markup Language (XML) is used to format messages used by SOAP to access and return data from Web Services. The use of XML Schemas to define the communication interfaces and to carry information between Web Services and invoking elements allows for a standard method that is independent of any firm or platform, is extensible and is language neutral. The nature of XML and SOAP allow this process to occur over a wide range of protocols including HTTP, SMTP, TCP, and even higher-level methods such as MQ Series messaging.

Directory Services (DAP and LDAP)

A *directory* is a data storage mechanism similar to a database, but it has several distinct differences designed to provide efficient data retrieval services compared to standard database mechanisms. A directory is designed and optimized for reading data, offering very fast search and retrieval operations. The types of information stored in a directory tend to be descriptive attribute data. A directory offers a static view of data that can be changed without a complex update transaction. The data is hierarchically described in a tree-like structure, and a network interface for reading is typical. Common uses of directories include e-mail address lists, domain server data, and resource maps of network resources.

To enable interoperability, the X.500 standard was created as a standard for directory services. The primary method for accessing an X.500 directory is through the **Directory Access Protocol (DAP)**, a heavyweight protocol that is difficult to completely implement, especially on PCs and more constrained platforms. This led to the **Lightweight Directory Access Protocol (LDAP)**, which contains the most commonly used functionality. LDAP can interface with X.500 services, and, most importantly, LDAP can be used over TCP with significantly less computing resources than a full X.500 implementation. LDAP offers all of the functionality most directories will need and is easier and more economical to implement, hence LDAP has become the Internet standard for directory services. LDAP standards are governed by two separate entities depending upon use. The International Telecommunication Union (ITU) governs the X.500 standard, and LDAP is governed for Internet use by the IETF. Many RFCs apply to LDAP functionality, but some of the most important are RFCs 2251 through 2256 and RFCs 2829 and 2830.

SSL/TLS LDAP
LDAP over TCP is a plaintext protocol, meaning data is passed in the clear and is susceptible to eavesdropping. Encryption can be used to remedy this problem, and the application of SSL/TLS-based service will protect directory queries and replies from eavesdroppers. SSL/ TLS provides several important functions to LDAP services. SSL/TLS can establish the identity of a data source through the use of certificates. SSL/TLS can also provide for the integrity and confidentiality of the data being presented from an LDAP source. As LDAP and SSL/TLS are two separate independent protocols, interoperability is more a function of correct setup than anything else. To achieve LDAP over SSL/TLS, the typical setup is to establish an SSL/TLS connection and then open an LDAP connection over the protected channel. To do this requires both the client and the server be enabled for SSL/TLS. In the case of the client, most browsers are already enabled. In the case of an LDAP server, this is a specific function that must be enabled by a system administrator. As setting this up initially is complicated, this is definitely a task for a competent system administrator.

Once an LDAP server is set up to function over an SSL/TLS connection, it essentially operates as it always has. The LDAP server responds to specific queries with the data returned from a node in the search. The SSL/TLS functionality operates to secure the channel of communication, and it is transparent to the data flow from the user's perspective. From the outside, SSL/TLS prevents observation of the data request and response, ensuring confidentiality.

File Transfer (FTP and SFTP)
One of the original intended uses of the Internet was for transferring files between machines. The ability to transfer files from one machine to another in a simple, secure, and reliable fashion was needed by scientific researchers. Today, file transfers represent the

downloading of music content, reports, and other data sets from other computer systems to a PC-based client. Until 1995, the majority of Internet traffic was file transfers. With all of this need, a protocol was necessary so that two computers could agree on how to send and receive data. As such, the File Transfer Protocol (FTP) is one of the older protocols.

FTP

FTP is an application-level protocol, allowing it to operate over a wide range of lower-level protocols. FTP is embedded in most operating systems and provides a method of transferring files from a sender to a receiver. Most FTP implementations are designed to operate both ways, sending and receiving, and can enable remote file operations over a TCP/IP connection. FTP clients are used to initiate transactions and FTP servers are used to respond to transaction requests. The actual request can be either to upload (send data from client to server) or download (send data from server to client).

Clients for FTP on a PC can range from an application program to the command line ftp program in Windows/DOS to most browsers. To open an FTP data store in a browser, entering ftp://url in the browser's address field indicates that you wish to see the data associated with the URL via an FTP session—the browser handles the details. File transfers via FTP can be either binary or in text mode, but in either case, they are plaintext across the network.

Blind FTP (Anonymous FTP)

To access resources on a computer, an account must be used to allow the operating-system–level authorization function to work. In the case of an FTP server, you may not wish to control who gets the information, so a standard account called *anonymous* exists. This allows unlimited public access to the files and is commonly used when you wish to have unlimited distribution. On a server, access permissions can be established to allow only downloading or only uploading or both, depending upon the system's function. As FTP can be used to allow anyone access to upload files to a server, it is considered a security risk and is commonly implemented on specialized servers isolated from other critical functions. As FTP servers can present a security risk, they are typically not permitted on workstations and are disabled on servers without need for this functionality.

SFTP

FTP operates in a plaintext mode, so an eavesdropper can observe the data being passed. If confidential transfer is required, Secure FTP (SFTP) utilizes both Secure Shell (SSH) protocol and FTP to accomplish this task. SFTP is an application program that encodes both the commands and the data being passed and requires SFTP to be on both the client and the server. SFTP is not interoperable with standard FTP—the encrypted commands cannot be read by the standard FTP server program. To establish SFTP data transfers, the server must be enabled with the SFTP program, and then clients can access the server provided they have the correct credentials. One of the first SFTP operations is the same as with FTP: an identification function that uses a username, and an authorization function that uses a password. There is no anonymous SFTP account by definition, so access is established and controlled from the server using standard access control lists, IDs, and passwords.

Vulnerabilities

Modern encryption technology can provide significant levels of privacy, up to military-grade secrecy. The use of protocols such as SSL/TLS provide a convenient method for end users to use cryptography without having to understand the methods and steps. This can result in complacency—the impression that once SSL/TLS is enabled, the user is safe, and this is not necessarily the case. If a Trojan program is recording keystrokes and sending the information to another unauthorized user, SSL/TLS cannot prevent this security breach. If the user is connecting to an untrustworthy site, the mere fact that the connection is secure does not prevent the other site from running a scam. Using SSL/TLS and other encryption methods will not guard against your credit card information being "lost" by the company you do business with, as in the egghead.com credit card hack of 2000. In December 2000, egghead.com's credit card database was hacked into, and as many as 3.7 million credit card numbers were exposed. Other similar stories include 55,000 credit card records being compromised by creditcards.com in 2000 and over 300,000 records being compromised by the CD Universe hack in 1999.

The key to understanding what is protected and where it is protected requires an understanding of what these protocols can and cannot do. The SSL/TLS suite can protect data in transit, but not on either end in storage. It can authenticate users and servers, provided that the certificate mechanisms are established and used by both parties. Properly set up and used, SSL/TLS can provide a very secure method of authentication, followed by confidentiality in data transfers and data integrity checking. But again, all of this occurs during transit, and the protection ends once the data is stored.

Code-Based Vulnerabilities

The ability to connect many machines together to transfer data is what makes the Internet so functional for so many users. Browsers enable much of this functionality, and as the types of data have grown on the Internet, browser functionality has grown as well. But not all functions can be anticipated or included in each browser release, so the idea of extending browser functions through plug-ins became a standard. Browsers can perform many types of data transfer, and in some cases, additional helper programs, or plug-ins, can increase functionality for specific types of data transfers. In other cases, separate application programs may be called by a browser to handle the data being transferred. Common examples of these plug-ins and programs include Shockwave plug-ins, RealOne player (both plug-in and stand-alone application), Windows Media Player, and Adobe Acrobat (both plug-in and stand-alone). The richness that enables the desired functionality of the Internet has also spawned some additional types of interfaces in the form of ActiveX components and Java applets. In essence, all of these are pieces of code that can be written by third parties, distributed via the Internet, and run on your PC. If the code does what the user wants, the user is happy. But the opportunity exists for these applications or plug-ins to include malicious code that performs actions not desired by the end user.

Buffer Overflows

The most common exploit used to hack into software is the buffer overflow. The **buffer overflow** is a result of poor coding practices on the part of software programmers—when any program reads input into a buffer and does not validate the input for correct length, the potential for a buffer overflow exists. The concept is simple. A hacker writes an executable program that performs some action on the target machine and appends this code fragment to a legitimate response to a program on the target machine. When the target machine reads through the too-long response, a buffer overflow condition causes the original program to fail. The extra malicious code fragment is now in the machine's memory, awaiting execution. If the hacker executed it correctly, the program will skip into the hacker's code, running it before failing.

Buffer overflows have been shown to be exploitable in a wide range of programs, from UNIX to Windows to applications such as Internet Explorer, Netscape Communicator, and many more. It has been estimated that 50 percent of the security incidents by type are from buffer overflow exploits. This is one of the most common hacks used, and the primary defense a user has is to keep their machine up-to-date with patches from software manufacturers. This has not proven to be a very effective method of protection. Many people don't keep up-to-date with the patches, as demonstrated by the Slammer worm attack, which took place over three months after Microsoft had released a patch for the vulnerability. Even with the patch widely available, both in a hot-fix and a service pack, many SQL servers had not received the patch and were affected by this worm, which used a buffer overflow to propagate.

Java and JavaScript

Java is a computer language invented by Sun Microsystems as an alternative to Microsoft's development languages. Designed to be platform independent and based on C, Java offered a low learning curve and a way of implementing programs across an enterprise, independent of platform. Although platform independence never fully materialized, and the pace of Java language development was slowed by Sun, Java has found itself to be a leader in object-oriented programming languages.

Java, and its close cousin JavaScript, operates through an interpreter called a Java Virtual Machine (JVM) on each platform that interprets the Java code and this JVM enables the program's functionality for the specific platform. This reliance on an interpretive step has led to performance issues, and Java is still plagued by poor performance when compared to most other languages. Security was one of the touted advantages of Java, but in reality, security is not a built-in function but an afterthought and is implemented independent of the language core. This all being said, properly coded Java can operate at reasonable rates, and when properly designed can act in a secure fashion. These facts have led to the wide dependence on Java for much of the server-side coding for e-commerce and other Web-enabled functionality. Servers can add CPUs to address speed concerns, and the low learning curve has proven cost efficient for enterprises.

Java was initially designed to be used in trusted environments, and when it moved to the Internet for general use, safety became one of its much hyped benefits. Java has many safety features, such as type checking and garbage collection, that actually improve a program's ability to run safely on a machine and not cause operating-system–level failures. This isolates the user from many common forms of operating system faults that can end in the "blue screen of death" in a Windows environment, where the operating system crashes and forces a reboot of the system. Safety is not security, however, and although safe, a Java program can still cause significant damage to a system.

The primary mode of a computer program is to interact with the operating system and perform functional tasks for a user, such as getting and displaying data, manipulating data, storing data, and so on. Although these functions can seem to be benign, when enabled across the Web they can have some unintended consequences. The ability to read data from a hard drive and display it on the screen is essential for many programs, but when the program is downloaded and run from the Internet and the data is, without the knowledge of the user, sent across the Internet to an unauthorized user, this enables a program to spy on a user and steal data. Writing data to the hard drive can also cause deletions if the program doesn't write the data where the user expects. Sun recognized these dangers and envisioned three different security policies for Java that would be implemented via the browser and JVM, providing different levels of security. The first policy is to not run Java programs at all. The second restricts Java program functionality when the program is not run directly from the system's hard drive—programs being directly executed from the Internet have severe restrictions that block disk access and force other security-related functions to be performed. The last policy runs any and all Java programs as presented.

Most browsers adopted the second security policy, restricting Java functionality on a client unless the program was loaded directly from the client's hard drive. Although this solved many problems initially, this also severely limited functionality. Today, browsers allow much more specific granularity on security for Java, based on security zones and user settings.

JavaScript is a form of Java designed to be operated within a browser instance. The primary purpose of JavaScript was to enable features such as validation of forms before they are submitted to the server. Enterprising programmers found many other uses for JavaScript, such as manipulating the browser history files, now prohibited by design. JavaScript actually runs within the browser (see Figure 17-9), and the code is executed by the browser itself. This has led to compatibility problems, and not just between vendors, such as Microsoft and Netscape, but between browser versions.

Although JavaScript was designed not to be able to directly access files or network resources, except through the browser functions, this has not proven to be as secure as desired. This fault traces back to a similar fault in the Java language, where security was added on afterwards, without the benefit of a comprehensive security model. So, although designers put thought and common sense into the design, the lack of a comprehensive security model left some security holes. For instance, a form could submit itself via e-mail to an undisclosed recipient, either eavesdropping, or worse spamming or causing other problems—imagine your machine sending death threat e-mails to high-level government officials from a rogue JavaScript implementation.

Figure 17-9
JavaScript

Further, most browsers do not have a mechanism to halt a running script short of aborting the browser instance, and even this may not be possible if the browser has stopped responding to commands. Malicious JavaScripts can do many things, including opening two new windows every time you close one, each with the code to open two more. There is no way out of this one, short of killing the browser process from the operating system. JavaScripts can also spoof a user into thinking they are communicating with one entity, when in fact they are communicating with another. For example, a window may open asking whether you want to download and execute the new update from "http://www.microsoft.com..../update.exe", and what is covered by the ellipsis (three dots (...)) is actually "www.microsoft.com.attacker.org/"—the user just assumes this is a Microsoft address that is cut short by space restrictions on the display.

The number of ways a JavaScript can interact with a system is so high, with so many opportunities for malicious code, that the best advice is not to run JavaScripts or Java applets unless you trust the source. Again, browsers have the ability to limit Java functionality, as shown in Figure 17-10 for Internet Explorer and Figure 17-11 for Netscape Communicator. A common recommendation for high-security clients is to disable JavaScript completely. Although this reduces the functionality, it also reduces the outside threat to a system.

As a browser scripting language, JavaScript is here to stay. Its widespread popularity for developing applets such as animated clocks, mortgage calculators, simple games, and the like will overcome its buggy nature and poor level of security. Similarly, Java as a development language is also here to stay, although it may never live up to its initial hype and will continue to have security issues. Both of these technologies boast many skilled developers, low learning curves (because of their heritage in the C language), and popularity in computer science courses. When viewed as a total package, the marketplace has decided that the benefits outweigh the drawbacks, and these two technologies will be a cornerstone for much Internet programming development.

Figure 17-10
Java configuration
options in
Microsoft
Internet Explorer

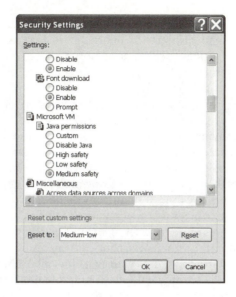

ActiveX

ActiveX is the name given to a broad collection of APIs, protocols, and programs developed by Microsoft to automatically download and execute code over an Internet-based channel. The code is bundled together into an ActiveX control and given an .ocx extension. These controls are referenced in HTML using the **<object>** tag. ActiveX is a tool for the Windows environment and can be extremely powerful. ActiveX can do simple things, such as enable a browser to display a custom type of information in a particular

Figure 17-11
Java configuration
options in
Netscape
Communicator

way, and it can also perform complex tasks, such as update the operating system and application programs. This range of abilities gives ActiveX a lot of power, but this power can be abused as well as used for good purposes.

Microsoft Internet Explorer has several options to control the execution of ActiveX controls, as illustrated in Figure 17-12.

To enable security and consumer confidence in downloaded programs such as ActiveX controls, Microsoft developed **Authenticode**, a system that uses digital signatures and allows Windows users to determine who produced a specific piece of code and whether or not the code has been altered. As in the case of Java, safety and security are different things, and Authenticode promotes neither in reality. Authenticode provides limited accountability at the time of download and guarantees that the code has not been changed since the time of signing. Authenticode does not identify whether a piece of code will cause damage to a system, nor does it regulate how code is used. A perfectly safe ActiveX control under one set of circumstances may be malicious if used improperly. As with a notary's signature, recourse is very limited—if code is signed by a terrorist organization and the code ruins your machine, all Authenticode did was make it seem legitimate. It is still incumbent upon the user to know from whom they are getting code and to determine whether or not they trust that organization.

Critics of Authenticode and other code-signing techniques are not against code signing, for this is a universally recognized good thing. What the critics argue is that code signing is not a panacea for security issues and that marketing it as doing more than it really does is irresponsible. Understanding the nuances of security is important in today's highly technical world, and leaving the explanations to marketing departments is not the ideal solution.

CGI

The **Common Gateway Interface (CGI)** was the original method of having a web server execute a program outside the web server process, yet on the same server. The intent was to pass information via environment variables to an independent program, execute

Figure 17-12

Some of the ActiveX control options in Microsoft Internet Explorer the program, and return the results to the web server for display. Web servers are presentation and display engines, and they have had less than stellar results when used in other fashions. For example, a web server instance may have numerous independent connections, and a program failure that results in a process bounce can affect multiple users if it is run within the web server process. Separating any time-consuming and more risky programming cores, such as database lookups and manipulation, complex calculations, and other tasks, into separate processes was and still is a prudent idea.

CGI offers many advantages to web-based programs. The programs can be written in a number of languages, although Perl is a favorite. These scripted programs embrace the full functionality of a server, allowing access to databases, UNIX commands, other programs, and so on. This provides a wide range of functionality to the web environment. With this unrestrained capability, however, come security issues. Poorly written scripts can cause unintended consequences at runtime.

The problem with poorly written scripts is that they are not always obvious. Sometimes scripts appear to be fine, but unexpected user inputs can have unintended consequences. The addition of extra elements on a command line, for example, can result in dramatically different outputs. The use of the Perl backquote function allows a user to programmatically encode user input to a UNIX shell, and this works properly given proper user input, but if the user appends **& /bin/ls -l** to a proper input, this could generate a directory listing of the cgi-bin directory, which in turn gives away script names for future exploitation attempts. Permitting users to execute other programs in such an uncontrolled fashion led many ISPs to prohibit the use of CGI scripts unless they were specifically approved by the ISP. This led to considerable overhead and code checking to ensure clean code and validated user inputs.

A variety of books have been written on how to code securely, and CGI has benefited. Properly coded, CGI offers no more and no less risk than any other properly coded solution. CGI's loss was that it was first and was abused first, and many developers learned by making mistakes early on CGI. On UNIX systems, CGI offers the ultimate in programmable diversity and capability, and now that security standard practices have been learned and put into use, the system is seeing new popularity.

Server-Side Scripts

CGI has been replaced in many web sites through newer server-side scripting technologies such as Java, Active Server Pages (ASP), and PHP. All of these technologies operate in much the same fashion as CGI: they allow programs to be run outside the web server and to return data to the web server to be served to end users via a web page. Each of these newer technologies has advantages and disadvantages, but all of them have stronger security models than CGI. With these security models comes reduced functionality and, as each is based on a different language, the learning curves are steeper. Still, the need for adherence to programming fundamentals exists in these newer technologies—code must be well designed and well written to avoid the same vulnerabilities that exist in all forms of code. Buffer overflows are still an issue, even with these newer technologies. Changing languages or technologies does not eliminate the basic security problems associated with incorporating open-ended user input into code. Understanding and qualifying user responses before blindly using them programmatically is essential to the security of a system.

Cookies

Cookies are small chunks of ASCII text passed within an HTML stream to temporarily store data in a web browser instance. Invented by Netscape, cookies pass back and forth between web server and browser and act as a mechanism to maintain state in a stateless world. *State* is a term that describes the dependence on previous actions. By definition, an HTTP session served by a web server is stateless—each request is completely independent of all previous requests, and the server has no memory of previous requests. This dramatically simplifies the function of a web server, but it also significantly complicates the task of providing anything but the most basic functionality in a site. Cookies were developed to bridge this gap. Cookies are passed along with HTML data through a Set-Cookie message in the header portion of an HTML transaction, or via script in the HTML body.

A cookie is actually a series of name-value pairs that is stored in memory during a browser instance. The specification for cookies established several specific name-value pairs for defined purposes. Additional name-value pairs may be defined at will by a developer. The specified set of name-value pairs include the following:

- **Expires=** This specifies when the cookie expires. If no value exists, then the cookie is only good during the current browser session and will not be persisted to the user's hard drive. Should a value be given, the cookie will be written to the user's machine and persisted until this datetime value occurs.

- **Domain=** This name-value pair specifies the domain where the cookie is used. Cookies were designed as memory-resident objects, but as the user or data can cause a browser to move between domains, say from comedy.net to jokes.org, then some mechanism needs to tell the browser which cookies belong to which domains.

- **Path=** This name-value pair further resolves the applicability of the cookie into a specific path within a domain. If path=/directory, the cookie will only be sent for requests within /directory on the given domain. This allows a level of granular control over the information being passed between the browser and server, and it limits unnecessary data exchanges.

- **Secure** The presence of the keyword [secure] in a cookie indicates that it is only to be used when connected in an SSL/TLS session. This does not indicate any other form of security, as cookies are stored in plaintext on the client machine. In fact, one browser-based security issue was the ability to read another site's cookies from the browser cache and determine the values by using a script.

Cookie management on a browser is normally an invisible process, but both Internet Explorer and Communicator have methods for users to examine and manipulate cookies on the client side. Communicator stores the cookies in a long text file (see Figure 17-13). Note the file location in the browser address line. This will vary based on user account, but is generally representative of a default Netscape Communicator installation.

Netscape, the inventor of cookies, has maintained a strong cookie management option within its Communicator product line. Users have the ability to examine, delete, and block individual cookies through this interface, as shown in Figure 17-14.

Figure 17-13   Netscape Communicator cookie file

Internet Explorer has a much simpler interface, with just a Delete Cookies option in the browser (see Figure 17-15). Additional cookie manipulation is done through the file processing system, because cookies are stored as individual files as shown in Figure 17-16. This combination allows easier bulk manipulation, a useful option, as cookies can become quite numerous in short order.

Figure 17-14

Netscape
Communicator
cookie
management
via browser

Cookie Manager		☒

Stored Cookies | Cookie Sites

View and Remove Cookies that are stored on your computer.

Site	Cookie Name	
aol.com	WA_TMCJ_ESK	
aol.com	MC_CMP_ESKX	
aol.com	MC_CMP_ESK	
aol.com	MCSS	
aol.com	MC_NPID	
aol.com	mcProfLastMod	

Information about the selected Cookie

Name:
Information:
Host:
Path:
Server Secure:
Expires:
Policy:

Remove Cookie | Remove All Cookies

☐ Don't allow removed cookies to be reaccepted later

OK | Cancel | Help

Figure 17-15
Microsoft
Internet Explorer
delete cookies
option

So what good are cookies? Disable cookies in your browser and go to some common sites that you visit—you will quickly learn the usefulness of cookies. Cookies store a variety of information, from customer IDs to data about previous visits. Because cookies are stored on a user's machine in a form that will allow simple manipulation, they must always be considered suspect and are not suitable for use as a security mechanism. They can, however, allow the browser to provide crucial pieces of information to a web server.

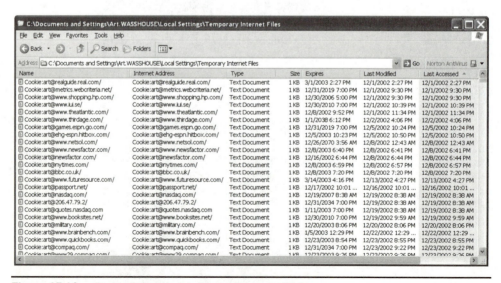

Figure 17-16   Cookie management in Microsoft Internet Explorer

Advertisers can use them to control which ads you are shown, based on previous ads, and regardless of ad location by site. Specific sites can use them to pass state information between pages, enabling functionality at the user's desired levels. Cookies can also remember your ZIP code for a weather site, your ID for a stock tracker site, the items in your shopping cart—these are all typical cookie uses. In the end analysis, cookies are a part of daily web experience, here to stay and useful if not used improperly (such as to store security data and to provide ID and authentication).

Disabling Cookies

If the user disables cookies in a browser, this type of information will not be available for the web server to use. IETF RFC 2109 describes the HTTP state-management system (cookies) and specifies several specific cookie functions to be enabled in browsers, specifically

- The ability to turn on and off cookie usage
- An indicator as to whether cookies are in use
- A means of specifying cookie domain values and lifetimes

Several of these functions have already been discussed, but to surf cookie-free requires more than a simple step. Telling a browser to stop accepting cookies is a setup option available through an options menu, but this has no effect on cookies already received and stored on the system. To prevent the browser from sending cookies already received, the user must delete the cookies from the system. This bulk operation is easily performed, and then the browser can run cookie-free. There are also several third-party tools that enable even a finer granularity of cookie control.

Signed Applets

Code signing was an attempt to bring the security of shrink-wrapped software to software downloaded from the Internet. Code signing works by adding a digital signature and a digital certificate to a program file to demonstrate file integrity and authenticity. The certificate identifies the author, and the digital signature contains a hash value that covers code, certificate, and signature to prove integrity, and this establishes the integrity of the code and publisher via a standard browser certificate check.

The ability to use a certificate to sign an applet or a control allows the identity of the author of a control or applet to be established. This has many benefits. For instance, if a user trusts content from a particular vendor, such as Sun Microsystems, the user can trust controls that are signed by Sun Microsystems. This signing of a piece of code does not do anything other than identify the code's manufacturer and guarantee that the code has not been modified since it was signed.

A signed applet can be hijacked as easily as a graphic, or any other file. The two ways an attacker could hijack a signed control are by in-line access or copying the file in its entirety and republishing it. *In-lining* is using an embedded control from another site with or without the other site's permission. Republishing a signed control is done much like stealing a GIF or JPEG image—a copy of the file is maintained on the unauthorized site and served from there instead of from the original location. If a signed control cannot be modified, why be concerned with these thefts, apart from the issue of intellectual property? The primary security concern comes from how the control is used. A hacker may be able to use a control in an unintended fashion, resulting in file loss or buffer overflow—conditions that weaken a system and may allow exploitation of other vulnerabilities. A common programming activity is cleaning up installation files from a computer's hard drive after successfully installing a software package. If a signed control is used for this task, and permission has already been granted, then improperly using the control could result in the wrong set of files being deleted. The control will still function as designed, but the issue becomes who it is used by and how. These are concerns not addressed simply by signing a control or applet.

Browser Plug-Ins

The addition of browser scripting and ActiveX components allows a browser to change how it handles data, tremendously increasing its functionality as a user interface. But all data types and all desired functionality cannot be offered through these programming technologies. Plug-ins are used to fill these gaps.

Plug-ins are small application programs that increase a browser's ability to handle new data types and add new functionality. Sometimes these plug-ins are in the form of ActiveX components, which is the form Microsoft chose for its Office plug-in, which enables a browser to manipulate various Office files, such as pivot tables from Excel, over the Web. Adobe has developed Acrobat Reader, a plug-in that enables a browser to read and display Portable Document Format (PDF) files directly in a browser. PDF files offer platform independence for printed documents and are usable across a wide array of platforms—they are a compact way to provide printed information.

Dynamic data such as movies and music can be manipulated by a wide variety of plug-ins, and one of the most popular comes from Real Networks. RealOne player can operate both as a stand-alone program or run video and audio files in a web page. QuickTime from Apple Computer provides the same type of functionality, and not just for Apple computers, but for Windows PCs as well. Microsoft has responded with their own viewer technology, the Windows Media Player, which also acts as a stand-alone application in addition to enhancing browser capabilities.

Two strikingly different plug-ins that few computers are without are the Flash and Shockwave plug-ins. These plug-ins from Macromedia can provide developers with the ability to develop striking graphic and cartoon animations that greatly enhance the look and feel of a web experience. The combination of a development environment for developers and plug-in enabled browsers that can display the content has caused these technologies to see widespread use. The result is a tremendous increase in visual richness in web communications, and this, in turn, has made the Web more popular and has increased usage in various demographic segments.

To date, these plug-ins have had a remarkable safety record. Although a plug-in changes a browser and how it can manipulate data, security holes have not been the norm in this area. This does not mean that all plug-ins are safe—far from it. There are as many plug-ins as one could imagine, most from small single-programmer shops, designed for specific purposes that may or may not be needed by most users. Your trust in plug-ins should, as usual, be based on knowing whom you are trusting. Major vendors, such as Macromedia, Adobe, and the like, with their history of product safety, encourage trust. When it comes to Joe's programming house offering a plug-in to enhance 3-D images in porn files—you get what you pay for.

Chapter Review

Chapter Summary

After reading this chapter and completing the exercises, you should understand the following about web components.

Current Web Components

- The Internet is built around common web components and protocols to enable interoperability.
- Security concerns include server security, security during data transport, and end-user machine security.

Protocols

- The commonest encryption protocol implementations are SSL and TLS.
- Web pages are delivered via HTTP and HTTPS.
- Directory services are delivered by DAP and LDAP, with LDAP being the commonest implementation.
- File transfers are typically accomplished using File Transfer Protocol (FTP).
- Web Services utilize technologies including SOAP, XML Schemas, and UDDI to allow remote procedure execution across the Web.

Code-Based Vulnerabilities

- The commonest code-based vulnerability is a buffer overflow.
- Java and JavaScript have specific security implications and must be properly configured to run securely.
- Cookies, properly employed, are not a security issue and can enhance a user's web experience.
- Plug-ins and applets, necessary for a content-rich web experience, have security concerns that can be mitigated through proper system setup and code signing.

Key Terms

ActiveX *(455)*
AuthentiCode *(456)*
Buffer overflow *(452)*
CGI (common gateway interface) *(456)*
Cookie *(458)*
DAP (Directory Access Protocol) *(449)*
FTP *(450)*
HTML (Hypertext Markup Language) *(439)*
LDAP (Lightweight Directory Access Protocol) *(449)*
Plug-in *(462)*
SOAP (Simple Object Access Protocol) *(448)*
SSL *(441)*
TLS *(441)*
URL (Uniform Resource Locator) *(439)*
Web Service *(447)*
XML (Extensible Markup Language) *(448)*

Key Terms Quiz

Use terms from the Key Terms list to complete the sentences that follow. Don't use the same term more than once. Not all terms will be used.

1. _____ is a small chunk of ASCII text passed within an HTML stream to temporarily store data in a web browser instance.

2. _____ is a series of functions to add message integrity and authentication functionality to TCP through the use of cryptographic methods.

3. _____ are small application programs that increase a browser's ability to handle new data types and add new functionality.

4. _____ is an application that is accessed via a standard set of remote procedure calls implemented over HTTP, where the content will be passed using XML over SOAP.

5. _____ forms a framework for generalized XML messaging between applications in a language-neutral and platform-independent fashion.

6. _____ is a streamlined set of commonly used directory access functionalities encapsulated in a standard protocol.

7. _____ are the commonest type of code-based exploit seen on the Internet today.

8. _____ is a protocol used to transfer files from one machine to another across a network.

9. _____ is the name given to a broad collection of APIs, protocols, and programs developed by Microsoft to automatically download and execute code over an Internet-based channel.

10. _____ is the original method of having a web server execute a program outside the web server process, yet on the same server.

Multiple-Choice Quiz

1. What is a cookie used for?

   A. To maintain state during a client web experience

   B. Server-side web programming

   C. To enhance a web page

   D. It was a favorite snack of web developers, so they named a program after it

2. SSL/TLS use of certificates is similar to…

   A. A receipt proving purchase

   B. Having a notary notarize a signature, providing proof of identity

   C. A historical record of a program's lineage, including authorship

   D. An end-user license

3. Web Services are a means of…

   A. Improving security through encryption technology

   B. Distributing program functions through remote procedure calls

   C. Developing customer loyalty through improved technology

   D. Employing Java through the Web

4. SFTP differs from FTP because it uses…

   A. SMTP

   B. SMNP

   C. SSH

   D. SSL

5. Who establishes security for JavaScript?

   A. The developer at the time of code development

   B. The user at the time of code usage

   C. The user through browser preferences

   D. Security for JavaScript is not necessary—the Java language is secure by design

6. ActiveX is used for which of the following purposes?

   A. To add functionality to a browser through scripting

   B. To update the operating system files on a client

   C. To run client-side scripts

   D. To run server-side scripts

7. Which of the following is a weakness of CGI implementations?

   A. It offers almost unlimited operating system access and functionality.

   B. It is limited to Windows operating systems only.

C. It is difficult to program in.

D. It is limited to the UNIX platform.

8. The keyword **[secure]** in a cookie…

    A. Causes the system to encrypt its contents

    B. Prevents it from passing over HTTP connections

    C. Tells the browser that the cookie is a security upgrade

    D. Is a Microsoft proprietary enhancement for security

9. A primary purpose of code signing is to…

    A. Allow authors to take credit for their hard work

    B. Provide a method to demonstrate code integrity

    C. Guarantee code functionality

    D. Enforce digital rights management through copy prevention

10. SSL provides which of the following functionalities?

    A. Data guarantee services

    B. User Authentication and confidentiality services

    C. Data streamlining services

    D. Anonymity for users and data

11. SSL uses which port to carry HTTPS traffic?

    A. TCP port 80

    B. UDP port 443

    C. TCP port 443

    D. TCP port 8080

12. SSL protocol is vulnerable to avoidance at what level of the OSI model?

    A. Application layer, level 7

    B. Session layer, level 5

    C. Network layer, level 3

    D. Transport layer, level 4

13. What must you do to establish an SSL connection for e-mail and HTTP across a firewall?

    A. Open specific TCP ports only

    B. Open specific TCP or UDP ports

    C. Open a TCP port of choice and assign it to all SSL traffic

    D. Do nothing; SSL tunnels past firewalls

14. LDAP directories are characterized by...

    A. Read-only data

    B. Attribute type data

    C. More functionality than a simple database

    D. A better security model than a database

15. What must a user do to prevent the use of cookies in a browser?

    A. Tell the browser to disable cookies via a setup option

    B. Disable cookies and delete all existing cookies on a client

    C. Disable cookies, delete existing cookies, and use only Netscape browsers

    D. The user need do nothing—by design, cookies are necessary and cannot be totally disabled

Essay Quiz

1. You are the security analyst for a company that is moving to Web Services as a method of distributed application deployment. Your boss has asked you to write a white paper covering the security issues associated with this new strategy. Be sure to include any existing security issues that may manifest themselves when this new strategy is implemented.

2. Your web site is completely encrypted using SSL. How does this enhance security? What will it *not* protect against?

3. What are cookies used for on a web site, and what problem do they specifically address? If your firm decides to go "cookieless," what are the implications for your ecommerce site?

4. What is code signing, and how does it enhance security?

5. Your boss has announced an initiative to change all the web pages to Java to enhance the security of the site. Explain the limitations of this decision with respect to your company's security goal.

Lab Projects

Lab Project 17.1
Connect to a SSL enabled web site and demonstrate that the security is session/application specific. How would you do this? (Hint: Use two browser instances and show that the security association from one instance does not extend to the other.)

Lab Project 17.2
Explore a site such as yahoo.com with cookies enabled and then again with cookies disabled. How does this affect functionality and the user experience? (Hint: Try logging into a my.yahoo.com account (you can create them for free).

Software Development

Upon completion of this chapter, you will be able to:

- Describe how security can be incorporated into the software development process
- List types of coding errors and their root cause
- Describe good software development practices and explain how they impact application security
- Describe how using a software development process enforces security inclusion in a project

Software engineering is the systematic development of software created to fill a variety of functions. Business, recreational, scientific, and educational uses are just a few things where software comes in handy. Regardless of the type of software, there is a universal requirement that the software works properly, performs the desired functions, and does so in the correct fashion. Its functionality ranges from spreadsheets that accurately add figures to pacemakers that stimulate the heart. Developers know that functional specifications must be met for the software to be satisfactory. Software engineering, then, fits as many requirements as possible into the project management schedule timeline. But with analysts and developers working overtime to get as many functional elements as they can correct, the issue of nonfunctional requirements often gets pushed to the back burner, or neglected entirely.

Security has been described as a nonfunctional requirement. This places it into a category of secondary importance for many people. If timelines, schedules, and budgets are all in the green, then maybe there will be time to devote to security programming. With computing becoming ubiquitous and our daily lives now supported by a wide assortment of computer programs, this viewpoint must change. Getting security right in a program is essential if we are going to rely on computing in our lives. Trust is built upon an expectation that the software will work, and keep working, meeting our needs and not changing its behavior or functionality because of outside influence. People do not get vaccinated to improve their health, they do so to prevent a downturn in their current well-being due to outside influence. As we depend more and more on computers driven by software, we will need systems to do the same—to not only function now, but be protected from malfunction in the future.

The Software Engineering Process

Software does not build itself. This is good news to software designers, analysts, programmers, and the like, for the complexity of designing and building software enables them to take on well-paying careers. To achieve continued success in this difficult work environment, software engineering processes have been developed. Rather than just sitting down and starting to write code at the onset of a project, a complete development process is used. There are several major categories of software engineering processes. The waterfall model, the spiral model, and the evolutionary model are major examples. Within each of these major categories, there are numerous variations, and each group then personalizes the process to their project requirements and team capabilities.

Traditionally, security is an add-on item that is incorporated into a system after the functional requirements have been met. It is not an integral part of the software development lifecycle process. This places it at odds with both functional and lifecycle process requirements. The resolution to all of these issues is relatively simple: incorporate security into the process model and build it into the product along with each functional requirement. The challenge is in how to accomplish this goal. There are two separate and required elements needed to achieve this objective. First, the inclusion of security requirements and measures into the specific process model being used. Second, the use of secure coding methods to prevent opportunities for security failures from being introduced into the software's design.

Process Models

There are several major software engineering process models, each with slightly different steps and sequences, yet they all have many similar items. The **waterfall** software engineering process model is characterized by a multistep process where steps follow each other in a linear, one-way fashion, like water over a waterfall. The **spiral model** has steps in phases that execute in a spiral fashion, repeating at different levels with each revolution of the model. The details of these process models are outside the scope of this book, and most of the detail is not significantly relevant to the issue of security. From requirements to system architecture to coding to testing, security is an imbedded property in all aspects of the process. There are several specific items of significance with respect to security. Four primary items are of interest, regardless of the particular model or methodology employed in software creation. Requirements should define the specific security requirements if there is any expectation of them being designed into the project. Regardless of the methodology employed, the process is all about completing the requirements.

System architecture acts to design a system that will meet the requirements that come forward from the requirements process. The division of the overall requirements of the software into systems and subsystems also acts to map the requirements to the systems and subsystems. The coding process for each component can have a significant impact on the security response of a system. The testing phase of the project is an opportunity to determine compliance with requirements and even discover unexpected behaviors that result in security issues. All of these opportunities exist regardless of the specific process model used. The key is to include security requirements in the requirements process, and security awareness during architectural design, coding, and testing.

The requirements process is a key component of security in software development. Security-related items enumerated during the requirements process are visible throughout the rest of the software development process. They can be architected into the systems and subsystems, addressed during coding and tested. For the subsequent steps to be effective, the security requirements need to be both specific and positive. Requirements such as "make secure code" or "no insecure code" are nonspecific and not helpful in the overall process. Specific requirements such as "prevent unhandled buffer overflows, or unhandled input exceptions" can be specifically coded for in each piece of code.

ROI and Error Correction

Developing a strong set of security requirements has a secondary result in the overall process: improved total cost of development. Correcting errors results in additional work and expense. The level of rework and extent of extra work are direct functions of how late in the development process the errors are detected. Errors that are not found until after development is complete are the most expensive. These errors require rework at several steps, including even design. Then there is coding rework, testing rework, and a new deployment cycle if the code is deployed. Compare the level of rework to an error discovered in the requirements or architecting process. Significantly less rework is required, and hence significantly lower expense in the rework process.

Developing a software engineering process should detect errors as early on in the process as possible. This detection implies a level of testing that is distributed throughout the development process. Also implied is that this distributed testing is guided by specific requirements that test each step of the development process. For security-related errors, these requirements, as you'd expect, focus on security. From a cost point of view, it doesn't matter the source or classification of an error, the cost to rework it is the measure. If the business objective is to lower total development cost, reducing errors through better requirements and the early detection and correction of remaining errors is what drives the cost reduction.

Secure Code Techniques

The point of implementation of designs is the coding step in the software development process. The act of instantiating an idea into code is a point where an error can enter the process. These errors are of two types: the failure to include desired functionality, and the inclusion of undesired behavior in the code. Testing for the first type of error is relatively easy if the requirements are enumerated in a previous phase of the process.

Testing for the inclusion of undesired behavior is significantly more difficult. Testing for an *unknown* unknown is a virtually impossible task. What makes this possible at all is the concept of testing for categories of previously determined errors. Several classes of common errors have been observed. The commonest of these is a type of error known as a buffer overflow. Other common types are code injections, privilege errors, and cryptographic failures.

Buffer Overflows

If there's one item that could labeled as the "Most Wanted" in coding security, it would be the **buffer overflow**. The CERT/CC at Carnegie Mellon University estimates that nearly half of all exploits of computer programs stem from some form of buffer overflow.

Finding a vaccine to buffer overflows would stamp out half of the security-related incidents, by type, and probably 90 percent by volume. The Morris finger worm in 1988 was an exploit of an overflow, as were recent big name events such as Code Red and Slammer. The generic classification of buffer overflows includes a wide variety of variants like static buffer overruns, indexing errors, format string bugs, Unicode and ANSI buffer size mismatches, and heap overruns.

The concept behind these vulnerabilities is relatively simple. The input buffer that is used to hold program input is overwritten with data that is larger than the buffer can hold. The root cause of this vulnerability is a mixture of two things: poor programming practice and programming language weaknesses. Programming languages such as C were designed for space and performance constraints. Many functions in C, like gets(), are unsafe in that they will permit unsafe operations, such as unbounded string manipulation into fixed buffer locations. The C language also permits direct memory access via pointers, a functionality that provides a lot of programming power, but carries with it the burden of proper safeguards being provided by the programmer.

The first line of defense is to write solid code. Regardless of the language used, or the source of outside input, prudent programming practice is to treat all input from outside a function as hostile. Validate all inputs as if they were hostile and an attempt to force a buffer overflow. Accept the notion that although during development, everyone may be on the same team, be conscientious and compliant with design rules, future maintainers may not be as robust. Designing prevention into functions is a foundational defense against this type of vulnerability.

A second, and equally important, line of defense is proper string handling. String handling is a common event in programs, and string-handling functions are the source of a large number of known buffer overflow vulnerabilities. Using strncpy() in place of strcpy() is a simple method of improving security. The function strncpy() requires an input length for the number of characters to be copied. Further validation before passing values to string functions, although they entail a performance penalty, can prevent buffer overrun problems. Proper use of functions to achieve program objectives is essential to prevent unintended effects such as buffer overflows. Use of the gets() function can probably never be totally safe since it reads from the *stdin* stream until a linefeed or carriage return. In most cases, there is no way to predetermine whether the input is going to overflow the buffer. A better solution is to use a C++ stream object or the fgets() function. The function fgets() requires an input buffer length, and hence avoids the overflow. Simply replace

```
{
    char buf[512];
    gets( buf );
    /* ... The rest of your code ... */
}
```

with

```
{
    char buf[512];
    fgets( buf, sizeof(buf), stdin );
    /*  ... the rest of your code ... */
}
```

Code Injection

Use of input to a function without validation has already been shown to be risky behavior. Another issue with unvalidated input is the case of **code injection**. Rather than the input being appropriate for the function, this code injection changes the function in an unintended way. A SQL injection attack is a form of code injection aimed at SQL databases. An example of this type of attack is where the function takes the user-provided inputs for username and password and substitutes them into a where clause of a SQL statement with the expressed purpose of changing the where clause into one that gives a false answer to the query.

Assume the desired SQL statement is

```
select count(*) from users_table where username = 'JDoe' and password = 'newpass'
```

The values JDoe and newpass are provided from the user and simply inserted into the string sequence. Though seemingly safe functionally, this can be easily corrupted by using the sequence

```
' or 1=1 --
```

since this changes the where clause to one that returns all records:

```
select count(*) from users_table where username = 'JDoe' and password = '' or 1=1 --'
```

The addition of the or clause, with an always true statement and the beginning of a comment line to block the trailing single quote alters the SQL statement to one in which the where clause is rendered inoperable.

The primary method of defense from this type of vulnerability is similar to that for buffer overflows: validate all inputs. But rather than validating towards just length, they need to be validated for content. Imagine a web page that asks for user input, and then uses that input in the building of a subsequent page. Now imagine that the user puts the text for a JavaScript function in the middle of their input sequence, along with a call to the script. Now, the generated web page has an added JavaScript that is called when displayed. Passing the user input through an HTML encode function before use can prevent such attacks.

Again, good programming practice goes a long way to prevent these types of vulnerabilities. This places the burden not just on the programmers, but on the process of training programmers, the software engineering process that reviews code and the testing process to catch programming errors. This is much more than a single person responsibility item, the software development process needs to be aware of the types and causes of these errors and have safeguards in place to prevent their propagation.

Least Privilege

One of the central paradigms of security is the notion of running a process with the least required privilege. **Least privilege** requires that the developer understand what privileges are required specifically for an application to execute and access all its required resources. Obviously, from a developer point of view, it would be easier to use administrative level permission for all tasks, for this is removing access controls from the equation, but this also removes the very protections that access level controls are designed to perform. The other end of the spectrum is software designed for operating systems without any built-in security, such as early versions of Windows and some mainframe OSs, where security comes in the form of an application package. When migrating these applications to platforms, the issue of access controls becomes an issue.

As developers move from developing where there is no security to an operating system with built-in security, the natural tendency is to code around this "new" security requirement, developing in the same fashion as before. This is commonly manifested as a program that runs only under an administrative level account, or runs as a service utilizing the SYSTEM account for permissions in Windows. Both of these practices are bad practices that reduce security, introduce hard to fix errors, and produce code that is harder to maintain and extend.

The key principle in designing and coding software with respect to access level controls is to plan and understand the nature of the software's interaction with the operating system and system resources. Whenever the software accesses a file, a system component, or another program, the issue of appropriate access control needs to be addressed. And although the simple issue of just giving everything root or administrative access may solve this immediate problem, it creates much bigger security issues that will be much less apparent in the future. An example is when a program runs correctly when initiated from an administrator account, but fails when run under normal user privileges. The actual failure may stem from a privilege issue, but the actual point of failure in the code may be many procedures away, and diagnosing these types of failures is a difficult and time-consuming operation.

The bottom line is actually simple. Determine what needs to be accessed and what the appropriate level of permission is, then use that level in design and implementation. Repeat this for every item accessed. In the end, it is rare that administrative access is needed for many functions. Once the application is designed, the whole process will need to be repeated with the installation procedure, because frequently, installing software will need a higher level of access than needed for executing the software. Design and implementation details must be determined with respect to required permission levels, not to a higher level such as administrative root access just for convenience.

The cost of failure to heed this can be two fold. First, you have expensive, time-consuming access violation errors that are hard to track down and correct. The second problem is when an exploit is found that allows some other program to use portions of your code in an unauthorized fashion. A prime example is the Sendmail exploit in the UNIX environment. Because Sendmail requires root level access for some functions, this exploit inserts foreign code into the process stream, thereupon executing its code at root level access because the Sendmail process thread itself has root level access. In this case, Sendmail needs the root level access, but this illustrates that the risk is real and will be exploited once found. Proper design can, in many cases, eliminate the need for such high access privilege levels.

Cryptographic Failures

Hailed as a solution for all problems, cryptography has as much chance of being the ultimate cure-all as the tonics sold by traveling salesman of a different era. There is no such thing as a universal solution, yet there are some very versatile tools that provide a wide range of protections. Cryptography falls into this very useful tool category. Proper use of cryptography can provide a wealth of programmatic functionality, from authentication to confidentiality, to integrity and non-repudiation. These are valuable tools and many programs rely on proper cryptographic function for important functionality. The need for this functionality in an application tempts programmers to roll their own cryptographic functions. This is a task fraught with opportunity for catastrophic error.

Cryptographic errors come from several common causes. One typical mistake is choosing to develop your own cryptographic algorithm. Development of a secure cryptographic algorithm is far from an easy task, and even when done by experts, weaknesses can occur that make them unusable. Cryptographic algorithms become trusted after years of scrutiny and attacks, and any new algorithms would take years to join the trusted set. If you instead decide to rest on secrecy, be warned that secret or proprietary algorithms have never provided the desired level of protection. One of the axioms of cryptography is that there is no security through obscurity.

Deciding to use a trusted algorithm is a proper start, but there still are several major errors that can occur. The first is an error in instantiating the algorithm. An easy way to avoid this type of error is to use a library function that has already been properly tested. Many sources of these library functions abound, and provide an economical solution to this functionality's needs. Once you have an algorithm, and have chosen a particular instantiation, the next item needed is the random number to generate a random key. Cryptographic functions use an algorithm and a key, the latter being a digital number.

The generation of a real random number is not a trivial task. Computers are machines that are renowned for reproducing the same output when given the same input, so generating a pure, non-reproducible random number is a challenge. There are random functions built into the libraries of most programming languages, but these are pseudorandom number generators, and although the distribution of output numbers appears random, it generates a reproducible sequence. Given the same input, a second run of the function will produce the same sequence of "random" numbers. Determining the seed and random sequence and using this knowledge to "break" a cryptographic function has been used more than once to bypass the security. This method was used to subvert an early version of Netscape's SSL implementation. Using a **cryptographically random** number generator resolves this problem, and again the use of trusted library functions designed and tested for this purpose is the proper methodology.

Now you've got a good algorithm and a good random number—so where can you go wrong? Well, storing private keys in areas where they can be recovered by an unauthorized person is the next worry. Poor key management has failed many a cryptographic implementation. A famous exploit of getting cryptographic keys from an executable and using them to break a cryptographic scheme is the case of hackers using this exploit to break DVD encryption and develop the DeCSS program. Tools have been developed that can search code for "random" keys and extract the key from the code or running process. A British firm, nCipher, has a variety of white papers detailing this type of attack on their web site, www.ncipher.com. The bottom line is simple: Do not hard-code secret keys in your code. They can, and will, be discovered. Keys should be generated, and then passed by reference, minimizing the travel of copies across a network or application. Storing them in memory in a non-contiguous fashion is also important to prevent external detection. Again, trusted cryptographic library functions come to the rescue.

You might have deduced by this point that the term "library function" has become synonymous with this section. This is not an accident. In fact, this is probably one of the best pieces of advice from this chapter: use commercially proven functions for cryptographic functionality.

Additional Failure Modes

What goes by a large name, *canonical representation issues,* is a simple concept: beware of names. Making a security decision based on the name of a resource, be it a file name or a URL, is a dangerous proposition. For a variety of reasons, there can be more than one way to represent the name of an object. A rose may always be a rose, but the same can be said of r%6fse, where one or more characters of the flower's name are represented by hexadecimal escape code representations. Canonicalization is the conversion of a name to its simplest form. Program errors from **canonicalization errors** can result in unexpected behaviors. Examples of this vulnerability include the IIS ::$DATA error, and a host of Unicode exploits to bypass checking based on URLs. The best method to avoid these errors is to not trust filenames when making decisions, and if you must use a filename, then run the resource through a canonicalization routine first.

Sometimes the failure mode is not to cause a program to operate differently, but to tie it up so that, even though it is running, it is not functioning. This is called a Denial-of-Service attack. Denial-of-Service attacks come in many types and each has its own mode of operation, but common to all is the desire to shut down the functionality of the program, and in some cases the entire server. Defending against Denial-of-Service attacks is complex, as it requires you to determine how the code is vulnerable and what safeguards will prevent the code from running forever. One major rule that will help is, again, don't trust input—validate all input before use in a module.

Good Practices

Good practices are common to many of the issues described earlier and it is best to focus on technical specifics, things directly related to coding or logic errors. Even then, an entire realm of opportunity exists in the software development process. Using a software development process that has security functionality built into the process will make a large difference in the end result. The process begins with requirements, and for functionality changes, ends with testing. Enumerating and defining the specific security requirements and how they are tested is a key element in building security into code.

Requirements

As mentioned before, security requirements are often the last ones included in a specific project, and then only as time and budget allow once the "business" functionality is completed. Turning this process upside down and having a default set of security requirements associated with all projects, and enumerating and defining them once (and in advance) greatly assists the development team in their quest to provide the largest amount of user-specified functionality within given time and budget constraints. Putting the security requirements first in an overhead role and having the corporate backing to maintain an acceptable level of security functionality as a baseline solves many of the problems.

Making system requirements such as "Never trust input" to a function, and "validate all buffer lengths" can be built into a template for all modules that are developed. Establishing a "code review" requirement, where a second programmer, or even a group of eyes, is walked through the functionality of code before it's released to testing can catch many errors. This is commonly referred to as a code walkthrough and is a very effective means of early error detection. This type of process addition, although it seems like management overhead, can make a tremendous difference in code quality. The closer this type of work is done to initial code generation, the lower will be the cost to correct any discovered errors. The **requirements phase** is the first step in a software development process model where the details for all end-product requirements are documented. Since it occurs at the beginning of the model, this ensures all future steps are aware of the specific requirements.

Testing

If requirements mark the beginning of the generation of security in code, then testing marks the other boundary. Although there are additional functions after testing, no one wants a user to validate errors in code. And errors discovered after the code has shipped are the most expensive to fix, regardless of the severity. Employing **use cases** to compare program responses to known inputs and then comparing the output to the desired output is a proven method of testing software. The design of use cases to test-specific functional requirements occurs based on the requirements determined in the requirements phase. Providing additional security-related use cases is the process-driven way of ensuring that security specifics are also tested.

The **testing phase** is the last opportunity to determine that the software performs properly before the end user experiences problems. Errors found in testing are late in the development process, but at least they are still learned about internally, before the end customer suffers. Testing can occur at each level of development: module, subsystem, system, and completed application. The sooner errors are discovered and corrected, the lower the cost and the less the impact will be to project schedules. This makes testing an essential step in the process of developing good programs.

Chapter Review

Chapter Summary

After reading this chapter and completing the exercises, you should understand the following about security issues related to software development.

The Software Engineering Process

- The requirements phase is the most important part of the software engineering process since it outlines the project's future requirements, thus defining its scope and limitations.

- Security is built into the software by including security concerns and reviews throughout the software development process.
- Regardless of the specific software engineering process model used, security can be included in the normal process by being input as requirements.

Good Practices

- The commonest coding error is buffer overflow conditions.
- Code injection errors can result in undesired code execution as defined by the end user.
- Input validation is the best method of ensuring against buffer overflows and code injection type errors.
- Early testing helps resolve errors at an earlier stage and results in cleaner code.
- Security-related use-cases can be used to test for specific security requirements.

Key Terms

Buffer overflow *(478)*
Canonicalization error *(476)*
Code injection *(473)*
Cryptographically random *(475)*
Least privilege *(473)*
Requirements phase *(477)*
Spiral model *(470)*
Testing phase *(477)*
Use case *(477)*
Waterfall model *(470)*

Key Terms Quiz

Use terms from the Key Terms list to complete the sentences that follow. Don't use the same term more than once. Not all terms will be used.

1. The _____ is a linear software engineering model with no repeating steps.

2. _____ cause an application to malfunction due to a misrepresented name for a resource.

3. An index overrun is an example of a _____.

4. A series of repeating cycles ever increasing in developing functionality describes the _____.

5. Replacing a SQL statement through false input to a function is an example of _____.

6. Using an administrator level account for all functions is a violation of the principle of _____.

7. The _____ is the first opportunity to address security functionality during a project.

8. The _____ is the last opportunity to address security functionality before shipping a product.

9. A _____ is a defined set of validated inputs and outputs used to test a module for correct functionality.

10. A random number suitable for an encryption function is called _____.

Multiple-Choice Quiz

1. Which of the following is not related to a buffer overflow?

   A. Static buffer overflow

   B. Index error

   C. Canonicalization error

   D. heap overflow

2. Which of the following is not involved with a code injection error?

   A. SQL statement building

   B. Input validation

   C. JavaScript

   D. A pointer in the C language

3. Input validation is important to prevent…

   A. Buffer overflow

   B. Index sequence error

   C. Operator overload error

   D. Unhandled exception

4. The term waterfall is associated with which of the following?

   A. Buffer overflow

   B. A software engineering process model

   C. Canonicalization error

   D. Code injection

5. It's most important to define security requirements during…

   A. Testing

   B. Use case development

    C. Code walkthroughs

    D. The requirements phase of the project

6. The largest class of errors in software engineering can be attributed to...

    A. Code injection

    B. Privilege violations

    C. Buffer overflows

    D. Canonicalization errors

7. The Morris worm exploited...

    A. A buffer overflow in Windows

    B. A buffer overflow in UNIX

    C. A code injection in both Windows and UNIX

    D. A canonicalization error in UNIX

8. Least privilege applies to...

    A. Only the application code

    B. Only to calls to operating system objects

    C. All resource requests from applications to other entities

    D. Applications under named user accounts

9. Common cryptographic failures include which of the following?

    A. Use of cryptographic random numbers

    B. Cryptographic sequence failures

    C. Poor encryption protocols

    D. Canonicalization errors

10. A cryptographically random number sequence is characterized by...

    A. Large value changes between successive numbers

    B. Normal probability distribution

    C. Intersequence randomness

    D. Pseudo

11. Testing is best accomplished...

    A. After all code is finished

    B. As early as possible in the process

    C. Using cryptographically random elements

    D. Using third-party testing software

12. Security requirements are best defined in...

    A. The requirements phase

B. The coding phase

C. The testing phase

D. During architectural review of the system

13. Code review by a second party is helpful to...

    A. Increase creativity of the junior programmer

    B. Cost—making for a better, cheaper method of testing

    C. Catch errors early in the programming process

    D. Ensure all modules work together

14. Virus and worm propagation can be achieved through exploiting...

    A. Buffer overflows

    B. Cryptographic random number failures

    C. The HTMLencode function

    D. Recursive functions

15. One of the most fundamental rules to good coding practice is...

    A. Code once, test twice

    B. Validate all inputs

    C. Don't use pointers

    D. Use obscure coding practices so viruses cannot live in the code

Essay Quiz

1. Describe the relationship of the requirements phase, testing phase, and use cases with respect to software engineering development and secure code.

2. Develop a list of five security-related issues to be put into a requirements document as part of a secure coding initiative.

3. Choose two requirements from the previous question and describe use cases that would validate them in the testing phase.

4. As the new programmer in a small firm that uses the C language, you have been asked to bring some security lessons learned from your university to the department's brown bag session. You choose to speak on buffer overflows. Explain how to detect buffer overflow errors and how to eliminate common sources for the errors from your coding practices.

5. You have been asked by your manager to develop a worksheet for code walkthroughs. This worksheet should include a list of common errors to look for during the examination, acting as a memory aid. You want to leave a lasting impression on the team as a new college grad. Outline what you would include on the worksheet related to security.

Lab Projects

Lab Project 18.1

Learn the specific software engineering process model used at a local firm (or you may be able to research a company online or find one in a software engineering textbook at a library). Examine where security is built in, or could be built into, the model. Provide an overview of the strengths and opportunities of the model with respect to designing secure code.

Lab Project 18.2

Develop an example of a SQL injection statement for a web page inquiry. List the web page inputs, what the projected backend SQL is, and how it can be changed.

CHAPTER 19

Disaster Recovery, Business Continuity, and Organizational Policies

Upon completion of this chapter, you will be able to:

- Describe the various ways backups are conducted and stored
- Explain different strategies for alternative site processing
- Describe the various components of a business continuity plan
- Explain how policies and procedures play a daily role in addressing the security needs of an organization

Much of this book focuses on avoiding the loss of confidentiality or integrity due to a security breach. The issue of availability is also discussed in terms of specific events, such as denial of service and distributed denial of service attacks. In reality, however, there are many things that can disrupt the operations of your organization. From the standpoint of your clients and employees, it makes little difference whether your organization's web site is unavailable because of a storm or an intruder—the site is still unavailable.

Disaster Recovery

Many types of disasters, whether natural or caused by people, can disrupt your organization's operations for lengthy periods. Such disasters are unlike the previously discussed threats to your computer systems and networks because the events that cause the disruption are not specifically aimed at your organization. Regardless of the source, there are many threats that may disrupt operations, including industrial espionage, hacking, attacks from disgruntled employees, and insider threats, which must all be considered important in planning for disaster recovery. The purpose of this chapter is to point out additional events that may not have been previously considered. How long your organization's operations are disrupted depends in part on how prepared it is for a disaster and what plans are in place to mitigate the effects of a disaster. Any of these events could cause a disruption in operations:

Fire	flood	tornado	hurricane
Electrical storm	earthquake	political unrest/riot	blizzard
gas leak/explosion	chemical spill	terrorism	war

Fortunately, these types of events do not happen too often. It is more likely that business operations will be interrupted due to employee error (such as accidental corruption of a database, or unplugging a system in order to plug in a vacuum cleaner—an event that has actually occurred to more than one organization). A good disaster recovery plan will prepare your organization for any type of organizational disruption.

Disaster Recovery Plans/Process

No matter what the event is that you are worried about—whether natural or not, targeted at your organization or not—there are certain preparations you can make to lessen the impact on your organization and the length of time that your organization will be out of operation. A **disaster recovery plan (DRP)** is critical for effective disaster recovery efforts. A DRP defines the data and resources necessary and the steps to take in order to restore critical organizational processes.

Put another way, what is it that is needed by your organization to perform its mission? Answer this question, and you have the beginning of a DRP, since you now know what needs to be quickly restored. When speaking of the resources, don't forget to include both the physical resources (such as computer hardware and software) and the personnel (you need somebody who knows how to run the systems that process your critical data).

A common way to begin creating your DRP is to answer the following questions for all critical functions:

- Who is responsible for the operation of this function?
- What do these individuals need to perform the function?
- When should this function be accomplished in relation to other functions?
- Where will this function be performed?
- How is this function performed (what is the process)?
- Why is this function so important or critical to the organization?

By answering these questions, you can create an initial draft of your organization's DRP. The name often used to describe the document created by addressing these questions is a **business impact assessment (BIA)**, or business impact analysis. This DRP, of course, will need to be approved by management, and it is essential that they buy into the plan—otherwise, your efforts will more than likely fail. That old adage, "those who fail to plan, plan to fail" certainly applies in this situation.

It is important in a good DRP to include the processes and procedures needed to restore your organization so that it is functioning again and to ensure continued operation. What specific steps will be required to restore operations? These processes should be documented and, where possible and feasible, they should be reviewed and exercised on a periodic basis. Having a plan with step-by-step procedures that nobody knows how to follow does nothing to ensure the continued operation of the organization. Exercising your disaster recovery plans and processes before a disaster occurs provides you with the opportunity to discover flaws or weaknesses in the plan when there is still time to modify and correct them.

Categories of Business Functions

It may be useful in developing your BIA and DRP to categorize the various functions your organization performs. This categorization is based on how critical or important the function is to your business operation. Those functions that are the most critical will be the ones that you want to restore first, and your DRP should reflect this. One possible categorization scheme might be to divide functions into the following categories:

- **Critical** The function is absolutely essential for operations. Without the function, the basic mission of the organization cannot occur.

- **Necessary for normal processing** The function is required for normal processing, but the organization can live without it for a short period of time (such as for less than 30 days).

- **Desirable** The function is not needed for normal processing but enhances the organization's ability to conduct its mission efficiently.

- **Optional** The function is nice to have but does not affect the operation of the organization.

An important aspect of this categorization scheme is understanding how long the organization can survive without the specific function. Asking yourself "how long can my organization operate without this function" will enable you to correctly place the function in the correct category. If the function is needed immediately, it is *critical*. If you can live without it for at most 30 days before severely impacting your organization, it falls into the *necessary for normal processing* category. If you can live without the function for more than 30 days, but it is a function that will eventually need to be accomplished when normal operations are restored, it falls into the *desirable* category (this implies some subsequent catch-up processing will need to be accomplished). If the function is not needed, and no subsequent processing will be required to restore this function, it falls into the *optional* category. If the function doesn't fall into any of these categories because it doesn't really affect the operation of your organization, it falls into a category not mentioned yet—*get rid of it*. You may want to consider eliminating this function, since it may not really be providing any useful purpose.

Business Continuity Plans

Another term that is often used when discussing the issue of continued organizational operations is **business continuity plan (BCP)**. You might wonder what the difference is between a DRP and a BCP—after all, isn't the purpose of the DRP the continued operation of the organization or business? In reality, these two terms are sometimes used synonymously, and for many organizations there may be no major difference in the two. There are, however, differences between a BCP and a DRP, one of which is the focus.

The focus of business continuity planning is the continued operation of the business or organization. The focus of a disaster recovery plan is also on continued operation, but that is in the face of a disaster. In a DRP, the protection of human life should be addressed and is a major focus of the document. Evacuation plans and system shutdown procedures should be addressed. The safety of employees should be a theme throughout a DRP. In a BCP, on the other hand, you may not see the same level of emphasis placed on protection of employees. In a BCP, you will often see a more significant emphasis placed on the critical systems the organization needs to operate. The BCP will describe the functions that are most critical, based on a previously conducted BIA, and will often describe the order in which functions should be returned to operation. In this situation, the two documents can be considered companion documents.

The difference between a DRP and BCP can be illustrated by imagining a disaster hitting an organization. The organization quickly assesses the situation and the amount of damage sustained. If systems can be restored within a maximum tolerable downtime, the DRP is executed. If not, both the DRP and BCP are executed. In cases where there are two separate plans, the DRP may be executed first, to ensure the safety of personnel, then the BCP is employed to bring operations back up in the appropriate order.

However you view these two plans, an organization that is not able to quickly restore business functions after an operational interruption is an organization that will most likely suffer an unrecoverable loss and may cease to exist.

Backups

A key element in any BCP or DRP is backups. This is true not only because of the possibility of a disaster but also because hardware and storage media will periodically fail, resulting in loss or corruption of critical data. Data backup is thus a critical element in DRPs and BCPs, as well as in normal operation. There are several factors to consider in an organization's data backup strategy:

- How frequently should backups be conducted?
- How extensive do the backups need to be?
- What is the process for conducting backups?
- Who is responsible for ensuring backups are created?
- Where will the backups be stored?
- How long will backups be kept?
- How many copies will be maintained?

Keep in mind that the purpose of a backup is to provide valid, uncorrupted data in the event of corruption or loss of the original file or the media where the data was stored. Depending on the type of organization you are part of, there may be legal requirements for conducting backups that will affect the factors mentioned previously.

What Needs to Be Backed Up

Backups are commonly thought of in terms of the data that an organization relies on to conduct its daily operations. While this is certainly true, a good backup plan will consider more than just the data; it will include any application programs needed to process the data, and the operating system and utilities that the hardware platform requires to run the applications. Obviously the application programs and operating system will change much less frequently than the data itself, so the frequency with which these items need to be backed up is considerably different. This should be reflected in the organization's backup plan and strategy.

The DRP should also address other items related to backups. Personnel, equipment, and electrical power must also be part of the plan. Somebody needs to have an understanding of the operation of the critical hardware and software used by the organization. If the disaster that destroyed the original copy of the data and the original systems also results in the loss of the only personnel that know how to process the data, having backup data will not be enough to restore normal operations for the organization. Similarly, if the data requires specific software to be run on a very specific hardware platform, then having the data without the application program or required hardware will also not be sufficient. As you can see, a DRP or BCP is an involved document that must consider many different factors and take into account many different possibilities.

Strategies for Backups

The process for actually creating a backup copy of data and software requires more thought than simply stating "copy all required files." The size of the resulting backup must be considered, as well as the time required to conduct the backup. Both of these will affect details such as how frequently the backup will occur and the type of storage media that will be used for the backup. Other considerations for backup strategies include who will be responsible for conducting the backup, where the backups will be stored, and how long they should be maintained. Short-term storage for those occasional accidentally deleted files that users need to have restored should probably be close at hand. Longer-term storage for backups that may be several months or even years old should occur in a different facility. It should be evident by now that even something that sounds as simple as maintaining backup copies of essential data requires careful consideration and planning.

Types of Backups   The amount of data that will be backed up, and the time it takes to accomplish this, has a direct bearing on the type of backup that will be performed. There are four basic types of backups that can be conducted, and the amount of space required for each, and the ease of restoration using each strategy, is outlined in Table 19-1.

The values for each of the strategies in the table are highly variable depending on your specific environment. The more files are changed between backups the more these strategies will look alike. What each strategy entails bears further explanation.

The easiest type of backup to understand is the **full backup**. In a full backup, all files and software are copied onto the storage media. Restoration from a full backup is similarly straightforward—you must copy all of the files back onto the system. While this is easy to understand, it may take a considerable amount of time. Consider the size of even the average home PC today, where storage is measured in tens and hundreds of gigabytes. Copying this amount of data takes time.

	Full	Differential	Incremental	Delta
Amount of Space	Large	Medium	Medium	Small
Restoration	Simple	Simple	Involved	Complex

Table 19-1   Characteristics of Different Backup Types

In a **differential backup**, only the files and software that have changed since the last full backup was completed need to be stored. This also implies that periodically a full backup needs to be accomplished. The frequency of the full backup versus the interim differential backups depends on your organization and is part of your defined strategy. Restoration from a differential backup requires two steps: the last full backup first needs to be loaded, and then the differential backup can be applied to update the files that have been changed since the full backup was conducted. Again, this is not a difficult process, but it does take some time. The amount of time to accomplish the actual periodic differential backup, however, is much less than a full backup, and this is one of the advantages of this method. Obviously, if the period of time between differential backups is long, or if your environment results in most files changing frequently, then the differential backup does not differ much from a full backup. It should also be obvious that in order to accomplish the differential backup, the system has to have a method to determine which files have been changed since some given point in time.

With **incremental backups**, even less information will be stored in each backup. The incremental backup is a variation on a differential backup, except that instead of copying all files that have changed since the last full backup, the incremental backup will only copy files that have changed since the last full or incremental backup occurred. Just as in the case of the differential backup, the incremental backup relies on the occasional full backup being accomplished. After that, you only back up files that have changed since the last backup of any sort was conducted. To restore a system using this type of backup method requires quite a bit more work. You first need to go back to the last full backup and reload the system with this data. Then you have to update the system with every incremental backup that has occurred since then. The advantage of this type of backup is that it requires less storage and time to accomplish. The disadvantage is that the restoration process is more involved. Assuming that you don't frequently have to conduct a complete restoration of your system, however, the incremental type of backup is a very valid technique.

The final type of backup that can be accomplished is the **delta backup**. The goal with the delta backup is to save as little information as possible each time you conduct a backup. As in the other strategies, an occasional full backup must be accomplished. After that, when a delta backup is conducted at specific intervals, only the portions of the files that have been changed will be stored. The advantage of this is easy to illustrate. If your organization maintains a large database with thousands of records that is several hundred megabytes in size, the entire database would be copied in the previous backup types even if only one record is changed. For a delta backup, only the actual record that changed would be stored. The disadvantage of this method should also be readily apparent—restoration is a complex process since it requires more than just loading a file (or several files). It requires application software be run to update the records in the files that have been changed.

There are advantages and disadvantages to each of the backup types described. Which type is best for your organization depends on a number of things, including the amount of data you routinely process and store, how frequently it changes, how often you expect to have to restore from a backup, and a number of other factors. The type you select, however, will greatly affect your overall backup strategy, plans, and processes.

Backup Frequency and Retention   What type of backup strategy an organization employs is often affected by how frequently the organization conducts the backup activity. The usefulness of a backup is directly related to how many changes have occurred since the backup was created, and this is obviously affected by how often backups are created. The longer it has been since the backup was created, the more changes will likely have occurred. There is no easy answer, however, to how frequently an organization should perform backups. Every organization should consider how long it can survive without current data from which to operate. It can then determine how long it will take to restore from backups, using various methods, and decide how frequently backups need to occur. This sounds simple, but it is actually a serious, complex decision to make.

Related to the frequency question is the issue of how long backups should be maintained. Is it sufficient to simply maintain a single backup from which to restore data? Security professionals will tell you the answer to this is easy—"no." Multiple backups should be maintained for a variety of reasons. If the reason for restoring from the backup is the discovery of an intruder in the system, it is important to restore the system to its pre-intrusion state. If the intruder has been in the system for several months before being discovered, and backups are taken weekly, it will not be possible to restore to a pre-intrusion state if only one backup is maintained. This would mean that all data and system files would be suspect and may not be reliable. If multiple backups were maintained at various intervals, then it is easier to return to a point before the intrusion (or before the security or operational event that is necessitating the restoration) occurred.

There are several strategies or approaches to backup retention. One common and easy to remember one is the "rule of three." This entails simply keeping the three most recent backups. When a new backup is created, the oldest copy is overwritten. Another strategy is to keep the most recent copy of backups for various time intervals. For example, you might keep the latest daily, weekly, monthly, quarterly, and yearly backups. It should be noted that in certain environments, regulatory issues may prescribe a specific frequency and retention period, so it is important to know your organization and its requirements when determining how often you will create a backup and how long you will keep it for.

If you are not in an environment where regulatory issues dictate the frequency and retention for backups, your goal will be to optimize the frequency. In determining the optimal backup frequency, there are two major costs that need to be considered. The first is the cost of the backup strategy you choose. The second is the cost of recovery if you do not implement this backup strategy (meaning if there were no backups created). Into this equation must also be factored the probability that the backup will be needed on any given day. The two figures to consider are

(probability the backup is needed) × (cost of restoring with no backup)

(probability the backup isn't needed) × (cost of the backup strategy)

The first of these two figures can be considered the probable loss you can expect if your organization has no backup. The second figure can be considered the price you are willing to pay (lose) to ensure that you can restore, should a problem occur (think of this as backup insurance—the cost of an insurance policy that may never be used but that you are willing to pay, just in case).

In order to optimize your backup strategy, you need to determine the correct balance between these two figures. Obviously, you do not want to spend more in your backup strategy than you face losing should you not have a backup plan at all. When working with these two calculations, you have to remember that this is a cost-avoidance exercise. The organization is not going to increase revenues with their backup strategy. All that you are trying to do is minimize the potential loss due to some catastrophic event by creating a backup strategy that will address your organization's needs.

When calculating the cost of the backup strategy, there are several elements that must be taken into consideration. These include:

- The cost of the backup media required for a single backup
- The storage costs for the backup media and the retention policy
- The labor costs associated with performing a single backup
- The frequency with which backups are created

All of these considerations can be used to arrive at an annual cost for implementing your chosen backup strategy, and this figure can then be used as previously described.

Storage of Backups One of the elements to be factored into the cost of the backup strategy is the expense of storing the backups. Backup storage is an important issue to consider. A simple strategy might be to store all of your backups together for quick and easy recovery actions. This is not, however, a good idea. Suppose the catastrophic event that made the restoration of backed-up data necessary was something like a fire that destroyed the computer system the data was processed on. In this case, any backups that were stored in the same facility might also be lost in the same fire.

The solution is to obviously keep copies of backups in separate locations. The most recent copy could be stored locally, as it is the most likely to be needed. Other copies can be kept at other locations. Depending on the level of security desired, the storage facility itself could be reinforced against possible threats in your area (such as tornados or floods). Another more recent advance is online backup services. There are a number of third-party companies that now offer high-speed connections for storing data in a separate facility on a frequent basis. Transmitting the backup data via network connections alleviates some other concerns with physical movement of more traditional storage media—concerns such as the care during transportation (tapes do not fare well in direct sunlight, for example) or the time that it takes to transport the tape data.

Alternate Sites An issue related to the location of backup storage is where the restoration services will be conducted. If the organization has suffered physical damage to a facility, having offsite storage of data is only part of the solution. This data will need to be processed somewhere, which means that computing facilities similar to those used in normal operations must be found. There are a number of ways to approach this problem, including hot sites, warm sites, cold sites, and mobile backup sites.

A **hot site** is a fully configured environment similar to the normal operating environment that can be operational within a few hours. A **warm site** is partially configured, usually having the peripherals and software but perhaps not the more expensive main processing computer. It is designed to be operational within a few days. A **cold site** will have the basic environmental controls necessary to operate but will have few of the computing components necessary for processing. Getting a cold site operational may take weeks. Mobile backup sites are generally trailers with the required computers and electrical power that can be driven to a location within hours of a disaster and set up to commence processing immediately.

All of these options can come with a considerable price tag, which makes another option, **mutual aid agreements**, a possible alternative. With mutual aid agreements, similar organizations agree to assume the processing for the other party in the event a disaster occurs. The obvious assumption here is that both organizations will not be hit by the same disaster and that both have similar processing environments. If these two assumptions are correct, then a mutual aid agreement should be considered. Such an arrangement may not be legally enforceable, even if it is in writing and organizations must consider this when developing their disaster plans. In addition, if the organization that the mutual aid agreement is made with also is hit by the same disaster, then both organizations will be in trouble. Additional contingencies need to be planned for even if a mutual aid agreement is made with another organization.

Issues with Long-Term Storage of Backups Depending on the media used for an organization's backups, degradation of the media is a distinct possibility and needs to be considered. Magnetic media degrade over time (measured in years). In addition, tapes can only be used a limited number of times before the surface begins to flake off.

Another consideration is advances in technology. The media you used to store your data two years ago may now be considered obsolete (5.25-inch floppy drives, for example). Software applications also evolve, and the media may be present but may not be compatible with current versions of the software.

Another issue is security related. If the file you stored was encrypted for security purposes, is there anybody remaining in the company who remembers the password to decrypt the file in order to restore the data?

Utilities

The interruption of power is a common issue during a disaster. Computers and networks obviously require power to operate, so emergency power must be planned for in the event of any disruption of operations. For short-term interruptions, such as what might occur as the result of an electrical storm, uninterruptible power supplies (UPSs) may suffice. These devices contain a battery that provides steady power for short periods of time—enough to keep a system running should power only be lost for a few minutes, or enough to allow administrators to gracefully halt the system or network. For continued operations that extend beyond a few minutes, another source of power will be required. Generally, this is provided by a backup emergency generator.

While backup generators are frequently used to provide power during an emergency, they are not a simple, maintenance-free solution. Generators need to be tested on a regular basis, and they can easily become strained if they are required to power too much equipment. If your organization is going to rely on an emergency generator for backup power, you must ensure that the system has reserve capacity beyond the anticipated load for the unanticipated loads that will undoubtedly be placed on it.

There are a number of other issues with generators. They take time to start up, so power will most likely be lost, even if only for a brief second, while they come on. This means that a UPS should also be used to allow for a smooth transition to backup power. Generators are also expensive and require fuel—when looking for a place to locate your generator, don't forget the need to deliver fuel to it or you may find yourself hauling cans of fuel up a number of stairs.

When determining the need for backup power, don't forget to factor in environmental conditions. Power to computer systems in a room with no air conditioning in the middle of the summer in the Southwest will result in an extremely uncomfortable environment for all to work in. Mobile backup sites, generally utilizing trailers, often rely on generators for their power but also factor in the requirement for environmental controls.

Power is not the only essential utility for operations. The most obvious other one is communications. Depending on the type of disaster that has occurred, telephone and Internet communication may also be lost. Wireless services may also not be available. Planning for redundant means of communication (such as using both land lines and wireless) can help with most outages, but for large disasters, your backup plans should include the option to continue operations from a completely different location while waiting for communications in your area to be restored. Telecommunication carriers have their own emergency equipment and are fairly efficient at restoring communications, but it may take a few days.

Secure Recovery

Several companies offer recovery services, including power, communications, and technical support that may be needed in the event that your organization's operations are disrupted. These companies advertise secure recovery sites or offices from which your organization can again begin to operate in a secure environment. Secure recovery is also advertised by other organizations that provide services that can remotely (over the Internet, for example) provide restoration services for critical files and data.

In both cases—the actual physical suites and the remote service—security is an important element. During a disaster, your data does not become any less important, and you will want to make sure that you maintain the security (in terms of confidentiality and integrity, for example) of your data.

High Availability and Fault Tolerance

Some other terms that may be used in discussions of continuity of operations in the face of a disruption of some sort are **high availability** and **fault tolerance**.

High availability is exactly what it seems. We earlier defined one of the objectives of security as the availability of data and processing power when an authorized user desires it. High availability refers to the ability to maintain availability of data and operational processing despite a disrupting event of any sort. Generally, this requires redundant systems, both in terms of power and processing, so that should one system fail, the other can take over operations without any break in service.

Fault tolerance basically refers to the same situation and is accomplished by the mirroring of data and systems. Should a "fault" occur, causing disruption in a device such as a disk controller, the mirrored system provides the requested data with no apparent interruption in service to the user.

Obviously, providing redundant systems and equipment comes with a price, and the need to provide this level of continuous, uninterrupted operation needs to be carefully evaluated.

Computer Incident Response Teams

Many of the issues discussed in this chapter illustrate the point that "if you fail to plan, you are planning to fail." One of the steps that should be taken to establish a plan to handle business interruptions as a result of a cyber event of some sort is the establishment of a **Computer Incident Response Team** (CIRT) or a **Computer Emergency Response Team** (CERT). This subject is covered in greater detail in Chapter 24 when the subject of incident response and forensics is covered. Not all computer incidents will threaten the organization's business operations and the level of response to computer incidents will not usually include activation of the BCP or DRP, but the possibility does exist that it could. At the very least, the organization's procedures to recover data from backup files may have to be exercised since computer intrusions may result in modified files or data. It will be the organization's CIRT that will conduct the investigation into the incident and make the recommendation on how to proceed. The CIRT will consist of both permanent and ad-hoc members who may be called upon to address special needs depending on the nature of the incident. The team will also include both individuals with a technical background as well as nontechnical personnel who provide guidance on ways to handle media attention, legal issues that may arise, and management issues regarding the continued operation of the organization. The CIRT should be created and team members notified before an incident occurs. Policies and procedures for the conducting of an investigation should also be worked out in advance of an incident occurring. It is also advisable to have the team periodically meet to review these procedures.

Test, Exercise, and Rehearse

Whether the plan covers the organization's BCP, DRP, backup procedures, or method to address computer incidents, it should periodically be taken off of the shelf and used. The time to find out that one of these plans has flaws in it is not when an actual event occurs and the recovery of data and information means the continued existence of the organization. The plans should be tested to ensure that they are sufficient and that all key individuals know what their role is in the specific plan.

A test implies a "grade" will be applied to the outcome. Did the organization's plan and the individuals involved perform as they should? Was the organization able to recover and continue to operate within the predefined tolerances set by management? If the answer is "no," then during the follow-up evaluation of the exercise, the failures should be identified and addressed. Was it simply a matter of untrained or uninformed individuals or was there a technological failure that necessitates a change in hardware, software, and procedures?

While a test implies a "grade," an exercise can be conducted without the stigma of a pass/fail grade being attached. Exercises are conducted to provide the opportunity for all parties to practice the procedures that have been established. It is important to actually perform as many of the recovery functions as possible, without impacting ongoing operations, to ensure that the procedures and technology will work in a real incident. You may want to periodically rehearse portions of the recovery plan which would include those aspects that are either more disruptive to actual operations or that have been identified as needing more frequent activation due to either the importance of them or the need for continual practice to ensure high levels of competency.

Policies and Procedures

Disaster recovery and business continuity plans are designed to address the needs of an organization in the event of a disruption of operations. What, however, governs the organization's operations on a daily basis? **Policies** are high-level statements made by management laying out the organization's position on some issue. Policies are mandatory but are not specific in their details. Policies are focused on the result, not the methods for achieving that result.

Standards are accepted specifications providing specific details on how a policy is to be enforced. **Procedures** are generally step-by-step instructions that describe exactly how employees are expected to act in a given situation or to accomplish a specific task. While there are standard policies that can be described in general terms that will be applicable to all organizations, standards and procedures are often more organizational specific and driven by specific organizational policies. This chapter will therefore concentrate on the higher-level general policy statements that every organization should have and will leave specific implementations to the individual organizations.

In security, there are several common policies that every organization should have in place. These policies include acceptable use policies, due care, separation of duties, and password management, and they will be addressed in the following sections. Other important policy-related issues that will also be covered include privacy, service level agreements, human resources policies, code of ethics, and policies governing incident response.

Security Policies

In keeping with the high-level nature of policies, the **security policy** is a high-level statement produced by senior management that outlines what security means to the organization and what the organization's goals are for security. Statements like "this organization will exercise the principle of least access in its handling of client information" would be an example of a security policy. The security policy may also describe how security is to be handled from an organizational point of view (it may describe which office and which corporate officer or manager oversees the organization's security program).

The security policy should include the other more specific policies just mentioned and spelled out next, and should be reviewed on a regular basis and updated as needed. Generally, policies will need to be updated less frequently than the procedures that implement them, since the high-level goals will not change as often as the environment in which they must be implemented. All policies should also be reviewed by the organization's legal counsel, and a plan should be outlined describing how the organization will ensure that employees will all be made aware of the policies. Policies can also be made stronger by including references to the authority who made the policy (for example, whether this policy comes from the CEO, or whether it is a department-level policy), and also refer to any laws or regulations that are applicable to the specific policy and environment.

Acceptable Use

An **acceptable use policy** (AUP) outlines what the organization considers to be the appropriate use of company resources, such as computer systems and networks. Organizations should be concerned with the personal use of organizational assets which does not benefit the company.

The goal of the policy is to ensure employee productivity while limiting organizational liability through inappropriate use of the organization's assets. The policy should clearly delineate what activities are not allowed. Issues such as the use of resources to conduct personal business, installation of hardware or software, remote access to systems and networks, the copying of company-owned software, and the responsibility of users to protect company assets, including data, software, and hardware should be addressed. Statements regarding possible penalties for breaking or ignoring any of the policies (such as termination) should also be included. Organizations should be careful, however, to not have the penalty outweigh the related offense.

Related to appropriate use of the organization's computer systems and networks by employees is the appropriate use by the organization. The most important of such issues is whether the organization will consider it appropriate to monitor the employee's use of the systems and network. If monitoring is considered appropriate, the organization will want to include a statement to this effect in the banner seen at login. This repeatedly warns employees, and possible intruders, that their actions are subject to monitoring and that any misuse of the system will not be tolerated. Should the organization have to use any information gathered during monitoring in a civil or criminal case, the issue of whether the employee had an expectation of privacy, or whether it was even legal for the organization to be monitoring, is simplified if the organization can point to a statement that is always displayed, stating that use of the system constitutes consent to monitoring. Before any monitoring is conducted, or the actual wording on the warning message is created, the organization's legal counsel should be consulted to determine the appropriate way to address this issue in the particular location.

Internet Usage Policy   In today's highly connected environment, employee use of access to the Internet is of particular concern. The goal for the **Internet usage policy** is to ensure maximum employee productivity and to limit potential liability to the organization from inappropriate use of the Internet in a workplace. The Internet provides a tremendous temptation for employees to waste hours as they surf the Web for the scores of the important games from the previous night, or conduct some quick online stock transactions, or read the review of the latest blockbuster movie everyone is talking about. Obviously, every minute they spend conducting this sort of activity is time they are not productively engaged in the organization's business, and their job. In addition, allowing employees to visit sites that may be considered offensive to others (such as pornographic or hate sites) may open the company up to accusations of condoning a hostile work environment and may result in legal liability.

The Internet usage policy needs to address what sites employees are allowed to visit, and what sites they are not. If the company will allow them to surf the Web during nonwork hours, the policy needs to clearly spell out what the acceptable parameters are, in terms of when they are allowed to do this and what sites they are still prohibited from visiting (such as the potentially offensive ones mentioned before). The policy should also describe under what circumstances an employee would be allowed to post something from the organization's network on the Web. A necessary addition to this policy would be the procedure for an employee to follow to obtain permission to post the object or message.

E-mail Usage Policy   Related to the Internet usage policy is the **e-mail usage policy**, which deals with what the company will allow employees to send in terms of e-mail. This policy should spell out whether non-work e-mail traffic is allowed at all or is at least severely restricted. It needs to cover the type of message that would be considered inappropriate to send to other employees (for example, no offensive language, no sex-related or ethnic jokes, no harassment, and so on). The policy should also specify any disclaimers that must be attached to an employee's message sent to an individual outside of the company.

Due Care

Due care and **due diligence** are terms used in the legal and business community to address issues where one party's actions may have caused loss or injury to another's. Basically, the law recognizes the responsibility of an individual or organization to act reasonably in relation to another. Reasonable precautions need to be taken that indicate that the organization is being responsible. In terms of security, it is expected that organizations will take reasonable precautions to protect the information that it maintains on other individuals. Should a person suffer a loss as a result of negligence on the part of an organization in terms of its security, a legal suit may be brought against the organization.

The standard applied—reasonableness—is extremely subjective and will often be determined by a jury. The organization will need to show how it had taken reasonable precautions to protect the information, and despite these precautions, an unforeseen security event occurred that caused the injury to the other party. Since this is so subjective, it is hard to describe what would be considered reasonable, but many sectors have "security best practices" for their industry, which provides a basis for organizations in that sector to start from. If the organization decides to not follow any of the best practices the industry agrees on, it needs to be prepared to justify its reasons in court should an incident occur.

Another element which can help establish due care from a security standpoint is developing and implementing the security policies discussed in this chapter.

Separation of Duties

Separation of duties is a principle employed in many organizations to ensure that no single individual has the ability to conduct transactions alone. This means that the level of trust in any one individual is lessened, and the ability for any individual to do catastrophic damage to the organization is also lessened. An example might be an organization where one person has the ability to order equipment, but it will be another individual who makes the payment. This would mean that an individual who wants to make an unauthorized purchase for their own personal gain would have to convince another person to go along with the transaction.

Separating duties as a security tool is a good practice, but it is possible to go overboard with this and break transactions up into too many pieces or require too much oversight. This results in inefficiency and may actually be less secure, since individuals may not scrutinize transactions as thoroughly, since they know others will also be reviewing them. The temptation is to hurry something along and assume that somebody else will or has examined it.

Another aspect of the separation of duties principle is that it spreads responsibilities out over an organization so no single individual becomes the indispensable individual with all of the "keys to the kingdom" or unique knowledge about how to make everything work. If there are enough tasks that have been distributed, having a primary and a backup person for each will ensure that the loss of any one individual will not have a disastrous impact on the organization.

Need to Know

Another common security principle is that of **need to know** and **least privilege**. The guiding factor here is that each individual in the organization is only supplied with the absolute minimum amount of information and privileges they need in order to perform their tasks. In order to obtain access to any piece of information, they must have a justified "need to know" it. In addition, they will only be granted the bare minimum number of privileges that are needed to perform their jobs.

A policy spelling out these two principles as guiding philosophies for the organization should be created. The policy should also address who in the organization can grant access to information or may assign privileges to employees.

Password Management

Since passwords are the most common authentication mechanism, it is imperative that organizations have a policy addressing them. The **password management policy** should address the procedures used for selecting user passwords (specifying what is considered an acceptable password in the organization in terms of the character set and length, for example), the frequency with which they must be changed, and how they will be distributed. Procedures for creating new passwords should an employee forget their old password also need to be addressed, as well as the acceptable handling of passwords (for example, they should not be shared with anybody else, they should not be written down, and so on). It might also be useful to have the policy address the issue of password cracking by administrators, in order to discover weak passwords that may have been selected by employees.

It should be noted that it is possible for the developer of the password management policy and procedure to go overboard and create an environment that leads to poorer security not better, and that negatively impacts employee productivity. If, for example, the frequency with which passwords are changed is too great, users will have a tendency to write them down or forget them. Neither of these is a desirable outcome, as the one makes it possible for an intruder to find a password and gain access to the system, and the other leads to too many people losing productivity as they have to wait for a new password to be created to allow them access again.

Disposal and Destruction

Many potential intruders have learned the value of "**dumpster diving**." This entails the potential intruder rummaging through the target organization's trash in order to find valuable information that may be used to penetrate the organization's security. The type of information that may be found includes documents, letters, scratch paper, old removable storage media, and even old equipment. Several government organizations have been embarrassed when old computers they had sold to salvagers proved to still contain sensitive documents on the hard drives. Other "dumpster diving" successes include finding e-mail or yellow sticky notes that contained passwords and user IDs. It is critical for the organization to have a strong **disposal and destruction policy** and related procedures.

Important papers should be shredded, and important, in this case, means anything that may be useful to a potential intruder. It is amazing what intruders can do with what appear to be the most innocent pieces of information.

Magnetic storage media need to have all files deleted, and then the media should be overwritten at least three times with all ones, all zeros, and then random characters. There are commercial products available to destroy files using this process. It is not sufficient to simply delete all files and leave it at that, since the deletion process only affects the pointers to where the files are stored and doesn't actually get rid of all of the bits in the file. This is why it is possible to "undelete" files and recover them after they have been deleted. A safer method for destroying files from a storage device is to magnetically destroy the data by using a strong magnetic field to degauss the media. This effectively destroys all data on the media, and there are several commercial degaussers that can be purchased for this purpose. Another method that can be used on hard drives is to take a file to them (the sort of file you'd find in a hardware store) and actually file off the magnetic material from the surface of the platter. Shredding floppy media is normally sufficient, but simply cutting a floppy into a few pieces is not enough—data has been successfully recovered from floppies that were cut into only a couple of pieces.

Privacy

Customers place an enormous amount of trust in organizations when they provide personal information to them. These customers expect their information to be kept secure so that unauthorized individuals will not gain access to it and so that authorized users will not use the information in unintended ways. Organizations should have a **privacy policy** that explains what their guiding principles will be in guarding personal data that they are given access to. In many locations, customers have a legal right to expect that their information is kept private, and organizations that violate this trust may find themselves involved in a lawsuit. In certain sectors, such as health care, federal regulations have been created that prescribe stringent security controls on private information.

It is a general practice today in most organizations to have a policy that describes very explicitly how information provided to the organization will be used (for example, it will not be sold to other organizations). Watchdog organizations have sprung up that monitor the use of individual information by organizations, and businesses can subscribe to services that will vouch for the organization to consumers, stating that the company has agreed to protect and keep private any information supplied to them. The organization is then granted permission to display a seal or certification on their web site where customers can see it. Organizations that then misuse the information they promised to protect will find themselves subject to penalties from the watchdog organization.

Service Level Agreements

Service level agreements (SLAs) are contractual agreements between entities describing specified levels of service that the servicing entity agrees to guarantee for the customer. These agreements not only clearly lay out what the expectations are in terms of the service provided and support expected, but also generally include penalties should the described level of service or support not be provided. An organization contracting with a service provider should remember to include in the agreement a section describing the service provider's responsibility in terms of business continuity and disaster recovery. The provider's backup plans and processes for restoring lost data should also be clearly described.

Human Resources Policies

It has been said that the weakest links in the security chain are the humans. Consequently, it is important to examine the policies that organizations have in place in relation to these employees. The first policies to be concerned with are those that relate to the hiring of individuals. You want to make sure that you hire individuals that you can trust with your organization's data and that of its clients. Once you've hired employees, you want to keep them from slipping into the category of "disgruntled employee." Finally, you need policies to address the inevitable point in the future when your employees leave the organization—either on their own or with the "encouragement" of the organization itself. There are security issues that must be considered at each of these points.

Employee Hiring and Promotions

It has increasingly become common for organizations to run background checks on prospective employees and check the references they supply. Drug tests, possible criminal activity in the past, claimed educational background, and reported work history are all elements that are frequently checked today. For highly sensitive environments, security background checks may also be required. You want to make sure that you hire the most capable and trustworthy employees, and your policies should be designed to ensure this.

Once you have made your selection and hired an individual, your organization needs to minimize the risk that the employee will "turn against you." Periodic reviews by supervisory personnel, additional drug checks, and monitoring of activity during work may all be considered by the organization. If there is an intent to accomplish any of these, they need to be specified in the organization's policies, and prospective employees should be made aware of these policies before being hired. What an organization can do in terms of monitoring and requiring of additional drug tests, for example, can be severely restricted if not spelled out in advance as terms of employment. New hires should be made aware of all pertinent policies, especially those applying to security, and documents should be signed by them indicating that they have read them and that they understand them.

Occasionally an employee's status will change within the company. If the change can be construed as a negative personnel action (such as a demotion), supervisors should be alerted to watch for changes in behavior that might indicate unauthorized activity is being contemplated or conducted. It is likely that the employee will be upset, and whether they act on this to the detriment of the company is something that needs to be guarded against. In the case of a demotion, the individual may also lose certain privileges or access rights, and these changes should be made quickly so as to lessen the likelihood that the employee can destroy previously accessible data if they become disgruntled and decide to take revenge on the organization. On the other hand, if the employee is promoted, privileges may still change, but the need to make the change to access privileges may not be as urgent, though it should still be accomplished as quickly as possible. If the move is a lateral one, there may still be changes that need to take place, and again they should be accomplished as quickly as possible. The organization's goals in terms of making changes to access privileges should be clearly spelled out in their policies.

Retirement, Separation, or Termination of an Employee

An employee leaving an organization can be either a positive or a negative action. Employees who are retiring by their own choice may announce their planned retirement weeks or even months in advance. Limiting their access to sensitive documents the moment they announce their intention may be the safest thing to do, but it may not be necessary. Each situation should be evaluated individually. Should the situation be a forced retirement, the organization must determine the risk to its data if the employee becomes disgruntled as a result of the action. In this situation, it may be the wisest choice to quickly cut off their access and simply provide them with some additional vacation time. This may seem like an expensive proposition, but the danger to the company of having a disgruntled employee may justify it. Again, each case should be evaluated individually.

When an employee decides to leave a company, generally as a result of a new job offer, continued access to sensitive information should be carefully considered. If the employee is leaving as a result of hard feelings for the company, it may be the wise choice to quickly revoke their access privileges. If they are leaving as a result of a better job offer, you may decide to allow them to gracefully transfer their projects to other employees, but the decision should be considered very carefully, especially if the new company can be considered a competitor.

If the employee is leaving the organization because they are being terminated, you have to plan on their becoming disgruntled. While it may not seem the friendliest thing to do, an employee in this situation should immediately have their access privileges to sensitive information and facilities revoked. Access cards, keys, and badges should be collected, the employee should be escorted to their desk and watched as they pack their personal belongings and then should be escorted from the building. It is better to give somebody several weeks of paid vacation rather than have a disgruntled employee trash sensitive files they have access to. Combinations should also be quickly changed once they have been informed of their termination.

No matter what the situation, the organization should have policies that describe the intended goals, and there should be procedures that detail the process to be followed for each of the described situations.

Code of Ethics

Numerous professional organizations have established codes of ethics for their members. Each of these describe the expected behavior of their members from a high-level standpoint. Organizations can adopt this idea as well. For organizations, a code of ethics can set the tone for how employees will be expected to act and to conduct business. The code should demand honesty from employees, and should require that they perform all activities in a professional manner. The code could also address principles of privacy and confidentiality and state how employees should treat client and organizational data. Conflicts of interest can often cause problems, so this could also be another item covered in the code of ethics.

By outlining a code of ethics, the organization can encourage an environment that will be conducive to integrity and high ethical standards. For additional ideas on possible codes of ethics, check professional organizations such as the Institute for Electrical and Electronics Engineers (IEEE), the Association for Computing Machinery (ACM), or the Information Systems Security Association (ISSA).

Incident Response Policies

No matter how careful an organization is, eventually a security incident of some sort will occur. When it happens, how effectively the organization deals with it will depend greatly on how prepared they are to handle incidents. An **incident response policy** and associated procedures should be developed to outline how the organization will deal with security incidents when they occur. Waiting until an incident happens is not the right time to establish your policies—they need to be designed in advance.

There are several phases that should be covered in an incident response policy: preparation, detection, containment and eradication, recovery, and any follow-on actions.

Preparation

Preparing for an incident is the first phase. Steps to be taken when an incident is discovered (or suspected) should be established. Points of contact should be determined. All employees should be trained so they understand the steps to take and who to call. An incident response team should be established, the equipment necessary to detect, contain, and recover from an incident should be acquired, and those who will use the equipment will need to be trained. Any additional training in areas such as computer forensics that are determined to be necessary should also be accomplished.

The incident response team is a critical part of the incident response plan. Team membership will vary depending on the type of incident or suspected incident, but there are some general points to think about. The team will need a leader, preferably a higher-level manager who will have the ability to obtain the cooperation from employees as needed. A computer or network security analyst will be useful to have as a member, since the assumption is that a security incident may have occurred. Specialists may be added to the team for specific hardware or software platforms as needed. The organization's legal counsel should be part of the team on at least a part-time or as-needed basis. The public affairs office should also be available on an as-needed basis, because it will be their responsibility to formulate the public response should the event become public. The organization's security office should also be kept informed, and there should be a point of contact for the team in case criminal activity is suspected. In this case, care must be taken to preserve evidence, should the organization decide to push for prosecution of the individuals.

This is by no means a complete list, as each organization is different and each will need to evaluate what the best mixture is for their own response team. Whatever the decision, the composition of the team, and how and when it will be formed, need to be clearly addressed in the incident response policy.

Detection

It goes without saying that before an incident response team can begin the investigation of an incident, there needs to be a suspected incident, which in turn implies that somebody needs to have detected what they believe may be an incident. Security incidents can take a variety of forms, and who discovers it will vary as well.

One of the most likely group of individuals to discover an incident will be the network and security administrators. These are the people who run devices such as the organization's firewalls and intrusion detection systems. So that this is not an ad hoc, hit-or-miss proposition, procedures need to be established that describe the process the administrators should use to check for possible security events. The tools for accomplishing this need to be identified during the preparation phase described previously, and any required training to operate the equipment should also be acquired.

Another common incident is a virus. There are several packages available that can help an organization discover potential virus activity or other malicious code. Administrators will often be the ones to notice something is amiss, but so might an average user who has been hit by the virus. Again, the appropriate hardware, software, and training needs to be acquired during the preparation phase.

A common technique used by potential intruders to acquire information that may be useful in gaining access to computer systems, networks, or the physical facilities that house them is social engineering. Anybody in the organization can be the target of a social engineering attack, so all employees need to know what to be looking for regarding this type of attack. In fact, it may not even be one of your organization's actual employees that is the target—it may be an "extended employee" of the company, such as somebody on the custodial staff or a night watchman. To thwart social engineering attacks, training is essential, and the organization should have a policy on who will be required to receive this type of training and how frequently they should receive it.

Whatever the type of security incident suspected, and no matter who suspects it, a reporting procedure needs to be in place for the employees to use. Everybody needs to know who to call should they suspect something, and everybody needs to know what to do. A common technique is to develop a reporting template that can be supplied to an individual suspecting an incident so that the necessary information is gathered in a timely manner.

One final word on detection remains. One of the first jobs of the incident response team will be to determine whether an actual incident has occurred. Many things can happen that may be interpreted as a possible incident but that may not be. A software bug in an application may cause a user to lose a file, and the user may blame this on a virus or similar malicious software. Each reported incident must be investigated and treated as a possible incident until it can be determined whether it is or isn't. This may mean that your organization may want to respond initially with a limited response team before wasting a lot of time having the full team respond.

Containment and Eradication

Once the determination has been made that an incident most likely has occurred, the team is going to want to quickly contain the problem. At this point, or very soon after containment begins, a decision will need to be made by management as to whether the organization will want to prosecute the individual who has caused the incident, or whether it is more important to simply restore operations. In certain circumstances there may not be a choice, such as if there are specific regulations or laws that require incidents in certain sectors to be reported. If the decision to prosecute has been made, specific procedures will need to be followed in handling potential evidence. Individuals trained in forensics should be used in this case.

Another decision that will need to be made quickly is how to address containment. If an intruder is on your system, one response is to disconnect from the Internet until the system can be restored and vulnerabilities patched. This, however, means that your organization may not be accessible to customers over the Internet anymore, and it may result in lost revenue. A decision will need to be made as to which is more important for your organization.

Other possible containment activities might include adding additional filtering rules or modifying existing rules on firewalls, routers, or intrusion detection systems, updating antivirus software, or removing specific pieces of hardware or halting specific software applications. If an intruder has gained access through a specific account, disabling that account or removing it may also be necessary.

Once the immediate problems have been contained, the cause of the incident needs to be addressed. If the incident is the result of a vulnerability that was not patched, the patch should be obtained, tested, and applied. Accounts may need to be deleted or passwords changed. It may also be necessary to completely reload the entire operating system if the intruder has been in the system for an unknown length of time or has been seen to have modified system files. Determining when an intruder first gained access to your system or network is critical in determining how far back to go in restoring the system or network.

Recovery

The major thrust of this chapter has been on business continuity and the quick recovery of operations. After the incident has been contained, and any malicious software or vulnerabilities have been taken care of, it is time to put the procedures described earlier into action. Again, the goal here is to quickly have the organization back to normal processing.

Follow-Up Actions

Once the excitement of the incident is over and operations have been restored to their pre-incident state, it is time to take care of a few last items. Senior-level management will need and want to be informed of what occurred and what was done to address it. An after-action report should be created to outline what happened and how it was addressed. Recommendations will most likely be made to improve processes and policies so that a repeat incident will not occur. If prosecution of the individual responsible is desired, there will be additional time that will be spent in helping law enforcement agencies and possibly testifying in court. Training material may also need to be developed or modified as part of the new, modified policies and procedures.

Chapter Review

Chapter Summary

After reading this chapter and completing the exercises, you should understand the following regarding disaster recovery, business continuity, and organizational policies.

Disaster Recovery

There are many types of disasters that can cause a disruption to an organization.

- A Business Impact Analysis can be conducted to identify the most critical functions for an organization.

- A disaster recovery plan is created to outline an organization's plans to recover in the event a disaster strikes.

- A business continuity plan is created to outline the order that business functions will be restored so that the most critical functions are accomplished first.

- One of the most critical elements of any disaster recovery plan is the creation and maintenance of system backups.

- Backups should include not only the organization's critical data but critical software as well.

- Exercises can play an important role by allowing personnel to practice the procedures established by the organization in the event of a security incident.

- Drills and exercises can play an important role by allowing personnel to practice procedures the organization has established in the event of a security incident.

Policies and Procedures

- Security policies are high-level statements produced by senior management to outline what security means to the organization.

- There are a number of standard policies that most organizations create including Acceptable Use, Internet Usage, and E-mail Usage policies.

- Human Resource policies are important to ensure that unacceptable risks are not taken in the event of an employee separating or being terminated.

- Incident Response Policies are critical in order to outline, in advance, the steps the organization will take to respond to a security incident.

Key Terms

Acceptable Use Policy *(495)*
Business continuity plan (BCP) *(485)*
Business impact assessment (BIA) *(484)*
Cold site *(490)*
Computer Emergency Response Team *(493)*
Computer Incident Response Team *(493)*
Delta backup *(488)*
Differential backup *(488)*
Disaster recovery plan (DRP) *(484)*
Disposal and destruction policy *(498)*
Due care *(496)*
Due diligence *(496)*
dumpster diving *(498)*
E-mail Usage Policy *(496)*
Fault tolerance *(492)*
Full backup *(487)*
High availability *(492)*
Hot site *(490)*
Incident Response Policy *(501)*
Internet Usage Policy *(495)*
Incremental backups *(488)*
Least privilege *(497)*
Mutual aid agreements *(491)*
Need to Know *(497)*
Password Management Policy *(497)*
Privacy Policy *(498)*
Policies *(494)*
Procedures *(494)*
Security Policy *(494)*
Service level agreements (SLAs) *(499)*
Standards *(494)*
Separation of duties *(496)*
Warm site *(490)*

Key Terms Quiz

Use terms from the Key Terms list to complete the sentences that follow. Don't use the same term more than once. Not all terms will be used.

1. Instructions that describe exactly how employees are expected to act in a given situation or to accomplish a specific task are known as _____.

2. A _____ is a partially configured backup processing facility usually having the peripherals and software but perhaps not the more expensive main processing computer.

3. A backup that includes only the files that have changed since the last full backup was completed is called a _____.

4. A _____ is an assessment of the impact that a loss of critical functions will have on the organization.

5. A rule used in many organizations to ensure that no single individual has the ability to conduct transactions alone is a _____.

6. _____ are accepted specifications providing specific details on how a policy is to be enforced.

7. An agreement in which similar organizations agree to assume the processing for the other in the event a disaster occurs is known as a _____.

8. The principle when each individual in an organization is only supplied with the absolute minimum amount of information and privileges they need in order to perform their tasks is called _____.

9. A _____ is a fully configured backup environment similar to the normal operating environment that can be operational within a few hours.

10. _____ is a method to ensure high availability that is accomplished by the mirroring of data and systems. Should a "fault" occur, causing disruption in a device, the mirrored system provides the requested data with no apparent interruption in service.

Multiple-Choice Quiz

1. Why is it important that security exercises be conducted?

   A. To provide the opportunity for all parties to practice the procedures that have been established to respond to a security incident.

   B. Determine if the organization's plan and the individuals involved perform as they should during a simulated security incident.

   C. Determine if processes developed to handle security incidents are sufficient for the organization.

   D. All of the above

2. A good backup plan will include which of the following?

   A. The critical data needed for the organization to operate

   B. Any software that is required to process the organization's data

   C. Specific hardware to run the software or to process the data

   D. All of the above

3. In which backup strategy are only those portions of the files and software that have changed since the last backup saved?

   A. Full

   B. Differential

   C. Incremental

   D. Delta

4. Which of the following is a consideration in calculating the cost of a backup strategy?

   A. The cost of the backup media

   B. The storage costs for the backup media

   C. The frequency with which backups are created

   D. All of the above

5. Which of the following is the name for a partially configured environment usually having the peripherals and software that the normal processing facility contains that can be operational within a few days?

   A. Hot site

   B. Warm site

   C. Online storage system

   D. Backup storage facility

6. Which of the following is considered an issue with long-term storage of magnetic media, as discussed in the chapter?

   A. Tape media can only be used a limited number of times before it degrades.

   B. Software and hardware evolve, and the media stored may no longer be compatible with current technology.

   C. Both of the above

   D. None of the above

7. What is the first phase in incident response?

   A. Detection of an incident

   B. Containment and eradication

   C. Preparation

   D. Recovery

8. What common utility or infrastructure is important to consider when developing your recovery plans?

   A. Transportation

   B. Oil and gas

   C. Communications

   D. Television/cable

9. Standards are...

    A. High-level statements made by management

    B. Statements that lay out the organization's position on some issue

    C. Mandatory but not specific in their details

    D. All of the above

    E. None of the above

10. For organizations that draw a distinction between a BCP and a DRP, which of the following is true?

    A. The BCP will detail the functions that are most critical and outline the order that critical functions should be returned to service to maintain business operations.

    B. The BCP will be a subset of the DRP.

    C. The DRP will outline the minimum set of business functions required for the organization to continue functioning.

    D. The DRP will always be developed first and the BCP will normally be an attachment to this document.

11. Which of the following is true concerning an organization's ability to monitor employee use of resources?

    A. It can generally be done, but a policy stating that it will be conducted should be created, and a warning message should be displayed when employees use the organization's resources (such as the network).

    B. It can be done without any policy or warning message since the corporation owns the resources in the first place.

    C. It cannot be done under any circumstances.

    D. It cannot be done except under extreme circumstances, such as when a person's life is in danger.

12. Due care and due diligence refer to:

    A. The situation in which one party's actions may have caused loss or injury to another's as a result of reasonable cautions not being taken

    B. The requirement to post safety notices about potentially hazardous situations

    C. The practice of determining what precautions should be taken by an organization to avoid financial responsibility for hazardous activities required of employees

    D. The responsibility placed on management to ensure that no corporate assets are lost as a result of a computer intrusion

13. What is the term for the ability to maintain availability of data and operational processing despite a disrupting event of some sort?

   A. Due care

   B. High availability

   C. Due diligence

   D. Secure recovery

14. In order for an organization to avoid problems with the activity known as dumpster diving, it is important that it has a(n)…

   A. Explicit privacy policy

   B. Strong disposal and destruction policy

   C. Disposal container investigative process

   D. Magnetic media destruction policy

15. In which of the following situations is it imperative that accounts be immediately and without question terminated for an employee?

   A. Termination of the employee

   B. Announced retirement of the employee

   C. Announced separation of the employee

   D. All of the above

Essay Quiz

1. Write a paragraph outlining the differences between a disaster recovery plan and a business continuity plan. Is one of the two more important than the other?

2. Write a brief description of the different backup strategies. Be sure to include a discussion of which of these strategies requires the greatest amount of storage space to conduct and which of the strategies involves the most complicated restoration scheme.

3. Your boss recently attended a seminar in which the importance of creating and maintaining a backup of critical data was discussed. He suggested to you that you immediately make a tape backup of all data, place it in a metal box, lock it, and bury it in your backyard. You're not really excited about this specific method but need to develop a plan that he will understand. Write a proposal describing your recommendations, making sure to include the issues involved with the long-term storage of backups.

4. Describe the difference in procedures an organization might use in the case of an employee retiring, an employing leaving to go to work with another organization, and an employee who is being terminated for poor performance. Using the Internet, research an example of a real-world instance where an employee or ex-employee caused damage to a company. Summarize your findings.

5. Write a brief essay outlining the steps an organization might take when responding to a computer incident.

Lab Projects

Lab Project 19.1

The Windows 2000 operating system provides administrators with the ability to set a number of security policies. Identify some of the more common security settings for the Windows environment. How do you set these policies in Windows 2000?

Lab Project 19.2

Obtain copies of the Acceptable Use, E-mail, and Internet policies for your school as well as its Privacy policy (you may be able to find them on the school's web site). Compare what they say with what you have learned in class. Do you consider them sufficient for your environment? If not, what suggestions might you have to improve them?

Risk Management

Upon completion of this chapter, you will be able to:

- Explain the purpose of risk management and describe an approach to effectively manage risk
- Describe differences between qualitative and quantitative risk assessment
- Explain, by example, how both approaches, qualitative and quantitative risk assessment, are necessary to effectively manage risk
- Define important terms associated with risk management
- Describe various tools related to risk management

Risk management can best be described as a decision-making process. In the simplest terms, when you manage risk, you determine what could happen to your business, you assess the impact if it were to happen, and you decide what you could do to control that impact as much as you or your management deems necessary. You then decide to act or not to act and, finally, evaluate the results of your decision. The process may then iterate. Industry best practices clearly indicate that an important aspect of effectively managing risk is to consider it an ongoing process. Effective risk management avoids costly oversights and unexpected problems.

An Overview of Risk Management

Managed risk creates value. You can't increase the value of your company without taking risk, and you can create exceptional value if you have strong risk management practices. Therefore, risk management is an essential element of management from the enterprise level down to the individual project. Risk management encompasses all the actions taken to reduce complexity, increase objectivity, and identify important decision factors. There has been, and will continue to be, discussion as to how complex risk management can be, and whether or not it should be done. Businesses must take risks to retain their competitive edge, and as a result, risk management must be done as part of managing any business, any program, or any project. To succeed, you don't need to take more risks, you just need to manage them better than your competition.

Risk management is both a skill and a task that all managers do, either deliberately or intuitively. It can be simple or complex, depending on the size of the project or business and the amount of risk inherent in an activity. Every manager, at all levels, must learn to manage risk. The required skills can be learned.

STUDY TIP This chapter contains several bulleted lists. These are designed for easy memorization in preparation for taking the Security+ exam.

Macro-Level Example of Risk Management: International Banking

The Basel Committee on Banking Supervision is composed of government central-bank governors from around the world. This body created a basic, global risk management framework for market and credit risk. They implemented internationally a flat 8 percent capital charge to banks to manage bank risks. In layman's terms, this means that for every $100 a bank makes in loans, it must possess $8 in reserve to be used in the event of financial difficulties. However, if banks can show they have very strong risk mitigation procedures and controls in place, that capital charge can be reduced to as low as $0.37 (0.37 percent). If a bank has poor procedures and controls, that capital charge can be as high as $45 (45 percent).

This example shows that risk management can be and is used at very high levels—the remainder of this chapter will focus on smaller implementations. It will be shown that risk management is used in many aspects of business conduct.

Key Terms Essential to Understanding Risk Management

There are a number of key terms that should be understood to manage risk. Some of these terms will be defined here because they are used throughout the remainder of the chapter. This listing is somewhat ordered according to the organization of this chapter. More comprehensive definitions and other pertinent terms are listed alphabetically in the glossary at the end of this book.

Risk The possibility of suffering harm or loss.

Risk management The overall decision-making process of identifying threats and vulnerabilities and their potential impacts, determining the costs to mitigate such events, and deciding what actions are cost-effective for controlling these risks.

Risk assessment (or risk analysis) The process of analyzing an environment to identify the threats, vulnerabilities, and mitigating actions to determine (either quantitatively or qualitatively) the impact of an event that would affect a project, program, or business.

Asset Resource or information an organization needs to conduct its business.

Threat Any circumstance or event with the potential to cause harm to an asset.

Vulnerability Characteristic of an asset that can be exploited by a threat to cause harm.

Impact The loss resulting when a threat exploits a vulnerability.

Control (also called countermeasure or safeguard) A measure taken to detect, prevent, or mitigate the risk associated with a threat.

Qualitative risk assessment The process of subjectively determining the impact of an event that affects a project, program, or business. Qualitative risk assessment usually involves the use of expert judgment, experience, or group consensus to complete the assessment. Often used to attach a potential monetary loss to a threat.

Quantitative risk assessment   The process of objectively determining the impact of an event that affects a project, program, or business. Quantitative risk assessment usually involves the use of metrics and models to complete the assessment.

Mitigate   Action taken to reduce the likelihood of a threat occurring.

Single loss expectancy (SLE)   The monetary loss or impact of each occurrence of a threat.

Exposure factor   A measure of the magnitude of loss of an asset. Used in the calculation of single loss expectancy.

Annualized rate of occurrence (ARO)   On an annualized basis, the frequency with which an event is expected to occur.

Annualized loss expectancy (ALE)   How much an event is expected to cost per year.

What Is Risk Management?

Three definitions relating to risk management show why it is sometimes considered difficult to understand. (See Figure 20-1.)

- The dictionary defines *risk* as the possibility of suffering harm or loss.
- Carnegie Mellon University's Software Engineering Institute (SEI) defines *continuous risk management* as "processes, methods, and tools for managing risks

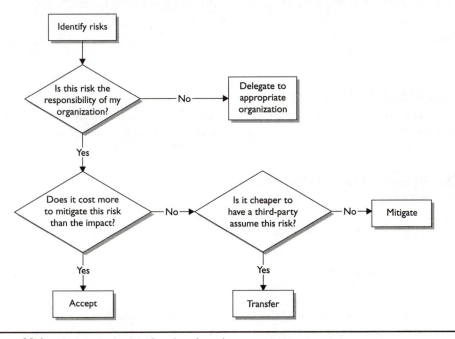

Figure 20-1   A planning decision flowchart for risk management

in a project. It provides a disciplined environment for proactive decision-making to 1) assess continuously what could go wrong (risks); 2) determine which risks are important to deal with; and 3) implement strategies to deal with those risks" (SEI, *Continuous Risk Management Guidebook* [Pittsburgh, PA: Carnegie Mellon University, 1996], 22).

- The Information Systems Audit and Control Association (ISACA) says, "In modern business terms, risk management is the process of identifying vulnerabilities and threats to an organization's resources and assets and deciding what countermeasures, if any, to take to reduce the level of risk to an acceptable level based on the value of the asset to the organization" (ISACA, *Certified Information Systems Auditor (CISA) Review Manual, 2002* [Rolling Meadows, IL:ISACA, 2002], 344).

These three definitions show that risk management is based upon what can go wrong and what action should be taken, if any. Figure 20-1, provides a high-level view of how to manage risk.

Transferring Risk

One possible action to manage risk is to transfer that risk. The most common method of transferring risk is to purchase insurance. Insurance allows risk to be transferred to a third party that manages specific types of risk for multiple parties, thus reducing the individual cost.

Business Risks

There is no comprehensive identification of all risks in a business environment. In today's technology-dependent business environment, risk is often simplistically divided into two areas: business risk and a major subset, technology risk.

Examples of Business Risks

The most common business risks include:

- Treasury management
- Revenue management
- Contract management
- Fraud
- Environmental risk management
- Regulatory risk management

- Business continuity management
- Technology

 NOTE It is important to understand that technology, itself, is a business risk. Hence, it must be managed along with other risks. Today, technology risks are so important they should be considered separately.

Examples of Technology Risks

The most common technology risks include:

- Security and privacy
- Information technology operations
- Business systems control and effectiveness
- Business continuity management
- Information systems testing
- Reliability and performance management
- Information technology asset management
- Project risk management
- Change management

Risk According to the Basel Committee

The Basel Committee referenced at the beginning of this chapter defined three types of risk specifically to address international banking:

- **Market Risk**   Risk of losses due to fluctuation of market prices
- **Credit Risk**   Risk of default of outstanding loans
- **Operational Risk**   Risk from disruption by people, systems, processes, or disasters

Risk Management Models

Risk management concepts are fundamentally the same despite their definitions, requiring similar skills, tools, and methodologies. There are several models for managing risk through its various phases. The models you choose should align with your business objectives and strategies. Two models will be presented: the first can be applied to managing risks in general, the second is tailored for managing risk in software projects.

General Risk Management Model

The following steps can be used in virtually any risk management process. Following these steps will lead to an orderly process of analyzing and mitigating risks.

Asset Identification Identify and classify the assets, systems, and processes that need protection because they are vulnerable to threats. This classification leads to the ability to prioritize assets, systems, and processes and to evaluate the costs of addressing the associated risks. A monetary value can be determined for a **tangible asset**, whereas a monetary value cannot be determined for an **intangible asset**. Assets can include:

- Inventory
- Buildings
- Cash
- Information and data
- Hardware
- Software
- Services
- Documents
- Personnel
- Brand recognition
- Organization reputation
- Goodwill

Threat Assessment Identify the possible threats and vulnerabilities associated with each asset and the likelihood of their occurrence. Threats can be defined as any circumstance or event with the potential to cause harm to an asset. Common classes of threats include:

- Natural disasters
- Man-made disasters
- Terrorism
- Errors
- Malicious damage or attacks
- Fraud
- Theft
- Equipment or software failure

Vulnerabilities are characteristics of resources that can be exploited by a threat to cause harm. Examples of vulnerabilities include:

- Unprotected facilities
- Unprotected computer systems

- Unprotected data
- Insufficient procedures and controls
- Insufficient or unqualified personnel

Impact Definition and Quantification　　An impact is the loss created when a threat exploits a vulnerability. When a threat is realized, it turns risk into impact. Impacts can be either tangible or intangible. For example, in a manufacturing facility, storing and using flammable chemicals creates a risk of fire to the facility. The vulnerability is that there are flammable chemicals stored there. The threat would be that a person could cause a fire by mishandling the chemicals (either intentionally or unintentionally). The impact would be the loss incurred (say $500,000) if a person ignites the chemicals and fire then destroys part of the facility.

Tangible impacts include:

- Direct loss of money
- Endangerment of staff or customers
- Loss of business opportunity
- Reduction in operational efficiency or performance
- Interruption of a business activity

Intangible impacts include:

- Breach of legislation or regulatory requirements
- Loss of reputation or goodwill (brand damage)
- Breach of confidence

Control Design and Evaluation　　Controls (also called countermeasures or safeguards) are designed to control risk by reducing vulnerabilities to an acceptable

Business Dependencies

An area often overlooked in risk assessment is the need to address business dependencies—each organization must assess risks caused by other organizations with which it interacts. This occurs when the organization is either a consumer of, or a supplier to, other organizations (or both). For example, if a company is dependent on products produced by a laboratory, then the company must determine the impacts that could be caused if that laboratory could not deliver the product when needed. Likewise, an organization must assess risks that can occur when it is considered a supplier to some other company dependent on its products.

> ### Can All Risks Be Identified?
> It is important to note that not all risks need to be mitigated or controlled; however, as many risks as possible should be identified and reviewed. Those deemed to have potential impacts should be mitigated by controls or countermeasures.

level. For use in this text, the terms *control*, *countermeasure*, and *safeguard* will be considered synonymous and will be used interchangeably.

Controls, countermeasures, or safeguards can be actions, devices, or procedures. They can be preventive or detective. *Preventive controls* are designed to prevent the vulnerability from being exploited by a threat, thus causing an impact. *Detective controls* are those that detect a vulnerability that has been exploited by a threat so that action can be taken.

Residual Risk Management   It is important to understand that risk cannot be completely eliminated. Any risks that remain after implementing controls are termed **residual risks**. Residual risks can be further evaluated to identify where additional controls are required to reduce risk even more. This leads us to the earlier statement that the risk management process is iterative. Business process reengineering or organizational changes can create new risks or weaken exitsting control acitivites.

Software Engineering Institute Model

In an approach tailored for managing risk in software projects, SEI uses the following paradigm (SEI, *Continuous Risk Management Guidebook* [Pittsburgh, PA: Carnegie Mellon University, 1996], 23). Although the terminology varies slightly from the previous model, the relationships are apparent, and either model can be applied wherever risk management is used.

1. **Identify**   Look for risks before they become problems.

2. **Analyze**   Convert the data gathered into information that can be used to make decisions. Evaluate the impact, probability, and timeframe of the risks. Classify and prioritize each of the risks.

3. **Plan**   Review and evaluate the risks and decide what actions to take to mitigate them. Implement those mitigating actions.

4. **Track**   Monitor the risks and the mitigation plans. Trends may provide information to activate plans and contingencies. Review periodically to measure progress and identify new risks.

5. **Control**   Make corrections for deviations from the risk mitigation plans. Correct products and processes as required. Changes in business procedures may require adjustments in plans or actions, as do faulty plans and risks that become problems.

These two example models define steps that can be used in any general or software risk management process. These risk management principles can be applied to any

Figure 20-2
Risk complexity
vs. project size

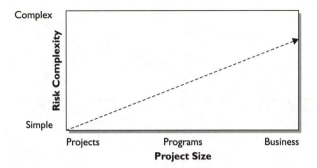

project, program, or business activity, no matter how simple or complex. Figure 20-2 shows how risk management can be applied across the continuum and that the complexity of risk management generally increases with the size of the project, program, or business to be managed.

Qualitatively Assessing Risk

Qualitative risk analysis allows expert judgment and experience to assume a prominent role. To qualitatively assess risk, you compare the impact of the threat with the probability of occurrence. For example, if a threat has a high impact and a high probability of occurring, the risk exposure is high and probably requires some action to reduce this threat (see darkest box in Figure 20-3). Conversely, if the impact is low with a low probability, the risk exposure is low and no action may be required to reduce this threat (see white box in Figure 20-3). Figure 20-3 shows an example of a *binary assessment*. There are only two possible outcomes each for impact and probability. Either it will have an impact or it will not (or it will have a low or high impact). And it can occur or it will not (or it will have a high probability of occurring or a low probability of occurring).

In reality, there are usually a few threats that can be identified as presenting high-risk exposure and a few threats that present low-risk exposure. The threats that fall somewhere between (see light gray boxes in Figure 20-3) tend to be those that will have to be evaluated by judgment and management experience. You may want to monitor these areas for a period of time or collect and analyze more data before deciding how to address these threats.

If the analysis is more complex, requiring three levels of analysis, such as low, medium, high or red-green-yellow, there are nine possible combinations, as shown in Figure 20-4. Again, the darkest boxes probably require action, the white boxes may not require action, and the gray boxes require judgment. (Note that for brevity, in Figures 20-4 and 20-5, the first term in each box refers to the magnitude of the impact, the second term refers to the probability of the threat occurring.)

Figure 20-3
Binary assessment

Impact	High Impact/Low Probability	High Impact/High Probability
	Low Impact/Low Probability	Low Impact/High Probability

Probability

Figure 20-4
Three levels of analysis

Impact

High	Low	High	Medium	High	High
Medium	Low	Medium	Medium	Medium	High
Low	Low	Low	Medium	Low	High

Probability

Figure 20-5
A 3 by 5 level analysis

Impact

Very high	Low	Very high	Medium	Very high	High
High	Low	High	Medium	High	High
Medium	Low	Medium	Medium	Medium	High
Low	Low	Low	Medium	Low	High
Very low	Low	Very low	Medium	Very low	High

Probability

Other levels of complexity are possible. If there are five levels of analysis, there will be 25 possible values of risk exposure. In this case, the possible values of impact and probability could take on the values: very low, low, medium, high, or very high. Also, note that the matrix does not have to be symmetrical. For example, if the probability is assessed with three values (low, medium, high) and the impact has five values (very low, low, medium, high, very high), the analysis would be as shown in Figure 20-5. (Again, note that the first term in each box refers to the impact, the second term in each box refers to the probability of occurrence.)

So far, the examples have focused on assessing probability versus impact. Qualitative risk assessment can be adapted to a variety of attributes and situations in combination with each other. For example, Figure 20-6 shows the comparison of some specific risks that have been identified during a security assessment. The assessment identified the risk areas listed in the first column (weak intranet security, high number of modems,

Qualitative Assessment of Findings

Legend
- Red
- Yellow
- Green

	Business impact	Probability of attack	Cost to fix	Difficulty to fix	Risk
Weak Intranet security	Red	Red	Red	Red	Red
High number of modems	Red	Red	Yellow	Green	Red
Internet attack vulnerabilities	Red	Red	Green	Yellow	Yellow
Weak incident detection/ response mechanism	Yellow	Red	Yellow	Red	Yellow

Figure 20-6   Example of a combination assessment

Internet attack vulnerabilities, and weak incident detection and response mechanisms). The assessment also identified various potential impacts listed across the top (business impact, probability of attack, cost to fix, and difficulty to fix). Each of the impacts has been assessed as low, moderate, or high (depicted using green (G), yellow (Y), and red (R), respectively). Each of the risk areas has been assessed with respect to each of the potential impacts, and an overall risk assessment has been determined in the last column.

Quantitatively Assessing Risk

Whereas qualitative risk assessment relies on judgment and experience, quantitative risk assessment applies historical information and trends to attempt to predict future performance. This type of risk assessment is highly dependent on the historical data, and gathering such data can be difficult. Quantitative risk assessment may also rely heavily on models. These models provide decision-making information in the form of quantitative metrics, which attempt to measure risk levels across a common scale.

It is important to understand that key assumptions underlie any model, and different models will produce different results even when given the same input data. Although significant research and development have been invested in improving and refining the various risk analysis models, expert judgment and experience must still be considered an essential part of any risk assessment process. Models can never replace judgment and experience, but they can significantly enhance the decision-making process.

Adding Objectivity to a Qualitative Assessment

Quantitative assessment can be as simple as just assigning numeric values to one of the tables shown in Figures 20-3 through 20-6. For example, the impacts listed in Figure 20-6 can be prioritized from highest to lowest and then weighted, as shown in Table 20-1 with Business Impact weighted the most and Difficulty to Fix weighted least.

Next, values can be assigned to reflect how each risk was assessed. Figure 20-6 can thus be made more objective by assigning a value to each color that represents an assessment. For example, a "red" assessment means there are many critical, unresolved issues and this will be given an assessment value of 3. Likewise, "green" means there are few unresolved issues, so it is given a value of 1. Table 20-2 shows values that can be assigned for an assessment using green, yellow, and red.

Table 20-1	Impact	Explanation	Weight
Adding Weights and Definitions to the Potential Impacts	Business impact	If exploited, would this have a material business impact?	4
	Probability of attack	How likely is a potential attacker to try this technique or attack?	3
	Cost to fix	How much will it cost in dollars and resources to correct this vulnerability?	2
	Difficulty to fix	How hard is this to fix from a technical standpoint?	1

Table 20-2	Assessment	Explanation	Value
Adding Values to Assessments	Red	Many critical, unresolved issues	3
	Yellow	Some critical, unresolved issues	2
	Green	Few unresolved issues	I

The last step will be to calculate an overall risk value for each risk area (each row in Figure 20-6) by multiplying the weights depicted in Table 20-1 times the assessed values from Table 20-2 and summing the products:

$$\text{Risk} = W_1 * V_1 + W_2 * V_2 + \ldots W_4 * V_4$$

The risk calculation and final risk value for each risk area listed in Figure 20-6 have been incorporated into Figure 20-7. The assessed areas can then be ordered from highest to lowest based on the calculated risk value to aid management in focusing on the risk areas with the greatest potential impact.

A Common Objective Approach

More complex models permit a variety of analyses based on statistical and mathematical models. A common method is the calculation of the annualized loss expectancy (ALE). This calculation begins by calculating a single-loss expectancy (SLE) with the following formula:

$$\text{SLE} = \text{asset value} * \text{exposure factor}$$

Qualitative Assessment of Findings

	Business impact (4)		Probability of attack (3)		Cost to fix (2)		Difficulty to fix (1)		Risk
Weak Intranet security	4*3	+	3*3	+	2*3	+	1*3	=	30
High number of modems	4*3	+	3*3	+	2*2	+	1*1	=	26
Internet attack vulnerabilities	4*3	+	3*3	+	2*1	+	1*2	=	25
Weak incident detection/ response mechanism	4*2	+	3*3	+	2*2	+	1*3	=	24

Figure 20-7   Final quantitative assessment of the findings

By example, to calculate the exposure factor, assume the asset value of a small office building and its contents is $2 million. Also assume that this building houses the call center for a business, and the complete loss of the center would take away about half of the capability of the company. Therefore, the exposure factor is 50 percent. The SLE is

$2 million * 0.5 = $1 million

The ALE is then calculated simply by multiplying the SLE by the number of times the event is expected to occur in a year, which is called the annualized rate of occurrence (ARO):

ALE = SLE * ARO

If the event is expected to occur once in 20 years, then the annualized rate of occurrence is 1/20. Typically, the ARO is defined by historical data, either from a company's own experience or from industry surveys. Continuing our example, assume that a fire where this business is located is expected to occur about once in 20 years. Given this information, the ALE is

$1 million * 1/20 = $50,000

The ALE determines a threshold for evaluating the cost/benefit ratio of a given countermeasure. Therefore, a countermeasure to protect this business adequately should cost no more than the calculated ALE of $50,000 per year.

STUDY TIP   It is always advisable to memorize these fundamental equations for tests or certifications such as Security+.

The examples in this chapter have been simplistic, but they demonstrate the concepts of both quantitative and qualitative risk analysis. There are more complex algorithms and software packages for accomplishing risk analysis, but these examples suffice for the purposes of this text.

Qualitative vs. Quantitative Risk Assessment

It is recognized throughout industry that it is *impossible* to conduct risk management that is purely *quantitative*. Usually risk management includes both qualitative and quantitative elements, requiring both analysis and judgment or experience. It is important to note that in contrast to quantitative assessment, it is *possible* to accomplish purely *qualitative* risk management.

It is easy to see that it is impossible to define and quantitatively measure all factors that exist in a given risk assessment. It is also easy to see that a risk assessment that measures no factors quantitatively but measures them all qualitatively is possible.

The decision of whether to use qualitative versus quantitative risk management depends on the criticality of the project, the resources available, and the management style. The decision will be influenced by the degree to which the fundamental risk management metrics, such as asset value, exposure factor, and threat frequency can be quantitatively defined.

Accepting Risk

In addition to mitigating risk or transferring risk, it may be acceptable for a manager to *accept* risk in that despite the potential cost of a given risk and its associated probability, the manager of the organization will accept responsibility for the risk if it does happen. For example, a manager may choose to allow a programmer to make "emergency" changes to a production system (in violation of good segregation of duties) because the system cannot go down during a given period of time. The manager accepts the risk that the programmer could possibly make unauthorized changes because of the high-availability requirement of that system. However, there should always be some additional controls such as management review or a standardized approval process to ensure the assumed risk is adequately managed.

Tools

Many tools can be used to enhance the risk management process. The following tools can be used during the various phases of risk assessment to add objectivity and structure to the process. More information on these tools can be found in any good project-management text.

Affinity grouping   A method of identifying items that are related and then identifying the principle that ties them together into a group.

Baseline identification and analysis   The process of establishing a baseline set of risks. It produces a "snapshot" of all the identified risks at a given point in time.

Cause and effect analysis   Identifying relationships between a risk and the factors that can cause it. This is usually accomplished using *fishbone diagrams* developed by Dr. Kaoru Ishikawa, former Professor of Engineering at the Science University of Tokyo.

Cost/benefit analysis   A straightforward method for comparing cost estimates with the benefits of a mitigation strategy.

Gantt charts   A management tool for diagramming schedules, events, and activity duration.

Interrelationship digraphs   A method for identifying cause-and-effect relationships by clearly defining the problem to be solved, identifying the key elements of the problem, and then describing the relationships between each of the key elements.

Pareto charts   A histogram that ranks the categories in a chart from most frequent to least frequent, thus facilitating risk prioritization.

> ## Risks Really Don't Change, But They Can Be Mitigated
> One final thought to keep in mind is that the risk itself doesn't really change, no matter what actions are taken to mitigate that risk. A high risk will always be a high risk. However, actions can be taken to reduce the impact of that risk if it occurs.

PERT (program evaluation and review technique) charts A diagram depicting interdependencies between project activities, showing the sequence and duration of each activity. When complete, the chart shows the time necessary to complete the project and the activities that determine that time (the critical path). The earliest and latest start and stop times for each activity and available slack times can also be shown.

Risk management plan A comprehensive plan documenting how risks will be managed on a given project. It contains processes, activities, milestones, organizations, responsibilities, and details of each major risk management activity and how it is to be accomplished. It is an integral part of the project management plan.

Chapter Review

Chapter Summary

After reading this chapter and completing the exercises, you should understand the following about risk management.

Risk Management Is an Essential Skill

- Risk management is a key management process that must be used at every level, whether managing a project, a program, or an enterprise.

- Risk management is also a strategic tool to more effectively manage increasingly sophisticated, diverse, and geographically expansive business opportunities.

- Managing risk is key to keeping a business competitive and must be done by managers at all levels.

Business Risks

- Common business risks include management of treasury, revenue, contracts, fraud, environment, regulatory issues, business continuity, and technology.

- Technology is a business risk that is so important it must be specifically managed.

- Technology risks include security, privacy, information technology operations, business systems control and effectiveness, information systems testing, and management of business continuity, reliability and performance, information technology assets, project risk, and change.

Two Risk Management Models

- A general model for managing risk includes asset identification, threat assessment, impact definition and quantification, control design and evaluation, and residual risk management.

- The SEI model for managing risk includes these steps: identify, analyze, plan, track, and control.

Qualitative and Quantitative Risk Assessment

- Both qualitative and quantitative risk assessment approaches must be used to effectively manage risk, and a number of approaches were presented in this chapter.

- Qualitative risk assessment relies on expert judgment and experience by comparing the impact of a threat with the probability of it occurring.

- Qualitative risk assessment can be a simple binary assessment weighing high or low impact against high or low probability. Additional levels can be used to increase the comprehensiveness of the analysis. The well-known red-yellow-green stoplight mechanism is qualitative in nature and is easily understood.

- Quantitative risk assessment applies historical information and trends to assess risk. Models are often used to provide information to decision-makers.

- A common quantitative approach calculates the annualized loss expectancy from the single loss expectancy and the annualized rate of occurrence.

- It is important to understand that it is impossible to conduct a purely quantitative risk assessment, but it is possible to conduct a purely qualitative risk assessment.

Risk Assessment Tools

- There are a number of tools which can be used to add credibility and rigor to the risk assessment process.

- Risk assessment tools help identify relationships, causes, and effects. They assist in prioritizing decisions and facilitate effective management of the risk management process.

Key Terms

Annualized loss expectancy (ALE) *(513)*
Annualized rate of occurrence *(513)*
Asset *(512)*
Control (also called countermeasure or safeguard) *(512)*
Countermeasure See *Control. (512)*
Exposure factor *(513)*
Impact *(512)*
Intangible asset *(516)*
Mitigate *(513)*
Qualitative risk assessment *(512)*
Quantitative risk assessment *(513)*
Residual risk *(518)*
Risk *(512)*
Risk assessment (or risk analysis) *(512)*
Risk management *(512)*
Safeguard (See *Control.) (512)*
Single loss expectancy (SLE) *(513)*
Tangible asset *(516)*
Threat *(512)*
Vulnerability *(512)*

Key Terms Quiz

Use terms from the Key Terms list to complete the sentences that follow. Don't use the same term more than once. Not all terms will be used.

1. asset value × exposure factor = _____.

2. A control may also be called a(n) _____ or a(n) _____.

3. When a threat exploits a vulnerability, you experience a(n) _____.

4. single loss expectancy × annualized rate of occurrence = _____.

5. If you reduce the likelihood of a threat occurring, you _____ a risk.

6. The _____ measures the magnitude of the loss of an asset.

7. Risk analysis is synonymous with _____.

8. Any circumstance or event with the potential to cause harm to an asset is a _____.

9. The characteristics of an asset that can be exploited by a threat to cause harm are its _____.

10. _____ is the overall decision-making process of identifying threats and vulnerabilities and their potential impacts, determining the costs to mitigate such events, and deciding what cost-effective actions need to be taken to control these risks.

Multiple-Choice Quiz

1. Which of the following correctly defines qualitative risk management?

   A. The process of objectively determining the impact of an event that affects a project, program, or business.

   B. The process of subjectively determining the impact of an event that affects a project, program, or business.

   C. The loss that results when a vulnerability is exploited by a threat.

   D. To reduce the likelihood of a threat occurring.

2. Which of the following correctly defines risk?

   A. The risks still remaining after an iteration of risk management.

   B. The loss that results when a vulnerability is exploited by a threat.

   C. Any circumstance or event with the potential to cause harm to an asset.

   D. The possibility of suffering harm or loss.

3. Single loss expectancy (SLE) can best be defined by which of the following equations?

   A. SLE = annualized loss expectancy × annualized rate of occurrence

   B. SLE = asset value × exposure factor

   C. SLE = asset value × annualized rate of occurrence

   D. SLE = annualized loss expectancy × exposure factor

4. Which of the following correctly defines annualized rate of occurrence?

   A. How much an event is expected to cost per year

   B. A measure of the magnitude of loss of an asset

   C. On an annualized basis, the frequency with which an event is expected to occur

   D. The resources or information an organization needs to conduct its business

5. Which of the following is a technology risk?

   A. Business continuity management

   B. Fraud

   C. Contract management

   D. Treasury management

6. The Basel Committee defines operational risk as which of the following?

   A. Risk from disruption by people, systems, processes, or disasters

   B. Risk of default of outstanding loans

   C. Risk of losses due to fluctuations of market prices

   D. The possibility of suffering harm or loss

7. Which of the following is *not* an asset?

   A. Equipment failure

   B. Hardware

   C. Inventory

   D. Cash

   For questions 8 and 9, assume the following: The asset value of a small distribution warehouse is $5 million, and this warehouse serves as backup capability. Its complete destruction by a disaster would take away about 1/5 of the capability of the business. Also assume that this sort of disaster is expected to occur about once every 50 years.

8. Which of the following would be the calculated single loss expectancy (SLE)?

   A. SLE = $25 million

   B. SLE = $1 million

   C. SLE = $2.5 million

   D. SLE = $5 million

9. Which of the following would be the calculated annualized loss expectancy (ALE)?

   A. ALE = $50,000

   B. ALE = $1 million

   C. ALE = $20,000

   D. ALE = $50 million

10. When discussing qualitative risk assessment versus quantitative risk assessment, which of the following is true?

    A. It is impossible to conduct a purely quantitative risk assessment, and it is impossible to conduct a purely qualitative risk assessment.

    B. It is possible to conduct a purely quantitative risk assessment, but it is impossible to conduct a purely qualitative risk assessment.

    C. It is impossible to conduct a purely quantitative risk assessment, but it is possible to conduct a purely qualitative risk assessment.

    D. It is possible to conduct a purely quantitative risk assessment, and it is possible to conduct a purely qualitative risk assessment.

11. Which of the following correctly defines residual risk?

    A. The risks still remaining after an iteration of risk management

    B. The possibility of suffering a loss

    C. The result of a vulnerability being exploited by a threat that results in a loss

    D. Characteristics of an asset that can be exploited by a threat to cause harm

12. Which of the following is a technology risk?

    A. Contract management

    B. Security and privacy

    C. Environmental risk management

    D. Revenue management

13. Which of the following statements about risk is true?

    A. A manager can accept the risk, which will reduce the risk.

    B. The risk itself doesn't really change. However, actions can be taken to reduce the impact of the risk.

    C. A manager can transfer the risk, which will reduce the risk.

    D. A manager can take steps to increase the risk.

14. Which of the following correctly defines a Gantt chart?

    A. A method of identifying items that are related and then identifying the principle that ties them together into a group

    B. A management tool for diagramming schedules events and activity duration

    C. A single page form used to document new risks as they occur

    D. A diagram depicting interdependencies between project activities, showing the sequence and duration of each activity

15. Which of the following is NOT a viable option when dealing with risk?

    A. A manager can take action to mitigate risk.

    B. A manager can take action to transfer risk.

    C. A manager can take action to increase risk.

    D. A manager can take action to accept risk.

Essay Quiz

1. You are drafting an e-mail to your risk management team members to explain the difference between tangible assets and intangible assets. Write a one- or two-sentence paragraph that explains the difference and include two examples of each.

2. You have been tasked to initiate a risk management program for your company. The CEO has just asked you to succinctly explain the relationship between impact, threat, and vulnerability. Think quick on your feet and state a single sentence that explains the relationship.

3. Your CEO now says, "You mentioned that risks always exist. If I take enough measures, can't I eliminate the risk?" Explain why risks always exist.

4. You are explaining your risk management plan to a new team member just brought on as part of a college internship program. The intern asks, "With respect to impact, what does a threat do to a risk?" How would you answer?

5. The intern mentioned in Question 4 now asks you to compare and contrast accepting risk, transferring risk, and mitigating risk. What's your response?

Lab Projects

Lab Project 20.1

The asset value of a distribution center (located in the midwestern United States) and its inventory is $10 million. It is one of two identical facilities (the other is in the southwestern United States). Its complete destruction by a disaster would thus take away half of the capability of the business. Also assume that this sort of disaster is expected to occur about once every 100 years. From this, calculate the annualized loss expectancy

Lab Project 20.2

You have just completed a qualitative threat assessment of the computer security of your organization with the impacts and probabilities of occurrence listed in the table that follows. Properly place the threats in a 3 by 3 table similar to that in Figure 20-4. Which of the threats should you take action on, which should you monitor, and which ones may not need your immediate attention?

Threat	Impact	Probability of Occurrence
Virus Attacks	High	High
Internet Hacks	Medium	High
Wireless Hacks	Low	High
Disgruntled Employee Hack	High	Medium
Weak Incidence Response Mechanisms	Medium	Medium
Theft of Information by a Trusted Third-Party Contractor	Low	Medium
Competitor Hack	High	Low
Dial-up Hack	Medium	Low
Inadvertent Release of Non-critical Information	Low	Low

Change Management

Upon completion of this chapter, you will be able to:

- Explain why change management is an important enterprise management tool
- Describe the key concept of segregation of duties
- Describe the essential elements of change management
- Describe a process for implementing change management
- List the concepts of the Capability Maturity Model

It is well recognized that today's software systems are extremely complex. It is obvious that inventory management systems for large international enterprises like Wal-Mart or Home Depot are probably as complex as an aircraft or skyscraper. Prominent operating systems like Windows or UNIX are very complex, as are computer processors on a chip. Even a Web-based shopping cart application is relatively complex.

It would be absurd to think of constructing an aircraft, large building, computer chip, or automobile in the informal manner we sometimes use to develop and operate software of equal complexity. Software systems have grown to be so complex and mission-critical that enterprises cannot afford to develop and maintain software in an ad hoc manner.

Change management procedures are one way to add structure and control to the development of large software systems as they move from development to operation. Change management, as discussed in this chapter, refers to a standard methodology for performing and recording changes during software development and operation. The methodology defines steps that ensure that system changes are required by the organization, and are properly authorized, documented, tested, and approved by management. In this chapter, the term *software configuration management* is considered synonymous with *software change management* and, in a more limited manner, *version control*.

The term *change management* is often applied to the management of changes in the business environment, typically as a result of business process reengineering or quality enhancement efforts. The term *change management* as used in this chapter is directly related to managing and controlling software development, maintenance, and operation.

Why Change Management?

In Chapter 20, risk management was presented as an essential decision-making process. In much the same way, change management is an essential practice for managing software during its entire lifecycle, from development, through deployment and operation, until it is taken out of service. In order to effectively manage the software development and maintenance processes, discipline and structure can help conserve resources and enhance effectiveness. Software change management, like risk management, is often considered expensive, nonproductive, unnecessary, and confusing—an impediment to progress. However, like risk management, it can be scaled to properly control and manage the development and maintenance of software effectively.

Change management should be used in all phases of software's life: development, testing, quality assurance (QA), and production. Short development cycles have not changed the need for an appropriate amount of management control over software development, maintenance, and operation. In fact, short turnaround times make change management more necessary because once a system goes active in today's Web-based environment, often it cannot be taken offline to correct errors—it must stay up and online or business will be lost and brand recognition damaged. In today's volatile stock market, even small indicators of lagging performance can have dramatic impacts on a company's stock value.

The following scenarios exemplify the need for appropriate change management policy and for procedures over software and data:

- The developers can't find the latest version of the production source code.
- A bug corrected a few months ago mysteriously reappeared.
- Fielded software was working fine yesterday but does not work properly today.
- Development team members overwrote each other's changes.
- A programmer spent several hours changing the wrong version of the software.
- A customer record corrected by the call center yesterday, shows the old, incorrect information today.
- New tax rates stored in a table have been overwritten with last year's tax rates.
- An application runs fine at some overseas locations but not at other locations.

Just about anyone with more than a year's experience in software development can relate to at least one of the preceding scenarios. However, each of these scenarios can be controlled, and impacts mitigated, through proper change management procedures.

NOTE All software can be placed under an appropriate software change management process, including:
Web pages
Service packs
Security patches
Third-party software releases
Test data and test scripts
Parameter files
Scripts, stored procedures, or job control language–type programs
Customized vendor code
Source code of any kind

The Key Concept: Segregation of Duties

A key foundation for software change management is the recognition that involving more than one individual in a process may reduce risk. Good business control practices require that duties be assigned to individuals in such a way that no one individual can control all phases of a process or the processing and recording of a transaction. This is called **segregation of duties** (sometimes called **separation of duties**). It is an important means by which errors and fraudulent or malicious acts can be discouraged and prevented. Segregation of duties can be applied in many organizational scenarios because it establishes a basis for accountability and control. Proper segregation of duties can safeguard enterprise assets and protect against risks. They should be documented, monitored, and enforced.

Information technology (IT) organizations should design, implement, monitor, and enforce appropriate segregation of duties for the enterprise's information systems and processes. Today's computer systems are rapidly evolving into an increasingly decentralized and networked computer infrastructure. In the absence of adequate IT controls, such rapid growth may allow exploitation of large amounts of enterprise information in a short time. Further, the knowledge of computer operations held by IT staff is significantly greater than that of an average user, and this knowledge could be abused for malicious purposes.

Some of the best practices for ensuring proper segregation of duties in an IT organization are as follows:

- Segregation of duties between development, testing, quality assurance, and production should be documented in written procedures and implemented by software or manual processes.

- Program developers' and program testers' activities should be conducted on "test" data only. They should be restricted from accessing "live" production data. This will assist in ensuring an independent and objective testing environment without jeopardizing the confidentiality and integrity of production data.

- End users or computer operations personnel should not have direct access to program source code. This control helps lessen the opportunity of exploiting software weaknesses or introducing malicious code (or code that has not been properly tested) into the production environment either intentionally or unintentionally.

- Functions of creating, installing, and administrating software programs should be assigned to different individuals. For example, since developers create and enhance programs, they should not be able to install it on the production system. Likewise, database administrators should not be program developers on database systems they administer.

- All accesses and privileges to systems, software, or data should be granted based on the principle of least privilege, which gives users no more privileges than are necessary to perform their jobs. Access privileges should be reviewed regularly to ensure that individuals who no longer require access have had their privileges removed.

- Formal software change management policy and procedures should be enforced throughout the enterprise. The number of changes in software components (including emergency changes) that are implemented after the product has been placed into production and that do not go through the approved formal change management mechanism should be minimized.

Managers at all levels should review existing and planned processes and systems to ensure proper segregation of duties. Smaller business entities may not have the resources to fully implement all of the preceding practices, but other control mechanisms, including hiring qualified personnel, bonding contractors, and using training, monitoring, and evaluation practices, can reduce any organization's exposure to risk. The establishment of such practices can ensure enterprise assets are properly safeguarded and can also greatly reduce error and the potential for fraudulent or malicious activities.

Change management practices implement and enforce segregation of duties by adding structure and management oversight to the software development process. Change management techniques can ensure that only correct and authorized changes, as approved by management or other authorities, are allowed to be made, following a defined process.

Elements of Change Management

Change management has its roots in system engineering, where it is commonly referred to as **configuration management**. For example, auto makers know that a certain amount of configuration management is necessary to efficiently and effectively build safe cars. Bolts and screws with proper strengths and qualities are used on every car, in specific places—employees don't just reach into a barrel of bolts, pull one out that looks about right, and bolt it on. The same applies to aircraft—for an aircraft to fly safely, it must be built of parts of the right size, shape, strength, and so on. Computer hardware and software development have also evolved over the last few decades. Proper management structure and controls must exist to ensure the products operate as planned.

Change management and configuration management have different terms for their various phases, but they can all fit into the four general phases defined under configuration management: configuration identification, configuration control, configuration status accounting, and configuration auditing.

Configuration identification is the process of identifying which assets need to be managed and controlled. These assets could be software modules, test cases or scripts, table or parameter values, major subsystems, or entire systems. The idea is that, depending on the size and complexity of the software project, an appropriate set of data and software (or other assets) must be identified and properly managed. These identified assets are called **configuration items** or **software configuration items**.

Related to configuration identification, and the result of it, is the definition of a baseline. A **baseline** serves as a foundation for comparison or measurement. It provides the necessary visibility to control change. In our case, a software baseline defines the software system as it is built and running at a point in time. As another example, network security best practices clearly state that any large organization should build their servers to a standard build configuration to enhance overall network security. The servers are the configuration items, and the standard build is the server baseline.

Configuration control is the process of controlling changes to items that have been baselined. Configuration control ensures that only approved changes to a baseline are allowed to be implemented. It is easy to understand why a software system, such as a Web-based order entry system, should not be changed without proper testing and control—otherwise the system might stop functioning at a critical time. Configuration control is a key step that provides valuable insight to managers. If a system is being changed, and configuration control is being observed, managers and others concerned will be better informed. This ensures proper use of assets and avoids unnecessary downtime due to the installation of unapproved changes.

Configuration status accounting consists of the procedures for tracking and maintaining data relative to each configuration item in the baseline. It is closely related to configuration control. Status accounting involves gathering and maintaining information relative to each configuration item. For example, it documents what changes have been requested; what changes have been made, when, and for what reason; who authorized the change; who performed the change; and what other configuration items or systems were affected by the change.

Returning to our example of servers being baselined, if the operating system of those servers is found to have a security flaw, then the baseline can be consulted to determine which servers are vulnerable to this particular security flaw. Those systems with this weakness can be updated (and only those that need to be updated). Configuration control and configuration status accounting help ensure systems are more consistently managed and, ultimately in this case, the organization's network security is maintained. It is easy to imagine the state of an organization that has not built all servers to a common baseline and has not properly controlled their systems' configurations. It would be very difficult to know the configuration of individual servers, and security could quickly become weak.

 NOTE It is important to understand that even though all servers may be initially configured to the same baseline, individual applications might require a system-specific configuration to run properly. Change management actually facilitates system-specific configuration in that all exceptions from the standard configuration are documented. All people involved in managing and operating these systems will have documentation to help quickly understand why a particular system is configured in this unique way.

Configuration auditing is the process of verifying that the configuration items are built and maintained according to the requirements, standards, or contractual agreements. It is similar to how audits in the financial world are used to ensure that generally accepted accounting principles and practices are adhered to and that financial statements properly reflect the financial status of the enterprise. Configuration audits ensure that policies and procedures are being followed, that all configuration items (including hardware and software) are being properly maintained, and that existing documentation accurately reflects the status of the systems in operation.

Configuration auditing takes on two forms: functional and physical. A *functional configuration audit* verifies that the configuration item performs as defined by the documentation of the software requirements. A *physical configuration audit* confirms that all configuration items to be included in a release, change, or upgrade are actually included and that no additional items are included—no more, no less.

Implementing Change Management

Change management requires some structure and discipline in order to be effective. The change management function is scalable from small to enterprise-level projects. Figure 21-1 illustrates a sample change management flow appropriate for medium to large projects. It can be adapted to small organizations, by having the developer only perform work on his/her workstation (never on the production system) and having the system administrator serve in the buildmaster function. The buildmaster is usually an independent person responsible for compiling and incorporating changed software into an executable image.

Figure 21-1 shows that developers never have access to the production system or data. It also demonstrates proper segregation of duties between developers, QA and test people, and production. It implies that there is a distinct separation between development, testing and QA, and production environments. This workflow is for major changes that have a major impact on production or the customer's business process. For changes that are minor or have minimal risk or impact on business processes, some of the steps may be omitted.

The change management workflow proceeds as follows:

1. The developer checks out source code from the code-control tool archive to the development system.

2. The developer modifies the code and conducts unit testing.

3. The developer checks the modified code into the code-control tool archive.

4. The developer notifies the buildmaster of changes and that they are ready for a new build and testing/QA.

5. The buildmaster creates a build incorporating the modified code and compiles the code.

6. The buildmaster notifies the system administrator that the executable image is ready for testing/QA.

7. The system administrator moves the executables to the test/QA system.

8. QA tests the new executables. If tests are passed, test/QA notifies the manager. If tests fail, the process starts over.

9. Upon manager approval, the system administrator moves the executable to the production system.

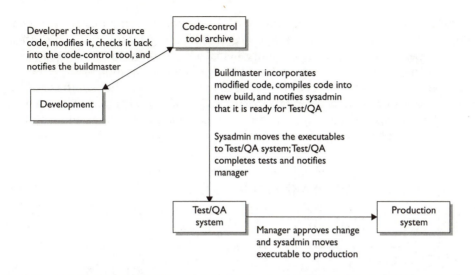

Figure 21-1   Software change control workflow

 NOTE   Observe the segregation of duties between development, test/QA, and production. The functions of creating, installing, and administrating are assigned to different individuals. Note also appropriate management review and approval. This implementation also ensures that no compiler exists on the production system.

The Purpose of a Change Control Board

To oversee the change management process, most organizations establish a **change control board** (CCB). In practice, a change control board not only facilitates adequate management oversight, it also facilitates better coordination between projects. The CCB convenes on a regular basis, usually weekly or monthly, and can be convened on an emergency or as-needed basis. Figure 21-2 shows the process for implementing and properly controlling software during changes.

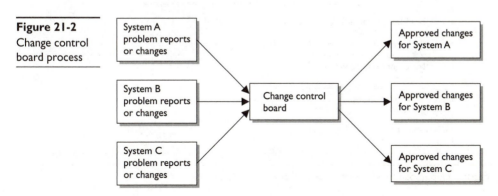

Figure 21-2
Change control
board process

The CCB's membership should consist of development project managers, network administrators, system administrators, test/QA managers, an information security manager, an operations center manager, and a help desk manager. Others can be added as necessary, depending on the size and complexity of the organization.

A **software problem report** (SPR) is used to track changes through the CCB. The SPR is used to document changes or corrections to a software system. It reflects who requested the change and why, what analysis must be done and by whom, and how it was corrected or implemented. Figure 21-3 shows a sample software problem report.

SOFTWARE PROBLEM REPORT (SPR)

❏ Error   SPR Number:_____

❏ Improvement   Originator:_____

----------------------------------- **Problem** -----------------------------------

System Affected:_____

Related Systems:_____

Classification: Problem Description:_____

❏ Software   _____

❏ Hardware   _____

❏ Documentation   _____

❏ Comment   _____

Analysis Assigned to:_____

----------------------------------- **Analysis** -----------------------------------

(Prepared by responsible software design organization)   Date Received:_____

Classification: Explanation:

❏ Design   _____

❏ Coding   _____

❏ Documentation   _____

❏ Environment   _____

Signatures

Analyst:_____ Date:_____ Originator:_____ Date:_____

----------------------------------- **Correction** -----------------------------------

Brief Description of Work and List of Modules Changed:

_____

_____

Documentation Changed:

_____

_____

Signatures

Developer:_____ Date:_____ Manager:_____ Date:_____

Figure 21-3   Sample software problem report

Code Integrity

One key benefit of adequate change management is the assurance of code consistency and integrity. Whenever a modified program is moved to the production source-code library, the executable version should also be moved to the production system. Automated change management systems greatly simplify this process and, hence, are better controls for ensuring executable and source-code integrity. Again, at no time should the user or application developer have access to production source and executable code libraries in the production environment.

Finally, in today's networked environment, the integrity of the executable code is critical. It is a common hacking technique to replace key system executable code with modified code that may contain backdoors, allowing unauthorized access or functions to be performed. Executable code integrity can be verified using a variety of host-based intrusion detection systems. These systems create and maintain a database of the size and content of executable modules. This is usually done by performing some kind of hashing or sophisticated checksum operation on the executable modules and storing the results in a database. The operation is performed on a regular schedule against the executable modules, and the results are compared to the database to identify any unauthorized changes that may have occurred to the executable modules.

The Capability Maturity Model

As an organization embarks upon implementing change management, an important concept to understand is the **Capability Maturity Model (CMM)** for software developed at Carnegie Mellon University's Software Engineering Institute (SEI). The CMM relies on configuration or change management as one of its fundamental concepts. It provides organizations with the capability to improve their software processes by providing an evolutionary path from ad hoc processes to disciplined software management processes.

The SEI's web page defines the five maturity levels:

- **Initial**   The software process is ad hoc.

- **Repeatable**   The software process is structured enough that success with one project can be repeated for another similar project.

- **Defined**   The software process is standardized and documented.

- **Managed**   Various aspects of the software process and products are measured and evaluated.

- **Optimizing**   Key business processes and their supporting software projects are continuously improved based on measurements and testing new ideas.

 STUDY TIP   To complete your preparations for the Security+ exam, it is recommended that you consult SEI's Web site (www.sei.cmu.edu/cmm/cmm.sum.html) for specific CMM definitions.

Change management is a key process to implementing the CMM in an organization. For example, if an organization is at CMM level 1, then it probably has no formal change management processes in place. At level 3, an organization has a defined change management process that is followed. At level 5, the change management process is a routine part of improving software products and implementing new ideas. In order for an organization to effectively manage software development, operation, and maintenance, then it should be using the CMM and must have effective change management processes in place.

Chapter Review

Chapter Summary

Explain Why Change Management Is an Important Enterprise Management Tool
After reading this chapter and completing the exercises, you should understand the following about change management.

- Change management should be used in all phases of the software lifecycle.
- It can be scaled to effectively control and manage software development and maintenance.
- It can prevent some of the most common software development and maintenance problems.

Describe the Key Concept of Segregation of Duties

- Segregation of duties ensures that no single individual or organization possesses too much control in a process.
- It helps prevent errors and fraudulent or malicious acts.
- It establishes a basis for accountability and control.
- It can help safeguard enterprise assets and protect against risks.

Describe the Essential Elements of Change Management
The elements of change management are
- Configuration identification to identify assets that need to be controlled
- Configuration control to keep track of changes to configuration items that have been baselined
- Configuration status accounting to track each configuration item in the baseline
- Configuration auditing to verify the configuration items are built and maintained appropriately

Describe a Process for Implementing Change Management

- A standardized process and a change control board provide management with proper oversight and control of the software development lifecycle.

- A good change management process will exhibit good segregation of duties and have clearly defined roles, responsibilities, and approvals.

- An effective change control board facilitates good management oversight and coordination between projects.

List the Concepts of the Capability Maturity Model

- Once proper management oversight exists, the company will be able to use the Capability Maturity Model to help the organization move from ad-hoc activities to a disciplined software management process.

- CMM relies heavily on change management to provide organizations with the capability to improve their software processes.

Key Terms

Baseline *(536)*
Capability Maturity Model *(541)*
Change management *(533)*
Change/configuration management *(536)*
Change control board *(537)*
Configuration auditing *(537)*
Configuration control *(537)*
Configuration identification *(536)*
Configuration item *(536)*
Configuration status accounting *(537)*
Segregation/separation of duties *(535)*
Software configuration item *(536)*
Software problem report *(540)*

Key Terms Quiz

Use terms from the Key Terms list to complete the sentences that follow. Don't use the same term more than once. Not all terms will be used.

1. The _____ is the body that provides oversight to the change management process.

2. _____, also known as _____, is a standard methodology for performing and recording changes during software development and operation.

3. _____ is the process of assigning responsibilities to different individuals such that no single individual can commit fraudulent or malicious actions.

4. Procedures for tracking and maintaining data relative to each configuration item in the baseline are _____.

5. A _____ describes a system as it is built and functioning at a point in time.

6. A structured methodology that provides an evolutionary path from ad-hoc processes to disciplined software management is the _____.

7. The process of verifying that configuration items are built and maintained according to requirements, standards, or contractual agreements is _____.

8. The document used by the change control board to track changes to software is called a _____.

9. When you identify which assets need to be managed and controlled, you are performing _____.

10. _____ is the process of controlling changes to items which have been baselined.

Multiple-Choice Quiz

1. The original developer of a web-based system has left the company, and the new developer assigned has been unable to find the latest source code for that system. This type of problem could have been prevented by:

    A. The system administrator making the changes instead of the developer

    B. Proper change management procedures over the object code

    C. The use of an object-oriented design approach rather than a rapid prototyping design approach

    D. Proper change management procedures over the source code

2. Why should developers and testers avoid using "live" production data to perform various testing activities?

    A. The use of "live" production data ensures a full and realistic test database.

    B. The use of "live" production data can jeopardize the confidentiality and integrity of the production data.

    C. The use of "live" production data ensures an independent and objective test environment.

    D. Developers and testers should be allowed to use "live" production data.

3. Software change management procedures are established to…

    A. Ensure continuity of business operations in the event of a natural disaster

    B. Add structure and control to the development of software systems

    C. Ensure changes in business operations caused by a management restructuring are properly controlled

    D. Identify threats, vulnerabilities, and mitigating actions that could impact an enterprise

4. Which of the following correctly defines the principle of least privilege?

   A. Access privileges are reviewed regularly to ensure that individuals who no longer require access have had their privileges removed.

   B. Authorization of a subject's access to an object depends on sensitivity labels.

   C. The administrator determines which subjects can have access to certain objects based on organizational security policy.

   D. Users have no more privileges than are necessary to perform their jobs.

5. Which of the following is *not* a principle of segregation of duties?

   A. Software development, testing, quality assurance, and production should be assigned to the same individuals.

   B. Software developers should not have access to production data and source-code files.

   C. Software developers and testers should be restricted from accessing "live" production data.

   D. The functions of creating, installing, and administrating software programs should be assigned to different individuals.

6. Configuration auditing consists of...

   A. The process of controlling changes to items that have been baselined

   B. The process of identifying which assets need to be managed and controlled

   C. The process of verifying that the configuration items are built and maintained properly

   D. The procedures for tracking and maintaining data relative to each configuration item in the baseline

7. Why should end users not be given access to program source codes?

   A. It could allow an end user to identify weaknesses or errors in the source code.

   B. It ensures testing and quality assurance perform their proper functions.

   C. It assists in ensuring an independent and objective testing environment.

   D. It could allow an end user to execute the source code.

8. Which position is responsible for modifying code in the system?

   A. System administrator

   B. Developer

   C. Manager

   D. Quality assurance

9. Configuration control consists of...

   A. The process of controlling changes to items that have been baselined

   B. The process of identifying which assets need to be managed and controlled

    C. The process of verifying that the configuration items are built and maintained properly

    D. The procedures for tracking and maintaining data relative to each configuration item in the baseline

10. Configuration identification consists of...

    A. The process of verifying that the configuration items are built and maintained properly

    B. The procedures for tracking and maintaining data relative to each configuration item in the baseline

    C. The process of controlling changes to items that have been baselined

    D. The process of identifying which assets need to be managed and controlled

11. Which position is responsible for approving the movement of executable code to the production system?

    A. System administrator

    B. Developer

    C. Manager

    D. Quality assurance

12. The purpose of a change control board (CCB) is to...

    A. Facilitate management oversight and better project coordination

    B. Identify which assets need to be managed and controlled

    C. Establish software processes that are structured enough that success with one project can be repeated for another similar project

    D. Track and maintain data relative to each configuration item in the baseline

13. Which computer security technology is used to ensure the integrity of executable code?

    A. Network-based intrusion detection systems

    B. Switches

    C. Routers

    D. Host-based intrusion detection systems

14. In the Software Engineering Institute's Capability Maturity Model (CMM), which of the following correctly defines Level 1, Initial?

    A. Various aspects of the software process and products are measured and evaluated.

    B. Key business processes and the supporting software are continuously improved based on measurements and testing new ideas.

C. The software process is standardized and documented.

D. The software process is ad hoc.

15. In the Software Engineering Institute's Capability Maturity Model (CMM), which of the following correctly defines Level 5, Optimizing?

    A. Various aspects of the software process and products are measured and evaluated.

    B. Key business processes and the supporting software are continuously improved based on measurements and testing new ideas.

    C. The software process is standardized and documented.

    D. The software process is structured enough that success with one project can be repeated for another similar project.

Essay Quiz

1. You are the project manager for a new web-based online shopping system. Due to market competition, your management has directed you to go live with your systems one week earlier than originally scheduled. One of your development team is a sharp, smart programmer with less than one year of experience. He asks you why your team is required to follow what he calls cumbersome, out-of-date change management procedures. What would you tell him?

2. Explain why managing operating system patches should use the change management principles discussed in this chapter.

3. Explain why a database administrator (DBA) should not be allowed to develop programs on the systems they administer.

4. Your company has just decided to follow the Capability Maturity Model. You manage a development shop of 15 programmers with four team leaders. You and your team have determined that you are currently at the CMM Initial level. Describe the actions you might take to move your shop to the Defined maturity level.

5. You have just been made Director of Ecommerce Applications over 30 programmers and ten major software projects. Your projects include multiple web pages on ten different production servers, system security for those servers, three development servers, three test/QA servers, and some third-party software. Which of those resources would you place under change management practices and why?

Lab Projects

Lab Project 21.1

Using a typical IT organization from a medium-sized company (100 developers/ managers/support personnel), describe the purpose, organization, and responsibilities of a change control board appropriate for this organization.

Lab Project 21.2

You are the IT staff auditor for the company mentioned in the first lab project. You have reviewed the change control board processes and found they have instituted the following change management process. Describe two major control weaknesses in this particular change management process. What would you do to correct these control weaknesses?

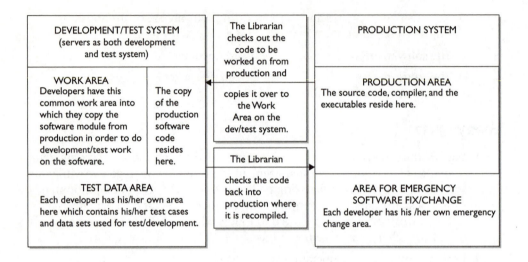

Privilege Management

Upon completion of this chapter, you will be able to:

- Describe the differences between user, group, and role management
- Explain the advantage of single sign-ons
- Compare and contrast centralized privilege management and decentralized privilege management
- Describe different auditing types (privilege, usage, and escalation)
- Describe methods of managing access (MAC, DAC, and RBAC)

Computer systems are in such wide use now that they touch almost every facet of our lives: they process credit card transactions, they handle airline reservations, they store a vast amount of personal information, and they manage car engines to ensure optimal fuel efficiency. Most of the time, computers—particularly the more complicated systems, such as PCs, servers and mainframes—require interaction from a human user. The user interacts with the applications and operating system of the computer to complete tasks and perform specific functions.

On single-user systems, such as PCs, the individual user typically has access to most of the system's resources, processing capability, and stored data. On multiuser systems, such as servers and mainframes, an individual user may have very limited access to the system and the data stored on that system. An administrator responsible for managing and maintaining the multiuser system may have much greater access. So how does the computer system know which users should have access to what data? How does the operating system know what applications a user is allowed to use?

On early computer systems, anyone with physical access had fairly significant rights to the system and could typically access any file or execute any application. As computers became more popular and it became obvious that some way of separating and restricting users was needed, the concept of users, groups, and privileges came into being. These concepts continue to be developed and refined and are now part of what we call *privilege management*.

Though privilege management has become a crucial part of modern operating systems and computer operations, it's really quite a simple concept. *Privilege management* is the process of restricting a user's ability to interact with the computer system. A user's interaction with a computer system covers a fairly broad area and includes items such as viewing, modifying and deleting data, running applications, stopping and starting processes, and controlling computer resources. Essentially, everything a user can do to or with a computer system falls into the realm of privilege management.

Privilege management occurs at many different points within an operating system or even within applications running on a particular operating system. While UNIX and Windows operating systems have a slightly different approach to privilege management, there are some similar approaches and concepts that we will cover in this chapter.

User, Group, and Role Management

In order to effectively manage the privileges of many different people on the same system, you must have a mechanism for separating people into distinct entities (users) so you can control things on an individual level. At the same time, it's convenient and efficient to be able to lump users together when granting many different people (groups) access to something at the same time. At other times, it's useful to be able to grant or restrict access based upon a person's job or function within the organization (role). While you can manage privileges on the basis of users alone, it is far more convenient and efficient to manage using the users, group, and role capabilities together.

User

The term "user" generally applies to any person accessing a computer system. In privilege management, a **user** is a single individual, such as "John Forthright" or "Sally Jenkins." This is generally the lowest level addressed by privilege management and the most common area for addressing things like access, rights, and capabilities. When accessing a computer system, each user is generally given a *userID*—a unique alphanumeric identifier they will use to identify themselves when logging in or accessing the system. UserIDs are usually based on some combination of the user's first, middle, and last name and will often include numbers. When developing a scheme for selecting userIDs, it is important to keep in mind that userIDs must be unique to each user, but must also be fairly easy for the user to remember and use.

Though there are some notable exceptions, in general a user wishing to access a computer system must first have a userid created for them on the system they wish to use. This is usually done by a system administrator, security administrator, or other privileged user, and this is the first step in privilege management—a user should not be allowed to create their own account.

Once the account is created and a userID is selected, the administrator may assign specific permissions to that user. **Permissions** control what the user is allowed to do on the system—which files they may access, which programs they may execute, and so on. While PCs typically only have one or two user accounts, larger systems such as servers and mainframes may have hundreds of accounts on the same system. Figure 22-1 shows the Users and Passwords screen from a Windows 2000 Professional system. Note that there are several user accounts on this system, each identified by a unique userID.

There are a few "special" user accounts that don't typically match up one-to-one with a real person. These accounts are reserved for special functions and typically have much more access and control over the computer system than the average user does. Two such accounts are the "administrator" account under Windows and the "root" account under

Figure 22-1

Windows 2000's
Users and
Passwords utility

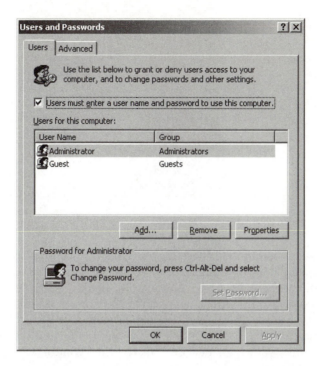

UNIX. The "administrator" and "root" accounts are known as **superusers**—if something can be done on the system, the superuser has the power to do it. These accounts are not typically assigned to a specific individual and are often shared, only being accessed when the full capabilities of that account are needed.

Due to the power these accounts possess, and the few, if any, restrictions placed on these accounts, they must be protected with strong passwords that are not easily guessed or obtained. These accounts are also the most common targets of attackers—if the attacker can become root or assume the privilege level associated with the root account, they can bypass most access controls and accomplish anything they want to on that system.

Groups

Under privilege management, a **group** is pretty much what you think it would be. A group is a collection of users with some common criteria, such as a need for access to a particular dataset or group of applications. A group can have one user or hundreds of users, and each user can belong to one or more groups. Figure 22-2 shows a common approach to grouping users—building groups based on job function.

By assigning a user membership in a specific group, it becomes much easier to control that user's access and privileges. For example, if every member of the Engineering department needs access to product development documents, administrators can place all the users in the Engineering department in a single group and then allow that group to access the necessary documents. Once a group is assigned permissions to access a particular resource, adding a new user to that group will automatically allow that user

Figure 22-2
Logical
representation
of groups

Sales

Engineering

Information
Technology

to access that resource. In effect, the user "inherits" the permissions of the group as soon as they are placed in that group. As Figure 22-3 shows, a computer system can have many different groups, each with their own rights and privileges.

As you can see from the description for the Administrators group in Figure 22-3, this group has complete and unrestricted access to the computer. This includes all files, applications, and datasets. Anyone who belongs to the Administrators group or is placed in this group will have a great deal of access and control over the system.

Role

The other common method of managing access and privileges is by roles. A **role** is usually synonymous with a job or set of functions. For example, the role of "backup operator" may be applied to someone who is responsible for making sure that the system and any data residing on the system is regularly and successfully saved (usually to some sort of removable media, such as tapes). Backup operators need to accomplish specific functions

Figure 22-3   Group management screen from a Windows 2000 system

and will need access to certain resources; for example, they may need the ability to read files on the system and save them to tape. In general, anyone serving in the role of backup operator will need the same rights and privileges as every other backup operator. For simplicity and efficiency, rights and privileges can be assigned to the role "backup operator," and anyone assigned to fulfill that role will automatically have the correct rights and privileges to perform their tasks.

Single Sign-On

In order to use a system, users must be able to access it, which they usually do by supplying their userid and corresponding password. As any security administrator knows, the more systems a particular user has access to, the more passwords that user must have and remember. The natural tendency for users is to select passwords that are easy to remember, or even the same password for use on the multiple systems they access. Invariably, users will forget the passwords they chose for infrequently accessed systems, which creates more work for system administrators who must assist users with password changes or password recovery efforts. Wouldn't it be easier for the user to just log in once and only have to remember a single, good password? This is made possible with a technology called **single sign-on**.

Single sign-on, often called SSO, is an authentication process where the user can enter a single userID and password and then be able to move from application to application or resource to resource without having to supply further authentication information. Put simply, you supply the right userID and password once and you have access to all the applications and data you're supposed to, without having to log in multiple times and remember many different passwords. From a user standpoint, single sign-on is much easier—you only need to remember one userID and one password. From an administration standpoint, single sign-on can be easier to manage and maintain. From a security standpoint, single sign-on may even be more secure, as the user who needs to remember only one password is less likely to pick something that is simple and easy or to write it down. Figure 22-4 shows a logical depiction of the single sign-on process:

1. The user signs in once, providing their userID and password to the single sign-on server.

2. The single sign-on server then provides authentication information to any resource the user accesses during that session. The server interfaces with the other applications and systems—the user does not need to log in to each system individually.

In reality, single sign-on is usually a little more difficult to implement than vendors would lead you to believe. To be effective and useful, all your applications need to be able to access and use the authentication provided by the single sign-on process. The more diverse your network is, the less likely this is to be the case. If your network, like most, contains multiple operating systems, custom applications, and a diverse user base, single sign-on may not even be a viable option.

Figure 22-4 Single sign-on process

Centralized vs. Decentralized Management

In the world of telecommunications and computers, there is almost always more than one way to accomplish the same goal. Coincidentally, there are usually several schools of thought as to why one method is better than the other. This is especially true of security and privilege management. Regardless of how vast or minute your computer deployment is, you will have to manage the rights and privileges of the users and processes using those systems, and the two main approaches to rights and privilege management are centralized and decentralized.

Centralized Management

Centralized management brings the authority and responsibility for managing and maintaining rights and privileges into a single group, location, or area. To illustrate, consider the employees of a bank. In a bank, the bank teller has certain rights and privileges: they can process withdrawals and deposits, count money, and process a specific set of transactions. But a bank teller can't approve your car loan, and they don't have unrestricted access to the bank vault. Even if they wanted to, the bank teller can't expand their privileges or give additional access to other tellers. In a bank, the bank manager is the central management authority—they decide who can approve loans, access the vault, and give away free toasters. In order to get elevated rights and privileges, the teller must go through the central authority, the bank manager. In a similar fashion, when it comes to managing and maintaining rights and privileges under the centralized model, there is a single group or person that creates and manages users, assigns rights and privileges, and controls access to information systems for the entire organization.

The centralized model has certain advantages and disadvantages.

Advantages

- It can be more efficient, especially for large organizations, to have a specialized, central capability for privilege management.

- Fewer people must be trained on tasks associated with privilege management.

- It is easier to implement new capabilities and processes centrally.
- Central control makes systems easier to audit and manage.
- A more consistent approach is ensured, as everyone "does it the same way."

Disadvantages

- Central management makes it more difficult to implement changes quickly.
- Functions at remote offices may be slowed down.
- It adds bureaucracy and is less flexible.
- Central control usually requires dedicated personnel and resources.

Most large corporations will use some form of centralized management, particularly at the local office level. For example, if a company has offices in Dallas, New York, and Seattle, each city may have its own centralized privilege management functions that perform all of the appropriate tasks for that location. In general, when dealing with a large number of users, it is better to use a centralized approach to privilege management.

Decentralized Management

Decentralized management spreads out the authority and capability to manage privileges and rights. While this may sound like a recipe for anarchy to some, it can be an effective model for the right organization. To illustrate, consider a police department. As a group, police officers are working toward a common goal—the "protect and serve" type of approach that makes our cities safer. Yet each individual police officer has a wide amount of latitude and authority: they can decide when to issue tickets and traffic citations, when to perform an arrest, what sort of activity is considered suspicious, and so on. In essence, individual police officers are constantly modifying their behavior and actions to fit the situation around them, sometimes using more authority and sometimes using less authority. With regard to computer systems, this is similar to each user or department controlling their own access to information systems and associated resources.

The decentralized model has certain advantages and disadvantages.

Advantages

- The decentralized model is highly flexible, as changes can be made whenever they are needed.
- It does not require a dedicated set of personnel and resources.
- Bureaucracy is reduced.

Disadvantages

- It produces very different approaches in each department and office.
- It is more difficult to manage, audit, and maintain.

- There is an increased risk of security breach and corruption.

- More users must be trained on the same tasks.

A decentralized model works well for rapidly changing environments where the tasks are constantly changing and the personnel are highly skilled and motivated. An academic research lab is a good example—in this environment, each researcher may need the capability to modify, manage, and maintain their own information systems without having to rely on a centralized authority.

The Decentralized, Centralized Model

In reality, most companies, and particularly the larger ones, use a combination approach. Imagine a company with 100,000 employees and offices in 52 locations around the world. It's not feasible to have a single person or group manage the rights and privileges of every user in an organization that large. It's much more efficient to decentralize control away from the main corporate office and let each office location handle their own privilege management tasks. Within each office, privilege management is usually centralized to a specific group of individuals (often the system administrators or security personnel). On a macro scale, the company as a whole is decentralized, while on a micro scale each office is centralized—it just depends on the level at which you're examining the organization.

Auditing (Privilege, Usage, and Escalation)

If you go through the trouble and effort to restrict access to certain resources and datasets, you will likely want to make sure only authorized individuals are able to gain access to those resources. Chances are, you'll also want to know who accessed what resources, when they accessed the resources, and what they did. When dealing with privilege management, **auditing** is the name given to any actions or processes used to verify the assigned privileges and rights of a user, as well as any capabilities used to create and maintain a record showing who accessed a particular system and what actions they performed. Records showing which users accessed a computer system and what actions they performed are called **audit trails**. In this section, we will discuss auditing as it pertains to three specific areas: privilege, usage, and escalation.

Privilege Auditing

Privilege auditing is the process of checking the rights and privileges assigned to a specific account or group of accounts. Each user account, group, and role is checked to see what rights and privileges are assigned to them. These results are then compared to the "expected" results to see where the actual results and expected results differ. Privilege auditing helps to find accounts with more privileges than they should have, as well as accounts that have fewer privileges than they should have. By comparing expected to actual results, the auditor can then determine which changes need to be made (like the removal of certain accounts, putting users into new groups or taking them out of other groups, and so on) and which rights and privileges need to be adjusted. Most organizations will perform some type of privilege auditing, either formally or informally, on a regular basis.

How does privilege auditing enhance security? Privilege auditing helps ensure that users have the correct privileges and rights to perform their jobs—not too much access and not too little access. Privilege auditing follows the "trust but verify" philosophy of double-checking each account, group, and role to ensure administrators have performed their jobs correctly. This is particularly important in large corporations or positions where there is a high rate of turnover or employee movement. As an employee leaves or changes positions, their privileges and rights must be revoked or modified to ensure their account is properly disabled (if they are leaving) or their account has been adjusted to reflect their new position (if they are changing positions).

Usage Auditing

Usage auditing is the process of recording who did what and when. Usage auditing creates a record showing who has accessed specific computer systems and what actions that user performed during a given period of time. Usage auditing can also be applied to datasets, specific applications, or databases, and it is very commonly used in accounting systems, transaction-based systems, and database management systems.

Usage auditing is usually performed by a process that records actions and stores them in a file for later analysis. These files can be in plain text or custom formats or can even be encrypted to prevent unauthorized access. Figure 22-5 shows an example of the usage-auditing process on a Red Hat Linux system.

In this example, you can see various processes starting, a user logging in, and actions being performed. Each of these pieces of information can help a system administrator determine what happened on that system during that given period of time. In this example, we see an entry indicating the root user logged in on January 3 at 16:21:48 (4:21 P.M.). This tells us several things:

- Someone with knowledge of the password for the root account has accessed the system.

- The login from 127.0.0.1 tells us that the user logged in on the system's console, so they had physical access to the system.

- The time of 4:21 P.M. tells us it was during business hours.

```
Jan  3 15:48:03 donald sshd[729]: Server listening on 0.0.0.0 port 22.
Jan  3 16:20:22 donald webmin[4086]: Webmin starting
Jan  3 16:20:40 donald xinetd[743]: START: sgi_fam pid=4142 from=<no address>
Jan  3 16:21:48 donald webmin[4212]: Successful login as root from 127.0.0.1
Jan  3 16:29:19 donald useradd[4323]: new group: name=mysql, gid=101
Jan  3 16:29:19 donald useradd[4323]: new user: name=mysql, uid=100, gid=101,
home=/var/lib/mysql, shell=/bin/bash
Jan  3 16:57:02 donald sshd[729]: Received signal 15; terminating.
Jan  3 16:58:03 donald sshd[728]: Server listening on 0.0.0.0 port 22.
Jan  3 16:58:14 donald webmin[917]: Webmin starting
Jan  3 16:58:40 donald xinetd[742]: START: sgi_fam pid=1024 from=<no address>
Jan  3 17:08:52 donald sshd[728]: Received signal 15; terminating.
```

Figure 22-5   Sample of a usage-auditing log from a Red Hat Linux system

Usage auditing is very common in both UNIX and Windows operating systems. Depending on the operating system and logging utility, the administrator can have a great deal of flexibility in what types of information are logged. Figure 22-6 shows the Audit Policy options available in the Windows 2000 operating system. As you can see, there are several audit policies that can be enabled with success and failure criteria. For example, you can audit the successful access to a particular file, or you can audit a logon failure. This type of customizable auditing allows the administrator to adjust the auditing process to suit their particular concerns and environment.

As you can see, this sort of information can be very useful when performing any sort of security investigation or incident response activities. With usage-auditing information, if there is a security incident, you can attempt to re-create the event: which accounts were compromised, what actions were performed, and so on. Having this type of information may enable you to spot the incident, correct any problems, address any issues, and return the machine to operational status. Without this type of information, you might be forced to completely rebuild the system as you would have no way of knowing what the attacker did or what they had access to on the system.

Escalation Auditing

Escalation auditing is the process of looking for an increase in privileges—a normal user suddenly switches to the administrator or root account or obtains admin-level access. Administrators normally operate using their own accounts and switch to the administrator or root account only when they need to perform specific operations that require that level of privilege. So, in the normal course of operations, you will see certain users elevating their privilege level, and this is acceptable behavior. However, this is usually a

Figure 22-6   Audit Policy settings under Windows 2000

small subset of the overall user community, and any privilege escalation by someone outside the administrator group is likely a security breach. Escalation auditing looks for those unexpected or unauthorized increases in rights or privileges and can help security administrators determine when they have happened.

Figure 22-7 shows a good example of escalation auditing. In this section of the auditing log file, you see the user "zack" log in to the system and attempt to switch to the root account. Zack fails once and then succeeds, becoming root and assuming all the rights and privileges associated with that account. As a security administrator, you would need to make sure Zack had legitimate access to the root account and is authorized to elevate his privileges accordingly.

Handling Access Control (MAC, DAC, and RBAC)

The last area of privilege management we will discuss deals with three methods for handling access control:

- **MAC** Mandatory access control
- **DAC** Discretionary access control
- **RBAC** Role-based access control

Mandatory Access Control (MAC)

Mandatory access control is the process of controlling access to information based on the sensitivity of that information and whether or not the user is operating at the appropriate sensitivity level and has the authority to access that information. Under a MAC system, each piece of information and every system resource (files, devices, networks, and so on) is labeled with its sensitivity level (such as Public, Engineering Private, Jones Secret). Users are assigned a clearance level that sets the upper boundary of the information and devices that they are allowed to access. For example, if the administrator defines a file as having an "Engineering Private" sensitivity level, then only the members of the engineering group with access to private information currently operating at a Private sensitivity level can access that file and its contents. A file with a Public sensitivity label would be available to anyone on the system.

The access control and sensitivity labels are required in a MAC system. Administrators define the labels and assign them to users and resources. Users must then operate within their assigned sensitivity and clearance levels—they don't have the option to

```
Jan 26 15:17:21 donald (pam_unix)[16605]: session opened for user zack
Jan 26 15:17:45 donald su(pam_unix)[16650]: authentication failure; logname=
uid=500 euid=0 tty= ruser=zack rhost=  user=root
Jan 26 15:17:51 donald su(pam_unix)[16651]: session opened for user root by
(uid=500)
Jan 26 15:17:53 donald su(pam_unix)[16651]: session closed for user root
Jan 26 15:17:54 donald su(pam_unix)[16605]: session closed for user zack
```

Figure 22-7   Escalation auditing example

modify their own sensitivity levels or the levels of the information resources they create. Due to the complexity involved, MAC is typically only run on systems and operating systems such as Trusted Solaris and OpenBSD where security is a top priority.

Figure 22-8 illustrates MAC in operation. The information resource on the right has been labeled "Engineering Secret," meaning only users in the Engineering group operating at the Secret sensitivity level or above can access that resource. The top user is operating at the Secret level but is not a member of Engineering and is denied access to the resource. The middle user is a member of Engineering, but is operating at a Public sensitivity level and is therefore denied access to the resource. The bottom user is a member of Engineering, is operating at a Secret sensitivity level, and is allowed to access the information resource.

Discretionary Access Control (DAC)

Discretionary access control is the process of using file permissions and optional access control lists to restrict access to information based on a user's identity or group membership. DAC is the most common access control system and is commonly used in both UNIX and Windows operating systems. The "discretionary" part of DAC means that a file or resource owner has the ability to change the permissions on that file or resource.

Under UNIX operating systems, file permissions consist of three distinct parts:

- Owner permissions (read, write, and execute)
- Group permissions (read, write, and execute)
- World permissions (read, write, and execute)

In a simplified view, a file's permissions are usually displayed as a series of nine characters with the first three characters representing the owner's permissions, the second three characters representing the group permissions, and the last three characters representing the permissions for everyone else, or for the "world." This concept is illustrated in Figure 22-9.

Figure 22-8
Logical representation of mandatory access control

Sales secret — Denied

Engineering public — Denied —

Granted

Engineering secret

Engineering Secret

Figure 22-9
Discretionary
file permissions
in the UNIX
environment

Owner	Group	World
rwx	**rw-**	**---**

For example, if you have a file called "design one" owned by Bob, group permissions for Engineering, and the permissions on that file are "rwx rw- ---" as in Figure 22-9, then

- Bob can read, write, and execute the file (rwx)

- Members of the Engineering group can read and write the file but not execute it (rw-)

- The world has no access to the file and can't read, write, or execute the file

Remember that under the discretionary model, the file's owner, Bob, can change the file's permissions anytime he wants.

Role-Based Access Control (RBAC)

Role-based access control is the process of managing access and privileges based on the user's assigned roles. RBAC is the access control model that most closely resembles an organization's structure. Under RBAC, you must first determine the activities that must be performed and the resources that must be accessed by specific roles. For example, the role of "backup operator" must be able to mount and write to removable media and must be able to read every file (in order to save it to tape). Once all the roles are created and the rights and privileges associated with those roles are determined, users can then be assigned one or more roles based on their job functions. When a role is assigned to a specific user, the user gets all the rights and privileges assigned to that role.

Chapter Review

Chapter Summary

After reading this chapter and completing the exercises, you should understand the following regarding privilege management.

User, Group, and Role Management

- *Privilege management* is the process of restricting a user's ability to interact with the computer system.

- Privilege management can be performed on an individual user basis, on membership in a specific group or groups, or on a function/role basis.

- The key concepts of privilege management are the ability to restrict and control access to information and information systems.

Single Sign-on

- Single sign-on requires a user to authenticate successfully once the validated credentials and associated rights and privileges are then automatically carried forward when the user accesses other systems or applications.

- Though it can be a very efficient method of controlling access, single sign-on can be difficult to implement.

Centralized vs. Decentralized Management

- Privilege management can be performed in a centralized or decentralized mode.

- In a centralized mode, control, along with modifications, updates, and maintenance, is performed from a central entity.

- In a decentralized mode, control is pushed down to a much lower and more distributed level.

Auditing (Privilege, Usage, and Escalation)

- Auditing is the process of tracking things such as logons, logoffs, file access, and process start or stop events.

- Auditing can be performed on a privilege-level, usage, or escalation basis.

- Privilege auditing is the process of checking the rights and privileges assigned to a specific account or group of accounts.

- Usage auditing is the process of recording who did what and when.

- Escalation auditing is the process of looking for an increase in privileges, such as when a "regular" user suddenly gains administrator level privileges.

Handling Access Control (MAC, DAC, and RBAC)

- The three main models of access control are mandatory access control, discretionary access control, and role-based access control.

- Mandatory access control is based on the sensitivity of the information or process itself.

- Discretionary access control uses file permissions and access lists to restrict access based on a user's identity or group membership.

- Role-based access control restricts access based on the user's assigned role or roles.

Key Terms

Discretionary access control *(560)*
Escalation auditing *(558)*
Group *(551)*
Mandatory access control *(559)*
Permissions *(550)*
Privilege auditing *(556)*
Role *(552)*
Role-based access control *(561)*
Single sign-on *(553)*
Superuser *(551)*
Usage auditing *(557)*
User *(550)*
UserID *(550)*

Key Terms Quiz

Use terms from the Key Terms list to complete the sentences that follow. Don't use the same term more than once. Not all terms will be used.

1. Checking the rights and privileges assigned to a specific account or group is called _____.

2. The "administrator" account in Windows is also known as a _____ account.

3. The process of looking for an increase in privileges, such as when an ordinary user obtains administrator-level privileges, is called _____.

4. _____ is an authentication process where the user can enter their user ID and password and then be able to move from application to application or resource to resource without having to supply further authentication information.

5. Managing and maintaining rights and privileges from a single group, location, or area is called _____.

6. An _____ is a set of records or events, generally organized chronologically, that record what activity has occurred on a system.

7. An access control mechanism in which the owner of an object can decide which other subjects may have access to the object, and what access these subjects may have is called _____.

8. The name given to any actions or processes used to verify the assigned privileges, rights, or actions of a user is _____.

9. _____ is an access control mechanism in which the security mechanism controls access to all objects (files), and individual subjects (processes or users) cannot change that access.

10. A _____ is a unique alphanumeric identifier that identifies individuals when logging in or accessing a system.

Multiple-Choice Quiz

1. Records showing what users accessed a computer system and what actions they performed are called:

   A. User rights

   B. System and event logs

   C. Permissions

   D. Audit trails

2. To find instances where users increased their privileges, you would use...

   A. Escalation auditing

   B. Discretionary access control

   C. UserID records

   D. User management

3. To make account management easier, a company might perform all administrative functions from a single area. This is known as:

   A. Consolidation

   B. Process control

   C. Centralized management

   D. Mandatory access control

4. If a user only has to provide their credentials once (userID and password) and can then access multiple resources and applications without having to authenticate again, this is known as:

   A. Privilege management

   B. Centralized user accounts

   C. Single sign-on

   D. Access control

5. The access control model where object owners can change the permissions of their own files is called:

   A. Mandatory access control

   B. Discretionary access control

   C. Distributed access control

   D. Dynamic access control

6. The process of examining what rights and capabilities a specific user or group of users has assigned to them is called:

   A. Escalation auditing

   B. Audit trails

    C. File access auditing

    D. Privilege auditing

7. When discussing privilege management, MAC stands for:

    A. Media Access Control

    B. Mandatory Access Control

    C. Mandatory Availability Criteria

    D. Modified Access Credentials

8. Privilege management applies to:

    A. Users, physical locations, and resources

    B. Users, physical locations, and processes

    C. Files, resources, and users

    D. Applications, systems, and security

9. Under the UNIX operating system, file permissions consist of what three parts?

    A. Open, Run, Modify

    B. Change, Delete, Execute

    C. Run, Write, Delete

    D. Read, Write, Execute

10. What are the three types of auditing?

    A. User, system, and application

    B. File, process, and media

    C. Memory, disk, application

    D. Privilege, usage, and escalation

11. A unique, alphanumeric identifier assigned to each user is called what?

    A. A userID

    B. Privilege

    C. Single sign-on

    D. Nickname

12. To assign and manage privileges by job function, you might use what?

    A. Role-based access control

    B. Mandatory access control

    C. Process-based access control

    D. Discretionary access control

13. Under which access control system is each piece of information and every system resource (files, devices, networks, and so on) labeled with its sensitivity level?

    A. Discretionary access control

    B. Resource access control

    C. Mandatory access control

    D. Media access control

14. The process of recording who did what and when on information systems is known as:

    A. Usage auditing

    B. Privilege auditing

    C. Process auditing

    D. Action auditing

15. The process of restricting a user's ability to interact with the computer system is called what?

    A. Privilege management

    B. Audit control

    C. Access restriction

    D. User management

Essay Quiz

1. Your company develops software for banks and has three separate office locations across the U.S. with approximately 5,000 users. The corporate office is examining two proposals for user management: one using centralized management and the other decentralized management. Your boss has asked you to compare the two approaches and recommend one for the company. Write up your recommendation and be sure to explain your choice.

2. Your boss just read an article about single sign-on technologies and wants to know how something like that would benefit an organization like yours. Summarize the benefits of single sign-on technologies and discuss how each benefit would affect your organization.

3. A training manager needs your help developing some new course material and wants to know if you can come up with a good discussion for how mandatory access control systems work.

4. An administrator from your company needs some help defining the company's new auditing policy. Define the basic types of auditing and describe how they could benefit your company.

5. A coworker with a strong Windows background is having difficulty understanding UNIX file permissions. Describe UNIX file permissions for them.

Lab Projects

Lab Project 22.1

Your company is considering turning on auditing for Windows desktops, but needs more information, especially information on Windows 2000 Professional auditing. Find a Windows 2000 Professional system and examine the options under "Audit Policy" in the Local Security Settings. Develop a list of which items to audit for your company (success or failure) and describe why each is important. For those items you have chosen not to audit, explain why they should not be audited.

Lab Project 22.1

Your system administrators are implementing a role-based access method and need your help defining the role of backup operator. Develop a list of privileges and capabilities the backup operator role should have and explain why each is important.

Computer Forensics

Upon completion of this chapter, you will be able to:

- List and describe the rules and types of evidence
- Describe issues involved with the collection of evidence
- Describe issues involved with the preservation of evidence
- Explain the importance of a viable chain of custody
- Describe the steps in investigating a computer crime or policy violation

Computer forensics is certainly one of the popular buzzwords in computer security. This chapter will address the key aspects of computer forensics. It is not intended to be a legal tutorial regarding the presentation of evidence in a court of law. The principles are of value in conducting any investigative processes, including internal or external audit procedures, but there are many nuances of handling legal cases that are far beyond the scope of this text.

The term **forensics** relates to the application of scientific knowledge to legal problems. Specifically, computer forensics involves the preservation, identification, documentation, and interpretation of computer data, as explained in Warren G. Kruse and Jay Heiser's *Computer Forensics: Incident Response Essentials* (Boston: Addison-Wesley, 2002). In today's practice, computer forensics can be performed for three purposes:

- Investigating and analyzing computer systems as related to a violation of laws
- Investigating and analyzing computer systems for compliance with an organization's policies
- Investigating computer systems that have been remotely attacked

This last point is often referred to as *incident response* and can be a subset of the first two points. If an unauthorized person is remotely attacking a system, laws may indeed have been violated. However, a company employee performing similar acts may or may not violate laws and may or may not violate corporate policies. So, any of these three purposes could ultimately result in legal actions. Therefore, it is important to note that computer forensics actions may, at some point in time, deal with legal violations, and investigations could go to court proceedings. It is extremely important to understand this concept, because even minor procedural missteps can have significant legal consequences.

Evidence

Evidence consists of the documents, verbal statements, and material objects admissible in a court of law. Evidence is critical to convincing management, juries, judges, or other authorities that some kind of violation has occurred. The submission of evidence is challenging, but it is even more challenging when computers are used because the people involved may not be technically educated and thus may not fully understand what's happened.

Computer evidence presents yet more challenges because the data itself cannot be sensed with the physical senses. You can see printed characters, but you can't see the bits where that data is stored—it is a magnetic pulse on a disk or some other storage technology. Therefore, it must always be evaluated through some kind of "filter" rather than sensed directly by human senses. This is often of concern to auditors, because good auditing techniques recommend accessing the original data or a version as close as possible to the original data.

Standards for Evidence

To be credible, especially if it will be used in court proceedings or in corporate disciplinary actions which could be challenged legally, evidence must meet these three standards:

- **Sufficient**   The evidence must be convincing or measure up without question.
- **Competent**   The evidence must be legally qualified and reliable.
- **Relevant**   The evidence must be material to the case or have a bearing on the matter at hand.

Types of Evidence

All evidence is not created equal. Some evidence is stronger and better than other, weaker evidence. There are several types of evidence:

- **Direct evidence**   Oral testimony that proves a specific fact (such as an eyewitness's statement). The knowledge of the facts is obtained through the five senses of the witness. There are no inferences or presumptions.
- **Real evidence** (also known as associative or physical evidence)   Tangible objects that prove or disprove a fact. Physical evidence links the suspect to the scene of a crime.
- **Documentary evidence**   Evidence in the form of business records, printouts, manuals, and the like. Much of the evidence relating to computer crimes is documentary evidence.
- **Demonstrative evidence**   Used to aid the jury and may be in the form of a model, experiment, chart, and so on, offered to prove that an event occurred.

For more information on the types of evidence, see Harold F. Tipton and Micki Krause's *Information Security Management Handbook*, 4th edition (Boca Raton: Auerbach Publications, 2000), p. 607.

Three Rules Regarding Evidence

There are some rules that guide the use of evidence, especially if they could result in court proceedings:

- **Best evidence rule**   Courts prefer original evidence rather than a copy to ensure that no alteration of the evidence (whether intentional or unintentional) has occurred. There are instances when a duplicate can be accepted, such as when the original is lost or destroyed by acts of God or in the normal course of business. A duplicate is also acceptable when a third party beyond the court's subpoena power possesses the original.

- **Exclusionary rule**   The Fourth Amendment to the United States Constitution precludes illegal search and seizure. Therefore, any evidence collected in violation of the Fourth Amendment is not admissible as evidence. Additionally, if evidence is collected in violation of the Electronic Communications Privacy Act (ECPA) or other related violations of the United States Code, it may not be admissible to a court. For example, if there is no policy regarding the company's intent to electronically monitor network traffic or systems, and the employee has not acknowledged this policy by signing an agreement, sniffing network traffic could be a violation of the ECPA.

- **Hearsay rule**   Hearsay is second-hand evidence—evidence not gathered from the personal knowledge of the witness. Computer-generated evidence is considered hearsay evidence—see Tipton and Krause's *Information Security Management Handbook*, p. 608–609.

 NOTE   The laws just mentioned are U.S. laws. Other countries and jurisdictions may have other laws that are similar and would need to be considered in a similar manner.

Collecting Evidence

When information or objects are presented to management or admitted to court to support a claim, that information or those objects can be considered as evidence or documentation supporting your investigative efforts. Senior management will always ask a lot of questions—second- and third-order questions that you need to be able to answer quickly. Likewise, in a court, credibility is critical. Therefore, evidence must be properly acquired, identified, protected against tampering, transported, and stored.

Acquiring Evidence

When an incident occurs, you will need to collect data and information to facilitate your investigation. If someone is committing a crime or intentionally violating a company policy, they will likely try to hide the fact that they were involved. Therefore, collect as much information as soon as you can. Obviously, as time passes, evidence can be tampered with or destroyed. Look around on the desk, on the Rolodex, under the keyboard, in desktop storage areas, and on cubicle bulletin boards for any information that might be relevant. Secure floppy disks, CDs, flash memory cards, USB drives, tapes, and other removable media. Request copies of logs as soon as possible. Most Internet service providers (ISPs) will protect logs that could be subpoenaed. Take photos (some localities require use of Polaroid photos, as they are harder to modify without obvious tampering) or video tapes. Include photos of operating computer screens and hardware components from multiple angles. Be sure to photograph internal components before removing them for analysis.

When an incident occurs and the computer being used is going to be secured, there are two facts to consider: should it be turned off, and should it be disconnected from the network? There has been much discussion concerning the reasons for turning a computer on or turning it off. Some forensics professionals state that the plug should be pulled in order to freeze the current state of the computer. However, this results in the loss of any data associated with an attack in progress from the machine. Any data in RAM will also be lost. Further, it may corrupt the computer's file system and could call into question the validity of your findings.

On the other hand, it is possible for the computer criminal to leave behind a software bomb that you don't know about, and any commands you execute, including shutting down or restarting the system, could destroy or modify files, information, or evidence. The criminal may have anticipated such an investigation and altered some of the system's binary files. This is trivial to do in UNIX systems and is now becoming common in Windows systems. Dr. Larry Leibrock at University of Texas, Austin, led a research project to quantify how many files are changed when turning a Windows workstation off and on. Their research documents that approximately 0.6 percent of the operating system files are changed each time a Windows XP system is shut down and restarted (http://praetor.bus.utexas.edu/leibrock/xpforensics/).

Further, if the computer being analyzed is a server, it is unlikely management will support taking it offline and shutting it down for investigation. So, from an investigative perspective, either course may be correct and either course may be incorrect, depending on the circumstances surrounding the incident. What is most important is that you are deliberate in your work, you document your actions, and you can explain why you took the actions you did.

 STUDY TIP For Security+ testing purposes, the memory should be dumped, the system powered down, and an image should be made and worked from.

There are many investigative methods. Figure 23-1 shows the continuum of investigative methods from simple to more rigorous.

Examine suspect system using its software without verification	Verify software on suspect system and use that software for investigation	Examine suspect system using external media with verified software	Build a new system that completely images suspect system	Boot suspect system with verified floppy, CD, kernel and tools	Use dedicated forensic workstation

Simple ◄──► Rigorous

Figure 23-1   Investigative method rigor

Figure 23-2 shows the relationship between the complexity of your investigation and both the reliability of your forensic data and the difficulty of investigation.

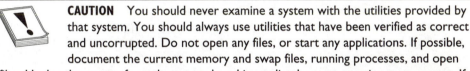

CAUTION   You should never examine a system with the utilities provided by that system. You should always use utilities that have been verified as correct and uncorrupted. Do not open any files, or start any applications. If possible, document the current memory and swap files, running processes, and open files. Unplug the system from the network and immediately contact senior management. If your organization has Computer Incidence Response Team (CIRT) procedures, follow them. Capture and secure mail, Domain Name Service (DNS), and other network service logs on supporting hosts. Unless you have appropriate forensic training and experience, consider calling in a professional.

Identifying Evidence

Evidence must be properly marked as it is collected so that it can be identified as the particular piece of evidence gathered at the scene. Properly label and store evidence. Be sure the labels can't be easily removed. Keep a log book identifying each piece of evidence (in case the label is removed), the persons who discovered it, the case number, the date, time, and location discovered, and the reason for collection. This information should be specific enough for recollection later in court. Log other identifying marks, such as device make, model, serial number, cable configuration or type, and so on. Note any type of damage to the piece of evidence.

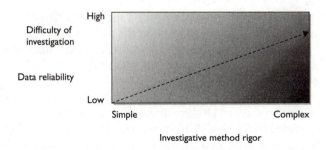

Figure 23-2   Rigor of the investigative method versus both data reliability and the difficulty of investigation

Being methodical is extremely important while identifying evidence. Do not collect evidence by yourself—have a second person who can serve as a witness to your actions. A sample log is shown here:

Item Description	Investigator	Case #	Date	Time	Location	Reason
Dell Latitude laptop computer, C600, Serial number: 62H5J25	Smith	C-25	30 Jan 2003	1325	Room 312 safe	Safekeeping

Protecting Evidence

Protect evidence from electromagnetic or mechanical damage. Ensure that evidence is not tampered with, damaged, or compromised by the procedures used during the investigation. Be careful not to damage the evidence to avoid potential liability problems later. Protect evidence from extremes in heat and cold, humidity, water, magnetic fields, and vibration. Use static-free evidence protection gloves as opposed to standard latex gloves. Seal the evidence in a proper container with evidence tape, and mark it with your initials, date, and case number.

Transporting Evidence

Properly log all evidence in and out of controlled storage. Use proper packing techniques, such as placing components in static-free bags, using foam packing material, and using cardboard boxes. Be especially cautious during transport of evidence to ensure custody of evidence is maintained and it isn't damaged or tampered with.

Storing Evidence

Store the evidence in an evidence room that has low traffic, restricted access, camera monitoring, and entry logging capabilities. Store components in static-free bags, foam packing material, and cardboard boxes. Computer devices that are subject to the effects of magnetism must not be stored on steel shelving or in steel cabinets unless precautions are taken to reduce the effects of magnetism from the steel.

Conducting the Investigation

When analyzing computer storage components, it is important to use extreme caution. A copy of the system should be analyzed—never the original system, as that will have to serve as evidence. A system specially designed for forensics examination should be used. Conduct analysis in a controlled environment with strong physical security, minimal traffic, controlled access, and so on.

Remember that witness credibility is extremely important. It is easy to imagine how quickly credibility can be damaged if the witness is asked, "Did you lock the file system?" and can't answer affirmatively. Or, "When you imaged this disk drive, did you use a new system?" and one can't answer that the destination disk was new or had been completely formatted using a low-level format before data was copied to it.

Unless you have tools specifically designed to take forensic images under Windows, your imaging process should use DOS instead of standard Windows. Boot it from a floppy disk or CD, and have only the minimal amount of software installed to preclude propagation of a virus or the inadvertent execution of a Trojan horse or other malicious program. Windows can then be used when examining copies of the system.

Although each investigation will be different, the following image backup process is a good example of a comprehensive investigation (see Tipton and Krause's *Information Security Management Handbook*, p. 634):

1. Remove or image only one component at a time.

2. Remove the hard disk and label it. Be sure to use an anti-static or static-dissipative wristband and mat before conducting forensic analysis.

3. Identify the disk type (IDE, SCSI, or other type). Log the disk capacity, cylinders, heads, and sectors.

4. Image the disk by using a bit-level copy, sector by sector. This will retain deleted files, unallocated clusters, and slack space.

5. Make either three or four copies of the drive: one replaces the drive removed if the system is to be returned to its owner and you don't want to divulge that the drive has been exchanged; one is marked, sealed, logged, and stored with the original, unmodified disk as evidence; one will be used for file authentication; the last is for analysis.

6. Check the disk image to make sure there were no errors during the imaging process.

7. Before analyzing the suspect disk, generate a message digest for all system directories, files, disk sectors, and partitions. MD5 and SHA are suitable and are superior to the older CRC32 or weaker hashing algorithms. Remember that even creating the message digest can change file access times, so it is important to have the files locked and to use the image, not the original evidence. Keep a good log of the hash values.

8. Inventory all files on the system.

9. Document the system date and time.

 TIP You should note that although this text describes the process and provides specific steps to be performed, they are to be used as guidelines. Any notes or record of results you make can end up being evidence in a court. Therefore, using a checklist and making notes on it could result in those lists and notes becoming evidence. Your credibility could be damaged if you have specific checklists and you skip a step or two because they aren't applicable—remember that you may need to explain why you skipped certain steps. While following the checklist, keep a log of all commands you issued on the system between the time you identified the incident and the time you imaged the disk. That way, if you are questioned in court about whether you changed anything on the disk, you can say, in effect, "Yes, but here is exactly what I did and here is how it would have changed things."

Chain of Custody

Evidence, once collected, must be properly controlled to prevent tampering. The chain of custody accounts for all persons who handled or had access to the evidence. The chain of custody shows who obtained the evidence, when and where it was obtained, where it was stored, and who had control or possession of the evidence.

The following is a list of the critical steps in a chain of custody:

- Record each item collected as evidence.
- Record who collected the evidence along with the date and time.
- Write a description of the evidence in the documentation.
- Put the evidence in containers and tag the containers with the case number, the name of the person who collected it, and the date and time.
- Record all message digest (hash) values in the documentation.
- Securely transport the evidence to a protected storage facility.
- Obtain a signature from the person who accepts the evidence at this storage facility.
- Provide controls to prevent access to and compromise of the evidence while it is being stored.
- Securely transport it to court for proceedings.

It is important to understand that even if no one tampers with the evidence, if the security of the evidence cannot be traced continuously from the time it was taken to the time it was presented in a court of law, then the chain of custody is broken and it will likely not be admitted.

Free Space vs. Slack Space

When a user deletes a file, the file is not actually deleted. Instead, a pointer in a file allocation table is deleted. This pointer was used by the operating system to track down the file when it was referenced, and the act of "deleting" the file merely removes the pointer and marks the sector(s) holding the file as available for the operating system to use. The actual data originally stored on the disk remains on the disk (until that space is used again); it just isn't recognized as a coherent file by the operating system.

Free Space

Since the "deleted" file is not actually completely erased or overwritten, it just sits there until the operating system needs to use that space for another file or application. Sometimes the second file that is saved in the same area does not occupy as many sectors as the first file, so there will still be a fragment of the original file.

The sector that holds the fragment of this file is referred to as **free space** because the operating system has marked it as usable when needed. As soon as the operating system stores something else in this sector, it is referred to as *allocated*. The unallocated sectors still contain the original data until the operating system overwrites those unallocated sectors. Looking at the free space might reveal information left over from files the user thought were deleted from the drive.

Slack Space

Another place that should be reviewed is **slack space**, which is different from free space. When a file is saved to a storage media, such as a hard drive, the operating system allocates space in blocks of a predefined size, called *sectors*. The size of all sectors is the same on a given system or hard drive. Even if your file contains only ten characters, the operating system will allocate a full sector of, say 1,024 bytes—there will be space left over in the sector. This is slack space.

It is possible for a user to hide malicious code, tools, or clues in slack space, as well as in the free space. You may also find information in slack space from files that previously occupied that same physical sector on the drive. Therefore, an investigator should review slack space using utilities that can display the information stored in these areas.

What's This Message Digest and Hash?

If files, logs, and other information are going to be captured and used for evidence, you need to ensure that the data isn't modified. In most cases, a tool that implements a hashing algorithm to create message digests is used.

 NOTE The mathematics behind these hashing algorithms has been researched extensively, and although it is possible that two different data streams could produce the same message digest, it is very, very improbable. This is an area of cryptography that has been rigorously reviewed, and the mathematics behind Message Digest 5 (MD5) and Secure Hash Algorithm (SHA) are very sound. (For more information about hashing and algorithms, see Chapter 5.)

A hashing algorithm performs a function similar to the familiar parity bits, checksum, or cyclical redundancy check (CRC). It applies mathematical operations to a data stream (or file) to calculate some number that is unique based on the information contained in the data stream (or file). If a subsequent analysis on the same data stream produces a different result, there is a very high probability that the data stream was changed.

The hash tool is applied to each file or log and the message digest value is noted in the investigation documentation. When the case actually goes to trial, the investigator may need to run the tool on the files or logs again to show that they have not been altered in any way. The logs may also need to be written to a write-once media, such as a CD-ROM.

 NOTE The number of files stored on today's hard drives can be very large, literally tens of thousands. Obviously, this is far too many for the investigator to analyze. However, if it were possible to know the message digests for most of the files installed by the most popular software products, and those message digests matched the message digests of the files on the drive being analyzed, approximately 90 percent of the files would not need to be analyzed by the investigator because they can be assumed to be unmodified. (See Dan Mares' "Using File Hashes to Reduce Forensic Analysis" in SC Online, May 2002, www.scmagazine.com/scmagazine/sc-online/2002/article/24/article.html. Also see www.nsrl.nist.gov.)

Analysis

After successfully imaging the drives to be analyzed and calculating and storing the message digests, the investigator will now begin the analysis. The details of the investigation will depend on the particulars of the incident being investigated. However, in general, the following steps will be involved:

- Check the Recycle Bin for deleted files.

- Check the web browser history files and address bar histories.

- Check the web browser cookie files. Each web browser stores cookies in different places. Some examples are provided. Browsers not listed here will require individual research. Netscape 7.0 for Windows stores them in a file called cookies.txt (click Tools | Cookie Manager, or search for files named cookies.txt). In Netscape 7.0 for Mac, click Netscape | Preferences | Privacy & Security | Cookies. Netscape for UNIX stores them in $HOME/netscape. Internet Explorer stores cookies in the Temporary Internet Files folder with all the other temporary Internet files. (Each cookie is stored in a separate file with the format "Cookie: <username>@URL," where <username> is the user who is logged into the Windows machine, and the URL is the address of the web server that set the cookie. Opening each cookie file will give you the details about that specific cookie. A handy tool for viewing Internet Explorer cookies is IECookiesView found at www.simtel.net/pub/dl/59299.shtml.)

- Check the Temporary Internet Files folders. Usually these are found in the Windows directory C:\Documents and Settings\<username>\Local Settings\ Temporary Internet Files. This location can be changed, so be sure to check where Internet Explorer is storing those files. In Internet Explorer, click Tools | Internet Options | General | Settings | View Files.

- Search files for suspect character strings. To conserve valuable time, be wise in the choice of words you search for, choosing "confidential," "sensitive," "sex," or other explicit words and phrases related to your investigation.

- Search the slack and free space for suspect character strings as described previously.

Chapter Review

Chapter Summary

After reading this chapter and completing the exercises, you should understand the following about incident response and forensics.

Evidence

- Evidence must meet the three standards of being sufficient, competent, and relevant if it is to be used in legal proceedings.

- There are four different types of evidence: Direct, Real, Documentary, and Demonstrative.
- There are three rules regarding evidence: the Best evidence rule, the Exclusionary rule, and the Hearsay rule.

Collecting Evidence

- Evidence must be properly collected, protected, and controlled to be of value during court or disciplinary activities.
- When acquiring evidence, one must be deliberate to ensure evidence is not damaged and operations are not negatively impacted.
- Evidence must be properly marked so that it can be readily identified as that particular piece of evidence gathered at the scene.
- Evidence must be protected so that it is not tampered with, damaged, or compromised.
- Evidence should be transported cautiously to ensure custody of the evidence is maintained and the evidence itself is not tampered with or damaged.
- Evidence should be stored in properly controlled areas and conditions.
- When conducting an investigation on computer components, one must be deliberate and cautious to ensure evidence is not damaged.

Chain of Custody

- A chain of custody that accounts for all persons who handled or have access to the evidence must be maintained to prevent evidence tampering or damage.

Free Space and Slack Space

- Information can be recorded and possibly hidden in various ways on a computer. Sometimes information will be hidden in either the free space or the slack space of the computer's disk drive.
- Free space is the space (sectors) on a storage medium that is available for the operating system to use.
- Slack space is the unused space on a disk drive created when a file is smaller than the allocated unit of storage, such as a sector.

Message Digest and Hash

- The use of a message digest or hashing algorithm is essential to ensure that information stored on a computer's disk drives has not been changed.
- A hashing algorithm applies mathematical operations to a data stream or file to calculate a number that is unique, based on the information contained in the data stream or file.

- A message digest is the result of applying the hash function to data. It is also known as a hash value.

- If the information in the data stream or file is changed, a different message digest will result, indicating the file has been tampered with.

Analysis

- Forensic analysis of data stored on a hard drive can begin once the drive has been imaged and message digests of important files have been calculated and stored.

- Analysis typically involves investigating the Recycle Bin, web browser and address bar history files, cookie files, temporary Internet file folders, suspect files, and free space and slack space.

- Experience and knowledge are your most valuable tools available when performing computer forensic activities.

Key Terms

Best evidence rule *(571)*
Competent evidence *(570)*
Demonstrative evidence *(570)*
Direct evidence *(570)*
Documentary evidence *(570)*
Exclusionary rule *(571)*
Evidence *(570)*
Forensics *(569)*
Free space *(576)*
Hearsay rule *(571)*
Real evidence *(570)*
Relevant evidence *(570)*
Slack space *(577)*
Sufficient evidence *(570)*

Key Terms Quiz

Use terms from the Key Terms list to complete the sentences that follow. Don't use the same term more than once. Not all terms will be used.

1. Evidence collected in violation of the Fourth Amendment of the United States Constitution, the Electronic Communications Privacy Act (ECPA), or other aspects of the United States Code may not be admissible to a court under the terms of the _____.

2. Evidence that is legally qualified and reliable is _____.

3. Documents, verbal statements, and material objects admissible in a court of law are called _____.

4. The rule whereby courts prefer original evidence rather than a copy to ensure that no alteration of the evidence (whether intentional or unintentional) has occurred is termed the _____.

5. Evidence that is convincing or measures up without question is _____.

6. _____ is the preservation, identification, documentation, and interpretation of computer data to be used in legal proceedings.

7. _____ is evidence that is material to the case or has a bearing on the matter at hand.

8. _____ is the unused space on a disk drive when a file is smaller than the allocated unit of storage.

9. _____ is oral testimony or other evidence that proves a specific fact (such as an eyewitness's statement, fingerprint, photo, and so on). The knowledge of the facts is obtained through the five senses of the witness. There are no inferences or presumptions.

10. _____ is the remaining sectors of a previously allocated file that are available for the operating system to use.

Multiple-Choice Quiz

1. Which of the following correctly defines evidence as being competent?

    A. The evidence is material to the case or has a bearing on the matter at hand.

    B. The evidence is presented in the form of business records, printouts, or other items.

    C. The evidence is convincing or measures up without question.

    D. The evidence is legally qualified and reliable.

2. Which of the following correctly defines evidence as being relevant?

    A. The evidence is material to the case or has a bearing on the matter at hand.

    B. The evidence is presented in the form of business records, printouts, or other items.

    C. The evidence is convincing or measures up without question.

    D. The evidence is legally qualified and reliable.

3. Which of the following correctly defines documentary evidence?

    A. Evidence in the form of business records, printouts, manuals, and other items

    B. The knowledge of these facts is obtained through the five senses of the witness.

    C. Used to aid the jury and may be in the form of a model, experiment, chart, or other item and be offered to prove an event occurred

    D. Physical evidence that links the suspect to the scene of a crime

4. Which of the following correctly defines real evidence?

   A. The evidence is convincing or measures up without question.

   B. The evidence is material to the case or has a bearing on the matter at hand.

   C. Used to aid the jury and may be in the form of a model, experiment, chart, or other item and be offered to prove an event occurred.

   D. Tangible objects that prove or disprove a fact.

5. Which of the following correctly defines the hearsay rule?

   A. The evidence is legally qualified and reliable.

   B. Tangible objects that prove or disprove a fact.

   C. Evidence not gathered from the personal knowledge of the witness.

   D. Evidence in the form of business records, printouts, manuals, or other items.

6. Which of the following is the LEAST rigorous investigative method?

   A. Using a dedicated forensic workstation.

   B. Verifying software on suspect system and using that software for the investigation.

   C. Examining the suspect system using its software without verification.

   D. Boot suspect system with verified floppy, CD, kernel, and tools.

7. Which of the following correctly defines slack space?

   A. The space on a disk drive that is occupied by the boot sector

   B. The space located at the beginning of a partition

   C. The remaining sectors of a previously allocated file that are available for the operating system to use

   D. The unused space on a disk drive when a file is smaller than the allocated unit of storage (as in a sector)

8. Which of the following correctly describes the minimum contents of an evidence control log book?

   A. Description, Investigator, Case # Date, Time, Location, Reason

   B. Description, Investigator, Case # Date, Location, Reason

   C. Description, Case # Date, Time, Location, Reason

   D. Description, Coroner, Case # Date, Time, Location, Reason

9. Which of the following correctly describes a message digest?

   A. An algorithm that applies mathematical operations to a data stream to calculate a unique number based on the information contained in the data stream

   B. A method of verifying that data has been completely deleted from a disk

C. A method of overwriting data with a specified pattern of 1s and 0s on a disk

D. A method used to keep an index of all files on a disk

10. Which of the following correctly describes the chain of custody for evidence?

   A. The evidence is convincing or measures up without question.

   B. Accounts for all persons who handled or had access to a specific item of evidence.

   C. Description, Investigator, Case # Date, Time, Location, Reason

   D. The evidence is legally qualified and reliable.

11. Which of the following correctly defines evidence as being sufficient?

   A. The evidence is convincing or measures up without question.

   B. The evidence is presented in the form of business records, printouts, and so on.

   C. The evidence is material to the case or has a bearing on the matter at hand.

   D. The evidence is legally qualified and reliable.

12. Which of the following correctly defines the exclusionary rule?

   A. Any evidence collected in violation of the Fourth Amendment is not admissible as evidence.

   B. The evidence consists of tangible objects that prove or disprove a fact.

   C. The knowledge of the facts is obtained through the five senses of the witness.

   D. The evidence is used to aid the jury and may be in the form of a model, experiment, chart, or the like, offered to prove an event occurred.

13. Which of the following correctly defines free space?

   A. The unused space on a disk drive when a file is smaller than the allocated unit of storage (such as a sector).

   B. The space on a disk drive that is occupied by the boot sector.

   C. The space located at the beginning of a partition.

   D. The remaining sectors of a previously allocated file that are available for the operating system to use.

14. If you are investigating a computer incident, and you need to remove the disk drive from a computer and replace it with a copy so the user doesn't know it has been exchanged, how many copies of the disk should you make, and how should they be used?

   A. Five copies: one is to replace the drive that will be removed; one is marked, sealed, logged, and stored with the original, unmodified disk as evidence; one is for file authentication; one is for analysis; and one is for holding message digests.

   B. Three copies: one is to replace the drive that will be removed; one to be used for file authentication; and one for analysis.

C. Four copies: one is to replace the drive that will be removed; one is marked, sealed, logged, and stored with the original, unmodified disk as evidence; one is for file authentication; and one is for holding message digests.

D. Four copies: one is to replace the removed drive; one is marked, sealed, logged, and stored with the original, unmodified disk as evidence; one is for file authentication; and one is for analysis.

15. Which of the following correctly defines the process of acquiring evidence?

A. Power down the system, dump the memory, create an image of the system, and analyze the image.

B. Create an image of the system, analyze the image, dump the memory, and power down the system.

C. Dump the memory, power down the system, create an image of the system, and analyze the image.

D. Dump the memory, analyze the image, power down the system, and create an image of the system.

Essay Quiz

1. A supervisor has brought a confiscated computer to your office which was allegedly used to view inappropriate material. He has asked you to look for evidence to support this allegation. Because you work for a small company, you do not have an extra computer you can dedicate to your analysis. How would you boot the system and begin forensic analysis? Provide a reason for your method.

2. Explain why you should always search the free space and slack space if you suspect a person has deliberately deleted files or information on a workstation that you are analyzing.

3. You are a member of your company's computer incident response team and have been called in after hours to investigate an attack in progress. The network engineers have identified the attack as coming from a workstation in an office area of your company. The attack is still in progress and needs to be terminated. You are in the office where the workstation is located and the computer is on with the hard disk light flashing occasionally. What steps would you take to terminate the attack and secure the computer for later forensic analysis?

4. Due to some suspected illegal activities involving a company employee and their company computer, a senior manager directed the company's workstation support personnel to remove the hard disk from the workstation, copy the disk, and replace the hard disk with the copy. The workstation support person entered the office after hours, removed the hard disk, took it to his lab (which he shares with another person), imaged the old drive onto a new drive, replaced the drive and then placed the original hard disk in his desk drawer. He then locked the lab and went home for the night. How will this evidence stand up in a court of law?

5. You have been asked by management to secure the laptop computer of an individual that was just dismissed from the company under unfavorable circumstances. Pretend that your own computer is the laptop that has been secured. Make the first entry in your log book and describe how you would start this incident off correctly by properly protecting and securing the evidence.

Lab Projects

Lab Project 23.1
Use an MD5 or SHA-1 algorithm to obtain the hash value for a file of your choice. Record the hash value. Change the file with a word processor or text editor. Obtain the hash value for the modified file. Compare the result.

Lab Project 23.2
In order to understand what information is stored on your computer, examine the contents of the Temporary Internet Files folders on your own computer as described in the text. Review the file names and examine the contents of a few of the files. Describe how this information could be used as evidence of a crime.

Lab Project 23.3
Visit www.ietf.org/rfc/rfc1321.txt and compile the MD5 algorithm from the information contained in Appendix A, "Reference Implementation," from the web site. Verify your results with another version of MD5.

CHAPTER 24

Security and Law

Upon completion of this lesson, you will be able to:

- List and describe laws and rules concerning importing and exporting encryption software
- List and describe laws that govern computer access and trespass
- List and describe laws that govern encryption and digital rights management
- List and describe laws that govern digital signatures
- List and describe laws that govern privacy in various industries with relation to computer security
- Explain the role of ethics in computer security
- List and describe laws that enforce ethical behavior

Computer security is no different than any other subject in our society; as it changes our lives, laws will be enacted to enable desired behaviors and prohibit undesired behaviors. The one substantial difference between this aspect of our society and others is that the speed of advancement in the information systems world as driven by business, computer network connectivity, and the Internet is much greater than in the legal system of compromise and law-making. In some cases, laws have been overly restrictive, limiting business options, such as in the area of importing and exporting encryption technology. In other cases, legislation has been slow in coming and this fact has stymied business initiatives, such as in digital signatures. And in some areas, it has been both too fast and too slow, as in the case of privacy laws. One thing is certain—you will never satisfy everyone with a law, but it does delineate the rules of the game.

Import/Export Encryption Restrictions

Encryption technology has been controlled by governments for a variety of reasons. The level of control varies from outright banning to little or no regulation. The reasons behind the control vary as well, and control over import and export is a vital method of maintaining a level of control over encryption technology in general. The majority of the laws and restrictions are centered around the use of cryptography, which was until recently mainly a military issue. The advent of commercial transactions and network communications over public networks such as the Internet has expanded the use of cryptographic methods to include securing of network communications. As is the case in most rapidly changing technologies, the practice moves faster than law. Many countries still have laws that are outmoded in terms of e-commerce and the Internet. Over time, these laws will be changed to serve these new uses in a way consistent with each country's needs.

United States Law

Export controls on commercial encryption products are administered by the Bureau of Industry and Security (BIS) in the U.S. Department of Commerce. The responsibility for export control and jurisdiction was transferred from the State Department to the Commerce Department in 1996 and most recently updated on June 6, 2002. Rules governing exports of encryption are found in the Export Administration Regulations (EAR), 15 C.F.R. Parts 730–774. Sections 740.13, 740.17, and 742.15 are the principal references for the export of encryption items.

Needless to say, violation of encryption export regulations is a serious matter and is not an issue to take lightly. Until recently, encryption protection was accorded the same level of attention as the export of weapons for war. With the rise of the Internet, widespread personal computing, and the need for secure connections for e-commerce, this position has relaxed somewhat. The United States updated its encryption export regulations to provide treatment consistent with regulations adopted by the **European Union** (EU), easing export and re-export restrictions among the 15 EU member states and Australia, the Czech Republic, Hungary, Japan, New Zealand, Norway, Poland, and Switzerland. The member nations of the Wassenaar Arrangement agreed to remove key length restrictions on encryption hardware and software that is subject to the certain reasonable levels of encryption strength. This action effectively removed "mass market" encryption products from the list of dual-use items controlled by the Wassenaar Arrangement.

The U.S. encryption export control policy continues to rest on three principles: review of encryption products prior to sale, streamlined post-export reporting, and license review of certain exports of strong encryption to foreign government end users. The current set of U.S. rules require notification to the BIS for export in all cases, but the restrictions are significantly lessened for "Mass Market" products as defined by all of the following:

- They are generally available to the public by being sold, without restriction, from stock at retail selling points by any of these means:
  - Over-the-counter transactions
  - Mail-order transactions
  - Electronic transactions
  - Telephone call transactions
- The cryptographic functionality cannot easily be changed by the user.
- They are designed for installation by the user without further substantial support by the supplier.
- When necessary, details of the items are accessible and will be provided, upon request, to the appropriate authority in the exporter's country in order to ascertain compliance with export regulations.

Mass-market commodities and software employing a key length greater than 64 bits for the symmetric algorithm must be reviewed in accordance with BIS regulations. Restrictions on exports by U.S. persons to terrorist-supporting states (Cuba, Iran, Iraq,

Libya, North Korea, Sudan, or Syria), their nationals, and other sanctioned entities are not changed by this rule.

As you can see, this is a very technical area, with significant rules and significant penalties for infractions. The best rule is that whenever you are faced with a situation involving the export of encryption-containing software, consult an expert and get the appropriate permission, or else a statement that permission is not required, first. This is one case where it is better to be safe than sorry; if in doubt, read the associated sidebar.

For Immediate Release
January 7, 2003

Silicon Graphics Settles Criminal and Civil Charges that Computer Shipments Violated U.S. Export Controls

The Department of Commerce's Bureau of Industry and Security (BIS) announced that Silicon Graphics, Inc. (SGI) of Mountain View, California pled guilty to two felony charges that the company violated Commerce Department regulations by illegally exporting high performance computers to a Russian nuclear laboratory in 1996. SGI agreed to pay $1 million in criminal fines to resolve the charges. In a related administrative case, SGI agreed to pay $182,000, the maximum penalty authorized by the Export Administration Regulations (EAR), to settle civil charges arising from the same exports to the Russian nuclear laboratory, as well as additional charges relating to illegal computer exports to Israel and for failure to meet reporting requirements for exports to China, Qatar, and the United Arab Emirates.

As part of the settlement of criminal charges, SGI admitted that, on two occasions in 1996, the company exported four Challenge L computer systems, upgrades, and peripheral equipment to the All-Russian Institute for Technical Physics (Chelyabinsk-70) in violation of U.S. export control regulations. Chelyabinsk-70, located in Snezhinsk, Russia, is a nuclear laboratory operated by Russia's Ministry of Atomic Energy and is engaged in research, development, testing, and maintenance of nuclear devices.

In addition to the monetary penalties, the civil settlement agreement provided that SGI's exporting privileges to Russia will be denied for a period of three years. The denial of export privileges will be suspended provided that SGI does not commit any export control violations involving Russia during the suspension period. SGI also agreed, for a period of three years, not to exercise its eligibility to use License Exception CTP for exports and re-exports to Russia, or to engage in any activity, such as repair or maintenance of computers, involving any military or nuclear end-user, or end-user in Russia without the prior written consent of BIS. Finally, SGI agreed to report to BIS, within 45 days, all of its exports to certain countries of concern during the last six months.

In announcing the settlement, Acting Assistant Secretary of Commerce for Export Enforcement Lisa Prager stated that this case demonstrates the Bureau's determination to rigorously enforce its controls over items that can be used in the proliferation of weapons of mass destruction. The Department of Commerce, through BIS, administers and enforces export controls for reasons of national security, foreign policy, anti-terrorism, nonproliferation, and short supply. Criminal penalties and administrative sanctions can be imposed for violations of the EAR.

http://www.bxa.doc.gov/press/2003/SiliconGraphics1_7.html

Non-U.S. Laws

Export control rules for encryption technologies fall under the Wassenaar Arrangement, an international agreement on export controls for conventional arms and dual-use goods and technologies. The Wassenaar Arrangement has been established in order to contribute to regional and international security and stability, by promoting transparency and greater responsibility in transfers of conventional arms and dual-use goods and technologies, thus preventing destabilizing accumulations. Participating states, of which the United States is one of 33, will seek, through their own national policies and laws, to ensure that transfers of these items do not contribute to the development or enhancement of military capabilities that undermine these goals, and are not diverted to support such capabilities.

Many nations have more restrictive policies than those agreed upon as part of the Wassenaar Arrangement. Australia, New Zealand, the U.S.A., France, and Russia go further than is required under Wassenaar and restrict general-purpose cryptographic software as dual-use goods through national laws. The Wassenaar Arrangement has had a significant impact on cryptography export controls, and there seems little doubt that some of the nations represented will seek to use the next round to move toward a more repressive cryptography export control regime based on their own national laws. There are ongoing campaigns to attempt to influence other members of the agreement toward less restrictive rules, and in some cases no rules. These lobbying efforts are based on e-commerce and privacy arguments.

Digital Signature Laws

On October 1, 2000, the Electronic Signatures in Global and National Commerce Act (commonly called the **E-Sign law**) went into effect in the United States. This law implements a simple principle: a signature, contract, or other record may not be denied legal effect, validity, or enforceability solely because it is in electronic form. Another source of law on digital signatures is the National Conference of Commissioners on Uniform State Laws' **Uniform Electronic Transactions Act** (UETA), which has been adopted in over 20 states. A number of the states have adopted a modified version of UETA, and the precise relationship between the Federal E-Sign law and UETA has yet to be resolved and will most likely be worked out through litigation in the courts over complex technical issues.

Many states have adopted digital signature laws, the first being Utah in 1995. The Utah law, which has been used as a model by several other states, confirms the legal status of digital signatures as valid signatures, provides for use of state-licensed certification authorities, endorses the use of public key encryption technology, and authorizes online databases called repositories, where public keys would be available. The Utah act specifies a negligence standard regarding private encryption keys and places no limit on liability. Thus, if a criminal uses a consumer's private key to commit fraud, the consumer is financially responsible for that fraud, unless the consumer can prove that they used reasonable care in safeguarding their private key. Consumers assume a duty of care when they adopt the use of digital signatures for their transactions, not unlike the care required for PINs on debit cards.

From a practical standpoint, the existence of the E-Sign law and UETA have enabled e-commerce transactions to proceed, and the resolution of the technical details via court actions will probably have little effect on consumers. It is worthy to note that consumers will have to exercise reasonable care over their signature keys, much as they must over PINs and other private numbers. For the most part, software will handle these issues for the typical user.

Non-U.S. Laws

The United Nations has a mandate to further harmonize international trade. With this in mind, the UN General Assembly adopted the United Nations Commission on International Trade Law (UNCITRAL) Model Law on E-Commerce. To implement specific technical aspects of this model law, further work on electronic signatures was needed. The UN General Assembly then adopted the United Nations Commission on International Trade Law (UNCITRAL) Model Law on Electronic Signatures. These model laws have become the basis for many national and international efforts in this area.

Canada

Canada was an early leader in the use of digital signatures. Singapore, Canada, and the State of Pennsylvania were the first governments to have digitally signed an interstate contract. This contract, digitally signed in 1998, concerned the establishment of a Global Learning Consortium between the three governments (source: *Krypto-Digest* Vol. 1 No. 749, June 11, 1998). Canada went on to adopt a national model bill for electronic signatures to promote e-commerce. This bill, the Uniform Electronic Commerce Act (UECA), allows the use of electronic signatures in communications with the government. The law contains general provisions for the equivalence between traditional and electronic signatures (source: *BNA ECLR*, May 27, 1998, p. 700) and is modeled after the UNCITRAL Model Law on E-Commerce (source: *BNA ECLR*, September 13, 2000, p. 918). The UECA is similar to Bill C-54 in authorizing governments to use electronic technology to deliver services and communicate with citizens.

Individual Canadian provinces have passed similar legislation defining digital signature provisions for e-commerce and government use. These laws are modeled after the UNCITRAL Model Law on E-Commerce to enable widespread use of e-commerce transactions. These laws have also modified the methods of interactions between the citizens and the government, enabling electronic communication in addition to previous forms.

The EU

The European Commission adopted a Communication on Digital Signatures and Encryption: "Towards a European Framework for Digital Signatures and Encryption." This communication states that a common framework at the EU level is urgently needed in order to stimulate "the free circulation of digital signature related products and services within the Internal market" and "the development of new economic activities linked to electronic commerce" as well as "to facilitate the use of digital signatures across national borders." Community legislation should address (1) common legal requirements for CAs, (2) legal recognition of digital signatures, and (3) international cooperation. This communication was debated, and a common position was presented to the member nations for incorporation into national laws.

On May 4, 2000, the European Parliament and Council approved the common position adopted by the Council. In June 2000, the final version of the directive, Directive 2000/31/EC, was adopted. The directive is now being implemented by member states. To implement the articles contained in the directive, member states will have to remove barriers, such as legal form requirements, to electronic contracting, leading to uniform digital signature laws across the EU.

Digital Rights Management

The ability to make flawless copies of digital media has led to another new legal issue: **digital rights management**. For years, the music and video industry has relied on technology to protect its rights with respect to intellectual property. It has been illegal for decades to copy information protected by copyright (except for specific exclusions permitted by the copyright statute). This has included items such as music and videos. Even with the law, people have for years made copies of music and videos to share, violating the basic copyright law. This has not had a significant economic impact in the eyes of the industry, as the copies were of lesser quality and that people would pay for original quality in sufficient numbers to keep the economics of the industry healthy. As such, legal action against piracy was typically limited to large scale duplication and sale efforts, commonly performed overseas and subsequently shipped to the U.S. as counterfeit items.

The ability of anyone with a PC to make a perfect copy of digital media has led to industry fears that individual piracy actions could lead to major economic issues in the recording industry. To protect the rights of the recording artists and the economic health of the industry as a whole, the music and video recording industry lobbied the U.S. Congress for protection, which was granted under the **Digital Millennium Copyright Act (DMCA)** on October 20, 1998. This law was stated, "To amend title 17, United States Code, to implement the World Intellectual Property Organization Copyright Treaty and Performances and Phonograms Treaty, and for other purposes." The majority of this law was well crafted, but one section has drawn considerable comment and criticism. A section of the law makes it illegal to develop, produce, and trade any device or mechanism designed to circumvent technological controls used in copy protection.

Although on the surface, this seems to be reasonable. The methods used in most cases are cryptographic in nature, and this provision had the ability to eliminate and/or severely limit research into encryption, and the strengths and weaknesses of specific methods. A provision, Section 1201(g) of the Digital Millennium Copyright Act, was included to provide for specific relief and allow exemptions for legitimate research. With this section, the law garnered industry support from several organizations such as the Software & Information Industry Association (SIIA), Recording Industry Association of America (RIAA), and Motion Picture Association of America (MPAA). Based on these inputs, the U. S. Copyright Office issued a report supporting the DMCA in a required report to the Congress. This seemed to settle the issues until the RIAA threatened to sue an academic research team headed by Professor Felten from Princeton. The issue behind the suit was the potential publication of results demonstrating that several copy protection methods were flawed in their application. This research came in response to an industry-sponsored challenge to break the methods. After breaking the methods developed and published by the industry, Professor Felten and his team prepared to publish their findings. The RIAA objected and threatened a suit under provisions of DMCA . After several years of litigation and support of Professor Felten by the Electronic Freedom Foundation (EFF), the case was eventually resolved in the academic team's favor, although no case law to prevent further industry-led threats was developed.

This may seem a remote issue; however, industries have been subsequently using the DMCA to protect their technologically inspired copy protection schemes in such industries as laser-toner cartridges and garage-door openers. It is doubtful that the U.S. Congress intended the law to have such effects, yet until they are resolved in court, the DMCA may have wide-reaching implications. The act has specific exemptions for research provided four elements are satisfied:

"(A) the person lawfully obtained the encrypted copy, phonorecord, performance, or display of the published work;

(B) such act is necessary to conduct such encryption research;

(C) the person made a good faith effort to obtain authorization before the circumvention; and

(D) such act does not constitute infringement under this title or a violation of applicable law other than this section, including section 1030 of title 18 and those provisions of title 18 amended by the Computer Fraud and Abuse Act of 1986."*

Additional exemptions are scattered through the law, although many were pasted in during various deliberations on the act and do not make sense when the act is viewed in whole. The effect of these exemptions upon people in the software and technology industry is not clear, and until restrained by case law, the DMCA gives large firms with deep legal pockets a potent weapon to use against parties who disclose flaws in encryption technologies used in various products. Actions have already been initiated against individuals and organizations who have reported security holes in products. This will be an active area of legal contention as the real issues behind digital rights management have yet to be truly resolved.

---

* Section 1201(g)(2) of DCMA

Privacy Laws

The advent of interconnected computer systems has enabled businesses and governments to share and integrate information. This has lead to a resurgence in the importance of privacy laws worldwide. Governments in Europe and the United States have taken different approaches in attempts to control privacy via legislation. There are many social and philosophical differences that have lead to these differences, but as the world becomes interconnected, understanding and resolving these differences will be important.

United States Laws

The **Electronic Communications Privacy Act (ECPA)** of 1986 was passed by Congress and signed by President Ronald Reagan to address a myriad of legal privacy issues that were resulting from the increasing use of computers and other technology specific to telecommunications. Sections of this law addressed e-mail, cellular communications, workplace privacy, and a whole host of other issues related to communicating electronically. A major provision was the prohibition against an employer's monitoring an employee's computer usage, including e-mail, unless consent is obtained. Other legal provisions protect electronic communications from wiretap and outside eavesdropping, as users were assumed to have a reasonable expectation of privacy and afforded protection under the Fourth Amendment to the Constitution.

A common practice with respect to computer access today is the use of a warning banner. These banners are typically displayed whenever a network connection occurs and serve four main purposes. First, from a legal standpoint, they establish the level of expected privacy (usually none on a business system) and serve as consent to real-time monitoring from a business standpoint. Real-time monitoring can be for security reasons, business reasons, or technical network performance reasons. The key is that the banner tells the user that their connection to the network signals their consent to monitoring. Consent can also be obtained to look at files and records. In the case of government systems, consent is needed to prevent direct application of the Fourth Amendment. And the last reason is that the warning banner can establish the system or network administrator's common authority to consent to a law enforcement search.

The **Patriot Act** of 2001, passed in response to the September 11 terrorist attack on the World Trade Center buildings in New York, substantially changed the levels of checks and balances in laws related to privacy in the United States. This law extended the tap and trace provisions of existing wiretap statutes to the Internet and mandated certain technological modifications at ISPs to facilitate electronic wiretaps on the Internet. The Act also permits the Justice Department to proceed with its rollout of the **Carnivore** program, an eavesdropping program for the Internet. There has been much stated on both sides of the controversy over Carnivore, but until changed, the Patriot Act mandates that ISPs cooperate and facilitate monitoring. The Patriot Act also permits federal law enforcement personnel to investigate computer trespass (intrusions) and enacts civil penalties for trespassers.

In November 1999, President Clinton signed the **Gramm-Leach-Bliley Act**, a major piece of legislation affecting the financial industry, and also one with significant privacy provisions for individuals. The key privacy tenets enacted in GLB included the establishment of an opt-out method for individuals to maintain some control over the use of the information provided in a business transaction with a member of the financial community. GLB is enacted through a series of rules governed by state law, federal law, securities law, and federal rules. These rules cover a wider range of financial institutions, from banks and thrifts, to insurance companies, to securities dealers. Some internal information sharing is required under the Fair Credit Reporting Act (FCRA) between affiliated companies, but GLB ended sharing to external third-party firms.

Identity privacy and the establishment of identity theft crimes is governed by the Identity Theft and Assumption Deterrence Act, which makes it a violation of federal law to knowingly use another's identity—identity theft. The collection of information necessary to do this is also governed by GLB, which makes it illegal for someone to gather identity information on another under false pretenses. Student records have even further protections under the **Family Education Records and Privacy Act of 1974**. On December 4, 2003, President Bush signed into law the Fair and Accurate Credit Transactions Act of 2003, which includes several major identity-theft provisions. These provisions are designed to be consumer-friendly and include a free credit report annually, require merchants to leave all but the last five digits of a credit card number off store receipts, and establish a national system of fraud detection allowing consumers to have a single number to call to receive advice, set off a nationwide fraud alert, and protect their credit standing.

Medical and health information also has privacy implications, which is why the U.S. Congress enacted the **Health Insurance Portability & Accountability Act** (HIPAA) of 1996. HIPAA calls for sweeping changes in the way health and medical data is stored, exchanged, and used. From a privacy perspective, significant restrictions of data transfers to ensure privacy are included in HIPAA, including security standards and electronic signature provisions. HIPAA security standards mandate a uniform level of protections regarding all health information that pertains to an individual and is housed or transmitted electronically. The standard mandates safeguards for physical storage, maintenance, transmission, and access to individuals' health information. HIPAA mandates that organizations that use electronic signatures will have to meet standards ensuring information integrity, signer authentication, and nonrepudiation. These standards leave to industry the task of specifying the specific technical solutions and only mandate compliance to significant levels of protection as provided by the rules being released by industry.

The latest movement in U.S. personal privacy with respect to computer records was started with **California Senate Bill 1386 (SB1386)**. This law was designed to help users fight identity theft through early notification of the loss of control of personal information stored in computer systems. The law is fairly complex in its restrictions, but in layman's terms, it is designed to force firms to notify users whenever their personal information has become compromised. Currently, this law only applies to California residents and lacks any strong enforcement provisions, but stronger laws are currently in the works. Though at first this law may not seem to be an issue for firms outside California, companies could still be found liable if a customer resides in California, and as the primary enforcement method is a civil class action suit, the business risk could be real for many firms.

European Laws

The governments of Europe have developed a comprehensive concept of privacy administered via a set of statutes known as data protection laws. These privacy statutes cover all personal data, whether collected and used by government or private firms. These laws are administered by state and national data protection agencies in each country. With the advent of the European Union (EU), this common comprehensiveness stands in distinct contrast to the patchwork of laws in the United States.

Privacy laws in Europe are built around the concept that privacy is a fundamental human right that demands protection through government administration. When the EU was formed, many laws were harmonized across the fifteen member nations, and data privacy was among those standardized. One important aspect of this harmonization is the Data Protection Directive, adopted by EU members, which has a provision allowing the European Commission to block transfers of personal data to any country outside the EU that has been determined to lack adequate data protection policies. The differences in approach between the U.S. and the EU with respect to data protection lead to the EU issuing expressions of concern about the adequacy of data protection in the U.S., a move that could pave the way to the blocking of data transfers. After negotiation, it was determined that U.S. organizations that voluntarily joined an arrangement known as Safe Harbor would be considered adequate in terms of data protection.

Safe Harbor is a mechanism for self-regulation that can be enforced through trade practice law via the Federal Trade Commission. A business joining the Safe Harbor Consortium must make commitments to abide by specific guidelines concerning privacy. Safe Harbor members also agree to be governed by certain self-enforced regulatory mechanisms, backed ultimately by FTC action.

Another major difference between U.S. and European regulation lies in where the right of control is exercised. In European directives, the right of control over privacy is balanced in such a way as to favor consumers. Rather than having to pay to opt out, as in unlisted phone numbers, consumers have such services for free. Rather than having to opt out at all, consumers get the option to opt in. The default privacy setting is deemed to be the highest level of data privacy, and users have to opt in to share information. This default setting is a cornerstone of the EU Data Protection Directive and is enforced through national laws in all member nations.

Computer Trespass

With the advent of global network connections and the rise of the Internet as a method of connecting computers between homes, businesses, and governments across the globe, a new type of criminal trespass can now be committed. Computer trespass is the unauthorized entry into a computer system via any means, including remote network connections. This has led to a new area of law, one that has both national and international consequences. For crimes that are committed within a country's borders, national laws apply. For cross-border crimes, international laws and international treaties are the norm. Enforcement actions stemming from these agreements have been rare, with most actions employing national laws where applicable.

Computer trespass is treated as a crime in many countries. National laws exist in many countries, including the EU, Canada, and the United States. These laws vary by state, but they all have similar provisions defining the unauthorized entry into and use of computer resources as a crime. Whether called computer mischief as in Canada, or computer trespass as in the U.S., unauthorized entry and use of computer resources can be a crime with significant punishments under any of these laws. With the globalization of the computer network infrastructure, or Internet, issues that cross national boundaries have arisen and will continue to grow in prominence. Some of these issues are dealt with through the application of national laws upon request of another government. In the future, an international treaty may pave the way for closer cooperation.

Convention on Cybercrime

The Convention on Cybercrime is the first international treaty on crimes committed via the Internet and other computer networks. The Convention is the product of four years of work by Council of Europe experts, but also by the United States, Canada, Japan, and other countries that are not members of the organization of the member states of the European Council. The current status of the convention is as a draft treaty, ratified by only two members. A total of five members must ratify it for it to become law.

The main objective of the convention, set out in the preamble, is to pursue a common criminal policy aimed at the protection of society against cybercrime, especially by adopting appropriate legislation and fostering international cooperation. This has become increasingly an issue with the globalization of network communication. The ability to write a virus anywhere in the world and escape prosecution because of lack of local laws has become a global concern.

The convention deals particularly with infringements of copyright, computer-related fraud, child pornography, and violations of network security. It also contains a series of powers and procedures covering, for instance, searches of computer networks and interception. It will be supplemented by an additional protocol making any publication of racist and xenophobic propaganda via computer networks a criminal offense.

Ethics

Ethics play a role in all aspects of human behavior. Entire books have been devoted to ethical behavior in various industries. Computer security is no stranger to the field of ethics, for as user behavior forms one of the basic elements of computer security, this part of the foundation is only as strong as the ethics behind the behavior generating this strength. Ethical behavior is seldom addressed directly in policies and procedures with respect to computer security. Many times, ethical behavior is tackled at a much higher level, one that applies to all aspects of an individual's work, including their work with computer systems.

Following some major lapses in senior executive ethical behavior, Congress passed the **Sarbanes-Oxley Act** in 2002. This law was targeted at curbing a series of financial reporting irregularities at the highest levels of corporate leadership. Although aimed at the senior executive's abuse of financial reporting systems (because these systems are major IT components of a firm), the inclusion of IT becomes a de facto standard event. Should tampering with electronic records that allow a company to perform accurate financial reporting occur, a violation of this statute is probable. Sarbanes-Oxley is still new and not yet fully explored by corporate management, but early indications are that this act will have significant ramifications through the chain of information used to report on current corporate financial conditions. Controls and oversight over all processes used to produce financial reports will include aspects of the Enterprise Resource

Planning (ERP) software and the business processes surrounding how it performs its specific functions in the enterprise. Validation and verification of the results from this software-driven process will be subject to review, and given the complexity of the process, reviews and audits of IS processes are sure to be used for monitoring compliance.

Chapter Review

Chapter Summary

After reading this chapter and completing the exercises, you should understand the following about ethics and law related to security.

Export Restrictions on Encryption Methods

- Export controls exist for most countries with respect to encryption technology.
- In the U.S., restrictions on exporting encryption technology are managed through the Department of Commerce.
- A wide range of international laws exist concerning importation/exportation of encryption technologies—laws that have practical significance on software firms trading overseas.

Digital Signatures

- Digital Signatures are governed by a wide range of laws, from the U.S. E-Sign Act, to individual state laws governing commerce.
- Digital signatures can have the same legal standing as normal handwritten signatures.

Digital Rights Management

- The application of technology to protect intellectual property and copyrighted material is called digital rights management.
- Digital rights management is much more than simple copy protection. It can have detailed control, including printing restrictions and length-of-possession restrictions.
- The Digital Millenium Copyright Act (DMCA) covers a wide range of legal issues surrounding the protection of intellectual property rights in a digital age.

Privacy

- The European Union is the unmistakable leader in data privacy and protection legislation.
- California SB1386 governs responsibilities for entities to notify Californians whenever personal information is compromised.
- Several federal acts, HIPAA, GLB, FERPA, and others cover industry-specific privacy regulation.

Computer Trespass and Cybercrime

- In the U.S., computer trespass is governed under Federal and State laws for the majority of situations.

- International regulation is spotty, with many countries having no laws at all governing this area of computer security.

Ethics

- Ethical issues in corporate governance now influence security issues through the stricter management controls surrounding corporate financial data integrity under Sarbannes-Oxley.

- Computer-related ethical issues are typically governed by high-level corporate policies that dictate acceptable employee behavior.

Key Terms

California Senate Bill 1386 (SB1386) *(595)*
Carnivore *(594)*
Digital Millenium Copyright Act (DMCA) *(592)*
Digital rights management *(592)*
Electronic Communications Privacy Act (ECPA) *(594)*
E-Sign law *(590)*
European Union (EU) *(588)*
Family Education Records and Privacy Act (FERPA) *(595)*
Gramm Leach Bliley Act (GLB) *(594)*
Health Insurance Portability Accountability Act (HIPAA) *(595)*
Patriot Act *(594)*
Safe Harbor *(596)*
Sarbanes-Oxley Act *(597)*
Senate Bill 1386 (SB1386) *(595)*
Uniform Electronic Transactions Act (UETA) *(590)*

Key Terms Quiz

Use terms from the Key Terms list to complete the sentences that follow. Don't use the same term more than once. Not all terms will be used.

1. _____ is the law that permits citizens to use digital signatures in transactions with government.

2. Reverse engineering or foiling of encryption mechanisms is prohibited under _____.

3. Personal information can receive data protection and privacy in the U.S. under _____ and _____.

4. _____ is the determination of specific allowable actions with respect to data (that is, play it once).

5. When a U.S. firm agrees to comply with EU data privacy regulations, it is typically done through the _____.

6. The use of digital signatures for medical records is required and covered under _____.

7. The legislation of ethical behavior can impact IT operations through the _____ act.

8. Identity theft is punishable under provisions of _____.

9. The collection of e-mail and other ISP-based records has been significantly enhanced under the _____.

10. Digital signatures in the United States are covered under provisions of the _____.

Multiple-Choice Quiz

1. To monitor user actions on a corporate computer network, what user notification is needed?

   A. A consent banner displayed upon login

   B. Written permission from a company officer

   C. Nothing; the system belongs to the company

   D. Written permission from the user

2. The compromise or loss of personal data in a financial institution's computer system to an unauthorized party is a violation of which of the following?

   A. The Social Security Act of 1934

   B. The Patriot Act of 2001

   C. The Gramm-Leach-Bliley Act

   D. HIPAA

3. Unauthorized use of a computer system in the U.S., even if you do not cause any damage, can result in prosecution according to which of the following?

   A. State law, under computer trespass statutes

   B. Federal law under the Identity Theft and Assumption Deterrence Act

   C. Federal law under the Electronic Communications Privacy Act (ECPA) of 1986

   D. SB 1386

4. In the United States, regulation and control over the import/export of encryption technology for commercial purposes is governed by which of the following?

    A. The U.S. State Department

    B. The U.S. Commerce Department

    C. The U.S. Department of Defense

    D. The National Security Agency

5. Carnivore is a software program designed to do what?

    A. Manage wiretaps on the Internet

    B. Scan specific user account e-mails for keywords and phrases

    C. Prevent loss of private data across a firewall

    D. Investigate computer trespass incidents

6. Digital signatures are…

    A. Valid for all transactions in which both parties agree to use digital signatures

    B. Valid only for non–real property transactions

    C. Valid only for ecommerce transactions

    D. Not yet valid since the necessary laws have not passed as of 2003

7. The primary factor(s) behind data sharing compliance between U.S. and European companies is/are…

    A. The Safe Harbor Provision and Privacy Laws

    B. The European Computer Security and Encryption Laws

    C. U.S. FCC enforcement actions

    D. The HIPAA

8. How accurate is the following statement? Writing malicious software (viruses and worms) and releasing them through the Internet is a violation of the law.

    A. Always True: All countries have reciprocal agreements under international law.

    B. Partially True: It depends upon current laws in the country of origin.

    C. False: Computer security laws do not cross international boundaries.

    D. Partially True: It depends upon the specific countries involved, both for the author of the virus and the recipient.

9. Reverse engineering of encryption technology in a software program is a potential violation of…

    A. HIPAA

    B. U.S. Commerce Department regulations

    C. DMCA

    D. National Security Agency regulations

10. Violation of the Digital Millenium Copyright Act (DMCA) can result in...

    A. Civil forfeiture of profits

    B. Jail time

    C. Loss of software license

    D. Export restrictions

11. The tampering of data that leads to false financial reporting is a potential violation of...

    A. UETA

    B. Sarbannes-Oxley

    C. Computer Trespass Act

    D. FERPA

12. Loss of personal financial information that could lead to identity theft is potentially reportable to the affected parties under which of the following?

    A. Sarbannes-Oxley

    B. GLB

    C. HIPAA

    D. SB1386

13. The Safe Harbor Provision is managed via which of the following?

    A. U.S. Federal Law

    B. It's self-imposed with government audits

    C. EU Law

    D. It acts as a contractual obligation between firms under UETA

14. Electronic eavesdropping on e-mail conversations is covered under what U.S. Federal law?

    A. The Patriot Act

    B. HIPAA

    C. ECPA

    D. UETA

15. Digital signatures are...

    A. Completely covered for all transactions by the E-Sign law

    B. Covered by a combination of federal and state laws

    C. Not yet legally valid; hand signatures are still required for legal records

    D. Not permitted for health records according to HIPAA

Essay Quiz

1. Describe the rules governing the exportation of encryption software from the United States to firms in other countries throughout the world.

2. Describe the main elements of the Digital Millennium Copyright Act. What was the purpose of these elements and what effect are they having in the computer industry?

3. What are the major laws governing healthcare records? What are the major components of these regulations and what is the specific purpose of their components?

4. What computer security regulations and laws apply to ISPs in the United States and what are these laws commonly used for?

5. What role does ethics play in computer security? How is this enforced? How does computer security affect compliance with portions of Sarbannes-Oxley?

Lab Projects

Lab Project 24.1

You have just been hired as a system administrator in a small college. Your servers are used for database storage and web sites serving the university community. Describe the laws that will potentially impact your job with respect to computer security. What actions will you take to ensure compliance with laws and regulations?

Lab Project 24.2

You recently joined a small doctor's group as their only system administrator. They have expressed concern over HIPAA compliance at the interview process, which you obviously successfully passed. What do you do to put in place a HIPAA-compliant solution?

Lab Project 24.3

You are joining a small firm as their primary IT person. This is a manufacturer that ships cosmetic products directly to customers (households) worldwide via a small web site that was home built. What are the main issues you need to develop policies for with respect to data security and data privacy? What legal considerations do you need to be prepared to brief senior management about regarding these issues? Outline your briefing for a 15-minute presentation.

About the CD-ROM

The CD-ROM included with this book comes complete with MasterExam and Session 1 of LearnKey's online training. The software is easy to install on any Windows 98/NT/2000 computer and must be installed to access MasterExam. To register for LearnKey's online training and a second bonus MasterExam, simply click the Online Training link on the Main Page and follow the directions to the free online registration.

System Requirements

The software requires Windows 98 or later and Internet Explorer 5.0 or later and 20MB of hard disk space for full installation. The Electronic book requires Adobe Acrobat Reader. To access the online training from LearnKey you must have RealPlayer Basic 8 or the Real1 plug-in, which will be automatically installed when you launch the online training.

LearnKey Online Training

The LearnKey Online Training link will allow you to access online training from mhteched.onlineexpert.com. The first session of this course is provided at no charge. Additional sessions for this course and other courses may be purchased directly from www.learnkey.com or by calling 800-865-0165.

The first time you run the training, you will be required to register with the online product. Follow the instructions for a first-time user, and make sure to use a valid e-mail address.

Prior to running the online training you, will need to add the Real1 plug-in and the RealCBT plug-in to your system. This will automatically be opened on your system when you run the training for the first time.

Installing and Running MasterExam

If your computer CD-ROM drive is configured to autorun, the CD-ROM will automatically start upon inserting the disk. From the opening screen, you may install MasterExam by pressing the *MasterExam* button. This will begin the installation process and create a program group named "LearnKey." To run MasterExam, choose Start | Programs | LearnKey. If the autorun feature does not launch your CD, browse to the CD and click the RunInstall icon.

MasterExam

MasterExam provides you with a simulation of the actual exam. The number of questions, the type of questions, and the time allowed are intended to be an accurate representation of the exam environment. You have the option to take an open-book exam, including hints, references, and answers, a closed-book exam, or the timed MasterExam simulation.

When you launch MasterExam, a digital clock display will appear in the upper-left corner of your screen. The clock will continue to count down to zero unless you choose to end the exam before the time expires.

Help

A help file is provided through the Help button on the main page in the lower-left corner. Individual help features are also available through MasterExam and LearnKey's Online Training.

Removing Installation(s)

MasterExam is installed to your hard drive. For *best* results when attempting to remove the MasterExam programs, choose Start | Programs | LearnKey | Uninstall options.

If you want to remove Real Player, use the Add/Remove Programs icon in the Control Panel. You may also remove the LearnKey training program from this location.

Technical Support

For questions regarding the technical content of the electronic book or MasterExam, please visit www.mhteched.com or send an e-mail to customer.service@mcgraw-hill.com. For customers outside the U.S., use the following e-mail: international_cs@mcgraw-hill.com.

LearnKey Technical Support

For technical problems with the software (installation, operation, removing installations), and for questions regarding LearnKey Online Training content, please visit www.learnkey.com or send an e-mail to techsupport@learnkey.com.

About the Security+ Exam

The Security+ exam is a vendor-neutral certification offered by the Computing Technology Industry Association (CompTIA). CompTIA developed this certification with the help of industry leaders and experts who came from various respected organizations in commercial, governmental, and academic areas. CompTIA took this material and then performed a multilevel review for accuracy, developing an exam series that is considered psychometrically sound.

The objective of the Security+ certification program is to provide an independent means of demonstrating knowledge in basic computer security. The body of knowledge covered by the certification examination consists of vendor-independent security-related knowledge that a professional with two years of computer system administration/network administration experience should have. The content can be viewed at www.comptia.org/certification/Security/objectives.asp.

The exam format is multiple choice, computer scored, and can be taken at several testing centers across the country. A total of 90 minutes is allowed for the 100-question exam, which is scored using a normalized scale of 100 to 900 points. A score of 764 or higher is required to pass. The Security+ certification does not expire, so an individual need never retake the exam once they have passed.

The 2004 Security+ exam objectives focus upon five domains. A mapping of these domains, their subdomains, and the chapters in this book are outlined in the following. The chapters listed are the main source of the material in the text, although additional references may be found in other chapters. As CompTIA is committed to maintaining a current body of knowledge for the exam objectives, potential examtakers are advised to obtain a current copy from CompTIA before taking the exam.

Domain 1.0—General Security Concepts (30 percent)	
1.1 Recognize, differentiate, and explain the following access control models	Chapter 2
MAC (Mandatory Access Control)	
DAC (Discretionary Access Control)	
RBAC (Role-Based Access Control)	

5.1 Understand application of the following concepts of physical security	Chapter 8
Access Control	
Physical Barriers	
Biometrics	
Social Engineering	
Environment	
Wireless Cells	
Location	
Shielding	
Fire Suppression	
5.2 Understand the security implications of the following topics of disaster recovery	Chapter 19
Backups	
Off-Site Storage	
Secure Recovery	
Alternate Sites	
Disaster Recovery Plans	
5.3 Understand the security implications of the following topics of business continuity	Chapter 19
Utilities	
High Availability / Fault Tolerance	
Backups	
5.4 Understand the concepts and uses of the following types of policies and procedures	Chapter 19
Security Policy	
Acceptable Use	
Due Care	
Privacy	
Separation of Duties	
Need-to-Know	
Password Management	
SLAs (Service Level Agreements)	
Disposal/Destruction	
HR (Human Resources) Policy	
Termination (Adding and revoking passwords and privileges, and so on)	
Hiring (Adding and revoking passwords and privileges, and other duties)	
Code of Ethics	
Incident Response Policy	

SSCP Exam

The System Security Certified Practitioner (SSCP) exam is an exam administered by the International Information Systems Security Certifications Consortium, Inc. (ISC)2. (ISC)2 is a global, not-for-profit organization involved in information security. (ISC)2 performs several functions in the community, including education, awareness, and certification programs. Information on (ISC)2 can be found on their web site, www.isc2.org.

(ISC)2 offers two certification exams, the SSCP exam and the CISSP exam. To obtain these credentials, one must pass the exam, subscribe to the (ISC)2 Code of Ethics, and have demonstrated experience in the field of information security. The material in this text can assist in preparing for the SSCP exam, and an analysis of the body of knowledge posted by (ISC)2 for the exam is listed next. The exam format is multiple choice, 125 questions; a period of three hours is given to complete the exam.

SSCP Body of Knowledge

The body of knowledge for the SSCP exam is broken into seven sections:

- Access Controls
- Administration
- Audit and Monitoring
- Risk, Response, and Recovery
- Cryptography
- Data Communications
- Malicious Code

An analysis of the details for each section and the corresponding material in this book is provided in the following table. Note that, because the exam structure is significantly different from the book structure, the mapping includes many chapter references for each section, and many book chapters apply to many sections of the exam.

Access Controls Section	
Overview: This section of the exam covers items related to the management of resource control on a system: What users can do, what resources are they allowed access to, and what is not allowed. The knowledge is based around how the access control systems function and how they are implemented in systems to control and protect data. Knowledge in how to defeat or go around these systems is expected as well as how to set them up and manage them.	
Identification, Authentication, Authorization, Accounting	Chapters 2, 11
Access Control Techniques	Chapters 2, 11
Best Practices for Access Control	Chapters 2, 11
Administration of Access Control	Chapters 2
Models, Methodologies, and Implementation	Chapters 2
Remote Authentication	Chapter 11
Methods of Attack	Chapters 2, 11
Intrusion Detection	Chapter 13
Penetration Testing	Chapters 2
Administration Section	
Overview: Security administration requires the identification of information assets and documentation-supporting policies, standards, procedures, and guidelines. Knowledge is expected in privacy issues, data integrity and classification, audit, organizational roles, and responsibilities.	

Principles of Security Administration	Chapter 2
Confidentiality, Integrity, Availability	Chapter 2
Policies, Standards, Guidelines, Baselines	Chapter 14
Privacy Issues	Chapter 24
Data Classification	Chapter 19
Documentation	Chapter 19
Security Architecture and Design	Chapter 14
Development Life Cycle	Chapter 18
Certification and Accreditation	Chapters 2, 4
Configuration Management	Chapter 21
Hardware Components	Chapter 10
Employment Practices	Chapters 2, 4
Security Awareness Training	Chapters 2, 4
Threats and Attacks	Chapter 15
Social Engineering	Chapter 4

Audit and Monitoring Section

Overview: Auditing is the main method for determining system operation within policies and procedures. Knowledge is expected in the areas of data collection, logging, sampling, and reporting with respect to audit records.

Types of Controls	Chapters 2, 22
Audit Processes	Chapter 22
Audit Log Review	Chapter 22
Incident Response and Analysis	Chapter 19
Media Protection	Chapter 10
Monitoring Devices and Techniques	Chapter 22

Risk, Response, and Recovery Section

Overview: Knowledge is expected in the identification, measurement, analysis, and control of loss associated with adverse events. Incident handling is the response to unauthorized events. Knowledge in business continuity, planning, and recovery operations.

Risk Management	Chapter 20
Threats, Vulnerabilities, Exposures	Chapter 19
Asset Identification and Evaluation	Chapter 19
Risk Analysis	Chapter 20
Safeguards and Countermeasures	Chapter 20
Incident Handling	Chapter 19
Incident Investigation	Chapter 19
Forensics	Chapter 23
Interviewing and Interrogation	Chapter 23
Business Impact Analysis	Chapter 19

Business Continuity Project Planning	Chapter 19
Evaluation of Recovery Alternatives	Chapter 19
System Backups, Processes, and Documentation	Chapter 19

Cryptography Section

Overview: Cryptography includes the techniques used to ensure confidentiality and integrity of data in storage and transfer. Knowledge is expected in cryptography, cryptanalysis, public and private key algorithms, key distribution and management, digital signatures, and PKI.

Algorithms	Chapter 5
Types and Uses of Cryptography	Chapter 5
Digital Signatures	Chapter 5
Public Key Infrastructure	Chapter 6
Certification	Chapters 5, 7
Hashing Functions	Chapter 5
Cryptographic Attacks	Chapter 5

Data Communications Section

Overview: Demonstrate an understanding of communications and data security, equipment, protocols, and techniques for preventing and detecting network-based attacks.

Types of Networks	Chapters 10,
Network Communication Protocols	Chapters 9, 10
Network Topologies	Chapters 9, 10
Physical Media Types	Chapter 10
Remote Access	Chapter 11
Network Components	Chapter 10
Network-Based Attacks	Chapter 15

Malicious Code Section

Overview: Demonstrate knowledge of the concepts and types of malicious code, how it is introduced to a system, protection, and recovery efforts.

Malicious Code Types	Chapters 2, 15
Countermeasure Techniques	Chapter 15
Mobile Code Threats	Chapter 15
Non-Technical Attacks	Chapters 15, 17, 18
Buffer Overflows	Chapters 15, 17, 18
Types of Attacks	Chapters 15, 17, 18
Software Copy/Download Protections	Chapter 15
Awareness Programs	Chapter 15

*-property   The security principle used in the Bell-LaPadula security model that states that no subject can write to an object with a lower security classification. (2)

2.4GHz band   The 2400MHz band that the FCC has allowed for unlicensed transmissions. (12)

802.1X   An IETF standard for performing authentication over networks. (11)

Access Control List   A list associated with an object (such as a file) that identifies what level of access each subject (such as a user) has, and what they can do to the object (such as read, write, or execute). (14)

Access controls   Mechanisms or methods used to determine what access permissions subjects (such as users) have for specific objects (such as files). (2)

Access tokens   Items carried by the user that allow them to be authenticated by the system. (8)

Active IDS   An intrusion detection system (IDS) that can react to the traffic it is analyzing. Reactions can be simple, such as running a script or sending a TCP reset, or complex, such as forcibly logging off offending users and terminating their processes. (13)

ActiveX   The name given to a broad collection of APIs, protocols, and programs developed by Microsoft to automatically download and execute code over an Internet-based channel. (17)

Address Resolution Protocol (ARP)   The protocol used to convert IP addresses into MAC addresses. (9)

Algorithm   A step-by-step procedure—typically an established computation for solving a problem within a set number of steps. (5)

Annualized loss expectancy (ALE)   How much an event is expected to cost the business per year, given the dollar cost of the loss and how often it is likely to occur. ALE = single loss expectancy * annualized rate of occurrence. (14)

Annualized rate of occurrence   On an annualized basis, the frequency with which an event is expected to occur. (20)

Anomaly detection model   A system that focuses on unusual or unexpected activity to detect attackers. (13)

AOL Instant Messenger   A popular instant messaging program distributed by America Online. (12)

Asset   Resources or information an organization needs to conduct its business. (20)

Audit files   Files containing records that show who accessed a computer system and what operations he or she has performed during a given period of time. (13)

Audit trail   A set of records or events, generally organized chronologically, that record what activity has occurred on a system. These records (often computer files) are often used in an attempt to re-create what took place when an incident occurred. They can also be used to detect possible intruders. (22)

Auditing   The name given to any actions or processes used to verify the assigned privileges and rights of a user, as well as any capabilities used to create and maintain a record showing who accessed a particular system and what actions they performed. (22)

Authentication Header (AH)   A portion of the IPSec security protocol that provides authentication services and replay-detection ability. AH can be used either by itself or with Encapsulating Security Payload (ESP). Refer to RFC 2402. (11)

Authentication   The process by which a subject's (such as a user's) identity is verified. (2)

AuthentiCode   A set of functions developed by Microsoft to enable code signing and content-integrity protection. (17)

Auto-run   A function by which a CD-ROM media that has been inserted into a machine gets automatically mounted and a program is executed. (8)

Availability   Part of the CIA of security. Availability applies to hardware, software, and data. All of these should be present and accessible when the subject (the user) wants to access or use them. (2)

Backdoor   Avenues that can be used to access a system while circumventing normal security mechanisms. (4)

Baseline   Describes a system or software as it is built and functioning at a point in time. Serves as a foundation for comparison or measurement, providing the necessary visibility to control change. (21)

Baselining   The process of establishing a system's security state. This process creates the "baseline." (14)

Beacon frames   The frames an access point sends out several times a second to let wireless clients know it exists. (12)

Bell-LaPadula security model   A security model developed by the U.S. military to enforce data confidentiality. (2)

Best evidence rule   Courts prefer original evidence rather than a copy to ensure that no alteration of the evidence (whether intentional or unintentional) has occurred. (23)

Biba security model   An integrity-based security model that prevents direct or indirect modification of information without authorization. (2)

Biometrics   An access control mechanism in which a physical characteristic, such as a fingerprint or the geometry of an individual's hand, is used to uniquely identify users. (3)

BIOS passwords   A password used to protect the computer's BIOS from being edited. (8)

Block cipher   An encryption method that separates input text into blocks before encrypting it. (5)

Bluetooth   A wireless technology designed as a short range (approximately ten meters) Personal Area Network (PAN) cable replacement technology that may be built into a variety of devices such as mobile phones, PDAs, and laptop computers. (3)

Bootdisk   A removable media from which a computer can be booted into an operating system. (8)

Bridge   A device used to segregate sections of a LAN based on layer 2 addresses. (10)

Buffer overflow   When a user or process supplies more data than was expected and the additional data overflows the intended storage area into other areas. (14)

Bus topology   The network topology where all network devices are connected to the same cable or media, called the bus. (9)

Business continuity plan (BCP)   A plan that details how an organization will continue operations when a disruption occurs. It will generally outline the order in which critical functions should be returned to service. (19)

Business impact assessment (BIA)   An assessment of the impact that a loss of critical functions will have on the organization. (19)

CA certificate   A certificate issued to a Certificate Authority. (6)

Canonicalization error   An error in determining the true name for a resource, derived from one of many representations. (18)

Capability Maturity Model   A structured methodology helping organizations improve the maturity of their software processes by providing an evolutionary path from ad hoc processes to disciplined software management processes. Developed at Carnegie Mellon University's Software Engineering Institutes. (21)

Carnivore   A software program developed by the U.S. government to implement tap and trace activity over the Internet at ISP locations. (24)

Centralized management   A type of privilege management that brings the authority and responsibility for managing and maintaining rights and privileges into a single group, location, or area. (22)

Certificate authority   An entity that is responsible for issuing and revoking certificates. CAs are typically third parties, although they exist for internal company use as well. This term is also applied to server software that provides these services. (6)

Certificate repository   A centralized storage location to maintain copies of digital certificates for use by authorized entities. (6)

Certificate revocation list   A digitally signed object that lists all of the current but revoked certificates issued by a given CA. This allows users to verify whether a certificate is currently valid even if the expiration date hasn't passed. This is analogous to a list of stolen charge card numbers that allows stores to reject bad credit cards. (6)

Certificate server   The actual service that issues certificates based on the data provided during the initial registration process. (6)

Certificates   A cryptographically signed object that contains an identity and a public key associated with this identity. The certificate can be used to establish identity, analogous to a notarized written document. (2)

CGI (common gateway interface)   The original method of having a web server execute a program outside the web server process, yet on the same server. (17)

Challenge Handshake Authentication Protocol (CHAP)   Used to provide authentication across point-to-point links using the Point-to-Point Protocol (PPP). (11)

Change control board   A body that oversees the change management process. Enables management to oversee and coordinate projects. (21)

Change/configuration management   A standard methodology for performing and recording changes during software development and operation. (21)

CHAP   See Challenge Handshake Authentication Protocol. (11)

Clark-Wilson security model   An integrity-based security model that centers its security on control of the processes that are allowed to modify critical data referred to as constrained data items. The model also enforces the principle of separation of duties to limit the ability of any one individual to modify critical data. (2)

Closed circuit television systems (CCTV)   Television systems where the camera and monitor are on a dedicated "closed" circuit; typically used in security systems. (8)

Code injection   A vulnerability where code is used for input to a computer application, causing the code to be executed instead of the input being acted upon. (18)

Cold site　A backup operating location that will have the basic environmental controls necessary to operate but will have few of the computing components needed for processing. (19)

Collision attack　An attack that attempts to find two input texts that hash to the same value. (5)

Competent evidence　Evidence that is legally qualified and reliable. (23)

Confidentiality　Part of the CIA of security. Refers to the security principle that states that information should not be disclosed to unauthorized individuals. (12)

Configuration auditing　The process of verifying that configuration items are built and maintained according to requirements, standards, or contractual agreements. (21)

Configuration control　The process of controlling changes to items that have been baselined. (21)

Configuration identification　The process of identifying which assets need to be managed and controlled. (21)

Configuration item　Assets identified during configuration identification which need to be managed or controlled. (21)

Configuration status accounting　Procedures for tracking and maintaining data relative to each configuration item in the baseline. (21)

Contactless access cards　A card that contains a radio frequency transmitter capable of sending a code. When passed near a reader, the code is transmitted, allowing the system to perform authentication. (8)

Content-based signatures　Signatures based on the contents of specific packets or groups of packets—for example, the phrase "/etc/passwd" inside a Telnet session. (13)

Context-based signatures　Signatures based on how a packet or group of packets fit together compared to the traffic around them—for example, a TCP port scan. (13)

Control (also called countermeasure or safeguard)　A measure taken to detect, prevent, or mitigate the risk associated with a threat. (20)

Cookie　Information stored on a user's computer by a web server to maintain the state of the connection to the web server. Used primarily so preferences or previously used information can be recalled on future requests to the server. (17)

Countermeasure　See Control. (20)

Critical infrastructures　Those infrastructures whose loss would have a severe detrimental impact on the nation. (1)

Cross-certificate　A mechanism through which one CA can issue a certificate allowing its users to trust another CA. (6)

Cryptanalysis   The process of attempting to break a cryptographic system. (5)

Cryptographically random   A random number from a sequence where the sequence itself is also random and cannot be duplicated or repeated. (18)

Cryptography   The art of secret writing that enables an individual to hide the contents of a message or file from all but the intended recipient. (5)

DAP (Directory Access Protocol)   The protocol for accessing directory-based data storage structures. (17)

Datagram   The name sometimes given to packets in an IP network. (9)

Decentralized management   A type of privilege management that spreads out the authority and capability to manage privileges and rights to multiple individuals and locations. (22)

Decision tree   A data structure where each element in the structure is attached to one or more structures directly beneath it. Making a decision carries you down a specific branch of the tree until you reach a structure with no more branches underneath it. (13)

Delta backup   A backup strategy where only the portions of the files that have been changed since the last delta or full backup will be stored. (19)

Demonstrative evidence   Used to aid the jury; may be in the form of a model, experiment, chart, and so on, offered to prove that an event occurred. (23)

Denial-of-Service (DoS) attack   An attack designed to prevent resources from being used for their intended purpose. (9)

DHCP (Dynamic Host Configuration Protocol)   A protocol used to dynamically configure IP addresses in networks. (10)

DIAMETER   The DIAMETER base protocol is intended to provide an authentication, authorization, and accounting (AAA) framework for applications such as network access or IP mobility. DIAMETER is a draft IETF proposal. (11)

Differential backup   A backup strategy in which only the files and software that have changed since the last full backup was completed are stored. (19)

Differential cryptanalysis   Compares the input plaintext and the output ciphertext to try and determine the key. (5)

Digital certificate   A digital document that establishes an association between a user and their public key. (6)

Digital Millenium Copyright Act (DMCA)   A law passed to update copyright issues; includes provisions restricting reverse engineering and the circumvention of encryption and security mechanisms. (24)

Digital rights management   A term used to denote the activities associated with the enforcement of copyright and owner rights with respect to digital works. (24)

Direct evidence   Oral testimony or other evidence that proves a specific fact (such as an eyewitness's statement, fingerprint, photo, and so on). The knowledge of the facts is obtained through the five senses of the witness. There are no inferences or presumptions. (23)

Direct-sequence spread spectrum (DSSS)   A method of distributing a communication over multiple frequencies to avoid interference and detection. (12)

Disaster recovery plan (DRP)   A written plan developed to address how an organization will react to a natural or man-made disaster in order to ensure business continuity. Related to the concept of a business continuity plan (BCP). (19)

Discretionary access control   An access control mechanism in which the owner of an object (such as a file) can decide which other subjects (such as other users) may have access to the object, and what access (read, write, execute) these objects may have. (2)

Discretionary access control   An access control mechanism in which the owner of an object (such as a file) can decide which other subjects (such as other users) may have access to the object, and what access (read, write, execute) these subjects may have. (22)

Diversity of defense   The approach of creating dissimilar security layers so that an intruder who is able to breach one layer will be faced with an entirely different set of defenses at the next layer. (2)

DMZ (demilitarized zone)   An area between the Internet and intranet, separated by firewalls. (10)

DOCSIS (Data Over Cable Service Interface Specification)   A standard for carrying digital traffic over cable TV circuits. (10)

Documentary evidence   Evidence in the form of business records, printouts, manuals, and the like. Much of the evidence relating to computer crimes is documentary evidence. (23)

Domain Name System (DNS)   The service that translates domain and system names, such as www.cnn.com, to IP addresses. (9)

Drive imaging   A technique that makes a complete bit-by-bit copy of a hard drive onto some other media. (8)

DSL (digital subscriber line)   A local phone circuit designed to directly carry digital communications. (10)

Dual control   The process of requiring more than one individual to recover a key. (6)

Due care   The legal duty for a party to act reasonably and responsibly to avoid causing loss or injury to another. (19)

Due diligence   The legal duty of investigating and ensuring that due care has been used. (19)

Dumpster diving   The process of going through a target's trash searching for information that can be used in an attack, or to gain knowledge about a system or network. (4)

Dynamic Host Configuration Protocol (DHCP)   A protocol for dynamically and temporarily assigning IP addresses to network devices. (9)

EAPOL   Extensible Authentication Protocol (EAPOL) over LAN is an encapsulated method of passing EAP messages over 802 frames. (11)

Electronic Communications Privacy Act (ECPA)   Congressional law designed to address the myriad legal privacy issues that resulted from the increasing use of computers and other technology specific to telecommunications, e-mail, cellular communications, workplace privacy, and various other electronic communication areas. (24)

Elite hackers   The most technically competent of individuals conducting intrusive activity on the Internet. These individuals not only can exploit vulnerabilities that are discovered but are also the ones that are usually responsible for finding these vulnerabilities. (1)

E-mail hoax   An e-mail that has a compelling story, seemingly true, but that is almost invariably false, and which requests you to send it to others. (16)

Encryption   The art of obscuring data by making it cryptic (as in scrambling data). (16)

Escalation auditing   The process of looking for an increase in privileges, such as when an ordinary user obtains administrator-level privileges. (22)

E-Sign law   Common name for the Electronic Signatures in Global and National Commerce Act, a law that enables digital signatures to be legally recognized when used with contracts. (24)

ESP   ESP is a portion of the IPSec implementation that provides for data confidentiality with optional authentication and replay-detection services. ESP completely encapsulates user data in the datagram. ESP can be used either by itself or in conjunction with Authentication Headers for varying degrees of IPsec services. (11)

European Union (EU)   A governmental association of the states that comprise the countries of Europe. (24)

Evidence   The documents, verbal statements, and material objects admissible in a court of law. (23)

Exclusionary rule   Evidence collected in violation of the Fourth Amendment of the United States Constitution, the Electronic Communications Privacy Act (ECPA), or other aspects of the United States Code, may not be admissible in court. (23)

Exposure factor A measure of the magnitude of loss of an asset. Used in the calculation of single loss expectancy (SLE). (20)

Extranet An extension of a company's intranet functionality to select groups of people for specific business purposes. (10)

False negatives Term used to define when a system denies the existence of an object that is there. The commonest use of the term concerns a biometric system that denies access to an authorized individual. (8)

False positive Term used when a security system makes an error and incorrectly reports the existence of a searched-for object. Examples include when an intrusion detection system misidentifies benign traffic as hostile, an antivirus program reports the existence of a virus in software that actually is not infected, or a biometric system allows access to a system to an unauthorized individual. (8)

Family Education Records and Privacy Act (FERPA) Congressional law created to protect student records in higher education. (24)

Fault tolerance A method to ensure high availability is accomplished through the mirroring of data and systems. Should a "fault" occur, causing disruption in a device, the mirrored system provides the requested data with no apparent interruption in service. (19)

File Transfer Protocol (FTP) File Transfer Protocol is an application level protocol used to transfer files over a network connection. (17)

Firmware update The process of updating software stored in non-volatile memory (such as EPROMS). The hardware and software used to run routers, switches, and many network devices is called firmware. (14)

Forensics The preservation, identification, documentation, and interpretation of computer data for use in legal proceedings. (23)

Free space Sectors on a storage medium that are available for the operating system to use. (23)

Full backup A backup strategy in which all files and software are copied onto the storage media. (19)

Gramm Leach Bliley Act (GLB) Congressional law dealing with privacy issues in the financial industry. (24)

Group A group of users with a common, shared criteria or trait. (22)

Guidelines Recommendations relating to a policy. They are not mandatory steps. (3)

Hacker The term used most often to refer to individuals who attempt to gain unauthorized access to computer systems or networks. An alternative term, offered by many in the security community, is cracker. (2)

Hacktivist   A hacker whose activities are motivated by a personal cause or position. (1)

Hardening   The process of securing and preparing a system for the production environment. (14)

Hash   Form of encryption that creates a digest of the data put into the algorithm. These algorithms are referred to as one-way algorithms because there is no feasible way to decrypt what has been encrypted. (5)

Health Insurance Portability Accountability Act (HIPAA)   Congressional law regulating privacy associated with medical records. (24)

Hearsay rule   Second-hand evidence not gathered from the personal knowledge of a witness. (23)

Hierarchical trust mode   A trust model in which CAs are subordinate to other CAs, forming a hierarchy. (6)

High availability   The ability to maintain availability of data and operational processing despite a disrupting event of any sort. (19)

Highly structured threat   Threats characterized by a much longer period of preparation (years is not uncommon), tremendous financial backing, and a large and organized group of attackers. It may include efforts to subvert insiders as well as plant individuals inside a potential target in advance of an attack. (1)

Honeypot/honeynet   A computer system or portion of a network that has been set up to attract potential intruders to it in the hope that they will leave the other systems alone. Since there is no legitimate user of this system, any attempt to access it is an indication of unauthorized activity and provides an easy mechanism to spot attacks. (13)

Host security   Takes a granular view of security by focusing on protecting each computer and device individually instead of addressing protection of the network as a whole. (2)

Host-based IDS   An intrusion detection system running on a single system that only examines and reports activity for that specific system. (13)

Hot site   A fully configured backup environment similar to the normal operating environment that can be operational within a few hours. (19)

Hotfix   A small software update designed to address a specific problem, such as a buffer overflow in an application that exposes the system to attack. (14)

HTML (Hypertext Markup Language)   The protocol designated for the transfer of hypertext-linked data over the Internet, from web servers to browsers. (17)

Hub   A device that makes connections between devices at the physical layer. (10)

HVAC   Heating, Ventilation, and Air Conditioning systems. (3)

Hybrid trust model A trust model that is a combination of hierarchical and peer-to-peer in nature. (6)

IEEE 802.11 A set of standards for wireless networks which are well suited for the local area network environment. The normal mode for this standard is to have computers with 802.11 network cards communicate with a wireless access point. (3)

IKE See Internet Key Exchange. (11)

Impact The result of a vulnerability being exploited by a threat, resulting in a loss. (20)

Incident response The process of responding to, containing, analyzing, and recovering from an incident. (13)

Incremental backups A backup strategy in which files that have changed since the last full or incremental backup occurred are stored. (19)

Inetd The master services daemon used by many UNIX operating systems. This daemon listens for incoming connections and then activates the appropriate service to handle those incoming connections. (14)

Information warfare Warfare conducted against the information and information processing equipment used by an adversary. (1)

initialization vector The initializing input for the algorithm, designed to enhance security by adding additional variance. (12)

Intangible asset An asset for which a monetary equivalent cannot be determined. Examples are brand recognition and goodwill. (20)

Integrity Part of the CIA of security, the security principle that requires that information is not modified except by individuals authorized to do so. (2)

Internet Control Message Protocol (ICMP) The protocol designed to carry error, network control and availability, and traffic flow messages. (9)

Internet Key Exchange (IKE) The protocol formerly known as ISAKMP/Oakley, defined in RFC 2409. A hybrid protocol that uses part Oakley and part of SKEME protocol suites inside the Internet Security Association and Key Management Protocol (ISAKMP) framework. IKE is used to establish a shared security policy and authenticated keys for services that require keys (such as IPSec). (11)

Internet Protocol (IP) The protocol responsible for moving packets around the Internet. (9)

Internet Security Association and Key Management Protocol (ISAKMP) A protocol framework that defines the mechanics of implementing a key exchange protocol and negotiation of a security policy. (7)

Internet The global connection of networks. (10)

Intranet   An internal network utilizing TCP/IP protocols, but limited to direct company personnel access. (10)

Intrusion detection system   A system to identify suspicious, malicious, or undesirable activity that indicates a breach in computer security. (13)

IPSec   IP Security, a protocol used to secure IP packets during transmission across a network. IPSec offers authentication, integrity, and confidentiality services. It uses Authentication Headers (AHs) and Encapsulating Security Payload (ESP) to accomplish this functionality. (7)

Key archiving system   A method of maintaining backups and historical records of private keys. (6)

Key escrow   A method to allow governmental access to your encrypted information with a court order, by which both you and the government have a copy of your private key. (5)

Key management   The name of the process that keeps the shared secrets from being exposed to unauthorized parties. (5)

Key recovery   The process or retrieving a key from a key escrow system. (6)

Key   In cryptography, a sequence of characters or bits used by an algorithm to encrypt or decrypt a message. (5)

Keyspace   The entire set of all possible keys for a specific encryption algorithm. (5)

Layer Two Tunneling Protocol (L2TP)   L2TP is a Cisco switching protocol that operates at the data-link layer. (11)

Layered access   The concept of making users pass through multiple types of security to reach critical assets that make those assets harder to attack. (8)

Layered security   An approach to security which provides multiple layers of protection so that if one layer is breached, other protective layers still exist to defeat the attacker. (2)

LDAP (Lightweight Directory Access Protocol)   A subset of DAP providing the most commonly used functionality. (17)

Least privilege   A security principle in which a subject is provided with the minimum set of rights and privileges that the subject needs in order to perform its function. The goal is to limit the potential damage that any subject can cause. (2)

Linear cryptanalysis   Puts the plaintext through a simple version of the algorithm to try and retrieve the key. (5)

Local Area Network (LAN)   A small, typically local network covering a relatively small area such as a single floor of an office building. (9)

Logic bomb   A piece of code that sits dormant for a period of time until some event invokes its payload. (15)

Low-Water-Mark policy   A policy useful in integrity-based security models that prevents subjects from modifying objects of a higher integrity level. This policy has the unfortunate side effect of lowering the subject's integrity level each time an object of a lower level is accessed, thus forcing the subject's level to the lowest possible on the system. (2)

Mail relaying   Many Internet e-mail servers, by default, allow any host to send e-mail to any other host—this is called using the server as a mail relay. E-mail servers should disallow this and only permit mail to be sent from their individual domain(s). (16)

Malware   Also known as malicious code, this refers to software that has been designed for some nefarious purpose. (15)

Mandatory access control   An access control mechanism in which the security mechanism controls access to all objects (files), and individual subjects (processes or users) cannot change that access. (2)

Man-in-the-middle attack   A type of attack that generally occurs when attackers are able to place themselves in the middle of two other hosts that are communicating in order to view and/or modify the traffic. (15)

Media Access Control (MAC) address   The hardware address used to uniquely identify each device on a network. (9)

Misuse detection model   A system that looks for suspicious activity or activity that violates specific policies or matches pre-defined, undesirable patterns. (13)

Mitigate   Action taken to reduce the likelihood of a threat occurring. (20)

Modem (modulator-demodulator)   A device used to convert digital to analog and back for signal transmission over analog circuits. (10)

Multifactor   Using more than one authentication mechanism at the same time. (2)

Multiple encryption   An encryption method that runs the input through the algorithm multiple times with different keys to improve security. (5)

Multiple-factor authentication   An authentication scheme in which a user must use a combination of something they have, something they know, and something they are (biometrics). (8)

Mutual aid agreements   An agreement in which similar organizations agree to assume the processing for the other in the event a disaster occurs. (19)

Mutual authentication   A process in which each side of an electronic communication verifies the authenticity of the other. (2)

Network Address Translation (NAT)   The protocol that allows the use of private, internal IP addresses for internal traffic and public IP addresses for external traffic. (9)

Network interface card (NIC)   The specific hardware interface for a network connection. (10)

Network operating system   An operating system that includes additional functions and capabilities to assist in connecting computers and devices, such as printers, to a local area network. (14)

Network operations center (NOC)   The point from which network functionality is monitored and controlled. (10)

Network security   Places an emphasis on controlling access to internal computers from external entities. (2)

Network   A group of two or more devices linked together to share data and resources. (9)

Network-based IDS   An intrusion detection system that collects network traffic, much like a sniffer, and analyzes it for suspicious, malicious, or anomalous activity. (13)

Nonrepudiation   The ability to verify that a message has been sent and received. This is a property of a system that prevents the parties to a transaction from subsequently denying involvement in the transaction. (2)

Operating system   The basic software on a computer that handles things such as input, output, display, memory management, and all the other highly detailed tasks required to support the user environment and associated applications. (14)

Operational model of computer security   Protection = Prevention + (Detection + Response) (2)

Packet   A small chunk of data transmitted from one device to another. (9)

Passive IDS   An IDS that merely monitors traffic and does not interact with, nor interfere with, the traffic it examines. (13)

Passphrase   A password created from a phrase, selection of text, song lyrics, and so on. (14)

Password policy   A policy that covers all aspects of password management, such as password selection criteria, aging, lockouts, rotation, and dissemination. (14)

Patch   A formal, usually large, software update that may address one or more software problems. (14)

Patriot Act   A law passed post-9/11 to increase government surveillance powers and facilitate the fight against terrorism. (24)

Peer-to-peer model   A trust model characterized by CAs trusting each other in a flat structure, where individual trust relationships occur at the same level. (6)

Permissions   Authorized actions a subject can perform on an object. See also access control. (22)

Phreaking   Used in the media to refer to the hacking of computer systems and networks associated with the phone company. See also cracking. (2)

Physical security   Consists of all mechanisms used to ensure that physical access to the computer systems and networks is restricted to only authorized users. (3)

Piggybacking   The simple tactic of following closely behind a person who has just used their own access card or PIN to gain physical access to a room or building. (4)

Ping sweep   The systematic "pinging" of IP addresses to determine which is assigned to a currently active computer system. (1)

Plug-in   Small application programs that increase a browser's ability to handle new data types and add new functionality. (17)

Policies and procedures   Written guidelines for employees. (8)

Policies   High-level statements made by management laying out the organization's position on some issue. (3)

Port scan   The systematic scanning of ports on a specific system to determine which ports currently are active/open with an application listening on it/responding to connection requests. (1)

Pretty Good Privacy (PGP)   A popular encryption program. It has the ability to encrypt and digitally sign e-mail and files. (16)

Preventative IDS   An intrusion detection system designed to detect and prevent malicious activity from occurring, usually by closing, rejecting, or resetting connections containing suspicious or malicious traffic. (13)

Privilege auditing   The process of checking the rights and privileges assigned to a specific account or group of accounts. (22)

Procedures   Step-by-step instructions that describe exactly how employees are expected to act in a given situation or to accomplish a specific task. (3)

Process identifier   A unique number given to each running process (or program). (14)

Protocol   An agreed-upon format for exchanging information between systems. (9)

PTPP   PPTP is a network protocol that enables the secure transfer of data from a remote PC to a server by creating a VPN across a TCP/IP network. (11)

Public Key Infrastructure (PKI)   Infrastructure for binding a public key to a known user through a trusted intermediary, typically a certificate authority. (6)

Qualitative risk assessment   The process of subjectively determining the impact of an event that affects a project, program, or business. Qualitative risk assessment usually involves the use of expert judgment, experience, or group consensus to complete the assessment. (20)

Quantitative risk assessment   The process of objectively determining the impact of an event that affects a project, program, or business. Quanitative risk assessment usually involves the use of metrics and models to complete the assessment. (20)

RADIUS   Remote Authentication Dial-In User Service is a standard protocol for providing authentication services. It is commonly used in dial-up, wireless, and PPP environments. (11)

RC4 stream cipher   Rivest's Cipher 4 (RC4) is a symmetric encryption method that works in a stream mode instead of a block mode. (12)

Real evidence   Also known as associative or physical evidence, real evidence consists of tangible objects that prove or disprove a fact. Physical evidence links the suspect to the scene of a crime. (23)

Realtime Blackhole List   A list of hosts known to relay or produce spam e-mails that is maintained in real time. This is used by many mail servers to auto-reject mail from hosts on the list. (16)

Registration authority (RA)   The component of a PKI that accepts a request for a digital certificate and performs the necessary steps of registering and authenticating the person requesting the certificate. (6)

Relaying   When a mail server handles a message and neither the sender nor the recipient is a local user. (14)

Relevant evidence   Evidence that is material to the case or has a bearing on the matter at hand. (23)

Replay attack   An attack in which the attacker captures a portion of network traffic between two parties and retransmits it at a later time. (15)

Requirements phase   A step in the software development process where all the requirements for the end product are documented. (18)

Residual risk   Risks remaining after an iteration of risk management. (20)

Reverse social engineering   This technique is similar to social engineering in that attackers are attempting to obtain information that can be used in an attack, but in this case, the attacker uses techniques to convince the target to initiate the contact. (4)

Ring policy   A policy useful in integrity-based security models that prevents subjects from modifying objects of a higher integrity level. It does not have the same side effect that the Low-Water-Mark policy has of lowering the subject's integrity level whenever the subject accesses an object with a lower integrity level. (2)

Ring topology   The network topology where each device is connected to two other devices so that all the devices are connected together in a ring. (9)

Risk assessment (or risk analysis)   The process of analyzing an environment to identify the threats, vulnerabilities, and mitigating actions to determine (either quantitatively or qualitatively) the impact of an event that would affect a project, program, or business. (20)

Risk management   Overall decision-making process of identifying threats and vulnerabilities and their potential impacts, determining the costs to mitigate such events, and deciding what actions are cost-effective to take to control these risks. (20)

Risk   The possibility of suffering harm or loss. (20)

Role   A job or set of job functions and responsibilities needed to carry out specific tasks (for example, backup operator). (22)

Role-based access control (RBAC)   An access control mechanism in which, instead of the users being assigned specific access permissions for the objects associated with the computer system or network, a set of roles that the user may perform will be assigned to each user. (2)

Router   A device used to direct traffic across a network based on layer 3 addresses (10)

Run level   The operating mode of a UNIX system such as single-user, multi-user without networking, or multi-user with networking. The run level determines what services are activated and available. (14)

Routing   The process of moving packets from the source to the destination across multiple networks. (9)

Safe Harbor   A mechanism for self-regulation of EU privacy concerns that can be enforced through trade practice law via the Federal Trade Commission. (24)

Safeguard   See Control. (20)

Sarbanes-Oxley Act   Congressional law designed to combat issues of corporate governance and responsibility. (24)

Script kiddies   Individuals who do not have the technical expertise to develop scripts or discover new vulnerabilities in software but who have just enough understanding of computer systems to be able to download and run scripts that others have developed. (1)

Secure Sockets Layer (SSL)   SSL is an encrypting layer between the session and transport layer of the OSI model designed to encrypt above the transport layer, enabling secure sessions between hosts. (7)

Secure/Multipurpose Internet Mail Extensions (S/MIME)   Secure/Multipurpose Internet Mail Extensions is an encrypted implementation of the MIME (Multipurpose Internet Mail Extensions) protocol specification. (7)

Security Association (SA)   An instance of security policy and keying material applied to a specific data flow. Both IKE and IPSec use SAs, although these SAs are independent of one another. IPSec SAs are unidirectional and they are unique in each security protocol, whereas IKE SAs are bidirectional. A set of SAs are needed for a protected data pipe, one per direction per protocol. SAs are uniquely identified by destination (IPSec endpoint) address, security protocol (AH or ESP), and security parameter index (SPI). (11)

Security topology   The layout of a computer network from a security perspective, frequently including a DMZ between two sets of firewalls, isolating the internal network from the outside Internet. (10)

Segregation/separation of duties   A basic control that prevents or detects errors and irregularities by assigning responsibilities to different individuals such that no single individual can commit fraudulent or malicious actions. (21)

Senate Bill 1386 (SB1386)   A California law with implications for identity theft. (24)

Separation of duties   A principle employed in many organizations to ensure that no single individual has the ability to conduct transactions alone. (19)

Server   A machine that provides services to multiple users on a network. (10)

Service level agreements (SLAs)   Contractual agreements between entities describing specified levels of service that the servicing entity agrees to guarantee for the customer. (19)

Service pack   A bundled set of software updates, fixes, and additional functions contained in a self-installing package. (14)

Service set identifier (SSID)   Identifies a specific 802.11 wireless network. It transmits information about the access point that the wireless client is connecting to. (12)

Shared secret   A key value that needs to be known by both parties for them to communicate with symmetric encryption. (5)

Shift cipher   A cipher in which every letter is moved a number of places down the alphabet. (5)

Shoulder surfing   A procedure in which attackers position themselves in such a way as to be able to observe the authorized user entering the correct access code. (4)

Signature   A predefined pattern of behavior used by an IDS to identify suspicious or malicious activity. (13)

Simple Security Rule   The security principle used in the Bell-LaPadula security model that states that no subject can read from an object with a higher security classification. (2)

Single loss expectancy (SLE)   Monetary loss or impact of each occurrence of a threat. SLE = asset value * exposure factor. (20)

Single sign-on   An authentication process where the user can enter a single user ID and password and then be able to move from application to application or resource to resource without having to supply further authentication information. (22)

Slack space   Unused space on a disk drive created when a file is smaller than the allocated unit of storage (such as a sector). (23)

Smart card   Card that possesses integrated circuits, allowing it to store information; especially useful for storing cryptographic information. (8)

SMTP   Simple Mail Transfer Protocol, the standard Internet protocol used to transfer e-mail between hosts. (16)

Sniffers   Software or hardware devices that are used to observe traffic as it passes through a network on shared broadcast media. (15)

SNMP (Simple Network Management Protocol)   The protocol used to control network devices and functionality across a network. (10)

SOAP (Simple Object Access Protocol)   A method of remote object access (17)

Social engineering   The art of deceiving another individual so that they reveal confidential information. This is often accomplished by posing as an individual who should be entitled to have access to the information. (3)

Software configuration item   See configuration item. (21)

Software exploitation   An attack that takes advantage of bugs or weaknesses in software. (15)

Software problem report   A document used by the change control board to track changes to software. (21)

Spam   E-mail that is not requested by the recipient and is typically of a commercial nature. Also known as unsolicited commercial e-mail (UCE). (16)

Spiral model   A software engineering process model characterized by a repeating series of steps. (18)

Spoofing   A type of attack in which data is made to look like it has come from a different source. (15)

SSH   SSH is a set of protocols for establishing a secure remote connection to a computer. This protocol requires a client on each end of the connection and can use a variety of encryption protocols. (11)

SSL   SSL is an encrypting layer between the session and transport layer of the OSI model designed to encrypt above the transport layer, enabling secure sessions between hosts. (17)

Standards   Accepted specifications providing specific details on how a policy is to be enforced. (3)

Standards   Accepted specifications providing specific details on how a policy is to be enforced. (19)

Star topology   The network topology where all network devices are connected to a single, central point. (9)

Stream cipher   An encryption method that encrypts information in a stream—that is, bit by bit. (5)

Structured threat   A threat characterized by a greater amount of planning, a longer period of time to conduct the activity, more financial backing to accomplish it, and the possible corruption of, or collusion with, insiders. Criminal organizations or well-organized "hacking" groups fall into this category. (1)

Subnet mask   A mask used to indicate how to interpret a given IP address; the mask tells how much of the IP address is being used for the network portion and how much is being used for the host portion. (9)

Subnet   The prefix potion of an IP address used to describe the network portion of the IP address. (9)

Sufficient evidence   Evidence that is convincing or measures up without question (23)

Superuser   A title associated with user accounts that have broad administrative capabilities, such as "administrator" under Windows or "root" under UNIX. (22)

Switch   A device used to direct traffic in a network based on layer 2 addresses. (10)

TACACS+   Terminal Access Controller Access Control System+ (TACACS+) protocol is the current generation of the TACACS family. (11)

Tangible asset   An asset for which a monetary equivalent can be determined. Examples are inventory, buildings, cash, hardware, software, and so on. (20)

TCP wrappers   Software filters that can compare incoming and outgoing network connections to lists or authorized and unauthorized connections and then allow or reject the connections based on a defined policy. (14)

TCP/IP hijacking   Also called session hijacking, this refers to attacks designed to take control of an already existing session between a client and a server. (15)

TEMPEST   Transient Electromagnetic Pulse Emanation Standard. (3)

Testing phase   The point in the software development process where the end product is compared to the input requirements to validate proper functionality. (18)

Threat   Any circumstance or event with the potential to cause harm to an asset. (20)

Three-way handshake The three-way packet exchange sequence (SYN, SYN/ACK, ACK) that initiates a TCP connection. (9)

Token A hardware device that can be used in a challenge-response authentication process. (2)

Topology The shape or arrangement of a network, such as bus, star, ring, or mixed. (9)

Transmission Control Protocol (TCP) A connection-oriented protocol that provides guaranteed, reliable delivery of data. (9)

Transport layer security (TLS) A newer form of SSL being proposed as an Internet standard. (17)

Transposition cipher A cipher where the same letters are used but the order has been changed. (5)

Trapdoor functions A type of math problem that is very difficult to solve unless you know a certain value. (5)

Trojan horse Sometimes known simply as Trojan, this is a piece of software that appears to do one thing (and may, in fact, actually do that thing) but which hides some other functionality. (15)

Uniform Electronic Transactions Act (UETA) Congressional law permitting the use of electronic signatures in communications with government. (24)

Uninterruptible power supplies Devices designed to provide power to essential equipment for a period of time when normal power is lost. (3)

Unsolicited commercial e-mail The more technical name for spam e-mail. It is e-mail trying to sell you something when you have not requested information about that particular product or service. (16)

Unstructured threat A threat that is generally short-term in nature, does not involve a large group of individuals, does not have large financial backing, and does not generally include collusion with insiders. Individual attackers fall into this category of threat. (1)

URL (Uniform Resource Locator) A unique Internet address for a resource. (17)

Usage auditing The process of recording who did what and when on an information system. (22)

USB devices Devices that utilize the Universal Serial Bus port to connect to the computer. (8)

Use case A set of sample inputs and known correct responses to use in the testing of a section of functionality, whether module, subsystem, system, or application. (18)

User Datagram Protocol (UDP)   A connectionless protocol that provides no error correction or reliability, but is very lightweight and efficient. (9)

User ID   A unique alphanumeric identifier that identifies individuals when logging in or accessing a system. (22)

User   An individual that uses a computer or information system. (22)

Vigenère cipher   An early polyalphabetic substitution cipher. (5)

Virtual local area network (VLAN)   A broadcast domain inside a switched system. (10)

Virtual private network (VPN)   An encrypted network connection across another network, offering a private communication channel across a public medium. (11)

Virus   A piece of malicious code that replicates by attaching itself to another piece of executable code. (15)

Vulnerability   Characteristic of an asset that can be exploited by a threat to cause harm. (20)

WAP GAP   The transition point between the wireless network's encryption and the Internet's encryption protocols, leaving any data in the "gap" in plaintext. (12)

Wardialing   The term used to describe an attacker's attempt to discover unprotected modem connections to computer systems and networks. (15)

WarDriving   The term used to refer to the activity where attackers wander throughout an area (often in a car) with a computer with wireless capability, searching for wireless networks they can access. (15)

Warm site   A partially configured backup processing facility usually having the peripherals and software but perhaps not the more expensive main processing computer. (19)

Waterfall model   A software engineering process model characterized by a linear series of steps in a sequential fashion. (18)

Web Service   A remote procedure invoked on a remote computer via common data formats and protocols. (17)

Wide area network (WAN)   A computer network that spans a large geographic area, such as a network connecting offices in different cities. (9)

Wired Equivalent Privacy (WEP)   The encryption scheme used to attempt to provide confidentiality and data integrity on 802.11 networks. (7)

Wireless Application Protocol (WAP)   A protocol for transmitting data to small handheld devices like cellular phones. (7)

Wireless Transport Layer Security (WTLS) The encryption protocol that is used on WAP networks. (7)

Workstation Typically, a client or end-user machine attached to a network. (10)

Worm A piece of code that attempts to propagate through penetration of networks and computer systems. (15)

X.509 standard The standard format for digital certificates. (6)

XML (Extensible Markup Language) A protocol for describing data. (17)

XOR Bitwise exclusive OR, an operation commonly used in cryptography. (5)

INDEX

See "Glossary" for a comprehensive list of terms.

INTERNATIONAL CONTACT INFORMATION

AUSTRALIA
McGraw-Hill Book Company
Australia Pty. Ltd.
TEL +61-2-9900-1800
FAX +61-2-9878-8881
http://www.mcgraw-hill.com.au
books-it_sydney@mcgraw-hill.com

CANADA
McGraw-Hill Ryerson Ltd.
TEL +905-430-5000
FAX +905-430-5020
http://www.mcgraw-hill.ca

**GREECE, MIDDLE EAST, & AFRICA
(Excluding South Africa)**
McGraw-Hill Hellas
TEL +30-210-6560-990
TEL +30-210-6560-993
TEL +30-210-6560-994
FAX +30-210-6545-525

MEXICO (Also serving Latin America)
McGraw-Hill Interamericana Editores
S.A. de C.V.
TEL +525-1500-5108
FAX +525-117-1589
http://www.mcgraw-hill.com.mx
carlos_ruiz@mcgraw-hill.com

SINGAPORE (Serving Asia)
McGraw-Hill Book Company
TEL +65-6863-1580
FAX +65-6862-3354
http://www.mcgraw-hill.com.sg
mghasia@mcgraw-hill.com

SOUTH AFRICA
McGraw-Hill South Africa
TEL +27-11-622-7512
FAX +27-11-622-9045
robyn_swanepoel@mcgraw-hill.com

SPAIN
McGraw-Hill/
Interamericana de España, S.A.U.
TEL +34-91-180-3000
FAX +34-91-372-8513
http://www.mcgraw-hill.es
professional@mcgraw-hill.es

**UNITED KINGDOM, NORTHERN,
EASTERN, & CENTRAL EUROPE**
McGraw-Hill Education Europe
TEL +44-1-628-502500
FAX +44-1-628-770224
http://www.mcgraw-hill.co.uk
emea_queries@mcgraw-hill.com

ALL OTHER INQUIRIES Contact:
McGraw-Hill Technology Education
TEL +1-630-789-4000
FAX +1-630-789-5226
http://www.mhteched.com
omg_international@mcgraw-hill.com

"Like the Book?" "You ll Love the Movie!"

IMAGINE . . .

Imagine Internet-based learning that allows you to engage in dynamic multi-media instruction for Windows XP Professional with a connection as low as 56.6 kbps.

Imagine learning from an expert through uninterrupted video instruction, full motion graphics and interactive lab exercises.

Imagine a Web-based learning environment that includes personal study plans, online mentoring, labs, references, testing, and all the resources you need for certification success.

Stop Imagining!
Insert the enclosed CD and experience it Today!

CD Contains:

- **Online Course Link**
- **Step-by-Step Video Clips**
- **Lab Simulations**
- **Test Prep**
- **Electronic Book**

1.800.865.0165 • learnkey.com

Learn From The Experts™